THE NEW INTERNATIONAL
GREEK TESTAMENT COMMENTARY

Editors
I. Howard Marshall
W. Ward Gasque (1978-93)
Donald A. Hagner

THE EPISTLES TO THE COLOSSIANS
AND TO PHILEMON

THE EPISTLES TO THE
COLOSSIANS
AND TO
PHILEMON

A Commentary on the
Greek Text

by

JAMES D. G. DUNN

Lightfoot Professor of Divinity
University of Durham

WILLIAM B. EERDMANS PUBLISHING COMPANY
GRAND RAPIDS, MICHIGAN

THE PATERNOSTER PRESS
CARLISLE

© 1996 Wm. B. Eerdmans Publishing Co.

First published 1996 jointly by Wm. B. Eerdmans Publishing Co.
255 Jefferson Ave. S.E., Grand Rapids, Michigan 49503 and by
The Paternoster Press Ltd.,
P.O. Box 300, Carlisle, Cumbria CA3 0QS England

Printed in the United States of America

01 00 99 98 97 96   7 6 5 4 3 2 1

Library of Congress Cataloging-in-Publication Data

Dunn, James D. G., 1939-
The Epistles to the Colossians and Philemon: a commentary on the
Greek text / by James D. G. Dunn
p.   cm.
— (The New International Greek Testament Commentary)
Includes bibliographical references and indexes.
ISBN 0-8028-2441-2 (alk. paper)
1. Bible. N.T. Colossians — Commentaries.   2. Bible. N.T.
Philemon — Commentaries.   I. Title.   II. Series: New International
Greek Testament Commentary (Grand Rapids, Mich.)
BS2715.3.D86   1996
227'.7077 — dc20   95-26758
                                                CIP

Paternoster Press ISBN 0 85364 571 X

To

Graham Stanton

friend and companion
for many years
in the quest
and questioning
which is
Christian scholarship

CONTENTS

Foreword	x
Preface	xii
Abbreviations	xiv

THE EPISTLE TO THE COLOSSIANS

BIBLIOGRAPHY	3
INTRODUCTION	19
THE SIGNIFICANCE OF THE LETTER	19
COLOSSAE AND THE ESTABLISHMENT OF CHRISTIANITY THERE	20
THE TROUBLE AT COLOSSAE	23
Presuppositions	24
Gnosticizing Syncretism . . . ?	27
. . . or Jewish?	29
The Colossian Philosophy	33
WHO WROTE COLOSSIANS?	35
WHERE AND WHEN WAS COLOSSIANS WRITTEN?	39
THE STRUCTURE OF COLOSSIANS	41
COMMENTARY	
ADDRESS AND GREETING (1:1-2)	43
EXTENDED THANKSGIVING (1:3-23)	53
Thanksgiving (1:3-8)	54
Prayer for the Colossian Recipients (1:9-14)	67
A Hymn in Praise of Christ (1:15-20)	83
Reconciliation and Response (1:21-23)	105
A PERSONAL STATEMENT (1:24–2:5)	113
Paul's Commitment to the Gospel (1:24-29)	113

Paul's Commitment to the Colossians (2:1-5)   128

THE THEME OF THE LETTER (2:6–4:6)   136

THE THEMATIC STATEMENT (2:6-7)   138

THE CROSS OF CHRIST RENDERS UNNECESSARY ANY
    FURTHER HUMAN TRADITIONS AND RULES (2:8-23)   144

The Scope of Christ's Accomplishments on the Cross (2:8-15)   145

*Beware of Claims That There Are More Important Practices
    and Experiences (2:16-19)*   171

*Life in Christ Does Not Depend on Observance of Jewish
    Practices (2:20-23)*   188

THE PATTERN OF LIVING THAT FOLLOWS FROM THE
    CROSS (3:1–4:6)   199

*The Perspective from Which the Christian Life Should Be
    Lived (3:1-4)*   202

General Guidelines and Practical Exhortations (3:5-17)   210

Household Rules (3:18–4:1)   242

Concluding Exhortations (4:2-6)   261

CONCLUSION (4:7-18)   269

Maintaining Communication (4:7-9)   271

Greetings (4:10-17)   274

A Final, Personal Greeting (4:18)   289

THE EPISTLE TO PHILEMON

BIBLIOGRAPHY   294

INTRODUCTION   299
    THE AUTHOR   299
    THE RECIPIENT   300
    THE OCCASION   301
    THE PLACE OF WRITING   307
    THE STRUCTURE OF THE LETTER   309

COMMENTARY
    ADDRESS AND GREETING (1-3)   310
    THANKSGIVING AND PRAYER (4-7)   315
    APPEAL TO PHILEMON (8-20)   322
    IN CONCLUSION (21-25)   343

INDEXES

Subjects 351
Modern Authors 355
Biblical and Other Ancient Works 362

FOREWORD

Although there have been many series of commentaries on the English text of the New Testament in recent years, very few attempts have been made to cater particularly to the needs of students of the Greek text. The present initiative to fill this gap by the publication of the *New International Greek Testament Commentary* is very largely due to the vision of W. Ward Gasque, who was one of the original editors of the series. (The present editors would like to place on record their recognition of Dr. Gasque's work in the establishment and development of the series until the pressure of other duties made it necessary for him to resign from his editorship). At a time when the study of Greek is being curtailed in many schools of theology, we hope that the *NIGTC* will demonstrate the continuing value of studying the Greek New Testament and will be an impetus in the revival of such study.

The volumes of of the *NIGTC* are for students who want something less technical than a full-scale critical commentary. At the same time, the commentaries are intended to interact with modern scholarship and to make their own scholarly contribution to the study of the New Testament. The wealth of detailed study of the New Testament in articles and monographs continues without interruption, and the series is meant to harvest the results of this research in an easily accessible form. The commentaries include, therefore, adequate, but not exhaustive, bibliographies and attempt to treat all important problems of history, exegesis, and interpretation that arise from the New Testament text.

One of the gains of recent scholarship has been the recognition of the primarily theological character of the books of the New Testament. The volumes of the *NIGTC* attempt to provide a theological understanding of the text, based on historical-critical-linguistic exegesis. It is not their primary aim to apply and expound the text for modern readers, although it is hoped that the exegesis will give some indication of the way in which the text should be expounded.

Within the limits set by the use of the English language, the series aims to be international in character, though the contributors have been chosen not primarily in order to achieve a spread between different countries but above all because of their specialized qualifications for their particular tasks.

The supreme aim of this series is to serve those who are engaged in the ministry of the Word of God and thus to glorify God's name. Our prayer is that it may be found helpful in this task.

I. Howard Marshall
Donald A. Hagner

PREFACE

I did not expect to find the writing of a commentary on Colossians quite so enjoyable. For one thing, it provides an unexpectedly interesting window into the character of Christianity in Asia Minor in the second half of the first century. Our knowledge of how Christianity developed in the second and third generations is very scanty, but it is fullest in regard to Asia Minor (given also not least the letters of Revelation and of Ignatius). Colossians provides a fascinating third perspective, and with the information it gives about the religious tensions within which emergent Christianity was caught up, not least those between Christianity and diaspora Judaism, we begin to gain more of an insight into the influences and factors which shaped the transition from apostolic to subapostolic Christianity in the region.

For another, the letter represents such a crucial stage in the development of Pauline theology. Whether it was written at the end of Paul's life or soon after his death (the two most likely alternatives), it indicates how Pauline theology retained its own vital character and did not die with Paul. As the margin between sea and land contains some of the most interesting natural phenomena, and the transition between epochs produces some of the most interesting people and cultural expressions, so the transition from Pauline to post-Pauline theology has a distinctive importance for our understanding of both what went before and what came after, able to throw light on both.

Another reason, I suppose, is that having written two large commentaries on earlier Pauline letters (Galatians and Romans) I had "gotten into the swing of it." More to the point, since this commentary is part of a larger project on Paul, who played a (probably the) decisive role in the spread, formation, and transformation of Christianity in the first decades of its existence, the interaction of this fresh material with the findings of the earlier commentaries was particularly stimulating and refreshing in the constant fine-tuning which it occasioned. My hope is that others will not be overwhelmed by the detailed workings of the commentary and experience something of the same stimulus and refreshment.

The first draft of the commentary was researched and written during my study leave in 1993. I remain grateful to my Durham colleagues, whose commitment to maintaining the tradition of a one-in-nine-term sabbatical policy makes such scholarship possible, particularly as it means more work for those covering for their sabbatical colleagues. The exegesis was "tried out" on successive final-year seminars during the academic years 1992-95, and I remain equally grateful to my students for the stimulus of our theological dialogue in and through exegesis. My hope here, too, is that the commentary will not only inform the exegesis of Colossians for its readers but also provide a productive partner for their own theological dialogue.

James D. G. Dunn
December 1995

ABBREVIATIONS

AB   Anchor Bible
ABD   *The Anchor Bible Dictionary,* ed. D. N. Freedman (6 vols.; New York: Doubleday, 1992)
AnBib   Analecta Biblica
ANRW   *Aufstieg und Niedergang der römischen Welt,* ed. H. Temporini and W. Haase (Berlin)
ATR   *Anglican Theological Review*
BAGD   W. Bauer, *A Greek-English Lexicon of the New Testament and Other Early Christian Literature,* ed. W. F. Arndt, F. W. Gingrich, and F. W. Danker (Chicago: University of Chicago, 1979)
BBB   Bonner biblische Beiträge
BDF   F. Blass, A. Debrunner, and R. W. Funk, *A Greek Grammar of the New Testament* (Cambridge University/University of Chicago, 1961)
Bib   *Biblica*
BibLeb   *Bibel und Leben*
BibSac   *Bibliotheca Sacra*
BJRL   *Bulletin of the John Rylands University Library*
BNTC   Black's New Testament Commentary
BR   *Biblical Research*
BU   Biblische Untersuchungen
BZ   *Biblische Zeitschrift*
BZNW   Beihefte zur *ZNW*
CBQ   *Catholic Biblical Quarterly*
CGT   *Cambridge Greek Testament*
CGTC   *Cambridge Greek Testament Commentary*
CIG   *Corpus Inscriptionum Graecorum*
CIJ   *Corpus Inscriptionum Judicarum*
CNT   Commentaire du Nouveau Testament
CTJ   *Calvin Theological Journal*
DPL   *Dictionary of Paul and His Letters,* ed. G. F. Hawthorne, et al. (Downers Grove and Leicester: InterVarsity, 1993)
DSS   Dead Sea Scrolls

ÉB	Études bibliques
EC	Epworth Commentary
EDNT	*Exegetical Dictionary of the New Testament,* ed. H. Balz and G. Schneider (3 vols.; Grand Rapids: Eerdmans, 1990-93)
EGGNT	Exegetical Guide to the Greek New Testament
EKK	Evangelisch-katholischer Kommentar
EvQ	*Evangelical Quarterly*
EvTh	*Evangelische Theologie*
ExpT	*Expository Times*
FRLANT	Forschungen zur Religion und Literatur des Alten und Neuen Testaments
FS	Festschrift
GLAJJ	M. Stern, *Greek and Latin Authors on Jews and Judaism* (3 vols.; Jerusalem: Israel Academy of Sciences and Humanities, 1976-84)
GNB	Good News Bible
GNTG	J. H. Moulton, *A Grammar of New Testament Greek.* Vol. 1: *Prolegomena* (Edinburgh: Clark, ²1908), vol. 3: *Syntax,* by N. Turner (Edinburgh: Clark, 1963)
HNT	Handbuch zum Neuen Testament
HTKNT	Herders theologischer Kommentar zum Neuen Testament
HTR	*Harvard Theological Review*
IB	*Interpreter's Bible*
ICC	International Critical Commentary
IDB	*Interpreter's Dictionary of the Bible,* ed. G. A. Buttrick (4 vols.; Nashville: Abingdon, 1962)
IDBS	*Supplementary Volume* to *IDB,* ed. K. Crim (1976)
Int	*Interpretation*
ITQ	*Irish Theological Quarterly*
JB	Jerusalem Bible
JBL	*Journal of Biblical Literature*
JETS	*Journal of the Evangelical Theological Society*
JJS	*Journal of Jewish Studies*
JR	*Journal of Religion*
JSNT	*Journal for the Study of the New Testament*
JSNTS	*JSNT* Supplements
JTS	*Journal of Theological Studies*
KEK	Kritisch-exegetischer Kommentar über das Neue Testament
LCL	Loeb Classical Library
LSJ	H. G. Liddell and R. Scott, *A Greek-English Lexicon,* rev. H. S. Jones (Oxford: Clarendon, ⁹1940; with supplement, 1968)
LTP	*Laval Théologique et Philosophique*
MM	J. H. Moulton and G. Milligan, *The Vocabulary of the Greek Testament* (London: Hodder, 1930)

MNTC Moffatt New Testament Commentary
NA *Novum Testamentum Graece,* ed. K. Aland, et al. (Stuttgart: Deutsche Bibelstiftung, [26]1979, [27]1993)
NCB(C) New Century Bible (Commentary)
NDIEC *New Documents Illustrating Early Christianity,* ed. G. H. R. Horsley, et al. (Macquarie University, 1981-)
NEB New English Bible
Neot *Neotestamentica*
NICNT New International Commentary on the New Testament
NIV New International Bible
NJB New Jerusalem Bible
NovT *Novum Testamentum*
NovTSup *NovT* Supplements
NRSV New Revised Standard Version
NRT Nouvelle Revue Théologique
NTD Das Neue Testament Deutsch
NTS *New Testament Studies*
NTTS New Testament Tools and Studies
OBO Orbis Biblicus et Orientalis
OCD N. G. L. Hammond and H. H. Scullard, ed., *Oxford Classical Dictionary* (Oxford: Clarendon, 1970)
OGIS *Orientis Graeci Inscriptiones Selectae,* ed. W. Dittenberger (3 vols.; 1903, 1905)
ÖTKNT Ökumenischer Taschenbuch-Kommentar zum Neuen Testament
OTP *Old Testament Pseudepigrapha,* ed. J. H. Charlesworth (2 vols.; London: Darton/Garden City: Doubleday, 1983, 1985)
PG *Patrologia Graeca,* ed. J. P. Migne (1844-)
PGL *Patristic Greek Lexicon,* ed. G. W. H. Lampe (Oxford: Clarendon, 1961)
QD Quaestiones Disputatae
RAC *Reallexikon für Antike und Christentum*
REB Revised English Bible
RevExp *Review and Expositor*
RevSR *Revue des sciences religieuses*
RGG *Religion in Geschichte und Gegenwart*
RHPR *Revue d'histoire et de philosophie religieuses*
RNT Regensburger Neues Testament
RSV Revised Standard Version
SBL Society of Biblical Literature
SBLDS SBL Dissertation Series
SBLMS SBL Monograph Series
SBLSP *SBL Seminar Papers*
SBM Stuttgarter biblische Monographien

SBS	Stuttgarter Bibelstudien
SEÅ	*Svensk exegetisk årsbok*
SJT	*Scottish Journal of Theology*
SNT	Studien zum Neuen Testament
SNTSMS	Society for New Testament Studies Monograph Series
SNTU	Studien zum Neuen Testament und seiner Umwelt
StTh	*Studia Theologica*
Str-B	H. Strack and P. Billerbeck, *Kommentar zum Neuen Testament* (Munich: Beck'sche, 1926-28)
SUNT	Studien zur Umwelt des Neuen Testaments
TDNT	G. Kittel and G. Friedrich, *Theological Dictionary of the New Testament,* 10 vols. (Grand Rapids: Eerdmans, 1964-76)
THNT	Theologischer Handkommentar zum Neuen Testament
ThViat	*Theologia Viatorum*
TLZ	*Theologische Literaturzeitung*
TNTC	Tyndale New Testament Commentary
TQ	*Theologische Quartalschrift*
TRE	*Theologische Realenzyklopädie* (1976-)
TS	Theologische Studien
TU	Texte und Untersuchungen
TynB	*Tyndale Bulletin*
TZ	*Theologische Zeitschrift*
UBS	*The Greek New Testament,* ed. K. Aland, et al. (New York/London: United Bible Societies, [3]1975, [3]corrected 1983, [4]1993)
USQR	*Union Seminary Quarterly Review*
v.l.	*varia lectio* = variant reading
WBC	Word Biblical Commentary
WC	Westminster Commentary
WD	*Wort und Dienst*
WMANT	Wissenschaftliche Monographien zum Alten und Neuen Testament
WTJ	*Westminster Theological Journal*
WUNT	Wissenschaftliche Untersuchungen zum Neuen Testament
ZBK	Zürcher Bibelkommentar
ZNW	*Zeitschrift für die neutestamentliche Wissenschaft*
ZKT	*Zeitschrift für katholische Theologie*
ZTK	*Zeitschrift für Theologie und Kirche*

COLOSSIANS

BIBLIOGRAPHY

COMMENTARIES

Abbott, T. K., *A Critical and Exegetical Commentary on the Epistles to the Ephesians and to the Colossians* (ICC; Edinburgh: Clark, 1897)

Aletti, J.-N., *Saint Paul Épître aux Colossiens* (ÉB; Paris: Gabalda, 1993)

Beare, F. W., "The Epistle to the Colossians," *IB*, vol. 11 (Nashville: Abingdon, 1955) 133-241

Bieder, W., *Der Kolosserbrief* (Zurich: Zwingli, 1943)

Bruce, F. F., *The Epistles to the Colossians, to Philemon, and to the Ephesians* (NICNT; Grand Rapids: Eerdmans, 1984) = revision of (with E. K. Simpson on Ephesians) *The Epistles of Paul to the Ephesians and to the Colossians* (NICNT; Grand Rapids: Eerdmans, 1958)

Caird, G. B., *Paul's Letters from Prison* (NCB; Oxford: Oxford University, 1976)

Carson, H. M., *The Epistles of Paul to the Colossians and Philemon* (TNTC; Grand Rapids: Eerdmans, 1960)

Conzelmann, H., "Der Brief an die Kolosser," in *Die kleineren Briefe des Apostels Paulus* (NTD 8; Göttingen: Vandenhoeck, [10]1965) 131-56

Dibelius, M., *An die Kolosser, Epheser, an Philemon,* revised by H. Greeven (HNT 12; Tübingen: Mohr, [3]1953)

Ernst, J., *Die Briefe an die Philipper, an Philemon, an die Kolosser, an die Epheser* (RNT; Regensburg: Pustet, 1974)

Gnilka, J., *Der Kolosserbrief* (HTKNT 10/1; Freiburg: Herder, 1980)

Harris, M. J., *Colossians and Philemon* (EGGNT; Grand Rapids: Eerdmans, 1991)

Houlden, J. L., *Paul's Letters from Prison* (Harmondsworth: Penguin, 1970)

Hugede, N., *Commentaire de l'Épître aux Colossiens* (Genève: Labor et Fides, 1968)

Leuken, W., "Die Briefe an Philemon, an die Kolosser und an die Epheser," *Die Schriften des Neuen Testaments,* vol. II (Göttingen: Vandenhoeck, [3]1917) 339-58

Lightfoot, J. B., *The Epistles of St Paul: Colossians and Philemon* (London: Macmillan, 1875)

Lindemann, A., *Der Kolosserbrief* (ZBK; Zurich: Theologischer Verlag, 1983)

Lohmeyer, E., *Die Briefe an die Philipper, an die Kolosser und an Philemon* (KEK 9; Göttingen: Vandenhoeck, [13]1964)

Lohse, E., *Colossians and Philemon* (Hermeneia; Philadelphia: Fortress, 1971) = *Die Briefe an die Kolosser und an Philemon* (KEK 9/2; Göttingen: Vandenhoeck, 1968)

3

Martin, R. P., *Colossians and Philemon* (NCBC; London: Marshall, Morgan, and Scott, 1973)

Masson, C., *L'Épître de Saint Paul aux Colossiens* (CNT 10; Neuchâtel: Delachaux, 1950)

Metzger, B. M., *A Textual Commentary on the Greek New Testament* (London: United Bible Societies, [2]1975)

Moule, C. F. D., *The Epistles to the Colossians and to Philemon* (CGTC; Cambridge: Cambridge University, 1957)

O'Brien, P. T., *Colossians, Philemon* (WBC 44; Waco: Word, 1982)

Peake, A. S., "The Epistle of Paul to the Colossians," in *Expositor's Greek Testament,* vol. 3 (1917) 475-547

Pokorný, P., *Colossians: A Commentary* (Peabody, Mass.: Hendrickson, 1987) = *Der Brief des Paulus an die Kolosser* (THNT 10/1; Berlin: Evangelische, 1987)

Radford, L. B., *The Epistle to the Colossians and the Epistle to Philemon* (WC; London: Methuen, 1931)

Schlatter, A., *Die Briefe an die Galater, Epheser, Kolosser und Philemon* (Erläuterungen zum NT, vol. 7; Stuttgart: Calwer, 1963)

Schmauch, W., *Beiheft* to Lohmeyer (KEK; Göttingen: Vandenhoeck, 1964)

Schweizer, E., *The Letter to the Colossians* (London: SPCK, 1982) = *Der Brief an die Kolosser* (EKK; Zurich: Benziger, 1976)

Scott, E. F., *The Epistle of Paul to the Colossians, to Philemon and to the Ephesians* (MNTC; London: Hodder, 1930)

Wall, R. W., *Colossians and Philemon* (The IVP New Testament Commentary; Downers Grove: InterVarsity, 1993)

Williams, A. L., *The Epistle of Paul the Apostle to the Colossians and to Philemon* (*CGT*; Cambridge: Cambridge University, 1907)

Wolter, M., *Der Brief an die Kolosser. Der Brief an Philemon* (ÖTKNT 12; Gütersloh: Mohn, 1993)

Wright, N. T., *The Epistles of Paul to the Colossians and to Philemon* (TNTC; Grand Rapids: Eerdmans, 1986)

Yates, R., *The Epistle to the Colossians* (EC; London: Epworth, 1993)

OTHER LITERATURE

Aletti, J.-N., *Colossiens 1:15-20. Genre et exégèse du texte. Fonction de la thématique sapientielle* (AnBib 91; Rome: Biblical Institute, 1981)

Anderson, C. P., "Who Wrote 'the Epistle from Laodicea'?" *JBL* 85 (1966) 436-40

Argall, R. A., "The Source of a Religious Error in Colosse," *CTJ* 22 (1987) 6-20

Arnold, C. E., "Jesus Christ: 'Head' of the Church (Colossians and Ephesians)," in *Jesus of Nazareth: Lord and Christ: Essays on the Historical Jesus and New Testament Christology,* I. H. Marshall FS, ed. J. B. Green and M. Turner (Grand Rapids: Eerdmans/Carlisle: Paternoster, 1994) 346-66

Arzt, P., "The 'Epistolary Introductory Thanksgiving' in the Papyri and in Paul," *NovT* 36 (1994) 29-46

Attridge, H. W., "On Becoming an Angel: Rival Baptismal Theologies at Colossae," in

Religious Propaganda and Missionary Competition in the New Testament World,
D. Georgi FS, ed. L. Bormann, et al. (Leiden: Brill, 1994) 481-98

Bahr, G. J., "Paul and Letter Writing in the First Century," *CBQ* 28 (1966) 465-77
Balch, D. L., *Let Wives Be Submissive: The Domestic Code in 1 Peter* (SBLMS 26; Chico: Scholars, 1981)
Balchin, J. F., "Colossians 1:15-20: An Early Christian Hymn? The Arguments from Style," *Vox Evangelica* 15 (1985) 65-94
———, "Paul, Wisdom and Christ," in *Christ the Lord,* D. Guthrie FS, ed. H. H. Rowdon (Leicester: Inter-Varsity, 1982) 204-19
Bammel, E., "Versuch zu Kol. 1:15-20," *ZNW* 52 (1961) 88-95
Bandstra, A. J., "Did the Colossian Errorists Need a Mediator?" *New Dimensions in New Testament Study,* ed. R. N. Longenecker and M. C. Tenney (Grand Rapids: Zondervan, 1974) 329-43
———, *The Law and the Elements of the World: An Exegetical Study in Aspects of Paul's Teaching* (Kampen: Kok, 1964)
———, "Pleroma as Pneuma in Colossians," in *Ad interim,* R. Schippers FS (Kampen: Kok, 1975) 96-102
Banks, R., *Paul's Idea of Community* (Grand Rapids: Eerdmans, 1980)
Barclay, W., *The All-Sufficient Christ: Studies in Paul's Letter to the Colossians* (London: Collins, 1963)
Bauckham, R. J., "Colossians 1:24 Again: The Apocalyptic Motif," *EvQ* 47 (1975) 168-70
Baugh, S. M., "The Poetic Form of Col. 1:15-20," *WTJ* 47 (1985) 227-44
Beasley-Murray, G. R., *Baptism in the New Testament* (London: Macmillan, 1962)
———, "The Second Chapter of Colossians," *RevExp* 70 (1973) 469-79
Beasley-Murray, P., "Colossians 1:15-20: An Early Christian Hymn Celebrating the Lordship of Christ," in *Pauline Studies,* F. F. Bruce FS, ed. D. A. Hagner and M. J. Harris (Exeter: Paternoster/Grand Rapids: Eerdmans, 1980) 169-83
Beker, J. C., *Heirs of Paul: Paul's Legacy in the New Testament and in the Church Today* (Minneapolis: Fortress, 1991)
Benoit, P., "Ἅγιοι en Colossiens 1:12: hommes ou anges?" in *Paul and Paulinism,* C. K. Barrett FS, ed. M. D. Hooker and S. G. Wilson (London: SPCK, 1982) 83-99
———, "Body, Head and *Pleroma* in the Epistles of the Captivity" (1956), in *Jesus and the Gospel* II (London: Darton, 1974) 51-92
———, "Colossiens 2:2-3," in *The New Testament Age,* B. Reicke FS, ed. W. C. Weinrich (Macon: Mercer University, 1984) 41-51
———, "L'hymne christologique de Col. 1:15-20. Jugement critique sur l'état des recherches," in *Christianity, Judaism and Other Greco-Roman Cults,* M. Smith FS, ed. J. Neusner (Leiden: Brill, 1975), vol. 1, 226-63
———, "The 'plèrôma' in the Epistles to the Colossians and the Ephesians," *SEÅ* 49 (1984) 136-58
———, "Rapports littéraires entre les épîtres aux Colossiens et aux Ephésiens," in *Neutestamentliche Aufsätze,* J. Schmid FS, ed. J. Blinzler, et al. (Regensburg: Pustet, 1963) 11-22
Best, E., *One Body in Christ* (London: SPCK, 1955)

Bieder, W., *Die kolossische Irrlehre und die Kirche von heute* (TS 33; Zurich: Evangelischer, 1952)

Blanchette, O. A., "Does the *Cheirographon* of Col. 2:14 Represent Christ Himself?" *CBQ* 23 (1961) 306-12

Bockmuehl, M., "A Note on the Text of Colossians 4:3," *JTS* 39 (1988) 489-94

―――, *Revelation and Mystery in Ancient Judaism and Pauline Christianity* (WUNT 2.36; Tübingen: Mohr, 1990)

Bornkamm, G., "The Heresy of Colossians," in Francis and Meeks, *Conflict* 123-45

―――, "Die Hoffnung im Kolosserbrief. Zugleich ein Beitrag zur Frage der Echtheit des Briefes," in *Geschichte und Glaube* 2 (*Gesammelte Aufsätze,* vol. 4; Munich: Kaiser, 1971) 206-13

Bouttier, M., "*Complexio Oppositorum.* Sur les Formules de 1 Cor. 12:13; Gal. 3:26-28; Col. 3:10, 11," *NTS* 23 (1976-77) 1-19

Bowen, C. R., "The Original Form of Paul's Letter to the Colossians," *JBL* 43 (1924) 177-206

Bowers, W. P., "A Note on Colossians 1:27a," in *Current Issues in Biblical and Patristic Interpretation,* M. C. Tenney FS, ed. G. F. Hawthorne (Grand Rapids: Eerdmans, 1975) 110-14

Brown, R. E., *The Semitic Background of the Term "Mystery" in the New Testament* (Philadelphia: Fortress, 1968)

Bruce, F. F., "Colossian Problems I: Jews and Christians in the Lycus Valley," *BibSac* 141 (1984) 3-15

―――, "Colossian Problems II: The 'Christ-Hymn' of Col. 1:15-20," *BibSac* 141 (1984) 99-111

―――, "Colossian Problems III: The Colossian Heresy," *BibSac* 141 (1984) 195-208

―――, *Paul: Apostle of the Free Spirit* (Exeter: Paternoster, 1977) = *Paul: Apostle of the Heart Set Free* (Grand Rapids: Eerdmans, 1977) 407-23

―――, "St. Paul in Rome. 3. The Epistle to the Colossians," *BJRL* 48 (1966) 268-85

Bujard, W., *Stilanalystische Untersuchungen zum Kolosserbrief als Beitrag zur Methodik von Sprachvergleichen* (SUNT 11; Göttingen: Vandenhoeck, 1973)

Burger, C., *Schöpfung und Versöhnung. Studien zum liturgischen Gut im Kolosser- und Epheserbrief* (WMANT 46; Neukirchen: Neukirchener, 1975)

Burney, C. F., "Christ as the APXH of Creation (Prov. 8:22, Col. 1:15-18, Rev. 3:14)," *JTS* 27 (1926) 160-77

Cannon, G. E., *The Use of Traditional Materials in Colossians* (Macon: Mercer University, 1983)

Carr, W., *Angels and Principalities* (SNTSMS 42; Cambridge: Cambridge University, 1981)

―――, "Two Notes on Colossians," *JTS* 24 (1973) 492-500

Carrez, M., "Souffrance et gloire dans les épîtres pauliniennes. Contribution à l'exégèse de Col. 1:24-27," *RHPR* 31 (1951) 343-53

Casey, P. M., *From Jewish Prophet to Gentile God: The Origins and Development of New Testament Christology* (Cambridge: James Clarke/Louisville: Westminster, 1991)

Cerfaux, L., *Christ in the Theology of St. Paul* (New York: Herder/London: Nelson, 1959)

————, *The Christian in the Theology of St. Paul* (London: Chapman, 1967)

————, *The Church in the Theology of St. Paul* (New York: Herder/London: Nelson, 1959)

————, "L'influence des 'mystères' sur les épîtres de S. Paul aux Colossiens et aux Éphésiens," in *Recueil Lucien Cerfaux: Études d'Exégèse et d'Histoire Religieuse,* vol. III (Gembloux: Duculot, 1962) 279-85

Coutts, J., "The Relationship of Ephesians and Colossians," *NTS* 4 (1957-58) 201-7

Craddock, F. B., " 'All Things in Him': A Critical Note on Col. 1:15-20," *NTS* 12 (1965-66) 78-80

Crouch, J. E., *The Origin and Intention of the Colossian Haustafel* (Göttingen: Vandenhoeck, 1972)

Daviau, P. T., "Une Lecture des Figures de l'Acteur Dieu dans *Colossiens*," *LTP* 48 (1992) 7-18

Davies, W. D., *Paul and Rabbinic Judaism: Some Rabbinic Elements in Pauline Theology* (Philadelphia: Fortress, [4]1980)

Deichgräber, R., *Gotteshymnus und Christushymnus in der frühen Christenheit. Untersuchungen zu Form, Sprache und Stil der frühchristlicher Hymnen* (SUNT 5; Göttingen: Vandenhoeck, 1967)

DeMaris, R. E., *The Colossian Controversy: Wisdom in Dispute at Colossae* (JSNTS 96; Sheffield: JSOT, 1994)

Dibelius, M., "The Isis Initiation in Apuleius and Related Initiatory Rites," in Francis and Meeks, *Conflict* 61-121

Doty, W. G., *Letters in Primitive Christianity* (Philadelphia: Fortress, 1973)

Duncan, G. S., *St. Paul's Ephesian Ministry* (London: Hodder, 1929)

Dunn, J. D. G., *Baptism in the Holy Spirit* (London: SCM/Philadelphia: Westminster, 1970)

————, "The 'Body' in Colossians," in *To Tell the Mystery: Essays on New Testament Eschatology,* R. H. Gundry FS, ed. T. E. Schmidt and M. Silva (JSNTS 100; Sheffield: JSOT, 1994) 163-81

————, *Christology in the Making* (London: SCM/Philadelphia: TPI, [2]1989)

————, *Galatians* (BNTC; London: A. and C. Black/Peabody: Hendrickson, 1993)

————, *Jesus and the Spirit* (London: SCM/Philadelphia: Westminster, 1975)

————, "Once More *PISTIS CHRISTOU*," *Society of Biblical Literature 1991 Seminar Papers* (Atlanta: Scholars, 1991) 730-44

————, *The Partings of the Ways between Christianity and Judaism* (London: SCM/Philadelphia: TPI, 1991)

————, *Romans* (WBC 38; Dallas: Word, 1988)

————, *Unity and Diversity in the New Testament* (London: SCM/Philadelphia: TPI, [2]1990)

Dupont, J., *Gnosis. La connaissance religieuse dans les épîtres de saint Paul* (Louvain: Nauwelaerts/Paris: Gabalda, 1949)

Easton, B. S., "New Testament Ethical Lists," *JBL* 51 (1932) 1-12

Eckart, K.-G., "Exegetische Beobachtungen zu Kol. 1:9-20," *ThViat* 7 (1959) 87-106

————, "Urchristliche Tauf- und Ordinationsliturgie (Col. 1:9-20; Act. 26:18)," *ThViat* 8 (1960) 23-37

Eitrem, S., "EMBATEYΩ. Note sur Col. 2:18," *StTh* 2 (1949-50) 90-94

Ellis, E. E., *Pauline Theology: Ministry and Society* (Grand Rapids: Eerdmans/Exeter: Paternoster, 1989)

————, *Prophecy and Hermeneutic in Early Christianity* (WUNT 18; Tübingen: Mohr/Grand Rapids: Eerdmans, 1978)

Eltester, F.-W., *Eikon im Neuen Testament* (BZNW 23; Berlin: Töpelmann, 1958)

Ernst, J., "Kolosserbrief," *TRE* 19, 370-76

————, *Pleroma und Pleroma Christi. Geschichte und Deutung eines Begriffs der paulinischen Antilegomena* (BU 5; Regensburg: Pustet, 1970)

Evans, C. A., "The Colossian Mystics," *Bib* 63 (1982) 188-205

————, "The Meaning of πλήρωμα in Nag Hammadi," *Bib* 65 (1984) 259-65

Fee, G. D., *God's Empowering Presence: The Holy Spirit in the Letters of Paul* (Peabody: Hendrickson, 1994)

Feuillet, A., *Le Christ sagesse de Dieu d'après les épîtres Pauliniennes* (ÉB; Paris: Gabalda, 1966)

————, "Le Création de l'univers 'dans le Christ' d'après l'Épître aux Colossiens (1:16a)," *NTS* 12 (1965-66) 1-19

Fiedler, P., "Haustafel," *RAC* 13 (1986) 1063-73

Findeis, H.-J., *Versöhnung — Apostolat — Kirche: Eine exegetisch- theologische und rezeptionsgeschichtliche Studie zu den Versöhnungsaussagen des Neuen Testaments (2 Kor, Röm, Kol, Eph)* (Würzburg: Echter, 1983)

Fiorenza, E. S., "Wisdom Mythology and the Christological Hymns of the New Testament," in *Aspects of Wisdom in Judaism and Early Christianity,* ed. R. L. Wilken (Notre Dame: University of Notre Dame, 1975) 17-41

Flemington, W. F., "On the Interpretation of Colossians 1:24," in *Suffering and Martyrdom in the New Testament,* ed. W. Horbury and B. McNeil (Cambridge: Cambridge University, 1981) 84-90

Foerster, W., "Die Irrlehrer des Kolosserbriefes," in *Studia Biblica et Semitica,* T. C. Vriezen FS (Wageningen: Veenman, 1966) 71-80

Fossum, J., "Colossians 1:15-18a in the Light of Jewish Mysticism and Gnosticism," *NTS* 35 (1989) 183-201

Fowl, S. E., *The Story of Jesus in the Ethics of Paul: An Analysis of the Function of the Hymnic Material in the Pauline Corpus* (JSNTS 36; Sheffield: JSOT, 1990)

Francis, F. O., "The Background of EMBATEUEIN (Col. 2:18) in Legal Papyri and Oracle Inscriptions," in Francis and Meeks, *Conflict* 197-207

————, "The Christological Argument of Colossians," in *God's Christ and His People,* N. A. Dahl FS (Oslo: Universitetsforlaget, 1977) 192-208

————, "Humility and Angel Worship in Colossae," in Francis and Meeks, *Conflict* 163-95

Francis, F. O. and Meeks, W. A., *Conflict at Colossae* (Missoula: Scholars, 1973)

Gabathuler, H. J., *Jesus Christus. Haupt der Kirche — Haupt der Welt. Der Christushym-*

nus Colosser 1:15-20 in der theologischen Forschung der letzten 130 Jahre (Zurich: Zwingli, 1965)

Gardner, P. D., " 'Circumcised in Baptism — Raised through Faith': A Note on Col. 2:11-12," *WTJ* 45 (1983) 172-77

Genest, O., "L'Actorialisation de Jésus dans l'Épître aux Colossiens," *LTP* 48 (1992) 19-30

Gibbs, J. G., *Creation and Redemption: A Study in Pauline Theology* (NovTSup 26; Leiden: Brill, 1971)

Gill, D. W. J. and Gempf, C., ed., *Graeco-Roman Setting*, vol. 2 of *The Book of Acts in Its First Century Setting*, ed. B. Winter, et al. (Grand Rapids: Eerdmans/Carlisle: Paternoster, 1994)

Glasson, T. F., "Col. 1:15, 18 and Sir. 24," *NovT* 11 (1969) 154-56

Gnilka, J., "Das Paulusbild im Kolosser- und Epheserbrief," in *Kontinuität und Einheit*, F. Mussner FS, ed. P. G. Müller and W. Stenger (Freiburg: Herder, 1981) 179-93

————, *Theologie des Neuen Testaments* (Freiburg: Herder, 1994)

Grant, R. M., "Les êtres intermediaires dans le judaisme tardif," *Le Origini dello Gnosticismo*, ed. U. Bianchi (Leiden: Brill, 1967) 141-54

Grässer, E., "Kol. 3:1-4 als Beispiel einer Interpretation secundum homines recipientes," *ZTK* 64 (1967) 139-68, reprinted in *Text und Situation* (Gütersloh: Gütersloher, 1973) 123-51

Gundry, R. H., *"Soma" in Biblical Theology* (SNTSMS 29; Cambridge: Cambridge University, 1976)

Gunther, J. J., *St. Paul's Opponents and Their Background* (NovTSup 35; Leiden: Brill, 1973)

Habermann, J., *Präexistenzaussagen im Neuen Testament* (Frankfurt: Peter Lang, 1990)

Hanson, A. T., "The Conquest of the Powers," in *Studies in Paul's Technique and Theology* (London: SPCK/Grand Rapids: Eerdmans, 1974) 1-12

————, "The Development of the Pauline Tradition," *The Paradox of the Cross in the Thought of St Paul* (JSNTS 17; Sheffield: JSOT, 1987) 157-82

Hanson, S., *The Unity of the Church in the New Testament: Colossians and Ephesians* (Uppsala: Almquist, 1946)

Hanssler, B., "Zu Satzkonstruktion und Aussage in Kol. 2:23," in *Wort Gottes in der Zeit*, K. H. Schelkle FS, ed. H. Feld and J. Nolte (Düsseldorf: Patmos, 1973) 143-48

Harrington, D. J., "Christians and Jews in Colossians," in *Diaspora Jews and Judaism*, A. T. Kraabel FS, ed. J. A. Overman and R. S. MacLennan (Atlanta: Scholars, 1992) 153-61

Hartman, L., "Code and Context: A Few Reflections on the Parenesis of Col. 3:6–4:1," in *Tradition and Interpretation in the New Testament*, E. E. Ellis FS, ed. G. F. Hawthorne and O. Betz (Grand Rapids: Eerdmans, 1987) 237-47

————, "Some Unorthodox Thoughts on the 'Household-Code Form'," in *The Social World of Formative Christianity and Judaism*, H. C. Kee FS, ed. J. Neusner, et al. (Philadelphia: Fortress, 1988) 219-34

————, "Universal Reconciliation (Col. 1:20)," *SNTU* 10 (1985) 109-21

Hegermann, H., *Die Vorstellung vom Schöpfungsmittler im hellenistischen Judentum und Urchristentum* (TU 82; Berlin: Akademie, 1961)

Helyer, L. R., "Colossians 1:15-20: Pre-Pauline or Pauline?" *JETS* 26 (1983) 167-79

Hengel, M., "Hymns and Christology," in *Between Jesus and Paul* (London: SCM/Philadelphia: Fortress, 1983) 78-96

Hemer, C. J., *The Letters to the Seven Churches of Asia in Their Local Setting* (JSNTS 11; Sheffield: JSOT, 1986) 178-82

Hinson, E. G., "The Christian Household in Colossians 3:18–4:1," *RevExp* 70 (1973) 495-506

Hockel, A., *Christus der Erstgeborene. Zur Geschichte der Exegese von Kol. 1:15* (Düsseldorf: Patmos, 1965)

Hollenbach, B., "Col. 2:23: Which Things Lead to the Fulfilment of the Flesh," *NTS* 25 (1978-79) 254-61

Hooker, M. D., "Were There False Teachers in Colossae?" in *Christ and Spirit in the New Testament*, C. F. D. Moule FS, ed. B. Lindars and S. S. Smalley (Cambridge: Cambridge University, 1973) 315-31, reprinted in *From Adam to Christ: Essays on Paul* (Cambridge: Cambridge University, 1990) 121-36

Hoppe, R., "Theo-logie in den Deuteropaulinen (Kolosser- und Epheserbrief)," in *Monotheismus und Christologie: Zur Gottesfrage im hellenistischen Judentum und im Urchristentutm*, ed. H.-J. Klauck (QD 138; Freiburg: Herder, 1992) 163-85

Hübner, H., *Biblische Theologie des Neuen Testaments: Band 2. Die Theologie des Paulus* (Göttingen: Vandenhoeck, 1993)

Hunt, J. P. W., "Colossians 2:11-12, the Circumcision/Baptism Analogy and Infant Baptism," *TynB* 41 (1990) 227-44

Hunter, A. M., *Paul and His Predecessors* (London: SCM, [2]1961)

Hurtado, L. W., *One God, One Lord: Early Christian Devotion and Ancient Jewish Monotheism* (Philadelphia: Fortress, 1988)

Jervell, J., *Imago Dei: Gen. 1:26f. im Spätjudentum, in der Gnosis und in den paulinischen Briefen* (FRLANT 76; Göttingen: Vandenhoeck, 1960).

Johnson, S. E., "Laodicea and Its Neighbors," *Biblical Archaeologist* 13 (1950) 1-18

Juel, D., *Messianic Exegesis: Christological Interpretation of the Old Testament in Early Christianity* (Philadelphia: Fortress, 1988)

Kamlah, E., "Ὑποτάσσεσθαι in den neutestamentlichen Haustafeln," in *Verborum Veritas*, G. Stählin FS, ed. O. Bocher and K. Haacker (Wuppertal: Brockhaus, 1970) 237-43

——, "Wie beurteilt Paulus sein Leiden? Ein Beitrag zur Untersuchung seiner Denkstruktur," *ZNW* 54 (1963) 217-32

Käsemann, E., "Kolosserbrief," *RGG*[3] 3.1727-28

——, "A Primitive Christian Baptismal Liturgy," in *Essays on New Testament Themes* (London: SCM, 1964) 149-68

Kehl, N., *Der Christushymnus im Kolosserbrief: Eine motivgeschichtliche Untersuchung zu Kol. 1:12-20* (SBM 1; Stuttgart: Katholisches Bibelwerk, 1967)

——, "Erniedrigung und Erhöhung in Qumran und Kolossä," *ZKT* 91 (1969) 364-94

Kertelge, K., ed., *Paulus in den neutestamentlichen Spätschriften* (QD 89; Freiburg: Herder, 1981)

Kiley, M., *Colossians as Pseudepigraphy* (Sheffield: JSOT, 1986)

Kippenberg, H. G., "Ein Vergleich jüdischer, christlicher und gnostischer Apokalyptik," in *Apocalypticism in the Mediterranean World and the Near East,* ed. D. Hellholm (Tübingen: Mohr, 1983) 751-68

Klauck, H.-J., *Hausgemeinde und Hauskirche im frühen Christentum* (SBS 103; Stuttgart: KBW, 1981)

Knox, J., *Philemon among the Letters of Paul* (Nashville: Abingdon, 1959/London: Collins, 1960)

————, "Philemon and the Authenticity of Colossians," *JR* 18 (1938) 144-60

Knox, W. L., *St Paul and the Church of the Gentiles* (Cambridge: Cambridge University, 1939)

Kraabel, A. T., "Paganism and Judaism: The Sardis Evidence," in *Paganisme, Judaïsme, Christianisme: Influences et affrontements dans le monde antique,* M. Simon FS (Paris: Boccard, 1978) 13-33, reprinted in *Diaspora Jews and Judaism,* A. T. Kraabel FS, ed. J. A. Overman and R. S. MacLennan (Atlanta: Scholars, 1992) 237-55

Kramer, W., *Christ, Lord, Son of God* (London: SCM, 1966)

Kremer, J., *Was an den Leiden Christi noch mangelt. Eine interpretations-geschichtliche und exegetische Untersuchung zu Kol. 1:24b* (BBB 12; Bonn: Hanstein, 1956)

Kümmel, W. G., *Introduction to the New Testament* (London: SCM/Nashville: Abingdon, [2]1975)

Kuschel, K.-J., *Born before All Time? The Dispute over Christ's Origin* (London: SCM, 1992)

Ladd, G. E., "Paul's Friends in Colossians 4:7-16," *RevExp* 70 (1973) 507-14

Lähnemann, J., *Der Kolosserbrief. Komposition, Situation und Argumentation* (SNT 3; Gütersloh: Gütersloher, 1971)

Lamarche, P., "Structure de l'épître aux Colossiens," *Bib* 56 (1975) 453-63

Langkammer, H., "Die Einwohnung der 'absoluten Seinsfülle' in Christus. Bemerkungen zu Kol. 1:19," *BZ* 12 (1968) 258-63

Larsson, E., *Christus als Vorbild. Eine Untersuchung zu den paulinischen Tauf- und Eikontexten* (Uppsala: Gleerup, 1962)

Legaré, C., "Figural et Figuratif dans l'*Épître aux Colossiens*," *LTP* 48 (1992) 31-42

Levison, J. R., "*2 Apoc. Bar.* 48:42–52:7 and the Apocalyptic Dimension of Colossians 3:1-6," *JBL* 108 (1989) 93-108

Lincoln, A. T., *Ephesians* (WBC 42; Dallas: Word, 1990)

————, *Paradise Now and Not Yet* (SNTSMS 43; Cambridge: Cambridge University, 1981)

Lindemann, A., "Die Gemeinde von 'Kolossä.' Erwägungen zum 'Sitz im Leben' eines deuteropaulinischen Briefes," *WD* 16 (1981) 111-34

————, *Paulus im ältesten Christentum* (Tübingen: Mohr, 1979)

Lohse, E., "Christologie und Ethik im Kolosserbrief," in *Apophoreta,* E. Haenchen FS (BZNW 30; Berlin: Töpelmann, 1964) 157-68, reprinted in *Einheit* 249-61

————, "Christusherrschaft und Kirche im Kolosserbrief," *NTS* 11 (1964-65) 203-16, reprinted in *Einheit* 262-75

————, *Die Einheit des Neuen Testaments. Exegetische Studien zur Theologie des Neuen Testaments* (Göttingen: Vandenhoeck, 1973)

————, "Ein hymnisches Bekenntnis in Kolosser 2:13c-15," *Einheit* 276-84

————, "Die Mitarbeiter des Apostels Paulus im Kolosserbrief," in *Verborum Veritas, G. Stählin FS*, ed. O. Bocher and K. Haacker (Wuppertal: Brockhaus, 1970) 189-94

————, "Pauline Theology in the Letter to the Colossians," *NTS* 15 (1968-69) 211-20

————, *Theological Ethics in the New Testament* (Minneapolis: Fortress, 1991)

Lona, H. E., *Die Eschatologie im Kolosser- und Epheserbrief* (Würzburg: Echter, 1984)

Löwe, H., "Bekenntnis, Apostelamt und Kirche im Kolosserbrief," in *Kirche, G. Bornkamm FS*, ed. D. Lührmann and G. Strecker (Tübingen: Mohr, 1980) 299-314

Lührmann, D., "Neutestamentliche Haustafeln und antike Ökonomie," *NTS* 27 (1980-81) 83-97

————, *Das Offenbarungsverständnis bei Paulus und in paulinischen Gemeinden* (WMANT 16; Neukirchen: Neukirchener, 1965)

————, "Wo man nicht mehr Sklave oder Freier ist. Überlegungen zur Struktur frühchristlicher Gemeinden," *WD* 13 (1975) 53-83

Lyonnet, S., "L'Épître aux Colossiens (Col. 2:18) et les mystères d'Apollon Clarien," *Bib* 43 (1962) 417-35

————, "Paul's Adversaries in Colossae," in Francis and Meeks, *Conflict* 147-61

————, "St. Paul et le gnosticisme: la lettre aux Colossiens," in *Le Origini dello Gnosticismo*, ed. U. Bianchi (Leiden: Brill, 1967) 538-50

MacDonald, M., *The Pauline Churches: A Socio-Historical Study of Institutionalization in the Pauline and Deutero-Pauline Writings* (SNTSMS 60; Cambridge: Cambridge University, 1988)

Mach, M., *Entwicklungsstudien des jüdischen Engelglaubens in vorrabbinischer Zeit* (Tübingen: Mohr, 1992)

Manns, F., "Col. 1:15-20: Midrash chrétien de Gen. 1:1," *RevSR* 53 (1979) 100-110

Marshall, I. H., "The Meaning of 'Reconciliation'," in *Unity and Diversity in New Testament Theology, G. E. Ladd FS*, ed. R. A. Guelich (Grand Rapids: Eerdmans, 1978) 117-32, reprinted in *Jesus the Saviour: Studies in New Testament Theology* (London: SPCK, 1990) 258-74

Martin, D. B., *Slavery as Salvation: The Metaphor of Slavery in Pauline Christianity* (New Haven: Yale University, 1990)

Martin, R. P., *Colossians: The Church's Lord and the Christian's Liberty* (Exeter: Paternoster, 1972)

————, "An Early Christian Hymn (Col. 1:15-20)," *EvQ* 36 (1964) 195-205

————, "Hymns in the New Testament: An Evolving Pattern of Worship Responses," *Ex Auditu* 8 (1992) 33-44

————, *Reconciliation: A Study of Paul's Theology* (Atlanta: John Knox, 1981)

————, "Reconciliation and Forgiveness in the Letter to the Colossians," in *Reconciliation and Hope, L. L. Morris FS*, ed. R. J. Banks (Exeter: Paternoster/Grand Rapids: Eerdmans, 1974) 104-24

————, "Some Reflections on New Testament Hymns," in *Christ the Lord,* ed. H. H. Rowdon (Leicester: Inter-Varsity, 1982) 37-49

Marxsen, W., *"Christliche" und christliche Ethik im Neuen Testament* (Gütersloh: Gütersloher, 1989) = *New Testament Foundations for Christian Ethics* (Minneapolis: Fortress, 1993)

Maurer, C., "Die Begründung der Herrschaft Christi über die Mächte nach Kolosser 1:15-20," *WD* 4 (1955) 72-93 *

McCarthy, J., "Le Christ cosmique at l'âge de l'écologie. Une lecture de Col. 1:15-20," *NRT* 116 (1994) 27-47

Meeks, W. A., *The First Urban Christians: The Social World of the Apostle Paul* (New Haven: Yale University, 1983)

————, "In One Body: The Unity of Humankind in Colossians and Ephesians," in *God's Christ and His People,* N. A. Dahl FS, ed. J. Jervell and W. Meeks (Oslo: Universitetsforlaget, 1977) 209-21

Merk, O., *Handeln aus Glauben. Die Motivierungen der paulinischen Ethik* (Marburg: Elwert, 1968)

Merklein, H., "Paulinische Theologie in der Rezeption des Kolosser- und Epheserbriefes," in *Paulus in den neutestamentlichen Spätschriften,* ed. K. Kertelge (QD 89; Freiburg: Herder, 1981) 25-69

Michaud, J.-P., "L'Ombre des *Autorités* et des *Pouvoirs.* La dimension polémique de l'*Épître aux Colossiens,"* LTP* 48 (1992) 43-52

Michl, J., "Die 'Versöhnung' (Kol. 1:20)," *TQ* 128 (1948) 442-62

Milot, L., Rivard, R., and Thériault, J.-Y., "Défi à la Lecture. Souffrances et Soumissions en *Colossiens,"* LTP* 48 (1992) 65-79

Mitchell, S., *Anatolia: Land, Men, and Gods in Asia Minor,* 2 vols. (Oxford: Clarendon, 1993)

Moir, I. A., "Some Thoughts on Col. 2:17-18," *TZ* 35 (1979) 363-65

Moore, G. F., *Judaism in the First Three Centuries of the Christian Era: The Age of the Tannaim,* 3 vols. (Cambridge, MA: Harvard, 1927-30)

Morray-Jones, C. R. A., "Paradise Revisited (2 Cor. 12:1-12): The Jewish Mystical Background of Paul's Apostolate," *HTR* 86 (1993) 177-217, 265-92

————, "Transformational Mysticism in the Apocalyptic-Merkabah Tradition," *JJS* 43 (1992) 1-31

Moule, C. F. D., " 'The New Life' in Colossians 3:1-17," *RevExp* 70 (1973) 481-93

Müller, K., "Die Haustafel des Kolosserbriefes und das antike Frauenthema. Eine kritische Rückschau auf alte Ergebnisse," in *Die Frau im Urchristentutm,* ed. G. Dautzenberg, et al. (QD 95; Freiburg: Herder, 1983) 263-319

Mullins, T. Y., "The Thanksgivings of Philemon and Colossians," *NTS* 30 (1984) 288-93

Munck, J., *Paul and the Salvation of Mankind* (London: SCM/Atlanta: John Knox, 1959)

Münderlein, G., "Die Erwählung durch das Pleroma. Bemerkungen zu Kol. 1:19," *NTS* 8 (1961-62) 264-76

Munro, W., "Col. 3:18–4:1 and Eph. 5:21–6:9: Evidences of a Late Literary Stratum?" *NTS* 18 (1971-72) 434-47

Nielsen, C. M., "The Status of Paul and His Letters in Colossians," *Perspectives in Religious Studies* 12 (1985) 103-22

Norden, E., *Agnostos Theos. Untersuchungen zur Formengeschichte religiöser Rede* (Berlin/Leipzig: Teubner, 1913, 1923)

O'Brien, P. T., *Introductory Thanksgivings in the Letters of Paul* (NovTSup 49; Leiden: Brill, 1977)
Ollrog, W.-H., *Paulus und seine Mitarbeiter* (WMANT 50; Neukirchen: Neukirchener, 1979)
O'Neill, J. C., "The Source of the Christology in Colossians," *NTS* 26 (1979-80) 87-100
Overfield, P. D., "Pleroma: A Study in Content and Context," *NTS* 25 (1978-79) 384-96

Percy, E., *Der Leib Christi in den paulinischen Homologumena und Antilegomena* (Lund: Gleerup, 1942)
————, *Die Probleme der Kolosser- und Epheserbriefe* (Lund: Gleerup, 1946)
Pierre, J., "Totalité et Plénitude: Une Stratégie de saturation de l'espace et du temps dans *l'Épître aux Colossiens*," *LTP* 48 (1992) 53-63
Pöhlmann, W., "Die hymnischen All-Prädikationen in Kol. 1:15-20," *ZNW* 64 (1973) 53-74
Polhill, J. B., "The Relationship between Ephesians and Colossians," *RevExp* 70 (1973) 439-50
Pollard, T. E., "Col. 1:12-20: A Reconsideration," *NTS* 27 (1980-81) 572-75
Porter, S. E., "P.Oxy. 744.4 and Colossians 3:9," *Bib* 73 (1992) 565-67

Ramsay, W. M., *Cities and Bishoprics of Phrygia*, I-II (Oxford: Oxford University, 1895-97)
Rapske, B., *The Book of Acts and Paul in Roman Custody*, vol. 3 of *The Book of Acts in Its First Century Setting*, ed. B. Winter, et al. (Grand Rapids: Eerdmans/Carlisle: Paternoster, 1994)
Reicke, B., "Caesarea, Rome and the Captivity Epistles," in *Apostolic History and the Gospel*, F. F. Bruce FS, ed. W. W. Gasque and R. P. Martin (Exeter: Paternoster/Grand Rapids: Eerdmans, 1970) 277-86
————, "The Historical Setting of Colossians," *RevExp* 70 (1973) 429-38
————, "Zum sprachlichen Verständnis von Kol. 2:23," *StTh* 6 (1953) 39-53
Richards, E. R., *The Secretary in the Letters of Paul* (WUNT 2.42; Tübingen: Mohr, 1991)
Robertson, A. T., *Paul and the Intellectuals* (Garden City, NY: Doubleday, 1928), revised by W. C. Strickland (Nashville: Broadman, 1956)
Robinson, J. M., "A Formal Analysis of Colossians 1:15-20," *JBL* 76 (1957) 270-87
Roloff, J., *Die Kirche im Neuen Testament* (NTD; Göttingen: Vandenhoeck, 1993)
Rowland, C., "Apocalyptic Visions and the Exaltation of Christ in the Letter to the Colossians," *JSNT* 19 (1983) 78-83
————, *The Open Heaven* (London: SPCK, 1982)

Sanders, E. P., "Literary Dependence in Colossians," *JBL* 85 (1966) 28-45
————, *Paul and Palestinian Judaism* (London: SCM, 1977)
Sanders, J. T., *Ethics in the New Testament* (Philadelphia: Fortress/London: SCM, 1975)

————, *The New Testament Christological Hymns: Their Historical Religious Background* (SNTSMS 15; Cambridge: Cambridge University, 1971)

————, *Schismatics, Sectarians, Dissidents, Deviants: The First One Hundred Years of Jewish-Christian Relations* (London: SCM, 1993)

Sappington, T. J., *Revelation and Redemption at Colossae* (JSNTS 53; Sheffield: JSOT, 1991)

Saunders, E. W., "The Colossian Heresy and Qumran Theology," in *Studies in the History and the Text of the New Testament, K. W. Clark FS*, ed. B. L. Daniels and M. J. Suggs (Salt Lake City: University of Utah, 1967) 133-45

Schenk, W., "Christus, das Geheimnis der Welt, als dogmatisches und ethisches Grundprinzip des Kolosserbriefes," *EvTh* 43 (1983) 138-55

————, "Der Kolosserbrief in der neueren Forschung (1945-1985)," *ANRW* 2.25.4 (1987) 3327-64

Schenke, H. M., "Die neutestamentliche Christologie und der gnostische Erlöser," in *Gnosis und Neues Testament,* ed. K.-W. Tröger (Gütersloh: Gütersloher, 1973) 205-29

————, "Der Widerstreit gnostischer und christlicher Christologie im Spiegel des Kolosserbriefes," *ZTK* 61 (1964) 391-403

Schmithals, W., "Corpus Paulinum und Gnosis," in *The New Testament and Gnosis, R. McL. Wilson FS* (Edinburgh: Clark, 1983) 107-24

Schnackenburg, R., "Die Aufnahme des Christushymnus durch den Verfasser des Kolosserbriefes," *EKKNT Vorarbeiten 1* (Neukirchen: Neukirchener, 1969) 33-50

————, *Baptism in the Thought of St. Paul: A Study in Pauline Theology* (New York: Herder, 1964)

————, *Die sittliche Botschaft des Neuen Testaments. Band 2: Die urchristlichen Verkündiger* (Freiburg: Herder, 1988)

Schneider, G., "Präexistenz Christi: Der Ursprung einer neutestamentlichen Vorstellung und das Problem ihrer Auslegung," in *Neues Testament und Kirche, R. Schnackenburg FS*, ed. J. Gnilka (Freiburg: Herder, 1974) 399-412

Scholem, G. G., *Jewish Gnosticism, Merkabah Mysticism and Talmudic Tradition* (New York: Jewish Theological Seminary of America, 1960)

Schrage, W., *The Ethics of the New Testament* (Philadelphia: Fortress/Edinburgh: Clark, 1988)

————, "Zur Ethik der neutestamentlichen Haustafeln," *NTS* 21 (1974-75) 1-22

Schubert, P., *Form and Function of the Pauline Thanksgivings* (BZNW 20; Berlin: Töpelmann, 1939)

Schulz, S., *Neutestamentliche Ethik* (Zurich: Theologischer, 1987)

Schürer, E. *The History of the Jewish People in the Age of Jesus Christ,* rev. and ed. G. Vermes, F. Millar, et al. (4 vols.; Edinburgh: Clark, 1973-87)

Schweizer, E., *Beiträge zur Theologie des Neuen Testaments* (Zurich: Zwingli, 1970)

————, "Christ in the Letter to the Colossians," *RevExp* 70 (1973) 451-67

————, "Christianity of the Circumcised and Judaism of the Uncircumcised: The Background of Matthew and Colossians," in *Jews, Greeks and Christians, W. D. Davies FS*, ed. R. Hamerton-Kelly and R. Scroggs (Leiden: Brill, 1976) 245-60

————, "Christus und Geist im Kolosserbrief," in *Christ and Spirit in the New Testament,*

C. F. D. Moule FS, ed. B. Lindars and S. S. Smalley (Cambridge: Cambridge University, 1973) 297-313, reprinted in *Neues Testament* 179-93

————, "Die 'Elemente der Welt.' Gal. 4:3, 9; Kol. 2:8, 20," in *Verborum Veritas*. G. Stählin FS, ed. O. Böcher and K. Haacker (Wuppertal: Brockhaus, 1970) 245-59, reprinted in *Beiträge* 147-63

————, "Die Kirche als Leib Christi in den paulinischen Antilegomena," *Neotestamentica* (Zurich: Zwingli, 1963) 293-316

————, "Kolosser 1:15-20," *Beiträge* 113-45

————, "Der Kolosserbrief — weder paulinisch noch nach-paulinisch," *Neues Testament* 150-63

————, "Zur neueren Forschung am Kolosserbrief (seit 1970)," *Neues Testament* 122-49

————, *Neues Testament und Christologie im Werden. Aufsätze* (Göttingen: Vandenhoeck, 1982)

————, "Slaves of the Elements and Worshippers of Angels: Gal. 4:3, 9 and Col. 2:8, 18, 20," *JBL* 107 (1988) 455-68

————, "Traditional Ethical Patterns in the Pauline and Post-Pauline Letters and Their Development (Lists of Vices and House-Tables)," in *Text and Interpretation,* M. Black FS, ed. E. Best and R. McL. Wilson (Cambridge: Cambridge University, 1979) 195-209

————, "Versöhnung des Alls. Kol. 1:20," in *Jesus Christus in Historie und Theologie,* H. Conzelmann FS, ed. G. Strecker (Tübingen: Mohr, 1975) 487-501, reprinted in *Neues Testament* 164-78

————, "Die Weltlichkeit des Neuen Testamentes: die Haustafeln," in *Neues Testament* 194-210

Scroggs, R., *The Last Adam: A Study in Pauline Anthropology* (Oxford: Blackwell, 1966)

Segal, A. F., *Paul the Convert: The Apostolate and Apostasy of Saul the Pharisee* (New Haven: Yale University, 1990)

Sheppard, A. R. R., "Pagan Cults of Angels in Roman Asia Minor," *Talanta* 12-13 (1980-81) 77-101

Stegemann, E., "Alt und Neu bei Paulus und in den Deuteropaulinen (Kol-Eph)," *EvTh* 37 (1977) 508-36

Steinmetz, F. J., *Protologische Heilszuversicht. Die Strukturen des soteriologischen und christologischen Denkens im Kolosser- und Epheserbrief* (Frankfurt: Knecht, 1969)

Stewart, J. S., "A First-Century Heresy and Its Modern Counterpart," *SJT* 23 (1970) 420-36

Suhl, A., *Paulus und seine Briefe. Ein Beitrag zur paulinischen Chronologie* (SNT 11; Gütersloh: Gütersloher, 1975)

Sumney, J., "Those Who 'Pass Judgment': The Identity of the Opponents in Colossians," *Bib* 74 (1993) 366-88

Tachau, P., *"Einst" und "Jetzt" im Neuen Testament* (FRLANT 105; Göttingen: Vandenhoeck, 1972)

Tannehill, R. C., *Dying and Rising with Christ: A Study in Pauline Theology* (BZNW 32; Berlin: Töpelmann, 1966)

Thraede, K., "Zum historischen Hintergrund der 'Haustafeln' des NT," in *Pietas*, B. Kötting FS, ed. E. Dassmann and K. S. Frank (Münster: Aschendorff, 1980) 359-68

Trebilco, P., *Jewish Communities in Asia Minor* (SNTSMS 69; Cambridge: Cambridge University, 1991)

Trudinger, L. P., "A Further Note on Colossians 1:24," *EvQ* 45 (1973) 36-38

Turner, N., *Grammatical Insights into the New Testament* (Edinburgh: Clark, 1965)

van der Horst, P. W., "Observations on a Pauline Expression," *NTS* 19 (1972-73) 181-87

Vawter, B., "The Colossians Hymn and the Principle of Redaction," *CBQ* 33 (1971) 62-81

Verner, D. C., *The Household of God: The Social World of the Pastoral Epistles* (SBLDS 71; Chico: Scholars, 1983)

Vogtle, A., *Das Neue Testament und die Zukunft des Kosmos* (Düsseldorf: Patmos, 1970)

Walter, N., "Die 'Handschrift in Satzungen' Kol. 2:14," *ZNW* 70 (1979) 115-18

Wedderburn, A. J. M., *Baptism and Resurrection: Studies in Pauline Theology against Its Graeco-Roman Background* (WUNT 44; Tübingen: Mohr, 1987)

———— in *idem* and Lincoln, A. T., *The Theology of the Later Pauline Letters* (Cambridge: Cambridge University, 1993)

Wegenast, K., *Das Verständnis der Tradition bei Paulus und in den Deuteropaulinen* (WMANT 8; Neukirchen: Neukirchener, 1962)

Weima, J. A. D., *Neglected Endings: The Significance of the Pauline Letter Closings* (JSNTS 101; Sheffield: JSOT, 1994)

Weiss, H., "The Law in the Epistle to the Colossians," *CBQ* 34 (1972) 294-314

Weiss, H.-F., "Gnostische Motive und antignostische Polemik im Kolosser- und im Epheserbrief," in *Gnosis und Neues Testament*, ed. K. W. Tröger (Gütersloh: Gütersloher, 1973) 311-24

————, "Taufe und neues Leben im deuteropaulinischen Schrifttum," in *Taufe und neue Existenz*, ed. E. Schott (Berlin: Evangelische, 1973) 53-70

————, *Untersuchungen zur Kosmologie des hellenistischen und palästinischen Judentums* (TU 97; Berlin: Akademie, 1966)

Wengst, K., *Christologische Formeln und Lieder des Urchristentums* (SUNT 7; Gütersloh: Gütersloher, 1972)

————, "Versöhnung und Befreiung. Ein Aspekt des Themas 'Schuld und Vergebung' im Lichte des Kolosserbriefes," *EvTh* 36 (1976) 14-26

Wessels, G. F., "The Eschatology of Colossians and Ephesians," *Neot* 21 (1987) 183-202

Williams, A. L., "The Cult of the Angels at Colossae," *JTS* 10 (1909) 413-38

Williamson, L., "Led in Triumph: Paul's Use of Thriambeuo," *Int* 22 (1968) 317-22

Wink, W., "The Hymn of the Cosmic Christ," in *The Conversation Continues: Studies in Paul and John*, J. L. Martyn FS, ed. R. T. Fortna and B. R. Gaventa (Nashville: Abingdon, 1990) 235-45

————, *Naming the Powers* (Philadelphia: Fortress, 1984)

Wischmeyer, O., "Das Adjective ΑΓΑΠΗΤΟΣ in den paulinischen Briefen. Eine traditionsgeschichtliche Miszelle," *NTS* 32 (1986) 476-80

Wright, N. T., "Poetry and Theology in Colossians 1:15-20," *NTS* 36 (1990) 444-68, substantially reprinted in *The Climax of the Covenant: Christ and the Law in Pauline Theology* (Edinburgh: Clark, 1991) 99-119

Yamauchi, E. M., *New Testament Cities in Western Asia Minor* (Grand Rapids: Baker, 1980)

————, "Sectarian Parallels: Qumran and Colossae," *BibSac* 121 (1964) 141-52

Yates, R., "Christ and the Powers of Evil in Colossians," *JSNT* 3 (1980) 461-68

————, "Col. 2:14: Metaphor of Forgiveness," *Bib* 71 (1990) 249-59

————, "Col. 2:15: Christ Triumphant," *NTS* 37 (1991) 573-91

————, "Colossians and Gnosis," *JSNT* 27 (1986) 49-68

————, "A Note on Colossians 1:24," *EvQ* 42 (1970) 88-92

————, "A Reappraisal of Colossians," *ITQ* 58 (1992) 95-117

————, "The Worship of Angels (Col. 2:18)," *ExpT* 97 (1985-86) 12-15

Zeilinger, F., *Der Erstgeborene der Schöpfung. Untersuchungen zur Formalstruktur und Theologie des Kolosserbriefes* (Vienna: Herder, 1974)

————, "Die Träger der apostolischen Tradition im Kolosserbrief," in *Jesus in der Verkündigung der Kirche,* ed. A. Fuchs (Freistadt: Plöchl, 1976) 175-90

INTRODUCTION

THE SIGNIFICANCE OF THE LETTER

Colossians could fairly be described as the most intriguing of the Pauline letters. This is primarily because it serves as a bridge between the undisputed Paulines and those members of the Pauline corpus that are generally considered post-Pauline. That is to say, on the one hand, it is remarkably close at many points to Ephesians, whose post-Pauline authorship is a matter of substantial consensus in Pauline scholarship. Yet at the same time, particularly in its christology and ecclesiology, it is significantly less developed than Ephesians and the Pastorals. In a post-Pauline trajectory, Colossians would have to be placed very close to the beginning. On the other hand, some of its detail locates it in close proximity to Philemon, whose Pauline authorship has been little questioned in the history of Christianity. Yet at the same time, again particularly in its christology and ecclesiology, and also its parenesis, it seems to be significantly developed beyond what we find in the undisputed Paulines. In any analysis of Paul's own theology it would have to be described as expressive of the late(r) Paul (see pp. 35ff. below).[1] In other words, either way Colossians shows us how Pauline thought developed, whether in the late phase of his own career or (presumably) among his close disciples after his death. By its position within the spectrum of Pauline theology it helps explain why the theology of the post-Pauline letters developed in the way it did and helps authenticate that theology as, in a quite proper sense, "Pauline."

It is worth making this point right at the beginning of our study of the letter because it helps put in perspective the introductory questions that must now be dealt with (in the tradition of modern commentaries). If what has just been said is true, the significance of a verdict "Pauline" as against "post-Pauline," or vice versa, is considerably lessened. And, more important, the questions themselves can be considered with greater dispassion, without

---

1. Both Lohse 166 n. 18 and Pokorný 4 allude approvingly to Käsemann's "Kolosserbrief" 1728: "The dating of the epistle presents two alternatives: If genuine, then because of content and style as late as possible; if not genuine, then as early as conceivable."

19

the reader feeling that historical integrity and theological value are being set in mutually antagonistic antithesis. But before we become involved in the more contentious issues it is well for us to begin with the basic data.

COLOSSAE AND THE ESTABLISHMENT
OF CHRISTIANITY THERE

There is no dispute regarding where and to whom the letter was addressed: "to the saints in Colossae" (1:2).

Colossae was in the southern part of the Roman province of Asia, which was the southern part of western Anatolia (Anatolia = Asia Minor = modern Turkey). The sites of settlements in the hinterland behind the Aegean coastline were principally determined by the easy access into the interior afforded by the several river valleys. One of the most important of these was the river Meander. About a hundred miles upstream, one of the Meander's main tributaries, the Lycus, joins it, providing the most accessible route from the coast to the central plateau (most directly to Apamea), and so forming the main artery of east-west communication during the Greek and Roman periods (Ramsay, *Cities* 5). The fertile Lycus valley also encouraged settlement, and three cities developed in close proximity to each other: Laodicea and Hierapolis on either side of the Lycus a few miles from the junction with the Meander, six miles apart and within sight of each other across the intervening plain, and Colossae about ten miles upstream on the southern bank of the Lycus.

Four or five centuries before the time of the New Testament Colossae had been populous, large, and wealthy (Xenophon *Anabasis* 1.2.6, cited by Lightfoot 15), its wealth due both to its position on the main road from Ephesus and Sardis to the Euphrates and to its wool industry. But by the earlier years of the Roman Empire its significance had been much reduced: both the later-founded Laodicea, which flourished under Roman rule and was by this time the administrative and financial center for the region (it was also noted for its textiles and medicines; see also on 4:13), and Hierapolis, with its hot mineral spring attracting many visitors, had steadily eclipsed Colossae in importance. How much we think it had declined depends on our assessment of texts in Strabo and the elder Pliny. Strabo 12.8.13 describes Colossae as a πόλισμα, which Lightfoot 16 and Ramsay, *Cities* 209 translate as "a small town," though the term was used elsewhere of such cities as Ecbatana and Athens (LSJ), and Strabo groups it with Aphrodisias, a major city (there is, however, a gap in the preserved text that renders the interpretation problematic). And there is equivalent disagreement over the significance of Pliny, *Historia Naturalis* 5.145 — "Phrygia . . . oppida ibi celeberrima praeter jam dicta (its most famous towns besides the ones already mentioned) . . . Colossae" — since the list excludes the really important cities that Pliny has mentioned earlier (5.105-6; Ramsay, *Cities* 209). Our ability to gain a clearer perspective on these questions is seriously diminished by the fact that, surprisingly, the site of Colossae has never been excavated, unlike Laodicea and Hierapolis (see, e.g., Yamauchi, *Cities* chs. 10-12). At all events, the cities were in such close proximity that they must have shared several features in common (not just textiles), and there must have been daily movement among them (cf. Col. 4:15-16).[2]

A significant feature of the Lycus valley cities, including presumably Colossae, was the presence of a substantial Jewish minority.[3] According to Philo, Jews were very numerous in every city in Asia Minor (*Legum Allegoriae* 245: Ἰουδαῖοι καθ' ἑκάστην πόλιν εἰσὶ παμπληθεῖς Ἀσίας). In the late third century BCE Antiochus the Great had settled two thousand Jewish families in Lydia and Phrygia to help stabilize the region (Josephus, *Antiquities* 12.147-53), and in the middle of the second century a sequence of letters sent by the Roman Senate to Asia Minor in support of Jews living there indicates a sizeable Jewish population (*Antiquities* 14.185-267; 16.160-78). Certainly we know that Hierapolis had a Jewish community (a κατοικία, a "colony," *CIJ* 2.775) from its earliest days as a city (the early second century BCE; see further Hemer 183 and n. 23). The same conclusion can be drawn from the attempt of Flaccus in 62 BCE to confiscate the gold collected by Jews in Asia Minor as their part of the temple tax: we learn from Cicero's defence of Flaccus (in 59) that "a little more than twenty pounds" of gold had been seized in Laodicea (*Pro Flacco* 28.68, in *GLAJJ* §68). That could represent as many as fourteen thousand adult males (Exod. 30:13-16; Neh. 10:32-33) paying the half-shekel (= 2 drachmae).[4] Evidently Laodicea was the central point for retaining the collection, presumably for the Lycus valley at least, so that would include the Jewish population of Colossae and Hierapolis.[5] And it is possible that more

2. See further Ramsay (with a still excellent map of the Lycus valley opposite p. 1); also Johnson. For the most recent map of the Roman road system in western Asia Minor see Mitchell 1.120. All the major commentaries rehearse the above and some other details concerning the history of Colossae.

3. For what follows see Bruce, "Jews and Christians" 4-8; Schürer 3.17-36; Trebilco; Mitchell 2.31-37; L. H. Feldman, *Jew and Gentile in the Ancient World: Attitudes and Interactions from Alexander to Justinian* (Princeton: Princeton University, 1993) 69-74; DeMaris 123-25.

4. See Trebilco 13-14. Other estimates are 7,500 (C. E. Arnold, *ABD* 1.1089), 9,000 (F. F. Bruce, *ABD* 4.230), over 9,000 (Bruce, *Colossians, Philemon, Ephesians* 10), more than 10,000 (Bruce 14), and more than 11,000 (Lightfoot 20-21, but he suggests that the Roman officials might not have succeeded in confiscating the complete sum gathered in the region; Gnilka, *Kolosserbrief* 3). We should also note that the social pressure on diaspora Jews to affirm their ethnic identity and continuing loyalty to their ancestral religion would probably ensure a high rate of participation.

5. Apamea, further up-country, was another collection point, where nearly one hundred pounds of gold (!) was seized. Cicero mentions only two other collection points further north in Asia Minor, but presumably there were collection points in the coastal cities such as Ephesus and

than one year's collection was involved (Trebilco 14). But when families are included we may have to allow a total Jewish population of Colossae during this period of as many as two or three thousand. Depending on how large Colossae still was by this time, that would make the Colossian Jews a substantial and possibly influential ethnic minority (as they certainly were later in other cities of the region — see n. 33 below).

It should be noted that the collection of the temple tax implies a fairly regular communication between the cities of the Lycus valley and the land of Israel. These would no doubt be facilitated by the good system of roads (see n. 2 above), which would probably bring a steady stream of Jewish travelers through a region where there were so many Jews resident.[6] In the same connection we should note that residents of Asia and Phrygia are reported among the crowd gathered in Jerusalem on the day of Pentecost in Acts 2:9-10. A further interesting confirmation is given by the tradition reported in Eusebius (*Historia Ecclesiastica* 3.31.2-5) that Philip the apostle (he must mean evangelist, unless the two were the same) settled in Hierapolis with his virgin daughters (see, e.g., Bruce, *Colossians, Philemon, and Ephesians* 16). The importance of this will become evident as we proceed.

The church in Colossae was evidently founded by Epaphras (Col. 1:6-7). Paul himself may have passed through the city, presumably without pausing to preach, some years earlier (about 52), since, as already noted, the Lycus and Meander valleys provided a natural route from Galatia and Phrygia through the interior or upper country to Ephesus (Acts 18:23; 19:1).[7] But the more northerly valley of the Hermus is perhaps more likely (Lightfoot 24; Bruce, *Colossians, Philemon, and Ephesians* 14),[8] and anyway it is fairly clear from Col. 2:1 that Paul was personally unknown to the Lycus valley churches. In accordance with his normal strategy, it would appear, Paul had made the major coastal city of Ephesus his center of operations for two years (according to Acts 19:10), and it was probably his policy to send associate workers to evangelize the surrounding districts (cf. Acts 19:26: "throughout all Asia").[9] Since the Lycus valley cities were only about 120 miles east of

---

Smyrna and other large centers of Jewish population like Sardis (Schürer 3.19-23). It is most unlikely that Laodicea functioned as a collection point for such cities as these. But it may well have covered other smaller settlements in the central Meander valley (Mitchell 2.35 notes that Jews would not have been confined to cities) and may have included Aphrodisias in the next valley.

6. Note also the rabbinic traditions cited by Hemer 183.

7. Johnson 4-5; Reicke, "Historical Setting" 432-33, noting the support provided by 4:10: the readers knew Barnabas, leader of the gospel campaign in Pisidian Antioch.

8. D. French, "Acts and the Roman Roads of Asia Minor," in Gill and Gempf 49-58 (here 55), suggests a still more northerly route through Pontus and Bithynia (?).

9. Ollrog 41-52, 111-61. O'Brien, *Colossians, Philemon* xxviii, notes that though Paul had not visited the Colossians personally he was able to speak of his commission as "to you" (1:25) and his sufferings as "for your sake" (1:24).

Ephesus, on the major road running up the Meander and Lycus valleys, and since Epaphras was a native of Colossae (Col. 4:12), it was natural that it should be Epaphras who assumed the responsibility for spreading the gospel among his own people, that is, presumably, with Paul's full support and commissioning. This would place the beginning of the Colossian church in the mid-50s.

We have no way of knowing how large the church in Colossae was by the time the letter was written to it. But if "the saints and faithful brothers" (Col. 1:2) are not to be simply identified with the church in the house of Philemon (Phm. 2) and/or with the church in the house of Nympha, we have to assume the existence of more than one house church in Colossae (see on 4:15). The same deduction from 4:15 can be made with regard to the churches in Laodicea. The lack of mention of Hierapolis in 4:15 presumably implies that Epaphras's mission there (4:13) had not been so successful; any believers who lived in Hierapolis may simply have made the double journey to Laodicea to attend gatherings there. In that case we have to envisage the Christians in the Lycus valley meeting in or as at least four small (house) churches.

The fact that the Lycus valley was ravaged by an earthquake in 60-61[10] might yield vital clues on all these matters, not least that of the date of the letter, were we in a position to evaluate its effects. Unfortunately there is no reference to damage suffered by Colossae (regarding Laodicea see Tacitus, *Annales* 14.27.1). And the odd fact that the site of Colossae has never been excavated means that we are unable to make informed guesses on this subject — not to mention other questions such as the size and likely population of the city at the time and whether there are any indications of a building that may have served as a synagogue at the time.

THE TROUBLE AT COLOSSAE

We now turn to the more contentious issue of why the letter was written. There is general agreement that one reason, probably the primary reason, was to counteract teaching that might become or already was either attractive or threatening to the baptized in Colossae, particularly with regard to their appreciation of the full significance of Christ. Beyond that, however, views vary quite considerably. Before we enter the debate, however, some preliminary comments are called for.

---

10. Wedderburn, *Baptism* 70, notes a seismologist's judgment that the earthquake took place in 60; Tacitus's report indicates 60 or 61; according to Lightfoot 38-40, the Armenian version of Eusebius, *Chronicle,* dates the earthquake subsequent to the burning of Rome in 64.

PRESUPPOSITIONS

There has been a long tradition of speaking of "the Colossian heresy" or "false teaching" as that which Paul sought to attack and refute, a tradition that continues to the present. The language is potentially misleading in the two assumptions that are bound up in the phrase.

One is that there was already a clear conception of "Christian orthodoxy," with clearly delineated boundaries marking off this "Christianity" from other religious groupings of the time and distinguishing it from all counterfeits and perversions ("heresy"). Such a view can no longer be sustained, at least in that simple form. The fact is that the term "Christianity" itself had not yet been coined (in our sources it does not appear for another half century or so).[11] And since the work of W. Bauer, it is much harder than once was thought to speak of "orthodoxy and heresy" as well-defined and uniform categories in the second century, let alone the first. This is true to such a degree that if one persists with the idea of "orthodoxy," it would be hard to deny that some of the forms of earliest "Christianity" would be better designated as "heresy," at least as judged by the subsequent course of theology.[12]

To say this is not to deny, of course, that there was already a system of belief and praxis that we with hindsight can properly call "Christian." It is rather to caution against the assumption that that system was already fully rounded and agreed upon and that its boundaries were already clearly defined. In contrast, all the evidence of the New Testament documents, Paul's letters in particular, indicates that the new movement centered on Christ Jesus was in process of defining itself, of developing its own self-understanding and drawing its boundaries. Of course there was already, more or less from the beginning, so far as we can tell, the primary identity marker and boundary of baptism in the name of this Jesus and confession of him as Lord. But this confession stood more at the *center* of Christian self-definition, whereas the *circumference* was still partial and vague (hence the problems confronting Christian communities such as those in Galatia and Corinth). Alternatively expressed, if the christological *unifying* factor of earliest "Christianity" was firmly stated and powerfully cohesive, the *diversity* of formulations in diverse situations and confrontations functioned as centrifugal forces to pull the same "Christianity" into a variety of forms that in effect left the question "Is this also Christianity?" not always clear or the answers agreed.[13]

11. It first appears in Ignatius, *Magnesians* 10:3; *Philippians* 6:1.
12. This is Bauer's principal thesis in *Orthodoxy and Heresy in Earliest Christianity* (Philadelphia: Fortress, 1971/London: SCM, 1972); cf. Caird 160-61.
13. See further my *Unity*.

We should also be alert to the fact that to describe the practitioners of the Colossian "philosophy" (2:8) as "heretics" or "errorists" may be totally to misrepresent them, the character of their "philosophy," and the threat they posed to the Colossian believers (cf. Schrenk 3350), and may indeed amount to little more than cheap and unworthy name calling. For titles like "heretic" or "errorist" reduce the system represented by those so labeled to the status of no more than a corrupt growth on Christianity as the main plant, their whole system of religion summed up and sweepingly dismissed solely as "error."[14] This may be effective populist demagoguery, but it is hardly responsible historical judgment. In more or less complete contrast, as will become clearer in the following paragraphs, the Colossian "philosophy" seems to have been quite separate from the Colossian Christian group, and probably much more established and influential on its own account. We do no justice to Christianity if we demean its early rivals by using such language and incapacitate our texts from serving as role models for a Christianity keen to respond to its contemporary challenges.

The second assumption often bound up in talk of "the Colossian heresy/false teaching" is that the Colossian church was in crisis with a vigorous group of teachers in Colossae attempting to subvert the gospel as preached by Paul and actively campaigning to draw the Colossian Christians (believers in Jesus) into a different system of belief.[15] This impression is probably a half-subconscious effect of two factors external to Colossians.

One of those factors is that Galatians seems to provide a model for the sort of confrontation that Paul had with "false teaching"; as Paul confronted what he saw as a virulent threat to the gospel in Galatia, so also, it is readily deduced, in Colossae.[16] Now there certainly were active "troublemakers" in the Galatian churches (probably other Jewish Christian missionaries) whom Paul denounces in no uncertain terms (see, e.g., my *Galatians*). But there is nothing in Colossians like the fierceness and explicitness of the denunciations that are such a feature of Galatians (Gal. 1:6-9; 3:1-3; 4:8-10; 5:2-12). Most striking is the contrast between the polemical epilogue to Galatians, summing up Paul's continuing deep anxieties (Gal. 6:11-17), and the relatively calm and untroubled conclusion to Colossians (Col. 4:7-17).

The other factor external to Colossians is the continuing influence of F. C. Baur's reconstruction of early Christian history a century and a half

14. Even Sappington in his otherwise fine study falls into this trap (ch. 6: "The Colossian Error"). "The Colossian heresy (or false teaching)" continues to serve as the most convenient shorthand for most commentators.

15. E.g., Lohse, *Colossians and Philemon* 127, speaks of a "teaching which threatened to engulf the community"; and Gnilka, "Paulusbild" 181, speaks of "an acute danger," "the acute threat."

16. E.g., Pokorný 106 speaks of "a passionate polemic against a heresy," and J. T. Sanders, *Schismatics* 190, 198, speaks of "a Jewish heresy" and "Judaizers."

ago. Baur saw that history as determinatively shaped by a massive and long-running confrontation between Jewish Christianity and Gentile Christianity, with Colossians in particular as a form of Christian Gnosticism confronting Ebionism.[17] In the present century the dominant tendency has been to understand the threat to the Colossian Christians more simply (!) in syncretistic terms, as we shall see shortly, but the idea of a confrontation with false teaching or "heresy" or "error" still persists.

In contrast, the mood in Colossians is surprisingly relaxed: a lengthy development section (1:9–2:7) before the first clear warning notes are sounded (2:8); a central section with firm rebuttal and relatively restrained polemic limited to 2:16-23; and a still longer concluding section with extensive parenesis, again giving no clear evidence of false teaching being countered (3:1–4:6), prior to the untroubled conclusion already mentioned.[18] Moreover, there is only one passage (2:19) that lends *prima facie* weight to the idea that the "philosophy" was already embraced by one or more of the Colossian Christians themselves (Wolter 149, 162-63; DeMaris 67), and even that is open to another interpretation (see on 2:19). Perhaps, then, as M. D. Hooker in particular has argued, the situation in Colossae, with its threat and potential trouble, was quite different[19] — not a "false teaching" targeted on and already winning support among the members of the church(es) in Colossae, but simply the temptation to conform to more traditional or pervasive ideas and practices, or the attractiveness of teachings on offer from one or more other groups in Colossae (2:4) that might for quite understandable reasons appeal to some of the Colossian baptized.[20]

In attempting to identify the character of the threat to the Colossian baptized, at least as viewed by the writer of the letter, it is inevitable that the discussion should focus on the only section where the warning and rebuttal is explicit, namely 2:8-23 (so also particularly Lähnemann 49-53; Sappington 144-49; DeMaris 43-45). This does not exclude other passages from consideration, but anything they add to the discussion will be at best allusive, and the strength of the allusion will depend on the clarity gained from that central section, where the outlines are clearest. Currently two main options are held by those who have studied the material most closely.

17. F. C. Baur, *Paul: His Life and Works,* vol. 2 (London: Williams and Norgate, 1875) 6-21, 26-31. See further my *Partings* ch. 1.

18. "More admonitory than argumentative and . . . most accurately characterized as a letter of exhortation and encouragement" (V. P. Furnish, *ABD* 1.1090).

19. Hooker, particularly 131-36, followed by Wright, *Colossians and Philemon* 27-28; cf. Yates, "Worship" 14. Cf. also Schenk, "Kolosserbrief" 3350: not a polemic but an attempt to immunize the Christian readers against the possibility of being misled.

20. As an interesting example of how features of a letter can be used to argue quite diverse cases we may note the argument of Kiley 63-65 and Nielsen 104-7 that the indefiniteness of the attack in Colossians is proof of its inauthenticity.

GNOSTICIZING SYNCRETISM . . . ?

One is the model of Hellenistic or pre-Gnostic syncretism. This is the continued outworking of the late nineteenth-century move away from Baur, in which, in reaction to Baur's overemphasis on Jew-Gentile tensions, the focus of research switched to the larger socioreligious context of the churches founded by Paul in Asia Minor and Greece — first the mystery religions[21] and then the syncretistic soup of religious philosophical ideas that cohered into the later Gnostic systems.

The most influential recent treatments have been those of Bornkamm ("Heresy") and Lohse.[22] For convenience we focus on the latter. Lohse sets out the case (*Colossians and Philemon* 127-31) by noting the various elements in the letter that, either by the frequency of their mention or more explicitly, can be linked to the Colossian "philosophy" (2:8). But in setting them out he also correlates them into a system that is his own construct and not part of the evidence. Thus he notes the emphasis in the letter on "wisdom" (1:9, 28; 2:3, 23; 3:16; 4:5), "insight" (1:9; 2:2), and "knowledge" (1:6, 9-10; 2:2-3; 3:10) and the references to "the elements of the universe" (2:8, 20), which, quite fairly, he associates with the angels of 2:18 and the cosmic powers of 2:10 and 15. But he further assumes that the knowledge is concerned with the latter (the cosmic elements, etc.), and that it is only by establishing a right relationship with the cosmic powers that one can "gain entry" to the "pleroma" (2:9) and participate in the divine fullness (2:10). "Man can be suffused with the divine 'fulness' only after he proves himself subservient to the angels and powers in the 'worship of angels'." Quite fairly he deduces that observance of regulations and ascetical practice is enjoined by the philosophy (2:16, 21, 23), but he further deduces that the philosophy took the form of a mystery cult, with talk of circumcision in 2:11 pointing to "a decisive act of initiation" and ἐμβατεύειν in 2:18 indicating initiatory mystery rites. And finally he suggests that the Colossian syncretism would have tried to find a place for Christ within this synthesis.

---

21. Most influential here has been Dibelius, "Isis Initiation," whose interpretation, however, hangs entirely on one word (ἐμβατεύων) in 2:18 (but see the comments below on that verse).

22. For their influence see Maurer; Conzelmann 148; Cerfaux, *Christian* 479-82; R. P. Martin, *Colossians and Philemon* 4-5, 9-19; Lähnemann *passim;* P. Vielhauer, *Geschichte der urchristlichen Literatur* (Berlin: de Gruyter, 1975) 195; G. Strecker, "Judenchristentum und Gnosis," in *Altes Testament — Frühjudentum — Gnosis,* ed. K.-W. Tröger (Gütersloh: Gütersloher, 1980) 261-82 (here 273); Gnilka, *Kolosserbrief* 163-69; Findeis 346-47; and Argall 14-20. It was popular in the 1960s and 1970s to characterize Colossians as countering the Gnostic soteriology/christology of the heretics with a more radically Gnostic soteriology/christology (Schenke, "Widerstreit" 403; Grässer 152; H.-F. Weiss, "Gnostische Motive" 315). Cf. Schmithals 120-21 and W. Marxsen's description of Colossians as "christianized" (near Gnostic) heresy (*Introduction to the New Testament* [Oxford: Blackwell/Philadelphia: Fortress, 1968] 177-86). Gunther 3-4 provides a fascinating list of no less than forty-four different suggestions regarding the identity of Paul's opponents in Colossae, two-thirds of them envisaging some sort of syncretistic or Gnostic mix.

It should be evident how much of the plausibility of the Gnostic/mystery cult hypothesis depends on the links thus postulated; the "syncretistic" (fusion of different elements) character of the philosophy is more the effect of the way Lohse has fused the various elements listed above than of actual connections indicated in the text of the letter. Thus, in particular, he ignores the fact that the wisdom/knowledge/insight motif is focused largely on the theme of God's "mystery" (1:25–2:3), which is thoroughly rooted in the Pauline conviction of God's purpose to include Gentiles in his saving purpose. Since the theme of divine fullness in 2:9 most probably depends on the earlier reference in the "hymn" of 1:15-20, Lohse's thesis requires the questionable corollary that the hymn was derived from (or at least expresses) the Colossian philosophy; besides which the idea of God filling all things is again thoroughly Jewish (see on 1:19). The circumcision-uncircumcision antithesis (2:11-13) presupposes a Jewish perspective and the characteristic Pauline concern to overcome that antithesis (3:11); in contrast to which the suggestion that "circumcision" indicates an act of initiation into a mystery cult is baseless (see further below, pp. 33f.). Likewise the suggestion that 2:18 has in view visions of angels seen during mystery rites in the Colossian cult (Lohse, *Colossians and Philemon* 114, 120) should probably be abandoned[23] since the verse can be more plausibly interpreted of entering the heavenly temple to worship with the angels (see on 2:18). Finally, and despite the widespread assumption to the contrary, nothing in the letter itself clearly indicates that the Colossian philosophy fitted Christ into its schema (2:19 hardly indicates this),[24] or that the Colossian "philosophy" should be regarded as some kind of corruption of Christian belief in Christ ("Christian heresy").[25] Given the popularity of the (pre-)Gnostic hypothesis, we should simply also note the lack of any clear indication of the dualism that is indispensable to the hypothesis of a Gnosticism properly so called and of any good reason to interpret verses like 2:11-12, 21 and 23, or even 1:13 and 3:2, in terms of ontological dualism.[26]

There is too much in all this that has to be abstracted from the context or read into the text. Only if a more plausible hypothesis is not forthcoming would it be necessary to return to the hypothesis of gnosticizing syncretism to look at it afresh and to see whether the weaknesses of Lohse's reconstruction could be remedied without introducing further stresses into the text.

---

23. Note also Pokorný's comment: "We are not able to demonstrate that the gnostics esteemed and venerated angels" (117-18). Despite this he speaks of the Colossian "gnostics" (112-20).

24. Cf. particularly Francis, "Christological Argument," who finds "nothing that urges the conclusion that the error itself was distinctly christological at all" (203); Sappington 174-76.

25. Contrast particularly Lindemann, *Kolosserbrief* 81-85, who compares the Colossian teachers with the German Christians of the Nazi period in Germany (7, 81-82, 88-89).

26. 1:13 and 3:2 could, however, quite properly be described as expressing an eschatological or apocalyptic dualism (see the comments below on 1:13).

... OR JEWISH?

In recent years the pendulum has begun to swing back toward recognition of more distinctively Jewish features in the Colossian threat, stimulated in large part by the continuing impact of the Dead Sea Scrolls.[27] This is the direction in which my own study of the text has led, and it is incumbent on me to explain why in a little more detail.

(1) First, we need to recall the information already provided above, that Colossae, and the other Lycus valley cities, probably had substantial Jewish ethnic minorities. This implies the presence of (probably) several synagogues in Colossae, bearing in mind that just as almost all churches at this time were house churches (see on Col. 4:15), so many Jewish gatherings for prayer must have been in private houses. If the pattern indicated in Acts and implied in Paul's letters applies here, we probably have to envisage a church made up initially of Jews and God-fearing Gentiles or proselytes (mostly the latter if 1:12, 27 and 2:13 are any guide), some of them drawn from (or indeed still members of) the synagogue (which would give the affirmations in 3:11 and 4:11 more point).

Moreover, we must avoid the later stereotype that Jews and Christians became clearly separate and distinct from each other almost from the first. On the contrary, there is clear evidence that many Christians, not least Gentile Christians, continued for a long time to regard the synagogue as equally their home and so to attend both church and synagogue. Over the next hundred years "Barnabas" had to warn Christians against becoming proselytes (*Barnabas* 3:6), Ignatius had to warn his Asia Minor readers further down the Meander against "living in accordance with Judaism" and against "judaizing" (*Magnesians* 8:1; 10:3), and Justin Martyr spoke likewise of Christians who had adopted Judaism and "gone over to the polity of the law" (*Dialogue* 47.4). So, too, we have to take serious note of the exhortations of such as Origen (*Homily on Leviticus* 5:8; *Selecta on Exodus* 12:46) and Chrysostom (*Homilia ad Judaeos* 1, *PG* 48.844-45) warning Christians against attending synagogue on Saturday and church on Sunday, not to mention the canons of the fourth-century Council of Laodicea (Canons 16, 29, 37, and 38) forbidding Christians to observe Jewish feasts and keep the sabbath (see, e.g., Trebilco 101).

---

27. See particularly Francis, "Humility"; for the influence of Francis see Kehl, "Erniedrigung," especially 371-74; Carr, "Notes" 496-500; Lincoln, *Paradise* 112; O'Brien, *Colossians, Philemon* 141-45; Evans, "Colossian Mystics"; Rowland, "Apocalyptic Visions"; Wink, *Naming* 80 n. 93; Bruce, *Colossians, Philemon, Ephesians* 22-26 (26: "an early form of *merkabah* mysticism"), who has changed his mind from his first edition (166: "a Judaism which had undergone a remarkable fusion with . . . an early and simple form of gnosticism"); Fowl 126-29; Yates, *Colossians* 55-56; Aletti, *Épitre aux Colossiens* 196-99, 211-13; and especially the whole thesis of Sappington.

In other words, the members of the different groups in Colossae —
synagogue and church — would probably not be strangers to each other or
ignorant of each other's beliefs and practices — to put the point no more
strongly.

(2) We know too little of diaspora Judaism in this period, but what we
do know gives us a number of clear pointers. First, there is a persistent record
of Jews being anxious to maintain their distinct religious identity and of
being given the right to do so. Most often mentioned are the rights of
assembly and places of prayer (synagogues), payment of the temple tax,
freedom from military service, and the right to live according to their own
laws, often with particular reference to sabbath and food laws. Laodicea
features in one of these decrees (Josephus, *Antiquities* 14.241-42), and a
Jewish inscription from Hierapolis (*CIJ* 777) also mentions the feasts of
Passover and Pentecost (Trebilco 12-19 and 199 n. 70; Feldman 70).

We cannot, however, assume from this that the Judaism of the Colossian
synagogues was wholly uniform — any more than was the Judaism (or
Judaisms) in the land of Israel, of which we have more information. Around
their common features, the "sects" of Palestinian Judaism displayed a striking
diversity of specific belief and halakhic practice.[28] So with diaspora Judaism
as well as with infant Christianity we should hesitate to envisage or speak of a
regular pattern of orthodoxy as the norm. Rather we might expect that something at least of the diversity of Palestinian Judaism was reflected in the
diaspora. This is not to suggest that there were flourishing groups of Pharisees
and Sadducees in Colossae, but it does suggest that the older idea of Lightfoot
that the Colossian "heresy" was a form of or shared characteristics with
Essenism may have more credibility than at first appears (cf. more recently
Foerster and Saunders). That the diversity of religious belief and practice in the
land of Israel could be transposed into the diaspora is confirmed by the presence
of a community of Samaritans on the island of Delos in the Aegean who called
themselves "Israelites who pay firstfruits to holy Mt. Gerizim" (Schürer 3.71).
And nearer home we should recall that Paul himself seems to have experienced
or practiced mystical ascent (2 Cor. 12:1-7 — a period of his life probably to
be located in Cilicia [Gal. 2:21; Acts 11:26]), that according to Acts 19:1-3 Paul
subsequently met a group in Ephesus who had received "John's baptism," and
that the seer of Revelation's characteristically Jewish apocalyptic visions are
said to have taken place in Patmos (Rev. 1:9; note the often observed parallel
between Rev. 3:14 and Col. 1:15).[29]

---

28. See, e.g., my *Partings* 12-13, 18.

29. *Sibylline Oracles* 4, which is sometimes thought to have originated in Asia Minor (4.107
refers to the destruction of Laodicea by earthquake and 4.150-51 to the Meander), has some curious
parallels with Colossians that may indicate that it underwent a sectarian Jewish redaction (6-7, 33-34,
165-70).

At the same time the evidence of Jewish syncretism in these diaspora communities is lacking, despite older claims to the contrary.[30] The easy both-and solution to the dispute about the Colossian "heresy" — viz. neither Jewish nor Hellenistic syncretism, but Jewish/Hellenistic syncretism — is not supported by the evidence regarding the Jewish communities in Asia Minor (see now Kraabel; Sanders, *Schismatics* 191-96). And one should hesitate to speak of "Jewish Gnosticism" or "Gnostic Judaism" at this period without firmer evidence than Colossians itself,[31] unless "gnostic" is being used in a diluted sense more closely equivalent to "apocalyptic" or "mystical."[32] The evidence we have from elsewhere in first-century Judaism is that, for example, while Jewish apologists were very willing to make use of Greek philosophies and categories like the figure of "wisdom," and while apocalyptists and mystics were keen to explore the revelations of the heavens, it was all done within circles who maintained a firm Jewish identity — and not least, or rather, particularly when they sought thereby to enhance the stature of Judaism in the eyes of others (see also below). Certainly, as we shall see, the categories used in Colossians itself have to be judged as consistently closer to those used in Jewish writings current at the time than to the later Gnostic texts from Nag Hammadi.

(3) Nor can we assume that the diaspora Jewish synagogues were closed off from the communities in which they lived, despised by their neighbors and living a sort of ghetto existence; here, too, we must avoid stereotypes drawn from later history. On the contrary, we know several cities in Asia Minor where the Jewish community and synagogue were well integrated into the social and civic life of the city.[33] And the few details we have from the Lycus valley cities, including a number of Jewish epitaphs in Hierapolis, only serve to strengthen the impression that the Jewish communities (some Jews at least) would have

30. See Bruce, *Colossians, Philemon, Ephesians* 12-13; Trebilco ch. 6; Feldman, *Jew and Gentile* 74. R. P. Martin, *Colossians and Philemon* 18-19, is quite unjustified in claiming that "the synagogues [of Phrygia] had a reputation for laxity and openness to speculation drifting in from the hellenistic world." Pokorný 20, 116; Wolter 160-61 are still influenced by the older view. Wedderburn 6-12 is more circumspect, drawing a parallel with the clearly syncretistic teaching of Elchasai, which emerged in Syria about fifty years later. Even so, it should be clear that a certain amount of social interaction between different ethnic groups within a society structured on the system of patronage should not be described as "syncretism" any more than the practice commended by Paul in 1 Cor. 5:10 and 10:27. On the famous Julia Severa inscription from Acmonia see Trebilco 58-60.

31. See, e.g., those cited by Lohse, *Colossians and Philemon* 129 n. 120.

32. It is this correlation that enables Scholem to speak of Jewish *merkabah* mysticism as a kind of "Jewish gnosticism" in *Jewish Gnosticism*.

33. Trebilco studies particularly Sardis, Acmonia, and Apamea, all within a 150-mile radius of Colossae. On Aphrodisias see particularly J. Reynolds and R. Tannenbaum, *Jews and Godfearers at Aphrodisias* (Cambridge Philological Society Supp. 12; Cambridge, 1987). On the level of social intercourse between Jews and Gentiles see, e.g., S. J. D. Cohen, "Crossing the Boundary and Becoming a Jew," *HTR* 82 (1989) 13-33; E. P. Sanders, "Jewish Association with Gentiles and Galatians 2:11-14," in *Studies in Paul and John*, J. L. Martyn FS, ed. R. Fortna and B. R. Gaventa (Nashville: Abingdon, 1990) 170-88; my *Galatians* 119-21.

been respected and well integrated into the business and community life of these cities (Schürer 3.27-28).

Conversely we should not assume that the Jews of Colossae would have been vigorously evangelistic. Here again the broader picture is clear: on the whole, Jewish communities were content to have their rights to practice their ancestral religion affirmed, without attempting to convert others to what was essentially an ethnic religion (the religion of the Jews); at the same time, however, they welcomed Gentiles who were attracted to Judaism (of whom there were many) and were pleased when such God-fearing Gentiles asked for circumcision and so became proselytes.[34] In some contrast, the compulsion to mission was a distinctive feature of the Jewish group that identified themselves by reference to Jesus the Christ.

This is not to say, however, that diaspora Jews were shy in explaining themselves. As already mentioned, we know of several apologies on behalf of Jews and Judaism, in which Jewish history (particularly Moses) and the peculiar beliefs and practices of the Jews are explained or expressed in categories and language more conducive to winning the respect of cultured Hellenists.[35] Philo is only the most striking example of a well-educated Jew who used Platonic and Stoic philosophy to demonstrate the rational and religious power of Judaism. And Josephus would not have been the only Jew writing in Greek to describe the different Jewish "sects" as "philosophies" (see on 2:8).[36] We may also assume that the tradition of a Jewish apologist engaging in dialogue with others neither began nor ended with

---

34. On God-fearers (or God-worshippers) in Asia Minor see Trebilco ch. 7, and on lack of missionary outreach (proselytizing zeal) within the Judaism of the period see S. McKnight, *A Light among the Gentiles: Jewish Missionary Activity in the Second Temple Period* (Minneapolis: Fortress, 1991); M. Goodman, "Jewish Proselytizing in the First Century," in *The Jews among Pagans and Christians in the Roman Empire,* ed. J. Lieu, et al. (London: Routledge, 1992) 53-78; also *Mission and Conversion: Proselytizing in the Religious History of the Roman Empire* (Oxford: Clarendon, 1994) ch. 4.

35. See particularly the wisdom and philosophical literature and fragments of lost Judeo-Hellenistic works in *OTP* 2.477-606, 775-919; C. R. Holladay, *Fragments from Hellenistic Jewish Authors* (4 vols.; Atlanta: Scholars, 1983, 1989, 1995, 1996); see also J. J. Collins, *Between Athens and Jerusalem: Jewish Identity in the Hellenistic Diaspora* (New York: Crossroad, 1983).

36. With reference to Schweizer's thesis that the Colossian philosophy was a kind of "Jewish Pythagoreanism" (*Colossians* 131-33; "Christ" 452-54; "Christianity"), which has influenced Wedderburn, *Colossians* 4-7, and Wolter 159-62, we should note: (a) the thesis depends too much on a particular interpretation of the στοιχεῖα in 2:8, 20 (see the comments below on 2:8), apart from which there is nothing distinctively Pythagorean about the features of the philosophy (listed by Schweizer, *Colossians* 133); and (b) Josephus was able to describe the Essenes as "a group that follows a way of life taught to the Greeks by Pythagoras" (*Antiquities* 15.371) as part of his commendation of the Jewish sects by presenting them in Greek garb (see further Schürer 2.589-90). Such considerations would explain why the Colossian philosophy might give the *impression* of Pythagoreanism without owing anything substantive to it in fact.

Trypho.[37] Apology, it should be noted, is not the same as evangelism or proselytism, and, more important, it serves as much the purpose of boosting the self-confidence of those who wish to win respect of neighbors and business associates as of explaining the unfamiliar to interested outsiders. At all events, it is more likely than not that the Jews of Colossae included those more than ready (and able) to explain their religious practices to inquirers and even to take some initiative in providing an apologetic exposition of Judaism in the public forum.

THE COLOSSIAN PHILOSOPHY

Against the background just sketched out, it has to be said, the threat to the church in Colossae makes perfect sense. The implications of 1:12, 21-22; 2:13; and 3:11-12 in particular are that the presuppositional framework of thought for both writer and recipients focuses on Jewish covenantal distinctiveness and privilege (see on these verses). Elements in 2:8-10, 15, 18, 20, and 23, which have seemed to some to require a hypothesis of Hellenistic or more explicitly (pre-)Gnostic syncretism, can more easily be seen to fit within Judaism (see on these verses), including the emphasis on wisdom (also in 1:9, 28; 2:3; 3:16; 4:5) and fullness (also in 1:9, 19, 25; 2:2; 4:12);[38] and indeed within a Judaism, somewhat surprisingly, given the different tone of its challenge and of the epistolary response, not so very different from that promoted in the Galatian churches (see pp. 136f. below). And, most striking of all, several other elements are so clearly Jewish that no other hypothesis will serve (see on 2:11-14, 16-17, 21-22).[39] In other words, the hypothesis of a syncretistic religious philosophy with only some Jewish elements is both unnecessary and highly implausible,[40] and easy talk of

37. See particularly R. L. Wilken, *Judaism and the Early Christian Mind* (New Haven: Yale University, 1971) 28-30, 35-38, 41-43, 50-53.

38. But can we deduce that the Colossian philosophy was laying claim to a *higher* wisdom (as, e.g., Lähnemann 33 suggests)?

39. Several, e.g., Lohse, *Colossians and Philemon* 129 n. 119, point out that the concept "law" is absent from Colossians. But since the law's most prominent features for diaspora Jews (circumcision, food laws, sabbaths, and purity regulations) are specifically mentioned (2:11, 13, 16, 20-21), the fact that the term "law" itself is lacking is of no great moment. See also Wright's more robust rebuttal of the point (*Colossians and Philemon* 25-26) and the comments below on 2:16.

40. Schweizer, *Colossians* 128: a "world view . . . with little more than Jewish trimmings"; Stegemann 530: "a few Jewish bits and pieces *(Versatzstücken),* nothing to do with Judaism itself"; Gnilka, *Kolosserbrief* 168: "a Jewish shell (Gehäuse) filled with an alien spirit." The most recent discussions of the opponents in Colossae pursue essentially the same line: ascetic visionaries who have drawn on Judaism for some aspects of their teachings (Sumney 386), or a syncretistic blend of "popular Middle Platonic, Jewish and Christian elements that cohere around the pursuit of wisdom" (DeMaris, here 17). Kiley 61-62 provides a useful enumeration of the options canvassed over the past hundred years. See also n. 34 on 2:18.

"Gnostic Judaism" at this stage is probably a sign of a too casual historical imagination.

None of the features of the teaching alluded to in 2:8-23 resist being understood in Jewish terms, and several can only or most plausibly be understood in Jewish terms (cf. particularly Wright, *Colossians and Philemon* 24-27). To be more precise, the division of the world into "circumcision and uncircumcision" (2:11-13; 3:11) and the observance of the sabbath (2:16) would generally be recognized in the ancient world as distinctively Jewish, as indeed also food and purity rules (2:16, 21) when set alongside circumcision and sabbath (see on 2:11, 16, 21); so distinctively Jewish are they, indeed, that any non-Jew adopting them would be said to be "judaizing" (adopting a Jewish way of life — see, e.g., my *Galatians* 129). As Schenk 3351-53 observes, calendar piety, food laws, and circumcision cannot be regarded as random elements of some syncretistic cult, but are the very norms that provide and confirm the identity of Israel (similarly Harrington 157-58 and J. T. Sanders, *Schismatics* 190). In other words, the number of distinctively and definitively Jewish features are such that it is scarcely possible to envisage the Colossian "philosophy" as a non-Jewish core that has attracted Jewish elements; at most we have to speak of an apocalyptic or mystical Judaism transposed into the diaspora that has been able to make itself attractive to those sympathetic to Judaism by playing on familiar fears and making more impressive claims.

The main proponents of the Colossian "philosophy," therefore, almost certainly have to be understood as belonging to one of the Colossian synagogues. If indeed there were Jews in Colossae confident in their religion (2:4, 8), above all in the access it gave them to the worship of heaven (2:18) through faithfulness to what were traditional (Jewish) observances (2:16, 21-23), then we should not be surprised if they professed such claims in dialogue and debate with other Colossians. And if there then grew up in their midst a new version of their own teaching, proclaiming the Jewish Messiah and the fulfillment of ancient Jewish hopes (note again particularly 1:12 and 3:12), then, again, it would hardly be a surprise if some of the more outspoken and self-confident members of the synagogues spoke dismissively of the beliefs, devotions, and praxis of the new movement as compared with their own.

In short, given the various factors outlined above, including the probable origin of the Colossian church from within synagogue circles, the likely presence of Israelite sectarianism within the diaspora, the lack of other evidence of Jewish syncretism in Asia Minor, and the readiness of some Jews to promote their distinctive religious practices in self-confident apology (see above), we need look no further than one or more of the Jewish synagogues in Colossae for the source of whatever influences were thought to threaten the young church there. The more relaxed style of the polemic in

Colossians and the absence there of anything quite like the fierceness of the reaction in Galatians further suggests that what was being confronted was not a sustained attempt to undermine or further convert the Colossians, but a synagogue apologetic promoting itself as a credible philosophy more than capable of dealing with whatever heavenly powers might be thought to control or threaten human existence. To describe this as a "heresy" is quite inappropriate, and to brand it simply as "false teaching" (maintained by Colossian "errorists"!) reduces that teaching to its controverted features while ignoring what must have been many points in common between the Jews and Christians in Colossae.[41]

WHO WROTE COLOSSIANS?

This is probably the most contentious of the introductory issues facing the student of Colossians. Although I have already indicated that the issue might not be quite so crucial for a full appreciation of the letter's significance (pp. 19f. above), it is still important. However, since I have little or no fresh insight to bring to the question I will simply refer to what seem to me the most decisive considerations and treatments of those considerations.

First, having studied the text with the care necessary for a commentary of this scope (the Introduction is, of course, written last!), I have to confirm the strong likelihood that the letter comes from a hand other than Paul's. This is not a mechanical judgment, based merely on vocabulary counts, sentence construction, and the like, but, as with all evaluations of literary style, is dependent also on the subjective appreciation of manner and mode of expression. The fact is that at point after point in the letter the commentator is confronted with features characteristic of flow of thought and rhetorical technique that are consistently and markedly different from those of the undisputed Paulines.[42] Of course it is possible that Paul's style changed over a few years (though if Colossians was written from Ephesus [see p. 40 below], the writing of it would fall in the midst of his other letters). But it is more probable (given the relative constancy of Paul's style elsewhere) that

---

41. For a fuller exposition of the case summarized above see my "The Colossian Philosophy: A Confident Jewish Apologia," *Biblica* 76 (1995) 153-81.

42. The most comprehensive and impressive study has been that of Bujard, whose findings Schweizer (*Colosssians* 18-19) thinks are decisive: "The letter can neither have been written nor dictated by Paul"; similarly Meeks, *Urban Christians* 125; see also the extensive summary treatments in Kiley 51-59 and Schenk, "Kolosserbrief" 3327-38. Cf. the documentation in Lohse, *Colossians and Philemon* 84-91, who is impressed most of all by "the peculiarity of the sentence structure and sequence" (89), but who thinks the evidence indecisive (a view echoed in favor of Pauline authorship by Percy, *Probleme* 16-66 and Kümmel 341-42; according to Aletti, *Épitre aux Colossiens* 208-9, the manner of reasoning in 2:6-23 is "typically Pauline").

the hand is different. In saying this we should recognize that it is not merely a matter of Paul dictating his letters to different secretaries. The differences come at the authorial level — the "fingerprint" differences of (unconscious) speech mannerisms and (second nature) patterns of composition.

Second, it is difficult to deny that the theological and parenetic content is significantly different from what we are accustomed to in all the undisputed Paulines.[43] The christology expressed in 1:15-20 and 2:9-10 and 15 looks to be further along the trajectory (which on any count stretches from what we find in the Synoptic Jesus tradition through John's Gospel to Ignatius and Irenaeus) than that of the undisputed Paulines; closest would be Rom. 10:6-13; 1 Cor. 8:4-6; and Phil. 2:6-11, but even so the thought of 1:19-20 and 2:9 is a step beyond any of those passages. So, too, the ecclesiology of 1:18, especially as correlated with 2:10, clearly reflects a development closer to Eph. 1:21-23 than to the ecclesiology of Rom. 12:4-8 or 1 Corinthians 12. There is a clear note of realized eschatology in 2:11-12 and 3:1, as compared with Rom. 6:4-5 and 8:11, though a note of future expectation is also maintained at other points (see on 1:5, 24, 27-28; 3:4, 6, 10, 24-25). And the parenesis using the "household rules" form in 3:18–4:1 is again much closer to Eph. 5:22–6:9 and the Pastorals than to anything we find earlier in Paul. Here again one could speak of the development of Paul's own thought, but again that would simply indicate that there is a later "Paulinism" that can be attributed to the late Paul or to a close Pauline disciple without altering the character of the "Paulinism" or its authentic character as "Pauline."

In addition, we cannot ignore the degree to which Colossians and Ephesians overlap, sufficiently often with very similar phraseology, structure, and content (cf., e.g., Col. 1:1-2/Eph. 1:1-2; Col. 1:4/Eph. 1:15; Col. 2:13/Eph. 2:5; Col. 2:19/Eph. 4:15-16; Col. 3:12/Eph. 4:32; Col. 3:16/Eph. 5:19-20; Col. 3:22–4:1/Eph. 6:5-9; Col. 4:7-8/Eph. 6:21-22).[44] This feature is best explained by Ephesians being written using Colossians as a kind of template (so most),[45] so discussion of its full significance belongs more to a treatment of Ephesians than of Colossians. Nevertheless, the fact that

43. See, e.g., Lohse's excursus on "The Letter to the Colossians and Pauline Theology" (*Colossians and Philemon* 77-83); Lindemann, *Paulus* 114-22; Merklein 37-62, though there is a tendency to exaggerate the differences (see, e.g., the comments below on 1:24). MacDonald sees in Colossians an example of "community-stabilizing institutionalization" (Part 2). For an alternative view see R. P. Martin, *Colossians and Philemon* 32-38; O'Brien, *Colossians, Philemon* xliv-xlix.

44. See particularly C. L. Mitton, *The Epistle to the Ephesians* (Oxford: Clarendon, 1951) 55-67, 279-315. The most comprehensive synoptic analysis has been provided by G. van Kooten, "The Literary Phenomenon of 'Conflation' in Paul's *Letter to the Colossians* by the Author of the *Letter to the Ephesians*" (M.A. Thesis, Durham, 1995).

45. See, e.g., those cited in Lohse, *Colossians and Philemon* 4 n. 2. For the alternative view that Colossians presupposes Ephesians see Coutts, and for more complex theories of canonical Colossians as the product of redaction and/or interpolation see the brief reviews in Kiley 42-43; Bruce, *Colossians, Philemon, Ephesians* 30-32.

(post-Pauline) Ephesians did make such use of Colossians suggests that Colossians itself may have provided something of a model for Ephesians — that is, as an expression of "late Paulinism" or as written by a Pauline disciple close to Paul.

On the other hand, thirdly, it is difficult to envisage a scenario where 4:7-17 can be easily explained on a full-blown post-Pauline (say, fifteen years after his death) hypothesis. It is not simply that the passage contains a sequence of personal references, as in 2 Tim. 4:9-21 and Tit. 3:12-13 (which anyway could be explained as brief private letters written during Paul's life and incorporated in the later Pastorals). It is more the fact that the references are so closely related to the Colossian church (see 4:7-9, 10, 12-13, 15-17; "to a concrete community," according to Gnilka, "Paulusbild" 181-83). What would the Colossians (or Laodiceans), receiving the letter *(ex hypothesi)* in, say, 70 or 75, make of such references? Are we to envisage an older Tychicus (and Onesimus) bearing the letter to Colossae as though from Paul, a letter written to boost their authority? But what then of the reference to the letter to the Laodiceans and the exhortation to Archippus (still in Colossae, or only then in Colossae)? Why would a pseudepigrapher, consciously free to create his own history and aware that Colossae was not strictly speaking one of Paul's churches, choose as the recipient of his putative letter, of all places, Colossae? And when we recall the possibility that Colossae was almost destroyed in the earthquake of 60 or 61, confidence in the hypothesis that the letter was first written to Colossae some years later takes a further knock (see Schweizer, *Colossians* 19-21), without making the suggestion that it was really written for the church in Laodicea (Lindemann, *Kolosserbrief* 12-13 = the thesis of his earlier "Gemeinde") or to a third unknown church (Wolter 36, 220-21) any more plausible. Occam's razor indicates that the most obvious solution is also the most trouble-free (see also pp. 269f. below).

Here the close overlap with Philemon at precisely the same point becomes a factor of some importance. The two letters name precisely the same authors (Paul and Timothy — Col. 1:1; Phm. 1) and more or less the same list of greeters (Epaphras, Aristarchus and Mark, Demas and Luke — Col. 4:10-14; Phm. 23-24). Such overlap can be the result only of deliberate contrivance (a later writer of Colossians simply copying Philemon, though with variations difficult to explain)[46] or of closeness of historical origin (both

---

46. The literary dependence of Colossians on Philemon is commonly assumed and commonly assumed to be a device to evoke the impression of Pauline authorship (e.g., Lohse, *Colossians and Philemon* 175-77; Lindemann, *Kolosserbrief* 72, 75; Yates, *Colossians* 85; Wolter 216-7; Aletti, *Épitre aux Colossiens* 268; otherwise Ollrog 238-39 n. 14). E. P. Sanders, "Literary Dependence," argues the more elaborate hypothesis that Colossians was contrived by someone taking phrases from Paul's seven letters; but such a "patchwork quilt" hypothesis is no more credible than the older source-critical theories of the Pentateuch or the Synoptic Gospels (explained solely in terms of

letters written at about the same time: Bruce, *Colossians, Philemon, and Ephesians* 177). On either theory Philemon's failure to mention Tychicus (who according to Col. 4:8-9 was the principal member of the party sent by Paul to Colossae) and the failure of Colossians to mention Philemon (especially when it does mention Archippus: cf. Col. 4:17 with Phm. 2) have to be explained. The puzzle is greater if Colossians was written later using Philemon's data (why include a reference to Onesimus but not to Philemon?). It could be explained, however, if there was a relatively brief time gap between the two letters (so that Paul's companions were more or less the same). If in the event the letters were brought to Colossae at the same time, Philemon by Onesimus to Philemon and his home church and Colossians by Tychicus to the other Colossian believers, that could be sufficient to explain why each did not mention a principal figure to do with the other. Alternatively, if Paul was imprisoned in not too distant Ephesus, we could certainly envisage a personal letter to Philemon, with the happy result that Onesimus was returned to Paul within a few days, only to be sent after an interval back to Colossae with Tychicus (who had come to Ephesus in the meantime) but after Philemon had himself left Colossae (on business).

The data are somewhat confusing, and no hypothesis fits it all with equal comfort. But on the whole the most plausible solution is probably that the letter was written at about the same time as Philemon but actually composed by someone other than Paul himself. We may, for example, envisage Paul outlining his main concerns to a secretary (Timothy) who was familiar with the broad pattern of Paul's letter-writing and being content to leave it to the secretary to formulate the letter with a fair degree of license, perhaps under the conditions of his imprisonment at that point able only to add the briefest of personal conclusions (see on 4:18). If so, we should perhaps more accurately describe the theology of Colossians as the theology of Timothy, or, more accurately still, the theology of Paul as understood or interpreted by Timothy. On the other hand, if Timothy did indeed write for Paul at Paul's behest, but also with Paul's approval of what was in the event written (prior to adding 4:18), then we have to call the letter "Pauline" in the full sense of the word, and the distinction between "Pauline" and "post-Pauline" as applied to Colossians becomes relatively unimportant.[47]

"literary dependence"). Kiley 76-91 argues the more limited hypothesis of a letter contrived using only Philippians and Philemon as its source; but the dependence in this case is not of the same character as in the more widely agreed examples of such usage (Ephesians on Colossians or Laodiceans on the basis of Col. 4:16) and is probably better explained as someone thinking in Pauline fashion, or indeed as Paul thinking similar but variant thoughts. As Richards 5 notes in reference to Cicero's practice, "It seems to have been quite acceptable to use the same material, theme, or argument in more than one letter, if the recipients were different."

47. I find myself thus pushed toward the same conclusion as Schweizer, *Colossians* 23-24 (see further his "Kolosserbrief — weder paulinisch noch nachpaulinisch?"; so also Ollrog 236-42; Wedder-

At all events, whatever the precise circumstances of its composition, Colossians strongly suggests that the distinctions between a Paul who himself changed in style and developed in theology, a Paul who allowed someone else to interpret his thought and concerns, and a Pauline disciple writing shortly after Paul's death but seeking to be faithful to what he perceived would be the master's thought and concerns in the situation envisaged in the letter become of uncertain and diminishing significance. In short, to repeat what I said earlier (p. 19), here we can see clearly the "bridge" character of Colossians.

In what follows I leave the issue fairly fluid, sometimes referring to the author as Paul and Timothy, sometimes simply as Paul to avoid tedious repetition.

WHERE AND WHEN WAS COLOSSIANS WRITTEN?

Of the introductory questions, this is the one I found most difficult to draw out to a clear and final answer. The one thing that is clear is that the letter was written from prison (4:3, 10, 18). If we can now sideline the hypothesis of a post-Pauline authorship written years after Paul's death (see above), these references must refer to a period of imprisonment of Paul during which the letter was written. That in turn pushes us to a choice between a largely hypothetical Ephesian imprisonment and the well-known imprisonment in Rome.[48] To choose between these, however, is very difficult.

The main elements of the problem have already been indicated. On the one hand, as we have seen, Colossians seems to locate itself on the trajectory of Pauline theology at or near the margin of the transition from "Pauline" to "post-Pauline" theology. Without forgetting what has just been said about that distinction, that location suggests a late date, that is, near the end of Paul's life, which points to a Roman imprisonment.[49] On the other

---

burn, *Baptism* 71; this view was foreshadowed by H. Ewald in 1857). A. Suhl, *Paulus und seine Briefe* (Gütersloh: Gütersloher, 1975) 168 n. 93, makes a similar suggestion regarding Epaphras. Lindemann, *Kolosserbrief* 11 and Pokorný 18 object that Paul would hardly have allowed the first-person references in 1:23-25; 1:29–2:5; and 4:3-18 to stand unaltered if Timothy was the actual author. But there is no real difficulty if Timothy saw himself as writing in Paul's name and so speaking with Paul's voice, as would an ambassador; Cicero's correspondence shows this to have been a quite accepted role for a secretary (Richards 49-56, 62; see earlier Bahr 475-76). But most still think of the letter as post-Pauline; so, e.g., Lohse, *Colossians and Philemon* 181; Kiley; Merklein 25-26; Gnilka, *Kolosserbrief* 19-26; Pokorný 10-19; Wolter 27-31; Yates, *Colossians* xi-xii; Furnish, *ABD* 1.1094.

48. E.g., Ephesus (R. P. Martin, *Colossians and Philemon* 22-32; Schweizer, *Colossians* 24-26; Wright, *Colossians and Philemon* 34-37), Rome (Moule, *Colossians and Philemon* 21-25; Bruce, *Colossians, Philemon, Ephesians* 32), and Caesarea (Reicke, "Historical Setting" 434-38). See also p. 307 below, n. 17.

49. In that case the likelihood that Colossae was seriously affected by the earthquake in 60-61 would point to a date not long prior to the earthquake (see also n. 10 above).

hand, given the close proximity of Colossians to Philemon (see pp. 37-38 above) and the strong case that can be made for setting Philemon in the context of an earlier Ephesian imprisonment (see pp. 307f. below), that would point to the same originating context for Colossians and a date in the mid 50s, that is, presumably prior to 2 Corinthians and Romans.[50]

An Ephesian scenario would not only explain the to-ing and fro-ing of Onesimus implied in Philemon (as also Paul's hope to visit Philemon on release, Phm. 22) but also allow for a further movement of Onesimus to Colossae (with the letter to Philemon), back to Paul, and back again to Colossae (with Tychicus and Colossians), one of the most plausible suggestions with regard to the relation of Colossians and Philemon. Moreover, the suggestion that Colossians was actually composed by Timothy (or someone else) could go some way toward explaining the developed character of the theology and parenesis: Timothy initiated (or developed Paul's thought further into) post-Pauline theology while Paul was still alive! Yet, we also suggested the likelihood that in such a case Timothy would have indicated or read to Paul what he had written, and Paul would have made it his own by adding his signature (4:18). It would be somewhat surprising if Paul then turned his back on such developed christology and ecclesiology and reverted in Romans to his earlier themes, only for them to be taken up and extended further in Ephesians (cf. Bruce, *Colossians, Philemon, and Ephesians* 32; Furnish, *ABD* 1.1094-95).

On the other hand, a later (Roman imprisonment) date for Colossians would certainly seem to best explain what I have called the bridge character of the letter. But an initial movement of Onesimus to Rome is more difficult to envisage, as is Paul's simply expressed hope to visit Philemon (why distant Colossae? see again the Introduction to Philemon, pp. 307f. below), and almost certainly rules out the possibility of Onesimus being returned to Paul and returning again to Philemon while Paul's support group was virtually unchanged. We would then be forced back to the hypothesis that the two letters were written within a few days of each other, but that while Paul was able to give more attention to the letter to Philemon, he chose (or some tightening of security forced him) to leave the composition of Colossians to someone else (Timothy?). Both situations are quite plausible to envisage, though the former (choosing to concentrate on Philemon and leaving Colossians to someone else) would suggest an interesting set of priorities for Paul (his personal obligation to Onesimus and Philemon overriding his concerns for the Colossian church as a whole) and strengthen the likelihood that the threat to the Colossian baptized was no great or pressing crisis.

50. In the later manuscript tradition some majuscules assert that Colossians was written from Rome (see Metzger 627); however, according to the Marcionite prologue to Colossians the letter was written from Ephesus ("Apostolus iam ligatus scribit eis ab Epheso," cited in Moule, *Colossians* 22 n. 1).

In the end the choice probably has to be made between two sets of plausibilities, each linked with sets of implausibilities. And to choose between them is a matter of fine judgment. Not much hangs on it, as I have repeatedly stressed, but on balance and for what it is worth I find myself inclining (55% to 45%, as it were) toward the more traditional hypothesis, that Colossians was written from Rome (similarly O'Brien, *Colossians, Philemon* xlix-liv) and was thus the last Pauline letter to be written with the great apostle's explicit approval.

THE STRUCTURE OF COLOSSIANS

Colossians is characteristically Pauline in its structure. By that I mean that Colossians has the typical structure of a Pauline letter, with its distinctively Pauline features in the opening (1:1-8) and closing (4:7-18), its thematic statement (2:6-7), and fully developed body comprising both theological argument (2:8-23) and parenesis (3:1–4:6). The features that cause most surprise for those familiar with the Pauline style and that strengthen the likelihood that another hand has been active in composing the letter are the substantial development of the thanksgiving (1:9–2:5) and the incorporation of household rules into the parenesis (3:18–4:1). For fuller details the introduction to each section should be referred to.

ADDRESS AND GREETING (1:1-2)

EXTENDED THANKSGIVING (1:3-23)
      Thanksgiving (1:3-8)
      Prayer for the Colossian Recipients (1:9-14)
      A Hymn in Praise of Christ (1:15-20)
      Reconciliation and Response (1:21-23)

A PERSONAL STATEMENT (1:24–2:5)
      Paul's Commitment to the Gospel (1:24-29)
      Paul's Commitment to the Colossians (2:1-5)

THE THEME OF THE LETTER (2:6–4:6)
      The Thematic Statement (2:6-7)
      The Cross of Christ Renders Unnecessary Any Further Human
      Traditions and Rules (2:8-23)
            The Scope of Christ's Accomplishments on the Cross (2:8-15)
            Beware of Claims That There Are More Important Practices and
                Experiences (2:16-19)
            Life in Christ Does Not Depend on Observance of Jewish
                Practices (2:20-23)

The Pattern of Living That Follows from the Cross (3:1–4:6)
>   *The Perspective from Which the Christian Life Should Be Lived*
>   *(3:1-4)*
>   *General Guidelines and Practical Exhortations (3:5-17)*
>   *Household Rules (3:18–4:1)*
>   *Concluding Exhortations (4:2-6)*

CONCLUSION (4:7-18)
>   *Maintaining Communication (4:7-9)*
>   *Greetings (4:10-17)*
>   *A Final, Personal Greeting (4:18)*

ADDRESS AND GREETING (1:1-2)

1 *Paul, apostle of Christ Jesus through God's will, and Timothy, the brother,*[1]
2 *to the saints in Colossae*[2] *and faithful*[3] *brothers*[4] *in Christ.*[5] *Grace to you*
and peace from God our Father.[6]

1:1 Παῦλος ἀπόστολος Χριστοῦ Ἰησοῦ διὰ θελήματος θεοῦ καὶ Τιμόθεος
ὁ ἀδελφός. In accordance with the conventions of the time[7] the first thing
the recipients of a letter would expect to read (or hear) is the name(s) of the
sender(s) and confirmation that the letter had been intended for them. So
here: "Paul . . . and Timothy . . . to . . . Colossians. . . ."

The name of Paul would be well known in all Christian gatherings in
the Roman province of Asia. News of Paul's work on the Aegean coast, in
Ephesus in particular (Acts 19:10), and of its impact (Acts 19:23-41!), would
no doubt have been familiar gossip among Christian evangelists and converts
as the gospel spread up the valleys into the Asian hinterland. And Epaphras
as a close associate of Paul (Col. 1:6-7; 4:13; Phm. 23) likely brought the
gospel to Colossae at Paul's behest; converts of Epaphras would certainly
know and honor the name of Paul, even though most of them would never
have met him personally (2:1; see also Introduction, pp. 22f.). At all events,
the Colossian recipients of the letter would have no doubt that the Paul
named at the head of the letter was the famous/infamous missionary who

1. NEB/REB translate "colleague," O'Brien "co-worker"; see n. 10 below.

2. Several, including RSV/NRSV, Masson, O'Brien, and Aletti, run the two phrases together:
"to the saints and faithful brethren in Christ at Colossae" (RSV). It would also be possible to take
ἁγίοις as an adjective: "holy and faithful brothers in Christ at Colosse" (NIV), but see, e.g., Dibelius,
Kolosser, Epheser, Philemon 4; Schweizer, *Colossians* 30; Bruce, *Colossians, Philemon, and Ephe-*
sians 39; Harris 9.

3. "Believing brothers" (as in effect by R. Bultmann, *TDNT* 6.214, followed by Lohse,
Colossians and Philemon 9; O'Brien, *Colossians, Philemon* 4) would be tautologous (Harris 9).
NEB's "brothers in the faith" and REB's "fellow-believers" are too far from the Greek.

4. To avoid the gender-specific "brothers," NRSV translates such references as "brothers
and sisters." In a historic text, however, it is better to retain the original usage, while noting that
women within these congregations would have understood that the term included them; to that extent
it was not gender specific.

5. Some manuscripts and versions add "Jesus," presumably because the scribes were accustomed to the fuller title, echoing 1:1, but forgetful of or less familiar with the regular Pauline usage
"in Christ."

6. Some prominent witnesses add "and the [or our] Lord Jesus Christ," to accord with the
fuller formula, which is an almost invariable feature of the earlier Pauline letters (Rom. 1:7; 1 Cor.
1:3; 2 Cor. 1:2; Gal. 1:3; Phil. 1:2; 2 Thes. 1:2; Phm. 3; also Eph. 1:2; 1 Thes. 1:1 is slightly different).

7. See, e.g., Doty 29-30; and more generally S. K. Stowers, *Letter Writing in Greco-Roman*
Antiquity (Philadelphia: Westminster, 1986); J. L. White, *Light from Ancient Letters* (Philadelphia:
Fortress, 1986); D. E. Aune, *The New Testament in Its Literary Environment* (Philadelphia: Westminster, 1987) 158-82; D. Pardee, P. E. Dion, and S. K. Stowers, *ABD* 4.282-93; P. T. O'Brien, *DPL*
550-53.

had brought the message of a Jewish Messiah/Christ so effectively to Gentiles.

Does any of this have any bearing on whether the letter was written/dictated by Paul himself or by one of his close disciples/associates in his name? The answer is unclear. A letter that claimed his authority and bore his signature (4:18) would carry great weight in all Gentile Christian congregations of the region. And if modern scholarship is persuaded by differences of style and emphasis that the letter cannot have been composed/dictated by Paul himself, that still leaves the possibility that Paul (incapacitated in prison) approved a letter written in his name and willingly appended his signature to a document whose central thrust and main outlines he approved of, even if the details were not stated quite as he would himself (see further p. 38 in the Introduction). Either way, the authority of the apostle lay behind the letter, and that would be sufficient to ensure that the letter was treasured by the Colossians and/or other of the other churches to which the letter was circulated (cf. 4:16), subsequently to be included in the earliest collection(s) of Paul's letters.

As usual in the Pauline letters, a descriptive phrase is attached to the name itself: "an apostle of Christ Jesus." In wider usage the term "apostle" could bear the sense "authorized emissary" (BAGD s.v. ἀπόστολος). This sense was familiar in the Pauline churches, as 2 Cor. 8:23 and Phil. 2:25 make clear: authorized emissary of particular churches. But as always in Paul's claims for his own apostleship, the claim is that his commission and authorization came directly from Christ Jesus. It is as a representative of and spokesman for Christ Jesus, therefore, that Paul would lay claim to a hearing — not simply as spokesman for some agreed tradition or some church council. And for Paul that meant a commission and authorization equal in weight to that of the earliest and most prominent Christian leadership (1 Cor. 15:5-11; 2 Cor. 12:11-12; Gal. 2:7-9). In other words, the added phrase is not merely a matter of providing fuller identification, as though the name "Paul" was insufficient. It is also and still more a claim to authority and respect. The earlier crisis in Galatia had called Paul's authority in question and had evidently persuaded him of the need to assert it forcefully (Gal. 1:1), so that in his subsequent letters where a strong display of authority was necessary he made a point of introducing himself by means of his Christ-authorized title "apostle" (Rom. 1:1; 1 Cor. 1:1; 2 Cor. 1:1). Given the various parallels with Galatians (see the introduction to 2:6–4:6), however, it is noticeable that, in contrast to Galatians, there is no hint here that Paul felt his apostolic authority to be in question.[8]

---

8. For bibliography on "apostle" see J. A. Kirk, "Apostleship since Rengstorf: Towards a Synthesis," *NTS* 21 (1974-75) 249-64; J.-A. Bühner, *EDNT* 1.142-46; F. Agnew, "The Origin of the NT Apostle-Concept: A Review of Research," *JBL* 105 (1986) 75-96; H. D. Betz, *ABD* 1.309-11;

This is all the more striking here if Paul was not in fact the founder of the Colossian church. For it indicates that Paul saw his authority as apostle extending more generally to Gentile churches (Rom. 11:13; Gal. 2:7, 9), even though an apostle's authority related most directly to the churches he/she had founded (1 Cor. 9:1-2; 2 Cor. 10:13-16). Here a comparison with Romans is relevant. For there, too, Paul was writing to churches that he had not founded. But in that case he was all too conscious that he could not claim the authority of the founder (Rom. 1:11-12). In contrast, in Colossians there is no similar sense of embarrassment at claiming the right to a hearing that others might question. This suggests therefore a sense of personal identification with evangelistic and pastoral work carried out by his immediate circle of associates, which again would help explain both how Paul could be introduced as apostle in relation to a church founded by one of his team (Epaphras, see on 1:7) and how a letter (perhaps) written for Paul by one of these associates (Timothy?) could quite properly bear his name and authority. In that case it is to be noted that the title "apostle" is reserved for Paul (contrast 1 Cor. 4:9; 1 Thes. 2:6-7); only Paul had that breadth of mandate ("apostle to the Gentiles") which gave him apostolic authority in reference to a church not founded by him.

That the authoritative and authorizing agent thus represented is named simply as "Christ Jesus" is significant. Christ Jesus was evidently the single most distinctive and characteristic identifying and bonding factor for these new groups. What could legitimately claim his authority ("apostle of Christ Jesus") had to be given first call on attention and obedience. Behind the two words "Christ Jesus," therefore, we must understand a whole body of preaching and teaching about Christ Jesus, on which the Colossian congregation was founded and which could be summed up in these two words (see further on 2:6). It is important to note then the surprising fact that this Jesus is here identified for both Paul and his Gentile audience simply by the epithet "Christ." The Jewish title "Messiah," translated into Greek as "Christ," had become so fixed as sufficient identification of who this Jesus was and what the message about him amounted to, that even for predominantly Gentile churches no further epithet was required. That is to say, the fundamentally Jewish character of this Jesus (a Jew) and of the message about him (Jewish Messiah) was one of the most basic axioms and presuppositions of the new movement, which was already beginning to bear the name "Christian" (Acts 11:26).

The importance of this observation is only partly diminished by the fact that "Christ" was already well on the way to becoming simply another name for Jesus (as usual, but not always in Paul, there is no definite article with "Christ"). In other words it is not clear how much the titular force of

---

P. W. Barnett, *DPL* 45-51. Nielsen 108-9 makes the surprising claim that absence of any reference to the Twelve amounts to an attack on them and rejection of their apostolic status.

the word Messiah would still be heard by people like the Colossians (though see p. 43 n. 5). Certainly it had been a fundamental concern for the first Christians to assert that Jesus, despite or rather precisely because of his suffering and death, was indeed God's Messiah, predicted by psalmist and prophet (particularly Psalms 22 and 69 and Isaiah 53), but it was an assertion which became so taken for granted already within the Gentile mission of Paul that only a few echoes of its controversial character remain in his letters (most notably 1 Cor. 1:23).[9] Nevertheless, it remains a striking fact that this designation of Jesus, whose significance could only be made clear by reference to distinctively Jewish beliefs and hopes and which in Jewish thought was typically bound up with nationalistic aspirations of the Jewish people, could thus function for Gentile Christians as the sole summary identification of the Jesus in whom they believed. That is to say, fundamental to their belief as Gentile Christians was their recognition and affirmation of Jesus as the Messiah of Israel.

In the same connection it may be relevant to note that in Colossians the word order is consistently "Christ Jesus," rather than "Jesus Christ" (but see on 1:3), whereas in the undisputed Paulines "Jesus Christ" is used regularly, in most of the letters more frequently than "Christ Jesus" (the precise statistics are greatly confused by textual variations). This is one of the small stylistic features that suggest a different hand than Paul's in Colossians. More to the above point, since "Jesus" would presumably be understood as the personal name, "Christ" would probably be heard as a descriptive or honorific epithet and thus have retained something at least of its titular force ("Messiah Jesus") even for Greek speakers. Perhaps, then, the titular significance of the name "Christ" resonated louder for the writer of Colossians than for Paul himself.

As in the two Corinthian epistles (and Ephesians) the rooting of Paul's apostolic authority in Christ Jesus is further clarified (or qualified) by the addition of "through the will of God," a legitimation formula (Wolter 47 compares Tob. 12:18). It is characteristic of the opening paragraphs of Paul's letters that he takes care to provide what we might call balancing mentions of Christ and God (cf. Rom. 1:1, 7-8; Gal. 1:1; Phil. 1:3-4; 1 Thes. 1:1-3). Christ Jesus is nowhere thought of as an authority independent of God. On the contrary, the fact that God is the ultimate source of reference and authority is repeatedly indicated. Of course, appeal to the will of God is something of a commonplace in Paul (e.g., Rom. 1:10; 15:32; Gal. 1:4; 1 Thes. 4:3; 5:18;

---

9. See particularly Juel chs. 4 and 5: "the confession of Jesus as Messiah is the presupposition for NT christology but not its content" (175, 177). Still justifiably influential are the essays by N. A. Dahl, "The Messiahship of Jesus in Paul" (1953) and "The Crucified Messiah" (1960), reprinted in *Jesus the Christ: The Historical Origins of Christological Doctrine* (Minneapolis: Fortress, 1991) 15-47.

see also on 1:9 and 4:12) as elsewhere (BAGD s.v. θέλω 2: "God/the gods willing"), but here the phrase rounds out a mutually reinforcing mesh of authority: Paul as apostle of Christ Jesus, Jesus as Christ owned and authorized by God, and God as the one God of Israel through whose Messiah and apostle good news is extending to the nations. Here not least is evoked the characteristic Jewish understanding of time and history as a process working out in accordance with a predetermined purpose of God, with the further particularly Christian inference that Messiah Jesus is the climax of that purpose and Paul his eschatological emissary (cf. 1 Cor. 4:9; see further on 1:25-26).

In this opening greeting Paul conjoins one other name: "Timothy." The formulation matches that of 2 Cor. 1:1 exactly. Timothy features more frequently in Paul's letters than any of Paul's other associates and is given special prominence in several of the greetings (Rom. 16:21; 2 Cor. 1:1; Phil. 1:1; 1 Thes. 1:1; 2 Thes. 1:1; Phm. 1). He also served as Paul's emissary in several delicate negotiations (1 Cor. 4:17; 16:10; Phil. 2:19; 1 Thes. 3:2, 6). All this is reinforced by the various Acts references (e.g., 17:14-15; 19:22) and the two letters to Timothy and leaves the strong impression that Timothy was widely known among the churches influenced by Paul (including, therefore, Colossae) as Paul's most trusted right-hand man. Nevertheless his prominence here is somewhat surprising. For in the other cases where he appears as coauthor he has been very actively involved with the churches addressed (Corinth, Philippi, Thessalonica), whereas here there is no hint that he had had any more personal involvement with the Colossians than Paul himself had. This could reinforce the possibility that in this case, of the two authors named, Timothy had in fact greater responsibility for composing the letter than Paul had, with Paul approving the content, adding his personal signature, and named first out of respect (cf. Schweizer, *Colossians* 23-24; Gnilka, *Kolosserbrief* 28; Wall 36; contrast, e.g., Yates, *Colossians* 5: "he is in no sense co-author of the letter"; see further above, p. 38).

The significance of the description of Timothy as "brother" is not entirely clear. It could reflect a sense of national kinship; Timothy was Jewish through his mother (Acts 16:1; cf., e.g., Lev. 19:17; Deut. 15:12; Isa. 66:20; Tob. 1:3). But religious associations in the wider Hellenistic world also spoke of their members as "brothers" (BAGD s.v. ἀδελφός 2; K. H. Schelkle, *RAC* 2.631-40; *NDIEC* 2:49-50), as at Qumran (Josephus, *War* 2.122; 1QS 6:10, 22; CD 6:20; 7:1-2; 1QSa 1:18; 1QM 13:1; 15:4, 7; see also on Phm. 2). Moreover, Jesus was remembered as in effect advocating a new model of family and kinship (Mark 3:31-35), and the sense of disciples as brothers gathered round Jesus in a new family unit is strong in the Gospels (e.g., Matt. 5:22-24, 47; 7:3-5; 18:15, 21, 35) as elsewhere in Paul (Rom. 1:13; 7:1, 4; 8:12, 29; etc.; but see also the introduction to the comments on 3:18–4:1). It is not surprising, therefore, that "brother" had become a title of respect ("the brother") and that Paul should so speak of several of his colleagues or particular Christians (Rom. 16:23; 1 Cor. 1:1; 16:12; Phil. 2:25; cf. 2 Cor. 8:18; 9:3, 5; 12:18). As such the term indicates warmth of fraternal feeling and common (spiritual) kinship rather than a title or office restricted to a few special individuals.[10]

1:2 τοῖς ἐν Κολοσσαῖς ἁγίοις καὶ πιστοῖς ἀδελφοῖς ἐν Χριστῷ, χάρις ὑμῖν καὶ εἰρήνη ἀπὸ θεοῦ πατρὸς ἡμῶν. Again as custom and common sense dictated, identification of author(s) is followed by designation of recipients. Although Colossae was clearly past the peak of its importance and was now overshadowed by its near neighbor Laodicea (see pp. 20f. in the Introduction), there was evidently a thriving Christian group there. That Epaphras was a native of the city (4:12) would also give it a particular claim on Paul's attention. Whether the challenges confronting the church there were more widespread (affecting also Laodicea? — cf. 4:16) we cannot say.

To address his readers as "saints" is another regular and distinctively Pauline feature of Paul's salutations (Rom. 1:7; 1 Cor. 1:2; 2 Cor. 1:1; Phil. 1:1; also Eph. 1:1; but here, as in Rom. 1:7 and Phil. 1:1, without describing them as "church"). The substantive ("the holy ones") derives from the cultic idea of holiness as a being "set apart from everyday usage, dedicated to God." That idea of holiness was familiar in Hellenistic cults, but otherwise it is a characteristic and overwhelmingly Jewish category. As applied to persons, the most obviously "holy" individuals were the priests and Levites (e.g., Lev. 21:7-8; Num. 16:5-7; 2 Chron. 35:3; Ps. 106:16), though Nazirites (Num. 6:5-8) and prophets (2 Kgs. 4:9) could also be so designated. In terms of "set-apartness" to God the most holy ones are angels (e.g., Job 15:15; Ps. 89:5, 7; Dan. 8:13; Zech. 14:5). Most relevant here, however, is the fact that the people of Israel as a whole were quite often called "the holy ones/saints" in Jewish literature (e.g., Pss. 16:3; 34:9; Dan. 7:18; 8:24; Tob. 8:15; Wis. 18:9; also Qumran: 1QSb 3:2 and 1QM 3:5; see further *ABD* 3.238-39). What is striking, therefore, is that Paul felt able to incorporate into this distinctively Jewish self-description small gatherings of predominantly Gentile believers in Christ Jesus (cf. Ernst, *Philipper, Philemon, Kolosser, Epheser* 153; Wright, *Colossians and Philemon* 47). The important inference is that Paul understood these Gentiles to have been incorporated into Israel, the people of God, through faith in and baptism in the name of Messiah Jesus — that is, without becoming Jewish proselytes (by being circumcised). And since there is no hint that this designation was offensive

---

10. As argued particularly by E. E. Ellis, "Paul and his Co-Workers," *NTS* 17 (1970-71) 437-52, reprinted in his *Prophecy* 3-22; also his *Pauline Theology* 97-98; followed by O'Brien, *Colossians, Philemon* 3; and see n. 1 above. For family images used by Paul see particularly Banks, *Idea* 61-71; see also R. P. Martin, *The Family and the Fellowship: New Testament Images of the Church* (Exeter: Paternoster, 1979) 123-25.

to local Jewish synagogues, we may further infer that there was a fair degree of toleration on the part of many such synagogues for these house groups meeting under the banner of Israel's diaspora — "the saints in Colossae, Laodicea, Ephesus, etc." In that case the situation seems to have deteriorated within a generation (cf. Rev. 2:9; 3:9).

In some contrast the further epithet "faithful brothers" is without parallel in Paul's greetings. "Brothers" he uses regularly as an address outside the salutation (see on 1:1), but "faithful" is a category he uses sparingly for humans (only five times in the undisputed Paulines) — perhaps because his theology focused so much on "faith" rather than on faithfulness (see my *Romans* 200-201, 238). It may be significant, then, that the term "faithful" occurs four times in this connection in Colossians (1:2, 7; 4:7, 9), twice in Ephesians, and nine times in the letters to Timothy (including "the faithful ones," 1 Tim. 4:3, 12). Given also that one of Paul's few usages refers to Timothy himself as "faithful" (1 Cor. 4:17), it raises again the question as to whether the letter was dictated by Paul or composed by Timothy, for whom "faithful" may have been a favorite epithet.

On the assumption that any departure from customary practice is probably significant, we may deduce here that Paul and Timothy chose to use this uncustomary address to reinforce their primary appeal. They wished to stress that these Christians, unknown to them personally, were nevertheless brothers just as much as Timothy himself was. And they complimented their addressees on their faithfulness, fearing that they might prove unfaithful (cf. Lightfoot 130; Masson 89). It was precisely the Colossians' continued commitment as brothers, members of the new family gathered around Christ Jesus, that the writers wanted to encourage and sustain (Aletti, *Épître aux Colossiens* 46). The two phrases in the address could be taken together (see n. 2), but even if we follow the natural phrasing of the Greek and take them separately there is no suggestion that two distinct or even overlapping groups are envisaged (as though not all the "saints in Colossae" were "faithful brothers in Christ"), simply an encouragement to the saints to demonstrate their continuing commitment and loyalty as brothers in Christ.

That should be all the more possible because their standing and persistence as brothers was "in Christ." Their brotherhood was not one of blood relationship, but rather the spiritual bond of the shared experience of believing in Christ Jesus and knowing that they were accepted by and through him. And this shared experience was itself a source of enabling for their persistence. The phrase "in Christ" is itself a classic expression of distinctive Pauline theology (occurring more than eighty times in the Pauline letters; elsewhere in the New Testament only in 1 Peter; see BAGD s.v. ἐν I.5d). It summed up the fact that for Paul the decisive factor in determining identity for the people of God was no longer the Temple cult ("set apart . . . in

Christ," not set apart by reference to the Jerusalem Temple) and no longer ethnic kinship, but that relation to Christ which the phrase epitomized.[11]

What that relation amounted to is less clear since the phrase itself is so brief. Some uses have become so formulaic that they could almost be translated "Christian" (as some in fact would translate passages like 2 Cor. 12:2; Gal. 1:22; 1 Thes. 2:14). But presumably the original and primary usage must have been more dynamic than that (Rom. 8:1-2; 12:5; 1 Cor. 4:15b; 2 Cor. 2:17; 5:17; 12:19, etc.). Nor can it denote simply the act of believing the message about Christ, otherwise the "in" would hardly have become so established. Rather at the root of the phrase there seems to be a sense of intimate and existential relationship with Christ, as the phrase "with Christ" also suggests — that is, with Christ as a living personality, risen from the dead (note especially Rom. 6:3-11; see 2:12-13, 20; 3:3-4). And the ἐν seems to indicate an integration of personal (and social) identity with this Christ (in some real sense "in" Christ; cf. Gal. 2:20), as the correlated phrase "into Christ" (Rom. 6:3; 1 Cor. 12:13; Gal. 3:27; and see on 2:5) and the image of "the body of Christ" (Rom. 12:4-5; 1 Cor. 12:12-27; see on 1:18) also imply (thus also a form of Adam christology — Ernst, *Philipper, Philemon, Kolosser, Epheser* 154). The frequency with which "in Christ/him/whom" appears is a feature of Colossians (1:2, 14, 16, 17, 19, 28; 2:3, 9, 10, 11, 12, 15).

That this involves a conception of "Christ" as one whose personal identity is retained but who is more than a human individual is clear enough, but analogies from human and social experience quickly prove inadequate. We may wish to speak of a mystical identity, so long as that is not seen as world-denying or as turning one's back on the world (the "in Christ" of Paul is also very much in the world — e.g., Rom. 15:17-19; Gal. 2:4; Phil. 1:13). The crucial feature of the phrase, however, is, as already indicated, that it enabled Paul to realign the identity of the people of God away from questions of ethnic descent and national custom to integration with this Jesus, who, even as Israel's Messiah, transcended such definitions and concerns (particularly Gal. 3:26-29). Assuming that Epaphras was a faithful exponent of Paul's gospel, all this would have been implicit for the Colossian recipients.

The greeting that follows is one of the most regular features in the Pauline letters (see n. 6). Only 1 Thes. 1:1 differs markedly (containing only the first part — "grace to you and peace" — perhaps an indication of its being Paul's first letter, composed before he settled on what became his established form), and 1 and 2 Timothy add "grace, mercy, and peace."

---

11. For the significance of the phrase see my *Jesus* 323-24; C. F. D. Moule, *The Origin of Christology* (Cambridge: Cambridge University, 1977) 47-96; A. J. M. Wedderburn, "Some Observations on Paul's Use of the Phrases 'in Christ' and 'with Christ,' " *JSNT* 25 (1985) 83-97.

1 Pet. 1:2; 2 Pet. 1:2; and Rev. 1:4 also probably reflect the influence of Paul's formulation. As all commentators rightly note, Paul seems deliberately to have adapted the regular Greek greeting, χαίρειν ("hail, greeting"), by replacing it with χάρις ("grace") and to have linked it with the characteristic Jewish greeting, *šalom* = εἰρήνη ("peace").[12] The more common Jewish association was "mercy" with "peace" (Num. 6:25-26; Ps. 85:10; Isa. 54:10; Tob. 7:12 v.l.; Sir. 50:23-24; 3 Macc. 2:19-20; *Jub.* 22:9; *1 Enoch* 5:5-6 Greek; *Shemoneh 'Esreh* 19).[13]

This was an effective way of underlining one of the most important features of the new Christian vocabulary. For though χάρις would be familiar enough in wider speech, in the sense particularly of "favor" (LSJ), the word had been taken up by Christians to epitomize the dynamic outreaching generosity of God which they had experienced through the gospel and the Spirit (see my *Jesus* 202-5; and further on 1:6 and 3:16). Here again Paul has clearly left his stamp on Christian thought, for 100 of the 155 New Testament uses of the word occur in the Pauline letters, and if the Pauline sections of Acts are included, we can say that more than two-thirds of New Testament usage is Pauline. His prayer in effect is that the grace that first set the Colossian Christians apart as "saints" will continue to enable them to remain faithful as "brothers."

The richness of the Jewish greeting "peace" should not be lost sight of since it denotes not simply cessation of war but all that makes for well-being and prosperity in the absence of war, and not simply individual or inner peace, but also the social wholeness of harmonious relationships (e.g., Pss. 72:1-7; 85; 147:14; Isa. 55:12; Zech. 8:12; see further W. Foerster and G. von Rad, *TDNT* 2.400-420). Like "grace" it is a characteristically Pauline term (43 of the 91 New Testament occurrences appear in the Pauline letters; see further on 3:15).[14] The greeting was particularly appropriate to a community where personal and corporate tensions were in danger of rending the community's harmony, as in most of the churches addressed by Paul. That Paul and Timothy could use it in a letter to an unknown Gentile church implies that such churches of the Pauline mission would be as familiar with such Jewish heritage as they were with the characteristic Pauline evocation of divine grace.

That God is the only source of this grace and peace could be taken for granted, as also that God is Father. In traditional Greek religious thought Zeus was regularly described as "Father of both men and gods," and the

12. All the extant Bar Kokhba letters (*ABD* 1.601-6) use the single word greeting, *šalom*.

13. See further K. Berger, "Apostelbrief und apostolische Rede. Zum Formular früh-christlicher Briefe," *ZNW* 65 (1974) 190-231, here 197-200.

14. There are no grounds for the suggestion that the epistolary usage here reflects a Hellenistic understanding of peace "and no longer the Pauline eschatological shalom" (*pace* V. Hasler, *EDNT* 1.397).

image of God/god as father was equally familiar in Greek philosophy and in the mystery cults (BAGD s.v. πατήρ 3a-c; G. Schrenk, *TDNT* 5.951-56). The appeal here, however, is, of course, not to this more widespread religious instinct within Hellenistic polytheism but to the one God of Israel. Here not least the modern reader has to hear the taken-for-granteds that do not need explicit expression. It was so axiomatic that the Christian gospel was good news of the one God of Israel that it need not be spelled out in Paul's letters (as it would have to be in a first preaching: cf. 1 Thes. 1:9-10 with Acts 14:15-17 and 17:22-31).

What is striking here, as in Paul's regular use of the phrase in his greetings, is that a relationship claimed particularly by Israel for itself (e.g., Deut. 32:6; Isa. 63:16; Jer. 31:9; Mal. 1:6; Tob. 13:3-4) and for the righteous within Israel (Wis. 2:13, 16, 18; *Pss. Sol.* 13:9) is appropriated also by Gentile believers: "*our* God." Paul's implicit claim is that by accepting the gospel of Christ and his Spirit Gentiles were incorporated into Israel/the family of God, now redefined as "the household of faith" (Gal. 6:10; see also on 1:3).

The omission of the regularly accompanying phrase "and of the Lord Jesus Christ" (see n. 6) is surprising. It cannot be that Paul and Timothy did not want to associate Christ as an equal source of the grace and peace (references in n. 6). That would hardly accord with the high status ascribed to Christ elsewhere in the letter (1:15-20; 2:9), and in the very next breath they speak of God as "the Father of our Lord Jesus Christ" (1:3). Nevertheless, it may be deliberate that before embarking on the exposition of Christ's full significance, the ultimate supremacy of the one God and Father is thus given prominence. The likelihood is strengthened by the formulation used in the thanksgiving in 1:3 (see on 1:3).

EXTENDED THANKSGIVING (1:3-23)

Paul's opening prayer follows no regular pattern. At most we can say that his usual but by no means constant custom was to assure his readers of his thanks and prayers for them (Rom. 1:8-9; Phil. 1:3-4; 1 Thes. 1:2; Phm. 4; so here in v. 3; also Eph. 1:15-16; cf. 1 Thes. 3:9-10). Beyond that, however, there is no fixed pattern. Here the opening announcement of thanksgiving and prayer (1:3) is expanded by the elaboration of each in turn. The closest parallels are in Philippians and Philemon and partly 2 Thessalonians (cf. the analysis in Schubert 54-55):

Col.		Phil.	Phm.	2 Thess.
1:3	statement of thanksgiving and prayer	1:3-4	4	
1:4-8	elaboration of thanksgiving	1:5-8	5	1:3-10
1:9-14	elaboration of prayer	1:9-11	6	1:11-12

Quite exceptional, however, is the further elaboration in the form of a hymn in praise of Christ (1:15-20) and its particular application to the Colossians (1:21-23), which maintains the spirit of praise and thanksgiving in a way unparalleled in the undisputed Paulines (cf. Schubert 14-16 and Pokorný 45; the extended thanksgiving in 1 Thessalonians is more closely parallel to the personal statement that follows in 1:24–2:5).

We may at once deduce that Paul's thanksgiving and prayer for his readers was by no means simply conventional. Rather, the variation of form and content must imply that he shaped his sentiments to reflect the real situations of his readers (as he knew them), even omitting them altogether in the case of Galatians (contrast 2 Cor. 1:3-7)! In other words, these are real prayers, however many conventional elements (see on 1:4) Paul or the one writing in his name incorporated.

The extended thanksgiving here is also significant in that it indicates that the writers had no urgency of anxiety regarding the situation confronting the Colossian church. Again in marked contrast to Galatians, where the crisis called for immediate attention, quite disrupting the normal epistolary pleasantries, Paul and Timothy here seem remarkably relaxed and in an expansive mood. However serious the threat posed to the Colossian believers it could be addressed at a more leisurely pace and the response built up to gradually.

Thanksgiving (1:3-8)

3 *We thank God, the Father of our Lord Jesus Christ,*[1] *always praying for*[2] *you,* 4 *having heard of your faith in Christ Jesus and of the love that you have for all the saints* 5 *on account of the hope laid up for you in the heavens.*[3] *Of this you heard earlier in the word of the truth of the gospel,* 6 *which has come to you, just as also in all the world it is bearing fruit and growing,*[4] *so also it is among you from the day on which you heard and came to know the grace of God in truth,* 7 *as you learned it from Epaphras, our beloved fellow slave. He is a faithful servant of Christ*[5] *on our*[6] *behalf,* 8 *and he has made clear to us your love in the Spirit.*

The beginning of the extended thanksgiving falls naturally into a chiastic pattern (Dibelius, *Kolosser, Epheser, Philemon* 5; cf. Lohse, *Colossians and Philemon* 14):

> (3) We thank God, the Father of our Lord Jesus Christ, always praying for you,
>> (4) having heard of your faith in Christ Jesus and of the love that you have for all the saints (5). . . .
>>> Of this you heard earlier in the word of the truth of the gospel, (6) which has come to you,
>>>> just as also in all the world it is bearing fruit and growing, so also it is among you from the day on which you heard and came to know the grace of God in truth, (7) as you learned it from Epaphras . . .
>> (8) and he has made clear to us your love in the Spirit.

> (9) That is why we also, ever since we heard, have not ceased to pray on your behalf and to ask that you . . .

---

1. The omission of "Christ" by B and a few others is probably accidental, since the full formula is characteristic of the formalities at the beginning and end of Paul's letters.

2. Some important manuscripts have changed the περί ("concerning") to ὑπέρ ("on behalf of"), presumably on the ground that it strengthens the intercessory character of the prayer, but the former is Paul's more regular usage (Rom. 1:8; 1 Cor. 1:4; 1 Thes. 1:2; 2 Thes. 1:3; ὑπέρ in Phil. 1:4; cf. 2 Cor. 1:11 and Eph. 1:16).

3. For different ways of taking the Greek see Harris 18. GNB engages in an elaborate reworking of vv. 5 and 6: "When the true message, the Good News, first came to you, you heard about the hope it offers. So your faith and love are based on what you hope for, which is kept safe for you in heaven. The gospel keeps bringing blessings and is spreading. . . ."

4. Some manuscripts omit "and growing," perhaps because it was judged to be tautologous.

5. The Greek could quite properly be translated here "servant of the Christ."

6. The more strongly attested and more difficult reading is undoubtedly ἡμῶν ("our," followed by most commentators and translations except NRSV; see Moule, *Colossians and Philemon*

As in the other Pauline letters, the themes and language of the thanksgiving are echoed in the rest of the letter (O'Brien, *Thanksgivings,* 69; Mullins 291), from which Mullins concludes that the structure and character of the thanksgiving are Pauline and provide no argument for post-Pauline authorship (against Lohse). "He might well be reproducing the kind of utterance he was accustomed to make in solemn liturgical gatherings of his churches. . . . the liturgical (or quasi-liturgical) utterances of a practical pastor and apostle" (Houlden 149).

1:3 εὐχαριστοῦμεν τῷ θεῷ πατρὶ τοῦ κυρίου ἡμῶν Ἰησοῦ Χριστοῦ πάντοτε περὶ ὑμῶν προσευχόμενοι. A characteristic feature of the ancient art of letter writing was the congratulatory thanksgiving.[7] In Paul, too, it follows a regular pattern: a thanksgiving (εὐχαριστεῖν) addressed to God; stressing his (unceasing) prayerful concern for the readers, with the subject of thanksgiving usually the faith they display (in 1 Corinthians their rich experience of grace rather than their faith). The closest parallel here is 1 Thes. 1:2-3 and, perhaps significantly, Phm. 4-5. The plural "we thank" may imply a consciously double authorship (Timothy and Paul), since elsewhere in Paul the singular is more usual (Rom. 1:8; 1 Cor. 1:4; Phil. 1:3; Phm. 4; but note also 1 Thes. 1:2 and 2 Thes. 1:3).[8]

The most interesting variation here is the insertion of the phrase "the Father of our Lord Jesus Christ." It is a phrase that Paul uses a number of times — usually in the form "the God and Father of our Lord Jesus Christ" (Rom. 15:6; 2 Cor. 1:3; 11:31; also Eph. 1:3, 17; 1 Pet. 1:3). Contained in it is the implicit Christian claim that God, the one God made known to Israel, is now to be understood no longer simply as Father of Israel, but most clearly as the Father of Jesus Christ, and only as such "our Father," Father of Gentiles as well as Jews (see on 1:2).

More to the point, here again, as in 1:2, there may be a deliberate attempt to stress the sole sovereignty of God at the beginning of a letter that focuses so much on the divine status of Christ (see again on 1:2). The significance is all the greater, the greater weight we see in the attachment of κύριος ("Lord") to "Jesus Christ" (see also on 2:6). Given the degree of heavenly majesty and divine authority that that title carried (particularly Rom. 10:13; 1 Cor. 8:5-6; Phil. 2:9-11; see further, e.g., my *Romans* 607-9), it is important to recognize that Paul and Timothy begin by reminding their readers that God is the Father of Jesus Christ the Lord, or in the fuller formula

27 n. 1; Pokorný 44 n. 50; Wolter 56), though NA and UBS prefer ὑμῶν/"your" because of the breadth of support for the latter and because early copyists may have been influenced by ἡμῶν and ἡμῖν in close proximity on either side (Metzger 619-20; Bruce, *Colossians, Philemon, and Ephesians* 40 n. 7).

7. Schubert 158-79; Doty 31-33; summary in Lohse, *Colossians and Philemon* 12; but see now Arzt. See also the introduction to Phm. 4-7 below.

8. "There is no reason to think that St. Paul ever uses an 'epistolary' plural, referring to himself solely" (Lightfoot 229; cf. Gnilka, *Kolosserbrief* 32).

Paul uses more often, that God is the *God* and Father of our *Lord* Jesus Christ. From the outset, therefore, Paul and Timothy wish it to be understood that the high christology to be enunciated shortly is kept within the constraints of Jewish monotheism. God the Father is the one to whom prayer should properly be offered (in 3:17, as in Rom. 1:8, the thanksgiving is directed to God *"through* him/Jesus Christ"; Conzelmann 134 thinks the mediatorship of Christ is implied also here), just as he is the ultimate source ("Father") of all creation and all being, including the dignity and authority of Jesus' Messiahship and Lordship.

The unceasing nature of this prayer (πάντοτε, "always, at all times") is one of the most characteristic features of Paul's opening assurance of his prayers for his readers, whether attached to the εὐχαριστεῖν ("thank" — 1 Cor. 1:4; 1 Thes. 1:2; 2 Thes. 1:3) or to the προσεύχεσθαι ("pray," as in Rom. 1:10 and Phil. 1:4). Phm. 4, as here, could be taken either way. Paul could have meant that every time he prayed he remembered his various churches. Perhaps he maintained the Jewish practice of prayer three times a day (cf. Dan. 6:11; Acts 3:1; 10:3; *Didache* 8:3), or perhaps he used the long hours of travel and of work in stitching to hold his churches before God (see also on 1:9 and 4:2). But not too much should be made of the language since it is an epistolary flourish characteristic of the period (O'Brien, *Colossians, Philemon* 10). The use of περί ("concerning") rather than ὑπέρ ("on behalf of"; see n. 2) is sufficient to indicate that Paul saw his prayers not as a substitute for their own prayers but as a natural expression of Christian love and concern.

1:4 ἀκούσαντες τὴν πίστιν ὑμῶν ἐν Χριστῷ Ἰησοῦ καὶ τὴν ἀγάπην ἣν ἔχετε εἰς πάντας τοὺς ἁγίους. The congratulatory element focuses as usual on their faith (Rom. 1:8) and love (1 Thes. 1:3; 2 Thes. 1:3; and, perhaps significantly, Phm. 5; also Eph. 1:15). That this is a matter of report rather than of personal knowledge confirms that Paul did not know the Colossian church personally (though cf. Rom. 1:8); the parallel with Phm. 5 is again worth noting. It also reminds us that news of his churches would reach Paul regularly along the trade routes, even to far-off Rome, though in this case Epaphras seems to have made a special point of keeping Paul informed (1:8). To be noted also is the degree to which the vertical ("faith in Christ") was integrated with the horizontal ("love for the saints"). Paul would never have wanted these two to fall apart.

Perhaps more than any other word, "faith" sums up the distinctive feature of the Christian gospel and life for Paul (see, e.g., G. Barth, *EDNT* 3.95). Rather like "grace" (see 1:2), Paul's use of "faith" dominates New Testament usage (142 of 243 occurrences). Its distinctive Pauline force is most evident in Romans 4, where he makes unforgettably clear the character of faith as sheer trust in the power and grace of God, as against a more typical traditional Jewish emphasis on faithfulness (see on 1:2, "faithful").

And in Gal. 2:16–3:26 he indicates by emphatic argument that this faith has now been given its eschatological focus in Christ to become the single most determinative characteristic of the new phase of God's saving purpose introduced by Christ. What Paul and Timothy commend here, therefore, is the way in which the Colossians received the message about Christ (as Abraham received the promise of a son, Gen. 15:6; Romans 4; Galatians 3) and committed themselves in trust to the one so proclaimed, making Christ the focus and determinant of their lives from then on (see on 1:2, "in Christ").

One of the most interesting divergences from normal Pauline usage comes in the phrase πίστις ἐν Χριστῷ 'Ιησοῦ ("faith in Christ Jesus"). For Paul never so speaks. Normally he uses the noun phrase in the form πίστις 'Ιησοῦ Χριστοῦ or an equivalent (Rom. 3:22, 26; Gal. 2:16, 20; 3:22; Phil. 3:9; see also 2:12). Some take this in the sense "the faith(fulness) of Jesus Christ," but almost certainly it denotes "faith in Jesus Christ" (see my *"Pistis Christou"* and *Galatians* 138-39). He also uses the verbal form πιστεύειν εἰς Χριστὸν 'Ιησοῦν ("believe in Christ Jesus," Gal. 2:16; so also Rom. 10:14; Phil. 1:29; see also 2:5). But nowhere does he use ἐν with the dative, as here (Gal. 3:26 is not an exception since the two prepositional phrases there are independent of each other, as is generally agreed).[9] In contrast the letters more frequently accepted as post-Pauline use phrases similar to what we have here in 1:4 a number of times (Eph. 1:15; 1 Tim. 3:13; 2 Tim. 1:13; 3:15; also *1 Clement* 22:1; 43:1). Here then is another suggestion that with Colossians we are already moving beyond Paul's own usage. There is, however, no significant difference in meaning (if anything, the ἐν formulation is more static), and the thought is otherwise wholly Pauline in character and emphasis.

The other element that draws the prayerful congratulation of Paul and Timothy is the Colossians' "love for all the saints." Here within the compass of three short verses we have a third word (after "grace" and "faith") to which Christianity, and again Paul in particular (75 out of 116 occurrences in the New Testament), gave distinctive weight as a carrier of one of the important and far-reaching emphases marking out Christianity among other religions of the time. For of the different Greek words for "love," ἀγάπη was little used at the time: it appears only rarely in nonbiblical Greek before the second or third century AD (C. Spicq, *Theological Lexicon of the New Testament* [Peabody: Hendrickson, 1994] 1.8-22) and is relatively rare in the

9. Despite strong support (e.g., Lightfoot 131; Dibelius, *Kolosser, Epheser, Philemon* 5; Moule 49; Lohse, *Colossians and Philemon* 16; Bruce, *Colossians, Philemon, and Ephesians* 41; Wall 44-45; cf. Masson 90 and n. 2), it is unlikely that ἐν Χριστῷ should be taken as referring to the sphere rather than the object of "your faith." Where Paul uses nouns with "in Christ" (as in Rom. 6:23; 8:39; 1 Cor. 1:4; Gal. 2:4; 3:14), he has in mind the blessing that derives from Christ and is given "in Christ," not faith directed to Christ; and the parallels in Ephesians and the Pastorals indicate clearly enough late Pauline or post-Pauline usage (cf. Mark 1:15).

LXX, usually used there in reference to conjugal love (though note Jer. 2:2; Wis. 3:9; 6:18). Most of Paul's references are to human love (e.g., Rom. 12:9; 13:10; 1 Cor. 13:1–14:1; 2 Cor. 2:4, 8; Gal. 5:6, 13, 22); so also in Colossians (1:8; 2:2; 3:14). But it is clear that for Paul the self-sacrifice of Christ is the definitive expression of this "love" (Rom. 5:6-8; 8:31-35; 2 Cor. 5:14-15; so also Col. 1:13-14; see further, e.g., G. Schneider, *EDNT* 1.10-11). Presumably, therefore, this is what was in mind here — an active concern for one another among the Colossian Christians which did not stop short at self-sacrifice of personal interests — and not just for one another, if the "all the saints" is to be taken seriously. Here may be indicated a network of mutual support and encouragement as Christians moved among the different towns in Asia Minor; a more specific reference to the collection for "the saints" in Jerusalem (Rom. 15:16; 1 Cor. 16:1 — as suggested by Ernst, *Philipper, Philemon, Kolosser, Epheser* 156) is less likely. Epaphras must have spoken very encouragingly of his Christian townsfolk. For "the saints" see on 1:2.

1:5 διὰ τὴν ἐλπίδα τὴν ἀποκειμένην ὑμῖν ἐν τοῖς οὐρανοῖς, ἣν προηκούσατε ἐν τῷ λόγῳ τῆς ἀληθείας τοῦ εὐαγγελίου. Given the fact that faith and love have already been given prominent mention, it should occasion no surprise that the third member of the characteristic Christian trio, ἐλπίς ("hope"), should immediately appear in close connection. For the linking of the three is another distinctive feature of Pauline teaching (1 Cor. 13:13; Gal. 5:5-6; 1 Thes. 1:3; 5:8; cf. Rom. 5:1-5; see further Hunter 33-35). "Hope" itself is almost as distinctively a Pauline feature in the New Testament (36 of 53 occurrences). In contrast to the more uncertain, fearful note typical of classical (and modern) usage, the sense here is characteristically Jewish: hope as expectation of good, confidence in God (R. Bultmann, *TDNT* 2.519-23). As such it is closely related to faith, confident trust in God.

The connection with v. 4, however, is slightly puzzling — "on account of the hope. . . ."[10] NEB/REB (and NIV similarly) resolve the puzzle by translating: "both [faith and love] spring from the/that hope. . . ." And that is probably a fair rendering, since the preposition must be taken to indicate that the faith and love are in some sense a response to, derived from, or in some way dependent on the hope. In which case, unusually in Paul, the hope is being presented as the basis for the faith and love, somewhat in contrast to 1 Cor. 13:13 and Gal. 5:5-6 (hope in God as the basis for faith in Christ and love to all). At all events, the formulation here serves to underline the eschatological and forward-looking character of the gospel message that called forth the Colossians' faith and stimulated their love for their fellow saints (cf. Wolter 52-53).

---

10. The older debate on the connection of these words is reviewed by Abbott 196 and Masson 90 n. 3.

This sense is reinforced by the description of the hope as "laid up (present tense) for you in the heavens." The verb has the basic sense of "be put away, stored up" (as in Luke 19:20). But it readily gathered to itself the richer sense of something held in reserve for someone or some occasion as a destiny (LSJ and BAGD s.v. ἀπόκειμαι; Lohse, *Colossians and Philemon* 18; so 4 Macc. 8:11; Heb. 9:27) and in Jewish and Christian thought of something retained by God for the appropriate time in God's foreordained plan (Gen. 49:10; Job 38:23; *Joseph and Asenath* 15:10: "your wedding robe . . . laid up in your chamber since eternity"), including eschatological reward (2 Macc. 12:45; 2 Tim. 4:8).[11] The imagery thus gives "hope" a less typically Pauline sense of "that which is hoped for" (rather than as the subjective experience of hope), which some regard as another mark of post-Pauline authorship (e.g., Bornkamm, "Hoffnung" 207; B. Mayer, *EDNT* 1.439), though the effect is the thoroughly Pauline one of expressing full confidence that the sure purpose of God, not yet fully unveiled, will be revealed and realized in God's good time. This emphasis on the forward-looking character of the gospel may well be a first counter to a too realized element in the teaching to be countered in the body of the letter (e.g., R. P. Martin, *Colossians and Philemon* 48; O'Brien, *Colossians, Philemon* 12), though the letter itself has a stronger realized emphasis than the earlier Paulines (see on 2:12 and the introduction to the comments on 3:1-4).

What precisely the hope is, or is directed to, is not mentioned here, but the picture becomes clearer with the other two references to hope in the letter, as to both its source ("the hope of the gospel," 1:23), its focus ("Christ in you"), and what is hoped for ("glory"; see on 1:27). The location of what is hoped for is, however, specified here: "in the heavens." What is hoped for, therefore, could be the exalted Christ ("their Lord in heaven," 4:1), making for an interesting tension with 1:27 ("Christ in you"), or the Colossian Christians' final salvation, consisting in their being taken up to heaven and transformed into heavenly/spiritual form ("glory"; cf. Rom. 8:17-25; 1 Cor. 15:44-49; 2 Cor. 5:1-5; 1 Thes. 4:14-17).

The plural form "heavens" should not be ignored, since it is hardly found in nonbiblical Greek and therefore reflects the common Jewish view that the heavenly realm above had a number of regions, if not many (note the repeated Old Testament phrase "heaven and the heaven of the heavens," Deut. 10:14; 1 Kgs. 8:27; 2 Chron. 2:6; 6:18; Neh. 9:6). If the usual topography is in mind here (anything from two to ten heavens; see H. Traub,

---

11. There is no thought here, however, of something stored up (in heaven) by human effort (as in Matt. 6:20; Luke 18:22; cf. Philo, *De praemiis et poenis* 104, cited by Dibelius, *Kolosser, Epheser, Philemon* 6) and no ground therefore for seeing here an echo of the apocalyptic idea of a treasure of (good) works laid up in heaven, which appears in *4 Ezra* 7:77 and *2 Baruch* 14:12 (as thought by Lohmeyer 24; Gnilka, *Kolosserbrief* 33; Ernst, *Philipper, Philemon, Kolosser, Epheser* 157).

TDNT 5.510-12), the implication would be that the lower reaches of heaven were populated by (normally hostile) "principalities and powers" (cf. particularly Eph. 6:12; see on 1:16), with God and his angels in the upper regions or beyond all the heavens (cf. 2 Cor. 12:2; Eph. 4:10; see on 2:18). The hope, then, would be for a destiny that outmaneuvers (cf. Rom. 8:38-39) and defeats these powers (see on 2:15) and reaches right into the presence of God. The sense that there are powers of evil abroad which are often strong enough to crush whole peoples as well as individuals is, of course, not dependent on the worldview presumed here. But however such realities are conceptualized, hope remains a constant feature of the Christian gospel.

In Greek the sentence runs on: "which [hope] you heard about earlier. . . ." The reference presumably is to their first hearing of the gospel from Epaphras. How much earlier is not stated. JB/NJB assume that the force of the προ- implies a hearing "recently," "not long ago." But neither the Greek nor 1:7 and 4:12-13 are so specific. This gospel came to them in the word of preaching (cf. 1 Cor. 1:18; 2:1-4; Phil. 1:14; Col. 4:3; 1 Thes. 1:5-8; 2:13). The eschatological focus implied in the centrality of the theme of hope (as in 1:23, "the hope of the gospel") suggests a preaching not unlike that of 1 Thes. 1:9-10, which is often taken as a summary of the gospel as preached directly to Gentiles.

"Gospel" is another word baptized into Christian vocabulary by Paul (60 of the New Testament's 76 occurrences are Pauline). It was known in wider Greek usage, but almost always in the plural, in the sense of "good tidings" (LSJ s.v. εὐαγγέλιον), and the singular is unknown in biblical Greek outside the New Testament. The reason that Paul, and presumably others among the first Christian missionaries, lighted upon it, however, is fairly obvious. For the related verb, "preach/announce good news," was prominent in the second half of Isaiah (40:9; 52:7; 60:6; 61:1), that is, in passages that are remembered as having influenced Jesus' own self-understanding of mission (Matt. 11:5/Luke 7:22) and as summing up his mission (Acts 10:36), just as they also influenced others in that time (*Psalms of Solomon* 11:1; 1QH 18:14; 11QMelch 18). It was natural, then, that the noun chosen by the first Christian preachers to encapsulate their message about Jesus was derived from this verb. Implicit in this developed vocabulary is the sense of eschatological hope (so powerful in the Isaiah passages) already fulfilled in the coming of Messiah Jesus (cf. again the *Psalms of Solomon* and DSS references). That the gospel is summed up here in terms of "hope" (as again in the only other use of "gospel" in the letter, 1:23) is a reminder of how closely its original eschatological force still clung to the word. We should also note in passing how much distinctively Christian vocabulary appears in these first five verses (grace, faith, love, hope, gospel).

To be more precise, 1:5 speaks of "the truth of the gospel." RSV/NRSV, NIV, and NJB put the two words in apposition, "the word of the truth, the gospel," and JB breaks the sentence after "truth" (cf. GNB in n. 3). These renderings probably reflect recognition that the Greek idea of "truth" is involved here, that is, of truth as the unveiling of the "full or real state of affairs" (R. Bultmann, *TDNT* 1.238). Here again the eschatological overtones of the word and the context are important: the claim being made is that the good news of Christ Jesus unveils the reality of human destiny in the sure hope that it holds forth (cf. again 1 Thes. 1:9-10; Acts 17:30-31). Equally, if "the word of truth" reflects a more Jewish assertion of the firm reliability *('emet)* of God's word (Ps. 119:43; *Testament of Gad* 3:1; *Odes of Solomon* 8:8), the effect is simply to reinforce the confidence in God's purpose for the future already evoked by the word "hope" (see further Lohse, *Colossians and Philemon* 18-19).

However, it is better to retain the fuller phrase, "the truth of the gospel," since it probably also contains an echo of the same phrase used in Gal. 2:5 and 14. That is to say, implicit in the language is the emphatic Pauline claim that the gospel is for Gentiles also, without requiring them to become proselytes; the echo is still more explicit in 1:25-27. It was this truth of the gospel (or the truth of *this* gospel) to which Paul dedicated his whole life as an apostle. At all events, there is probably a further implication (as in Galatians) that this is a truth that has to be stoutly maintained against teachings that (in this case) deny or diminish the eschatological thrust of the gospel's emphasis on hope (cf. pp. 33ff. above). This may lie behind NEB/REB's elision of the phrase into "the message of the true gospel" (cf. Bruce, *Colossians, Philemon, and Ephesians* 42: "the true message of the gospel"), with its implied warning against a false gospel.

1:6 τοῦ παρόντος εἰς ὑμᾶς, καθὼς καὶ ἐν παντὶ τῷ κόσμῳ ἐστὶν καρποφορούμενον καὶ αὐξανόμενον καθὼς καὶ ἐν ὑμῖν, ἀφ᾽ ἧς ἡμέρας ἠκούσατε καὶ ἐπέγνωτε τὴν χάριν τοῦ θεοῦ ἐν ἀληθείᾳ. The opening phrase could be translated "which is present among you," recognizing the force of the present tense (Lohse, *Colossians and Philemon* 19 nn. 53, 54). But in this case it can also mean "which has come to you" (and so is present among you). And that makes better sense of the preposition, which most naturally has the meaning "to or into" (Harris 19).

The congratulatory note continues: the gospel is (constantly) bearing fruit and growing among them; but since this is true all over the world, they should not feel particularly pleased with themselves. The implication may be that the Colossians should hesitate before making too much of the success of their own evangelism, and this prepares for the warning notes that become prominent from 2:8. Note should also be given to the dynamic, living character attributed to the gospel (cf. particularly Isa. 55:10-11): "just as a tree without fruit and growth would no longer be a tree, so a gospel that bore no fruit would cease to be a gospel" (Schweizer, *Colossians* 37).

The image of fruit-bearing is a natural one to indicate result, outcome (for good or evil), or success and was familiar in Greek and Jewish thought (F. Hauck, *TDNT* 3.614; Meeks, "One Body" 219 n. 26). In 1:10, as else-where, the fruit is thought of in terms of good moral character (the verb in Luke 8:15 and Rom. 7:4; the noun in Paul: Rom. 1:13; Gal. 5:22; Phil. 1:11). But here it could simply denote the success of the gospel in winning more and more to belief in Christ Jesus and in the hope offered. The unclarity is not helped by the ambiguity of the second verb, which can mean either that the gospel "is causing (its converts) to grow" (1 Cor. 3:6-7) — that is, in knowledge (1:10), righteousness (2 Cor. 9:10), or faith (2 Cor. 10:15) — or that the gospel "is (itself) growing," that is, like a plant (Matt. 13:32; Mark 4:8) spreading throughout the world (cf. Acts 6:7; 12:24; 19:20), with the benefit of its fruit-bearing implied.[12] Only here and in v. 10 are the two verbs thus associated in biblical Greek (though cf. Mark 4:8); the closeness of the two verses favors the idea of growth in character, but both ideas may be implied — the success of the gospel in producing so many mature and moral people. Either way, the note of triumphalism ("in all the world") is striking, as also the implied eschatological finality of Paul's apostolic mission (cf. particularly Munck 36-55, 275-79); and though hyperbolic (cf. Josephus, *Contra Apionem* 2.138-39, 284) it must reflect not only an amazing boldness of vision but also a considerable measure of success (already within three or four decades of Jesus' death), as in innumerable towns around the Med-iterranean small groups met in the name of Christ Jesus, drawn together by the gospel (so also Rom. 1:8; 1 Cor. 1:2; 1 Thes. 1:8).

The congratulatory thanksgiving continues with a fulsomeness that results in a rather cumbersome repetition of "just as" (καθὼς καί) and a second relative clause (1:5: "which you heard earlier"; 1:6: "from the day on which you heard"). The clause simply indicates that the process of growth and fruit-bearing has been continual since the day of the Colossians' con-version. This rhetorical courtesy would, of course, make it easier for the recipients to hear the subsequent exhortations more favorably.

The rhetorical flourish may also explain the use of the more elaborate form of the verb "to know" (ἐπιγινώσκειν) rather than the more common γινώσκειν, though some prefer to give the prefix more weight in intensifying the meaning ("understood," JB, RSV, NIV; "comprehended," NRSV). Either way the verb denotes the experience (Ernst, *Philipper, Philemon, Kolosser, Epheser* 159) as well as the intellectual apprehension of God's

---

12. The similar combination in the Old Testament (Gen. 1:22, 28; 8:17; 9:1, 7; 17:20, etc.) has clearly in mind increase in numbers. Despite Gnilka, *Kolosserbrief* 35 (cf. Meeks, "One Body" 219 n. 25), the imagery is sufficiently common that it need not be attributed specifically to influence from apocalyptic thought, nor, alternatively, to Gnostic thought (cf. W. L. Knox, *Gentiles* 149 n. 5). Lightfoot 133 capitalizes neatly on the somewhat surprising order of the verbs: "The Gospel is not like those plants which exhaust themselves in bearing fruit and wither away. The external growth keeps pace with the reproductive energy."

outreaching generosity ("grace") as transforming power (cf. Rom. 3:24; 5:15, 17; 1 Cor. 1:4-5; 15:10; 2 Cor. 6:1; Gal. 1:6, 15; see on 1:2, "grace"). The addition of "in truth" reinforces the overtones of 1:5 ("the truth of the gospel") that their encounter with the gospel was an opening of their eyes and lives to reality, what actually is God's purpose for humankind (see on 1:5), a purpose of grace, with the further implication that this truth first learned thus should continue to be the touchstone of their ongoing discipleship. NJB and REB catch the sense well when they translate: "recognised it for/learned what it [God's grace] truly is" (so also Moule, *Colossians and Philemon* 51). Lohse, *Colossians and Philemon* 21, notes that "knowledge of the truth" assumes much greater importance in the later New Testament writings (1 Tim. 2:4; 4:3; 2 Tim. 2:25; 3:7; Tit. 1:1; Heb. 10:26; 1 John 2:21; 2 John 1).

1:7 καθὼς ἐμάθετε ἀπὸ Ἐπαφρᾶ τοῦ ἀγαπητοῦ συνδούλου ἡμῶν, ὅς ἐστιν πιστὸς ὑπὲρ ἡμῶν διάκονος τοῦ Χριστοῦ. Paul and Timothy extend their note of congratulation to include the one who first brought them the gospel — Epaphras.[13] As a native of Colossae (4:12) he presumably first encountered Paul and was converted through his preaching during Paul's long stay in Ephesus (Acts 19:8-10), some 120 miles distant on the coast and directly accessible by road down the Lycus and Meander valleys (see further pp. 20f. above). Whether he became a regular member of Paul's mission team, as did so many others whose names are preserved for us in Paul's letters (see Ollrog ch. 2), we cannot say. But it may have been Paul's missionary strategy to concentrate his own energies in major cities, while sending out mission teams to towns in the region (Conzelmann 134-35; cf. Acts 19:10). It is not too fanciful to imagine Epaphras, anxious to share the good news with his own townsfolk, volunteering to evangelize Colossae and devoting himself to laboring for the gospel there and in the nearby cities of Laodicea and Hierapolis (4:13). In Paul's terms, therefore, Epaphras may be called "apostle of Colossae" (cf. 1 Cor. 9:1-2), though the fact that the letter to Colossae was then written by Paul and Timothy, without including Epaphras as fellow author, despite his recent (?) presence (1:8: cf. Phm. 23), presumably implies that Epaphras saw himself simply as Paul's emissary (see on 1:1), or that the letter writer (Timothy?) did not wish to diffuse Paul's apostolic authority too far. This is reinforced by the reading "on our behalf" (see n. 6), which again clearly implies that Epaphras's evangelization in Colossae was at Paul's behest: "the apostle gives his seal to the teaching of Epaphras" (Abbott 199). In view of the double commendation of Epaphras in 1:7-8 and 4:12-13, Paul and Timothy may have concluded that Epaphras

---

13. Epaphras is a shortened form of Epaphroditus, but it is most unlikely that Epaphras is to be identified with the Epaphroditus named in Phil. 2:25 and 4:18, who is as much identified with Philippi as Epaphras is with Colossae.

himself as well as his gospel needed some defense and support (Wall 42-43). At all events, 1:7-8 and Phm. 23 certainly seem to indicate someone who was eager to share the news of his success with Paul and who spent enough time with Paul to be imprisoned with him, but who remained deeply concerned for his townsfolk and fellow believers in Colossae.

The verb used ("as you learned") may imply that Epaphras had seen his task in Colossae not simply as winning them to faith but as instructing them in the traditions and parenesis without which they would have no guidelines in translating their faith into daily living (cf. Rom. 16:17; 1 Cor. 4:6; Phil. 4:9; see also on 2:6).

Ἀγαπητός ("beloved") is one of Paul's favorite words for fellow Christians (Rom. 1:7; 12:19; 16:8), converts (Rom. 16:5; 1 Cor. 4:14; 10:14; 15:58, etc.), and fellow workers (Rom. 16:9, 12; 1 Cor. 4:17; Col. 4:7, 9, 14; Phm. 1). It reinforces the sense of family belonging that seems to have been characteristic of the young Christian mission (see on 1:1, "brother"). Behind it probably lies Jewish election theology, the claim that the patriarchs, Jerusalem, and the whole people of God are loved and have been chosen by God (e.g., Deut. 33:12; Isa. 41:8; 44:1; Jer. 31:20; Dan. 3:35; Sir. 24:11) and therefore the sense that the first Christian churches shared in that election. If so, the term embodies an implicit claim first advanced by Paul and characteristic of a central thrust of his gospel (see particularly Wischmeyer).

"Fellow slave" (σύνδουλος) is a term that we might have expected to occur more often in Paul's letters, since he so delighted in the use of συν-compounds (W. Grundmann, *TDNT* 7.786-87, plus "fellow prisoner," "fellow worker," "yoke fellow," "fellow participant," "fellow imitator," "fellow soldier"), and he was quite prepared to use the term "slave" (of Christ) both for himself (Rom. 1:1; Gal. 1:10; Phil. 1:1) and for other Christians (1 Cor. 7:22; Col. 4:12; cf. Rom. 6:18, 22). In fact, however, "fellow slave" occurs only in Colossians (here and 4:7); Ephesians also has συν-compounds unique to it (2:19; 3:6; 5:7). On the basis of this evidence it is impossible to say whether this is the mark of a close disciple copying Paul's style or Paul himself simply extending his usage in coining ever more συν- compounds.

The slave metaphor was a potent one since the basic image was essentially negative in Greek thought — slavery as the antithesis of the freedom that the Greek mind cherished so dearly, since, by definition, the slave was completely at another's beck and call (K. H. Rengstorf, *TDNT* 2.261-65; H. Schlier, *TDNT* 2.493-96). Even so, "slave" could still be something of a honorific title, at least if one was slave of an important and powerful individual (D. B. Martin, *Slavery*), and this was reinforced by the more oriental tradition in which the devotee of the cult saw himself as slave of the god — not least in Jewish religious thought (e.g., Deut. 32:36; Josh. 24:29; Pss. 89:3; 105:26, 42; Mal. 4:4; see further my *Romans* 7). Implicit in the designation, therefore, is the readiness to hand over one's life completely to a master (to sell oneself into slavery was a policy of desperation, but not uncommon), but to a master (Christ Jesus) whose power and authority were greater than that in any other master-slave relation. Presumably also implicit is the Christian conviction that only such unconditional handing over of oneself can prevent one becoming enslaved by a more destructive power (Rom. 6:12-23).

Epaphras is further described as a "faithful [see on 1:2] servant of Christ on our [see n. 6] behalf." "Servant" (διάκονος) often retains overtones of its original sense, "waiter at table" (John 2:5, 9; cf. Mark 1:31; 15:41; Luke 10:40; 12:37; 17:8; Acts 6:2); and thus its range of meaning merges into "slave" as denoting obligation to offer humble service to a superior (note particularly Mark 9:35; 10:43-45). That the memory of Jesus' actions and teaching influenced Paul's idea and practice of service may be suggested by such passages as Gal. 2:17 and Rom. 15:8. At this stage the word seems to be still descriptive of an individual's sustained commitment (like "fellow worker") and not yet the title of a clearly defined office (cf. Rom. 16:1; 1 Cor. 3:5; 2 Cor. 3:6; 6:4; 11:23; Phil. 1:1; Col. 1:23, 25; 4:7; 1 Thes. 3:2). If there are conscious overtones of the use of the term for cultic and guild officials (LSJ s.v. διάκονος; H. W. Beyer, *TDNT* 2.91-92; cf. A. Weiser, *EDNT* 1.304) we must assume that, as with Paul's use of priestly language elsewhere (Rom. 12:1; 15:16; Phil. 2:25), the cult has been secularized and the terms appropriated for all ministry on behalf of the gospel and Christ (see also on 1:25).

1:8 ὁ καὶ δηλώσας ἡμῖν τὴν ὑμῶν ἀγάπην ἐν πνεύματι. The congratulatory thanksgiving is concluded with a final note of appreciation to Epaphras, which also serves to make clear to the readership that Paul is well informed about their situation. Presumably it was to Epaphras (cf. again Phm. 23) that Paul owed knowledge of the threatening circumstances at Colossae, to which the main thrust of the letter is directed (from 2:6 on). But here, as is appropriate in the letter opening, the note is all of praise, even though it involves repetition of what has already been said well enough in 1:4.

As hope is the main thrust of the gospel (1:5), so love (see on 1:4) is its main fruit (here cf. particularly 3:14). It is described more fully as "love in (or by) the Spirit" (NEB: "God-given love"; REB: "the love the Spirit has awakened in you"). This is another characteristic Pauline note (cf. particularly Rom. 5:5 and Gal. 5:22). The love that mirrors the love of God in Christ can only be aroused and sustained by the Spirit of God. The phrase carries overtones of an inspiration that wells up from within, charismatically enabled (Rom. 2:29; 1 Cor. 12:3, 9, 13; 14:16; 1 Thes. 1:5), and that depends on continued openness to the Spirit if its quality of unselfish service of others is to be maintained.

This is the only direct reference to the Spirit in Colossians — a surprising fact and further indication for many that the letter may not have been written/dictated by Paul himself. Schweizer, *Colossians* 38 and n. 19 notes several themes and phrases that attract reference to the Spirit (as a kind of reflex) in the undisputed Paulines but that do not do so in Colossians; he suggests therefore that ἐν πνεύματι here should be taken to mean "spiritual." But see Gnilka, *Kolosserbrief* 38; Fee 638-40; and below on 1:9.

Prayer for the Colossian Recipients (1:9-14)

9 *That is why we also,*[1] *from the day we heard, have not ceased to pray on your behalf and to ask*[2] *that you might be filled with the knowledge of his will in all wisdom and spiritual understanding,* 10 *that you might walk worthily of the Lord, wholly pleasing to him, bearing fruit in every good work and increasing in the knowledge of God,* 11 *being empowered with all power in accordance with his glorious might, for all patience and endurance, with joy*[3] 12 *giving thanks to the Father,*[4] *who has qualified*[5] *you*[6] *for the share of the inheritance of the saints in the light.* 13 *He has delivered us from the authority of darkness and has transferred us into the kingdom of the son of his love,* 14 *in whom we have redemption,*[7] *the forgiveness of sins.*

The second part of the extended thanksgiving elaborates the reassurance given in 1:3 that Paul and Timothy pray for the Colossians (see the introduction to 1:3-23). Lohse, *Colossians and Philemon* 24, notes how much of the language in 1:9-11 echoes that already used in 1:4-6: "all" (vv. 4, 6, 9-11), "from the day you/we heard" (vv. 6, 9), "came to know the grace of God/knowledge of his will/knowledge of God" (vv. 6, 9-10), "bearing fruit and growing/increasing" (vv. 6, 10).

Equally striking is the sequence of terms not characteristically Pauline in 1:12-14: "qualify" (v. 12 — only here and in 2 Cor. 3:6 in the New Testament), "share of the inheritance" (μερίς — elsewhere in Paul only in 2 Cor. 6:15, the Pauline authorship of which is also questioned), "saints in

---

1. Moule, *Colossians and Philemon* 52 takes the καί with the first two words: "this is precisely why." See also discussion in Aletti, *Épître aux Colossiens* 68-69.

2. "And to ask" (καὶ αἰτούμενοι) is omitted by one or two witnesses (including B), perhaps in recognition that it is both unusual in Paul (only 1 Cor. 1:22; but also Eph. 3:13 and 20) and tautologous here.

3. RSV, NEB, and JB follow the old verse division (supported by p⁴⁶, which adds "and" after "joy") by linking "with joy" to what precedes (e.g., NEB "with fortitude, patience, and joy"), but in each case the revisers (NRSV, REB, and NJB) have followed NA²⁶ and UBS³ in linking the phrase with what follows (e.g., REB "and to give joyful thanks"). Otherwise, see, e.g., Pokorný 50 n. 23; earlier discussion in Abbott 205. There is a similar problem in Phil. 1:4.

4. Some significant manuscripts and versions have evidently replaced the more strongly attested "the Father" (τῷ πατρί) with "God" (τῷ θεῷ), presumably because designation of God simply as the Father absolutely is unusual in the New Testament outside the Johannines (in the Paulines only Rom. 6:4; Eph. 2:18; 3:14) and unexpected here (Metzger 620).

5. The reading "who called" (ΤΩΚΑΛΕΣΑΝΤΙ) may have been the result of confusion (with ΤΩΙΚΑΝΩΣΑΝΤΙ) or the deliberate substitution of a better known word for one that occurs in only one other passage in the New Testament (Metzger 620).

6. In contrast to 1:7, the weight of evidence here favors "you" rather than "us" (preferred by RSV).

7. Some late witnesses have harmonized the text with Eph. 1:7 by adding "through his blood."

light" (v. 12), aorist tenses (v. 13), "transferred" (v. 13 — elsewhere in Paul only in the proverbial 1 Cor. 13:2), "authority," denoting domain (v. 13), "kingdom of the son of his love" (v. 13), and "forgiveness" (v. 14). Elsewhere Paul never rounds off his opening with a call to thanksgiving (v. 12; Lohmeyer 38).

This could suggest that 1:12 begins a fresh line of thought, with εὐχαριστοῦντες functioning as an imperatival participle and 1:12-14 drawing on preformed liturgical material as "a sort of introit which introduces the solemn hymn sung by the community" (Lohse, *Colossians and Philemon* 32-33).[8] But that would detach it from the preceding participles and run counter to the imperatival style used in the rest of the letter (see further O'Brien, *Thanksgivings* 71-75; Aletti, *Épître aux Colossiens* 76-77; Wolter 57-58, 61-62). Nor is it obvious that the setting envisaged for such liturgical usage would be baptism in particular (so, e.g., R. P. Martin, *Colossians and Philemon* 55; Ernst, *Philipper, Philemon, Kolosser, Epheser* 164-65; Pokorný 51, 54-55; Sappington 196): baptism was evidently a much more spontaneous affair in the earliest days of Christianity (Dunn, *Unity* 141-47); and no doubt, as now, congregations in their worship often recalled the spiritual blessings they had received, without particular reference to baptism as such (cf. O'Brien, *Colossians, Philemon* 25). The more elaborate suggestion of Käsemann that 1:12-20 is actually "a primitive Christian baptismal liturgy" has not won much support (Lohse, *Colossians and Philemon* 40 n. 63; Gnilka, *Kolosserbrief* 45-46; in contrast Eckart, "Exegetische Beobachtungen," in particular, wants to include vv. 9-12 as the "Eingangsparanese" of a three-part baptismal liturgy).

Perhaps most striking of all is the very Jewish character of the language: "knowledge of his will in all wisdom and spiritual understanding" (v. 9), "walk," "knowledge of God" (v. 10), "empowered with all power," "his glorious might" (v. 11), "the share of the inheritance of the saints in light" (v. 12), God as deliverer[9] from the authority of darkness, "the son of his love" (v. 13), and "redemption" (v. 14; in each case see the following commentary). This emphasis on (or assumption of) the Jewish character of the gospel to which the Colossian Christians were committed is unlikely to be accidental. It suggests that Paul and Timothy thought it desirable to emphasize just this fundamental feature of their common faith. The most obvious reason is that the Colossians were confronted by local Jews who were confident of the superiority of their own religious practice and who denigrated the claims of these Gentiles to share

---

8. Vawter suggests that 1:12-14 represent an earlier redaction of the christological hymn (1:15-20) prior to its use in Colossians.

9. Hoppe 168 notes the theo-logical emphasis in the section, with "the Father" as the subject of the three action verbs in vv. 12-13.

in their own Jewish heritage (see further pp. 29-35 in the Introduction, and on 2:8, 16, and 18).

1:9 διὰ τοῦτο καὶ ἡμεῖς, ἀφ' ἡμέρας ἠκούσαμεν, οὐ παυόμεθα ὑπὲρ ὑμῶν προσευχόμενοι καὶ αἰτούμενοι, ἵνα πληρωθῆτε τὴν ἐπίγνωσιν τοῦ θελήματος αὐτοῦ ἐν πάσῃ σοφίᾳ καὶ συνέσει πνευματικῇ. Having completed his thanksgiving (1:3-8) and in view of having had so much to give thanks for, Paul turns from thanksgiving to prayer, more or less repeating what he has already said in the second half of 1:3. "From the day we heard" is perhaps a deliberate echo of the same phrase already used in 1:6: as they were fruitful from the very day they heard the gospel, so Paul and Timothy have been prayerful from the very day they heard of their response to the gospel. Note again the plural, in contrast to Phil. 1:9 and Phm. 4-7 (but as in 1 Thes. 3:9-10 and 2 Thes. 1:11-12). The intensity of prayer is marked — *"from the day* we heard, we have *not ceased* to *pray* on your behalf and to *ask"* (cf. Rom. 1:9-10; 1 Thes. 1:2-3; and especially Eph. 1:15-16) — and introduces the "fill/fullness" motif that comes to be a feature of the letter (1:9, 19, 24, 25; 2:2, 9, 10; 4:12, 17; O'Brien, *Colossians, Philemon* 20). The middle voice αἰτεῖσθαι ("ask") appears elsewhere in the Paulines only in Eph. 3:20 (cf. 1 Cor. 1:22; Eph. 3:13).

It is not surprising that the prayer focuses on "knowledge of his (God's) will." [10] For a theist who believes that God's active purpose determines the ordering of the world, lies behind events on earth, and shapes their consequences, one of the most desirable objectives must be to know God's will. The corollary, spelled out in the following phrases, is that such knowledge gives insight into and therefore reassurance regarding what happens (often unexpected in human perspective) and helps direct human conduct to accord with that will. Such desire to know and do God's will is naturally very Jewish in character (e.g., Pss. 40:8; 143:10; 2 Macc. 1:3; *Testament of Issachar* 4:3) and was, not surprisingly, shared by Jesus (Matt. 6:10; 7:21; Mark 3:35; 14:36; Luke 12:47) and the first Christians (e.g., Acts 21:14; Eph. 5:17; 6:6; 1 Thes. 4:3; Heb. 10:36; 13:21; 1 Pet. 3:17; 1 John 2:17; see also on 1:1). No doubt the knowledge prayed for here included the teachings that follow in the letter (Wolter 59), but hardly need be limited to that.

A characteristic claim in Jewish tradition was that the necessary knowledge of God's will came through the law: "Happy are we, Israel, because we know what is pleasing to God" (Bar. 4:4); "you know his will and approve the things that matter, being instructed from the law" (Rom. 2:18; cf. Wis. 15:2-3; *4 Ezra* 8:12). But for Paul in particular there was now a better and surer way of knowing God's will and of discerning what really

---

10. On whether the prefix ἐπι- significantly strengthens the force of γνῶσις ("knowledge") see Lightfoot 136; Bruce, *Colossians, Philemon, and Ephesians* 46 n. 30; Harris 30; and above on 1:6. Note the more or less synonymous use of ἐπίγνωσις and γνῶσις in 2:2 and 3.

mattered: by the personal transformation that flowed from inward renewal (Rom. 12:2, probably set in deliberate contrast to Rom. 2:18), so that he can sum up the call to Christian conduct in terms of walking in accordance with the Spirit (Rom. 8:4, 13-14; Gal. 5:16, 18, 25).

However, there is no simple contrast here between Judaism and Christianity so far as the quality and stimulus for ethical conduct is concerned. For the recognition that obedience to the law must spring from inner consecration is familiar also in Jewish thought (e.g., Deut. 10:16; Jer. 4:4; 31:31-34; Ezek. 36:26-27). Even the claim that Paul's Spirit ethic was distinctively eschatological in character (the hopes of Jeremiah and Ezekiel now fulfilled) does not enable us to draw a clear line of contrast with his Jewish contemporaries, as the DSS remind us. For they, too, claim a knowledge (of God's will) given directly by the eschatological Spirit, though a knowledge that, as is also evident, focuses on a very sectarian interpretation of Torah (see, e.g., 1QH 4:9-12; 6:10-12; 11:7-10; 12:11-13; 16:11-12; 1QS 5:8-10; 9:13; 11:15-18; see further Lohse, *Colossians and Philemon* 25). Thus, although the orientation to Torah comes out differently in each case ("the law of Christ" facilitating Paul's inclusive gospel in contrast to Qumran's introverted and exclusivist interpretation), the eschatological-psychological dynamic is similar.

The spiritual source and character of this knowledge is reinforced by the qualifying phrase, "in all wisdom and spiritual understanding," which could equally well be rendered "in all spiritual wisdom and understanding" (RSV/NRSV, NIV, Harris), or "with all the wisdom and understanding that his Spirit gives" (GNB). The language and aspiration were widely shared by Greco-Roman philosophy, as classically expressed in Aristotle's numbering σοφία and σύνεσις ("wisdom" and "understanding") with φρόνησις ("prudence") as the highest virtues (*Ethica Nicomachea* 1.13).[11] But the more immediate background for the thought here is again, doubtless, Jewish, since the combination of "wisdom and understanding" is a repeated feature of Jewish writings.[12] Here, too, the wisdom in particular is understood as given through the law (Deut. 4:6; 1 Chron. 22:12; Sir. 24:23-26; Bar. 3:36–4:1), but it is equally recognized that such wisdom can come only from

11. Lightfoot's exposition (136) is still of value: he defines σοφία as "mental excellence in its highest and fullest sense"; "while σύνεσις is critical, φρόνησις is practical; while σύνεσις apprehends the bearings of things, φρόνησις suggests lines of action." See also H. Conzelmann, *TDNT* 7.889; Lohse, *Colossians and Philemon* 26.

12. Exod. 31:3; 35:31, 35; Deut. 4:6; 1 Chron. 22:12; 2 Chron. 1:10-12; Job 8:10; 12:13; 28:20; 39:17; Pss. 49:3; 111:10; Prov. 1:7; 2:2-3, 6; Isa. 10:13; 11:2; 29:14; Jer. 51:15; Dan. 1:17; 2:21; 5:14; Jdt. 8:29; Wis. 9:4-6; Sir. 1:4; 14:20; 15:3; 24:25-26; 37:22-23; 39:6, 9-10; 50:27; Bar. 3:23; *Testament of Zebulun* 6:1. For DSS see particularly 1QS 4:3 and further Lohse, *Colossians and Philemon* 25. Note the practical orientation of so much Jewish wisdom (see, e.g., G. Fohrer, *TDNT* 7.484-88).

above (as in Wis. 9:9-10). And particularly to be noted is the recognition
that wisdom and understanding come only from the Spirit (Exod. 31:3; 35:31;
Isa. 11:2; Wis. 9:17-19; Sir. 39:6; Philo, *De gigantibus* 22-27; *4 Ezra* 14:22,
39-40). It is certainly this thought that is taken up here ("spiritual" as given
by and manifesting the Spirit — cf. 1 Cor. 2:12-13; 12:1, 4; 14:1-2). Whether
there is an implied rebuke of an alternatively conceived or false wisdom[13]
is less clear since in that case we might have expected more emphasis on
the point (as in 1 Corinthians 1–2); but the allusion in 2:23 does indicate
that a claim to wisdom was part of the teaching in Colossae that called forth
the response of this letter (see also 2:2-3).

All this reflects the charismatic and eschatological character of Christian self-consciousness, not least in the transition from conviction to praxis:
charismatic in the sense of the immediacy of wisdom and insight that
Christians (or Paul in particular) expected to provide their lives with direction
and motivation (the parallel with Phil. 1:9-10 is very close)[14] and *eschatological* in that they (or Paul in particular) were convinced that this knowledge
of God's will was the outworking of the eschatological Spirit and renewal
looked for in the prophets (hence the enthusiastic "filled with" and "all";
cf. Isa. 11:2; 33:6).

1:10 περιπατῆσαι ἀξίως τοῦ κυρίου εἰς πᾶσαν ἀρεσκείαν, ἐν παντὶ
ἔργῳ ἀγαθῷ καρποφοροῦντες καὶ αὐξανόμενοι τῇ ἐπιγνώσει τοῦ θεοῦ. As
already implied, the object or value (the infinitive signifying object or result)
of knowledge of God's will, of wisdom and understanding, is that it enables
appropriate conduct. The metaphor "walk" denoting conduct in the walk of
life is untypical of Greek thought (BAGD s.v. περιπατέω; H. Seesemann,
TDNT 5.941) but characteristically Jewish (e.g., Exod. 18:20; Deut. 13:4-5; Ps.
86:11; Prov. 28:18; Isa. 33:15; 1QS 5:10; CD 19:4; the corresponding Hebrew
verb *halak* gives rise to the technical term "halakhah" to denote rabbinic
rulings on how the law should be interpreted in daily life). Similar exhortations
appear in other Pauline letters, but never quite as a standard formula: "conduct
yourselves (πολιτεύεσθε) in a manner worthy of the gospel of Christ" (Phil.
1:27), "walk worthily of God" (1 Thes. 2:12), and "walk worthily of your
calling" (Eph. 4:1; cf. Rom. 6:4; 8:4; 13:13; 1 Cor. 7:17; 2 Cor. 5:7; Gal. 5:16).
Here the thought is of conduct worthy of the Lord, that is, of Jesus (though see
Aletti, *Épître aux Colossiens* 72-73). That is particularly understandable in a
letter where the significance of Christ is so much in focus, but it also underlines
the degree to which Christian conduct was informed and directed by the
traditions regarding Jesus' own manner of life (see on 2:6).

13. As suggested, e.g., by Lightfoot 137; Abbott 202-3; Masson 93-94; Gnilka, *Kolosserbrief*
41; O'Brien, *Colossians, Philemon* 22.
14. Cf. particularly Dibelius, *Kolosser, Epheser, Philemon* 7; Percy, *Probleme* 122-27; see
further my *Jesus* 222-25; Fee 641-44.

Somewhat unnecessarily, but wholly in keeping with the continuing rather florid style ("all" occurs five times in 1:9-11), Paul adds "to all pleasing" (literally). The noun (ἀρεσκεία) occurs only here in the New Testament (in the LXX only in Prov. 31:30) and in wider Greek usage usually has a negative connotation ("obsequiousness"; cf. 3:22). But it does occur in a positive sense, and Philo uses it a number of times of pleasing God (BAGD s.v. ἀρέσκεια; Lohmeyer 34 n. 2; Lohse, *Colossians and Philemon* 27-28; Wolter 61). Paul also uses the verb in the same connection, usually with reference to God (Rom. 8:8; Gal. 1:10; 1 Thes. 2:4, 15; 4:1), but in 1 Cor. 7:32 with reference to pleasing "the Lord," as by implication here. It is worth noting how in several passages the thought is of conduct modeled on that of Christ (Rom. 15:1-2; 1 Cor. 10:33–11:1; 1 Thes. 4:1; see again on 2:6).[15]

The test of this conduct, as with all conduct, will be what it produces. The imagery of "bearing fruit and increasing" echoes 1:6, but this time clearly in reference to moral maturity (see on 1:6). Such is the intensity of some traditional Reformation polemic against the thought of any merit adhering to "good works" that it might come as a surprise that Paul should ever have spoken in commendatory fashion of "good works" (cf. Lindemann, *Kolosserbrief* 21; contrast Aletti, *Épître aux Colossiens* 74: "typically Pauline"). In fact, however, he does so on a number of occasions (Rom. 3:7; 13:3; 2 Cor. 9:8; Gal. 6:10; Phil. 1:6; 2 Thes. 2:17; also Eph. 2:10); Paul would think typically of almsgiving and hospitality (Rom. 12:8, 13). Any hint of post-Pauline authorship here derives not from the rather odd inference that Paul thought good works were displeasing to God but from the fact that the phrase became an intensive feature of post-Pauline usage (with fourteen occurrences in the Pastorals).

The basis from which or means by which the fruitbearing and growth "in every good work" is to come about is the "knowledge of God."[16] Repetition of the same possibly intensive form (ἐπίγνωσις) as in 1:9 doubles the insistence that such conduct can only grow from such knowledge. The term here includes "knowledge of his will" (see on 1:9), but is much larger in scope, including knowledge of God's grace (see on 1:6, which uses the equivalent verb; Eph. 1:17-23 is a rich elaboration of the theme). Another characteristic Jewish theme, "knowledge of God," includes experience of God's dealings (e.g., 1 Sam. 3:7; Ps. 9:10; Isa. 43:10; Mic. 6:5) and acknowl-

15. Wolter 60-61 prefers to take the clause in the sense of conduct that brings to expression the Colossians' belongingness *(Zugehörigheit)* to the Lord.

16. Taking τῇ ἐπιγνώσει τοῦ θεοῦ as an instrumental dative (so most, e.g., Abbott 203). Dibelius, *Kolosser, Epheser, Philemon* 8, and O'Brien, *Colossians, Philemon* 23, prefer to take it as a dative of reference: "in the knowledge of God"; but in that case the author could hardly have failed to complete the balance of the sentence by inserting ἐν ("in"), as several scribes realized in copying the text.

edgment of God in appropriate action (e.g., Deut. 4:39-40; Prov. 9:10; Dan. 11:32; Hos. 8:1-3).[17] According to Paul, failure thus to know and acknowledge God is at the root of human sin (Rom. 1:21; cf. Wis. 16:16). The interdependence of experience of the divine and practical conduct is a feature both of the phrase and of the present passage. Gal. 4:9 and 1 Cor. 13:12 are reminders that the initiative in this experiential knowledge is always God's, a point that Colossians immediately goes on to underline.

1:11 ἐν πάσῃ δυνάμει δυναμούμενοι κατὰ τὸ κράτος τῆς δόξης αὐτοῦ εἰς πᾶσαν ὑπομονὴν καὶ μακροθυμίαν. The sentence runs on with continued emphasis that such fruitful living is wholly dependent on divine enabling. The power of God is a familiar Pauline theme (e.g., Rom. 1:20; 9:17; 1 Cor. 1:18, 24; 6:14; 2 Cor. 13:4) and prominent in Ephesians (1:19; 3:7, 16, 20; 6:10). It is also deeply rooted in Jewish thought (see, e.g., W. Grundmann, *TDNT* 2.291-94; Wolter 63), and though there seems to have been a heightened interest in the theme in Greco-Roman religion of the period (C. E. Arnold, *ABD* 5.444-45), the Semitic doubling ("empowered with all power") is sufficient indication that the thought world here is still preeminently Jewish.[18] Particularly noticeable in Paul's usage is the claim actually to have experienced this power and to have been its instrument in his mission (Rom. 1:16; 15:19; 1 Cor. 2:4-5; 2 Cor. 4:7; 12:9; 1 Thes. 1:5).[19] It is this experience of sustaining, empowering grace ("the power of the Holy Spirit" — Fee 644) for which Paul prays for the Colossians (cf. again particularly Eph. 1:19; see also on 1:29).

As if the point were not already clear beyond doubt, the sense of complete dependence on divine enabling is reinforced with a further flourish: "according to the might of his glory" (a Semitism = "his glorious might"). κράτος ("might") is an understandable variant for δύναμις ("power"), though it appears only in the late (disputed) Paulines; its use in Eph. 1:19 strengthens the parallel with this verse. Still more characteristically Jewish is the talk of divine glory (δόξα), which hardly occurs in Greek writing apart from Jewish influence (see, e.g., BAGD s.v. δόξα 1a). Like Hebrew *kabod*, it denotes the awesome radiance of deity that is the visible manifestation of God in theophany (e.g., Exod. 16:10; 24:16-17; 40:34; Lev. 9:23; Pss. 63:2; 102:16; Isa. 6:3; 66:18-19). Particularly influential in Jewish thought was

---

17. "The pious life of the Jew consists in gift and task *(Gabe und Aufgabe)*, a continuous interaction *(Ineinander)* of recognition and act" (Lohmeyer 32).

18. "A devout Jew could request God his Father for a way of life pleasing to God no more clearly and intimately than does Paul here" (Lohmeyer 33). "If one were to remove the basis given for Christian conduct by means of the words 'worthy of the Lord,' then the rest of the passage could easily appear in a Jewish text" (Lohse, *Colossians and Philemon* 31 [my translation of the German original]).

19. Here again we may note a parallel with the Qumran community; see Lohse, *Colossians and Philemon* 30.

the theophany of Exod. 33:17-23, which served as a constant reminder that no one, not even Moses, can ever see God (cf., e.g., Deut. 4:12; Ps. 97:2; *1 Enoch* 14:21; *Apocalypse of Abraham* 16:3; Philo, *De specialibus legibus* 1:45; John 1:18; 6:46; see also on 1:15), despite the longings of the Jewish mystics influenced even more by Ezek. 1:26-28.

Particularly notable here is the thought of divine glory as a manifestation of power (like the radiant energy of the sun), a thought equally rooted in the folk memory of the fearful numinous power *(mysterium tremendum)* of such theophanies (Exod. 19:16-24; Num. 16:19-35; Isa. 6:4-5). In Paul this is understood as beneficial power, transforming for the better (Rom. 6:4; 2 Cor. 3:18; the parallel with Ephesians here is 3:16), though with double effect in 2 Thes. 1:9-10. Since transformation into heavenly splendor (glory) is part of the hope for heaven (see also on 1:27 and 3:4),[20] the prayer is in effect for that process to be forwarded already here on earth (cf. 2 Cor. 4:16–5:5; see also 1:27; H. Hegermann, *EDNT* 1.346-47). That this train of thought is in mind here is confirmed by the strong eschatological and realized eschatological note in the next two verses.

In the meantime, however, that is, in the circumstances of life in the present, one of the ways this powerful empowering of glorious might comes to most effective expression is in "all patience and endurance" (REB: "ample strength to meet with fortitude and patience whatever comes"). The two nouns are near synonyms. Both are included not so much because of their distinctive meanings but to reinforce the point that hope of heavenly glory in the future requires patience and endurance now (not least in the face of alternative religious claims) and that both the present patience and the future transformation are the outworking of the same glorious might. "Patience" (ὑπομονή) was highly prized both within wider Hellenism, particularly by the Stoics, as steadfast resistance of evil and fortitude under hardship (F. Hauck, *TDNT* 4.582-83), and in contemporary Judaism (frequently in 4 Maccabees to denote the steadfastness of the martyrs — 1:11; 7:9; 9:8, 30, etc.). In the later Greek translations the use of ὑπομονή in Job markedly increases (cf. Jas. 5:11). Paul, like other New Testament writers, gave it a prominent place among the Christian virtues, not least, as here, as a quality that those hoping for higher things must display (Rom. 2:7; 5:3-4; 8:25; Luke 21:19; Heb. 12:1 Jas. 1:3-4; Rev. 3:10; 13:10). "Endurance" (μακροθυμία)[21] is less frequently used in the New Testament, and

---

20. Note particularly Segal's thesis that Paul uses the language of transformation gained through contact with Jewish mystical apocalypticism to express the hope of ultimate salvation (*Paul* ch. 2; see also Morray-Jones, "Transformational Mysticism").

21. The Greek term means literally "the 'long breath' which can hold out in face of failure or opposition" (Schweizer, *Colossians* 44). On the importance of God's forbearance within Jewish thought see my *Romans* 552 and 558.

sometimes of divine forbearance (Rom. 2:4; 9:22; 1 Tim. 1:16; 1 Pet. 3:20; 2 Pet. 3:15). In Paul, more often the late Paul, it appears in lists of Christian virtues (2 Cor. 6:6; Gal. 5:22; Eph. 4:2; Col. 3:12; 2 Tim. 3:10; 4:2). Somewhat surprisingly, but presumably because these two words are such close synonyms, they appear only occasionally together (2 Cor. 6:4-6, 2 Tim. 3:10; Jas. 5:10-11; *1 Clement* 64; Ignatius, *Ephesians* 3:1).

1:12 μετὰ χαρᾶς (12) εὐχαριστοῦντες τῷ πατρὶ τῷ ἱκανώσαντι ὑμᾶς εἰς τὴν μερίδα τοῦ κλήρου τῶν ἁγίων ἐν τῷ φωτί. It is important to bear in mind that in the Greek this is not a new sentence and that the subject of the verb is not Paul and Timothy (repeating the opening note of 1:3). Rather, the subject is those being prayed for by Paul and Timothy. This prayer is not only for knowledge and wisdom, for conduct fruitful in good works, and for patient fortitude in the trying and testing circumstances of life, but that this may all be suffused by the experience of joy in thankfulness to the Father (so also 3:17). The implication is that these graces are all interdependent, that wisdom, conduct beneficial to others, and patience can only be sustained in that joyful honoring of Creator by creature which is the basis of all sound thinking and doing (Rom. 1:21).[22] On εὐχαριστοῦντες see the introduction to the comments on 1:3-23 and the comments on 1:3, and on God as Father (πατήρ) see on 1:2.

The experience of joy seems to have been common among the first Christians (e.g., Acts 2:46; Phil. 4:4-6; 1 Thes. 5:16-18), and not least in the midst of and despite hardship and suffering (2 Cor. 7:4; 8:2; 1 Thes. 1:6; Heb. 10:34; 12:2, 11; Jas. 1:2; so also Matt. 5:12; Rom. 5:3-4; 1 Pet. 1:6; 4:13). Paul evidently did not think of discipleship as a matter of grim endurance, nor is the experience described (joy in suffering) peculiarly Christian (cf. *Psalms of Solomon* 10:1-2; 1QH 9:24-25; *2 Baruch* 52:6; see also Lohse, *Colossians and Philemon* 34). However, the joy actually experienced and manifested must have been so real and sustaining as to be a factor in attracting others to the infant Christian groups (see also on 2:7).

The special cause for Christian thanksgiving is outlined in a sequence of clauses, each of them with striking features. The first underlines again, as clearly as anything in Colossians, the extent to which Paul and his Gentile converts understood their coming to faith in Christ Jesus as an act of divine grace whereby they were "qualified or made fit" (ἱκανώσαντι) to share in an inheritance for which they had previously been unqualified, that is, an inheritance thought to be exclusively Israel's (J. H. Friedrich, *EDNT* 2.299-300). Certainly the phrase "the share of the inheritance of the saints" is unmistakably Jewish in character. And for anyone familiar with the Jewish

---

22. "A Stoic in the stocks would have borne the discomfort calmly and uncomplainingly, but would he at the same time have been heard 'singing hymns to God,' as Paul and Silas did in the Philippian town jail (Acts 16:25)?" (Bruce, *Colossians, Philemon, and Ephesians* 48).

scriptures it would immediately evoke the characteristic talk of the promised land and of Israel as God's inheritance.[23] Particularly notable is the way the language could be transferred to the eschatological hope of share in the resurrection and/or life beyond death in the eternal life of heaven (Dan. 12:13; Wis. 5:5; *Shemoneh 'Esreh* 13; cf. *1 Enoch* 48:7). Most striking of all are the parallels in the DSS: 1QS 11:7-8: "God has given them (wisdom, knowledge, righteousness, power, and glory) to his chosen ones as an everlasting possession and has caused them to inherit the lot of the saints"; 1QH 11:10-12: "For the sake of your glory you have purified man of sin that he may be holy for you . . . that he may be one [with] the children of your truth and partake of the lot of your saints."[24]

The thought is so close that it must help illuminate the meaning here. "Light" here presumably denotes the light of heaven, that transcendent illumination that alone gives clarity of vision, including clarity of self-perception (e.g., John 1:4-5; 3:19-21; 2 Cor. 4:6; Eph. 5:13-14; 1 John 1:5, 7; 2:8). Those who have received this inheritance in the light[25] and live accordingly can be called "sons/children of the light" (as in Luke 16:8; John 12:36; 1 Thes. 5:15); the Qumran covenanters understood themselves in the same way. In both cases, the antithesis is explicit with the "sons of darkness," that is, those who by self-deception or demonic deception fail to understand the true nature of things (see further on 1:13).

There is some dispute, however, as to who is intended by the phrase "the saints in the light." They could be angels (as may well be intended in Wis. 5:5 and 1QS 11:7-8),[26] for "saints/holy ones" can be used of angels (BAGD s.v. ἅγιος 1bβ). And if the passage already has in view the claim to share in the worship of angels indicated in 2:18, the inference would be that, despite the disparagement of (some of) their fellow citizens in Colossae (2:18), the readers were *already* qualified to share with the angels their common inheritance (Lincoln, *Paradise* 119-20; Sappington 199).[27] On the other hand, it is doubtful whether "the saints" in Paul ever refer to any other

23. Num. 18:20; Deut. 10:9; 12:12; 18:1; 32:9; Josh. 14:3-4; 18:6-7; 19:9, 49, 51; Jer. 10:16; 12:9-10; 51:19; Sir. 24:12; 44:23; 45:22; cf. 2 Sam. 20:1; 1 Kgs. 12:16. See further W. Foerster and J. Herrmann, *TDNT* 3.759-61, 769-76; J. D. Hester, *Paul's Concept of Inheritance* (*SJT* Occasional Papers 14; Edinburgh: Oliver and Boyd, 1968).

24. For Qumran's more predestinarian use of the same language see again Lohse, *Colossians and Philemon* 35-36.

25. "In the light" probably goes with the whole phrase, not just with "the saints" (see Lohmeyer 39 n. 3).

26. So recently Lohse, *Colossians and Philemon* 36; Gnilka, *Kolosserbrief* 47; Pokorný 52; Wolter 65. But see Schweizer, *Colossians* 51; Benoit, "Col. 1:12"; O'Brien, *Colossians, Philemon* 26-27; Bruce, *Colossians, Philemon, and Ephesians* 49-50; Aletti, *Épître aux Colossiens* 79-80.

27. Compare, and contrast, R. P. Martin, *Colossians and Philemon* 54: "At a single blow he dispels this veneration of the angelic powers [Col. 2:18] by assuring the Colossians that they have attained a place shared by the angels" (cf. Dibelius, *Kolosser, Epheser, Philemon* 9).

than human saints (including 1 Thes. 3:13 and 2 Thes. 1:10). The closest parallels are certainly to be understood in that sense (Acts 26:18; Eph. 5:8; 1 Pet. 2:9; cf. Dan. 12:3; *1 Enoch* 1:8; 5:7; 104:2; *2 Baruch* 51:5, 10; Polycarp, *Philippians* 12:2). The thought, then, may rather be of heaven as the shared inheritance of the (human) saints, since both at Qumran and in the early Christian gatherings the joy of shared worship was understood as a foretaste of heaven (see further on 2:18). Certainly the closest parallels in the New Testament (just cited) imply a strong measure of realized eschatology. Either way, there is a strong sense of an inestimable privilege, previously understood as Israel's alone, and of a hope for choice companionship and social identity that will extend beyond death and whose quality can be experienced already in this mortal life.

1:13 ὃς ἐρρύσατο ἡμᾶς ἐκ τῆς ἐξουσίας τοῦ σκότους καὶ μετέστησεν εἰς τὴν βασιλείαν τοῦ υἱοῦ τῆς ἀγάπης αὐτοῦ. The note of realized eschatology becomes even stronger in the next two clauses, for what is described here would elsewhere be thought of as reserved for the end of history/time. The first verb, ῥύομαι ("rescue, deliver"), where it it is used of spiritual deliverance elsewhere in the New Testament, normally has such a final sense (Matt. 6:13 — in the final testing; Rom. 7:24 = 8:23; 11:26; 1 Thes. 1:10; 2 Tim. 4:18). To be noted also here is the fact that the deliverer is God (Findeis 366-68; so by implication in Rom. 7:24 = 8:11; but Jesus in Rom. 11:26; 1 Thes. 1:10; 2 Tim. 4:18), strengthening the echo of God's equally decisive act of deliverance of Israel from slavery in Egypt (e.g., Exod. 6:6; 14:30; Deut. 13:5; Judg. 6:9; *Psalms of Solomon* 9:1) already present in this context.[28] More striking still is the fact that elsewhere in the Pauline corpus talk of full sharing in the kingdom of God is always future (1 Thes. 2:12; 2 Thes. 1:5; 2 Tim. 4:1, 18; the formulaic phrase "inherit the kingdom of God" in 1 Cor. 6:9-10; 15:50; Gal. 5:21; cf. Eph. 5:5). There is nothing quite like this claim that believers in Christ Jesus have already (aorist tense) been transferred into the kingdom, like a whole people transported from their traditional territory to settle in a new region (Josephus, *Antiquities* 9.235 and 12.149 are cited appositely by several; see also on 2:12 and 3:1).[29]

The deliverance achieved has been from "the authority (ἐξουσία) of darkness." The antithesis between "light" and "darkness" is made explicit (see also on 1:12). In this context it is not simply the obvious moral antithesis familiar in Jewish wisdom (e.g., Eccl. 2:13; Wis. 17:20–18:4; though note the close parallel with *Joseph and Asenath* 8:10-11 and 15:12), but the eschatological dualism of apocalyptic (Amos 5:18, 20; *1 Enoch* 92:4-5;

28. For the typological significance of the liberation from Egypt in Jewish thought see, e.g., Str-B 4.860-64.

29. Hence Lightfoot's paraphrase: "He transplanted us thence, and settled us as free colonists and citizens in the kingdom of His Son."

108:11-15; *2 Baruch* 18:2).[30] Here again (as in 1:12) the parallel with Qumran's contrast between "the sons of light" and "the sons of darkness" is noticeable (1QS 1:9-10; 3:24-25; 4:7-13; 1QM, e.g., 1:1, 8-14; 13:5-16). Presumably the language was not intended to imply that deliverance from the power of darkness was complete and that transfer to the kingdom had been fully carried out. They were not yet in heaven! There is no hint in Colossians of any awareness of the danger of an overrealized eschatology (contrast 1 Cor. 4:8). The language is rather the exaggerated expression of rich spiritual experience and full confidence (hope) that what had already been done (aorist tense) would be completed without fail (cf. Phil. 1:6 with 3:20, and Eph. 1:3 with 1:13-14; cf. also Findeis 368-72). Taken in conjunction with 1:12 it may be a fair deduction that the Christian sense of already established privilege (1:12) was the converse of a sense of deliverance from dark powers and that reassurance of such deliverance was equally necessary to counter the overblown claims and disparaging attitudes stemming from the Colossian synagogue (2:16, 18).

The weight of ἐξουσία should also be noted. It denotes an executive authority, in this case a domination of darkness (though most take it in the sense "domain" or "dominion"; but cf. the same phrase in Luke 22:53). The implication, therefore, is not so much that the darkness has been already stripped of all its power and banished. Rather, the darkness can be legitimately and authoritatively resisted, as having had its license revoked (so Rom. 13:11-14; Eph. 5:8-11; 1 Thes. 5:4-8; 1 Pet. 2:9). Within a unitary kingdom (cf. 1 Cor. 15:24) subjects of the king can reject all other claims to final authority over them (see also 1:16 and 2:10, 15).

Does it make any difference that the kingdom here spoken of is "the kingdom of his [God's] beloved son"? In comparison with talk of "God's kingdom," the idea of Christ's kingdom occurs only infrequently in the New Testament (Matt. 13:41 and 25:31 — the Son of Man; 1 Cor. 15:24-28; also *1 Clement* 50:3; cf. Eph. 5:5: "the kingdom of Christ and of God") and lacks clarity of conception (U. Luz, *EDNT* 1.204-5). It was partly, no doubt, a consequence of the strong Jewish expectation of a royal Messiah: the identification of Jesus as Messiah carried with it the overtone that as Messiah he reigned as king (cf. Gnilka, *Kolosserbrief* 49; Schweizer, *Colossians* 52; the influence of 2 Sam. 7:14 was important here; see Joel 3). The disentangling of this notion from that of national ruler over Israel (Mark 15:26!) was a delicate business that probably was sufficiently hazardous to inhibit Christian development of a christology of kingship (cf. John 18:35-37). The other main root must have been Ps. 110:1 (note 110:2)

---

30. See also Lohmeyer 48 n. 2. The thought is not Gnostic as such, but the strong "already" emphasis of the passage no doubt gave scope to later Gnostic ideas (cf. Lightfoot 141; Gnilka, *Kolosserbrief* 48, 50; Pokorný 55).

and the talk of thrones (plural) in Dan. 7:9 — a fruitful source of speculation in Judaism of the time of the New Testament as to whom the extra throne(s) could be for (see my *Partings* 223-24). It was precisely the Christian claim that the full significance of Christ could be understood only if both passages were referred to him: he was the other "Lord" of Ps. 110:1 (see on 2:6); he shared sovereign rule with God (Rev. 7:17; 22:1, 3; see further on 3:1). As in 1:3, however, the thought of Christ's kingship here is carefully hedged around: the deliverer and actor is God, and as in 1 Cor. 15:24-28, so here, it is a subordinate kingship, as implied by talk of "the kingdom of his beloved son." Nevertheless, for Paul and Timothy it was a genuine kingship, requiring a proper submission from his servants, even if in the last analysis it is a devotion directed to God through his Son.

Perhaps the tension between the thought of Christ's kingdom and (by implication) God's kingdom in this text is itself a reflection of the eschatological tension characteristic of most New Testament writings. A somewhat similar tension is present in Jesus' teaching on the kingdom of God as preserved in the Synoptic Gospels; for example, Jesus bids his disciples pray "May your kingdom come" (Matt. 6:10/Luke 11:2), but he also claims that in his ministry of exorcism "the kingdom of God has come upon you" (Matt. 12:28/Luke 11:20). To that extent at least we may say that Jesus in his ministry embodied or enacted with executive authority the kingly rule of God. In turn, in the Paulines, the Spirit, that is, the Spirit of Christ, is understood as the first installment of the full share (inheritance) in God's kingdom (Rom. 8:15-17; 1 Cor. 6:9-11; 15:44-50; Gal. 3:29–4:7; 5:16-21; Eph. 1:13-14). The kingdom of Christ, insofar as it is to be distinguished from the kingdom of God, is a further way of expressing the tension between what has already been accomplished (the kingdom of Christ) and what is still to be accomplished (the kingdom of God). This also means that participation in Christ's kingship will always be experienced within the contradiction of a world that does not yet own the sovereign rule of God (hence, again, the joy and the need for patience and endurance, as in 1:11-12; see also 4:11).

This is the only time in the letter that Christ is explicitly described as God's Son, and in the unusual formula, "Son of his love," a Semitic form[31] equivalent to "beloved son" (cf. Eph. 1:6: "the beloved"). The nearest equivalent comes in the Gospels' talk of Jesus as God's "beloved son" (Mark 1:11; 9:7; cf. 12:6; also Matt. 22:2 and Luke 22:29). The usage reflects something of the range of relationship to God that could be expressed by this category, including especially Israel, Israel's king, or the righteous (e.g., Deut. 33:12; Neh. 13:26; Isa. 41:8; 43:4; Wis. 4:10; Sir. 17:18; *Psalms of Solomon* 13:8; 18:4). That is to say, the metaphor of

31. BDF §165; questioned by Dibelius, *Kolosser, Epheser, Philemon* 9.

sonship to God denoted different degrees of closeness to God or favor and acknowledgment given by God, with the added "beloved" indicating a further degree of closeness. In the case of Jesus, initially this also may have been no more than a matter of degree (believers could share in Christ's sonship: Rom. 8:14-17; Gal. 4:6-7). But very quickly a note of qualitative distinction emerged, particularly through the identification of Jesus with Wisdom (see on 1:15), heightened still further in John's Gospel by the distinction of Christ as God's "only or unique (μονογενής) Son," with υἱός ("son") reserved for Jesus. "Son" was the metaphor that most effectively "caught" the relationship between God and Jesus and so became the standard way of referring to Christ in classical christology. See further my *Christology* ch. 2 and *Partings* 245-47.

1:14 ἐν ᾧ ἔχομεν τὴν ἀπολύτρωσιν, τὴν ἄφεσιν τῶν ἁμαρτιῶν. In the final clause of this striking sequence the focus switches directly to Christ, leading into the powerful "Christ hymn" of 1:15-20. The "in whom" (the second occurrence of the "in Christ" phrase, which is used so frequently in this letter; see on 1:2) may indicate that a more established formula is being cited or echoed here (cf. Rom. 3:24; Eph. 1:7). Accordingly, "we" now embraces not only Paul and Timothy and those prayed for (1:9) but all who are "in Christ." ἔχομεν ("we have") continues the note of realized eschatology, whereas in Rom. 8:23 and Eph. 1:14 and 4:30 the "redemption" still lies clearly in the future. In every case, however, the crucial fact is that the redemption is dependent solely on Christ ("in him"; cf. 1 Cor. 1:30: "God has made him [our] redemption"). So the eschatological tension could be implicit, similar to that between 1:27 ("Christ in you, the hope of glory") and 3:4 ("When Christ who is our life appears . . ."): being "in Christ" we have the (future) redemption (assured).

The word "redemption" (ἀπολύτρωσις), "release" (NEB/REB), "freedom" (JB/NJB) is comparatively rare, but would be well enough known to denote the ransom of a captive or prisoner of war from slavery (BAGD s.v.). Understandably, the antithesis between light and darkness (1:12-13) could be readily translated into the idea of those who belonged to the light held as prisoners or slaves by an alien power. Hence such exhortations as Rom. 6:13 and 13:12, in which the reality of the eschatological tension (that which needs yet to be done as the outworking of what has already been accomplished) becomes clear. Given the clear echo of the settlement of the promised land in 1:12, the compound word would probably evoke thought of Israel's ransom from slavery in Egypt and from captivity in Babylon, which were usually described with the uncompounded verb λυτροῦν ("deliver, ransom," e.g., Deut. 7:8; 9:26; 15:15; Isa. 43:1, 14; 44:22-24; 51:11; 52:3). In that case the great acts of Israel's redemption are being understood typologically as foreshadowing the eschatological redemption of Gentile as well as Jew to share in the new promised land ("the kingdom of God's beloved Son").[32]

In many ways the most astonishing feature of this passage is the final phrase, which further describes the "redemption" as "the forgiveness of sins," that is, pardon for failure, expunging of offense from memory and conscience. The idea and language were familiar enough in the wider Greek world (e.g., BAGD s.v. ἄφεσις; R. Bultmann, *TDNT* 1.509), and of course it was wholly familiar in Jewish thought. This latter point perhaps needs some emphasis since it has sometimes been suggested that Jesus brought forgiveness to a legalistic Judaism to which the theology and experience of forgiveness had become foreign (see, e.g., details in my *Partings* 44-51). But forgiveness was at the heart of the sacrificial cult centered in Jerusalem (note, e.g., the repeated refrain in Lev. 4:20, 26, 31, 35; 5:6, 10, 13, 16, 18; see further J. S. Kselman, *ABD* 2.831-33). And forgiveness continued to be a regular theme in the Judaism of Paul's time.[33] Equally it was a familiar theme in early Christianity (e.g., Mark 1:4; Luke 24:47; Acts 2:38; 10:43; Heb. 9:22; 10:18; Jas. 5:15; 1 John 1:9; *Barnabas* 6:11; 16:8; Hermas, *Mandates* 4.3.1).

The surprising feature is rather that forgiveness of sins seems to be a very minor element in Paul's theology and gospel (only in a quotation in Rom. 4:7 in the undisputed Paulines). The related theme of repentance fares only a little better (Rom. 2:4; 2 Cor. 7:9-10; 12:21). This lack of interest in such prominent features of Jewish theology (repentance and forgiveness) has caused great puzzlement to many scholars attempting to understand Paul from a Jewish perspective (e.g., Moore, *Judaism* 3.151). The usual deduction made is that Paul's metaphor of "justification" and his theology of being "in Christ" absorbed within them such alternative ways of describing the blessings of the gospel — though even so their absence remains a puzzle. That the phrase occurs here, and in very close parallel in Eph. 1:7, adds strength to the view that this is the work of a close disciple of Paul, glossing a more familiar Pauline motif and anxious, *inter alia,* to relate Pauline thought more closely to the other main streams of Christian (and Jewish) thinking.[34] At all events, the phrase serves as a

32. For the older debate as to whether the idea of payment of a ransom price is implicit in the use of ἀπολύτρωσις here, see L. Morris, *The Apostolic Preaching of the Cross* (London: Tyndale/Grand Rapids: Eerdmans, 1955) 43 (yes) and D. Hill, *Greek Words and Hebrew Meanings* (SNTSMS 5; Cambridge: Cambridge University, 1967) 73-74 (no). See also K. Kertelge, *EDNT* 1.138-40.

33. See, e.g., 1QS 11:11-14; CD 3:18; 1QH 4:37; *Psalms of Solomon* 9:7; *Testament of Job* 42:8; *Testament of Abraham* 14:12, 14; *Joseph and Asenath* 11:18; *Shemoneh ʿEsreh* 6; see also Sanders, *Paul* index s.v. "forgiveness"; J. H. Charlesworth, *ABD* 2.833-35.

34. Aletti, *Épître aux Colossiens* 81-82, notes the close parallel here (1:12-14) with Acts 26:18 (darkness, light, authority, forgiveness of sins, lot, saints) and wonders whether it points to Lukan authorship for Colossians. Percy, *Probleme* 85-86, however, notes that ἄφεσις τῶν ἁμαρτιῶν has a liturgical ring more suited to the passage and that Paul was presumably familiar with the

reminder of how easily translatable are the more common Pauline categories into the more traditional Jewish ones.

The one step clearly taken beyond Jewish thinking on forgiveness
is the location of forgiveness no longer in the cult, or even simply in
directness of prayer to God, but once again "in Christ." As particularly
in Galatians, it is the possibility of Gentiles being "in Christ" that brings
them within the sphere of God's gracious forgiveness. "In Christ" is the
key to all.

Lord's Prayer. See also Bruce, *Colossians, Philemon, and Ephesians* 54 n. 68; Wolter 69 ("an early
Christian tradition which . . . reflects the saving effect of baptism").

A Hymn in Praise of Christ (1:15-20)

15 *He is the image of the invisible God,*
   the firstborn of all creation.

16 *For in him were created all things*
   in the heavens and on the earth,
   the visible and the invisible,
   whether thrones or dominions
   or principalities or authorities;
   all things were created through him and for him.

17 *He himself is before all things,*
   and all things hold together in him;

18 *and he is the head of the body, the church.*
   He is the beginning,[1] the firstborn from[2] the dead,
   in order that he might be in all things preeminent.

19 *For in him all the fullness of God was pleased to dwell,*

20 *and through him to reconcile all things to him,[3]*
   making peace through the blood of his cross (through him),[4]
   whether the things on the earth or the things in the heavens.

It is generally agreed that at this point the writer(s) have included an already formed hymn.[5] The marks of hymnic or poetic form are clear enough (cf. particularly Wolter 72):

1. NEB/REB's "origin" is acceptable, but GNB moves too far away from the Greek: "the source of the body's life. He is the first-born Son, who was raised from the dead."

2. p⁴⁶ and ℵ* omit the ἐξ ("from") to give the sense "firstborn *of* the dead," that is, strengthening the sense of identification between Christ and "the dead": he was first of the dead to be resurrected.

3. It would be possible to read the original ΕΙΣΑΥΤΟΝ (written without accents or breathings) as εἰς αὐτόν = εἰς ἑαυτόν ("to himself"), that is, to God (cf. 2 Cor. 5:19), rather than as εἰς αὐτόν (see, e.g., Moule, *Colossians and Philemon* 169-70); but that would break the triple parallel of "in him," "through him," "to him" (1:16/1:19-20).

4. The manuscript attestation is equally weighty for omission as for inclusion of "through him" (δι᾽ αὐτοῦ). It could have been included by scribal reflex in view of the repeated use of the phrase in 1:16 and 20 or omitted by accident (the scribe's eye jumping directly from the immediately preceding αὐτοῦ) or design (because it is so awkward for the sense). The presence of the phrase must count as the more difficult reading and so it should probably be included (cf. Metzger 621).

5. There have been several reviews of the debate (Schmauch 47-55; Gabathuler; R. P. Martin, *Colossians and Philemon* 61-66; Benoit, "Hymne"; Burger 3-53; O'Brien, *Colossians, Philemon* 32-37; on the history of the hymn's theological interpretation see Gnilka, *Kolosserbrief* 77-87). The most common division is of two strophes (1:15-18a and 1:18b-20), as suggested originally by Norden 252, or of two main strophes (1:15-16c, 1:18b-20) with transitional lines in 1:17-18a (marked by paralleling of "and he is" in 17a and 18a) or in 1:16d-18a (marked also by paralleling of "all things" in 16d and 17b), as suggested first by Schweizer, "Kirche" 295 (see also Burger 12-15; Balchin,

(1) a relative clause beginning with "who" (ὅς), presupposing an opening line that identified the object of praise and evoked the hymnic response, and introducing a sustained description of the one so designated (cf. Phil. 2:6; 1 Tim. 3:16; Heb. 1:3; 1 Pet. 2:22);

(2) a sequence of clauses and phrases that fall easily into matching rhythmic units;

(3) a clear structure of two strophes (1:15-18a, 18b-20), marked by paralleling of key motifs —

1:15	"who is the firstborn"	1:18b
1:16	"because in him"	1:19
1:16	"all things, through him, to him"	1:20

— by the thematic repetition of "all things" (twice each in vv. 16 and 17, once each in vv. 18 and 20), and by a movement from the creation of "all things in the heavens and on the earth" (1:16) to a climax of reconciliation of "the things on the earth and the things in the heavens" (1:20; see, e.g., discussion in Kehl, *Christushymnus* 28-49);

(4) resulting in a rounded unit whose meaning is self-contained and not dependent on its immediate context but which nevertheless appears to have been "nested" between two passages functioning as introduction (1:12-14: "in whom . . . who") and corollary (1:21-23: "to reconcile all things . . . and you he has now reconciled"), even though it disrupts the context to the extent that it interposes a third person sequence into a more personal "we/you" sequence;

(5) not to mention (the least decisive consideration) the appearance of various terms (particularly "visible," "thrones," "hold together," "beginning," "be preeminent," "making peace," "the blood of the cross") that are not found elsewhere in Paul (Deichgräber 153 is overconfident on this point).

Nevertheless, it can never be finally proved that preformed material has been taken up here. It is always possible that Paul himself became lyrical at the thought of all that Christians owed Christ (1:13-14) or simply struck a purple passage.[6] Moreover, it cannot be denied that the second strophe (1:18b-20) does not fall into such a natural or matching rhythmic pattern as the first (1:15-18a; so Burger 8-9). And there is some tension between a first

---

"Colossians 1:15-20" 78-79; Aletti, *Épître aux Colossiens* 89-93). Habermann 235-37 regards 1:17-18a as the earliest redaction. Baugh rightly warns against any assumption that a Semitic-style composition would necessarily have formed perfectly balanced symmetrical strophes.

6. A persistent minority continue to deny the presence of pre-Pauline material here and thus to affirm that the "hymn" was composed by Paul himself (e.g., Feuillet, *Christ Sagesse* 246-73; Kümmel 342-43; Caird 174-75; Helyer; Balchin, "Colossians 1:15-20").

strophe that sees the cosmos as sustained "in him" (1:17) and a second that begins from the presupposition of a cosmos disrupted and alienated (1:20; cf., e.g., Ernst, *Philipper, Philemon, Kolosser, Epheser* 172-73), which is presumably why NA²⁶ prints only 1:15-18a in poetic lines.

An alternative hypothesis would be, then, that a one-verse hymn/poem in praise of Christ's role in creation has been supplemented by a second hand (the author's) to bring out in echoing terms the significance of Christ's redemptive work (particularly Benoit, "Hymne" 248-50; cf. H. Langkammer, *EDNT* 3.49; Yates, *Colossians* 15, 19, 26). The difficulty with this is the doubt whether at that stage the first Christians would have composed a hymn solely in honor of Christ's role in creation (cf. 1 Cor. 8:6, though that, more properly speaking, is an adaptation of the Jewish creed, the *Shema;* contrast Heb. 1:1-4). This in turn raises the question of whether 1:15-18a was in fact a *pre*-Christian hymn (in praise of Wisdom or Logos; apart from the last two words, nothing in 1:15-18a need refer to Christ), which was taken over by Paul and Timothy and elaborated to indicate both Christ's "takeover" of Wisdom's role (see the exegesis below) and the completion of that role by his work of redemption (cf. O'Neill). The difficulty with this understanding is that, at least in Jewish circles, such a hymn to Wisdom would have an immediate practical application to daily life or a reference to the Torah (Prov. 8:22-36; Sir. 24; Bar. 3:9–4:4) equivalent, in fact, to the elaboration here in Colossians by reference to Christ's work of reconciliation.

The issue is further complicated by the question whether in taking over preformed material the authors of Colossians have added their own explanatory glosses. The most commonly agreed glosses are: (1) lines 5-7 in the above translation ("the visible . . . authorities") or lines 6-7 ("whether thrones . . . authorities"), which were introduced presumably because of the importance of their theme for the letter (cf. particularly 2:15) and without which the "in him, through him, to him" parallels would be much tighter; (2) "the church" (1:18a), by which a pre-Christian hymn to Wisdom could have been "christianized; and (3) "through the blood of his cross" (1:20), which would then explain how the awkwardness of the second "through him" arose (see n. 4).⁷

At all events, whether taken over in part or in whole, whether from

---

7. The range of suggested additions and their varying support have been documented in tabular form by Benoit, "Hymne" 238; Burger 9-11, 15-16; Gnilka, *Kolosserbrief* 53-54; and Balchin, "Colossians 1:15-20" 79; for this list of three additions see also R. P. Martin, *Colossians and Philemon* 56-57. For fuller discussion see Lohse, *Colossians and Philemon* 42-44, and Gnilka 54-58, who conclude that only the last two of the three need be regarded as insertions (the earlier analysis of Käsemann, "Liturgy," has been influential on these points), and Schweizer, *Colossians* 58-63. Wengst argues that only "the church" need be regarded as an addition (*Formeln* 172-75). Wright offers a balanced analysis in which nothing is omitted ("Poetry" 99-106); see also n. 25 below.

pre-Christian or Christian material, whether composed entirely by Paul and Timothy or merely glossed by them, the passage can be quite properly classified as an early Christian hymn in which Christ is praised in language used commonly in Hellenistic Judaism in reference to divine Wisdom.[8] The hymn, it should be noted, is not addressed to Christ, but is in praise of Christ. The complementarity (rather than antithesis) between God's creative activity and redemptive activity is in a most striking way brought out and maintained by the crucial middle term, Christ, in, through, and to whom God has accomplished both his creative and his redemptive purposes.

That Christians at such an early stage should be willing to use such language of Christ tells us much of "the intellectual vitality of the early Christian communities" (Houlden 170) and of their willingness to use categories fundamental to wider philosophical thought in their attempts to explicate the significance of Christ and to communicate it to a wider audience. The hymn is itself a sharp reminder that there were front-rank thinkers among the first Christians eager to engage with their contemporaries in the attempt to explain reality. It is also salutary to recall that such christological innovation came in the context of worship and through the medium of hymns (cf. Hengel 95). However, again despite Käsemann, "Liturgy" (cf. Schnackenburg, "Aufnahme" 42-45; Wengst, Lieder 179; Löwe 302; Meeks, "Body" 211), there is no particular reason why it should be designated a "baptismal" hymn.

It remains unclear what light the passage sheds on the situation at Colossae. Why should this hymn be cited, and why here? Paul does tend to cite christological formulas at the beginnings of his letters (Rom. 1:3-4; Gal. 1:3-4; 1 Thes. 1:9-10; cf. 1 Cor. 1:7-9, 23-24, 30; 2 Cor. 1:19-20), but nothing so extensive as here and nothing that causes quite such a modification of the normal thanksgiving. Nor is the hymn and its framework (1:12-23) particularly polemical in character, in contrast to Gal. 1:6-9 or in comparison even with the closest christological parallel (1 Cor. 8:4-6).[9] We may fairly deduce that Paul and Timothy thought the preeminence of Christ, in terms both of creation and redemption, needed to be emphasized. But the absence of polemic suggests that Christ's status and significance were being devalued rather than attacked, that an alternative religious system was being exalted, so that any disparagement of the Colossian Christians' faith and praxis was more of a corollary than a central objective (cf. Hooker 122, 135; see also

8. The Wisdom character of the hymn is a matter of broad consensus; see, e.g., Percy, Probleme 70-71; Fiorenza; Aletti, Colossiens 1:15-20 148-52; Hurtado 41; Sappington 172-74; Habermann 247, 262; and Wolter 76. We may speak with hindsight of a developing trajectory toward a/the Gnostic redeemer myth (so Sanders, Hymns 75-87; Fiorenza), but not yet of a Gnostic formation.

9. The list in 1:16 ("the visible . . . authorities") is often assumed to be derived from "the Colossian heresy" (e.g., Dibelius, Kolosser, Epheser, Philemon 10; Robinson 283).

on 2:8, 16, 18, 20). At any rate, it is worth noting again that any confrontation intended by the authors was not so serious that it needed to be pursued in urgent or immediately explicit terms. It was evidently sufficient for their purpose to assert (or recall) the high status and full significance of God's Son as of central importance for the Colossians' own confidence and persistence (1:23).[10]

1:15 ὅς ἐστιν εἰκὼν τοῦ θεοῦ τοῦ ἀοράτου, πρωτότοκος πάσης κτίσεως. The ἐν ᾧ ("in whom") of 1:14 switched the focus from God (ὅς, 1:13) to Christ and thus made it possible to attach the lengthy hymnic description of Christ (running to six verses) by means of a further simple ὅς ("who"). The language used is unlike other traditional formulaic summaries of the gospel introduced elsewhere by the same relative pronoun (such as Rom. 3:25; 4:25; 8:34), which focus on the cross and resurrection of Christ. But the same phrase ("who is the image of God") is used in 2 Cor. 4:4.

Here it is important to note the description of God as "invisible" (ἀόρατος). The adjective is used of God in four of the five New Testament occurrences (here and in Rom. 1:20; 1 Tim. 1:17; Heb. 11:27) and nowhere else in biblical Greek, but is common in Philo (see W. Michaelis, *TDNT* 5.368; note also *Adam and Eve* 35:3; *Testament of Abraham* 16:3-4). It is, of course, a central Jewish theologoumenon that God cannot be seen (see also on 1:11). Hence the figure of "the angel of the Lord" in the patriarchal narratives (e.g., Gen. 16:7-12; 22:11-12; Exod. 3:2-6; 14:19-20) and the importance of the commandment against idolatry (Exod. 20:4-6; Deut. 5:8-10). In the wider Hellenistic world this chimed in with the basic Platonic distinction between the world of sense perception (κόσμος αἰσθητός/ὁρατός) and the world of ideas accessible only to the mind (κόσμος νοητός/ἀόρατος), fundamental also to Philo's religious cosmology.

In each case the consequent crucial question was: How then can God be known? How may one gain knowledge of or access to this higher world, which is inaccessible to the senses? A common answer was found in the term "image," εἰκών, which had a range of meaning embracing "representation, reflection, likeness" (H. Kleinknecht, *TDNT* 2.388-89) and which Plato had used in that sense, both for the cosmos as the visible "image" of God (*Timaeus* 92c) and for the sun as the "image" of the "idea of the good" (*Republic* 6.509a; see further Kleinknecht 389; Lohse, *Colossians and Philemon* 47). The thought of man (human being) as "image of god" was also familiar (BAGD s.v. εἰκών 1b), and it is this rather than reference to the cosmos that characterized Jewish usage of the word, though the theme did not feature prominently across the spectrum of Jewish

---

10. Fowl 152-54, however, struggles to understand the hymn in terms of an exemplary christology.

theology.[11] None of this seems to be in mind here, however,[12] although Adam christology is prominent elsewhere in Paul's theology (see also on 1:18b and particularly on 3:10).

More to the point here is the importance in Hellenistic Judaism of the thought of divine Wisdom as the "image of God" (particularly Wis. 7:26; Philo, *Legum allegoriae* 1:43); also of the divine Logos in Philo (*De confusione linguarum* 97, 147; *De fuga et inventione* 101; *De somnis* 1.239; 2.45; Eltester 110). The invisible God makes himself visible in and through his wisdom (Feuillet, *Sagesse* 173-74). The importance of this in Hellenistic Judaism was that "image" could thus bridge the otherwise unbridgeable gulf between the invisible world and God on the one side and visible creation and humanity on the other — denoting both that which produces the divine image and the image thus produced.[13] In Jewish theology Wisdom and Logos (the two are often equivalent) thus become ways of safeguarding the unknowability of God by providing a mode of speaking of the invisible God's self-revelatory action (his "image/likeness" being stamped, his "word" spoken) by means of which he may nevertheless be known ("the knowledge of God"; see on 1:9 and 10). The Wisdom and Logos of God could thus function in effective Jewish apologetic within a wider Hellenistic milieu, where other similarly functioning terms were less suitable ("glory of God" too Jewish, "Spirit of God" too nonrational).

This means also that Wisdom (and Logos) should not be understood in simplistic or mechanical terms as "intermediaries" between God and his world. Nor is a term like "hypostasis" appropriate, since only in later centuries did it gain the distinctive meaning that was necessary for it to function in resolving otherwise intractable problems for the Christian understanding of God.[14] Rather, these terms have to be understood as ways of speaking of God's own outreach to and interaction with his world and his people, ways, in other words, of speaking of God's immanence while safeguarding his transcendence — in a word, "personifications" of God's

11. Gen. 1:26-27; 5:1; 9:6; Sir. 17:3; Wis. 2:23; *Testament of Naphtali* 2:5; *Apocalypse of Moses* 10:3; 12:1; 33:5; 35:2; *Adam and Eve* 14:1-2; 37:3; 4 Ezra 8:44; 2 *Enoch* 65:2. So also in early Christianity: 1 Cor. 11:7; cf. Jas. 3:9.

12. Despite Masson 98-99; Bruce, *Colossians, Philemon, and Ephesians* 58; and Pokorný 74. In a famous article Burney saw here an exposition of Gen. 1:1 by means of Prov. 8:22 (followed by Davies, *Paul* 150-52; Caird 175; adapted by Wright, "Poetry" 110-13); Manns 101-2 draws particular attention to the Targums on Gen. 1:1; but see Lohse, *Colossians and Philemon* 46 n. 101; Schweizer, *Colossians* 65 n. 25; and Aletti, *Colossiens* 115; other bibliography in Sappington 172 n. 3; Aletti 98 n. 43.

13. This factor will also be the source of the confusion between Wisdom christology and Adam/Man christology here (as illustrated by Fossum).

14. "The statement that hypostasis ever received 'a sense midway between "person" and "attribute," inclining to the former' is pure delusion, though it derived ultimately from Harnack." So G. L. Prestige, *God in Patristic Thought* (London: SPCK, ²1952) xxviii.

wisdom rather than "intermediaries" or "hypostases" (see further Weiss, *Untersuchungen* 318-31; Dunn, *Christology* 168-76, 217-30). The character and effectiveness of this divine Wisdom become clear in wider Jewish usage, both in the affirmation of its unknowability, unless God takes the initiative (Job 28; Bar. 3:28-36), and in the claim that God has expressed his wisdom most clearly in the Torah (Sir. 24:23; Bar. 3:36–4:1).

As the sequence of parallels with motifs characteristically used of Jewish Wisdom in these verses will confirm, the writer here is taking over language used of divine Wisdom and reusing it to express the significance of Christ, if not, indeed, taking over a pre-Christian hymn to Wisdom. That is to say, he is identifying this divine Wisdom with Christ, just as ben Sira and Baruch identified divine Wisdom with the Torah (so also Heb. 1:3; cf. particularly Davies, *Paul* 168-75; Weiss, *Untersuchungen* 306-8). The effect is the same: not to predicate the actual (pre)existence of either Torah or Christ prior to and in creation itself, but to affirm that Torah and Christ are to be understood as the climactic manifestations of the preexistent divine wisdom, by which the world was created.[15] It is Christ in his revelatory and redemptive significance who is the subject of praise here;[16] "the description is revelatory, more than ontological" (Martin, *Colossians and Philemon* 57). And the praise is that his redemptive work (1:14: "in whom we have the redemption") is entirely continuous and of a piece with God's work in creation. It is the same God who comes to expression in creation and definitively in Christ; "he who speaks of Christ speaks of God" (Gnilka, *Kolosserbrief* 61). In short, there is no dualism here. Quite the contrary: this is christology set *within* Jewish monotheism and predicated on the Jewish theological axiom that the one God has chosen to reveal himself in and through his creative power (cf. Hegermann 101: "dynamic monism"; Wright, "Poetry" 114: "christological monotheism").[17]

The Wisdom parallel is extended in the second phrase, "firstborn of

15. Cf. particularly Caird 175-78; Dunn, *Christology* 194-96; Kuschel 331-40; also Yates, *Colossians* 18-19, 23. "Christ is the visible icon of the invisible God" (Hübner 351).

16. The present tense "shows that St. Paul is speaking of Christ in His present glorified state" (Abbott 209-10), "the exalted Christ" (Lohse, *Colossians and Philemon* 46); similarly Kehl, *Christushymnus* 81; Pokorný 76; Habermann 239, 260, 262; Wolter 77). In some contrast Steinmetz 75 ("radically protological") and Schneider 409-10: the Lordship of Christ over the principalities and authorities is grounded not only in his death and resurrection but also in his work as creator in the beginning. Jervell understands Christ as εἰκών in the light of 1:19 and 2:9: "The Eikon of Christ means that God himself dwells in Christ" (224-26).

17. See further Dunn, *Partings* chs. 10-11; Hurtado; Kuschel. Contrast Balchin, "Paul": "The plain meaning here is that Christ pre-existed the creation of the world. . . . The dangerous implications would have been obvious to Paul's monotheistic countrymen" (215; cf. Manns 107-10). But there is no hint whatsoever at this stage that monotheistic Jews were troubled by this language (cf. P. M. Casey, *From Jewish Prophet to Gentile God: The Origins and Development of New Testament Christology* [Cambridge: Clarke/Louisville: Westminster, 1991] 116).

all creation," where again the antecedent for use of the word πρωτότοκος ("firstborn") in relation to creation is most obviously Wisdom (Prov. 8:22, 25; Philo, *De ebrietate* 30-31; *Quaestiones in Genesin* 4.97; cf. *De virtutibus* 62); it is "a commonplace of the Hellenistic synagogue" (W. L. Knox 159 n. 3).[18] Here, however, we should note the ambiguity attaching to the imagery, since "firstborn" can mean first created being and/or that which has precedence over creation (NEB/REB use the similarly ambiguous phrase "primacy over"). The former sense, first created being, gave scope to subsequent Arian christology (the Son as created by God; see, e.g., Lightfoot 146-48; Feuillet, *Sagesse* 178-85; Schweizer, *Colossians* 250-52). But we should recognize that the categories at this stage were not at all so precise (see also my *Christology* 189). Just the same ambiguity attaches to earlier Jewish talk of Wisdom, sometimes spoken of as created by God (Prov. 8:22; Sir. 1:4; 24:9) and at other times as the agency through which God created (see on 1:16). The reason is presumably the same as in the case of εἰκών; that is, both concepts were able to bridge the gulf between Creator and created, and both try to put into words the self-revelation (becoming visible) of the invisible God (Schweizer, "Kol. 1:15-20" 123). In other words, precisely the ambiguity that allows the words to serve their bridge function allows both meanings to be embraced. It is important theologically, therefore, to maintain that transcendent-immanent tension, precisely as expressing the continuum between the unknowable God and his self-revelation in creation and in other all too human categories. When the choice between "begotten" and "created" later became an issue, the Fathers were no doubt correct to insist that the force of the word here falls on the side of transcendence (see, e.g., Aletti, *Épître aux Colossiens* 96-98; history of interpretation in Hockel); but the continuum is then lost sight of and the danger is that the Son's deity becomes part of a transcendence distinct and even remote from his immanence.

1:16 ὅτι ἐν αὐτῷ ἐκτίσθη τὰ πάντα ἐν τοῖς οὐρανοῖς καὶ ἐπὶ τῆς γῆς, τὰ ὁρατὰ καὶ τὰ ἀόρατα, εἴτε θρόνοι εἴτε κυριότητες εἴτε ἀρχαὶ εἴτε ἐξουσίαι· τὰ πάντα δι᾽ αὐτοῦ καὶ εἰς αὐτὸν ἔκτισται. That "firstborn" must denote primacy over creation, and not just within creation, is indicated by the conjunction linking the two verses: he is "firstborn of all creation *because* in him were created all things (τὰ πάντα)," that is, everything, the universe, the totality of created entities (see BAGD s.v. πᾶς 2ad), including, as the appended phrases make clear, everything within that totality, however it be subdivided — both "in the heavens" (see on 1:5) "and on the earth,"

18. Philo preferred to speak of the Logos as πρωτόγονος ("first born, first created": *De agricultura* 51; *De confusione linguarum* 146; *De somnis* 1:215). The use of πρωτότοκος of the Davidic king in Ps. 89:27 (LXX 88:28) or elsewhere of Israel (Exod. 4:22; Jer. 31:9; *Psalms of Sololomon* 18:4; *4 Ezra* 6:58; πρωτόγονος in *Prayer of Joseph* 3) is less relevant here.

"the visible and the invisible" (see also on 1:15). Likewise in the final clause of the verse, if "everything (τὰ πάντα) was created and exists [perfect tense; see Turner, *Insights* 125] through him and for him," that presumably also distances him from creation as creation's means and end (see also Harris 44).

The "in him" is the beginning of a sequence of prepositional phrases by means of which the creation of "all things" is described: "in him, through him, to him." Such use of the prepositions "from," "by," "through," "in," and "to" or "for" was widespread in talking about God and the cosmos. So particularly pseudo-Aristotle, *De mundo* 6: ὅτι ἐκ θεοῦ πάντα καὶ διὰ θεοῦ συνέστηκε; Seneca, *Epistulae* 65.8: "Quinque ergo causae sunt, ut Plato dicit: id ex quo, id a quo, id in quo, id ad quod, id propter quod"; Marcus Aurelius, *Meditations* 4.23: ἐκ σοῦ πάντα, ἐν σοὶ πάντα, εἰς σὲ πάντα; so also Philo, *De cherubim* 125-26: τὸ ὑφ᾽ οὗ, τὸ ἐξ οὗ, τὸ δι᾽ οὗ, τὸ δι᾽ ὅ; and already in Paul (Rom. 11:36 and 1 Cor. 8:6, as partially also in Heb. 2:10).[19]

Once again, however, we may deduce that the primary influence is the Jewish Wisdom tradition, within which such language had already been used of divine wisdom (Feuillet, *Sagesse* 206-11). So, e.g., Ps. 104:24 (LXX 103:24):"you made all things by wisdom (πάντα ἐν σοφίᾳ ἐποίησας)," a very close parallel; Prov. 3:19:"The Lord by wisdom (τῇ σοφίᾳ) founded the earth"; Wis. 8:5:"wisdom that effects all things (τῆς τὰ πάντα ἐργαζομενης)"; Philo, *Quod deterius* 54:"Wisdom, by whose agency the universe was brought to completion (δι᾽ ἧς ἀπετελέσθη τὸ πᾶν)"; similarly *Heres* 199 and *Fuga* 109.

What does such language mean when applied to Messiah Jesus? Not, presumably, that the Christ known to his followers during his ministry in Palestine was as such God's agent in creation; in the first century no less than the twentieth that would be to read imaginative metaphor in a pedantically literal way. It must mean rather that that powerful action of God, expressed by the metaphor of the female Wisdom, in and through whom the universe came into being, is now to be seen as embodied in Christ, its character now made clear by the light of his cross and resurrection (1:18, 20). The subsequent desire to distinguish more clearly God as the final cause (ἐκ) from Wisdom/Christ as the means or agent (διά) is already evident in 1 Cor. 8:6 (cf. John 1:1-3), as it had been important in equivalent terms for Philo (*De cherubim* 125).[20]

19. The parallels were already noted by Norden 240-43, 347-48. See also particularly Pöhlmann. Such parallels make it clear that the reference is to the old creation, not to "the eschatological new creation" (despite Zeilinger, *Erstgeborene,* particularly 195-200; Schweizer, *Colossians* 263, notes that this interpretation of 1:15-17 goes back to Theodore of Mopsuestia).

20. The ἐν αὐτῷ therefore probably reflects the Hellenistic Jewish idea of the Logos as the "place" in which the world exists (particularly Philo, *De somnis* 1.62-64; Lohmeyer 57; Schweizer, *Colossians* 69; Wolter 79; Aletti, *Colossiens* 99 n. 48; see also my *Christology* 333 n. 118) and

What of the least common of the three prepositions, the εἰς ("for, to") in the last line of v. 16 (never used in such contexts in reference to Jewish Wisdom)?[21] If the prepositional sequence was simply adapted from the wider philosophic usage it need not be indicative of eschatological purpose (cf. Rom. 11:36; 1 Cor. 8:6; δι' ὅν in Heb. 2:10).[22] Even as christianized, the two strophes seem to be structured on a protology/eschatology, old cosmos/new cosmos distinction, with the future eschatological emphasis limited to the second. Nevertheless, because of the hymn's present context, the redemptive work also accomplished "in Christ" (1:14) is presented as the key that unlocks the mystery of the divine purpose. "In Christ" creation and redemption are one. In the cross and resurrection (1:18, 20) both past and future find the clue to their ultimate significance (cf. Schweizer, *Colossians* 70-71; Gnilka, *Kolosserbrief* 66; Wolter 79-80; Aletti, *Épître aux Colossiens* 102-3).

The addition of "thrones or dominions, or principalities or authorities" does disrupt what would otherwise be a more compact and better balanced sequence of lines, unless we envisage a more complex structure in which the middle two refer to the invisible things in the heavens and the outer two to visible things on the earth (Bammel 88-95, followed by Houlden 163). But that is unlikely. Rather, we should suppose a hierarchy of heavenly powers — "thrones" superior to "lordships," and so on (see particularly Lightfoot 151-52). The "thrones" are assuredly to be located in heaven (cf. Dan. 7:9; Rev. 4:4; though cf. Wis. 7:8), not least because the word is used for heavenly beings in *Testament of Levi* 3:8 (in the seventh heaven, with "authorities"); *2 Enoch* 20:1; and *Apocalypse of Elijah* 1:10-11. Likewise the "dominions" (κυριότητες) are almost certainly to be taken as referring to heavenly powers, in the light of Eph. 1:20-21 (also *1 Enoch* 61:10 and *2 Enoch* 20:1; F. Schröger, *EDNT* 2.332). But the same must be true of the "principalities" (ἀρχαί) and "authorities" (ἐξουσίαι) in the light of 2:10 and 15, not to mention the other New Testament parallels (1 Cor. 15:24; Eph. 1:21 again; 3:10; 6:12; see also on 2:10). The fact that all four terms thus refer only to the invisible, heavenly realm[23] and the repeated emphasis on Christ's supremacy and triumph over the "principalities and powers" in 2:10 and 15 do therefore strengthen the likelihood that the two lines were inserted by the author(s) of the letter, sacrificing the balance of the hymn in

---

coheres with the use of the same phrase in 1:17 An instrumental sense, "by" (Hegermann 96; Lohse, *Colossians and Philemon* 50 n. 129; Fowl 109; cf. Wedderburn, *Theology* 26), would cause confusion with an ἐκ reserved for God.

21. That the hymn goes beyond previous talk of Wisdom should make us hesitate before simply identifying Christ with Wisdom (Aletti, *Colossiens* 16-17).

22. Though see Eltester 145-46, referred to also by Dibelius, *Kolosser, Epheser, Philemon,* 13-14; Lohse, *Colossians and Philemon* 51 n. 137.

23. Cf. REB: ". . . not only things visible but also the invisible orders of thrones, sovereignties, authorities, and powers."

order to add a further reference to Christ's superiority over all beings in heaven as well as on earth. Despite Carr, *Angels* 48-52, followed by Yates, *Colossians* 24-25 with some reserve, the most obvious inference of 1:20 taken in conjunction with 1:13 and 2:15 is that these powers are understood as somehow threatening or hostile to God's cosmos. Wink 66 offers quite an effective demythologization of the four powers: "whether seats of power or spheres of influence, whether incumbents-in-office or the legitimations and sanctions that keep them there." See further on 2:10 and 15; and for a brief bibliography see C. E. Arnold, *ABD* 5.467.

1:17 καὶ αὐτός ἐστιν πρὸ πάντων καὶ τὰ πάντα ἐν αὐτῷ συνέστηκεν. The thematic emphasis on τὰ πάντα and on Christ's ultimacy in relation to τὰ πάντα is continued.[24] Once again the theme reflects Jewish reflection on Wisdom. According to Sir. 1:4 "wisdom was created before all things" (προτέρα πάντων ἔκτισαι σοφία), and the second-century-BCE Jewish philosopher Aristobulus notes Solomon's observation (Prov. 8:22-31) that "wisdom existed before heaven and earth" (Eusebius, *Praeparatio Evangelica* 13.12.11). Likewise, although the thought of the universe as held together by divine agency is characteristic of wider Greek philosophic thought (see, e.g., pseudo-Aristotle, cited above in 1:16; W. Kasch, *TDNT* 7.897), in Jewish thought this is attributed particularly to the divine Logos: thus Sir. 43:26 maintains that "by his word all things hold together" (ἐν λόγῳ αὐτοῦ σύγκειται τὰ πάντα) and similarly in Philo (*Quis rerum divinarum heres* 23, 188; *De fuga* 112; *De vita Mosis* 2.133; *Quaestiones in Exodum* 2.118) and in Wis. 1:6-7 Wisdom, God, and Spirit are merged into each other with the description τὸ συνέχον τὰ πάντα ("that which holds all things together").

Here again conceptuality from contemporary cosmology seems to be loaded in an undefined way on Christ. But again it is important to realize that this is not the language of clinical analysis but of poetic imagination, precisely the medium where a quantum leap across disparate categories can be achieved by use of unexpected metaphor, where the juxtaposition of two categories from otherwise unrelated fields can bring an unlooked for flash of insight. In this case the language is that of Platonic-Stoic cosmology, the belief that there is a rationality (Logos) which pervades the universe and

---

24. As with πρωτότοκος (1:15), there is some uncertainty as to whether πρo ("before") should be taken to denote temporal priority (Moule, *Colossians and Philemon* 66-67; Ernst, *Philipper, Philemon, Kolosser, Epheser* 168; Wedderburn, *Theology* 28; Aletti, *Colossiens* 103) or superiority in status (Masson 101 n. 3; Lohse, *Colossians and Philemon* 52; Caird 179). As with πρωτότοκος, the implication of the immediately attached clauses favors the former (so most translations: NEB "he exists before everything"; similarly JB/NJB and GNB), though the present tense (ἐστιν) suggests the latter (Gnilka, *Kolosserbrief* 66), and with κεφαλή (1:18) again suggesting a similar double sense we might be wiser to conclude that hymn and letter writer(s) were happy to leave the ambiguity, deliberately choosing to exclude neither sense (cf. Harris 46-47).

bonds it together (cf. Heb. 1:3) and which explains both the order and
regularity of natural processes and the human power of reasoning resonates
with this rationality. In the modern era Newtonian physics and the scientific
investigation of "the laws of nature" were premised on a similar axiom. The
hymn could say this of divine Wisdom, precisely because, as a personification of God's wisdom in creating, it could be thought of both as personal
and as pervading the whole world (Wis. 1:6-7; 7:22–8:1). In identifying this
function with Christ ("in him") the intention presumably was not to reduce
the person of Christ to a personification, but to shed the further light of
Christ on that personification: paradoxical as it may seem, the wisdom which
holds the universe together is most clearly to be recognized in its distinctive
character by reference to Christ. This will mean, among other things, that
the fundamental rationale of the world is "caught" more in the generous
outpouring of sacrificial, redemptive love (1:14) than in the greed and grasp-
ing more characteristic of "the authority of darkness" (1:12).

1:18a καὶ αὐτός ἐστιν ἡ κεφαλὴ τοῦ σώματος τῆς ἐκκλησίας. The
hymn or its first strophe ends with a switch in imagery from the traditional
"in, through, and for" language expressing divine agency in creation. If the
last two words, "the church," were added to the line,[25] then the original
meaning would be clear, and entirely consistent with what has gone before.
For the likening of the cosmos to a body is very ancient in Greek thought,
the cosmos understood as an ensouled and rationally controlled entity. Most
often cited are the *Timaeus,* where Plato speaks of God constructing τὸ τοῦ
παντὸς σῶμα (31b, 32a) and of τὸ τοῦ κόσμου σῶμα (32c), and the Orphic
fragment 168, which describes Zeus as the "head" (κεφαλή) of the cosmos.[26]
As might be expected, this way of envisaging the cosmos also penetrated
Hellenistic Judaism, or at least Philo's philosophical theology, influenced as
he was to such an extent by Platonic-Stoic thought in every aspect of his

25. O'Brien, *Colossians, Philemon* 48-50 prefers to follow Feuillet, *Christ Sagesse* 217-28,
and Kehl, *Christushymnus* 41-45 (also Helyer 173-74; Wright, "Poetry" in n. 7 above; cf. n. 27
below), in taking these last two words as part of the original line, thus beginning the second,
soteriological section of the hymn with 1:18a, despite the obvious parallel of 1:18b with 1:15, and
explaining the abrupt introduction of the head/body imagery by reference to the now largely
discredited idea of "corporate personality" (but see J. W. Rogerson, "The Hebrew Conception of
Corporate Personality: A Re-Examination," *JTS* 21 [1970] 1-16).

26. O. Kern, *Orphicorum Fragmenta* (Berlin: Weidmann, 1922) 201. See Lohmeyer 62 n. 1;
Dupont 431-35; Hegermann 53, 62-63, 94; Lohse, *Colossians and Philemon* 53; Kehl, *Christushymnus* 94; Gnilka, *Kolosserbrief* 68; Wedderburn, *Theology* 17. E. Schweizer, *TDNT* 7.1029-30, 1032,
1035, 1037-38, sums up his careful analysis of the data: "Undoubtedly, then, in NT days there is
identification of the cosmos and God, and undoubtedly too the cosmos is regarded as the body which
is directed by the supreme God as world-soul or head" (1037-38). For later Gnostic parallels see,
e.g., Pokorný 82. The later Jewish mystical speculation on the fantastic size of the divine body
(notably *Shi'ur Qomah*) is not the same as speculation about the bodily character of the cosmos
(despite Fossum 197-201).

reflections on reality. So, for example, humankind, like the world, "consists of body and reasonable soul" (*Quis rerum divinarum heres* 155); heaven in the cosmos is like a soul in a body (*De Abrahamo* 272). And the Logos (divine reason) is the head of this body, of all things (*De Somnis* 1.128; *Quaestiones in Exodum* 2.117).[27]

In the original hymn (lacking "the church"), then, the imagery would be a variation on what has already been said, identifying the one praised as being over the body, ruler of the cosmos,[28] without posing that idea as in any degree of tension with the correlated thought of the Logos as pervading the body. With this applied to Christ, the significance attached to Christ would be little different from that already discussed in 1:15-17; and once again the motivation seems to be not so much a speculative interest in the world's beginnings as an attempt to make sense of the world and its rationale in the light of Christ (Kuschel 339; Wolter 82).

However, at some point the last two words have, in fact, been added, whether in an original Christian adaptation of older language or by the author(s) of the letter. And thereby the thought of the hymn has been abruptly wrenched from a consistent and rounded theme by identification of "the body" not with τὰ πάντα but with "the church," ἡ ἐκκλησία. The wrenching in fact is twofold. For prior to this, in the earlier Paulines, "the church" denoted simply the assembly or coming together of Christians in particular houses or cities (Rom. 16:1, 4, 5, 16; 1 Cor. 1:2; 4:17, etc.; so also Col. 4:15-16). This usage of the word took over the usage in which ἐκκλησία denoted the assembly of Yawheh (BAGD s.v. ἐκκλησία 3), as expressed most clearly in the phrase "the church(es) of God" (e.g., 1 Cor. 1:2; 11:16, 22; 15:9; 1 Thes. 2:14) — each church as an assembly of Israel. And even when the same body imagery was used (Christ likened to a body with many members, 1 Cor. 12:12; "we the many are one body in Christ," Rom. 12:5), the thought was clearly of the particular church as the body of Christ in these particular localities (so explicitly in 1 Cor. 12:27: "you [Corinthians] are the body of Christ [that is, in Corinth]").

Here, however, in what seems a rather forced fashion, "the church" is

27. Hegermann 58-59, 64-66, 149; Lohse, *Colossians and Philemon* 54. Schweizer, *TDNT* 7.1054-55 is more cautious on the latter point (also his *Colossians* 58 n. 9); P. Beasley-Murray 179-82 is entirely skeptical; similarly Arnold 347-49.

28. The observation is regularly made that in the LXX κεφαλή often translates *r'š* in the sense of "ruler" or "leader" interchangeably with ἀρχή (e.g., Deut. 28:13; Jdg. 10:18; 11:11; 2 Sam. 22:44; 1 Kgs. 20:12; Isa. 7:8-9; see, e.g., H. Schlier, *TDNT* 3.674-75). It is possible that the idea of κεφαλή = ἀρχή ("beginning, principle") is also in play; see S. M. Bedale, "The Meaning of κεφαλή in the Pauline Epistles," *JTS* 5 (1954) 211-15; P. Beasley-Murray 175, 180-81; and particularly Aletti, *Colossiens* 104-5 (bibliography n. 62); Arnold 350-58. As in 1 Cor. 11:7, the "image" is also "head," precisely as being "the image of God" (Käsemann, "Liturgy" 156-57; Schweizer, "Kirche" 313 n. 56).

equated with the cosmic body. Or, should we rather say, the cosmic body is transposed by the addition of these words into the more familiar Christian conception of the church in Colossae?

In the former case the way is opened up to the idea of the church as the church universal, and not only so, but identified, moreover, with the cosmic body of which Christ is head. This certainly is the line which Eph. 1:22-23 follows. In that case we have to speak here, too, of the church under Christ's headship being depicted as the microcosm which mirrors (or should mirror) the divinely ordered cosmos, the assembly of Israel's wilderness wanderings anticipatory of and preparatory for the new state of society in the eschatological promised land, the church as the greenhouse in and by means of which the green shoots of God's purpose in and for creation are brought on.[29]

But in the latter case, if, that is, "the church" transposes the cosmic body into the church in Colossae, then the transition from cosmos to local assembly comes at the beginning of the line, and the two thoughts (Christ's supremacy over all things and his headship over each individual church as his body in a particular place) are simply juxtaposed (cf. Yates, *Colossians* 26). The implication may then be similar: the coherence of Christ's headship over the church and his priority over all things suggesting that one ought to reflect the other or provide a model for the other. As the creative power of divine wisdom is now defined in terms of Christ, so the cosmos of divine purpose can (or should) now be defined in terms of the church.

Either way the assertion of 1:18a does not evacuate the cosmic claims of 1:15-17 of their christological significance: to assert that Christ is head of the church does not narrow his cosmic mediatorial role; rather, it expands the significance of the claims made for the church.[30] And either way a significant shift has been taken beyond the earlier *church = body = (in) Christ* imagery. For in 1 Corinthians 12 the head is simply one among all the members of the body (12:21). But here it denotes Christ and his relation over the body.

Whatever the hymn writer may have intended, no firm decision can be made between these two alternatives so far as the author(s) of Colossians are concerned. For the first is given support by 2:10 — Christ as "the head of all rule and authority" (cf. 1:16 with 1:18). And the latter is taken up in 2:19, with the older *church = body* imagery retained also in 3:15. 1:24 comes somewhere in between, with 1:22 and 2:11 providing a further distinctive use of "body" in its talk of "the body of (his) flesh." A fuller exposition of

---

29. On Eph. 1:22-23 see particularly Lincoln, *Ephesians* 66-82.

30. But to say that "creation . . . happened for the sake of the church" (Hübner 352) pushes the point too far.

the theology of the body in Colossians must therefore await treatment of these subsequent verses (see also my "Body").

1:18b ὅς ἐστιν ἀρχή, πρωτότοκος ἐκ τῶν νεκρῶν, ἵνα γένηται ἐν πᾶσιν αὐτὸς πρωτεύων. The obviously deliberate repetition of ὅς ἐστιν . . . πρωτότοκος is clearly intended to parallel the opening of the hymn (1:15) and thus to introduce either a second strophe or an echoing supplement to it. Either way the possibility that this, too, in its original form, could be the work of a pre-Christian writer is simply not present: the πρωτότοκος ἐκ τῶν νεκρῶν ("firstborn from the dead") is both integral to the second strophe or echoing supplement and inescapably Christian (see below).[31]

In this second strophe or supplement the focus swings emphatically from a cosmology of creation to a cosmology of reconciliation, from the divine purpose that shaped creation in the beginning to the divine purpose that retrieves creation for its intended end, from first creation to re-creation beyond death. Implicit is the apocalyptic conviction that the original creation has fallen under the authority of darkness (1:13) and needs to be rescued from the malevolent domination of the principalities and authorities (2:15). But in both cases, as the hymn writer or his first commentator makes emphatically clear, the principal actor is the same, the "in him," "through him," and "for him" emphasizing the essential coherence and continuity of divine purpose, as now recognized in Christ, through both epochs and spanning all time and creation from beginning to end, from primal time to final time.

Given this switch it is initially a little surprising that the first descriptive word used is ἀρχή ("beginning, origin, first cause"). For this is still language that reflects Jewish reflection on Wisdom (Prov. 8:22: wisdom is "the beginning of his ways or work"; Philo, *Legum Allegoriae* 1.43: God "calls it [wisdom] 'beginning' and 'image' . . ."); note also Rev. 3:14, "the beginning of God's creation," in a letter written, perhaps significantly, to neighboring Laodicea. But that simply underlines the extent to which the hymn writer or its first expositor has determined to integrate the themes of the two strophes. For the "beginning," which is now expounded, is the new beginning of resurrection: πρωτότοκος ἐκ τῶν νεκρῶν, "firstborn from the dead."[32] The phrase was, or became, an identifying title for Christ, significantly in the first Christian apocalypse (Rev. 1:5). As with the preceding use of πρωτότοκος, but more clearly,

---

31. As is now generally recognized (see, e.g., Deichgräber 153; Gnilka, *Kolosserbrief* 70; O'Brien, *Colossians, Philemon* 38), against particularly Käsemann, "Liturgy" 154-59. Wedderburn, *Baptism* 212-18 documents subsequent Gnostic discomfort with the idea of resurrection.

32. In Gen. 49:3 LXX πρωτότοκος and ἀρχή are used synonymously: "Reuben, my firstborn, you are my strength and first of my children." Wedderburn, *Theology* 30 n. 14, notes that in Philo, *De vita Mosis* 2:60, Noah is described as the ἀρχή of a second γένεσις ("beginning, generation") of human beings.

the word has a double force. For it echoes the earlier Pauline talk both of Christ's resurrection as temporally prior to the resurrection of all in Christ, first in order, firstfruits (1 Cor. 15:23; cf. Acts 26:23), and of Christ as the πρωτότοκος among many brothers, eldest in a family destined to share his archetypal image (Rom. 8:29). In both senses it nicely encapsulates what appears to have been the earliest Christian understanding, namely that with Christ's resurrection the end-time resurrection itself had begun (Rom. 1:4: "the resurrection of the dead"; see also n. 2). The sense of a new beginning for creation could hardly be clearer, that with Christ's death and resurrection what had been expected as the end of all things and renewal of creation in a new age was already operative in and through this same Christ.[33]

In a hymn in praise of Christ, the focus is naturally on the significance of the resurrection for Christ himself, though always with a view to the consequences for creation. It is important, then, to note that the immediate outcome of the resurrection is "that he might be in all things preeminent" (πρωτεύων, the only occurrence in the New Testament). And we should also note that the clause is introduced with ἵνα, indicating that the purpose of Christ's resurrection from the dead was precisely that he might become (γένηται, aorist) preeminent, "that he might come to have first place in everything" (BAGD s.v. πρωτεύω; NRSV), "to become in all things supreme" (REB).

This clause stands in striking tension with the emphasis throughout the first strophe, where the equivalent is "he is the head of the body" (Hegermann 103, 106, 115-16).[34] There the emphasis was on Christ's (divine Wisdom's) *primordial* primacy, a becoming firstborn before time. Here, in contrast, Christ's primacy over all things is the consequence, the divinely intended outcome of his resurrection, a becoming firstborn beyond (the other end of) time (Jervell 224 sees two christological schemes that do not quite fit each other). It would be unjustified to ignore this feature,[35] since the tension is already implicit in the double use of πρωτότοκος (1:15, 18). We must therefore assume that it was intentional from the first Christian use of the material. That is to say, it was always intended that the full hymn should speak of a double, or two-stage becoming of the Christ thus praised — a becoming (the Fathers would say "begotten") as Wisdom in the power of

---

33. Schenk, "Christus" 147-51, argues the strained thesis that πρωτότοκος ἐκ τῶν νεκρῶν here describes the baptism of Jesus (comparing 2:12).

34. Glasson, however, draws attention to a neglected observation of J. Rendel Harris, that πρωτεύων corresponds to "primatum habere" in the Latin version of Sir. 24:6 ("In every people and in every race I had the primacy"), as does 1:15 to the Latin of Sir. 24:3 ("primogenita ante omnem creaturam").

35. The view that this line, too, is an addition to the hymn is also quite popular (see those listed by Burger 15-16).

creation, but also a becoming as resurrected one in new creation.[36] In the balanced, two-strophe form of the passage, it cannot be said that one becoming is more important than the other: the one as necessary for creation as the other for the work of reconciliation and (by implication) completion; at the same time, since the cross and resurrection provide the key to the whole, the primary theological weight rests on the second strophe (Wolter 89). Overall we might speak of the inextricable complementarity of Paul's Adam christology with his Wisdom christology, both emphasizing the divine purpose of creation and Christ's supremacy over (the rest of) creation, but the one in terms of creation (Wisdom) and the other in terms of creation redeemed (last Adam).[37]

1:19 ὅτι ἐν αὐτῷ εὐδόκησεν πᾶν τὸ πλήρωμα κατοικῆσαι. The assertion of 1:18b is further explained: this resurrection preeminence was also the result or effect (ὅτι) of a previous divine act (εὐδόκησεν, aorist). As we shall see, the imagery (πλήρωμα) is consistent with the emphasis of the first strophe. But the repetition of the sequence of prepositional phrases begun here (ἐν αὐτῷ) is obviously intended to set out the second phase of Christ's work in correspondence to the first; and this line is bracketed by references to Christ's resurrection (1:18) and his peace-making work (on the cross — 1:20). Both facts clearly indicate that the reference here is to Christ's ministry climaxing in his death and resurrection. As in the last line of 1:18, therefore, we have to acknowledge a deliberate attempt to explain Christ's present preeminence as the result, not of his primordial role in the figure of Wisdom, but in his role as depicted more by the Synoptic tradition.

What was it, then, about Jesus' ministry in Galilee and Jerusalem that, in addition to his resurrection, could explain the high praise now offered to him? The answer lies in the key word πλήρωμα ("fullness"). In itself it denotes completeness, as in the regular Greek use of it for a ship's crew (a full complement, LSJ s.v. 3) or in the repeated phrase in LXX, "the earth and its fullness (all that is in it)" (e.g., Ps. 24:1 [LXX 23:1]; Jer. 8:16; Ezek. 19:7; 30:12). A more cosmological usage as such is not attested before this time; the word is never taken up in this connection by Philo, usually a sure guide to contemporary philosophical usage in the wider Hellenistic world. However, the idea of God or his Spirit as filling the world is another way of expressing the divine rationality that permeates the world in Stoic thought (Seneca, *De beneficiis* 4.8.2: "nihil ab illo vacat, opus suum ipse implet" ["nothing is void of him (God); he himself fills all his work"]; Aelius

---

36. Cf. Lightfoot 156 ("The γένηται here answers in a manner to the ἔστιν of ver. 17. Thus ἔστιν and γένηται are contrasted as the absolute being and the historical manifestation") with Caird 180 ("What Christ is de jure in God's decree, he must become de facto; and the resurrection, by which he has become head of the church, is the beginning of the process"). See also n. 16 above.

37. See further my "Pauline Christology: Shaping the Fundamental Structures," in *Christology in Dialogue*, ed. R. F. Berkey and S. A. Edwards (Cleveland: Pilgrim, 1993) 96-107.

Aristides, *Orationes* 45.21: Zeus τὸ πᾶν πεπλήρωκε). And again, as we might now expect in the light of our findings in the first strophe, the same language was used in Hellenistic Judaism of divine Wisdom. Thus in Wis. 1:6-7: "Wisdom is a kindly spirit. . . . Because the Spirit of the Lord has filled the world (πεπλήρωκεν τὴν οἰκουμένην)." And Philo quite frequently uses similar phrases, "God (who) has filled/fills all things" (πάντα πεπλήρωκεν ὁ θεός, πάντα πεπληρωκὼς ὁ θεός; e.g., *Legum Allegoriae* 3:4; *De gigantibus* 47; *De confusione linguarum* 136; *De Vita Mosis* 2.238). At the same time, we should not attribute the conceptuality solely to the influence of wider (Stoic) thought, since it is already present in Jer. 23:24 (" 'Do I not fill heaven and earth?' says the Lord") and Ps. 139:7; cf. also *Aristeas* 132 ("God is one and his power is manifest through all things, every place filled with his sovereign power").[38] And the thought of divine indwelling (κατοικέω) in human beings is also familiar in Jewish thought (Wis. 1:4 — wisdom; *Testament of Zebulun* 8:2 and *Testament of Benjamin* 6:4 — God/the Lord; *1 Enoch* 49:3 — the Spirit; so also Eph. 3:17 — Christ).

The theme, then, is traditionally Jewish and is wholly of a piece with the Wisdom tradition, which was so powerfully influential in the first strophe. The only difference is one of emphasis and metaphor, "wisdom" denoting the mature, personal rationality that permeates creation and "fullness" the impersonal completeness of that permeation, that is, completeness both of God's commitment to creation and of the extent of his presence throughout creation. It was the potency of this imagery ("fullness") that presumably made the term πλήρωμα so attractive to later Gnostic use to denote the completeness of spiritual being emanating from the hidden God, the perfection of the highest spiritual realm (see G. Delling, *TDNT* 6.300-301; Ernst, *Pleroma* ch. 4; Lohse, *Colossians and Philemon* 57).

In Colossians we are at the beginning of this development in the use of this term, but only the beginning. It would be quite unjustified on the basis of the evidence to conclude that the usage here is "Gnostic"; the line of influence and development most obviously runs from the undeveloped usage here to the much more developed language of the later Valentinian Gnosticism (cf. particularly Overfield; Evans, "Meaning"). Nor is it likely that the usage is dependent on a proto-Gnostic syncretistic teaching current in Colossae,[39] since the use of πλήρωμα here would effectively have en-

38. See further Dupont 469-70; G. Delling, *TDNT* 6.288-89; Kehl, *Christushymnus* 116-25; Ernst, *Pleroma* 26-40; also Feuillet, *Sagesse* 236-38, for Wisdom/πλήρωμα parallels. This background is sufficient to explain why the term can be introduced here without explanation (despite Dibelius, *Kolosser, Epheser, Philemon* 18).

39. It is a common view that the affirmation here is in reaction to a "Colossian heresy" that envisaged a range of intermediate powers between God and the cosmos (so, e.g., Bruce, *Colossians, Philemon, and Ephesians* 73-74; see further Pokorný 64-69; but see also Percy, *Probleme* 77; Moule, *Colossians and Philemon* 166-67; and pp. 27f. above).

couraged the very syncretism against which *(ex hypothesi)* the letter sets itself. In contrast, there is no real reason why we should not attribute to the author of Colossians the small step of development from use of the verb πληρόω in the perfect tense to the noun πλήρωμα (Cerfaux, *Christ* 427; Benoit, "Plèrôma" 137-42; so also 2:9).

In the light of the above discussion the solution to another contentious issue becomes clearer: how the clause should be translated. Grammatically the subject of the verb must be πᾶν τὸ πλήρωμα; but the more impersonal "fullness" does not sit easily with a verb, εὐδόκησεν, that more naturally presupposes a personal subject. Moreover, this verb is used regularly in the LXX and elsewhere in the New Testament with God as subject to describe his good pleasure (e.g., Ps. 68:16: "God was pleased to dwell in it [Zion]"; 3 Macc. 2:16; other examples in G. Schrenk, *TDNT* 2.738; Mark 1:11; 1 Cor. 10:5). We could assume, therefore, that the personal subject is "God in all his fullness" (Moule, *Colossians and Philemon* 70-71; Ernst, *Pleroma* 83-87; REB; Harris). Or if we want to respect the degree of distinction present in the use of such a surrogate, as in all talk of divine immanence which also respects God's transcendence,[40] it may be better to stay closer to the Greek with a slightly expanded translation like NEB ("the complete being of God, by God's own choice, came to dwell") or NRSV ("all the fullness of God was pleased to dwell"; cf. H. Hübner, *EDNT* 3.111; Hoppe 169-72: "theological christology").[41] A similar note of reserve comes in the other occurrence of πλήρωμα in the letter, in 2:9: "all the fullness of deity [not God; θεότης, not θεός] dwells in him" (see on 2:9).

Either way, the importance of the language is to indicate that the completeness of God's self-revelation was focused in Christ, that the wholeness of God's interaction with the universe is summed up in Christ. Here the thought reaches well beyond that of Wisdom or even God "dwelling in" a good and compassionate person (Wis. 1:4; *Testament of Zebulun* 8:2; *Testament of Benjamin* 6:4) to grasp at the idea of the wholeness of divine immanence dwelling in Christ. As Christian devotion reflected on the significance of Messiah Jesus' work, it evidently could not rest content short of assessing him in the highest possible terms, of God's self-expression in and through him. To be sure, the imagery was hazardous in its imprecision

40. The Targum of Ps. 68:17 shows this to be a genuinely Jewish concern: "It pleased Yahweh's Word to cause his Shekinah to dwell upon it (Sinai)." Cf. also *1 Enoch* 49:3-4: "In him (the Elect One) dwells the spirit of wisdom, the spirit that gives thoughtfulness, . . . For he is the Elect One before the Lord of the Spirits according to his good pleasure."

41. Other translations open up the distinction between God and his fullness too much: NJB — "because God wanted all fullness to be found in him"; NIV — "God was pleased to have all his fullness dwell in him"; with GNB still more remote and incorporating patristic terminology anachronistically — "it was by God's own decision that the Son has in himself the full nature of God."

of definition. As the use of the figure of Wisdom, first creation of God, subsequently gave scope to Arianism (see on 1:15), so now with the idea of a man significant because of an act of divine choice to indwell him, scope was given to later Adoptionism[42] and Nestorianism.[43] But to press either corollary would be unfair to the Christians who used or composed the hymn. The object here is simply to claim that divine fullness is evident in Christ's ministry on earth, above all in his death and resurrection, and that that is another way of explaining his preeminence in all things (1:18). The thought is not yet of incarnation, but it is more than of inspiration; rather, it is of an inspiration (in Greek, "God-possessed" — ἔνθεος, ἐνθουσιασμός) so complete ("all the fullness") as to be merging into the idea of incarnation.

1:20 καὶ δι᾿ αὐτοῦ ἀποκαταλλάξαι τὰ πάντα εἰς αὐτόν, εἰρηνοποιήσας διὰ τοῦ αἵματος τοῦ σταυροῦ αὐτοῦ, [δι᾿ αὐτοῦ] εἴτε τὰ ἐπὶ τῆς γῆς εἴτε τὰ ἐν τοῖς οὐρανοῖς. That the thrust of this second strophe or supplementary expansion is directed to this as the climactic point (Findeis 392-95), to the work of redemption accomplished in Christ (1:14), is made clear beyond dispute by the two verbs used here ("reconcile," "make peace"). The clause is still governed by the ὅτι at the beginning of 1:19; that is, 1:20 continues the explanation of why the risen Christ is preeminent in all things (1:18). And the subject therefore is still πᾶν τὸ πλήρωμα, further emphasizing the personal character of "the fullness" as the completeness of God's presence throughout creation (see on 1:19); in contrast, the repetition of the controlling subject and verb in some translations ("and through him God was pleased to . . . ," NRSV, similarly NEB) both modifies the subject (not "the fullness of God") and unwisely implies a second act of divine choice.

The act of reconciliation is described in the uniquely compounded verb ἀποκαταλλάσσω, which is used in literary Greek only here, in 1:22, and in Eph. 2:16 and was therefore quite possibly coined by Paul (F. Büchsel, *TDNT* 1.258). Like the simpler form, καταλλάσσω (Rom. 5:10; 1 Cor. 7:11; 2 Cor. 5:18-20), it presumes a state of estrangement or hostility. In other words, between the two strophes, and the two phases of divine activity in Christ, there is presupposed an unmentioned event or state, that is, presumably the falling of the cosmos under the domination of the heavenly powers created as part of τὰ πάντα (1:16), the state already spoken of in 1:13 ("the power

---

42. Given the parallels with Ps. 139:7 and Wis. 1:7 on the one hand and with the account of Jesus' baptism (Mark 1:11) on the other, the thought of the Spirit's descent into Jesus at the Jordan may well lie in the background here (cf. Münderlein 271-73; Houlden 172; Aletti, *Colossiens 1:15-20* 30-32; Pokorný 85-86; Schenk, "Kolosserbrief," 3342-44). Others (Kehl, *Christushymnus* 124; Gnilka, *Kolosserbrief* 73; P. Beasley-Murray 177-78; Fowl 116; Wedderburn, *Theology* 33; Wolter 85), however, maintain that the context requires a reference rather to the resurrection (for which we may compare Acts 13:33; Rom. 1:4; and Heb. 5:5). See also on 2:9.

43. See my *Christology* 192, with reference to the objections of Benoit, "Body" 81.

of darkness"),[44] an ongoing crisis now resolved in the cross (see on 2:15). The defeat of these powers is also the means of reconciling heaven and earth,[45] unusually "to him" (see n. 3), in some contrast to Eph. 2:16, which has in view specifically the reconciliation of Jew and Gentile to God, more typical of Paul (cf. Rom. 11:15; 2 Cor. 5:18-20). The thought is coherently Jewish (cf. Isa. 11:6-9; 65:17, 25; *Jubilees* 1:29; 23:26-29; *1 Enoch* 91:16-17; Philo, *De specialibus legibus* 2.192: God as "peace-maker" among the various parts of the universe; a similar role is attributed to the Logos in *De plantatione* 10 and *Quis rerum divinarum heres* 206; see further Hartman, "Reconciliation") and in sharp contrast to later Gnosticism, for which such a reconciliation would be unthinkable. The implication is that the purpose, means, and manner of (final) reconciliation have already been expressed by God, not that the reconciliation is already complete.[46]

Almost as infrequent is the word εἰρηνοποιέω ("make peace"; only here in the New Testament; in LXX only in Prov. 10:10; the adjective only in Philo, *De specialibus legibus* 2.192; Matt. 5:9), though, of course, the idea of peace as the cessation of war would be more familiar. The phrase is almost unnecessary, particularly if the following six words were lacking in the original, leaving simply "making peace through him," since it simply repeats the thought of the preceding verb, though it adds the richness of the Jewish concept of "peace" (see on 1:2). But the appended phrase "through the blood of his cross" does make explicit what was implicit, that the act of peacemaking was accomplished by Christ's death. In its elements it is strongly Pauline, but the phrase itself is unique in Paul. Moreover, the combination of the elements ("blood" and "cross") and the present context put them at some remove from the more characteristic Pauline usage: the "blood" of Christ in Paul more naturally evokes the thought of his death as a bloody sacrifice (Rom. 3:25; 1 Cor. 11:25; and cf. Eph. 2:13-18 with Heb. 10:19), whereas here the imagery of warfare and triumph (2:15) suggests rather the blood of battle. And in Paul the "cross" usually evokes thought of shame and embarrassment because of the shamefulness of death on a

---

44. Schweizer thinks that the background lies in the idea of cosmic strife current in Greco-Roman thought of the period ("Versöhnung"; also "Slaves," followed particularly by Wolter 86-87). Findeis 348-49, 443-45, indicates how readily this can be reexpressed in more contemporary existential terms of the experience of disorientation.

45. That cosmic reconciliation is in view (and not just human creation) is implied by the thematic τὰ πάντα. Moule, *Colossians and Philemon* 62, regards this as the most difficult to accommodate to the rest of Paul's thought (similarly Marshall 126); but cf. Rom. 8:19-23; Phil. 2:10-11. See further particularly Gnilka, *Kolosserbrief* 74-76; for the older debate (only animate or also inanimate creation, angels as well as humans) see Abbott 221-24 and Michl; and for more recently posed alternatives see O'Brien, *Colossians, Philemon* 53-56.

46. Lohmeyer 43-47, 67-68 makes "reconciliation" the key to the whole hymn and attempts to interpret it against the background of the Day of Atonement; but see Lohse, *Colossians and Philemon* 45-46 (cf. Schweizer, *Colossians* 74-75).

cross (1 Cor. 1:17-18; Gal. 5:11; 6:12; Phil. 2:8; cf. Heb. 12:2), whereas here it is itself an instrument of warfare by which peace is achieved (see on 2:14-15). Here again, then, we either have to hypothesize a Paul who has modified his own characteristic motifs, and so speak of the early and late Paul, or we can speak of a close disciple who has modulated his master's voice to express his own adaptations and emphases. Either way we can hardly avoid the adjective "Pauline" in describing the theology expressed.

It is obviously no accident that the verse echoes the "all things through him and to him" of 1:16 —

1:16: τὰ πάντα δι' αὐτοῦ καὶ εἰς αὐτὸν ἔκτισαι
1:20: δι' αὐτοῦ ἀποκαταλλάξαι τὰ πάντα εἰς αὐτόν —

nor that the last line echoes the earlier phrase of 1:16 —

1:16: τὰ πάντα ἐν τοῖς οὐρανοῖς καὶ ἐπὶ τῆς γῆς
1:20: εἴτε τὰ ἐπὶ τῆς γῆς εἴτε τὰ ἐν τοῖς οὐρανοῖς.

What is being claimed is quite simply and profoundly that the divine purpose in the act of reconciliation and peacemaking was to restore the harmony of the original creation, to bring into renewed oneness and wholeness "all things," "whether things on the earth or things in the heavens" (see on 1:16). That the church has a role in this is implied in the correlation of 1:18a with 1:20. And when we include the earlier talk of the gospel "in all the world (κόσμος) bearing fruit and growing" (1:6), and the subsequent talk of the ages-old mystery being made known among all the nations (1:27), the implication becomes clear: it is by its gospel living (1:10) and by its gospel preaching (1:27) that the cosmic goal of reconciled perfection will be achieved (1:28; cf. Findeis 405-15, 422-26).

The vision is vast. The claim is mind-blowing. It says much for the faith of these first Christians that they should see in Christ's death and resurrection quite literally the key to resolving the disharmonies of nature and the inhumanities of humankind, that the character of God's creation and God's concern for the universe in its fullest expression could be so caught and encapsulated for them in the cross of Christ (cf. already1 Cor. 1:22-25, 30). In some ways still more striking is the implied vision of the church as the focus and means toward this cosmic reconciliation — the community in which that reconciliation has already taken place (or begun to take place) and whose responsibility it is to live out (cf. particularly 3:8-15) as well as to proclaim its secret (cf. 4:2-6).

Reconciliation and Response (1:21-23)

21 *And you, once alienated and enemies in mind in works that are evil,* 22
he has now reconciled[1] *in the body of his flesh through his death, to present
you holy and unblemished and blameless before him,* 23 *provided that you
remain in the faith established and steadfast and not shifting from the hope
of the gospel which you heard, proclaimed in all creation under heaven, of
which I Paul became servant.*[2]

The impression that 1:15-20 was in large measure a preformed unit that Paul
and Timothy took over for their own purposes is strengthened by the way
in which 1:21-23 seem deliberately to pick up the final theme of the hymn
and to repeat and elaborate it, bringing the cosmic vision of the hymn (in
third person) down to earth by relating it immediately to the readers. Hence
the emphatic opening "and you. . . ." Moreover, Aletti, *Épître aux Colossiens* 119-22, shows how pivotal 1:21-23 are in that they gather up earlier
emphases (vv. 22a/20, 22b/12b, 21-22/13, 23/4-6) and in effect indicate the
themes to be subsequently developed:

$$
\begin{array}{ccc}
21\text{-}22 & 23a & 23b \\
1:24\text{-}2:5 & 2:6\text{-}23 & 3:1\text{-}4:1
\end{array}
$$

1:21 καὶ ὑμᾶς ποτε ὄντας ἀπηλλοτριωμένους καὶ ἐχθροὺς τῇ διανοίᾳ
ἐν τοῖς ἔργοις τοῖς πονηροῖς. It is now made clear that the state of alienation
and hostility implied in 1:20 had been a fact in the readers' own past, the
verb "to be" with the perfect participle expressing a persisting state of affairs.
The verb which the participle is from, ἀπαλλοτριόω ("estrange, alienate"),[3]
appears only here and in Eph. 2:12 and 4:18, but the passive (used in all
three cases) would be familiar in reference to human estrangement (Ps.
69[LXX 68]:8; Sir. 11:34), and to alienation from God by sin and idolatry
(Ps. 58[LXX 57]:3; Ezek. 14:5, 7; Hos. 9:10). That human guilt and hostility
are in view, and not nameless fate or inscrutable destiny, is clear from the
supplementary description: "enemies in mind" and "in works that are
wicked." Paul previously had not hesitated to speak in such terms ("enemies

---

1. The passive form ἀποκατηλλάγητε meets all the criteria to be counted as original: it is
well supported (p[46] B), it explains the other readings, and it is the most difficult (following ὑμᾶς;
Metzger 621-22). But since the second person passive fits so badly we may be justified in concluding
that the early correction/improvement was wholly justified (cf. Lightfoot 249-50; Moule, *Colossians
and Philemon* 72).

2. ℵ* reads κῆρυξ καὶ ἀπόστολος ("herald and apostle") instead of διάκονος ("servant"),
presumably since the latter seemed too inadequate to express the status of Paul.

3. The passive participle means literally "having been given over to strangers," so
"estranged," not "being foreigners," as JB implies.

[of God]," Rom. 5:10; 11:28), though διάνοια (like ἀπαλλοτριόω) occurs only here and in Eph. 2:3 and 4:18 in the Pauline corpus. In this case διάνοια has the force of "mind (as a kind of thinking), disposition, thought," hence "hostile in attitude" (BAGD s.v. διάνοια 2), "in heart and mind" (NEB/REB). It reflects the determined and self-sustained attitude illuminated in Rom. 1:21, where human creation, having disowned its creatureliness, finds a self-satisfying mode of existence in ignorance of God (1:21-32; the thought is close to Bar. 1:22). Consequently the "deeds" (see on 1:10) which such an attitude produces are "wicked" (cf. *Testament of Dan* 6:8 and *Testament of Asher* 6:5), where the stronger adjective πονηρός ("wicked, evil"; cf. Rom. 12:9 and 1 Thes. 5:22) is used rather than κακός ("bad"; as in Rom. 13:3).

If we take the parallel with Ephesians seriously we will have to recognize the words written here from a Jewish perspective (a conceptuality taken over from Jewish polemic against Gentiles; so Wolter 92). For in Ephesians the alienation is "from the body politic of Israel" and "the covenants of promise" (Eph. 2:12) as well as "from the life of God" (Eph. 4:18). Consequently the "evil deeds" in mind can be characterized in terms of the indictment of Rom. 1:18-32 (see also on 3:5, 8; cf. *Psalms of Solomon* 17:13). At the same time we should recall that it is a cosmic alienation which is implied in 1:20 and that Paul elsewhere labored to persuade his fellow Jews that they, too, were guilty of defection from God's way of making righteous (Rom. 2; 11:28).[4] Nevertheless, here the thought is directed specifically at "you (Gentiles)," with the implication that Israel's relation with God models the relation to which all creation should aspire, as now the church (as the body of Christ) provides that model (1:18a, 24). At all events, it is not surprising that Gentile converts looking back to their old way of life should characterize it in strongly negative terms. Such an evaluation need not be self-justification by means of biographical reconstruction, but here presumably reflects the sense of having shifted from one realm (where the dominant force was evil and dark) to another (1:13; cf. Gal. 1:4). In such a decisive, final (eschatological) shift, the relative brightness and richness of life newly experienced "in Christ" would naturally make the old days seem much darker and illuminate their character as alienation (cf. Phil. 3:7-8).

1:22 νυνὶ δὲ ἀποκατήλλαξεν ἐν τῷ σώματι τῆς σαρκὸς αὐτοῦ διὰ τοῦ θανάτου παραστῆσαι ὑμᾶς ἁγίους καὶ ἀμώμους καὶ ἀνεγκλήτους κατενώπιον αὐτοῦ. The darker the past, the more dramatic the transition

---

4. Cf. Ezek. 14:5, 7, one expression of a regular warning that idolatry/following other gods results in Israel's estrangement from God. It is precisely in this context that we might have expected some use of the alternative metaphor of justification/making righteous, since that metaphor so dominates Paul's earlier presentation of a Jewish gospel for Gentiles (Romans 3–4; Galatians 3; Philippians 3; cf. even Eph. 2:8; 4:24).

(see Lona 99-100). "But now" (νυνὶ δέ) is a genuine Paulinism to express this moment of divine reversal (Rom. 3:21; 6:22; 7:6; 11:30; 1 Cor. 15:20; Phm. 11; see also Col. 3:8 and Eph. 2:13; Heb. 9:26; see further Tachau). The theme of cosmic reconciliation is picked up from 1:20 (with the same verb; see on that verse) and personalized: "he (this same one 'in whom all the fullness of God was pleased to dwell') has reconciled you." Unlike 1:20, where the maintenance of the pattern of "in, through, to" resulted in the thought of reconciliation "to him" (that is, to Christ), the language here, freed from the poetic constraints of the hymn, reverts to the more typical Pauline thought of reconciliation through Christ to God (Rom. 5:10; 2 Cor. 5:18-20; see also Marshall 125-27; Martin, *Reconciliation* 125-26), but here with Christ as subject (though see n. 1), as in Eph. 2:16 (Findeis 432-33). As in 1:13, the aorist tense ("has reconciled") indicates the decisiveness of what happened on the cross, not the completion of the whole work of reconciliation (1:20). The reconciliation of Gentiles (to be also the church) is the first stage in the reconciliation of the world; note also the "not yet" note implied in the following παραστῆσαι, which is the objective of the act of reconciliation, as also in 1:28.

In this elaboration of the imagery of 1:20 the means of reconciliation are explained, as already alluded to in the (likely) addition in 1:20 ("through the blood of his cross"). Reconciliation happened "in the body of his flesh through (his) death." This is the second occurrence of σῶμα ("body") in the letter (after 1:18a), the second of one of the most fascinating kaleidoscopes of usage that we can imagine in a key Pauline category (see Dunn, "Body"). Here it clearly denotes the human body of Christ on the cross, though the "in" may be locative and not merely instrumental (cf. Bruce, *Colossians, Philemon, and Ephesians* 78 n. 181), denoting, that is, not merely the means of identification but also that identification with Christ which is at the heart of Paul's "in Christ" (see on 1:2) and "suffering with Christ" motif (see on 1:24). The most striking variation at this point is the addition "of flesh" (as in the other reference to Christ's body on the cross, 2:11), resulting in a phrase (τὸ σῶμα τῆς σαρκός, "body of flesh") that occurs only in Colossians in the Pauline corpus.

The two words σάρξ and σῶμα are characteristically Pauline (each occurs more than ninety times in the letters attributed to Paul, more than 60% of the New Testament usage of these words). And they never appear linked together elsewhere in Paul simply because their ranges of meaning overlap to such an extent. The basic distinction is that σῶμα denotes the fact of embodiment, that aspect of human (and other) existence which gives it place in its world and makes it possible for embodied entities to interact upon each other (so, e.g., 1 Cor. 6:16-18; 7:4), while σάρξ is the material substance of which the body is composed in this world. It is always important in trying to understand Paul to remember that σῶμα does not mean "physical body" as such. Thus, most clearly, the distinction he makes in 1 Cor. 15:44, between the body of this age, σῶμα ψυχικόν ("natural body"), and the resurrection body, σῶμα πνευματικόν ("spiritual body"), shows that different embodiments are necessary for different environments. Since in Hebrew anthropology disembodied existence was scarcely conceivable, transformation of the "body" was simply the means by which transition from this world to the next takes place (cf. Phil. 3:21). In contrast, "flesh" remains rootedly of this world, inextricably part of it, so that "flesh and blood" cannot inherit the kingdom (1 Cor. 15:50). Nevertheless, since the embodiment of which Paul speaks most frequently is that within this world, a physical (three-dimensional) world, the individual σῶμα in Paul does in fact usually denote physical body. A fair degree of overlap between "body" and "flesh" is therefore inevitable (see also on 2:1).

From the other side of the overlap between the two words in Paul, σάρξ in its range of meaning quickly gathers to itself a characteristically negative note. The degree to which σάρξ belongs to and is part of this world means that it shares this world's weak, ephemeral character (contrast σῶμα, 2:17) and that its corruptibility leaves it ready prey to the powerful enticements of sin (classically expounded in Rom. 7:7–8:3). This negative tone is at its sharpest in Paul's blunt antithesis between "flesh" and "Spirit" (Rom. 8:4-8; Gal. 5:16-17).[5] In contrast, σῶμα as such is characteristically neutral and only rarely negative (Rom. 8:13 is exceptional).

The usage here, then, is unusual in that the unprecedented combination of these two terms looks almost tautologous. Almost as striking is the degree to which the second term, σάρξ ("flesh"), initially and more frequently in this letter denotes mere physical presence or existence (1:22, 24; 2:1, 5, 11), with the negative notes more characteristic of Paul coming only in 2:13, 23 and 3:22, though "mind of flesh" in 2:18 is equally unprecedented in Paul (see on 2:18 end). Why then the unusual formulation here? Clearly, in Pauline terms, we can say that the more neutral term "body" is being qualified by the traditionally more negative term. However, that may mean here simply a heightening of the sense of mere physicality. In contrast to a heavenly existence in the form of Wisdom (1:15-17) and to a σῶμα identified either with the universe as a whole or with the church in particular (1:18a), the σῶμα with which Christ achieved his act of reconciliation was merely that of one single frail human being. "Of flesh" ensures that this σῶμα could never be confused with the σῶμα of 1:18. The negative here, then, would be the sharpness of the antithesis between glorious cosmic body and individual human frame stretched out in the agonizing humility of crucifixion (cf. the similar usage in 1QpHab 9:2; also 4QpNah/4Q169 2:6 = "corpse,

---

5. See further my "Jesus — Flesh and Spirit: An Exposition of Rom. 1:3-4," *JTS* 24 (1973) 40-68.

carcass").[6] At any rate, intentional or not, such an emphasis would have been a bulwark against any Gnostic tendencies that attempted to question the reality of Christ's death:[7] the firstborn of all creation attained his status as firstborn from the dead by experiencing the full reality of physical death.

The divine act of reconciliation had two phases: the means ("in the body of his flesh through death") and the objective ("to present you holy . . ."). The repetition of "you" underscores how personalized was the divine condecension; of course, it does not mean "you alone" but "you" among all the other "you"'s, all of whom could count themselves the beneficiaries of personally characterized and directed grace. The imagery is drawn from cult and law court and reflects the degree to which these two powerful features of daily life in classical society were interwoven.

Παρίστημι ("present") here signifies a formal bringing before and presentation in the implied hope of acceptance and acknowledgment (as in 2 Cor. 4:14; 11:2; Eph. 5:27; 2 Tim. 2:15; see also 1:28). Thus it could be used both of offering a sacrifice (hence Rom. 12:1) and of bringing someone before a judge (hence Rom. 14:10; see BAGD s.v. 1d, e). Ἅγιος ("holy"), as we have already seen (1:2), also derives from the cult, denoting that which has been set apart, consecrated to God. Ἄμωμος ("without blemish or blame") is used most commonly in the LXX of the physical perfection required of the sacrificial animal (e.g., Exod. 29:1; Lev. 1:3, 10, etc.; Num. 6:14, etc.; Ezek. 43:22-25; 45:18, 23; 46:4-6, 13), though naturally such perfection became a metaphor for blamelessness before God (2 Sam. 22:24; Pss. 15:2; 18:23; 19:13, etc.). The same overtone carries over into New Testament use (Eph. 5:27; Phil. 2:15; Jude 24; Rev. 14:5; explicitly in Heb. 9:14 and 1 Pet. 1:19). The parallel is particularly close with Eph. 1:4: ἁγίους καὶ ἀμώμους κατενώπιον αὐτοῦ (κατενώπιον only in these two passages in the Pauline letters). Ἀνέγκλητος, though much less common in Jewish tradition (only 3 Macc. 5:31), is drawn directly from legal procedure: ἐγκαλέω is a legal technical term, "accuse, bring charges against" (BAGD s.v. ἐγκαλέω); so ἀνέγκλητος denotes one free of accusation or charge, hence "irreproachable, blameless" (cf. particularly 1 Tim. 3:10 and Tit. 1:6-7; elsewhere in Paul only in 1 Cor. 1:8).

There is implicit, then, an interplay between the idea of Christ's death as sacrifice (1:20) and the presentation of those who are as unblemished as

6. The phrase also occurs in the Greek of Sir. 23:17 (ἄνθρωπος πόρνος ἐν σώματι σαρκὸς αὐτοῦ) and 1 Enoch 102:5 (τῷ σώματι τῆς σαρκὸς ὑμῶν). See further Lohse, *Colossians and Philemon* 64 n. 20. Since the contrast with 1:18 would be sufficient to explain "of flesh" here, it is less certain that a polemical overtone is present, directed against teaching current in Colossae (so Lightfoot 160; otherwise Abbott 226; Bruce, *Colossians, Philemon, and Ephesians* 78; R. P. Martin, *Colossians and Philemon* 67; O'Brien, *Colossians, Philemon* 68).

7. According to Tertullian, *Adversus Marcionem* 5.19.6, Marcion did not include "of flesh" in his reading of Col. 1:22 and took "his body" to refer to the church.

a sacrifice to God. In other words, there is an echo of the Pauline idea of sacrificial interchange, where the spotless sacrifice by dying as a sin offering is somehow interchanged with the blameworthy sinner and its spotlessness transferred to the sinner (so most explicitly in 2 Cor. 5:21). This has been taken up in the imagery of formal presentation to judge or king or emperor, where it is the irreproachable character of those presented that guarantees their acceptance (the two elements nicely caught in NIV's "without blemish and free from accusation"). But it is clearly implicit that this acceptability has been made possible and guaranteed by the death of Christ. The sacrificial imagery is one way of explaining how that came about, but others will be offered shortly (see 2:11-15, 20; 3:1).

Also implicit is the suggestion that the presentation has not yet taken place and that it will be the final climax of God's saving purpose through Christ (otherwise Lightfoot 160-61; Lohse, *Colossians and Philemon* 65; Aletti, *Épître aux Colossiens* 125). This is borne out by the immediately following note of caution (1:23) and the otherwise surprising indication in 1:24 that Christ's sufferings (on the cross) are as yet somehow incomplete.

1:23 εἴ γε ἐπιμένετε τῇ πίστει τεθεμελιωμένοι καὶ ἑδραῖοι καὶ μὴ μετακινούμενοι ἀπὸ τῆς ἐλπίδος τοῦ εὐαγγελίου οὗ ἠκούσατε, τοῦ κηρυχθέντος ἐν πάσῃ κτίσει τῇ ὑπὸ τὸν οὐρανόν, οὗ ἐγενόμην ἐγὼ Παῦλος διάκονος. The confidence in the effectiveness of the divine provision made for those estranged from God by their evil and for the blameworthy by Christ's death is qualified by a matching emphasis on human responsibility. Such emphasis on the need for persistence in Christian belief and conduct is a regular feature in Paul (e.g., Rom. 8:13, 17; 11:22; 1 Cor. 9:27; 10:11-12; Gal. 5:4) and should not be ignored. Εἴ γε may denote confidence more than doubt (cf. its use in 2 Cor. 5:3; Eph. 3:2; 4:21),[8] but final acceptance is nevertheless dependent on remaining in the faith. The parenetic and pastoral point is that however such persistence must be and is enabled by God through his Spirit (1:11), there must be such persistence (cf. O'Brien, *Colossians, Philemon* 69).

That the persistence (see BAGD s.v. ἐπιμένω 2; the same verb as in Rom. 11:22) is here described as "with reference to the faith" (τῇ πίστει) may be significant. On the one hand it catches the authentic Pauline emphasis on "faith" (see on 1:4), perhaps in some contrast to the more typically Jewish emphasis on "faithfulness" (see again my *Romans* 200-201, 238). Whereas Jewish parenesis focused on the ongoing responsibilities of the covenant people, without (in Paul's view) sufficient recall to the foundational character

---

8. See, e.g., Harris 60; J. M. Gundry Volf, *Paul and Perseverance* (WUNT 2.37; Tübingen: Mohr/Louisville: Westminster/JohnKnox, 1990) 197 n. 231. Contrast Wall 81: "Paul does not teach a 'once saved, always saved' kind of religion; nor does he understand faith as a 'once for all' decision for Christ."

of election by grace (Romans 4; 9:6-11; 11:20), Paul always insisted that the ongoing "walk" (1:10) of the Christian should be in direct continuity with and continuingly expressive of the faith by which the Christian first entered upon that walk (the main thrust of Galatians; so, e.g., Gal. 3:2-3; 5:4-6; Rom. 14:23). It is probably that faith by which the Colossians first received the gospel which is referred to here: without that same basic conviction and openness to the grace of God they would be unable to persist (Aletti, *Épître aux Colossiens* 126). On the other hand, the definite article could denote an early example of the objectification of faith ("the faith"; Houlden 175; O'Brien, *Colossians, Philemon* 69) which begins to characterize post-Pauline usage (1 Tim. 3:9; 4:1, 6; 5:8; 6:10, 21; etc.), though it could equally denote "your faith." Pokorný 93 thinks both meanings are involved here.

The point is reinforced by a sequence of strengthening images. "Established" (τεθεμελιωμένοι) uses the image of a "foundation" (θεμέλιος). The verb occurs only here and in Eph. 3:17 in the Pauline corpus, but Paul liked to think of himself as a master builder laying a foundation of the gospel or of faith in Christ (Rom. 15:20; 1 Cor. 3:10-12). The image of Christ as the "foundation" on which Christians are established (1 Cor. 3:11) was presumably drawn from Isa. 28:16 (cf. particularly Rom. 9:33; Eph. 2:20; 1 Pet. 2:6).[9] The passive here could imply Paul or Epaphras as the builder: as elsewhere, the "provided that" takes its force from the gospel in which the Colossians first believed (1 Cor. 15:2; Gal. 5:4-5). Ἑδραῖος ("firm, steadfast"; elsewhere in the New Testament only in 1 Cor. 7:37 and 15:58; but also in Ignatius, *Ephesians* 10:2; *Polycarp* 3:1) comes from ἕδρα or ἕδρη, meaning a "place where one sits": the addressees are to remain as firmly seated on the gospel as a god in his temple or a skillful rider on a spirited horse. The third image is simply that of movement, shifting from one place to another (μετακινοῦμαι; only here in the New Testament but echoing the imagery in 1 Cor. 15:58; cf. Deut. 19:14; not quite "drift away," as in JB/NJB). This they must avoid, remaining firmly attached to "the hope of the gospel," a neat phrase summarizing the earlier emphasis (1:4-5), with "hope" again prominent as characterizing the "gospel" (see on 1:5).

The recollection of the opening thanksgiving is continued with the further relative clause, "proclaimed in (= throughout) all creation (better than "to every creature" in RSV/NRSV, NJB, NIV) under heaven." This is simply a variation on 1:6, using the verb κηρύσσω, "proclaim (as a herald)" (cf., e.g., Rom. 10:8, 14-15; 1 Cor. 1:23; 15:11), "creation" instead of "cosmos" (perhaps in echo of 1:15), and the singular "heaven" instead of the plural (as in 1:5, 16, 20; but "under heaven" is not otherwise used by

9. On the imagery of God's building in Jewish thought see, e.g., Lohmeyer 72 n. 3; Lohse, *Colossians and Philemon* 66 and nn. 33 and 34.

Paul). The aorist tense (against the present tenses of 1:6) may reflect the perspective of Paul at the end of his missionary career, conscious of the flickering pinpoints of candle flame that he (and others) had kindled in so many cities of the Mediterranean world (cf. Gnilka, *Kolosserbrief* 92; Wolter 96). But a degree of hyperbole can hardly be denied. However, the purpose evidently is not to convey any fresh thought but to round off the great sequence of thanksgiving and to provide a link into the next section in the closing words of the preceding section (another characteristic of Pauline style).

In this case the transition is to a personal statement about Paul's own involvement in the preaching of the gospel and in his concern for the Colossians (1:24–2:5). The link is provided by the affirmation that this is the gospel of which he himself (ἐγὼ Παῦλος, with some emphasis; cf. Gal. 5:2 and 1 Thes. 2:18) became "servant" (διάκονος; see on 1:7), a thought that is repeated with reference to the "church" in 1:25. Paul and his immediate circle could never forget that he had been given a special and decisive mission as "apostle to the nations" (Rom. 11:13). But here it is not his apostolic status which is emphasized (that was not under threat at Colossae; see n. 2); rather, the privileged but hard service which his calling involved (cf. 1 Cor. 3:5; see also O'Brien, *Colossians, Philemon* 71).

A PERSONAL STATEMENT (1:24–2:5)

Paul's Commitment to the Gospel (1:24-29)

24 *Now[1] I rejoice in my sufferings for your sake and I fill up what is lacking of the afflictions of the Christ in my flesh for the sake of his body, which is the church,* 25 *of which I became servant in accordance with the commission which was given to me for you, to make the word of God fully known,* 26 *the mystery which has been hidden from the ages and from the generations. But now it has been revealed to his saints,* 27 *to whom[2] God wished to make known what is the wealth of the glory[3] of this mystery among the nations, which[4] is, Christ in you, the hope of glory.* 28 *Him we proclaim, warning everyone and teaching everyone in all wisdom, in order that we might present everyone complete in Christ.[5]* 29 *For this I also labor, striving in accord with his energy which operates effectively in me with power.*

It was Paul's custom to write about his own missionary labors and personal involvement with his readers, most naturally after the opening thanksgiving (Rom. 1:11-15; 1 Thes. 2:17–3:11; cf. the lengthy *narratio* in Gal. 1:10–2:21), but elsewhere also (Rom. 15:14-32; 1 Cor. 16:1-11; Phm. 21-22). The irregularity of such features is simply a reminder that Paul treated matters of structure and format as completely adaptable to what he wanted to say. So after the lengthy thanksgiving (cf. 1 Thes. 1:2–2:16), Paul picks up the final clause of the last section ("of which I Paul became a minister") and fills it out.

Aletti, *Épître aux Colossiens* 132-33, notes the prominence of revelation/knowledge language in 1:24–2:5 (μυστήριον in 1:26, 27; 2:2; φανερόω in 1:26; γνωρίζω in 1:27; καταγγέλλω in 1:28; σοφία in 1:28; 2:3; οἶδα in 2:1; σύνεσις in 2:2; ἐπίγνωσις in 2:2; γνῶσις in 2:3). Again, this need not imply a strong "Gnostic" or hidden knowledge content in the teaching and praxis being confronted at Colossae; of the words cited, only σοφία (2:23) appears within the explicitly polemical section (2:8-23), and, somewhat surprisingly, ἀποκαλύπτω/ἀποκάλυψις not at all. The inspiration for this language comes from Paul's own self-awareness rather than that of the Colossians. Here the objective was possibly to boost further the Colossian

---

1. "Now" can mean "as I review my part in all this" (similarly Lightfoot 164) or "imprisoned as I am" (similarly Masson 109-10). But it could be simply resumptive, as it often is in common speech today (Moule, *Colossians and Philemon* 75).

2. Bowers's suggestion that τοῖς ἁγίοις αὐτοῦ is the *antecedent* of οἷς ("whom," not "to whom": the saints as the divinely intended agency for the Gentile mission) has gained no support.

3. p[46] omits "of the glory."

4. A natural correction was to change the "which" to "who."

5. Another case where later scribes thought it appropriate to add "Jesus."

believers' self-esteem by reinforcing their appreciation of the riches of insight and glory given to them in Christ (the focus of the whole paragraph: 1:24, 27-28; 2:2-3, 5) and at such cost to Paul (1:24, 29; 2:1). They should not allow others to denigrate the Christians' privileges (2:4, 8) or to compare these privileges unfavorably with their own (2:16, 18).

1:24 νῦν χαίρω ἐν τοῖς παθήμασιν ὑπὲρ ὑμῶν καὶ ἀνταναπληρῶ τὰ ὑστερήματα τῶν θλίψεων τοῦ Χριστοῦ ἐν τῇ σαρκί μου ὑπὲρ τοῦ σώματος αὐτοῦ, ὅ ἐστιν ἡ ἐκκλησία. The initial statement echoes a characteristic Pauline theme, that of rejoicing in suffering (Rom. 5:3 — boasting in afflictions [cf. 12:12]; 8:18 — sufferings not worth comparison with the coming glory [similarly 2 Cor. 4:17-18]; 2 Cor. 1:5-7 — abundance of sufferings matched by abundance of comfort; 2 Cor. 7:4 — "I am overflowing with joy in our affliction"; 1 Thes. 1:6 — "you received the word in much affliction with joy of the Holy Spirit"). As these texts show, such suffering is characteristic of apostolic ministry (also 1 Cor. 4:9-13; 2 Cor. 11:23-27; Gal. 6:17), but not distinctive of it either (over against that of other Christians). Nor indeed is it a distinctively Pauline theme, since positive evaluation of suffering is to be found in Stoic sources (such as Seneca's *De Providentia* 4), as also in contemporary Jewish sources (e.g., 1QH 9:24-25; *Psalms of Solomon* 10:1-2; *2 Baruch* 52:6, cited in my *Romans* 250). Rather, it is the response of those who recognize that suffering positively reacted to can be a maturing experience, as also of those convinced of the rightness of their cause, which conviction functions as an inner source of strength and transforms the sufferings into a confirmation of that rightness. At this point the line between blind fanaticism and unflinching devotion can become very thin.

Here at least we can say that Paul accepted suffering on behalf of others (ὑπὲρ ὑμῶν) — a reminder that the sufferings were not sought in anything like a masochistic spirit, but were accepted, indeed welcomed, as the unavoidable consequence of the all-important objective of preaching the gospel. What the sufferings in view here might have involved is documented in 2 Cor. 11:23-28.

Paul's theology of suffering, however, was still richer. For Paul suffering meant suffering with Christ, sharing Christ's sufferings (Rom. 8:17; 2 Cor. 1:5; 4:10-11; Phil. 3:10-11). It is clearly this theme which is taken further here in the surprising sentence, "I fill up what is lacking of the afflictions of the Christ in my flesh." The words have caused bewilderment to generations of translators[6] and commentators.[7] But in fact they are simply

---

6. NEB: "This is my way of helping to complete, in my poor human flesh, the full tale of Christ's afflictions still to be endured"; REB: "I am completing what still remains for Christ to suffer in my own person"; NJB: "in my own body to make up all the hardships that still have to be undergone by Christ."

7. The one thing on which most are clear is that there can be no thought here of Christ's

the extension of Paul's complete eschatological schema. It contains several elements: (1) Christ's sufferings and death as the eschatological tribulation expected as the antecedent to the new age — Paul's adaptation, reflected particularly in Rom. 8:18-23, of an older Jewish theme;[8] (2) participation in the death of Christ as itself the means of transition from old age to new (Rom. 6:3-11; 8:18-23 prefaced by 8:17; 2 Cor. 4:10-12 leading into 4:16–5:5; Phil. 3:10-11; Heb. 2:9-10 offers a different model with equivalent effect); and, consequently, (3) Christian existence as a lifelong process in which dying with Christ leads to a share of his final resurrection (Rom. 6:5; Gal. 2:19; 6:14 — still nailed to the cross with Christ [note the perfect tenses]; Rom. 6:5; 8:11, 23; Phil. 3:11 — resurrection still future; see further my *Jesus* 326-38).

Col. 1:24 is clearly building on this theme.[9] In particular, the thought that Paul's sharing in Christ's death was essential to the well-being of his converts is already present in 2 Cor. 4:10-12. To be sure, the schema is modified in Colossians in the thought that resurrection with Christ is already past (see on 2:12). On the other hand, the retention or at least echo of the titular force of Christ ("the Christ") reinforces the Jewish character of the schema (so we can speak already of "the messianic woes"; see G. Bertram, *TDNT* 9:671-72). But Paul here has also made a unique addition to the theme by adding the (implied) thought that Christ's afflictions lack something (ὑστέρημα, "lack, deficiency")[10] and need to be completed in Paul's flesh

vicarious sufferings being inadequate or insufficient, not least since Paul never calls Christ's sufferings "afflictions" (see particularly discussion in Schweizer, *Colossians* 101-3; Aletti, *Épître aux Colossiens* 134-36). Almost as unanimous is the view that the category of "mystical union with Christ" is inappropriate, particularly since it leaves unexplained the "lack in Christ's afflictions" (see particularly Lohmeyer 77-78). For exegetical alternatives see Kremer 174-95; Gnilka, *Kolosserbrief* 95-96; O'Brien, *Colossians, Philemon* 77-78; and Pokorný 96-99; and for the earlier history of interpretation see Kremer 5-152.

8. Dan. 7:21-22, 25-27; 12:1-3; *Jubilees* 23:22-31; 1QH 3:28-36; *Testament of Moses* 5-10; Matt. 3:11/Luke 3:16 (drawing on Isa. 30:27-28); Mark 10:38; Acts 14:22. See further Str-B 4.977-86.

9. Cf. Dibelius, *Kolosser, Epheser, Philemon* 22-23; Best 130-36; Moule, *Colossians and Philemon* 76-79; Kamlah, "Wie beurteilt Paulus sein Leiden?"; Bauckham; O'Brien, *Colossians, Philemon* 78-80. As Lightfoot 163 noted, " 'the afflictions . . . which Christ endured' . . . seems to be the only natural interpretation of the words." Schweizer, *Colossians* 104, however, resists this whole train of thought when he insists that "one can understand 'Christ's afflictions' only as the sufferings endured in the community for the sake of Christ, or 'in Christ' "; similarly A. Wikenhauser, *Pauline Mysticism: Christ in the Mystical Teaching of St Paul* (Freiburg: Herder, 1960) 159-62. The motif is only partially grasped also by Gnilka, *Kolosserbrief* 98 (also *Theologie* 340), and Pokorný 99-100. Thus the latter: "The apostle struggles and suffers in order that people may 'realize' that their salvation in Jesus Christ is already completed. . . . What is still 'lacking' is the appropriation of the already complete salvation."

10. The fact that ὑστέρημα also became a Gnostic technical term (see, e.g., Moule, *Colossians and Philemon* 79) simply underlines the danger of reading the outlines of "the Colossian heresy" back from these later sources, since it is very hard to conceive what use the "false teaching" would have been making of the concept to which Paul would then be responding.

(ἀνταναπληρῶ, literally "fill up in place of"; cf. the similar phrase in 1 Cor. 16:17 and Phil. 2:30; see Abbott 229-30; Lohse, *Colossians and Philemon* 71 n. 25). This again is partly a reflection of the cosmic scope of the reconciliation envisaged and of Paul's awareness that it is not yet complete; therefore the decisive sufferings of the Christ cannot yet be complete. Foreshadowed is the apocalyptic thought that there is an appointed sum of suffering that must be endured in order to trigger (as it were) the final events of history (Rev. 6:9-11; *4 Ezra* 4:33-43);[11] the thought then is that the death of Christ has (as it were) activated the first trigger, but those sufferings are not yet complete, otherwise the second and final trigger would have been activated too.

Central to this further thought is the claim that these remaining afflictions are being experienced by Paul himself ("in my flesh").[12] The claim is not megalomanic, as though Paul thought he could supplement the work of divine Wisdom-Christ's act of cosmic reconciliation ("a theologically untenable glorification of the apostle by one of his followers," according to H. Hübner, *EDNT* 3.110; similarly Löwe 313; Nielsen 111-14; Beker, *Heirs* 68; Roloff 225-26). It is rather the most striking expression of a conviction which Paul seems to have had from the beginning of his apostolic ministry, namely that his mission was to fulfill or complete that of the Servant of Yahweh, that is, also of the suffering Servant of deutero-Isaiah.[13] This underlines in turn the degree to which Paul understood his apostleship in eschatological terms as the last act on the stage of this world before (as we would say) the final curtain (particularly 1 Cor. 4:9).[14] It was because Paul saw himself as a major actor in the final drama of God's reconciling purpose that he could also see his all too real sufferings as somehow bringing to completion what was still outstanding of the suffer-

11. See further R. Stuhlmann, *Das eschatologische Mass im Neuen Testament* (FRLANT 132; Göttingen: Vandenhoeck, 1983), here 99-101; otherwise Nielsen 112.

12. Not "the afflictions of Christ-in-my-flesh" (Houlden 180), which would require τοῦ Χριστοῦ τοῦ ἐν τῇ σαρκί μου. Flemington also insists on the importance of taking "in my flesh" in close conjunction with the preceding words: "the afflictions of Christ as they are reflected and reproduced in the life and behaviour of Paul his apostle" (87; cf. Wolter 101-2). But he does not give enough weight to ὑστερήματα and to the ὑπέρ clause, neither of which, however, need detract from the finished and decisive character of the cross (see also n. 7 above).

13. Note particularly Rom. 15:20-21 (= Isa. 52:15); 2 Cor. 6:1-2 (= Isa. 49:8); Gal. 1:15-16 (echoing Isa. 49:1-6); Phil. 2:16 (cf. Isa. 49:4). The same conviction impressed itself on the Acts material: 13:47 (= Isa. 49:6); 26:16-18 (cf. Isa. 42:7); also 18:9-10 (cf. Isa. 41:10; 43:5). Cf. Bruce, *Colossians, Philemon, and Ephesians* 82-83.

14. See further my *Jesus* 111-13, referring particularly to O. Cullmann, "Le caractère eschatologique du devoir missionaire et de la conscience apostolique de S. Paul. Étude sur le κατέχον(-ων) de 2 Thes. 2:6-7," *RHPR* 16 (1936) 210-45; A. Fridrichsen, *The Apostle and His Message* (Uppsala: Lundequistaka, 1947); Munck 36-42. Paul is himself part of the mystery he proclaims (Merklein 29-30). In contrast, A. T. Hanson, "Development" 160-65 sees the delay in the parousia as the key to the thought here.

ings of Christ ("crucified with Christ") by which the world was redeemed and transformed.

One interesting corollary is that for such a theology to be realistically put forward it was almost essential that Paul was still alive. If he was dead, then his sufferings were complete, and so also (the most obvious corollary to this verse) were Christ's afflictions; and where then was the end of all things? Here is a further slight indication that the letter was probably written while Paul was still alive, not by him, but with his approval. It follows further (despite most) that the sense of eschatological expectancy in the letter must have been still high if Paul's missionary work was nearly over. Nor should his subsequent death be allowed to devalue the whole line of thought overmuch. For at its heart is the double claim that the suffering and dying of Christ provides a key insight into the way the cosmos is constituted and into its reclamation (1:15-20) and that it is only by identification with this Christ in the way of suffering that those who serve the church can help it truly to be his body, the body which mirrors the cosmos as it was intended to be.

To be noted, finally, is the further change rung on the use of σῶμα. As just implied, the thought of 1:18a is deliberately echoed in the last two phrases of the verse: "on behalf of his body, which is the church" (see on 1:18a). But the addition of "his" ("his body") also echoes 1:22 ("the body of his flesh"). We may say then that the embodiment of Wisdom-Christ, which was more impersonal in the cosmos (1:18), was succeeded by an embodiment in the particularity of human flesh (1:22), to be succeeded in turn by an embodiment in the (universal) church (1:24), but now characterized by the personality known in and as Jesus Christ. While the cosmos does not cease to be pervaded by the divine Wisdom, which sustains it (how could it then continue to hold together?), the means by which the world encounters and interacts with this Wisdom now recognized as Christ is primarily through his body, the church, just as the means by which Christ encounters and acts upon the world of humanity is primarily through his body, the church. The privilege, but also obligation, of the church so conceived is staggering. In the same vein we should not ignore the further interplay with 1:22: the act of reconciliation took place ἐν τῷ σώματι τῆς σαρκὸς αὐτοῦ; Paul fills up what is lacking of the afflictions of Christ ἐν τῇ σαρκί μου ὑπὲρ τοῦ σώματος αὐτοῦ. There is a degree of continuity between Christ's body of flesh and Paul's flesh for Christ's body (cf. Ernst, *Philipper, Philemon, Kolosser, Epheser* 183).

1:25 ἧς ἐγενόμην ἐγὼ διάκονος κατὰ τὴν οἰκονομίαν τοῦ θεοῦ τὴν δοθεῖσάν μοι εἰς ὑμᾶς πληρῶσαι τὸν λόγον τοῦ θεοῦ. The astonishing claim just made is at once balanced and modified by repetition and variation of the claim made already in 1:23, "the church, of which I became a servant." Despite the attractive simplicity of translating "the church of which I became deacon (διάκονος)," we are clearly not yet at the stage where the term has become a formal and uniform title for a recognized office in the Pauline churches (as subsequently in 1 Tim. 3:8, 12; but evidently not yet in Rom. 16:1 and Phil. 1:1).[15] Paul, who was so insistent on his apostolic status, would hardly wish to be thought to lay claim to what subsequently was understood as a much lower function. The thought here in fact is both much grander and more humble. For on the one hand, the church of which Paul has claimed to be servant is the church, Christ's body, microcosm of the cosmic world body of Stoic speculation (1:18). But on the other, it is the church in Colossae and other places, small groups of believers in the cities of the eastern Mediterranean region, and it is the humble role of table servant to which Paul has laid claim (see on 1:7). Here again we should take seriously Paul's concern to spend himself in the service and for the benefit of others; the love in which he was held by so many testifies to the real benefit he succeeded in bringing.

This service was in accord with the οἰκονομία of God that had been given to Paul, that is, by God, "with you in view" (maintaining the personal touch toward a congregation he had not yet met). The verbal phrase echoes one of Paul's regular ways of speaking of his commission, "the grace of God given to me" (Rom. 12:3; 15:15; 1 Cor. 3:10; Gal. 2:9). The noun would normally designate the administration or stewardship carried out by the οἰκονόμος ("steward or administrator" of an estate); it is consonant with the train of thought here that in the Roman Empire as a whole at this time the οἰκονόμοι were usually of servile origin (whether slave or freed; D. B. Martin, *Slavery* 15-17). But Paul applied the language to his own work: he saw himself as commissioned by his master, like a good steward having received his orders for the master's absence; hence 1 Cor. 9:17, and cf. Eph. 3:2 with here (cf. Ignatius, *Ephesians* 6:1 and *Diognetus* 7:1). The thought is already developing into the fuller and still more distinctive Christian idea of "God's plan of salvation" (as in Eph. 1:10; 3:9), as the transition to 1:26 here indicates,[16] but "commission" is still adequate here (so also NIV and NRSV, though NEB/REB's "task assigned to me by God" and NJB's "responsibility" are too light for the context and RSV's "divine office" too heavy).

All this is confirmed by the description of the commission as "to fulfill (literally) the word of God," the latter a regular phrase to denote the gospel, delivered as it was by word of mouth (see BAGD s.v. λόγος 1bβ). The verb is unusual in this context, but must mean "complete" (the preaching of) the

15. Schweizer finds here a mark of post-Pauline authorship: "Paul never describes himself as a minister of the church" (*Colossians* 106; cf. Wolter 102-3; Yates, *Colossians* 31). But we should recall how often Paul spoke of his work as "ministry" (διακονία, Rom. 11:13; 15:31; 1 Cor. 16:15; 2 Cor. 3:7-9; 4:1; 5:18; 6:3; διακονέω, Rom. 15:25; 2 Cor. 3:3; 8:19-20).

16. See particularly J. Reumann, "Οἰκονομία-Terms in Paul in Comparison with Lucan *Heilsgeschichte*," *NTS* 13 (1966-67) 147-67, here 162-63.

gospel (BAGD s.v. πληρόω 3). As in the only close parallel use, in Rom. 15:19, there is an eschatological overtone: Paul's commission as apostle (to the Gentiles) was intended as a decisive factor in completing the inbringing of the Gentiles and so facilitating the final climax of God's purpose (Rom. 11:13-15, 25-32; cf. 2 Tim. 4:17).[17] Certainly it is such an awesome sweep and scope of divine purpose which is in view in the continuation of the sentence in the next two verses (see also on 1:24 end).

1:26 τὸ μυστήριον τὸ ἀποκεκρυμμένον ἀπὸ τῶν αἰώνων καὶ ἀπὸ τῶν γενεῶν — νῦν δὲ ἐφανερώθη τοῖς ἁγίοις αὐτοῦ. "The word of God" to which Paul had been commissioned is further defined as "the mystery hidden from the ages and from the generations." Ἀπό ("from") could indicate those from whom the mystery had been hidden. In that case the αἰῶνες and the γενεαί would have to be understood as further names of heavenly powers (cf. 1:16). Some would argue so in regard to the first of these terms, "the Aions" (see BAGD s.v. αἰών 4; Dibelius, *Kolosser, Epheser, Philemon* 24-25; Lohmeyer 82; Scott 33), the powers that rule over each age (*aion;* cf. 1 Cor. 2:6, 8; 2 Cor. 4:4). The issue is even sharper in Ephesians, which besides the closely parallel Eph. 3:9 also speaks of "the αἰῶν of this world" (2:2). Even in this latter case, however, it is probably better to take αἰῶν simply in its more common meaning of "age" (see particularly T. Holtz, *EDNT* 1.44-46; Lincoln, *Ephesians* 94-95). And here the case is even clearer since γενεαί simply means "generations" and most obviously denotes the time spanned by numerous generations.[18] It is typically semitic, as repeated phrases like "from generations to generations" make clear (e.g., Exod. 17:16; Pss. 10:6; 49:11; 77:8; Is. 34:17; Joel 2:2; so also Lk. 1:50 and Eph. 3:21). And αἰῶνες is regularly used in the New Testament to denote time understood as a sequence of ages: so particularly "this age" (e.g., Matt. 12:32; Luke 16:18; Rom. 12:2; 1 Cor. 1:20; Eph. 1:21; 2 Tim. 4:10) and "the age to come" (Matt. 12:32; Mark 10:30; Eph. 1:21; Heb. 6:5); and in echo of regular Old Testament phrases, "to the age(s)" = "forever," and "from the age" = "from everlasting" (Lohmeyer 82 n. 1). Lohmeyer also notes how often the words are linked (as in Exod. 40:15; Esth. 10:3; Isa. 51:9; Tob. 1:4; Sir. 24:33). So here ἀπό is best taken in a temporal sense and the phrase as meaning "from (and so throughout) the ages and generations" (so NRSV; NEB/REB's "for long ages and through many generations" weakens the stark strength of the phrase).

The term μυστήριον heightens still further the already eschatological

17. Cf. particularly Gnilka, *Kolosserbrief* 99. Others take it of a full (dynamic and effective) preaching (O'Brien, *Colossians, Philemon* 83; NEB: "to deliver his message in full"; REB: "to put God's word into full effect"), but this ignores the apocalyptic eschatological context.

18. A. T. Hanson, "Development" 165-68, follows Houlden in suggesting that the phrase means "from angels and men."

and apocalyptic sense of being privileged to see the whole sweep of human history from God's standpoint. For here it is clearly dependent on Jewish apocalyptic usage, where "mystery" refers not so much to undisclosed secrets (as it is used in regard to the rituals of contemporary Hellenistic mystery cults)[19] as to secrets of the divine purpose now revealed by divine agency. This usage begins with the first classic Jewish apocalypse, Daniel (Dan. 2:18-19, 27-30): "God is . . . a revealer of mysteries." And it recurs regularly in subsequent apocalypses (e.g., *1 Enoch* 103:2; 106:19; *2 Enoch* 24:3; *4 Ezra* 10:38; 14:5; Rev. 10:7), as also in the DSS (e.g., 1QS 3:23; 4:18; 1QpHab 7:5; 1Q27). It is indeed at the heart of the apocalyptic rationale: what has been "revealed" to the apocalyptist is precisely the "mystery" of how the cosmos functions and particularly of how God's purpose will achieve its predetermined end.[20]

What is claimed here, then, is the basic Jewish apocalyptic credo, which goes beyond the Platonic-Stoic (and apocalyptic) axiom that the cosmos is rationally ordered (1:15-20) and claims further that not only the three dimensions of spatial existence but also the fourth dimension of time is firmly under divine control. The movement of world history is a linear progression which has also been directed by a secret purpose determined from the beginning by the one God. It is a secret purpose, hitherto "hidden" by divine intention (as in Luke 10:21; 1 Cor. 2:7; Eph. 3:9). But "now" (the eschatological νῦν, similar to 1:22), as that purpose nears or reaches its climax (the typical apocalyptic perception), it has been revealed, "disclosed" (NEB/REB, NIV; not the classical apocalyptic term ἀποκαλύπτω, but the near synonym φανερόω; cf. particularly Rom. 16:26). This is what gives apocalypticism its character: the claim to have been privileged "now" with an insight into God's purpose for creation not given to others.[21]

In this case the recipients of the revelation are called "his saints" (see on 1:2).[22] Elsewhere the emphasis is more on Paul as the one who has been given the privilege (Rom. 11:25; Eph. 3:3, 4, 8-9; 6:19); but since he saw his task precisely as making this mystery known to others (cf. Eph. 1:9), it

---

19. See, e.g., C. Kerényi, "The Mysteries of the Kabeiroi" (1944), in *The Mysteries: Papers from the Eranos Yearbooks* (Princeton: Princeton University, 1955) 32-61 (here 41-42).

20. For bibliography on "mystery" see, e.g., Lohse, *Colossians and Philemon* 74 n. 44; H. Krämer, *EDNT* 2.446. Particularly valuable is Brown.

21. N. A. Dahl, "Form-Critical Observations on Early Christian Preaching," *Jesus in the Memory of the Early Church* (Minneapolis: Augsburg, 1976) 30-36, found in Paul's talk of a previously hidden mystery now revealed a regular "revelation pattern" and suggested that the language here might indicate an underlying fixed formulation (followed by Lührmann, *Offenbarungsverständnis* 124-33: "das Revelationsschema"; cf. Lona 110-12).

22. Whatever "saints" refers to in 1:12, there can be little doubt here (despite Lohmeyer 82-83) that it refers to believers in Christ (cf. Eph. 1:8-9: "to us"). For Paul to use "the saints" for ecclesiastical leaders alone (Bockmuehl, *Revelation* 183-85) would fly in the face of Paul's ecclesiology and his identification of Gentile believers as a whole with Israel's heritage (1:2; 3:12)

comes to the same thing. At all events, the implication here, as 4:3-4 confirms, is that the revelation to the saints took place particularly through Paul's preaching (Lührmann, *Offenbarungsverständnis* 121; Aletti, *Épître aux Colossiens* 140): his gospel was itself an apocalypse (cf. Rom. 16:25; Gal. 1:12; Eph. 3:3).

1:27 οἷς ἠθέλησεν ὁ θεὸς γνωρίσαι τί τὸ πλοῦτος τῆς δόξης τοῦ μυστηρίου τούτου ἐν τοῖς ἔθνεσιν, ὅ ἐστιν Χριστὸς ἐν ὑμῖν, ἡ ἐλπὶς τῆς δόξης. But what is this mystery? The answer is provided somewhat tautologously as the writer continues, "to whom God wished (but the aorist tense indicates more of a decision made, so 'willed, resolved, chose') to make known what is the wealth of the glory of this mystery." Τὸ πλοῦτος τῆς δόξης ("the wealth/riches of the glory") has something of a liturgical ring (Rom. 9:23; Phil. 4:19; Eph. 1:18; 3:16; cf. Rom. 2:4; Eph. 1:21; 2:7) and again heightens the sense both of divine condescension and that what has been revealed is itself a manifestation of the heavenly majesty of God (see on 1:11).[23]

In other Pauline writings the "mystery" of God's purpose is primarily his intention from the first to include at the last Gentiles together with Jews as his people. In Rom. 11:25-26 it is the mystery of Israel's partial hardening till the full number of the Gentiles has come in, leading in turn to the salvation of all Israel. In the addendum of Rom. 16:25-26 it is "the mystery concealed for long ages, but now made manifest and . . . made known for the obedience of faith for all the nations." In Eph. 1:9-10 it is the divine purpose in Christ "to sum up all things in Christ, things in heaven and things on earth, in him." And again in Eph. 3:3-6 it is "the mystery of Christ . . . that the Gentiles should be joint heirs and joint members of the body and joint participants in the promise in Christ Jesus." Here there is a further variation, whose closest parallel is Rom. 16:25-26: that the mystery is to be made known "among the Gentiles." And only then the mystery is identified, in a phrase similar to that in Eph. 3:4 ("the mystery of Christ"), as the mystery "which is Christ in you, the hope of glory."[24]

These, however, should not be taken as alternatives, and Col. 1:27 should not be taken as an ignoring of or departure from the earlier thought (so Hübner 355; cf. Lona 113-15). For as Eph. 3:4-6 shows, the two thoughts (the mystery of Jew and Gentile together as recipients of God's saving grace and the mystery of Christ) are two aspects of the same larger divine plan as Paul had come to see it. It was Paul's assertion from the beginning, and

23. As Lohmeyer 84 n. 1 and Lohse, *Colossians and Philemon* 75 n. 62, observe, the "richness" and "glory" of God are often mentioned together in the Old Testament. But Gnilka, *Kolosserbrief* 102 n. 56, points out that the references there are to earthly wealth and honor.

24. Brown 55-56 compares the Similitudes of Enoch, where it is the Elect One, the Son of Man, who, having been concealed from the beginning, is now revealed to the saints (*1 Enoch* 48:6; 62:7).

based precisely on the "revelation" given him on the Damascus road (Gal. 1:15-16), that the gospel was also for non-Jews, that the blessing of Abraham had always had the future benefit of the nations in view from the first (Gal. 3:8) and that Gentiles were now able to share in this Jewish heritage precisely by being "in Christ" (Gal. 3:14, 16, 26-29). The theology is elaborated in striking terms in Eph. 2:11-22, the letter closest to Colossians, in its similar emphasis on the divine "mystery." And that double aspect of the mystery is still in view here in the assertion that the mystery was not only to be made known "among the Gentiles," but precisely as the mystery of "Christ (again the overtone of Jewish Messiah) in you," that is, in you Gentiles (cf. Moule, *Colossians and Philemon* 82-83).

Here again we should recall the cosmic and apocalyptic context within which this understanding of divine mystery is formulated. The fact is that Paul saw the reconciliation of Gentile to Jew and both as one to God as an act of cosmic and eschatological significance. It was precisely this breaking down of one of the fundamental dividing lines in human society (between Jew and Gentile; see also on 3:11) that Paul saw as the climax of the divine purpose for creation. Such breaking down of barriers of nation and race, often so impenetrable to human resources, must therefore be for him one of the primary goals of the gospel. Indeed, we might even say that such reconciliation between the diversity of nationalities and races was one of the main tests for the church, one of the most crucial signs of the effectiveness of the gospel. Without the reconciliation of nation to nation, of race to race, of social group to social group, the reconciliation of all things "to him" (1:20) has not even begun.

The specific description of the mystery here as "Christ in you" is a shift in focus from the goal (reconciliation of Jew and Gentile) to the means ("Christ"). In Galatians and Ephesians the means is expressed rather by the "in Christ" formula (Gal. 3:14, 26, 28; Eph. 2:13, 15-16, 21-22). But the reverse formula is appropriate here in the light of 1:15-20: as Stoicism in particular saw an identity between individual rationality and the rationality pervading the cosmos, so this divine Wisdom now identified with Christ can be seen as an immanent power within the personality. In a similar way in Galatians Paul had personalized devotional talk of Christ's self-giving and the apocalyptic idea of rescue from the present evil age (1:4): "Christ lives in me . . . , who loved me and gave himself for me" (2:20). So here the mystery of how the cosmos was created and holds together is personalized: "Christ in (each of) you" (cf. also Rom. 8:10; 2 Cor. 13:5; Eph. 3:17). Strictly speaking the divine presence indwelling individual humanity should be expressed in terms of the Spirit of God; hence the more typical Pauline balance between "us in Christ" (see on 1:2) and "the Spirit in us" (e.g., Rom. 8:9, 11, 15-16, 23, 26). But given the overlap between Wisdom and Spirit as ways of speaking of divine immanence, a degree of interchange between "in Christ" and "Spirit in" formulations is no problem. That a person should be spoken of as indwelling another no doubt poses something of a conceptual difficulty, but the idea of divine immanence in an individual is simply an aspect of the larger concept of divine immanence (see on 1:19), and generations of Christian believers have evidently found no problem in using such language to describe the experience of personal communion with God understood in terms of Jesus Christ and the inner strengthening which comes through it. All this tells against the common assumption that the phrase must mean "Christ *among* you,"[25] which weakens the train of thought and makes the phrase add hardly anything to the preceding "among the nations."

This mystery of "Christ in you" is further defined as "the hope of glory" (cf. Ignatius, *Ephesians* 21:2 and *Magnesians* 11: "Jesus Christ, our [common] hope"). It is striking that for the third time in these opening paragraphs the theme of hope is given central place in the gospel (1:5, 23, 27; see on 1:5). This is an appropriate note on which to wind up this brief reference to the mystery of God's purpose shaped from before the ages and generations and now moving toward its eschatological climax. "Christ in you" spans the full sweep of time, God's creative power in Christ determining end as well as beginning and blending the individual into the harmony of the divine composition. The hoped-for "glory" again ties the whole process into God: such glory can only be God's ("the wealth of his glory"). It is the radiant energy which first accomplished creation and which will accomplish its consummation. It is the glory which Adam first shared and then lost (Rom. 3:23) and to which it is the divine intention to restore humanity (Rom. 8:17-21). "Christ in you" is "the hope" of that "glory" because retransformation into the divine image and glory is a lifelong process already underway in the person of faith (see also on 1:11; 3:4, 10).

1:28 ὃν ἡμεῖς καταγγέλλομεν νουθετοῦντες πάντα ἄνθρωπον καὶ διδάσκοντες πάντα ἄνθρωπον ἐν πάσῃ σοφίᾳ, ἵνα παραστήσωμεν πάντα ἄνθρωπον τέλειον ἐν Χριστῷ. As in 1:23 the line of thought trails off in a sequence of more conventional descriptions. Καταγγέλλω is not simply a variation on εὐαγγελίζομαι ("preach the gospel") and κηρύσσειν ("proclaim," 1:23). From its usage elsewhere, it carries overtones of a solemn intimation, as in the proclamation of a sacred festival or of imperial rule (J. Schniewind, *TDNT* 1.70-71). Hence the use in 1 Cor. 2:1 and 9:14; and hence the use here, appropriate in speaking of a divine mystery which spans

25. Particularly Lohse, *Colossians and Philemon* 76; Gnilka, *Kolosserbrief* 102; Wolter 105; and Aletti, *Épître aux Colossiens* 141-42; otherwise Dibelius, *Kolosser, Epheser, Philemon* 25; Lohmeyer 85; Conzelmann142; and Lindemann, *Kolosserbrief* 34. In contrast, the English language tradition tends to favor "in you" (exceptions are Abbott 235; Moule, *Colossians and Philemon* 83; Yates, *Colossians* 35; JB/NJB).

both space and time. "The frequency of expressions of communication (cf. 2:2) is perhaps intended as deliberate emphasis that the time of obscurity and silence has passed" (Pokorný 104). The reversion to plural form ("whom *we* proclaim") is typical of the way Paul catches himself every so often to ensure that the scope of what is being said is not being taken in too restricted a sense: the responsibility of evangelism and its corollary is not his alone (otherwise Lohse, *Colossians and Philemon* 76). At the same time it may be a further indication of a letter consciously written by or on behalf of more than Paul.

Νουθετέω and διδάσκω are near synonyms, both meaning "instruct." The former carries the implication of exhortation, warning, and correction,[26] hence "admonish, warn" and its use in Jewish literature with reference to God's chastening (Job 40:4; Wis. 11:10; 12:2, 26; *Psalms of Solomon* 13:9). Paul saw it as a characteristic ministry to be exercised widely within his churches (Rom. 15:14; 1 Thes. 5:12, 14; 2 Thes. 3:15). The latter, διδάσκω, more characteristically refers to the skill of the teacher in imparting practical and theoretical knowledge to the pupil (hence such usage elsewhere in Paul as Rom. 2:21; 12:7; 1 Cor. 11:14; Gal. 1:12). Paul uses it of his own instruction of his churches earlier only in 1 Cor. 4:17, though the most natural way of taking Acts 13:1 designates Saul/Paul still earlier as a teacher of the Antioch church. The two terms are often linked in wider Greek writing (J. Behm, *TDNT* 4.1019; Lohse, *Colossians and Philemon* 77 n. 72), but only here and in 3:16 in the Pauline corpus (perhaps another small feature in the fingerprint of the author). It should be noted that the idea of proclaiming Christ is thus supplemented, or indeed explained, by a double emphasis on instruction: the two belong together, and presumably the former without the latter would be dangerously lacking in content and guidance for everyday praxis. The addition of "in all wisdom" recalls the same phrase in 1:9 (see on that verse) and reiterates the indispensability of divinely given wisdom for daily living. It also reflects the link between practical wisdom and the figure of divine Wisdom in the Jewish wisdom tradition. So here the wisdom necessary is that Wisdom displayed in the cosmos (the implicit Wisdom christology of the hymn in 1:15-20) and on the cross. The warning and teaching in all wisdom is also the proclamation of Christ.

The goal of such instruction is stated in terms which have already been used: presentation, that is, before God (see on 1:22). This is another repetition of theme not quite in Pauline style as we know it from his earlier correspondence. Here, however, the context strengthens the eschatological note of

---

26. In Greek moral philosophy νουθεσία "was defined as the instilling of sense in someone and teaching him what should and should not be done." So A. J. Malherbe, " 'Pastoral Care' in the Thessalonian Church," *NTS* 36 (1990) 375-91 (here 383-84).

presentation in the final judgment (otherwise Lohse, *Colossians and Philemon* 78 n. 80; Gnilka, *Kolosserbrief* 104).

The threefold repetition of "everyone" (πάντα ἄνθρωπον) should not be taken too quickly as meaning "everyone of you in Colossae" (NEB/REB "each one of you"). Following so soon after the eightfold repetition of "all" in the hymn in praise of cosmic Wisdom-Christ, it presumably expresses the confident hope not only that those now believing "in Christ" (1:2, 4) will be able thus to be presented before God, but also that "every person" (the human segment of the "all things," 1:20) will in the end be found "in Christ." Here again the tie-in between the cosmic Wisdom christology of 1:15-20 and the historical particularity of the Christian gospel is important. The focusing of divine Wisdom in Christ should not be thought of as a narrowing of the divine purpose for the cosmos to a particular people or group. As in Galatians and Romans and given the usual content of the "mystery" (see on 1:27), "all" means particularly "everyone — Jews as well as Gentiles, Gentiles as well as Jews" (e.g., Rom. 1:16; 3:22; 4:11; 10:4, 11; Gal. 3:8, 26, 28). As Christ brought to focus both divine Wisdom and the divine mystery, so the reconciliation of Jew and Gentile in Christ brings to focus the reconciliation of "all things" and "everyone."[27] The church that forgets this has lost sight of the Pauline gospel. For "in Christ," the seventh occurrence of the motif in the letter, see on 1:2.

The desired state for those to be thus presented is described in a rich word, τέλειος ("whole, complete"; so "mature" in RSV/NRSV, NEB/REB, GNB; "perfect" in JB/NJB, NIV; see H. Hübner, *EDNT* 3.342-43 for bibliography). (1) In wider Greek usage this word could denote the quality of sacrificial victims, entire and without blemish (LSJ s.v. 1), and is so used of the Passover lamb in Exod. 12:5. In view of the similar imagery in 1:22 such overtones are probably present here as well. (2) By natural extension it can denote the equivalent quality of moral character, of which blameless Noah was a classic example (Gen. 6:9; Sir. 44:17; Philo, *De Abrahamo* 34). The DSS use the Hebrew equivalent *(tamim)* frequently of the blameless conduct required of community members, the perfection of their "walk" (see 1:10) being dependent on the degree to which they observe the community's own interpretation of Torah (1QS 2:2; 3:9-11; 9:9-10, 19; see further Lohmeyer 88 n. 3; G. Delling, *TDNT* 8.73) and presumably also the degree to which they accept the Teacher's interpretation of the mysteries of the words of the prophets (1QpHab 7:1-5).[28]

---

27. The double echo of 1:15-20 and of "all" = Gentile as well as Jew is sufficient explanation for the triple "everyone." The emphasis is not quite what we would expect had the letter been directed against a form of spiritual elitism (as, e.g., Lightfoot 168; Abbott 235; Bruce, *Colossians, Philemon, and Ephesians* 87; Sappington 186) or "heretical conventicles" (Gnilka, *Kolosserbrief* 103).

28. Cf. particularly B. Rigaux, "Révélation des Mystères et Perfection à Qumrân et dans le Nouveau Testament," *NTS* 4 (1957-58) 237-62.

That the equivalent moral quality of character and conduct is also in view here is implicit in the talk of "warning and teaching" (cf. 1:10). (3) The word is also prominently used of someone whose instruction is "complete," one who has advanced to "maturity" and become "perfect" in mastery of subject or craft. The "perfect man" was a theme in Greek philosophy, including, not least Philo (see Delling 69-72). This is probably the principal note here (as in most of Paul's other usage: 1 Cor. 2:6; 14:20; Phil. 3:15; see also Col. 4:12; cf. Matt. 5:48; 19:21). Here again there may be a gentle reminder that any of the Colossian recipients tempted to look elsewhere for a "fuller" experience and wisdom need to look, and should look, no further than Christ for their "completion."[29] The vision is again eschatological, with a view to the last judgment (Sappington 189, with bibliography). The hope is for the restoration of wholeness throughout creation ("everyone"). As creation only came to existence "in him," so the final restoration is possible only "in Christ." The onward drive of creation toward ever greater refinement ("maturity, perfection") depends on a similar growing to maturity of humankind, of which the growing maturity of those "in Christ" is the microcosm which should mirror the destiny of the macrocosm.

1:29 εἰς ὃ καὶ κοπιῶ ἀγωνιζόμενος κατὰ τὴν ἐνέργειαν αὐτοῦ τὴν ἐνεργουμένην ἐν ἐμοὶ ἐν δυνάμει.   Again, as in 1:23, Paul rounds off this vision of eschatological and universal completeness by affirming his own personal commitment to its realization. In wider Greek κόπος means "beating," so the weariness that results from being repeatedly struck, and so by analogy the physical tiredness caused by work and exertion. Consequently the verb can mean both "become weary" and "work hard, labor, strive" (F. Hauck, *TDNT* 3.827-28). Paul uses it regularly for the hard work of ministry and preaching (Rom. 16:6, 12; 1 Cor. 4:12; 15:10; 16:16, etc.). The emphasis is strengthened (as in 1 Tim. 4:10) by the complementary imagery of engaging in an athletic contest (ἀγωνίζομαι, as in 1 Cor. 9:25), with its equivalent implication of giving oneself in the utmost effort, with all the self-discipline required to achieve the goal (hence REB's "toiling strenuously").[30] The imagery is extended into 2:1, and the image of hard training to achieve the peak ("perfection") required for success in the contest of life is repeated in 4:12, though again with the transposition that Paul/Epaphras thus applies himself for *the Colossians'* perfection/maturity.

---

29. It does not necessarily follow, however, that this reference is directed against a form of Colossian "perfectionism" (the "philosophy" of 2:8 [?], as suggested, e.g., by Dibelius, *Kolosser, Epheser, Philemon* 25; Lohse, *Colossians and Philemon* 78), which, were it a serious threat, would presumably have required a fuller rebuttal (as in 1 Cor. 2:6–3:4). Attempts to deduce the outlines of the "false teaching" at Colossae require a more controlled "mirror reading" with clearer reflection of polemical intent if they are to carry weight.

30. See further V. C. Pfitzner, *Paul and the Agon Motif* (NovTSup 16; Leiden: Brill, 1967), who notes that Paul's striving is not for his own honor but in service of others (194).

As in 1:10-11, however, the balance between human effort and divine enabling is clearly struck. Ἐνέργεια means basically "activity," and so also the "energy" that accomplishes activity; similarly the verb ἐνεργέω, "be at work" and so "produce, be effective." In normal usage the word group usually refers to the activity of God or other supernatural forces (BAGD s.v. ἐνέργεια; G. Bertram, *TDNT* 2.652-53). Similarly in Paul (e.g., verb in 1 Cor. 12:6, 11; Gal. 2:8; Phil. 2:13; noun in Phil. 3:21; Eph. 3:7), with the Semitic doubling of noun and verb (as in Eph. 1:19-20; cf. the similar doubling in 1:11) reinforcing the point. Lest the implication of the effectiveness of this divine "activity" be lost, ἐν δυνάμει ("in power") is added (NRSV "all the energy that he powerfully inspires within me"). As in 1:11 no room for doubt is left as to Paul's own utter dependence on God's enabling for the exhausting schedule that he followed, or as to its effectiveness (see also on 1:11).

Paul's Commitment to the Colossians (2:1-5)

1 *For I want you to know how great is the struggle I have on your behalf and on behalf of those in Laodicea[1] and as many as have not seen my face in the flesh, 2 that their hearts might be encouraged, united[2] in love, and[2] for all[2] riches of full assurance of understanding, for knowledge of the mystery of God, of Christ,[3] 3 in whom all the treasures of wisdom and knowledge are hidden. 4 I say this[4] that no one might deceive you by plausible arguments. 5 For though I am absent in flesh, yet I am with you in spirit, rejoicing at seeing your good order and the firmness of your faith in Christ.*

There is disagreement as to where the main section of the letter begins. Lohmeyer and Gnilka see it beginning at 2:1, despite the continuation of the personal style from 1:24 to 2:5. Others prefer to make the break after 2:3 (e.g., Moule, Harris, Wall). But the τοῦτο λέγω which begins 2:4 is best taken as referring to what has just been said (see particularly Bandstra, "Errorists" 340 and Sappington 177), and 2:4-5, therefore, as the conclusion to the paragraph begun at 1:24. Aletti also notes the chiastic structure embedded in 1:24–2:5:

1:24	χαίρω	2:5
1:27	γνωρίσαι/ἐπίγνωσιν	2:2
1:27	πλοῦτος . . . μυστηρίου	2:2
1:29	ἀγωνιζόμενος/ἀγῶνα	2:1

The fact that 2:6 follows more naturally from 1:23 than from 2:5 confirms the unified nature of the unit (1:24–2:5), without necessarily implying that the paragraph was a late insertion.

2:1 θέλω γὰρ ὑμᾶς εἰδέναι ἡλίκον ἀγῶνα ἔχω ὑπὲρ ὑμῶν καὶ τῶν ἐν Λαοδικείᾳ καὶ ὅσοι οὐχ ἑόρακαν τὸ πρόσωπόν μου ἐν σαρκί. Paul's

1. Some late witnesses introduced "and of those in Hierapolis," no doubt in echo of 4:13.

2. Various attempts were made by later scribes to tidy up the awkwardness of the syntax and grammar at these points. On the first see, e.g., Harris 80.

3. This phrase clearly caused scribes much perplexity, as the range of modifications indicates: "of God" (alone), followed by Lohmeyer 91 n. 1; Benoit, "Colossiens 2:2-3"; and JB/NJB; "of (the) Christ" (alone); "of God, which is Christ"; "of God, who is in Christ"; "of God the Father of Christ"; "of the God and Father of Christ"; "of (our) God and Father and of Christ" (details also in Lohse, *Colossians and Philemon* 82). But these can all be most easily explained as attempts to ease the awkwardness of the text, which has the strong support of p[46] and B; for detailed treatment see B. M. Metzger, *The Text of the New Testament* (New York: Oxford University, [2]1968) 236-38; cf. also Bockmuehl, *Revelation* 187-88. Other modern translations understandably polish by translating "that is, Christ himself" (NRSV), "which is Christ himself" (REB), or "namely, Christ" (NIV).

4. The abruptness of τοῦτο λέγω caused some scribes to insert δέ to improve the style.

depth of concern for his churches must have been well known. The ups and downs of his relations with the church in Corinth in particular would probably have been familiar to the churches of the Lycus valley, since so much of his time at Ephesus had been spent agonizing over the problems of the Corinthian Christians and his relationships with them (1 Cor. 4:17; 16:8, 10; 2 Cor. 1:23–2:4; 7:8; 12:14). Lest it be inferred that Paul was concerned only for those churches founded by himself, the writer(s) hasten to assure the Colossians that Paul was equally concerned for those churches founded by his associates.

The formulation is a natural one — "I want you to know," "I do not want you to be unaware" — but characteristic of Paul (Rom. 1:13; 11:25; 1 Cor. 10:1; 11:3; 12:1; 2 Cor. 1:8; 1 Thes. 4:13).[5] The metaphor of the athletic contest (ἀγών) is continued from the preceding verse — an image which Paul and his circle used to express the concentrated and sustained effort that his ministry demanded (Phil. 1:30; 1 Thes. 2:2; 1 Tim. 6:12; 2 Tim. 4:7; also Heb. 12:1). Hence NEB/REB: "how strenuous are my exertions for you." One specific contest (martyrdom [Lohmeyer 92], against "false teaching") is not necessarily implied (cf. O'Brien, *Colossians, Philemon* 92).

Paul makes a point of mentioning also "those in Laodicea," which was just about ten miles downstream from Colossae. These two cities, together with Hierapolis (some fifteen miles away), made a natural grouping, as Epaphras's evangelistic efforts in all three confirms (4:13). The failure to mention Hierapolis here, however (see n. 1), and the further information of 4:15-16 probably indicate that the mission in the nearer and more important Laodicea had been the more successful (cf. Revelation 2–3, where Laodicea is the only one of the three to be mentioned) and that there were quite close relations between the two churches. Tacitus notes the earthquake devastation to Laodicea in 60 or 61 and that it was able to be rebuilt from its own resources without state assistance (*Annales* 14.27.1), which confirms its greater importance (see also F. F. Bruce, *ABD* 4.229-30; p. 23 above, and the comments below on 4:13).

The metaphor of "seeing someone's face" naturally expresses the immediacy of personal encounter (cf. 1 Cor. 13:12; 2 Cor. 10:1, 7; Gal. 1:22; 2:11; 1 Thes. 2:17; 3:10; see also E. Lohse, *TDNT* 6.776; K. Berger, *EDNT* 3.181; NEB/REB "never set eyes on me"; NIV "not met me personally"). The addition of ἐν σαρκί is unnecessary: how else would they "see his face"? It reinforces the merely physical sense of σάρξ which predominates in these early references in Colossians (see on 1:22), and though ἐν σαρκί in itself is Pauline enough (2 Cor. 10:3; Gal. 2:20; Phil. 1:22, 24), there is nothing here of the antithesis implied in these passages. The extension of

---

5. A regular phrase in Greek letters (Lohmeyer 91 n. 4).

Paul's concern to "as many as have not seen my face" (not every believer in the area — he may have passed through Colossae earlier and would probably have come to know some of the Colossian Christians during his time in Ephesus) confirms that in his city bases he was at the center of a network of expanding and successful mission undertaken by such as Epaphras. Schenk, "Kolosserbrief" 3334, finds here a conscious indication that the letter had a universal circle of addressees in view (but see also Wolter 109-10).

2:2 ἵνα παρακληθῶσιν αἱ καρδίαι αὐτῶν συμβιβασθέντες ἐν ἀγάπῃ καὶ εἰς πᾶν πλοῦτος τῆς πληροφορίας τῆς συνέσεως, εἰς ἐπίγνωσιν τοῦ μυστηρίου τοῦ θεοῦ, Χριστοῦ. Since Paul cannot be present with them personally, the letter must serve in his place. The hope is that the assurance which it brings of his personal commitment to them will provide the encouragement which the visible proof of his own presence would have demonstrated. That his readers might be "encouraged" or "comforted" was one of Paul's most frequent objectives in so writing (Rom. 15:4-5; 2 Cor. 1:4, 6; 13:11; 1 Thes. 3:2; 4:18; see also O'Brien, *Colossians, Philemon* 92-93). Talk of "hearts" being encouraged is confined to the disputed Paulines (Eph. 6:22; Col. 2:2; 4:8; 2 Thes. 2:17), though it is typical of Paul to hope that spiritual effects would reach to the depth of their experience, where not only emotions were rooted, but also thought and decision ("heart"; see, e.g., Rom. 1:21, 24; 8:27; 9:2; 2 Cor. 9:7).[6]

Unlike the previous prayer for the Colossians, which could be understood simply in individual terms (1:9-14), the hope here is also for their well-being as a community. The encouragement is thought of not in terms of a sequence of individuals being individually encouraged but of an encouragement which facilitates and is facilitated by their experience of being "held together in love." The verb is not very common, but elsewhere includes the thought of being brought together and of being reconciled (G. Delling, *TDNT* 7.763; Lohse, *Colossians and Philemon* 81 n. 103); in this sense only here, and of the body held together in 2:19 and Eph. 4:16. Dibelius, *Kolosser, Epheser, Philemon* 26, Scott 36 and O'Brien, *Colossians, Philemon* 93, prefer the sense here of "instruct, teach" (as in its only other Pauline use, 1 Cor. 2:16), but "in love" is more appropriate to an implied plea for harmony (cf. particularly Rom. 14:15; 1 Cor. 16:14; Phil. 2:1-2; 1 Thes. 3:12; 5:13; so also 3:14: "love, the bond of perfection"; Aletti, *Épître aux Colossiens* 149). Only a love which penetrates to the heart and wells up from the heart can sustain the sort of unity that Paul sought (see also on 1:4).

---

6. In the Old Testament the heart is "the principle and organ of man's personal life . . . the focus of his being and activity as a spiritual being . . . the source and seat of his moral and religious life" (J. Behm, *TDNT* 3.609). See further Behm 611-13; R. Jewett, *Paul's Anthropological Terms* (Leiden: Brill, 1971) 305-33; A. Sand, *EDNT* 2.249-51.

The further hope of the letter's beneficial effect is expressed in awkward echo of the prayer already offered in 1:9-10, with a somewhat tautologous alliterative piling up of the thought of completeness (πᾶν πλοῦτος τῆς πληροφορίας, "all riches of full assurance"). There is nothing quite the same in the rest of Paul (though cf. the only other use of πληροφορία in Paul — 1 Thes. 1:5: πληροφορία πολλῇ — and the use of the verb in Col. 4:12). Nevertheless it is wholly in line with Paul's earlier thought that assurance was not simply a matter of cerebral conviction but something deeply felt (cf., e.g., Rom. 8:15-16; 1 Cor. 2:1-4; 1 Thes. 1:5; also Heb. 10:22). That the thought here is of "full assurance of understanding" does not change the sense of existential confidence, since "understanding" (σύνεσις) is the same word used in 1:9, that is, an understanding granted by the Spirit (see on 1:9). The integration between (as we would say) mind and heart is an important feature of Paul's understanding of how the salvation process works out in the individual and group. That is why he can speak here of the "riches" that come from such confidence, "the full wealth of conviction that understanding brings" (NEB/REB).

The same double thrust (mind and heart) is sustained in the next phrase. This assured understanding also brings with it a growing recognition (ἐπίγνωσις; see on 1:9 and 10) of "the mystery of God" (see on 1:26). But since this mystery has already been defined as "Christ in you" (see on 1:27), the integration of content and motivating conviction is still a major factor. It is this identification of Christ himself with the mystery (not with God) which has been reiterated here, but with surprising awkwardness (see n. 3). Given the train of thought running through to 2:5, there is probably an implication that with such "full assurance" in their understanding of this mystery, the attractiveness of the "seductive speech" of other religious philosophers (2:4) will be all the less. But there is no reason to see here the vocabulary of such false teaching itself (as, e.g., Ernst, *Philipper, Philemon, Kolosser, Epheser* 190).

2:3 ἐν ᾧ εἰσιν πάντες οἱ θησαυροὶ τῆς σοφίας καὶ γνώσεως ἀπό-κρυφοι. The awkward insertion of "Christ" at the end of 2:2 has the effect (no doubt deliberate) of focusing attention back onto Christ, thus introducing what is a very tight and effective summary of the main emphases of the distinctive christology so far put forward in the letter (Sappington 178-79; Aletti, *Épître aux Colossiens* 151-52). The eighth "in him" recalls the sustained repetition of the motif in 1:14-19, and with talk once again of "wisdom" recalls not only 1:9 (again), but also the thoroughgoing Wisdom character of the hymn in praise of Christ (1:15-20).[7] The imagery of "hidden treasures or treasuries of wisdom and knowledge" also evokes Jewish wis-

---

7. "All the powers and activities formerly attributed to the personified Wisdom of God must now be attributed to Christ" (Caird 187).

dom tradition (Prov. 2:3-6; Sir. 1:24-25; Wis. 6:22; 7:13-14; Bar. 3:15; D. Zeller, *EDNT* 2.151). But in the wake of talk of the "mystery," the imagery also evokes apocalyptic ideas of heavenly treasuries, hidden from human eye but revealed to the visionary or heavenly traveler (particularly *1 Enoch* 18:1: "the storerooms [Greek θησαυρούς] of all the winds"; 46:3: "the Son of Man . . . will open all the hidden storerooms"; cf. Isa. 45:3). No doubt part of the attractiveness of the Christian message regarding Christ was the degree to which Jewish wisdom and apocalyptic traditions were thus combined (as they had only occasionally been previously — as in *1 Enoch* 42). It was this assurance that they, too, were "in Christ," together with *all* the treasures of divinely given insight into the mysteries of the cosmos and of human destiny (cf. Rom. 11:33; 1 Cor. 2:7: λαλοῦμεν θεοῦ σοφίαν ἐν μυστηρίῳ τὴν ἀποκεκρυμμένην) and the riches of the experience of the wise in successful living, that was to give them the confidence they needed (see also 3:3).

In view of the further reference to "wisdom" in 2:23 the language here may well tell us something further about teaching on offer in Colossae (e.g., Sumney 380-81; Lindemann, *Kolosserbrief* 37 is confident that the "false teachers" were Christians from within the community). Certainly the "all" may anticipate and devalue equivalent enticements which other religious practitioners held out to interested parties (as may be alluded to in 2:18). At the same time, the hypothesis going back to Lightfoot 172, that ἀπόκρυφοι was "a favourite term of the Gnostic teachers," is unnecessary, given the play between hiddenness and revelation both in Jewish wisdom tradition (and already in the Jesus tradition: Matt. 11:25 and Mark 4:22) and in Jewish apocalyptic tradition (already in Paul's use of μυστήριον). Moreover, Dupont, *Gnosis* 16-18, may well be justified in seeing some counter to the more widely prevalent Jewish view that hidden wisdom had already been fully revealed in the Torah (cf. Sir. 24:23-26 — law, wisdom, understanding; Bar. 3:15–4:1 — wisdom's "treasuries," hiddenness, identification with Torah; *2 Baruch* 44:14-15 — "treasures of wisdom," "stores of insight," "truth of the Law"; 54:13-14 — "treasures of wisdom," law; see further Bandstra, "Errorists" 339-43; O'Brien, *Colossians, Philemon* 96-97).[8] And Gnilka, *Kolosserbrief* 111-12, appropriately notes that the range of terms (mystery, secret knowledge, hidden treasure) has again and again proved itself attractive to "sectarian mentality," referring to Gnostic circles, but also to the Qumran scrolls, where again the claims focus on Torah.

2:4 τοῦτο λέγω, ἵνα μηδεὶς ὑμᾶς παραλογίζηται ἐν πιθανολογίᾳ. Paul and Timothy are now ready to launch into the main theme of their letter. But, in line with Pauline style elsewhere, they wind up the preceding section

---

8. Bockmuehl, *Revelation* 189 is concerned about some self-contradiction in view of the claim already made in 1:26-27, but ignores the πάντες.

by indicating the direction they are about to take. The abruptness of "this I say" (see n. 4) is a modest attempt to catch attention and to reinforce the importance of the point being made (cf. 1 Cor. 1:12; 7:29; 15:50; Gal. 3:17; 1 Thes. 4:15), so much so that we might speak of 2:4 as a thematic statement of what follows, though the main thematic statement is more obviously 2:6-7.

For the first time it becomes clear that Paul and Timothy had some concerns regarding the Colossians. These concerns can hardly have been serious; otherwise they would have come to the fore much more quickly (as in 1 Cor. 1:10; Gal. 1:6; 1 Thes. 2:1). Given the evident lack of urgency, we have been hesitant to identify too many echoes of a clear-cut "false teaching." But here there is a clear warning against the possibility of being "deceived" or "deluded" — παραλογίζομαι, a well-known word in wider speech (Lohse, *Colossians and Philemon* 83 n. 121; elsewhere in the New Testament only in Jas. 1:22).

The danger, however, is posed in terms of πιθανολογία. This term and its cognates denote the persuasiveness and plausibility particularly of popular speakers (LSJ s.v. πιθανός). But in an interesting passage Plato distinguishes πιθανολογία from ἀπόδειξις, "demonstration," a technical term in rhetoric for a compelling conclusion drawn from acccepted premises (*Theaetetus* 162E; similarly Aristotle, *Ethica Nicomachea* 1.3.4; cf. Epictetus 1.8.7; Philo, *De cherubim* 9). Thus the term easily gains, as here, the overtone of plausible (sounding) but actually "specious arguments" (NEB/REB, JB/NJB). Clearly implied is the claim that there is a power of conviction in the gospel of Paul (the "this" referring back to 2:2-3; see also the introduction to the comments on 2:1-5) which specious arguments of popular rhetoricians and religious philosophers in the marketplace cannot match. The line of attack is obviously similar to that in 1 Cor. 2:1-4 and raises the question whether an older argument of Paul is in effect being rehashed (cf. Rom. 16:17-20 and my *Romans* 901-7).

As the first clear allusion to an alternative religious system confronting the Colossian believers, the verse need imply no more than the sort of popular religious teaching which must have often been heard in the marketplaces of that region, much of which might have been beguilingly attractive to truth-seeking young converts (cf. Hooker). It will become clearer that Paul and Timothy had in mind teaching and praxis particularly of the Colossian synagogue(s) (see pp. 23-35 in the Introduction, and on 2:16 and 18), so the implication here is that the Colossian Jewish community was not lacking in skilled apologists, but was well able to express the appeal of their worship and code of behavior in beguiling terms (see also 2:8). Moreover, the cautious and unspecific way in which the confrontation of 2:16-23 is approached continues to strengthen the likelihood that this was the level of the threat from the synagogue — that is, a more general marketplace apology which was proving quite appealing to God-worshipping Gentiles, who, after all, were claiming a share in the same heritage (1:12); "a critical situation" (Ernst, *Philipper, Philemon, Kolosser, Epheser* 189) would have called forth a less leisurely response.

2:5 εἰ γὰρ καὶ τῇ σαρκὶ ἄπειμι, ἀλλὰ τῷ πνεύματι σὺν ὑμῖν εἰμι, χαίρων καὶ βλέπων ὑμῶν τὴν τάξιν καὶ τὸ στερέωμα τῆς εἰς Χριστὸν πίστεως ὑμῶν. The concern nevertheless is real. Paul wishes he could be present "in the flesh" — the fourth "merely physical" use of σάρξ in thirteen verses. At first it seems that the more traditional Pauline antithesis between "flesh" and "Spirit" should have given "flesh" a more negative note. But the implication could equally be that Paul's "spiritual presence" is a less adequate substitute for his physical presence. Although closely parallel to the equivalent concern expressed in 1 Cor. 5:3 (ἀπὼν τῷ σώματι παρὼν δὲ τῷ πνεύματι), there we see a much stronger assertion of a powerful "spiritual presence" (1 Cor. 5:4). Nevertheless, the parallel does raise the question whether the claim was intended to be understood as something more than the weak modern conventional "I will be with you in spirit" (so Gnilka, *Kolosserbrief* 114: "a rhetorical flourish *[floskelhaften Aussage]*"),[9] that is, whether Paul did not in fact think of being somehow really present with the Colossians, in the spiritual realm by means of the Spirit (see my *Jesus* 73; so also Fee 646; cf. O'Brien, *Colossians, Philemon* 98; Wall 102). In neither case is there any suggestion that the πνεῦμα is the real person (escaped from the body); rather, that the only means of communion with the Colossians was in the realm of the Spirit (hence a degree of ambiguity between human spirit and divine Spirit).[10] At the very least the claim reflects the intensity of Paul's prayers for the Colossians (1:3, 9) and presumably implies a more effective presence than simply the letter itself provided.

The implication that Paul can actually see the state of affairs at Colossae ("rejoicing and seeing your good order . . .") is, of course, intended more as an expression of what he would hope to see were it possible. The note of rejoicing echoes the theme of thanksgiving with which the letter opened (1:3-8). What Paul sees (would like to see) is the "good order (τάξις) and firmness (στερέωμα)" of their faith. The former denotes an "arrangement," something set in orderly fashion (hence the English "taxonomy," principles of classification); hence the only other Pauline use, 1 Cor. 14:40. The latter term, στερέωμα, means basically "what is made firm or thick," hence "basis, foundation, or solid body." LXX usage is largely influenced by the Genesis 1 account of creation, where it translates "firmament" (*raqîaʿ* = the solid vault of heaven; see further G. Bertram, *TDNT* 7.609-11). But the less

---

9. For contemporary examples see G. Karlson, "Formelhaftes in den Paulusbriefen," *Eranos* 54 (1956) 138-41.

10. Cf. Masson 119. Lohse, *Colossians and Philemon* 83; Schweizer, *Colossians* 119-20; Dibelius, *Kolosser, Epheser, Philemon* 26; and Pokorný 108 think simply of the Holy Spirit.

specific use of "firmness" is sufficiently indicated by the cognates in Acts 3:7 (ankles able to bear his weight) and 2 Tim. 2:19 ("firm foundation"); with reference to faith cf. Acts 16:5 and 1 Pet. 5:9. Both words could be used in military contexts: τάξις = rank and file of soldiers, drawn up in battle order (LSJ s.v. I; Lohse, *Colossians and Philemon* 84 n. 128); στερέωμα = the solid part, the strength of an army (1 Macc. 9:14; see further Bertram, *TDNT* 7.614); so that analogy may be in mind here.[11] But if so, the allusion is at most somewhat casual and does not call for a particular (military) discipline (cf. Scott 38-39), and the confidence expressed hardly implies a pressing crisis and numerous defections.

That which is to remain in good order and firm is their "faith in (εἰς) Christ." This is the only occasion in the Pauline corpus where this noun phrase occurs, though it reflects the more familiar verbal phrase πιστεύειν εἰς Christ (see on 1:4), and the noun phrase does appear in three "Pauline" passages in Acts (20:21; 24:24; 26:18; cf. also Phm. 5: τὴν πίστιν, ἣν ἔχεις πρὸς τὸν κύριον Ἰησοῦν, and Phm. 6: εἰς Χριστόν). Thoroughly Pauline, however, is the conviction that the whole Christian position (rank and solidity) stands or falls with faith in Christ, with the further implication, again characteristically Pauline, that anything which claims to be an advance upon that faith is in fact a retreat from it (cf. Conzelmann 143). This final recall to faith forms an inclusio with 1:4 and thus brackets the whole of the intervening thanksgiving and personal statement as an exposition of that faith (see also on 2:6).

---

11. Lightfoot 174; Lohmeyer 95; Moule, *Colossians and Philemon* 89; R. P. Martin, *Colossians and Philemon* 76-77; Caird 188; Ernst, *Philipper, Philemon, Kolosser, Epheser* 190; Wright, *Colossians and Philemon* 96; REB: "your unbroken ranks and the solid front"; but NRSV's "morale" is too remote from τάξις.

THE THEME OF THE LETTER (2:6–4:6)

The main thrust of the letter, forming the letter's body, extends from 2:6 to 4:6. It is thematically stated in 2:6-7, a passage which indicates clearly the integration of faith and praxis and which suggests that the main threat to the Colossians was failure both to recognize all that was already theirs in the faith they had accepted and expressed in the beginning and to translate their faith into an appropriate pattern of living. This explains the structure and character of the following sections, which cannot be simply analyzed into doctrinal and practical parts.[1]

The first main section is 2:8-23. It consists of a threefold warning to the Colossians: (1) to recognize the full scope of what Christ accomplished on the cross (2:8-15), (2) to beware of claims that there are further spiritual experiences in the light of which the significance of the cross may be discounted (2:16-19), and (3) to resist any suggestion that life in Christ depends on observance of traditional Jewish laws and customs (2:20-23).

The second main section takes up the challenge of what then should be the appropriate lifestyle for believers in Christ (3:1–4:6). This consists of four sections: (1) a statement of basic principle, the perspective from which all their ethical conduct should flow (3:1-4), (2) a sequence of general guidelines and practical exhortations (3:5-17), (3) some specific household rules (3:18–4:1), and (4) some further, concluding appropriate exhortations (4:2-6).

It thus begins to become clear how closely parallel the situations in Galatia and Colossae were (Colossae was not much further from Antioch in Roman Galatia than from Ephesus, though the route was more difficult; see further pp. 20f. above). Not that the crisis was anything as sharp in Colossae as it was in Galatians, as the different tone and pace of Colossians indicate. Nevertheless, a number of common features stand out in this section.

(1) It is clearly implied that the philosophy which threatened to seduce some of the Colossians did not see itself as challenging the basic gospel, but, presumably, as supplementing it. In contrast, as in Galatians (particularly Gal. 2:19–3:1; 6:12-14), Paul insists that the other teaching has failed to understand the gospel of the cross properly (Col. 2:8-15).

(2) Part of the attractiveness of the other teaching was that it gave rules of conduct (the law in Galatians; Col. 2:16, 20-23), which required Paul in response to make a clear statement of how the starting point of faith provided the pattern for going on. In Galatians the appeal could be particularly to the Galatians' experience of the Spirit, which Paul himself could recall so clearly

---

1. Lähnemann 111-15 and Wolter 114-16 prefer to take the introductory unit as 2:6-8; but 2:8 is better seen as the opening statement of what follows (see the introduction to the comments on 2:8-15).

(Gal. 3:1-5; 5:16-26). In Colossians also the appeal is to the Christians' starting point (Col. 2:6-7), but the corollary is drawn in more directly christological than pneumatological terms (perhaps the Colossians' conversion had been less attended by charismatic experience than that of the Galatians).

(3) Also common to the two letters is the strongly Jewish character of the "human tradition" (2:8; cf. Mark 7:8) against which warning is given, notably the Jewish festivals (Gal. 4:10; Col. 2:16) and even the "elemental forces" (Gal. 4:3, 9; Col. 2:8, 20). Circumcision was evidently not a major factor of enticement in what was being offered to the Colossians (as it had been in Galatia — Gal. 5:2-12; 6:12-15), but the play on the metaphor of circumcision in Col. 2:11, the echo of a characteristically Jewish view of Gentiles (2:13: "dead in . . . the uncircumcision of your flesh"), and the discounting of any distinction between "circumcision" and "uncircumcision" (3:11), similar to what is in Gal. 5:6 and 6:15, all suggest that circumcision was an element in the makeup of the package being held out before the Colossians. Similarly with food laws in both letters (Gal. 2:11-14; Col. 2:21). Also striking is the suggestion common to both letters that halakhic rules were being presented as the means of controlling the flesh but were having the opposite effect (Gal. 5:13-19; 6:12-13; Col. 2:20-23). Even the distinctive element of "worship of angels" (Col. 2:18) has parallels in the similarly ambiguous references to angels in Gal. 3:19.

All this suggests a stronger Jewish element in the teaching being offered in Colossae than has been commonly recognized in recent decades (see, e.g., Hübner 356-57).

THE THEMATIC STATEMENT (2:6-7)

6 *As therefore you received the tradition of Christ Jesus as Lord, walk in him,* 7 *rooted and being built up in him and confirmed in faith, just as you were taught, overflowing[2] in thanksgiving.*

Paul had already alluded to his fears for the Colossians — the danger of them being deluded by specious arguments used by plausible religious salesmen (2:4). Now he prepares to confront the danger head-on, beginning with a positive statement of his objective. As in Rom. 1:16-17 and Gal. 1:11-12, these two verses provide a brief summary sentence of the main point to be made in the body of the letter, to serve as a heading to what follows (cf. Lähnemann 49; Meeks, "Body" 210). As such, the emphases which the sentence strikes are of particular importance for our understanding of the letter.

2:6 ὡς οὖν παρελάβετε τὸν Χριστὸν Ἰησοῦν τὸν κύριον, ἐν αὐτῷ περιπατεῖτε. In untypically Pauline style (ὡς οὖν) the recall to faith is reexpressed ("as you received Christ Jesus as Lord") and the appropriate conclusion ("therefore") drawn: "walk in him." The allusion is not simply to the immediately preceding reference to "faith" in 2:5, which summed up the intent of the opening section as a whole (see on 2:5). Included therefore is a congratulation to the Colossians on their faith (1:4), a reminder of its amazing content (1:13-22, 26-27), and an encouragement to remain firm on its foundation (1:23, 28; 2:3).

It is significant, then, that this summarizing and summary statement is expressed in the term παραλαμβάνω. For, as is generally recognized, this word is more or less a technical term for the receiving of tradition, and it is most often used by Paul in this sense (1 Cor. 11:23; 15:1, 3; Gal. 1:9, 12; Phil. 4:9; 1 Thes. 2:13; 4:1; 2 Thes. 3:6). As such it is twin with παραδίδωμι ("hand over"), as again used by Paul (1 Cor. 11:2, 23; 15:3). Such "handing on" and "receiving" was crucially important in the ancient world, when the continuation of so much received wisdom and knowledge depended on oral transmission. Indeed, this was a principal function of teaching, the teacher handing on and the next generation receiving what the community or school valued as its formative tradition (Plato, *Theaetetus* 198B; Philo, *De cherubim* 68; see further BAGD s.v. παραδίδωμι 3; G. Delling, *TDNT* 4:11-12; A. Kretzer, *EDNT* 3:29-30). Precisely the same balance is struck by the Hebrew terms *qibbel* and *masar*, with the same emphasis on the importance of passing on and receiving tradition (as in Mishnah *Aboth* 1:1; see, e.g., O'Brien, *Colossians, Philemon* 105).

---

2. There is strong support for the addition of "in it" (that is, in faith), but it was probably inserted in conscious or unconscious echo of the full phrase in 4:2 (see Metzger 622).

The clear implication is that what was in mind was the founding traditions on which new churches were built (Meeks, *Urban Christians* 126-27). So Moule, *Colossians and Philemon* 89: "As, therefore, you received as tradition (the account) of Jesus as Christ and Lord." In other words, the thought is not of the reception of Christ's Lordship in baptism (Wegenast 126-29; cf. Ernst, *Philipper, Philemon, Kolosser, Epheser* 192), far less the thought of receiving Christ into their lives (cf. 1:27), for which παρα-λαμβάνω is never used by Paul (see my *Baptism* 95) and for which (προσ)δέχομαι (as, e.g., in Gal. 4:14 and Rom. 16:2) would have been more suitable. Rather, Paul refers his readers back to their experience of hearing and receiving the gospel (aorist tense),[3] as he had in responding to the equivalent situation in Galatia (Gal. 3:1-5). As in Galatians, this first decisive experience provides a norm and a starting point for what should follow: their ongoing life of faith should be in accord with the faith with which it began.

What these traditions were in the case of the Colossians we can deduce from the actual object of the verb — literally "the Christ Jesus the Lord." As both the Wisdom and "mystery" spoken of earlier could be simply identified with "Christ" (1:15-18; 1:27; 2:2), so here the preaching/teaching received could be summed up as focused in Christ. The phrase itself could be taken in different ways: "the Christ, Jesus the Lord," "the Christ Jesus, the Lord," "(the previously referred to) Christ Jesus as (the one who is =) Lord"; hence JB "the Christ you have received — Jesus the Lord," and NEB "since Jesus was delivered to you as Christ and Lord" (see further Harris 88-89). Probably the formulation was chosen to bring out the two strands of the preaching/teaching (Abbott 244).

The one strand was kerygmatic tradition, summed up by the phrase "the Lord" (BAGD s.v. παραλαμβάνω 2bγ: "the proclamation of him as Lord"). This way of speaking of Jesus goes back to the earliest days of Christianity. It reflects the impact of the resurrection of Jesus on the beginnings of christology proper (Acts 2:36; Phil. 2:11),[4] the significance of Ps. 110:1 as one of the main Old Testament texts to shape the earliest faith (see on 3:1), and the importance of the title in earliest Christian devotion (such that it was preserved in an Aramaic formulation in Greek-speaking churches [1 Cor. 16:22]). 2 Cor. 4:5 indicates that the proclamation of Jesus as Lord was one of Paul's principal emphases in preaching; by general consent Rom. 10:9 probably reflects one of the earliest baptismal confessions ("Jesus is Lord");[5] and the title "Lord" was Paul's favorite (about 230 occurrences in

---

3. Cf. Gnilka, *Kolosserbrief* 116: "Christian traditions do not emerge in the controversy with heresy, but are given precision through it."

4. See particularly P. Pokorný, *The Genesis of Christology: Foundations for a Theology of the New Testament* (Edinburgh: Clark, 1987).

5. On kerygmatic/confessional traditions see further particularly Wengst, *Formeln* 27-129.

the Pauline corpus). Receiving (the proclamation of) Christ Jesus as Lord was thus one of the most effective summaries of the gospel as it had been understood from the beginning and had been preached particularly in the Pauline mission.

Since the basic sense of κύριος is that of superior to inferior (master to slave; king to subject; god to worshiper), with formally acknowledged rights of the former to command or dispose of the latter (see also 3:22 and 4:1), all would have recognized that acceptance of Christ Jesus as Lord included within it submission of the believer to this Christ and unconditional readiness to act in obedience to him. The title had further overtones of considerable significance for christology (see on 1:3), but here it is the practical outworkings of its acceptance which are to the fore. Hence the accompanying urge to shape conduct accordingly (περιπατεῖτε), which echoes the practical exhortation of 1:10 ("walk worthily of the Lord"; see on that verse; κύριος is used nine or ten times in the parenesis of 3:12–4:1). And the "in him" in this case is equivalent to "in the Lord," the more common "in" formulation in ethical exhortations (see also 3:18, 20). In itself the phrase ("in him") is sufficient reminder that the "walking" was not to be thought of simply as a following of received tradition, but also as something motivated from within and from the living relation with Christ as Lord which it expressed (Lähnemann 113). Ἐν αὐτῷ περιπατεῖτε here, then, is equivalent to the πνεύματι περιπατεῖτε of Gal. 5:16 (*pace* Pokorný 111). This combination of "receiving tradition of Christ Jesus as Lord" and "walking in him" is thus a neat summary of the mutual check and balance between outward guideline and inward motivation which was a feature of the Pauline ethic (as in Gal. 5:25–6:2).

The other strand of the preaching/teaching alluded to here is probably tradition about Jesus' own ministry and teaching, summed up in the phrase "the Christ." The point is much less clear and more disputed.[6] But the echo of the titular usage ("the Christ" — Moule, *Colossians and Philemon* 89; N. Turner, *GNTG* 3.167) probably at least includes a reminder to the Colossians that this Jesus was first and foremost Jewish Messiah. For this to make sense to Gentiles in Asia Minor, and not forgetting the likelihood of a large Jewish colony in Colossae (see pp. 21f. in the Introduction), it would have been necessary for some information to be given about this Jesus and his ministry in the Jewish homeland. Because Paul makes so few explicit references to the Jesus tradition that it is generally argued that he had no interest in the life and ministry of Jesus, apart from his death and resurrection. But such a hypothesis makes little sense of what we know of the sociology of

---

6. Though see particularly O. Cullmann, "The Tradition," *The Early Church* (London: SCM, 1956) 59-75; C. H. Dodd, "Ἔννομος Χριστοῦ," *More New Testament Studies* (Manchester: Manchester University, 1968) 134-48.

new movements. It is scarcely credible, in other words, that a new movement could be gathered round a single name without a story being told to identify that name and explain its significance and thus to provide foundation (note the metaphor used in 2:7) and identity for the movement itself. And to Gentiles living in Asia Minor, but aware of Judaism and perhaps attracted to its practices (cf. particularly 2:16), that story must have included a fair amount about Jesus' life and ministry (which had taken place less than thirty years earlier) and not just the bare fact of his death and resurrection.

This a priori speculation is sufficiently confirmed by (1) references to traditions being passed on as part of the process of founding a new church, which clearly include ethical traditions (particularly 1 Thes. 4:1 and 2 Thes. 3:6), (2) indications of the importance of the role of teachers in the earliest Christian communities (Acts 13:1; 1 Cor. 12:28; Gal. 6:6 — surely not simply repeating the bare account of Jesus' death and resurrection; see also 2:7), and (3) allusions to the teaching and example of Jesus (e.g., Rom. 12:14; 13:9; 14:14; 15:1-5; Gal. 5:14; 6:2; here Col. 2:22).[7] Here we might simply note that for traditions of Jesus as (the) Christ to provide any kind of guidelines for the Colossians' "walk," they must at least have included illustrations of what Jesus said and did — the "in him," in other words, including relationship to the earthly Christ as well as to the heavenly Lord (see also on 1:2).[8] By including so many of these traditions in their Gospels the Synoptic evangelists later simply formalized what must have been an already long-standing practice in church founding and catechetical formation.

2:7 ἐρριζωμένοι καὶ ἐποικοδομούμενοι ἐν αὐτῷ καὶ βεβαιούμενοι τῇ πίστει καθὼς ἐδιδάχθητε, περισσεύοντες ἐν εὐχαριστίᾳ. The point is reinforced by a sequence of forceful metaphors. These traditions of Jesus as Christ and Lord provide for the new community both a root for the new plant and a foundation for the new building. The verb ῥιζόω ("cause to take root," only here and in Eph. 3:17 in the New Testament) vividly images the preaching/teaching as an effective sowing that results in a well-rooted plant (perfect participle; cf. Sir. 24:12 — of wisdom; *Psalms of Solomon* 14:4; *Odes of Solomon* 38:17-22). The importance of deep roots was well under-

7. See further my "Paul's Knowledge of the Jesus Tradition: The Evidence of Romans," in *Christus Bezeugen,* W. Trilling FS, ed. K. Kertelge, et al. (Leipzig: St. Benno, 1989) 193-207; also "Jesus Tradition in Paul," in *Studying the Historical Jesus: Evaluations of the State of Current Research,* ed. B. Chilton and C. A. Evans (NTTS 19; Leiden: Brill, 1994) 155-78, where I point out that explicit citations of Jesus tradition would probably have been less effective than the allusions to shared tradition, whose very character as allusions affirmed and strengthened the bond which the founding traditions formed.

8. It is an interesting fact that the first half of the letter is characterized by the frequent use of "in Christ" (fourteen or fifteen occurrences), which does not appear after 2:15, and the second half by "in the Lord" (four occurrences), which does not appear before 3:18.

stood in Jewish tradition (e.g., Jer. 17:8; Ezek. 31:7; Sir. 40:15). Naturally the image is complementary to the "fruit-bearing" metaphor of 1:10, which follows the same emphasis on a "walk" determined by reference to "the Lord." Equally it makes a natural partner in Jewish tradition with the following metaphor (particularly in Jeremiah, e.g., 1:9-10; 18:7-9; 24:6; 31:28; 42:10; Aletti, *Épître aux Colossiens* 161 n. 4).

The prefix ἐπι- in ἐποιχοδομέω ("build on") likewise emphasizes the importance of the starting point (the foundation; cf. Josephus, *Antiquities* 11.79; Philo, *De somnis* 2.8) as ensuring the viability and strength of what is "being built (present participle) on" it. Paul used the metaphor intensively in 1 Cor. 3:10-14 (otherwise in Paul only in Eph. 2:20). In both cases the metaphors underline the importance of the founding traditions (see on 2:6), with the tenth "in him" in Colossians here again implying (as in 2:6) a balance between the guidelines provided by the traditions of which "he" was the focus and the living experience of a community "in him" (see again on 1:2).

The third metaphor is drawn from the marketplace. Βέβαιος and βεβαιόω were commonly used to denote the formal or legal guarantee required in the transfer of property or goods (MM; H. Schlier, *TDNT* 1:602-3). This technical sense is probably echoed also in Paul's other uses of these words (Rom. 4:16; 15:8; 1 Cor. 1:6, 8; 2 Cor. 1:7, 21). Here the guarantee or confirmation is τῇ πίστει, "with reference to your faith" (for alternative ways of taking the dative see Harris 90). Once again the emphasis is on the message (traditions) which the Colossian Christians first received and their acceptance of it as providing the basis and guarantee of the transfer they made in baptism to Christ as Lord (Rom. 10:9).[9] And once again typically Pauline is the insistence that this faith (in Jesus as Christ and Lord, 2:5) is the sum and heart of their ongoing life and walk.

"As you were taught" confirms the root-digging, foundation-laying, guarantee-providing character of the teaching in the establishing of a new church. The teaching was not something additional to or less important than the gospel. It was basic to and constitutive of a new community of faith (see further on 2:6). Hence its importance also in 1:28 and 3:16.

With a characteristic Pauline flourish the thematic statement is rounded off. Περισσεύω, "be more than enough," and with persons "have in abundance," was one of the words Paul quite often reached for to express the rich, overflowing character of the experience of himself and his converts (Rom. 15:13 — hope; 2 Cor. 1:5 — Christ's comfort; 4:15 and 9:8 — grace; Phil. 1:9 and 1 Thes. 3:12 — love). Here the thought is of "thanksgiving"

---

9. "One must not at this stage draw a sharp distinction between faith as the way a person acts and faith as the content of a confessional formula which is believed" (Schweizer, *Colossians* 124).

(εὐχαριστία), echoing the prayer of 1:12 (NEB/REB: "let your hearts over-flow with thankfulness"). As there, so here, the implication is that a characteristic and fundamental feature of their relation with Jesus as Christ and Lord should be gratitude for what God has done in and through him. As rootedness and foundation depends on the faith called forth by the gospel, so growing from the root and building up on the foundation can be successful only in an atmosphere of thankfulness to God (see also on 1:12).

THE CROSS OF CHRIST RENDERS UNNECESSARY ANY FURTHER HUMAN TRADITIONS AND RULES (2:8-23)

This section forms the theological and polemical heart of the letter, balancing the more intensively parenetic section that follows (3:1–4:6). 2:8 functions as a heading and initial statement of the section's theme, in chiastic form:

> 8a polemical denunciation   16-23
> 8b in accordance with Christ   9-15

After the slow buildup of the letter thus far, in which the warnings have been nonspecific, the challenge confronting the Colossian believers is brought more clearly into the open and begins to become more clearly identifiable as a coherent alternative. However, the possibility continues to remain open that as well as the more specific religious system and praxis referred to, the writers recognized the possibility of other philosophies or cults proving attractive to their readers and framed their warnings in more general terms in consequence. At all events, if the Colossian alternative (usually denoted as "false teaching") is to be given any clear identity, the issue will be resolved from 2:8-23 or not at all (see also pp. 23ff. in the Introduction).

The Scope of Christ's Accomplishments on the Cross (2:8-15)

8 *Watch out lest there be someone who tries to captivate you through philosophy and empty deceit in accordance with human tradition, in accordance with the elemental forces of the world, and not in accordance with Christ.*

9 *For in him dwells all the fullness of the deity in bodily form,*
10 *and in him you are fulfilled,*
       who[1] is the head of all rule and authority.
11 *In him also you were circumcised with a circumcision not*
       performed by human hand
       in the stripping off of the body of flesh,
       in the circumcision of the Christ,
12 *having been buried with him in baptism.[2]*
    In whom also you were raised with him
       through faith in the effective working of God,
       who raised him from the dead.

13 *And though you were dead in the transgressions and uncircumcision of your flesh, he made you[3] alive with him, when he forgave us[3] all our transgressions.* 14 *He canceled the bond that stood against us with its decrees, which was opposed to us, and removed it by nailing it to the cross.* 15 *He stripped off the rulers and the authorities, exposing them to public disgrace, leading them in triumph in him.[4]*

After the initial warning (2:8) Paul proceeds to fill out the foundational importance of the faith in and by which the Colossians had first received Jesus as Christ and Lord and the principal cause for their continuing thankfulness. His first concern is to explain (or recall) the full significance of what happened on the cross of Christ (the central element in the founding traditions), in relation particularly to the heavenly powers and to the question of circumcision's continuing relevance.

From 2:9 the language assumes a semi-poetic quality: most notably,

---

1. An early grammatical correction changed masculine ὅς to neuter ὅ to agree with neuter πλήρωμα in 1:9.

2. The less usual Christian word for baptism, βαπτισμός ("washing"; cf. Mark 7:4; Heb. 6:2; 9:10) is probably original, having been altered by many in transmission to the more usual word βάπτισμα (Metzger 623). See further Lightfoot 182.

3. There was an understandable tendency to change ὑμᾶς to ἡμᾶς (an early change with some strong support) or ἡμῖν to ὑμῖν (less well attested) to avoid the awkward shift in persons ("you," "us").

4. ἐν αὐτῷ could be taken as "in it," referring to the cross (so NIV, NRSV; Lightfoot 190; R. P. Martin, *Colossians and Philemon* 88; Yates, *Colossians* 53). But it is more appropriate to read it as a final chord of the "in him" theme (so most).

2:9-12 is structured around a sequence of "in him/whom" phrases (four in all) and 2:13c-15 on a striking sequence of participles (five in all). This has resulted in suggestions that underlying 2:9-15 as a whole,[5] or 2:11-15 (Zeilinger, *Erstgeborene* 54), or 2:13c-15,[6] or 2:14-15 (Martin, "Reconciliation" 116-24) in particular,[7] can be detected a Christian hymn or hymnic confession. But attempts at reconstruction have gained very little support (see Deichgräber 167-69; Lähnemann 126 n. 67; Gnilka, *Kolosserbrief* 120-21; Pokorný 136-37; Sappington 205-7). The character of the Greek, including its awkward links, may simply be the result of an attempt to describe the effectiveness of Christ's death by using a sequence of metaphors, some of them already traditional, which, however, do not sit comfortably together:

11 circumcision
12 burial and resurrection
13 death and (new) life
14 expunging the record
15 stripping off and public triumph.

2:8 βλέπετε μή τις ὑμᾶς ἔσται ὁ συλαγωγῶν διὰ τῆς φιλοσοφίας καὶ κενῆς ἀπάτης κατὰ τὴν παράδοσιν τῶν ἀνθρώπων, κατὰ τὰ στοιχεῖα τοῦ κόσμου καὶ οὐ κατὰ Χριστόν. For the first time a specific danger is referred to. The imperative βλέπετε can mean simply "look at," but followed by μή has a clear note of warning: "look out, beware" (BAGD s.v. βλέπω 6; in Paul 1 Cor. 8:9; 10:12; Gal. 5:15; and Phil. 3:2). Paul regularly refers to known opponents in a somewhat diminishing allusion as "some, certain people" (Rom. 3:8; 1 Cor. 4:18; 15:12, 34; 2 Cor. 3:1; 10:2; Gal. 1:7; 2:12; Phil. 1:15). But here the singular (τις), followed by the future tense (ἔσται), suggests in contrast that a possibility is being envisaged rather than a current state of affairs described: "Take heed! Perhaps there will be someone who . . ." (J. H. Moulton, *GNTG* 1:192-93; cf. Masson 121 n. 3; Bruce, *Colossians, Philemon, and Ephesians* 97; otherwise Lightfoot 176; O'Brien, *Colossians, Philemon* 109).

This suggests in turn that the participle συλαγωγῶν should be taken as a conative present, "who tries to . . . , who wants to . . ." (BDF §319). The verb itself, συλαγωγέω, is little known (only here in biblical Greek),

5. Particularly G. Schille, *Frühchristliche Hymnen* (Berlin: Evangelische, [2]1965) 31-37; cf. Cannon 37-49: a hymn created by the author out of traditional materials.

6. Schenke, "Gnostische Erlöser" 222-23: from a Christian Gnostic hymn, with 2:15 a "typically Gnostic presentation of a public and triumphal return of the Redeemer through the spheres of the Archons."

7. See further Lohse, "Bekenntnis"; also his *Colossians and Philemon* 106; Wengst, *Formeln* 186-90; Burger 79-114.

but as a stronger form of ἄγω and from its two other known occurrences (set out in Lohse, *Colossians and Philemon* 94 n. 18) the meaning "carry off as booty or captive" is clear enough. Here then, given the fuller description that follows, the thought is of some popular rhetorician (2:4) or philosopher captivating (so NJB; REB "capture your minds") some in his audience by the power of his rhetoric or the impressiveness of his claims. The visual metaphor is of such a marketplace preacher gathering together those impressed by his discourse and taking them off for a fuller exposition and induction. If indeed, then, the challenge to the Colossian believers stemmed primarily from the synagogue, as appears to be the case (see pp. 29ff. in the Introduction), this allusion confirms the likelihood that the Colossian Jews included some effective apologists and rhetoricians in their number, well able to hold their own in learned debate.[8]

The further description, however, is still not specific. Φιλοσοφία (again only here in biblical Greek) means literally "love of wisdom," but had long been used of a systematic treatment of a theme, practical as well as speculative, and so also for various schools of "philosophy" (see O. Michel, *TDNT* 9.172-79). Jewish apologists made free use of it in this more technical sense in commending their own religious system. Thus, for example, *Aristeas* 256 provides a definition of "philosophy" which begins: "To have a well-reasoned assessment of each occurrence and not to be carried away by impulses." 4 Maccabees is set out as a philosophical discourse which begins by commending "philosophy" as "a subject necessary to everyone for understanding" (1:1-2) and which later defines the value of "our (Jewish) philosophy" as teaching the virtues of "sound judgment or self-control," "manliness," "justice," and "godliness" (5:22-24). Josephus, in turn, did not hesitate to commend the different sects of Judaism (Essenes, Sadducees, and Pharisees) to his intellectual readers as φιλοσοφίαι. Philo, too, found no difficulty in presenting biblical teaching and Jewish piety as a kind of philosophy (see Michel 181-82; DeMaris 48-49). A century later Justin Martyr presented Christianity as "the true philosophy."

The term as it is used here, then, is in no way disparaging or specific in its reference in itself. It is a term which many apologists for all sorts of religious and pseudo-religious teaching would use because of its distinguished pedigree, as subsequently in relation to the mysteries (Lohse, *Colossians and Philemon* 95; see also G. Bornkamm, *TDNT* 4.808-10). The association with the next phrase, "the (so-called) philosophy and empty deceit," still leaves it open that what was in mind here were the sort of popular religious speculations which must often have appeared in marketplace discourses by self-styled "philosophers" (see also 2:23: "a reputation

---

8. Wright, *Colossians and Philemon* 100 suggests that "a contemptuous pun with the word synagogue" (συναγωγή/συλαγωγῶν) is intended.

of wisdom"). The judgment as to whether Paul and Timothy had a particular "philosophy" in mind is dependent on the greater clarity provided by what follows, particularly 2:16-23; but even so, Paul may have left his warning vague so that it could cover a wider range of possible alternatives to his gospel than the more specific challenge at Colossae.

"Empty deceit" (κενῆς ἀπάτης) is doubly condemnatory (cf. Eph. 5:6). Κενός signifies "without content, without any basis, without truth, without power" (BAGD s.v. 2; cf. particularly 1 Cor. 15:14; Jas. 2:20), and ἀπάτη "deception or deceitfulness." But again it tells us no more about the "philosophy" envisaged. The language, of course, is pejorative and expresses the contempt which Paul, confident in the rootedness and firmness of his own gospel, evidently felt for the teachings masquerading as philosophies which competed for the ear of his own audiences when he spoke in the open,[9] including probably what he (now) regarded as the fanciful claims of Jewish mystics (see on 2:18).

This "empty deceit," or better the whole phrase "philosophy and empty deceit" (governed by a single definite article), is given a further dismissive shrug as being "in accordance with human tradition." The use of παράδοσις ("tradition") no doubt glances back to the tradition received (παραλαμβάνειν) according to 2:6 (cf. 1 Cor. 11:2; 2 Thes. 2:15; 3:6). The tradition on which the Colossian church was founded was divinely authenticated (Jesus the Christ was also the divine Wisdom and mystery); in contrast, any "philosophy" that discounted that tradition could only be of human origin. The term "tradition" and the importance of tradition were familiar in wider Greek usage, including the mystery cults (BAGD s.v. παράδοσις 1; Lohse, *Colossians and Philemon* 95-96), but Paul the Pharisee would be bound to think of the importance of "traditions" in the "philosophy" of the Pharisees, as he recalled his own devotion to them (Gal. 1:14). Most striking is the fact that the very same phrase, "the tradition of human beings" (τὴν παράδοσιν τῶν ἀνθρώπων), occurs in Mark's account of Jesus' denunciation of such pharisaic traditions (Mark 7:8; Mark 7:3-13/Matt. 15:2-9). This adds strength to the likelihood that the sort of "philosophy" in mind here was essentially a form of Jewish thought being presented as a "philosophy" by Jewish apologists (Wright, *Colossians and Philemon* 101). At all events, Paul obviously envisages a "philosophy" that could claim respect by virtue of its ancient tradition.[10]

The final description, κατὰ τὰ στοιχεῖα τοῦ κόσμου ("according to

9. Lightfoot 177 notes how little use Paul made of such highly valued terms as φιλοσοφία and ἀρετή ("virtue"): "the Gospel had deposed the terms as inadequate to the higher standard, whether of knowledge or of practice, which it had introduced."

10. "The argument from antiquity plays a great role in religious controversy" (Gnilka, *Kolosserbrief* 122, appositely citing Josephus, *Contra Apionem* 1, subtitled "On the Antiquity of the Jews"; see particularly 1.2-3).

the elemental forces of the cosmos"), is also enigmatic and has spawned a huge debate (see bibliography in G. Delling, *TDNT* 7.670; Bandstra, *Law* 5-30; Schweizer, "Elemente" 147-48; O'Brien, *Colossians, Philemon* 129-32; Sappington 164-68). The basic meaning of στοιχεῖον is "element," and here, where the immediate context is dominated by cosmic categories (2:9-10, 15), the most obvious reference in the full phrase is to the elemental substances of which the cosmos was thought to be composed (earth, water, air, and fire — as the term is used in Wis. 7:17 and 2 Pet. 3:10, 12), by far the most common usage in literature prior to Paul.[11] However, as Philo knew well, these substances could be understood (mythologized or personified) as spirits or given the names of deities (*De vita contemplativa* 3; *De decalogo* 53). "The divinization of the elements was a commonplace in the whole Graeco-Roman period" (Wink 74).[12]

Whether στοιχεῖα was at this time actually being used of heavenly bodies, the stars understood as heavenly powers that influence or determine human destiny, is still unclear. The usage is not attested until after the time of the New Testament; the earliest explicit references are usually taken to be those in *Testament of Solomon* 8:2-4, where seven demonic spirits identify themselves as στοιχεῖα ("rulers of this world of darkness. . . . Our stars in heaven look small, but we are named like gods"), and Diogenes Laertius 6.102, who calls the twelve signs of the zodiac "the twelve στοιχεῖα" (cf. *Corpus Hermeticum* 13.12). But it is a natural extension of the more established use, since stars were understood to be composed of one of the elements, fire. Thus, in condemnatory tone, Wis. 13:2: "they (Gentiles in general) supposed that either fire or wind or swift air, or the circle of the stars, or turbulent water, or the luminaries of heaven were the gods that rule the world." Philo describes the στοιχεῖα as "powers" (*De aeternitate Mundi* 107-9), and Hermas (*Visions* 3.13.3) speaks of the world as controlled (κρατεῖται) through the four στοιχεῖα (cited also by DeMaris 53-55). And both here and in Galatians there is a clear implication that the στοιχεῖα were closely associated with heavenly

11. A minority continues to uphold the traditional interpretation: rudimentary ideas or "elementary teaching," as in Heb. 5:12 (so Moule, *Colossians and Philemon* 91-92; Carr, *Angels* 75-76; Sappington 169; Yates, *Colossians* 40, 54-55; "the basic forces of the world, namely the law and the flesh," according to Bandstra, *Law* 68-72). Despite the evidence, which he himself notes, DeMaris argues rather woodenly for the meaning "first principles" (73, 79-83), sets the Colossian usage speculatively within the context of Middle Platonism, and compounds implausibility by hypothesizing a discipline (2:23) "fostered by the close scrutiny (ἐμβατεύω) of the στοιχεῖα . . ." (114-18).

12. See further particularly J. Blinzler, "Lexikalisches zu dem Terminus τὰ στοιχεῖα τοῦ κοσμοῦ bei Paulus," in *Studiorum Paulinorum Congressus Internationalis Catholicus 1961* (AnBib 17-18; Rome: Pontifical Biblical Institute, 1963) 2.429-43; Schweizer, "Elemente" 149-63; "Slaves" 456-64; D. Rusam, "Neue Belege zu den στοιχεῖα τοῦ κοσμοῦ (Gal. 4:3, 9; Kol. 2:8, 20)," *ZNW* 83 (1992) 119-25; summary of Philo's usage in Wink 69.

beings (Gal. 4:8-9 — gods as popularly understood; Col. 2:10 — rulers and authorities).[13]

It is important here to note that the issue does not turn on any distinction of personal versus impersonal: it was commonplace, not least within Judaism, to think of the stars as living beings (Judg. 5:20; Job 38:7; Dan. 8:10; *1 Enoch* 86; Philo, *De opificio mundi* 73; *De plantatione* 12; Rev. 1:20; 9:1); likewise "fate" could be personified ("the Fates") or attributed to a personal δαίμων (*OCD* s.v. "Fate"; LSJ s.v. δαίμων). The allusion, in other words, is to the belief that was no doubt then common (as still among not a few today) that human beings had to live their lives under the influence or sway of primal and cosmic forces, however precisely conceptualized (for an effective summary of the case see Martin, *Colossians and Philemon* 10-14). Hence the translation "elemental forces" or "elemental spirits of the universe" (RSV/NRSV, NEB/REB); but "principles of this world" (JB/NJB; cf. NIV) is too vague.

It is particularly interesting that precisely the same phrase is used in Gal. 4:3 and 9 (as again in Col. 2:20). There it is clearly linked into the Jewish law, understood as itself a kind of power set in charge over Israel like a slave-custodian or guardian (Gal. 3:23-25; 4:1-3, 9-10) and given "through angels" (3:19). The close association of the thought here with talk of Jewish festivals (Col. 2:16; cf. Gal. 4:10) and "worship of angels" (Col. 2:18) strongly suggests that we are moving in the same realm of thought and association as with the same phrase in Galatians. Here it needs to be remembered that Jewish apocalyptic also spoke of spirits controlling the elements: for example, *Jubilees* 2:2: "the angels of the spirit of fire, the angels of the spirit of the winds . . ."; *1 Enoch* 75:1: "the leaders of the chiefs of thousands who are in charge of all the stars"; *2 Enoch* 4:1: "the rulers of the stellar orders . . . , the angels who govern the stars"; *Testament of Abraham* 13:11: "the archangel Purouel, who has authority over fire" (Lohse, *Colossians and Philemon* 98, cites *1 Enoch* 43:1-2 and *2 Enoch* 19:1-4). *1 Enoch* 18:14-16 also speaks of stars bound and imprisoned for their transgression, and the Greek fragment of *Jubilees* 2:8 links "the plac-

---

13. For further details see BAGD s.v. στοιχεῖον 2-4; G. Delling, *TDNT* 7.672-83; Lohse, *Colossians and Philemon* 96-99; Gnilka, *Kolosserbrief* 124-26. Schweizer, *Colossians* 131-33 draws attention particularly to the importance of the elements in the Pythagorean texts of the first century BC, and concludes that the Colossian philosophy was a form of Jewish Pythagoreanism (critiqued and developed by DeMaris 88-96, 103-4; but *pace* DeMaris see n. 11 above and comments below on 2:18). Bruce, *Colossians, Philemon, and Ephesians* 99-100 suggests that use of the phrase in relation to heavenly bodies may have been "an original Pauline contribution to religious vocabulary" (cf. E. Plümacher, *EDNT* 3.278), a possibility for which most recently Wolter 123-24 makes no allowance ("it is hardly possible to identify the 'rulers and authorities' or 'angels' mentioned in 2:15, 18 with the *stoicheia* . . . any more than with the four elements . . . that bind humankind to the world").

ings of the stars" with τὰ στοιχεῖα (καὶ τὰς τῶν ἄστρων θέσεις καὶ τὰ στοιχεῖα). We might also note that some fragmentary horoscopes have been discovered among the DSS (4Q186 and 4QMessAr), that one of the ways in which Hellenistic Jewish apologists sought to commend Judaism was by presenting the Jewish patriarchs as the discoverers of astrology (Artapanus and pseudo-Eupolemus in Eusebius, *Praeparatio Evangelica* 9.18.1 and 9.17.8-9), and that Josephus could describe the Pharisees and the Essenes in particular as believers in Fate (*Antiquities* 13.172) and could even claim that the Essenes prayed to the sun (*War* 2.128). It is quite possible, then, to conceive of an essentially Jewish "philosophy" in Colossae that drew on such traditions as a way of commending their religious practices to their fellow citizens (see further on 2:18).

The key test of such systems for the letter writer(s), however, was whether they accorded with Christ (κατὰ Χριστόν). Here the credit built up in 1:15-20 and 26-27 is now drawn on. The Christ who embodies the secret of both cosmos and history must obviously serve as the yardstick by which all other claims to religious insight (not least claims regarding human relationships with and within the cosmos) should be measured. It was precisely the failure of such speculation to grasp the significance of Christ and of his death that demonstrated their emptiness and deceitfulness.

2:9 ὅτι ἐν αὐτῷ κατοικεῖ πᾶν πλήρωμα τῆς θεότητος σωματικῶς. The force of κατὰ Χριστόν is explained (ὅτι) by a sequence of "in him" clauses (2:9-12) which build into a powerful exposition of the cross. Initially, however, these clauses pick up the theme of the hymn in praise of Christ, recalling first the hymn's second strophe (1:19) in very similar words ("in him," "all the fullness," "dwells"), and then (2:10) the thought of the first strophe (1:18a — "head"; 1:16 — "rule and authority").

In 2:9, apart from the change in tense, the only modification to the language of 1:19 is the addition of τῆς θεότητος and σωματικῶς, both *hapax legomena* in biblical Greek. The former was sufficiently familiar in literary Greek to denote the nature or essence of deity, that which constitutes deity (BAGD s.v. θεότης; for the distinction from θειότης see Lightfoot 179). The later christology of "divine nature" and "essence" is clearly prepared for but is by no means yet present (Ernst, *Philipper, Philemon, Kolosser, Epheser* 199-200). The thought is no different in substance from the earlier formulation (see on 1:19), only that the divine fullness which indwelled and continues to indwell Christ is expressed in more abstract terms. As Lona 133-34, 141 and Pokorný 121 n. 71 note, this dependence on the earlier phrase (assuming that 1:19 was part of the original "hymn") calls into question the more popular suggestion that the concept πλήρωμα was derived from "the Colossian philosophy" (as, e.g., Dibelius, *Kolosser, Epheser, Philemon* 29; Lohmeyer 105; Lähnemann 117; Fowl 128-29, 136-37; but see again Benoit, "Plèrôma" 137-42).

The latter addition, σωματικῶς, reinforces the encounterable reality of the indwelling: as the human σῶμα is what enables a person to be in relationship with other persons, so the somatic character of this indwelling meant that God could be encountered directly in and through this particular human being, Christ. Here, as in 1:19 (and as with the use of the adjective in Luke 3:22), σωματικῶς underscores the accessibility (come-at-ableness) of the divine epiphany (cf. the data in Lohse, *Colossians and Philemon* 100 n. 46; H. Balz, *EDNT* 3.325) and can hardly refer to anything other than Jesus' life on earth, though including his death (as the next few verses imply). At the same time the present tense indicates this function of Jesus as ongoing: Christ in his historical embodiment still brings the character of deity fully to focus. Hence NIV, "in Christ all the fullness of the Deity lives in bodily form," and GNB, "the full content of divine nature lives in Christ, in his humanity" (see also Lightfoot 180; Moule, *Colossians and Philemon* 92-94; Wall 110-13). In all this a common concern for access to the ultimate of reality is presupposed (Fowl 137); to be a Christian is to recognize Christ as the point and means of that access.

Not to be ignored is the further variation on the theme of "body," again no doubt in deliberate counterpoint with "the body of flesh" (2:11): in terms that foreshadow the Fourth Evangelist's theology of Christ's glorification, the embodiment of divine fullness is presented as one with the crucified body of flesh. To take the word as a reference to the body = the church (Masson 124; Lohse, *Colossians and Philemon* 101; Gnilka, *Kolosserbrief* 129; but see Best, *Body* 117-20; Aletti, *Épître aux Colossiens* 169) is a too simple solution which diminishes the richness of the play on the term (cf. Benoit, "Plèrôma" 145-49; though cf. also the amazing Eph. 1:22-23). Alternatively, that the word here already reflects the use of σῶμα in 2:17 (as Pokorný 122 in particular argues) is less likely since the latter is so unusual and could hardly be anticipated by the hearers; though doubtless the full impact of 2:17 depends on an awareness of the preceding "body" language (see also Wedderburn, *Theology* 37-38).

2:10 καὶ ἐστὲ ἐν αὐτῷ πεπληρωμένοι, ὅς ἐστιν ἡ κεφαλὴ πάσης ἀρχῆς καὶ ἐξουσίας. The immediate corollary to this understanding of Christ is that those "in Christ" (the twelfth occurrence; see on 1:2) share in that fullness. The language is, of course, rhetorical and hyperbolic (see also 2:9). It presumably means simply that in Christ they have been granted a completeness and fulfillment which they could not find or achieve anywhere else: "you have come to fullness of life in him" (RSV/NRSV); "he is able to bring their life to its destination" (Pokorný 123).[14] That is why any thought of seeking out higher or more fulfilling experiences is fanciful and self-delusive (but it is unclear

14. For those who take the "bodily" of 2:9 as a reference to the church the carryover of thought from 2:9 is even closer: "you (= the church) are fulfilled in him" (so Gnilka, *Kolosserbrief* 130). But that leaves 2:10a simply as a weaker variation or repetition of 2:9.

whether language current in the Colossian "philosophy" is echoed here). The tense ("to be" + perfect passive participle) indicates a state of fullness accomplished in the past and sustained since then. The implication, therefore, is that in receiving the tradition of Jesus as Christ and Lord and believing in(to) him (2:5-7), the Colossian Christians already had all that is necessary for fullness of life, unrestricted access to the divine power which will shape them, too, into the divine image (3:10). It is no contradiction to such thought that Eph. 3:19 can pray "that you may be filled with all the fullness of God," for such imagery can be both affirmative and hortatory (cf., e.g., Gal. 3:27 with Rom. 13:14); hence the equivalent balance between indicative and imperative in the next main section (3:3-5 and 10-12).

The language is inflated, but the cash value would come in the daily walk of conduct and relationships. As with the "philosophy" illustrated above (see on 2:8), concern with affairs of heaven usually had the consequences for everyday life very much in view. So here, too, the reaffirmation of Christ's headship over the cosmos (1:18a; but cf. Wolter 127), including the heavenly powers mentioned in the hymn (1:16), is explicitly stated with regard to "every rule and authority," not as a matter of idle cosmic speculation, but as a matter of vital interest to an understanding of the way heavenly forces determined earthly conduct. For these "rule(r)s and authorities" were presumably another way of speaking about the "elemental forces" (2:8), also understood as exercising rule and authority over and within the world of humanity (hence their names; see also on 1:16). To know that Christ was above the addressees and was their head (see on 1:18a) was therefore important, partly for the confidence with which other claims to access to such heavenly powers could be confronted and partly for the "full assurance of understanding" out of which they sought to live their own daily lives.

The resumption of the "head" imagery is a further element in the varied "body" theology which is such a mark of this letter. In particular, it is unlikely that Paul and Timothy felt any tension between this continued cosmic headship and the headship of the body (= church, 1:18a) resumed in 2:19. The point implicit in the "body" theology is precisely that a recognition of the "fullness of deity" in Christ enables a harmony between the cosmos and human society which would otherwise be impossible (since he is head of both).

2:11 ἐν ᾧ καὶ περιετμήθητε περιτομῇ ἀχειροποιήτῳ ἐν τῇ ἀπεκδύσει τοῦ σώματος τῆς σαρκός, ἐν τῇ περιτομῇ τοῦ Χριστοῦ. In what follows (2:11-15) the main thrust and chief emphases are clear, but the detail and the syntax allow a variety of interpretations. The principal difficulty for both translator and exegete is that the piling up of phrases seems excessive and unnecessarily redundant and encourages them to consider renderings which reduce the redundancy by broadening the focus of meaning. But the key to what the authors were after is probably to recognize that the redundancy is deliberate, that is, that they were using this technique precisely to focus with greater intensity on the significance of the act of redemption and reconciliation already spoken of (1:14, 20, 22). The impression of hymnic form is sustained (see the introduction to the comments on 2:8-15), with the language continuing to express something of the extravagance of worship and with the "in him" structuring maintained into 2:12, where it is supplemented with a sequence of συν- compounds (2:12-13). In short, 2:11-15 were probably intended as an elaborate attempt to describe the importance of what Christ accomplished on the cross and in his resurrection by means of a sequence of vivid metaphors (circumcision, burial and resurrection, death and giving life, forgiveness and cancellation of legal bond, public triumph).[15]

The linking "in whom" (ἐν ᾧ καί) introduces the first image: "you were circumcised with a circumcision not performed by human hand." Why this image? The answer depends on the significance of circumcision. Here at once we must note the almost inescapably Jewish dimension which the image introduces. The simple fact of the matter is that in the world of this time circumcision was regarded by both Jews and Gentiles as distinctively and characteristically Jewish. This is at first surprising since others were known to practice the rite (Egyptians and others: Herodotus 2.104.2-3; Strabo 17.2.5). But circumcision had always been central to Israel's self-understanding as the people of God (at least from the formulation of Gen. 17:9-14). And the Maccabean crisis had made it a crucial mark of national and religious identity, the mark which most clearly distinguished Judaism from Hellenism (1 Macc. 1:15, 48, 60-61; 2:46; 2 Macc. 6:9-10; Josephus, *Antiquities* 12:241). Thus Josephus saw circumcision as God's way of preventing Abraham's posterity "from mixing with others" (*Antiquities* 1:192). And the point was well taken by outsiders such as Tacitus: "They adopted circumcision to distinguish themselves from other peoples by this difference" (*Historiae* 5.5.2).

It is not surprising, then, that Paul could simply translate the Jew versus Gentile classification of the world into "circumcision" versus "uncircumcision" (Rom. 2:25-27; 3:30; 4:9-12; Gal. 2:7-8), each group defined by their most distinctive characteristic in relation to each other, circumcision providing the fundamental principle of classification. This perspective, be it also noted, is thoroughly Jewish. It was Jews who regarded circumcision as a positive factor which could serve as a badge of identity; for the typical Hellenist circumcision seemed more like a form of bodily mutilation (see R. G. Hall, *ABD* 1.1027). And it was certainly not Gentiles who chose to identify themselves as "the uncircumcision (foreskin)."

---

15. Pokorný 126-33 surprisingly picks out 2:12-13 as containing the argument of the entire epistle, thus giving undue prominence to two out of the sequence of metaphors.

This is the characteristically Jewish attitude which lies behind the other references to circumcision in Colossians. The disparaging note of 2:13 — "the uncircumcision of your flesh" — should not be taken as "the uncircumcision which is your flesh," with "flesh" understood as a moral category (NEB "morally uncircumcised," NIV "the uncircumcision of your sinful nature"; so most). Rather, it echoes the classic description of circumcision as marking God's covenant with Israel (Gen. 17:11-14: "So shall my covenant be in your flesh an everlasting covenant"), a characteristic echo in Pauline usage (Rom. 2:28; Gal. 6:12-13; Phil. 3:3-5). "The uncircumcision of your flesh" means simply "your status as Gentiles," primarily an ethnic distinction.[16] The thought is precisely that of Eph. 2:11: "Gentiles in the flesh, those called 'uncircumcision' by the so-called 'circumcision' made by human hand in the flesh." So, too, Col. 3:11 repeats the distinctively Pauline claim that with Christ "there is no 'circumcision' and 'uncircumcision,' " where again it is a matter of removing labels which categorized non-Jews into a disadvantaged status by definition, and where again it is circumcision versus noncircumcision which provided the primary and crucial differentiation.

These considerations immediately restrict our options in interpreting 2:11. Indeed, they leave us with only one or both of two answers: (1) The language simply reflects the strongly Jewish character of earliest Christianity, including the Pauline mission among Gentiles. So fundamental to Paul was the conviction that faith in Christ was the outworking of the promise to Abraham and of the covenant with Israel, and so deeply impressed on his formulation of the gospel had been his earlier disputes with his fellow Jews on the need for Gentiles to be circumcised (Gal. 2; 5–6; Rom. 4), that a thoroughly Pauline expression of the gospel was bound to use and echo the characteristic Pauline attitude to circumcision and spiritualization of circumcision. In that case, these references would tell us nothing of the "philosophy" which was in danger of leading the Colossians astray.

(2) However, the unusualness of the reference here indicates that it is not simply a matter of echoing older formulations, and the frequency with which the circumcision versus uncircumcision motif recurs in Colossians, and the intensity of 2:11 itself, is probably best explained by the hypothesis that circumcision was indeed a factor in the threatening situation in Colossae. Moreover, the evidence clearly indicates that this factor included Jews as such, with their distinctive attitude to Gentiles as "the uncircumcision" (2:13; 3:11). Such language cannot be explained on the assumption that the rite of circumcision had been abstracted from Judaism and thrown as a separate item into some proto-Gnostic, syncretistic melting pot of ideas and

16. This is recognized by GNB; cf. JB/NJB; Abbott 253; Masson 127 and n. 3; Wright, *Colossians and Philemon* 109; Harris 106.

rites (cf. Foerster 73 against Lohse, *Colossians and Philemon* 102; Lindemann, *Kolosserbrief* 42; and see p. 33 n. 40 above). For the attitude expressed in the distinction of circumcision versus uncircumcision is one of ethnic identity, and not some individualistic or syncretistic ritualism.

At the same time the contrast with Galatians at this point cannot be ignored. Here there is no polemic against circumcision as such (contrast Gal. 5:2-12). We cannot deduce, therefore, a form of vigorous Jewish or Christian-Jewish proselytizing in Colossae (as in Galatians and Philippians 3); there is no evidence of strong pressure being brought on the Colossians to be circumcised "in the flesh." At most we need only envisage a form of Jewish apologetic (rather than evangelism) in which the rationale of circumcision was explained, perhaps as Philo does in *De specialibus legibus* 1:1-11 and *Quaestiones in Genesin* 3:46-62. This at least would explain the double feature in the letter's treatment of circumcision: on the one hand it echoes the typically Jewish distinctiveness as "the circumcision" over against "the uncircumcision" (Gentile "uncircumcision" is still understood as a disadvantaged state); on the other hand the authors use circumcision as a positive image. In short, in view of the lightness of the polemic and the positiveness of the understanding of the imagery of circumcision, all that may be implied or envisaged here is some debate with Jews in Colossae (probably not just Christian Jews) on the spiritual significance of circumcision.

What then is meant by "you were circumcised with a circumcision not made with hand"? The adjective ἀχειροποίητος clearly rules out literal circumcision (NEB/REB "not in a physical sense"). For though it occurs only in the New Testament (Mark 14:58; 2 Cor. 5:1; and here) its meaning is obvious, as the opposite of χειροποίητος ("made with hands"), used characteristically in the LXX of idols (E. Lohse, *TDNT* 9.436). It denotes what human hands cannot make, but only natural or divine agency (see Schweizer, *Colossians* 140), and so in this context "wrought by God" or "spiritual."[17] Here, then, the language is presumably an adaptation of the long-standing recognition in Jewish circles that circumcision "in the flesh" had to be matched by circumcision of the heart (e.g., Deut. 10:16; Jer. 4:4; 1QpHab 11:13; 1QS 5:5; *Jubilees* 1:23; Philo, *De specialibus legibus* 1:305). That is to say, it probably contains a reference to conversion ("you were circumcised," aorist tense), the circumcision of the heart wrought by the Spirit, referred to elsewhere in Paul (Rom. 2:28-29; 2 Cor. 3:3; Phil. 3:3;

17. It is just possible that the very unusual ἀχειροποίητος here reflects a local Jewish apologetic (cf. P. W. van der Horst, "A New Altar of a Godfearer?" *JJS* 43 [1992] 32-37, reprinted in his *Hellenism — Judaism — Christianity: Essays on Their Interaction* [Kampen: Kok, 1994] 65-72); for all the Jewish insistence on the ἀχειροποίητος character of their cultural religious claims (God as one and unrepresentable by a χειροποίητον idol) their continued high regard for the very χειροποίητον ritual of circumcision ran counter to their apologetic and undermined it in some degree.

also *Odes of Solomon* 11:2; *Gospel of Thomas* 53).[18] However, given what follows, including the strong sequence of συν- compounds (2:12-13), it is also possible that what was in mind was the image of Christ's death on the cross as itself a kind of circumcision in which believers have been included. In that case we might have expected the coining of a further compound, in typical Pauline style, συμπεριετμήθητε. But equally it might have been thought that the remainder of the verse made the point clearly enough.

There is a similar ambiguity in the next phrase, "in the stripping off of the body of flesh." Ἀπέκδυσις is not attested outside Paul's writings, but is obviously drawn from the verb meaning "take off, strip off (clothes)" (as in 2:15). The lack of an αὐτοῦ, "his flesh," would normally indicate that the phrase should be rendered "the body of the (= your) flesh." But all the "flesh" references so far have denoted physical flesh (1:22, 24; 2:1, 5), and the most obvious way to take the combination "body of flesh" is once again as a way of emphasizing the physicality of the body (see on 1:22).[19] "Stripping off the body of flesh," therefore, can hardly mean anything other than literal death (cf. again 1:22). If then the phrase was chosen precisely to emphasize the physical nature of the death, it is difficult to see it being referred primarily to something that had already happened to the readers. For there is no suggestion that believers have already stripped off the flesh or the body of flesh (to the contrary, 2:1, 5).[20]

More likely the phrase is an adaptation of the description of physical circumcision — a stripping off of the flesh (of the foreskin) — applied to Jesus' death in deliberate echo of 1:22: in this case the flesh which was stripped away

18. Despite the assumption of many (Dibelius, *Kolosser, Epheser, Philemon* 30; Moule, *Colossians and Philemon* 94; Houlden 189 — "for a believer in Christ, circumcision means baptism"; Ernst, *Philipper, Philemon, Kolosser, Epheser* 202; Lona 149, 151-53; Gnilka, *Kolosserbrief* 131; Bruce, *Colossians, Philemon, and Ephesians* 103; O. Betz, *EDNT* 3.80; W. Rebell, *EDNT* 3.464; Pokorný 124 — "to begin with, the writer explains that baptism is the true circumcision"; Wolter 130 — *"Taufbeschneidung"*; Aletti, *Épître aux Colossiens* 172), it is unlikely that a reference to baptism as such is intended. Despite Gnilka, *Theologie* 345, Paul nowhere rejects circumcision on the grounds that Christians have a more effective ritual act (Dunn, *Baptism* 153-54). Cf. also Wedderburn, *Theology* 49-50.

19. This is lost sight of by several translations which seem to want to avoid using "flesh" at all cost and which produce unjustifiably tendentious translations (NEB "lower nature," REB "old nature," NJB "your natural self," NIV "sinful nature," GNB "sinful self"). Wright, *Colossians and Philemon* 106, leaves the phrase itself much too far behind when he translates "in the stripping off of the old human solidarities."

20. This conclusion represents a change of mind from my earlier *Baptism* 153, though it strengthens its argument that the imagery of circumcision spoke directly of spiritual realities and not of baptism. In *Baptism* I followed the consensus (e.g., Lightfoot 182; Masson 126-27; Tannehill 49; Schweizer, *Colossians* 143; Wolter 131) that "body of flesh" was in effect synonymous with "body of sin" (Rom. 6:6) and "body of death" (Rom. 7:24) — "a slogan of the false teachers [about transcending one's physical body in mystical experience] which Paul has turned against them" (Fowl 140-41).

was the whole physical/fleshly body.[21] We might translate, "in the stripping off of the body, the flesh/as the flesh." This likelihood is strengthened when we look ahead to 2:15 (where the equivalent verb is used, "strip off") and realize that we are caught up in a further play on the body of Christ theme. On the cross there was a double "stripping off": his physical body in death and the rulers and authorities in triumph (see on 2:15). If there is a moral note in "flesh" here, it probably reflects a variation of Paul's Adam christology at this point. It was not simply "his" flesh that Christ stripped off, but the flesh of the first Adam (cf. Rom. 8:3), representing "all things" in their domination by the powers, this being necessary before he could assume his Adamic reign over "all things" (cf. 1 Cor. 15:27, 45, 50). A cosmic circumcision of human flesh was a necessary preliminary to cosmic rule.

The final phrase, "in the circumcision of Christ," is best seen, then, simply as a summary expression of the larger imagery of the preceding phrases. That is, what is in view is not primarily a circumcision effected by Christ (NEB/REB; NIV; GNB; e.g., Scott 45; Pokorný 124-25; in the earlier Paul the "circumcision of the heart" is always attributed to the Spirit — Rom. 2:29; 2 Cor. 3:3; Phil. 3:3) but a concise description of the death of Christ under the metaphor of circumcision. It is clearly implied, of course, from the first phrase, that conversion-initiation could consequently be understood as a sharing in that circumcision, but it is precisely a sharing in *his* circumcision-death, not an independent act of Christians' own circumcision-death. It is because they share in a body which transmutes, as it were, from cosmic body ("head over all rule and authority," 2:10), through body of flesh done to death, to his body the church, that their conversion has cosmic and eschatological implications. And even more astonishing corollaries can be drawn out for the church subsequently in Eph. 1:22-23.

2:12 συνταφέντες αὐτῷ ἐν τῷ βαπτισμῷ, ἐν ᾧ καὶ συνηγέρθητε διὰ τῆς πίστεως τῆς ἐνεργείας τοῦ θεοῦ τοῦ ἐγείραντος αὐτὸν ἐκ νεκρῶν. The second metaphor for what was accomplished by means of the cross is burial and resurrection. The sequence of συν- compounds (2:12-13) is characteristically Pauline,[22] and its beginning clearly echoes the earlier and most power-

---

21. So also Moule, *Colossians and Philemon* 95-96; G. R. Beasley-Murray, *Baptism* 152-53; R. P. Martin, *Colossians and Philemon* 82-83; O'Brien, *Colossians, Philemon* 116-17; Yates, *Colossians* 42. Wolter 130-31 notes that the idea of the body or flesh as a "garment" of the soul or of something "put off" was quite familiar in Greek and Jewish thought (e.g., Philo, *Legum Allegoriae* 2.55; *Quis rerum divinarum heres* 54; *De fuga et inventione* 110; *Quaestiones et solutiones in Genesin* 1.53; *2 Enoch* 22:8-9). Failure to appreciate the allusion to circumcision and the force of "body" and "flesh" thus combined (see on 1:22), which retains the neutral force of σῶμα as such and makes possible the positive play on σῶμα which is such a feature of the letter, must lie behind Bornkamm's otherwise surprising judgment that "stripping off the body of flesh" is wholly un-Jewish and must presuppose a Gnostic context of thought ("Heresy" 128).

22. See, e.g., my *Romans* 313; on the σὺν Χριστῷ formula and for bibliography see, e.g., Lohse, *Colossians and Philemon* 104-5 and n. 76; O'Brien, *Colossians, Philemon* 169-71.

ful sequence of such compounds in Rom. 6:4-6 (συνετάφημεν αὐτῷ διὰ τοῦ βαπτίσματος . . .), though whether we should speak of Paul reworking a familiar theme or of a close collaborator echoing his master's voice is less clear. The imagery is forceful, of sinking below the waters of baptism as a kind of burial. Baptism, presumably by immersion, represented mimetically the commitment to enter the tomb with Jesus after he has been taken down from the cross. Since burial was understood as the conclusion of the event of dying,[23] this commitment meant the enacted willingness to identify oneself with the complete event of Jesus' death. The passive tense indicates also the yielding of those being baptized to the baptizer as indicative of their surrender to God. Here again the initial focus is on the event of conversion-initiation, but also in view is the effectiveness of what Christ's death accomplished. It is because his death was a kind of circumcision of old humanity (cf. 3:9) that such an identification with it engages its spiritual energy in effective operation in believers' lives, both individually and corporately.

To what extent we can speak already of a "baptismal theology" or a "sacramental theology" here is also unclear. Certainly the power of the symbolic, ritual action is in view: baptism as the means by which or at least occasion in which this powerful spiritual conjunction ("buried with him") takes place. And a reference back to baptism would be important for a community which needed to affirm its boundaries (cf. Meeks, *Urban Christians* 166-67). But the passage is not intended as an exposition of baptism; "in baptism" is mentioned almost incidentally in a sequence of vigorous metaphors.[24] Moreover, it is doubtful whether we can yet speak of baptism as accomplishing spiritual circumcision (the preceding metaphor),[25] since that is always linked directly with the action of the Spirit (see on 2:11), usually remembered because of its vivid experiential character, without any reference to baptism (e.g., Rom. 5:5; 8:15-16; 1 Cor. 2:12; 2 Cor. 1:22; Gal. 3:2-5; 1 Thes. 1:5-6; see further my *Baptism*). And the prominence given in the exposition above to the idea of baptism as expressive of the commitment of the one being baptized is supported by the next clause, which links a second συν- passive verb with faith as the means (διὰ τῆς πίστεως, equivalent to the διὰ τοῦ βαπτίσματος of Rom. 6:4) by which its action was accomplished.

Nor is there any need to invoke precedent in contemporary mystery cults to explain how a powerful symbolic action could have appeared in

---

23. "The event of dying, of departure from this world, was first really concluded by burial" (E. Stommel, cited by Schnackenburg, *Baptism* 34; similarly Wedderburn, *Baptism* 368-69).

24. Against, e.g., Larsson 80-84; Pokorný 133; and MacDonald 143 it needs to be pointed out that the subject of the section is not baptism.

25. Cf. Conzelmann 144: "baptism actualizes this event for us" (cited also by Gnilka, *Kolosserbrief* 134).

Christianity (*pace* Argall 18-20). In point of fact, in the little we know of the mysteries, there is nothing quite like baptism as an initiatory (as distinct from preparatory) rite, and there seems to be no clear idea of identification with the cult deity. In other words, the two vital features in 2:12 lack obvious parallel in the mysteries (see further my *Romans* 308-11; Wedderburn, *Baptism*).[26] In contrast we need look no further than a Baptist tradition which spoke of water baptism as a metaphor for the action of the Spirit (Mark 1:8 pars.) and a Jesus tradition which spoke of Jesus' suffering and baptism (of death) as something which his disciples could share (Mark 10:38-39). If Jesus spoke of his coming death as a shared baptism, it is little surprise that his disciples should speak of their baptism as a sharing in his death.

The matching metaphor is that of resurrection — resurrection, that is, with Christ. The initial ἐν ᾧ looks at first as though it should be referred to baptism ("in which" or "by which"; so most translations).[27] This is an understandable deduction, since it appears natural to associate sinking under the water with burial and rising out from the water with resurrection. The problem is that the term "baptism" did not yet denote the whole action, but properly speaking only the act of immersion as such.[28] And in the closest parallel (Rom. 6:4) it evidently did not occur to Paul to make any such association between Christ's resurrection and baptism; the association is exclusively with burial. What appears obvious to us, with a long history of sacramental theology,[29] was then not yet obvious.

A further factor in 2:12 is that ἐν ᾧ καί is the fourth of the sequence of "in him, in whom" phrases around which this hymn-like snatch has been composed, matching the ἐν ᾧ καί of 2:11. When set out in lines, as I have above, it becomes clearer that βαπτισμῷ is best seen, then, not as the antecedent of ἐν ᾧ, but as the end of the preceding segment, with ἐν ᾧ serving as the final structural link back to "Christ" in 2:8. The resulting combination of "in him" and "with him" is stylistically but not theologically awkward: they are both common and overlapping ideas in Paul anyway; and precisely

---

26. Attridge 483-89 claims to find in several Nag Hammadi texts "a theology of or rationale for baptism, a rationale that conceives baptism as a transformation of the baptizand into a heavenly state that enables 'vision' of the divine such as that accorded to angels"; but it is hardly clear that baptism played a significant part in the Colossian philosophy.

27. This is the majority view in commentaries written in English (O'Brien, *Colossians, Philemon* 118-19, and Gardner are exceptions); but elsewhere opinion is strongly against it (see my *Baptism* 154-55 and n. 7), with Schweizer, *Colossians* 145-46, and Lona 156-58 exceptions the other way.

28. Schweizer, *Colossians* 145 n. 33, notes that Josephus uses βαπτίζειν frequently in the sense " drown" or "dive in," as also of dipping hyssop in a stream and in the passive of a ship sinking. Contrast Meeks, "Body" 213: "the picture of baptism as initiating into a life 'above,' " dramatizing "the believers' anticipatory enthronement in heaven."

29. Already in the fourth-century *Apostolic Constitutions* 3.17.

the same awkward combination occurs in the parallel Eph. 2:6 — συνήγειρεν
. . . ἐν Χριστῷ Ἰησοῦ.

The idea that Christ's resurrection was something also shared by believers is, again, a natural corollary to the idea of sharing his burial. Here, however, we can see that something of a development has taken place. For prior to this Paul saw such a sharing in Christ's resurrection as belonging to the future, part of the "eschatological not yet," so that the Christian life could be understood as a kind of long, drawn-out process between Christ's death (in which they [had] already shared; hence the perfect tenses in Gal. 2:19 and 6:14) and Christ's resurrection (sharing in which would mark the completion of the process of salvation; Rom. 6:5; 8:11; 1 Cor. 15:47-49; Phil. 3:10, 21). But here, as in 3:1 and as with the preceding verb, the tense is aorist passive; that is, for the author of Colossians, resurrection with Christ also belongs to the "already" of Christian beginnings. That of itself does not mean that the formulation is post-Pauline (cf. Percy, *Probleme* 109-13): Paul was quite capable of such variations, as with other metaphors like redemption (cf. Rom. 3:24 with 8:23) and adoption (cf. Rom. 8:15 with 8:23; cf. Moule, "New Life" 484-85). Nor need we assume that such a variation meant that Paul's theology of an ongoing sharing in Christ's sufferings was being abandoned (see on 1:24).[30]

In fact, the shift in emphasis is in line with the loftier cosmic vision of the letter; that is, it reflects a still higher evaluation of what happened on the cross. That event meant not only that the sentence of death on the old epoch, its rule(r)s and its practices, had already been passed, but also that believers were able to share already in the resurrection life of the new epoch. The reason for this double emphasis on shared death and shared resurrection probably becomes clear in the parenesis beginning at 2:20.[31] That is to say, it was evidently thought necessary to draw in the new emphasis as a way of encouraging positive embrace of the power of the new creation and not just renunciation of the old (note 2:20; 3:1, 5, 9-10, 12).[32] In the event, then, the shift in emphasis does not amount to much (cf. O'Brien, *Colossians, Philemon* 120): it strengthens the force of the indicative (what God has already done in Christ), but it does so as a means of strengthening the resolve necessary if the imperative is to be obeyed and the work of salvation completed (cf. Lona 164-66).

---

30. Contrast G. Sellin, " 'Die Auferstehung ist schon geschehen.' Zur Spiritualisierung apokalyptischer Terminologie im Neuen Testament," *NovT* 25 (1983) 220-37 (here 230-32).

31. Since the assertion that "the resurrection is already past" is treated as an error and usually attributed to a form of proto-Gnosticism (2 Tim. 2:18; cf. 1 Cor. 15:12; see also Pokorný 130) we may deduce that such a Gnostic emphasis was *not* prominent in the Colossian "philosophy" (but cf. Conzelmann 145 and n. 28).

32. Cf. Wolter 133: the author seeks "to immunize the community against the bacillus of uncertainty of salvation."

The final phrase, "through faith in the effective working of God who raised him from the dead," like ἐν τῷ βαπτισμῷ in the preceding clause, maintains the balance between what happened in cross and resurrection and its appropriation in the believers' present. It is the openness of faith to divine grace, the commitment of mind and life to that which is confessed about the resurrection, that makes it possible for faith to serve as the conduit through which the divine energy (without which all human endeavor would be in vain) flows to energize the commitment and make more effective its translation into action. The divine working is the same (cf. the parallel with Rom. 8:11), and its proof is the resurrection of Christ. The "faith" formula is the more customary Pauline πίστις + genitive = "faith in" (Abbott 252; see further on 1:4 and 2:5). For ἐνέργεια see on 1:29 and cf. Eph. 1:19.

"God who raised him from the dead" is a piece of confessional formula regularly echoed in Paul (Rom. 4:24; 8:11; 10:9; 1 Cor. 6:14; 15:15; 2 Cor. 4:14; Gal. 1:1; 1 Thes. 1:10; Eph. 1:20; Kramer 20-26; Wengst, *Formeln* 27-48). As such it reminds us how fundamental belief in the resurrection of Christ was for the first Christians. Moreover, as itself an essentially apocalyptic category (initially formulated in Dan. 12:2), "resurrection" is a further reminder of how much this letter was influenced and shaped by a Jewish apocalyptic thought world.

2:13 καὶ ὑμᾶς νεκροὺς ὄντας [ἐν] τοῖς παραπτώμασιν καὶ τῇ ἀκροβυστίᾳ τῆς σαρκὸς ὑμῶν, συνεζωοποίησεν ὑμᾶς σὺν αὐτῷ, χαρισάμενος ἡμῖν πάντα τὰ παραπτώματα. The third metaphor drawn in to describe the transition effected by the cross and resurrection and by the Colossians' participation therein is death and (new) life. The impression that it jars slightly with the preceding metaphor (conversion-initiation as the event of dying; pre-Christian condition as the state of already being dead) is of little consequence. With the kaleidoscope of metaphors which Paul used to express these fundamental transformations (of cosmos and history as well as of individuals) some overlap and inconsistency was inevitable. Confusion only arises if the metaphors are treated as literal statements. The jarring, however, is not so great as at first appears.[33] For talk of God (now the subject) making alive the dead is another way of speaking of the resurrection, as the New Testament parallels show (John 5:21; Rom. 8:11; 1 Cor. 15:22, 45; 1 Pet. 3:18); and its formulation in a further συν- compound ("he made you alive together with him") is simply a variation of the preceding συν- compound ("you were raised together [with him]").[34] Lona 96-98 also notes that

---

33. Wedderburn, *Baptism* 63, notes that death as a figure for a life of wickedness was quite familiar in Stoic and Hellenistic Jewish thought.

34. We might also note that circumcision as a metaphor for conversion and ζωοποίησις are both explicitly attributed to the Spirit in the New Testament (cf. Rom. 2:28-29 and Phil. 3:3 with John 6:63 and 2 Cor. 3:6).

the thought is structured on the typical Pauline "once — now" formula, even though νυνί is lacking.

More to the point, the confession of God as he "who gives life to the dead" was a typical definition of God in contemporary Judaism (*Shemoneh 'Esreh* 2; *Joseph and Asenath* 20:7; hence Paul's use of it in Rom. 4:17; also John 5:21),[35] an application no doubt of the more basic recognition that God "gives life to all things" (Neh. 9:6; *Joseph and Asenath* 8:3, 9; 12:1). Initially this confession presumably was said in reference to the resurrection, as in *Shemoneh 'Esreh* and the main New Testament parallels (cf. also Tob. 13:2; Wis. 16:13; 2 Macc. 7:22-23; *Testament of Gad* 4:6); the image of being brought up from Sheol as a metaphor of deliverance from despair (Pss. 30:3; 88:3-6; Jonah 2:6; 1QH 3:19) is an earlier version. But *Joseph and Asenath* 20:7 shows how readily the confession of God as he "who gives life to the dead" could be adapted to the idea of Gentiles as living in a state of death and being made alive by conversion to proselyte status.

It is this last that is the governing thought here. The "you" are the Gentile believers in Colossae (as more explicitly in the immediate parallel in Eph. 2:1-2, 11). Their "being dead" refers to their status outside the covenant made by God with Israel (cf. again Eph. 2:12). That is to say, their "transgressions" (παραπτώματα, usually violations of God's commands) would be those referred to already in a similar passage (1:21), the transgressions of the law that from a Jewish perspective were typical of lawless Gentiles (see on 1:21). The Jewish perspective is put beyond question with the complementary phrase "you being dead (NEB/REB "although you were dead") in . . . the uncircumcision of your flesh."[36]

The significance of this should not be lost sight of, especially in view of the indications, some of them already noted (see on 2:11), that the most likely threat from an alternative philosophy in Colossae was perceived to be basically Jewish in character (see also on 2:16-18, 21-22 and pp. 29-35 above). The significance is that Paul does not attempt to avoid such a Jewish characterization and perspective; he makes no attempt, as it were, to outflank the alternative philosophy by ignoring or striking clear of the Jewish character of Christianity's message. On the contrary, he reaffirms the Christian-Jewish starting point, that Israel was in an advantaged position over other nations by virtue of God's choice of Israel to be his special people. The difference is that the disadvantaged state of "uncircumcision" has been remedied by a "circumcision not performed by human hand" (2:11) rather

---

35. "Around the beginning of our era 'He who gives life to the dead' had become all but a definition of God in Judaism" (C. Burchard, *OTP* 2.234 n.).

36. Despite Wolter 134, "flesh" is not to be understood here as a power which compels individuals to sin (cf. Rom. 7:5, 14); the phrase "uncircumcision of your flesh" functions in a quite different context. See on 2:11.

than by "circumcision in the flesh." The point, however, is not made with anything like the sharpness of the polemic in Galatians, indicating a situation in Colossae in which the proselytizing option was not being posed with anything like the same forcefulness as earlier in Galatia. Nevertheless, it is important to note again that the categories of debate remain Jewish through and through, with God as the initiator and subject of the saving action throughout (or at least to 2:15).

The final clause, "having forgiven us all our transgressions," adds the same qualification as the concluding phrase in 1:14. The difference is only that a rather more Pauline verb is used, χαρίζομαι ("remit, forgive, pardon"), which we find in Paul in this sense at least in 2 Cor. 2:7-10 (cf. Luke 7:42-43; *Testament of Job* 43:1; Josephus, *Antiquities* 6:144; K. Berger, *EDNT* 3.457; see also Col. 3:13 and Phm. 22). The awkward transition to "us" (see n. 3) is characteristically Pauline, betraying here (as in Eph. 2:5) an element of self-correction: it constitutes not a denial that such transgressions are to be attributed to Gentiles but rather a recognition that all, Jews as well, are equally guilty of such transgressions and equally in need of forgiveness. The point is not developed here, but behind it we can see the fuller argument of Rom. 1:18–3:20; 5:12-21 (where "transgression" occurs six times); 7:7-12.

2:14 ἐξαλείψας τὸ καθ' ἡμῶν χειρόγραφον τοῖς δόγμασιν ὃ ἦν ὑπεναντίον ἡμῖν, καὶ αὐτὸ ἦρκεν ἐκ τοῦ μέσου προσηλώσας αὐτὸ τῷ σταυρῷ. The fourth metaphor is quite different again. It is drawn from the legal world. Χειρόγραφον, only here in the New Testament, meant literally a document written by the person responsible, a holograph, so "receipt," as in its only occurrence in the LXX (Tob. 5:3 and 9:5). But here it has the further sense of "a certificate of indebtedness, bond," as in *Testament of Job* 11:11 and *Life of Aesop* 122 (in A.-M. Denis, *Concordance Grecque des Pseudepigraphes d'Ancien Testament* [Louvain-la-Neuve: Institut Orientaliste, 1987] 875 and 908; see further MM). The metaphor is probably adapted to the earlier Jewish idea of a heavenly book of the living (Exod. 32:32-33; Ps. 69:28; Dan. 12:1; Rev. 3:5) as developed in apocalyptic circles into that of books wherein deeds of good and evil were recorded with a view to the final judgment (Dan. 7:10?; *1 Enoch* 89:61-64, 70-71; 108:7; *Apocalypse of Zephaniah* 7:1-8; *Testament of Abraham* (A) 12:7-18; 13:9-14; (B) 10:7–11:7; *2 Enoch* 53:2-3; Rev. 20:12). In *Apocalypse of Zephaniah* 3:6-9 and *Apocalypse of Paul* 17, *chirographum* (= χειρόγραφον) itself is used for these heavenly books (M. R. James, *The Apocryphal New Testament* [Oxford: Clarendon, 1924] 534; E. Lohse, *TDNT* 9.435 n. 2; Sappington 100-108, 216-17).[37] This is most obviously the background of thought here, with

---

37. For later rabbinic development of the theme see Str-B 3:628; but this is not to be simply assumed as the background to the thought here, as many do.

καθ' ἡμῶν ("against us") confirming that the document in question was one of condemnation, that is, presumably the record of their "transgressions" (repeated for emphasis in the following relative clause), "which was opposed, hostile (ὑπεναντίον, another Pauline *hapax*) to us."[38]

Quite what the intervening and awkward τοῖς δόγμασιν adds to the picture is not so clear.[39] However, in the context the δόγματα must be formal "decrees or ordinances or regulations" (BAGD s.v. δόγμα 1; *NDIEC* 4.146), "binding statutes" (Lohse, *Colossians and Philemon* 109), "legal demands" (RSV/NRSV, REB). They presumably, therefore, refer to that which constituted the record of transgression as condemnatory ("against us," "hostile to us"). That is, they must refer to the divinely decreed ordering of cosmos and society and judgment consequent upon such behavior. The thought, in other words, is close to that of Rom. 1:32. In Hellenistic Judaism these "decrees, regulations" were, not surprisingly, the law, the commandments of Moses (3 Macc. 1:3; Philo, *Legum allegoriae* 1:55; *De gigantibus* 52; Josephus, *Contra Apionem* 1:42). Thus, although τὸ καθ' ἡμῶν χειρόγραφον itself cannot be identified with the law as such (as by Abbott 255; Wright, *Colossians and Philemon* 112; the otherwise unarticulated dative, τοῖς δόγμασιν, leaves the precise relationship obscure), behind it lie the decrees of the law giving the χειρόγραφον its condemnatory force (*pace* Weiss, "Law" 310-12; cf. the clearer formulation in Eph. 2:15, the only other occurrence of δόγμα in the Pauline corpus). At all events this probably alludes to the halakhic rulings about to be denounced in 2:16, 21-22, which includes talk of "judgment" (2:16) and uses the verbal equivalent (δογματίζω in 2:20; Lightfoot 185; Dibelius, *Kolosser, Epheser, Philemon* 32; Schweizer, *Colossians* 150-51; Gnilka, *Kolosserbrief* 139; Sappington 218-20; Yates, *Colossians* 48; cf. N. Walter, *EDNT* 1.340; Aletti, *Épître aux Colossiens* 179).

This is important, since the act of redemption on the cross under this imagery effects a wiping out of the χειρόγραφον. The verb ἐξαλείφω is the natural one to use in the context, since it denotes the erasure of an entry in

---

38. Walter, "Kol. 2:14"; also *EDNT* 3.464, makes the unnecessary and less persuasive suggestion that the χειρόγραφον is the sinner's own confession of guilt (*Schuldbekenntnis*). Carr, "Notes" 492-96; *Angels* 55-58, suggests a reference to penitential *stelae* set up to confess guilt (a practice attested in Asia from the early second century); but the key term here is lacking, and such a reference does not fit most naturally with the term itself or its accompanying imagery, namely erasure (ἐξαλείψας) and nailing to the cross (προσηλώσας κτλ.). For a recent survey of alternative interpretations see Yates, *Colossians* 45-48; more fully his "Col. 2:14."

39. For attempts to explain the awkwardness see, e.g., Masson 128 n. 1; Lohse, *Colossians and Philemon* 109-10; and Harris 108-9. The old suggestion that "a pact with the devil" is in view is still defended by Lohmeyer 116-17, but has no contemporary support. Lindemann, *Kolosserbrief* 44, attempts an explanation in traditional Lutheran terms: "Our self-accusation (χειρόγραφον) is based on our opinion that in our relation to God we must commit ourselves to norms, to firm prescriptions" (cf. NEB "the bond which pledged us to the decrees of the law").

a book, and is so used in several of the above contexts (Exod. 32:32-33; Ps. 69:28; *1 Enoch* 108:3; *Apocalypse of Zephaniah* 7:8 [*chirographum* as the object]; *Testament of Abraham* [E] 11:10; Rev. 3:5). The expunging of the record confirms that none of these transgressions is any longer held "against us." That does not mean, however, that the underlying decrees or regulations cease to have force, that is, that the law no longer functions as God's yardstick of right and judgment; there is no contradiction here with Rom. 2:12-16. It is simply that the record of the transgressions has been erased — another way of saying "he forgave us all our transgressions" (cf. Martin, *Colossians and Philemon* 83-85; for a review of the range of interpretations see Aletti, *Épître aux Colossiens* 179-81).

How this was done is vividly described within the imagery being used. He "took away, removed, destroyed" (BAGD s.v. αἴρω 4)[40] the record of transgression. And he did so "by nailing it to the cross," another way of saying "by crucifying it" (BAGD s.v. προσηλόω). There may be a play on the practice of attaching a crucified man's indictment to his cross to indicate to onlookers what his crime was (cf. Mark 15:26; Dibelius, *Kolosser, Epheser, Philemon* 31). But that would hardly be described as "removing" the indictment. The thought is rather of the indictment itself being destroyed by means of crucifixion, as though it was the indictment which was itself nailed to the cross in execution.[41] The play, then, is rather with the thought of Christ as himself the condemnatory bond and his death as its destruction. The metaphor is convoluted, but presumably reflects again the idea of Christ's death as a sin offering and thus of Christ as embodying the sins of the offerer and destroying them in his death.[42] Once again we should just note that it is not the law which is thought of as thus destroyed, but rather its particular condemnation (χειρόγραφον) of transgressions, absorbed in the sacrificial death of the Christ (cf. Rom. 8:3).

2:15 ἀπεκδυσάμενος τὰς ἀρχὰς καὶ τὰς ἐξουσίας ἐδειγμάτισεν ἐν παρρησίᾳ, θριαμβεύσας αὐτοὺς ἐν αὐτῷ. The fifth and final metaphor to describe the significance of the cross is a complete reversal of the imagery of the cross in the precedingverse. From the idea of the cross as a symbol of destruction, the thought is transformed into the image of public triumph.

---

40. ἐκ τοῦ μέσου, "from the midst," simply strengthens the verb ("removed out of the way, completely") and was a familiar idiom (examples in Lohse, *Colossians and Philemon* 110 nn. 121, 122).

41. Cf. *Gospel of Truth* 20:24-25: "he put on that book; he was nailed to a tree." *Gospel of Truth* 20:24-34, as Bruce, *Colossians, Philemon, and Ephesians* 110 n. 92 points out, seems to be an early Valentinian interpretation of this section of Colossians (see also Yates, "Gnosis" 61-62).

42. Cf. Blanchette; Bandstra, *Law* 158-63; R. P. Martin, *Colossians and Philemon* 85-86; Schweizer, *Colossians* 149; for the theology see my "Paul's Understanding of the Death of Jesus as Sacrifice," in *Sacrifice and Redemption: Durham Essays in Theology,* ed. S. W. Sykes (Cambridge: Cambridge University, 1991) 35-56.

The first clause is somewhat puzzling. The verb ἀπεκδύω is the cognate of the noun ἀπέκδυσις, which appears in 2:11, and is repeated in 3:9. It is most naturally understood as an intensive form of the more widely used ἐκδύω, "strip, take off" or in the middle voice (ἐκδύομαι) "undress oneself," as indeed is confirmed by 2:11 and 3:9, as well as by the occasional possibly contemporary use (*Testament Abraham* 17:12; Josephus, *Antiquities* 6.330 v.l.; see also on 3:9). The same understanding here would result in the ungainly image of God stripping off (like a set of clothes) the rulers and authorities.[43] Or should we assume that unconsciously the subject has shifted to Christ himself, thus giving more weight to the middle form (so Lightfoot 183, 187; Moule, *Colossians and Philemon* 100-101; Hanson, *Studies* 8-10)? Such a change of subject would be more easily explained if these clauses were quoting from some preformed hymnic material in praise of Christ (see the introduction to the comments on 2:8-15). The unresolved problems have encouraged commentators to regard the middle as active in force, meaning "disarm, despoil" (BDF §316.1; BAGD s.v. 2; M. Lattke, *EDNT* 1.409; NIV, REB; see, e.g., discussion in Abbott 258-61; Percy, *Probleme* 95-97; Bruce, *Colossians, Philemon, and Ephesians* 107 n. 82; Gnilka, *Kolosserbrief* 141-42; Sappington 209-12).[44] But this meaning is not attested for some time yet, and, more significantly, the early Greek commentators seem to have followed the more obvious sense of the middle (taking Christ as the subject; cf. also *Gospel of Truth* 20:30-31: "having stripped himself of the perishable rags"), with the interpretation "despoil" not clearly understood prior to Severianus Gabalensis in the late fourth or early fifth century (*PGL* s.v.).[45] We should therefore probably stick with the most natural meaning ("stripped off"), despite its awkwardness (see particularly Lightfoot 187-89).

The image then has to be understood as an extension of the cosmic vision of the earlier hymn (1:15-20) and a further variation on the "body" metaphor. The spiritual powers spoken of there (see on 1:16) could be likened to a kind of garment draped over the cosmos, lying upon it and dominating it (cf. Philo, *De fuga et inventione* 108-10 — the cosmos as garment of the Word; *De vita Mosis* 2.117-35 — the different features of the high priest's

43. It is most natural to take "the rulers and authorities" as the object of the verb, given the flexibility of the imagery (cf. 3:9-10; Gal. 3:27). A repetition of the idea of "stripping off the body of flesh" (2:11) is still less appropriate in the immediate context, including the suggestion of an allusion to Colossian talk of " 'stripping off the flesh' in mystical visionary experiences" (Yates, *Colossians* 52). The attempt to tie the metaphor to the image of the triumph ("the triumphator divests himself of his battle dress"), with the metaphor reduced to the sense "preparing himself" (Carr, *Angels* 61), simply adds to the awkwardness of the text (cf. Aletti, *Épître aux Colossiens* 181-83).

44. Lohmeyer 119, however, suggests that the imagery is rather of public officials being degraded by being stripped of their dignity.

45. Wedderburn, *Theology* 45, also appropriately asks: "how likely is it that the author would introduce a pair of seeming new coinages," namely ἀπέκδυσις and ἀπεκδύομαι, "but in different senses?"

robe representing the elements, στοιχεῖα).[46] But the cosmos could also be likened to the body of Wisdom-Christ, so that the cross could be likened in turn to a stripping off of that garment from Christ's body in order to discard it. The image is certainly grotesque, but so was the image of the cross as a kind of circumcision, a discarding of the body of flesh (2:11).[47] Perhaps we should not press the detail[48] and simply allow the powerful imagery of old and wasted garments being discarded to work its effect. For the Colossians at any rate the point would be clear: the spiritual powers, including the elemental forces (2:8), should be counted as of no greater value and significance than a bunch of old rags.

The second verb, δειγματίζω, is another rare word. It could simply have the sense "publicize" (cf. particularly Lähnemann 131-32; Carr, *Angels* 63); but in its only other New Testament usage (Matt. 1:19) it clearly has the sense "expose to public shame, make an example of, disgrace." The practice would be like that envisaged in a Cyprian law, to which Dio Chrysostom 64.3 refers, according to which an adulteress's hair was cut off and she was treated as a prostitute by the community (so BAGD s.v.). Vettius Valens 43.25-26 also used the cognate noun in association with "scandal" (περιβοησίας καὶ δειγματισμοὺς ἀναδέχονται). Associated, as the term is here, with the idea of "stripping off" and "triumph," it is hard to avoid a pejorative note.[49] The addition of ἐν παρρησίᾳ, "openly, in public," simply reinforces the note of public shame, though the phrase could also mean "boldly."

Θριαμβεύω is the best known of the three verbs, though it occurs elsewhere in biblical Greek only in 2 Cor. 2:14. It means to "celebrate a triumph," or more specifically "lead in triumph," as a victorious general leading his army with his defeated enemies in his train (LSJ and BAGD s.v.; cf. the imagery in Eph. 4:8).[50] In a manner anticipating the Fourth Gospel's theology of glory, the cross and the ascension are merged into a single thought of triumph. "The cross on which Christ died is compared to the chariot in which the victor rode in triumph" (Scott 49).

46. For the idea of God's cosmic garment in later Jewish mysticism see Scholem 58-64.

47. Here, too, it is unnecessary to think of a Gnostic or proto-Gnostic source for this imagery (rightly Ernst, *Philipper, Philemon, Kolosser, Epheser* 205). The evidence of *Gospel of Truth* 20:24-34 points the other way (see n. 41 above); see also E. H. Pagels, *The Gnostic Paul* (Philadelphia: Fortress, 1975) 139.

48. Bandstra, *Law* 164-66, attempts to demonstrate a connection of thought between vv. 14 and 15 by identifying the body of flesh put off here with the χειρόγραφον wiped out in 2:14.

49. But the use of παραδειγμάτισον in Num. 25:4 hardly provides evidence for A. T. Hanson's thesis that "behind Col. 2:14-15 lies the LXX of Nu. 25:1-5" (*Studies* 4).

50. See particularly L. Williamson, "Led in Triumph," *Int* 22 (1968) 317-22; C. Breytenbach, "Paul's Proclamation and God's 'Thriambos' (Notes on 2 Corinthians 2:14-16b)," *Neot* 24 (1990) 257-71 (here 260-65). There is little to be said for the suggestion, as in G. Dautzenberg, *EDNT* 2.155-56, that it means simply "make known, expose."

Carr, *Angels* 61-63, and Yates, *Colossians* 49-50 (more fully "Colossians 2:15"), argue that there is no thought of triumph *over* the rulers and authorities or of the rulers and authorities as hostile and evil. But the 2 Cor. 2:14 parallel does not help much, since the thought there is probably of the apostles as prisoners of the triumphant Christ, their sufferings (which feature so prominently in 2 Corinthians) being likened to the humiliation of the defeated foe (cf., e.g., 4:17-18; 6:4-10).[51] More decisive is the contemporary usage which indicates that the object of θριαμβεύω would most naturally refer to those over whom the triumph was celebrated.[52] The flow of the discussion has been: (1) talk of "deliverance from the authority of darkness" (1:13; Sappington 213, 221-22), (2) the implication of a state of cosmic warfare which the cross brought to reconciliation (1:20), (3) the implication that the στοιχεῖα are a force opposed to Christ (2:8), from which believers need to escape (2:10), and (4) the sustained impression in the immediate context of a fatally disadvantaged, condemned status from which the cross has provided deliverance (2:11-15). Given this, it would be surprising if the authors' intention were simply to describe Christ's triumph here without any thought of what had been triumphed over or what, by implication, the Colossian believers had been delivered from. Oddly enough, Wall 118 thinks that certain *Christian* powers and authorities, perhaps in Colossae itself, might be in view.

The final ἐν αὐτῷ (the fifteenth "in him" in the letter and the fifth since 2:9) raises another puzzle (see n. 4), but it probably is simply Paul's attempt to retain the focus on what has been done "in Christ" on the cross. With such a kaleidoscope of metaphors in 2:11-15 it is hardly surprising that they trip over each other and leave an impression of some confusion. This applies also to the tension between this image and the earlier talk of Christ's death as the means of "reconciling all things" (1:20), where the primary undergirding thought is that God is and in the end will be seen to be "all in all" (1 Cor. 15:28).

It is clear, however, that Paul and Timothy wanted to end the sequence of metaphors on a note of triumph and to build up to this climax as a way of preparing the ground for the practical advice to follow. The force of the sequence of images of what happened on the cross is powerful: a spiritual circumcision achieved and body of flesh stripped off, a burial with Christ and resurrection with Christ, a being made alive with Christ from a state of

51. See discussion particularly in S. J. Hafemann, *Suffering and the Spirit: An Exegetical Study of 2 Cor. 2:14–3:3* (WUNT 2.19; Tübingen: Mohr, 1986) 18-39; Breytenbach (see n. 50 above); P. B. Duff, "Metaphor, Motif, and Meaning: The Rhetorical Strategy behind the Image 'Led in Triumph' in 2 Corinthians 2:14," *CBQ* 53 (1991) 79-92.

52. As best illustrated by Strabo 12.3.35.6: Καῖσαρ θριαμβεύσας τὸν Ἀδιατόριγα μετὰ παίδων καὶ γυναικός . . . ; and Plutarch, *Comparatio Thesei et Romuli* 4.4.3: ἔθνη προσηγάγετο πολέμῳ καὶ πόλεις κατεστρέψατο καὶ βασιλεῖς ἐθριάμβευσε καὶ ἡγεμόνας.

death, and a wiping out of the record of transgression and destruction of that record. But the final one is boldest of all: a stripping off of the rulers and authorities as discarded rags, putting them to public shame and triumphing over them in him. This is a piece of theological audacity of the same order as deutero-Isaiah's proclamation of the God of a small, devastated nation as the one and only God.

To treat the cross as a moment of triumph was about as huge a reversal of normal values as could be imagined, since crucifixion was itself regarded as the most shameful of deaths (M. Hengel, *Crucifixion* [London: SCM, 1977]). But in this letter it is simply of a piece with the theological audacity of seeing in a man, Jesus the Christ, the sum and embodiment of the divine wisdom by which the world was created and is sustained (1:15-20). The key can only be to recognize that for Paul, as for the first Christians generally, the cross and resurrection of Christ itself constituted such a turning upside down of all that had previously determined or been thought to determine life that only such imagery could suffice to express its significance. The unseen powers and invisible forces that dominated and determined so much of life need no longer be feared. A greater power and force was at work, which could rule and determine their lives more effectively — in a word "Christ." Triumph indeed!

Beware the Claims That There Are More Important Practices and Experiences (2:16-19)

16 *Therefore do not let anyone pass judgment on you over food and drink or in the matter of festival, new moon, or sabbaths.* 17 *These things are a shadow of what was to come, but the reality belongs to the Christ.*[1] 18 *Let no one disqualify you, taking pleasure in humility and the worship of the angels,*[2] *which things*[3] *he had seen on entering,*[2] *made arrogant without cause by his mind of flesh,* 19 *and not holding to the head, from whom*[4] *the whole body, supported and held together by joints and ligaments, grows with the growth of God.*

2:16 μὴ οὖν τις ὑμᾶς κρινέτω ἐν βρώσει καὶ ἐν πόσει ἢ ἐν μέρει ἑορτῆς ἢ νεομηνίας ἢ σαββάτων. Having built up to such an impressive climax regarding the significance of Christ's death, Paul and Timothy proceed to draw out the immediate corollary (οὖν). Clearly what is envisaged is a situation where the Colossian believers were being (or might be) criticized for their conduct in respect of dietary rules and festival days. Equally clearly the line of reply is that a proper understanding of the significance of Christ's death would render such criticism unnecessary, irrelevant, or wrong. By implication those who made such criticism were themselves failing to grasp the significance of the cross.

Can we be more specific? Τις could be unspecific, as in 2:8. But with the present imperative here and the following more detailed indications of the issues over which the "someone" was likely to level criticism (2:16, 18), the readers were probably being told "you know who." That is to say, reports to Paul from Colossae had given a clear enough idea of where the (likely) trouble was coming from. Here again the details which follow point with greatest consistency to an essentially Jewish teaching.[5]

It is presumably not a matter of coincidence that the first issue men-

---

1. Moir makes the unnecessary and implausible suggestion that v. 17b should be attached to v. 18: "But let no one deprive/defraud you of . . . the body of Christ."

2. Gnilka, *Kolosserbrief* 144 (accidentally?) omits the first phrase ("the worship of angels") and Masson 130 the second ("which things he had seen on entering"; cf. Moule, *Colossians and Philemon* 106), which rather takes Conzelmann's opening comment — "this section cannot be translated" (146) — too literally!

3. The more weakly attested reading adds "not" ("things not seen"), probably indicative of some confusion on the part of scribes as to whether "things seen" was itself a claim that ought to be disputed (Metzger 623). On further emendations and attempts to make sense of ἐμβατεύων see Moule, *Colossians and Philemon* 105-6; Bruce, *Colossians, Philemon, and Ephesians* 120 n. 130.

4. The Greek has masculine here rather than feminine (which would be in agreement with "head"), presumably because the identification of the head as Christ is taken for granted.

5. As recognized by Dupont 490-91. "Everything here [ch. 2] calls to mind Judaism" (Lyonnet, "Adversaries" 148; see also his "Saint Paul et le gnosticisme").

tioned over which the "someone" might take the addressees to task is the question of food and drink. The use of the verb κρίνω ("criticise" in NJB, "condemn" in NRSV) also indicates clearly enough that what would be under attack was failure to observe certain dietary rules. Both features at once suggest the importance which traditional Judaism laid on the food laws and the fierceness with which traditional Jews insisted on maintenance of their practice as a vital test case of Jewish identity and faithfulness to God's covenant with Israel. At the root of this concern were the important rules regarding clean and unclean food in Lev. 11:1-23 and Deut. 14:3-21. These had been given a much heightened significance by the Maccabean crisis, where resistance on this issue was one of the make-or-break points. "Many in Israel stood firm and were resolved in their hearts not to eat unclean food. They chose to die rather than to be defiled by food or to profane the holy covenant; and they did die" (1 Macc. 1:62-63). Thereafter observance of the food laws was counted a fundamental mark of loyalty to nation and religion, as we may see in popular Jewish tales of the time, in which the heroes or heroines are presented as models of piety acknowledged by God precisely in terms of their refusal to eat the food of Gentiles (Dan. 1:3-16; 10:3; Tob. 1:10-12; Jdt. 12:2, 19; Add. Est. 14:17; *Joseph and Asenath* 7:1; 8:5). Such Jewish scruples were well known in the ancient world (see, e.g., *GLAJJ* §§63, 196, 258, 281, 301). Further factors affecting Jewish eating were the kosher laws requiring that the blood be properly drained from an animal fit for food (e.g., Lev. 7:26-27; Deut. 12:16, 23-24)[6] and the fear prominent among diaspora Jews of eating meat from animals sacrificed in Gentile temples, which was contaminated by idolatry (see, e.g., Schürer 2.81-83). In short, observance of various restrictions on food was essential to Jewish identity and to a Jewish way of life in the diaspora.

The importance of such concerns is equally clear in the history of the earliest Christian mission. According to Acts it was precisely at this point that the barrier had to be broken down in the case of Cornelius. Peter's response to the vision in Joppa speaks for itself: "No, Lord! for I have never eaten anything that is common or unclean" (Acts 10:14). And the subsequent point of criticism leveled against him is that he had eaten with uncircumcised men (Acts 11:3). So also in Galatians, even after and despite the agreement that Gentile believers need not be circumcised (Gal. 2:1-10), the issue of what one could eat with whom resulted in a much more damaging confrontation and split (Gal. 2:11-14). In 1 Corinthians the issue of food offered to idols betrays the same essentially Jewish fear of idolatry (1 Corinthians 8–10, where βρῶσις appears at 8:4). And in Romans Paul felt it necessary to devote the major part of his parenesis to the problem of how local churches could

---

6. Josephus, *Antiquities* 14.261 indicates that provision for dietary observances would require special permission.

live in mutual respect where there were different attitudes to and practice regarding clean and unclean food.

It is true that restrictions on diet were not confined to Jews in the ancient world (see, e.g., Wolter 141-42). But it is clear from the very use of the words "clean" and "unclean" (Rom. 14:20, 14) that it was Jewish sensibilities which were primarily in view in Romans 14, since the latter term in particular (κοινός) is distinctively Jewish (see further my *Romans* 799-801, 818-19). And though drink was not such an issue as clean versus unclean food, it was quite natural for scrupulous Jews (particularly in the diaspora) to exercise restraint there as well because of the possibility of being given wine which had been offered in libation to the gods and which was therefore also contaminated by idolatry (Dan. 1:3-16; 10:3; Add. Est. 14:17; *Joseph and Asenath* 8:5; Mishnah *'Abodah Zarah* 2:3; 5:2).[7] In *Testament of Reuben* 1:10 and *Testament of Judah* 15:4 avoidance of wine and meat is an expression of repentance. Of the devout Christian Jew James, the brother of Jesus, it was said that "he drank no wine or strong drink, nor did he eat meat" (Eusebius, *Historia Ecclesiastica* 2.23.5). Hence Paul's expressed willingness neither to eat meat nor to drink wine if it would help the scrupulous Jewish brother to maintain his integrity (Rom. 14:21).

In the present case, the significant factor is the closeness of the parallel to Romans 14. There not only βρῶσις and πόσις are used as one of the variant ways of posing the issue of Christian Jewish sensitivities over food and drink (14:17, the only other Pauline use of the latter term). There, too, as here, the question of (feast) days is bound up with that of food and drink (Rom. 14:5-6). More noteworthy still is the use of the verb κρίνω, as in Rom. 14:3-4, where it clearly indicates the tendency of the more scrupulous to pass judgment on others who do not live according to their scruples (cf. its use elsewhere, e.g., Rom. 2:1, 3, 12; 1 Cor. 5:3; 2 Thes. 2:12). Those who insist on a more restricted lifestyle for themselves do so because they think it an essential expression of their belief and identity as believers. They observe because they think God requires such observance. That conviction will inevitably result in them criticizing or even condemning those who claim the same fundamental faith loyalty but who practice a less restricted lifestyle. If God requires observance, then he disapproves of nonobservance, and those who ignore God's requirements are to be con-demned and avoided, despite their claim to the same fundamental faith. Such was the logic of the devout Jewish traditionalist, including the tradi-tionalist Christian Jew. It is this attitude which is most probably in view here, judged to be more dangerous than the equivalent attitude critiqued in

---

7. As Wink notes, the Essenes regarded drink as more susceptible to contamination than food (*Naming* 80 n. 91).

Romans 14 but requiring less forceful response than in Galatians, presumably because the circumstances in each case were different.

In short, the first item of the particularities envisaged here points fairly firmly to an essentially Jewish faction in Colossae who were deeply critical of Gentile Christian failure to observe the Jewish food laws. From this we may make a further deduction: that they should be thus critical is equally indicative of the fact that the Gentile believers in Colossae must have regarded themselves as heirs of Israel's inheritance, in effect part of an expanding Judaism (see also on 1:2 and 12, and the introduction to the comments on 1:9-14). Only if such claims were being made, only if Gentiles were assuming identity markers which Jews had always understood as distinctively theirs, would Jews, who otherwise lived (for the most part) in mutual respect with their Gentile fellow citizens, have found it necessary to be so critical and condemnatory. The criticism here is that of the traditionalist devout Jew against would-be fellow religionists whose claims he could not really or fully accept.

The already strong implication that the Colossian "philosophy" was basically Jewish in character is further strengthened by the other items over which the Colossian believers might be criticized or condemned and which we may likewise deduce were central to the Colossian "philosophy": "in the matter of [see BAGD s.v. μέρος 1c] a festival or new moon or sabbath." The first of these three terms, "festival" (ἑορτή), is unspecific: such feasts, festivals, and holidays were common to all societies (LSJ s.v.), and though elsewhere in the New Testament the "feast" in question is one of the traditional Jewish feasts (Passover or Tabernacles), the term itself occurs only here in the Pauline corpus. The second term (νεομηνία) is equally imprecise: the new moon was reckoned to have a religious significance and celebrated accordingly in most ancient societies, though here again that included the Jewish cult (e.g., Num. 10:10; 2 Kgs. 4:23; Ps. 81:3; Isa. 1:13; Ezek. 46:3, 6; see further G. Delling, *TDNT* 4:639-41).

However, the issue is put beyond doubt by the third element, the "sabbath." The sabbath was another Jewish tradition which marked out Jews as distinctive from Gentiles, another essential mark of Jewish identity and covenant belonging (Exod. 31:16-17; Deut. 5:15; Isa. 56:6). Even before the Maccabean crisis, "violating the sabbath" was ranked with "eating unclean food" as one of the two chief marks of covenant disloyalty (Josephus, *Antiquities* 11:346). And its increasing importance for Judaism is indicated by the developing sabbath law, as attested both within other Jewish groups of the time (*Jubilees* 2:17-33; 50:6-13; CD 10:14–11:18) and by the Gospels (Mark 2:23–3:5 pars.). Characteristically Jewish also is the practice of referring to the "sabbath" in the plural, τὰ σάββατα, as here (Lightfoot 192; BAGD s.v. σάββατον 1bβ). It is true that the most unusual practice of maintaining one day in seven as a day of rest proved attractive to sympathetic

Gentiles (Philo, *De vita Mosis* 2:21; Josephus, *Contra Apionem* 2:282; Juvenal, *Satirae* 14:96), but a critical or judgmental attitude on the subject, as here, is much more likely to express a traditional Jewish attitude, defensive of identity and covenant distinctiveness.

But if sabbath is so clearly a distinctively Jewish festival, then the probability is that the "festival" and "new moon" also refer to the Jewish versions of these celebrations. The point is put beyond dispute when we note that the three terms together, "sabbaths, new moons, and feasts," was in fact a regular Jewish way of speaking of the main festivals of Jewish religion (1 Chron. 23:31; 2 Chron. 2:3; 31:3; Neh. 10:33; Isa. 1:13-14; 1 Macc. 10:34; Ezek. 45:17, and Hos. 2:11 in reverse order, as here; see, e.g., Sappington 163; Aletti, *Épître aux Colossiens* 193 n. 112). In view of later discussion we should also note that the Essenes claimed to have received special revelation regarding "the holy sabbaths and glorious feasts" and also the new moon (CD 3:14-15; 1QS 9:26–10:8). We must conclude, therefore, that all the elements in this verse bear a characteristically and distinctively Jewish color, that those who cherished them so critically must have been the (or some) Jews of Colossae, and that their criticism arose from Jewish suspicion of Gentiles making what they would regard as unacceptable claims to the distinctive Jewish heritage without taking on all that was most distinctive of that heritage.[8]

That circumcision is not also mentioned is puzzling, but the issue clearly lay in the background, and the silence here may be sufficiently explained if the Jewish posture overall was more apologetic than evangelistic (see on 2:11). In contrast to those who think the absence of any mention of the law is a decisive impediment to identifying the Colossian philosophy too closely with a traditional Judaism (so Lohse, *Colossians and Philemon* 115-16 n. 11; Martin, *Colossians and Philemon* 91), it should be noted that circumcision, food laws, and sabbath were recognized by both Jew and Gentile as the most distinctive features of the Jewish way of life based on the law (cf., e.g., Justin, *Dialogue* 8:4; see also p. 33 n. 39 above).[9] And those who think the link with "the elemental forces" likewise diminishes the case for seeing traditional Jewish concerns here[10] need simply recall the same link in Gal. 4:9-10.

---

8. The more this concern for observance of days is linked to a lifestyle determined by reference to the "elemental forces" (2:8, 20; so Lohse, *Colossians and Philemon* 115-16), the closer the parallel with Gal. 4:9-10.

9. Cf. Houlden 193: "These are Jews teaching strict obedience to the Jewish law (vv. 16, 21, 23)"; Caird 197: "This asceticism is the product of an exaggerated and puritanical form of Judaism"; Wright, *Colossians and Philemon* 26: "The regulations referred to in 2:16 fit the Jewish law and nothing else"; Schenk, "Kolosserbrief" 3351.

10. Lohmeyer 122 n. 2; Conzelmann 146; Ernst, *Philipper, Philemon, Kolosser, Epheser* 208; Gnilka, *Kolosserbrief* 146.

2:17 ἅ ἐστιν σκιὰ τῶν μελλόντων, τὸ δὲ σῶμα τοῦ Χριστοῦ. The response to such Jewish criticism is brief and to the point. Such practices are but "a shadow of things to come, but the reality is with Christ." The language is ultimately Platonic, but here is probably drawn from the Hellenistic Judaism which we find most clearly expressed in Philo. Basic to Plato's view of reality was the distinction between the heavenly original and the earthly copy, the former being the true reality, the latter, even in its physical objectivity, only a "shadow" of the idea(l) or archetype. Philo makes a fair use of the term "shadow" (σκιά) in a number of variations of this Platonic distinction (e.g., *Legum allegoriae* 3.100-103; *De plantatione* 27; *De Abrahamo* 119-20). Most significant is the fact that he sets σκιά over against σῶμα as the name over against that which it represents (πρᾶγμα) (*De decalogo* 82), or as copy to archetype (ἀρχετύπος, *De migratione Abrahami* 12), or again: "the letter is to the oracle as the shadow to the substance (σκιάς τινας ὡσανεὶ σωμάτων) and the higher values therein are what really and truly exist" (*De confusione linguarum* 190, LCL translation; see also S. Schulz, *TDNT* 7.396; Lohse, *Colossians and Philemon* 116; Gnilka, *Kolosserbrief* 147).

The contrast intended here is evidently along similar lines,[11] but with two important modifications. The first is signaled by τῶν μελλόντων, "the things to come" (for this use of the participle see BAGD s.v. μέλλω 2). This no doubt is a reflection of Jewish eschatology, in which the longed for new age can be described as ὁ αἰὼν μέλλων, "the age to come" (as in Isa. 9:6 LXX v.l.; Matt. 12:32; Eph. 1:21). By the addition of this phrase, an essentially static Platonic dualism (between heaven and earth) has been transformed into an expression of Jewish eschatological hope. The strongest parallel is in Hebrews, where precisely the same amalgam of Platonic cosmology and Jewish eschatology has been carried through most effectively. So most noticeably in Heb. 10:1: "For the law has a shadow of the good things to come instead of the (true) form of these things (σκιὰν τῶν μελλόντων ἀγαθῶν, οὐκ αὐτὴν τὴν εἰκόνα τὼν πραγμάτων)" (see also 2:5; 6:5; 9:11; 12:14).[12]

---

11. Francis, "Argument" 205-6, suggests that the whole of v. 17 is "a quotation from the opponents," with σκιά used positively. But the context clearly indicates that the two halves of the verse are set in contrast.

12. Schweizer, *Colossians* 156-57, has no doubt that "Paul, in speaking of the law, could never use the relatively innocuous image of the shadow of that which is to come." But the images of the law in Gal. 3:23-24 and 4:1-7 are not so negative as is usually assumed to be the case (see my *Galatians*) and in fact quite complementary to the image here. See further my "Was Paul against the Law? The Law in Galatians and Romans: A Test-Case of Text in Context," in *Texts and Contexts: Biblical Texts in their Textual and Situational Contexts,* L. Hartman FS, ed. T. Fornberg and D. Hellholm (Oslo: Scandinavian University Press, 1995) 455-75. See also Lohmeyer 122-23; Scott 52; Ernst, *Philipper, Philemon, Kolosser, Epheser* 209; Bruce, *Colossians, Philemon, and Ephesians* 116.

The second modification is christological: the reality, the substance thus foreshadowed, is "of Christ, belongs to the Christ." The Christ (the definite article should be given due weight here) is the fulfillment of Jewish eschatological hope. Here the closest parallel is in Paul, in Rom 5:14: Adam as the "type of the one to come (τύπος τοῦ μέλλοντος)," namely, of Christ. In contrast to Platonic-Philonic thought, it is the Christ in all the concrete bloodiness of the cross who is the true reality. The amalgam thus echoes the christology of the earlier hymn (1:15-20): Christ embodies the heavenly reality which lies beyond and sustains the percep- tible cosmos. But, as in Hebrews, it also affirms that Christ is the substance to the shadow of Jewish food laws and feasts: he is the reality which casts its shadow backward in time; they are the provisional, inferior copies whose inadequacy is now evident in the light of the real. The claim is again bold and, it should be noted, only makes sense as a response to and rebuttal of essentially Jewish claims. Only as a claim that Christ is the fulfillment of Jewish eschatological expectation, which provides a Jewish answer to a Jewish alternative, does the rebuttal make sense (cf. Foerster 74).

We should also note the further variation on the σῶμα motif, which is such a prominent feature of this letter. Here it relates most closely to the earlier play on the body of the cosmos (1:18a; 2:10 — "head of every rule and authority"): as Christ embodies the ultimate reality, the divine wisdom and rationality which holds the cosmos together, so he is the reality reflected imperfectly in the rules and festivals by which Jewish social life and time are structured. Presumably there is also a play on σῶμα = church (1:18a, 24; 2:19), though NJB's "the reality is the body of Christ" is too free. The implication, then, as in 1:18a, is that the church's role now is to embody the same reality (cf., e.g., those cited by Pokorný 145 n. 12; but note also the reservations of Best, *Body* 121; Bruce, *Colossians, Philemon, and Ephesians* 116-17; O'Brien, *Colossians, Philemon* 141).

2:18 μηδεὶς ὑμᾶς καταβραβευέτω θέλων ἐν ταπεινοφροσύνῃ καὶ θρησκείᾳ τῶν ἀγγέλων, ἃ ἑόρακεν ἐμβατεύων, εἰκῆ φυσιούμενος ὑπὸ τοῦ νοὸς τῆς σαρκὸς αὐτοῦ. The cautionary warning of 2:16 is repeated in similar terms: "Let no one . . . ." The verb used this time is again drawn from the arena (cf. 1 Cor. 9:24-27 and Phil. 3:14): βραβεύω has the primary meaning of "award a prize (a βραβεῖον)" in a contest (see 3:15); hence καταβραβεύω (only here in biblical Greek and not much attested elsewhere) means "decide against" as an umpire, "deprive of the prize" (BAGD), or simply "disqualify." The force of the warning at first seems stronger than in 2:16 (Abbott 265-66), but since κρίνω there can have the force of "con- demn," the warnings are probably of similar weight.

Why and of what might they be deprived? The imagery, as usual with such metaphors, suggests both a prize aimed at and the effort required to achieve it. Furthermore, it paints the picture of some individual in Colossae judging that others were achieving the goal (of religious practice, 2:16) more successfully than the Colossian believers.[13] What this goal and successful practice were must be given in the words which follow. But here we enter a nest of problems which have never ceased to test exegetical skill. It is probably wisest to take the phrases step by step.[14]

The potential judgmental attitude is attributed to one "who delights in ταπεινοφροσύνη and θρησκεία τῶν ἀγγέλων." To be noted at once is the fact that the verb θέλων indicates something desired or wanted by the subject of the verb. In the absence of a following personal pronoun (ὑμᾶς or ὑμῖν) together with an appropriate verb (infinitive or subjunctive), θέλων cannot signify something imposed on the Colossian Christians or required of them; the translation "insisting on self-abasement" (RSV/NRSV; Harris 121; Wall 122) is therefore misleading.[15] In fact, as Lightfoot 193 and others have noted, θέλων ἐν is a Hebraism, reflecting the familiar *hapes beʾ* ("delight in"), as also in LXX (1 Sam. 18:22; 2 Sam. 15:26; 1 Kgs. 10:9; 2 Chron. 9:8; Pss. 111:1; 146:10; *Testament of Asher* 1:6; see also Bruce, *Colossians, Philemon, and Ephesians* 118 n. 115). In other words, what is about to be described is what the other sets as *his own* goal or relishes as the means of achieving that goal, not a goal or means of achieving it which he sets before or wishes to impose on the Colossian Christians (*pace* Sappington 162). The attitude is simply that "my way is superior to yours; it achieves goals which you fall short of." It is, we might say, an essentially sectarian attitude which is so confident of its rightness and success that any other systems, especially those most closely related to it, must be judged at best inadequate if not dangerously defective.

What then does this critic delight in? Ταπεινοφροσύνη usually means "humility," but most follow the observation that the LXX uses the repeated phrase "to humble (ταπεινόω) one's soul" in the sense of "to mortify oneself" (Lev. 16:29, 31; 23:27, 29, 32) or more specifically "to fast" (Ps. 35:13; Isa. 58:3, 5; Jdt. 4:9; see also Ps. 69:10; *Psalms of Solomon* 3:8); ταπεινοφροσύνη is clearly used in this latter sense in Hermas, *Visions* 3.10.6 and *Similitudes*

13. Aletti, *Épître aux Colossiens* 195, notes the irony of those who prized humility (ταπεινο-φροσύνη) acting as judges over others to disqualify them.

14. The disputes regarding this verse are indicated in the range of translations: e.g., REB — "You are not to be disqualified by the decision of people who go in for self-mortification and angel-worship and access to some visionary world"; NJB — "Do not be cheated of your prize by anyone who chooses to grovel to angels and worship them, pinning every hope on visions received"; NIV — "Do not let anyone who delights in false humility and the worship of angels disqualify you for the prize. Such a person goes into great detail about what he has seen."

15. Dibelius, *Kolosser, Epheser, Philemon* 34-35 preferred an old minority view that θέλων should be treated as an adverbial modification of the preceding verb ("let no one willfully disqualify you"), but his advocacy has not won it any more support.

5.3.7. This suggests a fair degree of ascetic practice as part of the Colossian "philosophy" (see also 2:21, 23; cf. 1 Tim. 4:3).[16]

"Worship of angels" is more problematic, but a wholly natural rendering would take it as worship given to angels (objective genitive).[17] It is true that there is no close parallel to the phrase, but popular religion in the Greco-Roman world did reckon with ἄγγελοι, "messengers" both from heaven and from the underworld (W. Grundmann, *TDNT* 1.75). And there is some evidence for worship of angels in western Asia Minor, first adduced by W. Ramsay (BAGD s.v. θρησκεία; Sheppard; Trebilco 132-33; DeMaris 62), though it may equally suggest pagan borrowing of only half-understood Jewish concepts (NDIEC 5.72-73, 136; Sheppard 86-87; Trebilco 137; Mitchell 2.45-46; see also pp. 29ff. above).[18] A plausible picture can thus emerge, one which envisages the Colossian "philosophy" as a syncretistic religious mix involving ascetic practices and worship of angels. Linked with the talk of rulers and authorities (1:16; 2:15), these angels could be seen within the "philosophy" as either benevolent, and therefore to be worshiped to attain their blessing, or malevolent, and therefore to be appeased.[19]

How does this fit with the strongly Jewish character which has been evident in earlier allusions to the Colossian "philosophy"? "Humility" as fasting is certainly Jewish enough. But worship of angels is something one would not expect in any of the forms of Judaism known to us for this period. It is true that various second-century sources describe (or accuse) Jews of worshiping angels: *Kerygma Petri* (in Clement of Alexandria, *Stromata* 6.5.41.2); *Apology of Aristides* 14:4; and Celsus, in Origen's *Contra Celsum* 1:26 and 5:6 (also Origen himself in *Comm. in Joann.* 13:17); but none of these can be described as a friendly witness.[20] Pseudo-Philo 13.6 also speaks of "an

16. So, e.g., Percy, *Probleme* 147-49; W. Grundmann, *TDNT* 8.22; Schweizer, "Elemente" 161-62; Caird 198; Lincoln, *Paradise* 111; otherwise H. Giesen, *EDNT* 3.334. Lohse, *Colossians and Philemon* 118 takes ταπεινοφροσύνη as "readiness to serve": "It describes the eagerness and docility with which a person fulfills the cultic ordinances." DeMaris brushes aside the evidence cited and simply asserts that ταπεινοφροσύνη here is a distinctively Christian virtue (63, 71, 74-75).

17. So, most recently, Wolter 146-47 — "without doubt the angels are in view here as the object of the worship"; DeMaris 59-62.

18. On whether the recently published inscription from northeast of Ankara (late second or third century CE), in which the dedication is "to the great God Most High (Θεῷ Ὑψίστῳ)" and "his holy angels," indicates Jewish syncretism or pagan borrowing see Sheppard 94-99; Trebilco 137; and Mitchell 2.46. Lightfoot 65-66 already observed the interesting coincidence that the canons of the fourth-century Council of Laodicea warn against Christians "judaizing," observing the sabbath and other festivals, and going off to "name angels" (ἀγγέλους ὀνομάζειν) in other gatherings (29, 35, 37, 38).

19. For the role of angels in later Gnostic systems see A. Szabó, "Die Engelvorstellungen vom Alten Testament bis zur Gnosis," in *Altes Testament — Frühjudentum — Gnosis,* ed. K.-W. Tröger (Gütersloh: Gütersloher, 1980) 143-52.

20. But M. Simon, *Verus Israel* (Oxford: Oxford University, 1986) 345-47, is not alone in seeing in these reports evidence of Jewish syncretism.

offering for your watchers (= guardian angels?)"; *1 Enoch* 48:5 and 62:6, 9 envisage worship given to the Son of Man; and later Tosefta *Hullin* 2:18 alludes to angel worship within popular Judaism (*GLAJJ* 2.295).[21]

More characteristic of Judaism, however, was warning against worship of the host of heaven (Deut. 4:19; 17:3; Jer. 8:2; 19:13; Zeph. 1:5), including the repeated warnings in first-century Judaism against the worship of angels (*Apocalypse of Zephaniah* 6:15; *Apocalypse of Abraham* 17:2; Philo, *De fuga et inventione* 212; *De somnis* 1.232, 238; similarly Rev. 19:10 and 22:9; *Ascension of Isaiah* 7:21);[22] in *Adam and Eve* 13–15 angels are commanded by Michael to worship Adam as the image of God; in pseudo-Philo 34:2 sacrifice to angels is linked with magic and condemned; and when in the early second century Elisha ben Abuyah hailed a second divine power in heaven, he was completely disowned as apostate by his fellow rabbis (for details see, e.g., Rowland, *Open Heaven* 331-39). Were the Colossian "philosophy" Jewish in character, on this hypothesis, we would have to envisage a very syncretistic form of Judaism, unlike anything else we know of. This, however, hardly squares well with the evidence of a Jewish character for the "philosophy" which relished not simply odd bits and pieces abstracted from Judaism but the identity markers which marked out ethnic Jews anxious to maintain their ancestral traditions (circumcision, food laws, and sabbath in particular; see on 2:11 and 2:16).[23]

However, an alternative hypothesis has been put forward, particularly by F. O. Francis, which has proved influential and has been helpfully elaborated by others (see p. 29 n. 27 above). This starts from the neglected observation that θρησκεία τῶν ἀγγέλων can also be taken as a subjective genitive (as in 4 Macc. 5:7; Josephus, *Antiquities* 12.253), denoting worship offered *by* angels to God. Such worship is implicit already in the great visions of Isa. 6:2-3; Dan. 7:10; and *1 Enoch* 14:18-23 and explicit in *1 Enoch* 36:4, 39-40; 61:10-12; *2 Enoch* 20–21; *Apocalypse of Abraham* 17–18; *Testament of Levi* 3:3-8, not to mention the Christian evidence of Luke 2:14; Phil. 2:10-11; Revelation 4–5; and *Ascension of Isaiah* 7–9.[24] But more to the point here is the evidence of a desire particularly within apocalyptic and mystical circles of first-century Judaism to join in with the worship of angels

21. See also Mach 296-300. Lyonnet, "Adversaries" 151-53 is willing to speak of veneration of the names of the angels at Qumran.

22. See also Williams, "Cult of Angels," particularly 420-32; Percy, *Probleme* 149-55; Hurtado 82-85.

23. Particularly unsatisfactory is DeMaris's hypothesis of a kind of Jewish Middle Platonism which advocated demon worship (particularly 104-8), whose points of contact with the text of Colossians are hardly obvious and at best tangential and seem to result from a tendentious reading of the text.

24. H. Bietenhard, *Die himmlische Welt im Urchristentum und Spätjudentum* (WUNT 2; Tübingen: Mohr, 1951) 123-42; see further Mach 209-28.

in heaven. It is implicit already in such Psalms as 29:1-2 and 148:1-2. But it is most strikingly attested in *Testament of Job* 48–50, where the three daughters of Job speak in the language of angels, praising and worshiping God. Similarly, in *Apocalypse of Abraham* 17 Abraham is taught a hymn of praise by the angel who joins with him in reciting it. The same motif is a feature of *Ascension of Isaiah* 7:13–9:33 (particularly 8:17 and 9:28, 33). And in *Apocalypse of Zephaniah* 8:3-4 the seer sees the angels praying and prays with them, knowing their language (see further Sappington 90-94; Mach 239-40; Morray-Jones, "Paradise Revisited" 182; cf. Attridge).

Most interesting of all is the evidence that such worship was coveted at Qumran.[25] According to 1QSa 2:8-9 the rules for the congregation of the last days would have to be strict, "for the Angels of Holiness are [with] their [congregation]." But the implication of other references is that these rules were already in operation, indicating that the Qumran community saw itself as a priestly community whose holiness was defined by the presence of the angels (cf. particularly 4QCD[b] and 1QM 7:4-6 with Lev. 21:17-21). So explicitly in 1QH 3:21-22: "Thou hast cleansed a perverse spirit of great sin . . . that it may enter into community with the congregation of the Sons of Heaven" (similarly 1QH 11:10-13). More to the immediate point, in 1QSb 4:25-26 one of the blessings of the priest is: "May you be as an Angel of the Presence in the Abode of Holiness to the glory of the God of [hosts]. . . . May you attend upon the service in the Temple of the Kingdom and decree destiny in company with the Angels of the Presence." Most interesting of all are the recently published complete (but often fragmentary) texts of the *Songs of the Sabbath Sacrifice* (4Q400-405), which contain songs of praise to be offered to God by angels in the heavenly temple during the first thirteen sabbaths of the year and in which it is clear enough (since the *Songs* presumably belonged to the community's liturgy) that the community itself (or at least its priests) joined with the angels in reciting these songs of heavenly worship.[26]

It is quite possible, therefore, to envisage a Jewish (or Christian Jewish) synagogue in Colossae which was influenced by such ideas and which delighted in their worship sabbath by sabbath as a participation in the worship of the angels in heaven (cf. 1 Cor. 11:10). In this case the "humility" associated with this worship could very well denote the spiritual discipline and mortification (particularly, but not only, fasting; see above) regarded as essential to maintain the holiness required to participate with the holy ones and the holy angels (see also 1:12). The association of fasting and heavenly

---

25. For the sake of convenience the following quotations of the DSS are all taken from G. Vermes, *The Dead Sea Scrolls in English* (London/New York: Penquin, [3]1987).

26. See C. Newsom, *Songs of the Sabbath Sacrifice: A Critical Edition* (Atlanta: Scholars, 1985), particularly 59-72; Vermes 221.

revelation is stressed in such passages as Dan. 10:2-3; *Apocalypse of Abraham* 9:7-10; 12:1-2; *Testament of Isaac* 4:1-6; 5:4; *4 Ezra* 5:13; 6:35; and *2 Baruch* 5:7; and Philo notes that Moses heard the strains of heavenly worship as a result of having fasted for forty days and nights (*De Somnis* 1.35-37; *De vita Mosis* 2.67-69).[27] But it would be equally possible to take both nouns as referring to the angels — "delighting in the humility and worship of the angels" — as may be implicit in the very fact that such glorious beings also fall down in worship before God.[28] Despite Lohse, *Colossians and Philemon* 119 n. 36; Martin, *Colossians and Philemon* 94; Schweizer, *Colossians* 159; also "Christ" 452; W. Radl, *EDNT* 2.155; and DeMaris 77-79, reference to 2:23 by no means rules out this line of interpretation (see on 2:23). And (*pace* Bockmuehl, *Revelation* 180) it is not so much interest in angelic worship which Paul finds "reprehensible" as the attitude of dismissive superiority which it evidently engendered among its practitioners (μηδεὶς ὑμᾶς καταβραβευέτω . . .).

The further clause, "which things[29] he had seen on entering (ἃ ἑόρακεν ἐμβατεύων)," if anything strengthens the above hypothesis. To be sure, the most influential interpretation for most of the present century has been that put forward by Dibelius, most fully in 1917.[30] He argued on the basis of inscriptions found at the site of the sanctuary of Apollo at Klaros (a few miles northwest of Ephesus) that ἐμβατεύων here is drawn from the language of the mysteries, a technical term for initiation into a mystery cult, so that the phrase refers to visions seen preparatory to initiation; hence the translation of Lohse, *Colossians and Philemon* 114: "visions of them [angels] during the mystery rites" — a catchword quoted from the Colossian cult (Lohse 120). But since neither "the elemental forces" (see on 2:8) nor the talk of burial with Christ (see on 2:12) need evoke thought of mystery cults,

27. Francis, "Humility" 167-71. See also Kehl, "Erniedrigung" 368-74, 383-88; Bandstra, "Errorists" 335-38; I. Gruenwald, *Apocalyptic and Merkabah Mysticism* (Leiden: Brill, 1980) 99-102; Lincoln, *Paradise* 111; Sappington 65-66, 150-53. The clear implications of the evidence are determinedly resisted by DeMaris 75-77. Against Bandstra's thesis that the Colossians' error was thinking they could participate in angelic liturgies without the assistance of a mediator, Evans, "Colossian Mystics" 199, rightly points out that there is no hint that the need of a mediator was an issue in the writings cited (see also Argall 7-14).

28. Str-B 3.629, referring to *Aboth de-Rabbi Nathan* 12; see also Rowland, "Apocalyptic Visions" 75; Sappington 160; Sumney 376-77.

29. This is the most natural way of taking the relative ἃ (e.g., Schweizer, *Colossians* 160-61). Col. 3:6 provides another example of a neuter plural relative following feminine nouns (Rowland, "Apocalyptic Visions" 77).

30. Dibelius, "Isis Initiation": the Colossian mystery cult, "the earliest certainly datable and historically recognizable case of an early and germinal Christian-gnostic formation" (91); briefly his *Kolosser, Epheser, Philemon* 35-36. The link was first posited by W. Ramsay early in 1912; his account of the matter is in his *The Teaching of Paul in Terms of the Present Day* (London: Hodder, 1913) 286-305.

this single reference (ἐμβατεύων) is a very limited base on which to build such a theory.[31] Nor, once again, does it make sense of the strong ethnic character of the Jewish features of the Colossian "philosophy" so far analyzed (2:11, 16).

In fact, however, it is dubious whether ἐμβατεύω was, strictly speaking, a technical term, at least for entry into a mystery cult. Its basic meaning is simply "enter," and the word was regularly used in legal papyri of entering into possession of an inheritance.[32] So in the two Old Testament (LXX) occurrences (Josh. 19:49, 51), where the thought is of entering into possession of the promised land. So, too, in the Klaros inscriptions the basic thought seems to be of entering into the sanctuary to consult the oracle (Francis, "Background" 199-204). And the Fathers seem unaware that the term could have such sensitive overtones (*PGL* s.v.). Moreover, when we set the usage here against the background already sketched out above, we cannot but be aware that the revelations described usually involved a visionary or mystical ascent to (entry into) or through the heavens (e.g., *1 Enoch* 14:8-13; *2 Enoch* 3; *3 Baruch* 2:2; 3:1-2; *Testament of Levi* 2:5-7; Rev. 4:1-2). It was when Elisha ben Abuyah "entered a garden" (= paradise = heaven) that he committed the heresy of recognizing a second divine power in heaven.[33] Indeed, ἐμβατεύειν itself is attested in the sense of "enter heaven."[34] Most interesting of all are the clear indication in the *Songs of the Sabbath Sacrifice* that heaven was seen as a temple where the angelic worship took place and the prominence given to doorways of the temple (probably on the basis of Ezekiel 40–41; see Newsom 39-59) and to the theme of entering in 4Q405 14-15i:3-4 ("their wonderful praise is for the God of gods . . . and they sing . . . the vestibules by which they enter, the spirits of the most holy inner Temple") and 4Q405 23i:8-10 ("When the gods of knowledge enter by the doors of glory, and when the holy angels depart towards their realm, the entrance doors and the gates of exit proclaim the glory of the King, blessing and praising all the spirits of God when they depart and enter by the gates").

When we add the echo of Josh. 19:49, 51 in Col. 1:12, the inference

31. Dibelius, *Kolosser, Epheser, Philemon* 75, draws attention to the language of "entering" *(pervaderem)* in Apuleius, *Metamorphoses* 11.21, but also has to point out that "never is there a suggestion that the initiate suffers the same fate as Osiris" (77). The Nag Hammadi references cited by Pokorný 147 lack any "entering" motif.

32. Francis, "Background" 198-99. Less likely is the sense suggested by H. Preisker, *TDNT* 2.535-36, and Lyonnet, "Col. 2:18" 432-33, and strongly advocated by DeMaris 64-66: the verb means "investigate closely," since the thought in the two parallels cited (2 Macc. 2:30; Philo, *De plantatione* 80) is primarily that of "enter (deeply) into (a subject)."

33. Rowland, *Open Heaven* ch. 12. See further A. F. Segal, "Heavenly Ascent in Hellenistic Judaism, Early Christianity and Their Environment," *ANRW* 2.23.2 (1980) 1333-94; Sappington 73-75.

34. Francis, "Background" 197; Evans, "Colossian Mystics" 198 n. 45; see also Carr, "Notes" 498-99; Lincoln, *Paradise* 112-13; Sappington 155-58.

becomes strong that there was a prominent strand among the Colossian Jews who thought of heaven either (or both) as a promised land into which they should aspire even now to enter, or particularly as the temple of God into which they could now enter by means of appropriate spiritual disciplines in order to share the worship of the angels in heaven. It was their delight thus to "enter" sabbath by sabbath (note the present tense). This would also make the best sense of the other part of the phrase (ἃ ἑόρακεν), which Dibelius treated too lightly. For it is precisely the characteristic of the apocalyptic and mystical Jewish traditions documented above to give prominence to "the things seen" (e.g., *1 Enoch* 14; *Testament of Abraham* 10; Revelation 4–5); we should recall that Paul himself enjoyed such a visionary or mystical journey (2 Cor. 12:2-4). This no doubt was why the Colossian Jews so "delighted in" these practices, so rich were the audiovisual experiences which they had enjoyed at least once in the past (the force of the perfect tense is not wholly clear).[35] And if they were persuasive word-spinners on the subject (2:4, 8), it is no wonder that Paul and Timothy were concerned that they might well captivate the Colossian believers by the descriptions they gave and fearful lest Epaphras's converts feel that they were indeed in danger of being disqualified and deprived of the prize of their new faith.

The description of Colossian teaching in 2:18 has thus far been neutral. But now the writers show what they think of it. Such claims to enter into the very presence of God and hymn him in the company of angels was an idle self-deceit. Anyone who made such a claim was "puffed up with conceit, putting on airs" (BAGD s.v. φυσιόω), a term used by Paul several times to rebuke Corinthian arrogance (1 Cor. 4:6, 18-19; 5:2; 8:1; 13:4). Such conceit was "without cause" and "to no avail" (εἰκῇ can have both senses; cf. Rom. 13:4 and Gal. 3:4). A contrast with the delighted in "humility" earlier in the verse is obviously intended.

The most stinging part of the rebuke, however, would have been the final phrase, "by his mind of flesh." For in a Hellenistic context, as Philo again well illustrates, it was precisely the "mind" which would have been the medium by means of which the person could enter the higher realms,

---

35. The weakest point of this thesis is the difficulty of correlating it with the implication in 2:8, 10, 15, 20 that the Colossian philosophy included belief in heavenly powers that were threatening or hostile. This might provide the best evidence that the beliefs and practices of the Colossian synagogue(s) were syncretistic in some measure (see pp. 27ff. above). But the issue may equally be resolved by the observation of Morray-Jones, "Paradise Revisited" 182-83, that heavenly ascents could be frightening and dangerous; he speaks of "a genre of horror stories" in Jewish mystical tradition which warn against ill-advised attempts to hazard such ascents as "terrifyingly dangerous and forbidden." We may note in particular the famous warning tale of the four sages (190-208). This line of reflection gives added significance to Paul's reference to the ἄγγελος σατανᾶ (2 Cor. 12:7) in his own recollection of such experiences (Morray-Jones 281-83). So also in the DSS we read of "the angel of darkness," the "angel of perdition," and not least the frightening appearances in vision of Melkiresha (1QS 3:17-21; 4Q286; 4QAmram).

the *logos* of human rationality, itself part of the medium of the divine Logos that interpenetrated the cosmos (see, e.g., J. Behm, *TDNT* 4.954-56). In such a scheme "mind" and "flesh" were quite antithetical since it was impossible for the divine substance to mingle with the material. To speak of "the mind of flesh" was therefore in effect to deny that this Colossian worshiper with angels could ever have "lifted off" from earth: even his mind was "flesh," fast bound to earth. The phrase, in fact, is unique in Paul[36] and suggests once again that in this letter the more strongly moral note which is such a strong feature of "flesh" in the earlier Pauline letters has been largely displaced by a predominantly "flesh = physical substance" sense (see further on 1:22). Most, however, assume that "flesh" here retains its more typical Pauline sense: thus RSV "his sensuous mind," NRSV/NJB "a human way of thinking," NEB/REB "worldly minds."

2:19 καὶ οὐ κρατῶν τὴν κεφαλήν, ἐξ οὗ πᾶν τὸ σῶμα διὰ τῶν ἀφῶν καὶ συνδέσμων ἐπιχορηγούμενον καὶ συμβιβαζόμενον αὔξει τὴν αὔξησιν τοῦ θεοῦ. In some ways the most striking notice of the Colossian "philosophy" is the likely implication here that the one just described as "delighting in" the angel worship, etc., was himself a Christian (disputed by Foerster 72).[37] This is probably the force of οὐ κρατῶν, since it most naturally has the sense of "not holding fast," that is, failing to remain closely united to (so BAGD s.v. κρατέω 2eβ; cf. the only other Pauline use, 2 Thes. 2:15; also Mark 7:3; Heb. 4:14; Rev. 2:13-15; so most translations). The alternative sense of "take hold, grasp" usually has an implication of some force which would be inappropriate here. Does this imply, then, that the main proponent of the Colossian philosophy was a Christian Jew who had attempted to blend his faith in Christ with more mystical practices? Or does it imply rather the assumption that a Jew by virtue of his own heritage was part of that corporate body of which the Christ (Messiah) was head and that to look to other means to enter the presence of God was to fail to hold to Christ? Either is possible, though on the former we might have expected a more forceful denunciation. At least, however, we must allow for the possibility (on the basis of this verse) that there was some overlap in membership or attendance in synagogue and church in Colossae (see further pp. 29f. above).

The image of Christ (clearly implicit; see n. 4) as the "head" is one more variation of the body-head metaphor. For whereas the earlier references emphasized the idea of the "head" in the sense of source and/or authority (see on 1:18a), here the thought is more of the body's complete dependence on the head

36. Rom. 8:6 appears to be close (τὸ φρόνημα τῆς σαρκός), but is in fact an abbreviation of the fuller description in 8:5: οἱ . . . τὰ τῆς σαρκὸς φρονοῦσιν ("those who set their minds on the things of the flesh").

37. The subject of κρατῶν must be the same as the subject of θέλων. Too many assume that the subject of 2:19 has shifted to the Christian in danger of being seduced by the Colossian "philosophy." So, e.g., Lohse, *Colossians and Philemon* 121.

for its nourishment and growth. Although that idea could follow from the background already sketched out (1:18a), the head as the controlling organ ultimately determining all that happens in the body (so E. Schweizer, *TDNT* 7.1076), the description of how this control operates here assumes a physiological understanding of the body (Lightfoot 198-99; Gnilka, *Kolosserbrief* 153; Arnold, "Head" 350-61). Ἀφή (only here and in Eph. 4:16 in the New Testament) is a medical technical term meaning "joint, ligament," and as its companion here, σύνδεσμος (literally "a fastening, that which binds together") is almost synonymous, denoting "sinews, ligaments" (see particularly Lightfoot 196-98). Through these the whole body is supported, supplied with what it needs (ἐπιχορηγέω; cf. 2 Cor. 9:10 and Gal. 3:5) and thus held together (συμβιβάζω, used already in 2:2); the whole image is taken further in Eph. 4:15-16. The emphasis seems to be more on the interconnectedness of the members of the body than on the joints and ligaments as actually channels of nurture. At the same time the end note is one of growth, which presumably includes both growth in size (numbers becoming Christian) and character (cf. 1:6, 10). The growth is "the growth of God" ("from God" in RSV/NRSV, "given by God" in NJB) because the head is the same Wisdom-Christ as in 1:15-20. "It should not be overlooked that God is and has the last word in this section" (Gnilka, *Kolosserbrief* 144).

The emphasis on the interconnectedness and thus interdependence of the members of the body is characteristically Pauline (particularly 1 Cor. 12:14-26).[38] And though the identification of the head (obviously Christ) as the most important part of the body is a step beyond the earlier Pauline theology of the church as body (see on 1:18a), there is no other sense of hierarchy within the body apart from that of the head.[39] The supply and bonding are provided to all and through all by the head. All are equally dependent on each other for that support; by implication, if any joints or ligaments fail, other members of the body will suffer. And the growth is corporate: there is no thought of some members growing independently or out of step with the rest. The sense of mutual interdependence remains strong. It was presumably the failure of the individual who had let go of Christ that he had gone in for flights of individual mystical experience, glorying in the company of angels, without regard to the other members of the body. And his advocacy of such experiences, criticizing and disqualifying those who saw their spirituality in more humdrum terms, must have been the very opposite of supportive of the Christian community.

38. Cf. Percy, *Leib* 54. For the development in thought from the earlier letters see my " 'The Body of Christ' in Paul," in *Worship, Theology and Ministry in the Early Church*, R. P. Martin FS, ed. M. J. Wilkins and T. Paige (JSNTS 87; Sheffield: Sheffield Academic Press, 1992) 146-62.

39. It is hardly the intention of the metaphor to identify the "joints and ligaments" as particular ministries or offices; see Schweizer, *Colossians* 164-65; Wolter 150.

It is noticeable that the response to the spirituality outlined in 2:18 is not to emphasize again Christ's headship over the rulers and authorities, as we might have expected. The worshiping angels as such were evidently not a threatening factor like the elemental forces, and the two categories should not be simply lumped together; at most we need to assume a recognition on the part of the Colossian mystics that venturing into the heavens took them into regions where other heavenly agencies exercised authority (see also n. 35 above). The danger at this point, however, was not so much a diminishing of Christ as a weakening of the link between Christ and his church. "As he fought in 2:9-15 for the wholeness of redemption, so now he fights for the wholeness of the community (πᾶν τὸ σῶμα), the one body of Christ" (Lähnemann 143). In other words, the concern here is more ecclesiological than christological: failure to hold to Christ is destructive of the body's unity and growth. At the same time, the play on the head-body theme probably implies the same movement of thought as in 1:18a (cf. Dibelius, *Kolosser, Epheser, Philemon* 36; Ernst, *Philipper, Philemon, Kolosser, Epheser* 211-12; Gnilka, *Kolosserbrief* 152; Roloff 227-29): the church is the place where Christ's headship over the cosmos should be most clearly evident, precisely because it is the church which is most fully "plugged into" (connected with) the source of supply and growth.

Life in Christ Does Not Depend on Observance of Jewish Practices (2:20-23)

20 *If* [1] *you died with Christ from the elemental forces of the world, why do you submit to regulations as though living in the world?* 21 *Do not touch, do not taste, do not handle,* 22 *things which are all meant for destruction by being consumed, in accordance with human commandments and teachings.* 23 *Such things have a reputation of wisdom in self-chosen worship and humility* [2] — *severe treatment of the body, not of value to anyone in regard to the gratification of the flesh.*

The reversion in a single compact sentence to talk of "dying with Christ" (cf. 2:12), "elemental forces" (cf. 2:8), regulations (cf. 2:14), food taboos (cf. 2:16), human traditions (cf. 2:8), and "self-chosen worship and humility" (cf. 2:18) indicates both that the teaching in view in Colossae was an integrated "package" and that this sentence functions as a conclusion to the section 2:6-23. The double emphasis of 2:12 ("buried with him . . . and raised with him") is now divided into two sections (2:20 — "If you died with Christ . . ."; 3:1 — "If you were raised with Christ . . ."); this suggests that the intention is to round off the critique of the Colossian "philosophy" by emphasizing what the Colossians have been rescued from (2:20-23) before going on to spell out what is involved in the new way of life (3:1–4:6). In both cases it is clear that what was in mind in such metaphors was not simply some mystical experience of initiation but the transition and transformation from one way of life to another quite different in character (see further on 3:1).

2:20 εἰ ἀπεθάνετε σὺν Χριστῷ ἀπὸ τῶν στοιχείων τοῦ κόσμου, τί ὡς ζῶντες ἐν κόσμῳ δογματίζεσθε; For the first time a note of appeal seems to enter (as distinct from a warning or instruction). And for the first time the suggestion is made that (many/some? of) the Colossian Gentile believers were finding, or beginning to find, the teaching of the Colossian Jews attractive and were (in danger of) being drawn into their practices. Hooker 123, however, may be right in translating "Why submit?" rather than "Why *do* you submit?" so that the clause is still a warning against a possibility rather than an accusation in reference to already adopted practices. Either

---

1. A natural impulse among later witnesses was to add a conjunction to smooth the link with 2:19: "If *therefore* you died. . . ."

2. The "and" inserted here by ℵ A C D and others disrupts what would otherwise be a close echo of the same combination (worship and humility) in 2:18. It should probably be omitted, therefore, with p⁴⁶ B and others, so that the third item of the list ("severe treatment of the body") becomes not a separate item, but a further description of the first two: "self-chosen worship and humility [that is], severe treatment of the body" (see on 2:23). The addition of the "and" no doubt was an attempt to make better sense of a difficult text.

way, this would not have been the first time that Gentile believers in Christ found the clearer lines of definition provided by traditional Judaism more attractive (Gal. 4:9-10), and it would not be the last (see pp. 29ff. above).

The appeal is the same as in 2:12, to that decisive event of baptism in which they identified themselves with Christ in his death, taking his death as marking the end of their identification with the world to which Christ died (cf. Gal. 6:14), and yielding themselves to the power of that death to old ways and to the power of his life from the dead (see on 2:12-13). The clause here is a direct echo of Rom. 6:8 (εἰ δὲ ἀπεθάνομεν σὺν Χριστῷ), a particularly Pauline adaptation of the more common summary of the Christian gospel, "Christ died for . . ." (Rom. 5:6, 8; 14:15; 1 Cor. 8:11; 15:3; 2 Cor. 5:15; 1 Thes. 5:10; 1 Pet. 3:18; see also Rom. 8:34; 14:9; Gal. 2:21; 1 Thes. 4:14).

The obvious construction to follow the intransitive verb to indicate what one has "died" to is the dative (as in the otherwise closely parallel context, Rom. 6:2 and 10; also Gal. 2:19). Here, however, ἀπό plus the genitive has been chosen (cf. Rom. 9:3; BDF §211). The intention is clearly to indicate that "from" which death has set free (GNB; NEB/REB try to capture the implication by translating "pass beyond reach of"); the alternative ἐν ᾧ construction of Rom. 7:6 is more awkward. Here the reference is to "the elemental forces of the world" (see on 2:8; though Wink, *Naming* 76-77, surprisingly argues that in 2:20 στοιχεῖα has a quite different sense). The implication is also clear. These are the powers and authorities which were so decisively routed on the cross (2:15). They therefore have no more authority over those "in Christ."

The conclusion is equally clear: there is no need to live any longer "in the world." That can hardly mean that the Colossian Christians should try to live as though physically abstracted or cut off from the world (cf. 1 Cor. 5:10); believers are as much still "in the world" in that sense as they are still "in the flesh." It must mean that they are no longer to live under the authority of "the elemental forces" which rule "the world," living lives determined by reference to these forces (cf. Lohmeyer 127; Lindemann, *Kolosserbrief* 50; Wolter 151), living as though the world itself was ultimately determined by such factors, as though the values and conduct which they stood for were what really counted in daily life.[3] The death of Christ spelled the end of all such systems; his death and resurrection provided the key insight into the reality of the world.[4] Why look anywhere else for the basis of daily living (cf. Phil. 3:18-20)?

---

3. Hence RSV/NRSV "still belonged to the world"; NEB/REB "still living the life of the world."

4. Cf. the whole three-volume project by W. Wink, *The Powers* (Minneapolis: Fortress, 1984, 1986, 1992), of which *Naming* is the first volume.

What "living in the world" amounts to in this case is given by the final verb δογματίζεσθε. It is the passive of δογματίζω, "decree by ordinance, issue a decree (δόγμα)," and thus presumably denotes the response of those to whom the decrees have been issued, that is, "submit to decrees or regulations" (LSJ), "let yourself be regulated" (BDF §314). There can be no doubt that a reference back to the "regulations" (δόγμασιν) of 2:14 is intended (the passive used of persons is attested only here, so we are dealing with a special formation). The decrees are thus those of "the rulers and authorities" (2:15), that is, of "the elemental forces." They are what might be called "the laws of nature." Or to be more precise, they are rules which order the cosmos and which need to be followed for life "in the world." This at any rate would be the rationale of those who pressed such regulations, of diaspora Jew as well as Gentile. What they meant for daily life is indicated by the examples following.

2:21 μὴ ἅψῃ μηδὲ γεύσῃ μηδὲ θίγῃς. The regulations quoted (they could be put in quotation marks) are all to do with purity and food. It is striking that just these are chosen to illustrate the decrees/regulations by which the Colossian "philosophy" thought it necessary to regulate this life, and not great moral rules such as those listed in 3:5 and 8. However, they should not be denigrated as indicating a primitive attitude to the cosmos and its controlling forces. On the contrary, they are a reminder of the importance attributed to ritual in all religions as a means of accessing and maintaining harmony with the spiritual forces behind perceptible reality. This is the Colossian philosophy's version of a "sacramental universe." On the other hand, the emphasis on the *via negativa* (life lived by "Do not"s) is probably indicative of a somewhat defensive and introverted group self-understanding.[5]

What precisely is in view in the three commands is not clear. Ἅπτομαι, "touch, take hold of," must denote a purity concern (Lohmeyer 128); behind it lies fear of defilement by physical contact with something forbidden, fear of impurity being transferred by physical contact (as regularly in Lev. 5:2-3; 7:19, 21; 11:8, 24-28, etc.; also Isa. 52:11, cited in 2 Cor. 6:17; Lohse, *Colossians and Philemon* 123 n. 77, cites Lucian, *De Syria dea* 54, evidencing the same concern). It can also mean "touch food," and so "eat" (BAGD s.v. ἅπτω 2a), or "touch (a woman)," denoting sexual intercourse (Gen. 20:6; Prov. 6:29; 1 Cor. 7:1; cf. 1 Tim. 4:3).[6] But here, without an object, the more general sense is presumably intended. Even so, purity concerns are usually

---

5. Abbott 273 notes: "It is a singular illustration of the asceticism of a later date, that some Latin commentators (Ambrose, Hilary, Pelagius) regarded these prohibitions as the apostle's own."

6. The latter is favored by Gnilka, *Kolosserbrief* 158; cf. Aletti, *Épître aux Colossiens* 202 n. 136. Sappington 68-69 notes the possibility that sexual abstinence was regarded as a preparation for receiving heavenly revelation.

at the root of food taboos, so the next regulation is no surprise: γεύομαι, "taste, partake of" food (BAGD; as in Matt. 27:34; Luke 14:24; John 2:9; Acts 10:10; 20:11; 23:14; only here in Paul). The third prohibition could again refer to food (see again BAGD s.v. ἅπτω 2a), but again probably means "touch" (with the hand, LSJ s.v. θιγγάνω 1), so that "handle" becomes a way of distinguishing the two nearly synonymous words. Most translations, however, prefer the sequence "handle, taste, touch," following Lightfoot 201; but it is the sense "touch" which is appropriate for ἅπτομαι in this context (as the Leviticus references make clear), not the stronger sense "take hold of."

These regulations could indicate the ritual practices of more than one of the ancient religions and cults. But here again the echo of characteristically Jewish concerns is strong, and particularly purity concerns, though that is missed by almost all commentators.[7] We have already noted the fundamental importance of observing the distinction between clean and unclean food within Jewish tradition (see on 2:16); here we might simply underline the fact that a distinction between "clean" and "unclean" is essentially a purity distinction. According to Jewish law one became impure by touching what was impure, particularly a corpse (Num. 19:11-13), but also through physical contact with (touching) a menstruant, or someone with a discharge of blood (Leviticus 15), or a leper (implied by the rules of Lev. 13:45-46). In short, touching human impurity of whatever sort made one impure (Lev. 5:3).[8] Such concerns were widely shared by Jews of the late Second Temple period, as the discovery of many *mikwaot* (immersion pools for ritual purification) in pre-70 Jerusalem and Judea clearly attests (Sanders, *Jewish Law* 214-27). They lie behind such episodes as Mark 5:1-34 and Luke 10:30-32 in the Gospels. Pharisees seem to have been still more concerned with purity, as their very nickname (Pharisees = "separated ones") indicates, a concern focused most sharply on the meal table.[9]

With the Essenes the concern was accentuated to an extreme degree, with strict regulations in place to ensure and safeguard "the purity of the Many" (1QS 6–7).[10] In view of the discussion of 2:18 above, it is particularly notable here that at Qumran we see precisely the same combination of purity concerns and heavenly worship as is implied for the Colossian "philosophy." Since the Dead Sea sect saw itself as a priestly community (hence the accentuated concern for purity), anticipating the eschatological congregation

7. Ernst, *Philipper, Philemon, Kolosser, Epheser* 213 is an exception. Pokorný 153 does at least note that "the observance of food regulations was not characteristic of the Gnostics."

8. For full details see E. P. Sanders, *Jewish Law from Jesus to the Mishnah* (London: SCM, 1990) 137-39.

9. This is the consensus view, though challenged by Sanders; see my *Partings* 41-42.

10. See further M. Newton, *The Concept of Purity at Qumran and in the Letters of Paul* (SNTSMS 53; Cambridge: Cambridge University, 1985), particularly 10-26.

in the presence of the holy angels, and encouraged also a mystical entrance into the heavenly temple (see on 2:18), it is no surprise that purity was as important for entry into the one as for the other. As we see in 11QT 47: "The city which I will sanctify, causing my name and sanctuary to abide [in it], shall be holy and pure of all impurity with which they can become impure. Whatever is in it shall be pure. Whatever enters it shall be pure." And the emphasis on holiness in the *Songs of the Sabbath Sacrifice* is likewise strong: "there is no unclean thing in their holy places" (4Q400 1.i.14 Newsom).

Such emphasis on purity would, of course, be more prominent among those who lived in the "holy" land. But concern among diaspora Jews regarding corpse impurity is attested in Philo, *De specialibus legibus* 3.205-6, and for regular purification in *Sibylline Oracles* 3.592-93. Most striking here is the explanation given by *Aristeas* 142 for the law of Moses: "So, to prevent our being perverted by contact with others or by mixing with bad influences, he hedged us in on all sides with purifications connected with meat and drink and touch (περιέφραξεν ἀγνείαις καὶ διὰ βρωτῶν καὶ ποτῶν καὶ ἀφῶν) and hearing and sight in terms of the law (νομικῶς)." The same combination of food and touch as here is notable. Also notable is the almost stereotyped criticism in Jewish literature of other Jews for their hypocrisy in claiming to be pure while acting impurely. Most striking here is Isa. 65:5 LXX: "They say 'Keep away from me; do not come near me, for I am pure.' " To similar effect, the attack by one group (probably within Judea) against another faction of Second Temple Judaism in *Testament of Moses* 7:9-10: "They, with hand and mind, will touch impure things, yet their mouths will speak enormous things, and they will even say, 'Do not touch me, lest you pollute me in the position I occupy . . . ,' " where again the combination of "Do not touch" with the criticism of high-sounding speech (as in Col. 2:4, 8, 18d) is striking. See also Mishnah *Makshirin* 3:7-8, cited by Str-B 3.629.

The likelihood, then, once again, is that the Colossian regulations in view in 2:21 are those of Colossian Jews who are anxious to maintain the purity they regard as necessary both to maintain their status as God's people, set apart by such purity rules from other nations, and for entry into the heavenly temple in their worship. The implication is not so much that these Colossian Jews were trying to enforce such regulations on all the Christians, simply that they were effective and forceful in explaining the theological rationale of their own lifestyle and worship. The overlap between the two groups was evidently such that several Gentile Christians were being enticed by these explanations to copy or join with the Colossian Jews in their ritual purity rules with a view to sharing their access to heaven (cf. again pp. 29ff. above). Paul and Timothy wrote in the hope of putting a stop to such an erosion of distinctive Christian faith and identity (cf. particularly Rom. 14:17).

2:22 ἅ ἐστιν πάντα εἰς φθορὰν τῇ ἀποχρήσει, κατὰ τὰ ἐντάλματα καὶ διδασκαλίας τῶν ἀνθρώπων. To counter this over-concern with purity of things, an effective response would seem to be to point out the relative unimportance of the things themselves. The trouble is that in a sacramental theology certain material things do assume a central importance, precisely because they have been found to afford that point of intersection with and access to the spiritual. Such were the purity regulations for many or most Jews. The writers, in contrast, had found that the cross and resurrection were the only effective point of intersection and access, so that anything which facilitated that (such as baptism) was to be promoted, but whatever diminished the effectiveness of the cross and resurrection was to be disowned.

The response here could call on the precedent which Jesus himself was remembered as having set. Ἔστιν εἰς has the sense "be destined for" (cf. Acts 8:20; 2 Pet. 2:12); ἀπόχρησις, another biblical *hapax*, is simply a stronger form of χρῆσις ("use"), to give the sense "using up, consumption"; and φθορά denotes dissolution and destruction of the material particularly in decay and death (as in Rom. 8:21 and 1 Cor. 15:42, 50; see LSJ and BAGD). "All which things" therefore focuses the purity issue on food and drink: they are "destined for destruction by being used up," that is, in consumption. The echo is of Mark 7:19/Matt. 15:17: unclean food should not be a matter of great concern because it goes into the stomach only to be thence expelled into the latrine (cf. 1 Cor. 6:13).

The echo becomes still stronger with the next phrase, which closely parallels the argument of Mark 7:7/Matt. 15:9, both quoting almost verbatim from Isa. 29:13, God's rebuke of his people:

Isa. 29:13	μάτην δὲ σέβονταί με διδάσκοντες
Mark 7:7/Matt. 15:9	μάτην δὲ σέβονταί με διδάσκοντες

Isa. 29:13	ἐντάλματα ἀνθρώπων καὶ διδασκαλίας
Mark 7:7/Matt. 15:9	διδασκαλίας ἐντάλματα ἀνθρώπων
Col. 2:22	τὰ ἐντάλματα καὶ διδασκαλίας τῶν ἀνθρώπων

It is most unlikely that either echo is accidental; apart from anything else ἔνταλμα ("commandment") occurs only in these three passages in the New Testament and only in one other passage in the LXX as a translation of Hebrew (Job 23:11-12); outside the Pauline corpus διδασκαλία ("teaching") appears in the New Testament only in Mark 7:7/Matt. 15:9, and again rarely in the LXX (from the Hebrew Bible only in Prov. 2:17 and Isa. 29:13); and the definite article here strengthens the sense of an allusion to a well-known phrase (cf. Masson 137 n. 3). Almost certainly, then, Paul and Timothy here were deliberately alluding to the rebuke of Isaiah. This at once provides a further confirmation of the essentially Jewish character of the threat to the

Colossian Christians: the allusion to a rebuke to Israel would only be effective if it came as a rebuke to those who understood themselves as the people of Israel. These regulations of which the Colossian (Christian?) Jews made so much were the very commandments and teachings which Isaiah had long ago warned against.

More striking still is the fact that the quotation of Isa. 29:13 in the Jesus tradition comes once again in the context of the dispute between Jesus and the Pharisees about purity (Mark 7:1-23/Matt. 15:1-20). This second echo of the same tradition again should be sufficient to remove most doubts (Lightfoot 202-3; *pace* Gnilka, *Kolosserbrief* 159) that the writers here were aware of this Jesus tradition (in its Greek form), including both its major thrust (regarding purity) and its detail, and that they deliberately echoed it in order to give their argument more bite with those who identified themselves religiously by their relation to Jesus (see also 2:8 — "the tradition of human beings"). It was Jesus who showed the relative unimportance (according to Mark 7:19 the complete irrelevance) of the purity laws as they affected food. This presumably is one of the traditions about the Christ which the Colossians had "received" from Epaphras (2:6). Paul's echo of the same Jesus tradition in Rom. 14:14 is hedged around with more qualification, no doubt because of the different circumstances among the Christians in Rome (note also *1 Clement* 15:2 and Justin, *Dialogue* 48, 78, 140).

2:23 ἅτινά ἐστιν λόγον μὲν ἔχοντα σοφίας ἐν ἐθελοθρησκίᾳ καὶ ταπεινοφροσύνῃ καὶ ἀφειδίᾳ σώματος, οὐκ ἐν τιμῇ τινι πρὸς πλησμονὴν τῆς σαρκός. The rebuke just delivered by means of the allusion to Isa. 29:13 was strong enough, but Paul and Timothy were probably well enough aware of the attractiveness of such regulated religious discipline, both as a mark of commitment and because of the rich spiritual experiences which it promised. This claim could not be ignored. The writers certainly go on to address it, but to what precise effect is unclear. Here again the text becomes difficult ("hopelessly obscure" according to Moule, *Colossians and Philemon* 108), as a result of a sequence of unusual terms (most assume that terms used in the Colossian "philosophy" are being cited) and syntax,[11] and again we need to proceed phrase by phrase before trying to put the whole together.

With "such things" (the force of ἅτινα), the reference is still to 2:21, "have a reputation of wisdom." The latter phrase (λόγον ἔχειν + genitive) is unusual, but there are sufficient indications of its use in the sense "have a reputation (for something)" (see Lightfoot 203; Lohse, *Colossians and Philemon* 126 n. 96), where the context allows the usually positive term (λόγος) to have a more querulous tone. The reference to "wisdom" confirms what was implicit in the frequency of the earlier references, including the

---

11. For attempts to "mend" the text see, e.g., Lohse, *Colossians and Philemon* 124-26; O'Brien, *Colossians, Philemon* 151-52.

use of the hymn to Wisdom-Christ (1:9, 15-18, 28; 2:3), namely that desire for wisdom and desire to practice wisdom was a prominent element in the Colossian Jewish religious praxis in view (see on 1:9 and 2:3).

The link back into the visionary piety of 2:18 is clear in the next phrase. The rules of 2:21 appear wise as a means of promoting ἐθελοθρησκία καὶ ταπεινοφροσύνη. The latter term obviously refers back to the "humility" seen as integral to either preparation for or participation in the angel worship (see on 2:18). And the former is obviously a special coinage for the occasion (it is not found anywhere else). As noted on 2:18, some commentators think that the reference here rules out the possibility of taking θρησκεία τῶν ἀγγέλων as subjective genitive. But an ἐθελο- compound simply denotes an action or status taken voluntarily or deliberately (see LSJ s.v. ἐθελο-). The implied criticism here, then, like the preceding "reputation of wisdom," which governs the phrase, is dressed in an acknowledgment of good intent; the "worship (of angels)" was freely chosen.[12] Alternatively, given its coinage to suit the occasion, the word could be a play on the θέλων ἐν . . . θρησκείᾳ of 2:18, denoting "delighted-in worship," or it could be intended to convey the sense "wished-for worship," implying that participation in angel worship was a figment of an overimaginative desire.[13] And if the next phrase, ἀφειδίᾳ σώματος, is in apposition (see below) there could be a still stronger negative note: severity to the body as an expression of the strength of the desire.

Ἀφειδία is yet one more biblical *hapax,* and it was not much used elsewhere. But it comes from the verb ἀφειδέω, "be unsparing," and thus can be given the sense of unsparing discipline ("severity"), as well as the better-attested unsparing giving ("generosity, liberality," LSJ s.v.). The equivalent verbal expression ἀφειδεῖν τοῦ σώματος is not uncommon in the sense of courageous exposure to hardship and danger in war (Lightfoot 204; see also Lohmeyer 129 n. 5). Since the term ἀφειδία would normally occur in a eulogistic context (*NDIEC* 2.106), we should note that once again the riposte of 2:23 is disguised in terms of compliment; the severity of the self-discipline practiced by the others in Colossae is not as such a matter for criticism.[14]

Now the problems become severe.[15] The phrase ἐν τιμῇ τινι is again highly unusual, but τιμή in the sense of "value, worth" is well enough known

---

12. See also Francis, "Humility" 181-82; Kehl, "Erniedrigung" 390; Carr, "Notes" 500; H. Balz, *EDNT* 1.381; Rowland, "Apocalyptic Visions" 76-77; O'Brien, *Colossians, Philemon* 153.

13. NEB/REB's "forced piety" and GNB's "forced worship of angels" introduce an unjustifiably strong negative note, as does Wolter's "self-made worship" (153-54).

14. DeMaris 58 oddly regards "severe treatment of the body" as one of the "aims" or a "goal" of the Colossian philosophy and as therefore indicating a teaching and practice that has gone beyond typically Jewish concerns.

15. For options at this point see, e.g., Schweizer, *Colossians* 169.

(Lightfoot 204; LSJ s.v. II), and the phrase itself may be a Latinism (BAGD s.v. 1). It is doubtful, however, whether οὐ . . . τινι means "not any" (Abbott 277), and Gnilka, *Kolosserbrief* 161, attempts to retain τιμή in its normal sense of "honor": "to no one does it bring honor!" (cf. H. Hübner, *EDNT* 3.359). For πρός in the sense of "for," that is, to check or prevent or cure, see again Lightfoot 204-5. If the phrase should be taken together, a translation "not of any value to anyone in regard to" seems best.

We are still not out of the woods, however, since the next term, πλησμονή, is yet one more New Testament *hapax*. But it clearly means "being filled, satiety," particularly with regard to food and drink, and so "gratification" (BAGD). And the most obvious implication here is that "gratification of the flesh" is something undesirable. If we compare its use in the LXX, a neutral sense predominates (satisfaction of hunger, usually in the equivalent prepositional phrase, εἰς πλησμονήν, e.g., Exod. 16:3, 8; Lev. 25:19; Prov. 3:10; Lam. 5:6); but a negative note is probably present in Ezek. 16:49 ("surfeit of food") and Hos. 13:6 (εἰς πλησμονήν).[16]

How then should the pieces be put together into a single sentence? The most common interpretation in effect makes the understandable assumption that the sentence is structured around the contrast provided by the two ἐν phrases: "Such things have a reputation of wisdom in (ἐν) . . . but are not in value (ἐν τιμῇ, i.e., "of worth") to anyone. . . ."[17] The difficulty here is the absence of an adversative before the οὐκ ("but," ἀλλά, or δέ to balance the earlier μέν). It is true that the omission of an adversative is not exceptional (BDF §447.2, 3; Moule, *Colossians and Philemon* 108, suggests the rather different 2 Tim. 2:14 as a parallel; Hanssler 145 argues that the concessive force of the first clause renders a δέ superfluous); but the absence of an adversative here is so striking (it would leave Paul's conclusion critically ambiguous) that the attempt should be made to make sense of the text without reading one in. A well-argued alternative takes everything from λόγον μέν . . . ἐν τιμῇ τινι as a parenthesis, leaving "which things are for gratification of the flesh" as the main clause, itself a rebuke to the attitude expressed in 2:21;[18] but the lack of an adversative at the same point is still a problem and the whole remains awkward.

Perhaps a better key to structure is to note the further play on the concepts σῶμα and σάρξ, since this has been such a feature of the letter so far (1:22, 24; 2:11, 17-19). That is to say, the contrast between ἀφειδίᾳ

---

16. It is possible to argue that πλησμονὴ τῆς σαρκός takes a backward glance (by way of contrast) to πλήρωμα τῆς θεότητος σωματικῶς (2:9; so Lähnemann 148-49).

17. The most striking attempt here is that of NJB: "In these rules you can indeed find what seems to be good sense, the cultivation of the will, and a humility that takes no account of the body; but in fact they have no value against self-indulgence."

18. Reicke, "Verständnis"; Hollenbach, followed by O'Brien, *Colossians, Philemon* 151-52; Pokorný 154-55; Fowl 149.

σώματος and πλησμονὴν τῆς σαρκός needs to be given more weight. When we add in the likelihood that the original text did not have an "and" linking ἀφειδίᾳ σώματος to what went before (see n. 2 above), we are left with the possibility that ἀφειδίᾳ σώματος . . . is attached to the preceding context in apposition to the antecedent datives (Masson 138 n. 1). This would diminish the problem of the lack of an adversative, since the contrast between the two main phrases would be sufficient of itself to make the point. The following sense is the result: "which things have a reputation of wisdom in self-chosen worship and humility — severe treatment of the body, not of value to anyone in regard to the gratification of the flesh."

The remaining problem is how to assess the force of the contrast — between a commendatory (even if qualified) reference to "severity of the body" and the implied condemnation of "gratifying the flesh." The most obvious answer, as commentators usually argue, is that "flesh" is being used with the negative, moral force so characteristic of the earlier Paul (cf. Rom. 13:14 and Gal. 5:16-17: the desires of the flesh); hence NEB/REB "in combating sensuality."[19] The difficulty is that the phrase itself suggests gratification of physical needs in terms of food and drink, as the Fathers clearly understood (BAGD s.v. πλησμονή; G. Delling, *TDNT* 6.133). But if that sense of the phrase were pressed it would reduce the contrast of this final clause to something of an absurdity: the practice of severity to the body, including self-mortification and fasting (ταπεινοφροσύνη), does not make any difference to the satisfaction of physical appetites.

It may be, therefore, that we need to look for a third option, one which gives more weight to the physical sense of "flesh," in line with the consistent emphasis of the word in the letter. Such a sense is given in the use of σάρξ to refer to physical and ethnic identity (as regularly in the phrase κατὰ σάρκα: Rom. 1:3; 4:1; 9:3, 5, 8; 1 Cor. 10:18; Gal. 4:23, 29). And similarly negative phrases are used elsewhere by Paul to denote too much value being placed in that flesh, ethnic flesh rather than moral flesh, as we might say — in particular, "boasting in the flesh" in Gal. 6:12-13 and "confidence in the flesh" in Phil. 3:3-4, which in Pauline terms were as much a distortion of the terms of grace and a pandering to the flesh as any physical greed or overindulgence. "Gratification of the flesh" should possibly, therefore, be taken as referring to satisfaction felt by the Colossian Jews in their ethnic (fleshly, κατὰ σάρκα) identification as Jews, the people chosen by the one God to be his own elect. And in view of our repeated findings that the most clearly discernible features of the Colossian "philosophy" are Jewish in character, the likelihood becomes still stronger that what is being critiqued here is an assumption on the part of (many of) the Colossian Jews that rules

19. " 'Flesh' is humankind in its own resources (*Selbstmächtigkeit*) and thereby in its opposition (*Widerspruch*) to God" (Lindemann, *Kolosserbrief* 52).

for living and worship practices were ways of expressing (maintaining and marking out) their distinctiveness as Jews.

In short, the line of criticism at this point is probably to acknowledge much that appears admirable in the religious praxis of the Colossian Jews here in view, but with the added final reminder that severity to the body can be just another form of pandering to the flesh (cf. 1 Cor. 13:3). It is the extent to which the maintenance of Jewish identity, as also providing the possibility of such heavenly worship, depended on the rules and regulations of 2:16 and 21, which is the main focus of attack. And the line of attack is the earlier Pauline one (particularly in Galatians), that such a concern for Jewish identity and Jewish privilege as Jewish is at the end of the day just another form of self-indulgence or national indulgence.

THE PATTERN OF LIVING THAT FOLLOWS FROM THE
CROSS (3:1–4:6)

The main line of argument so far (2:8-23), following from the thematic statement of 2:6-7, has been primarily a response, more and more specific and emphatic, to what Paul and Timothy regarded as a threat posed to the Colossian believers by members of the Colossian synagogues who had developed a forceful apologetic rhetoric (2:8). These Jews probably included some who associated with the Gentile believers in the alternative (Christian) gathering (2:19), or at least their apologetic was proving attractive (2:16, 18) and effective (2:20) among at least some of the Gentile believers in Christ. Their religious praxis, where their appeal was most direct (2:14, 16, 18, 21), evidently blended the characteristic Jewish appeal to the distinctiveness of Israel's ancestral traditions (2:8, 22 — circumcision, food laws, sabbath, ritual purity) with an observance of such regulations that in effect was (in the writers' view) as dependent on the elemental forces as any Hellenistic cult (2:8, 14-15, 20). In pandering to Jewish pride their praxis simply re-channeled the "fleshliness" which their asceticism was designed to over-come (2:23). Worst of all, it diminished the status of the Christ, who was the focus of the Christian community and the reason for its distinctive existence, by failing to grasp the full significance of the cross and resurrection in particular (2:11-15) and thus also the unimportance of practices regulated by reference to the cosmic elements (2:15, 20). In this way the significance of the Colossian believer's acceptance of Christ Jesus as Lord (2:6) has been expounded.

But once the authors have disowned the lifestyle and religious practices of traditional and mystical Judaism, there is more to be said. The other clause of 2:6 must also be expounded — what it means to "walk in him." It was not enough to remind the recipients of the letter of the ways of life and worship which they should have left behind and/or should not be adopting now. It was equally important, if not more important, to give a clear indication of the characteristic features of Christian living and worship, the positive alternative to be pursued over against the negative alternative to be avoided. The change of emphasis is indicated by the opening term (3:1 — "Since you have been raised with Christ"), balancing the reminder of what they had left behind (2:20 — "Since you died with Christ"). After a statement of principle, the perspective from which all their ethical conduct should flow (3:1-4), there follows a sequence of general guidelines and practical exhortations, relating also to worship (3:5-17), then some specific household rules (3:18–4:1) and some further, concluding exhortations (4:2-6).

Two important issues have caused some dispute regarding this section. First, it looks as though a sequence of general exhortations (3:1-4), traditional motifs ("put off/put on"), and standard forms (vice and virtue lists, household rules) have simply been lumped together. This is in line with the original observation of M. Dibelius, *From Tradition to Gospel* (London: Nicholson and Watson, 1934) 238, that "the hortatory sections of the Pauline letters . . . lack an immediate relation with the circumstances of the letter" (so here, e.g., Lohmeyer 131; Hunter 55-56; Pokorný 158-59; cf. J. T. Sanders, *Ethics* 79-80). But while the use of familiar themes is obvious, the adaptation of the material to the context is also evident: 3:1 picks up the themes of resurrection with Christ (2:12) and of Christ's triumph (2:10, 15), just as the talk of having died in 3:3 echoes 2:12 and 20; the exhortation to "seek/set your minds on" τὰ ἄνω (3:1-2) is obviously playing in some way upon the Colossian philosophy's delight in heavenly worship (2:18), just as the commendation of ταπεινοφροσύνη within the list of virtues in 3:12 can hardly be without a backward glance to 2:18 and 23; and the theme of hiddenness and (future) unveiling in 3:3-4 clearly echoes the prominence of these themes earlier in 1:26-27 and 2:2-3. Similarly at the end of the section the attempt to summarize earlier themes is obvious:

4:2-3	prayer and thanksgiving	1:3, 9
4:3	mystery of Christ	1:26-27; 2:2
4:5	walk in wisdom	1:9-10; 2:6-7.

It is equally if not more striking how much the whole parenesis has been Christianized. This is most obvious in the complete christocentricity of the opening paragraph (3:1-4). And though the vice lists include standard terms (3:5-8), the correlated "put off/put on" exhortation (3:9-11) brings us back at once to the motif of renewed creation where Christ is all in all, in echo of the earlier hymn (1:15-20). Likewise, the following virtue list climaxes with the characteristic Christian encouragement to forgive as forgiven, with love and the peace of Christ undergirding the whole and the unity of the body (3:12-15), just as it is the word of Christ which issues in worship with "all things in the name of the Lord Jesus" as its desired outworking (3:16-17). And in the household rules (3:18–4:1) it is the sevenfold reference to "the Lord" which infuses and transforms all. Despite this, Schulz, *Ethik* 560-63, presses the Colossian parenesis into a works-faith dialectic and accuses it of a moralism which has left behind the characteristic Pauline emphasis on justification by faith. At the same time, the degree to which the focus on Christ has removed the Spirit from view (contrast Romans 8 and Galatians 5) remains a puzzle, explained by Schweizer, "Geist," as a reaction to Colossian enthusiasm, but without real support from the text.

In regard to the second disputed issue, it is regularly assumed that the parenesis, while following Paul's typical indicative-imperative pattern (e.g., Moule, "New Life"; Schrage, *Ethics* 244-46; Marxsen, *Ethik* 236-39), nevertheless gives clear evidence of a later perspective in which the "already" has swamped the "not yet" (resurrection with Christ has already happened, 3:1), so that a kind of Platonic or Gnostic above-below timelessness (3:1-2, 5) has replaced the more typically apocalyptic forward-looking emphasis of the earlier Paul, the writer perhaps thus trying to "out-Gnosticize" the opposition.[1] But neither is this sufficiently accurate. The "not yet" is strongly present in 3:3-4, 10, 24-25 and 4:2, the apocalyptic character of 3:3-4 being particularly noticeable (cf. Percy, *Probleme* 116). Even more notable is the strongly Jewish cast to the whole, particularly in the list of vices ("idolatry"), the double emphasis given in 3:11 to the ending of the distinction between Greek and Jew, circumcision and uncircumcision, the echo of Jewish covenant self-identity in 3:12 ("elect, holy, and beloved"), and the various allusions to characteristic Jewish principles in the household rules (concern for the weaker members in the threefold pairing, honoring parents as pleasing to God, fearing the Lord, inheritance from the Lord, and no favoritism with God).

In short, this section is clearly of a piece with what has gone before, confirms the Jewish character of the Colossian opposition, and maintains a characteristically Pauline balance between teaching and parenesis, "already" and "not yet," heavenly perspective and everyday responsibility.

---

1. With varying emphases: Dibelius, *Kolosser, Epheser, Philemon* 40; Bornkamm, "Hoffnung"; Grässer; J. T. Sanders, *Ethics* 69-73; Stegemann 528-30; Schulz 559; Schnackenburg, *Botschaft* 2.75; Lohse, *Ethics* 148; Hübner 360-61; only "traces of future eschatology" according to Steinmetz 29-32.

The Perspective from Which the Christian Life Should Be Lived (3:1-4)

1 *If then you have been raised with Christ, seek what is above, where the Christ is,*[2] *seated on God's right.* 2 *Set your minds on what is above, not on what is on the earth.* 3 *For you died and your life has been hidden with Christ in God.* 4 *Whenever the Christ, who is our*[3] *life, has been revealed, then you also will be revealed with him in glory.*[4]

As noted above, 3:1-4, particularly 3:2, has encouraged the view that the writer has adopted a Hellenistic mystical or Gnostic perspective (Grässer, etc.: see n. 1 above). But this ignores the fact that τὰ ἄνω can as readily denote an apocalyptic perspective, which fits much more consistently with the apocalyptic-mystical character of the Colossian philosophy (cf. Findeis 421 n. 162). Levison, indeed, makes a persuasive case for seeing the thought of the paragraph as more consistently expressive of apocalyptic perspective, closely similar to that evident in 2 *Baruch* 48:42–52:7, where the "things above" (3:2) are synonymous with the "life hidden" of Col. 3:3-4. Either way this attempt to outflank the Colossian philosophy was somewhat hazardous — the key difference, and the main reason for its prominence, presumably being the sustained focus on Christ throughout 3:1-4 (Lincoln, *Paradise* 125-28).

Wolter 164-65 takes 3:1-4 as the *peroratio,* summing up the considerations of the *argumentatio* (2:9-23) and drawing the reader to a favorable reception of the following more specific *exhortatio* (3:5–4:6).

3:1 εἰ οὖν συνηγέρθητε τῷ Χριστῷ, τὰ ἄνω ζητεῖτε, οὗ ὁ Χριστός ἐστιν ἐν δεξιᾷ τοῦ θεοῦ καθήμενος.   As 2:20 took up what we might call the "down side" of 2:12 ("you were buried with Christ"), so now Paul and

2. Almost all agree that a comma should be inserted here, the verb ("is") introducing a more established description ("seated on God's right"); see, e.g., Harris 137.

3. ὑμῶν is more strongly attested (Metzger 624), but it is more likely that ἡμῶν was altered (deliberately or unconsciously) to conform with the consistent second person plural usage of the paragraph. It was evidently a Pauline characteristic to move awkwardly from second to first person to ensure that his readers did not think that what was said applied exclusively to them (see, e.g., Lightfoot 184 and 208). Translators and commentators are as divided as the textual considerations between "our" (RSV, NEB/REB; e.g., Abbott 279-80; Lohmeyer 131 n. 2; O'Brien, *Colossians, Philemon* 157) and "your" (JB/NJB, GNB, NIV, NRSV; Dibelius, *Kolosser, Epheser, Philemon* 40; Masson 140 n. 1; Pokorný 162).

4. Note the neat structural parallel between 3:3 and 3:4 (O'Brien, *Colossians, Philemon* 159):

For you died	Whenever the Christ
and your *life*	who is our *life*
has been hidden *with Christ*	has been manifested, then you also will
	be manifested *with him*
in God.	*in* glory.

Timothy take up the "up side" of the same verse ("you were raised with him"). The event of death-and-resurrection was two-sided for Christ himself (2:15); a message of the cross without the resurrection would not be gospel, and a call to embrace the implications of the cross without a call also to embrace the implications of the resurrection would be poor teaching. So here: it was not enough to remind the Colossian recipients of the lifestyle and religious praxis that they no longer do or need follow out; that would have been too much like the "Do not"s characteristic of the Colossian Jews' praxis (2:21). The message of the resurrection has equally positive corollaries for the believer's daily life, which have to be spelled out to provide a sufficient counterweight to the evident attractiveness of the more traditional Jewish lifestyle: "If, therefore, . . ." in the sense of "Since it is the case that. . . ."

As in 2:12, the language is metaphorical and not literal. The resurrection with Christ in a resurrection like Christ's still lay as much in the future as it had in the earlier treatment in Romans 6 (see on 2:12, and note the prominence of "hope" in 1:5, 23, and 27). The very fact that an exhortation to "seek what is above" was required and needed to be repeated ("set your minds on what is above," 3:2) is sufficient indication that what was in mind was a change of perspective, not (yet) a (complete) ontological change (see also Lohmeyer 132-33; Gnilka, *Kolosserbrief* 171-72; and Lincoln, *Paradise* 122-23, 131-34, against Grässer's overemphasis on the "already" dimension: baptism understood as ascension to heaven [150-53]). It is the sort of change which follows from complete identification with another person or cause, when the service of that person or cause becomes all-consuming, the basic determiner of all priorities, the bubbling spring of a motivation, resolution, and application which perseveres despite even repeated setbacks. In the ancient world such self-identification would normally be with a patron and his or her cause or with a club or cult. Today we might think of a mother with her handicapped child or an artist with his or her calling. What the Pauline gospel offered and emphasized by means of its passive formulations was the promise that the change was not self-contrived but rather enabled and brought about by divine grace, the same divine grace which had raised Jesus from the dead (cf. again 2:12 with Rom. 8:11).

The key factor in this new perspective is the fact that Christ has been raised and exalted (the two are not distinguished here) to sit on God's right in heaven. The language is formulaic, clearly echoing Ps. 110:1: "The LORD said to my Lord, 'Sit on my right' (Κάθου ἐκ δεξιῶν μου), till I make your enemies a stool for your feet."[5] This was a passage which featured greatly in earliest Christian apologetic, since it provided such a good explanation of

5. The lack of other specific allusions to particular Old Testament passages in Colossians is striking and as puzzling as the equal lack of clear references to the Spirit (apart from 1:8).

what had become of the resurrected Jesus. It is explicitly cited in Mark 12:36 pars.; Acts 2:34-35; and Heb. 1:13 and clearly alluded to elsewhere (Mark 14:62 pars.; Rom. 8:34; 1 Cor. 15:25; Eph. 1:20; Heb. 1:3; 8:1; 10:12-13; 12:2; 1 Pet. 3:22). That makes it the Old Testament text most often alluded to in the New Testament.[6]

The picture is clear. God sits on a throne in heaven (so explicitly in Heb. 8:1 and 12:2), with the exalted Christ sitting on a throne beside him. The imagery was almost certainly drawn from Dan. 7:9-14: the human-like figure ("one like a son of man") apparently takes the other throne (7:9 — plural "thrones"). This is the implication of Matt. 19:28 and 25:31, the only references to Christ's throne outside the Christian apocalypse (Rev. 3:21a), both linked to the Son of Man. What made Christ's throne different from other thrones (Luke 22:30; Rev. 4:4; 11:16; 20:4) is its proximity to God's throne (hence the confusing picture in Rev. 3:21b; 5:6; 7:17; 22:1, 3).

The exalted Christ sat on God's immediate right (ἐν δεξιᾷ τοῦ θεοῦ). The image is one of power. The right (hand) of God (ἡ δεξιὰ θεοῦ) was a way of expressing strength, powerful protection, and favor in Hebrew poetry (e.g., Exod. 15:6, 12; Pss. 16:11; 17:7; 20:6; 44:3; 60:5; 73:23; 98:1; 118:15-16), and to sit at the king's right was a sign of special recognition and authorization (1 Kgs. 2:19; 1 Esdr. 4:29; Sir. 12:12; Mark 10:37). Speculation in some Jewish circles about who should sit on God's right evoked considerable fear among the early rabbis that the unity of God was being infringed (the "two powers heresy"); and there is a rabbinic tradition of the great rabbi Akiba at that time being rebuked for his suggestion that the second throne in heaven was for the Messiah (Babylonian Talmud *Hagigah* 14a).[7] But there is no indication at this stage that Jews in general perceived the Christian claim regarding Jesus as such a threat, even though Christians were already in effect making the same assumption as Akiba (we could translate "where the Messiah is, seated . . ."). On the contrary, the problem for Colossian Christian Jews was likely to be the reverse, that the visionary worship envisaged in 2:18 was itself in danger of postulating too many heavenly powers, of whom Jesus was only one. It was the Christian belief that Christ had to be recognized as having distinctive, indeed unique, significance among the powers of heaven which was having to be asserted at this stage and which resulted a generation after the probable date of this letter in Jewish authorities accusing Christians of abandoning the unity of God with their claims regarding Christ (John 5:18; 10:33).

---

6. The main specialist studies of Ps. 110:1 are still D. M. Hay, *Glory at the Right Hand: Psalm 110 in Early Christianity* (SBLMS 18; Nashville: Abingdon, 1973); W. R. G. Loader, "Christ at the Right Hand — Ps. 110:1 in the New Testament," *NTS* 24 (1977) 199-217; M. Gourges, *À la droite de Dieu* (Paris: Gabalda, 1978); Juel ch. 6.

7. See A. F. Segal, *Two Powers in Heaven: Early Rabbinic Reports about Christianity and Gnosticism* (Leiden: Brill, 1977), particularly ch. 2.

The consequences for the Christian perspective are thus also clear. If Jesus, the Christ, is so highly favored and acknowledged to be God's "right-hand man," with all the power and authority to effect God's will and to protect his own which is implicit in that claim, then Christian life should be entirely oriented by reference to this Christ. This is summed up in the exhortation τὰ ἄνω ζητεῖτε, in which τὰ ἄνω ("the things above") is a shorthand way of referring to heaven (as in John 8:23; in Paul cf. Gal. 4:26 and Phil. 3:14). Ζητεῖτε (present tense) probably has the force not so much of "try to obtain, desire to possess" (BAGD s.v. ζητέω 2a; NEB/REB "aspire to the realm above") as of "keep looking for" that which is of Christ or from heaven in the situations of daily living (cf. Matt. 6:33; Rom. 2:7; 1 Cor. 10:24; Heb. 11:14; 13:14; NIV's "set your hearts on" is not quite right). What is in view is a complete reorientation of existence (Wolter 166). The theological worldview implied is that of 2:17, including some degree of merging of Platonic (but not yet Gnostic) cosmology and Jewish apocalyptic (see above on 2:17, and see Lincoln, *Paradise* 117-18, 123-24). Such Jewish-Christian adaptation of more widespread Hellenistic cosmologies is already an indicator of how readily a spatial conceptuality (heaven as above) can be translated into a different conceptuality where "higher" retains its positive significance.

3:2 τὰ ἄνω φρονεῖτε, μὴ τὰ ἐπὶ τῆς γῆς. For the sake of emphasis the exhortation is in effect repeated, again in the present tense to denote a sustained effort or perspective (GNB "keep your minds fixed").[8] Φρονέω means not merely to think but to have a settled way of understanding, to hold an opinion, to maintain an attitude (Rom. 8:5; 14:6; 1 Cor. 13:11; 2 Cor. 13:11; Phil. 2:2, 5; 3:19). The fuller phrase τά τινος φρονεῖν is well known in the sense "take someone's side, espouse someone's cause" (BAGD s.v. φρονέω 2). This underscores the point, therefore, that what is commended is not an apocalyptic or mystical preoccupation with the fur-niture of heaven, as 3:1 could be taken to imply (that might have conceded the ground already contested in 2:18 and 23), but a cast of mind, a settled way of looking at things, a sustained devotion to and enactment of a life cause.

The alternatives are posed simply and starkly. There is an orientation and manner of living which is firmly rooted to the ground (cf. Phil. 3:19: οἱ τὰ ἐπίγεια φρονοῦντες), which looks no higher than satisfaction of physical appetites and social manipulation, however much it may be dressed up in fine phrases and high sentiments. This was probably the charge brought against the adherents to the Colossian "philosophy" in 2:23, and it is equally polemical here: their claim to participate in the worship of

---

8. NEB's "let your thoughts dwell" and JB/NJB's "let your thoughts be" are not strong enough.

heaven in fact betrayed a very earthbound perspective, not least in its practical outworkings (2:20-23). The alternative commended is not to abandon a heavenly perspective, but to maintain one which results in a less earthly outcome, to foster and follow a way of living and of practicing religion which always and again takes its starting point from the true reality (Christ, 3:1, 3-4) in heaven (τὰ ἄνω).[9] It is the latter alone which the Colossian Christians should cherish and seek to live from. The key, once again then, is recognition of the crucial turn of events and transformation of perception of reality effected by Christ's death and resurrection; it is this Christ-perspective which should mark out the Colossian Christians' heavenly spirituality and enable them to see through the alternative spirituality of the Colossian philosophy.

3:3 ἀπεθάνετε γὰρ καὶ ἡ ζωὴ ὑμῶν κέκρυπται σὺν τῷ Χριστῷ ἐν τῷ θεῷ. The importance of gaining firm hold on this new perspective is so important that Paul and Timothy restate the point afresh, summing up once again the twofold consequence of the Colossian believers' identification with Christ. "You died!" "With Christ" (2:20) is not included here, though clearly implied, in order that the point can be made in all its starkness. Here again there is, of course, no suggestion that a literal death has taken place (other than Christ's). The aorist is simply a powerful metaphor for the fact that when they believed in Christ in baptism they were putting their previous way of life to death and having it buried out of sight. Consequently, it should no longer be a factor in their new way of life. They have been freed by that one act to live a quite different kind of life, determined not by their old fears and loyalties but by their new and primary loyalty to Christ and by the enabling which comes from on high (1:11, 29). The fact that no irreversible change has taken place (begun but not completed) is sufficiently indicated by the exhortations which immediately follow (3:5). The rhetorical character of the bare aorist formulation here, as also at the beginning of chapters 6, 7, and 8 of Romans, needs to be recognized. Its object is to ensure that the change of perspective marked by conversion-initiation is final and fixed. Nevertheless, throughout this section the balance between past act, ongoing outworking, and future completion is maintained (cf. Lona 179-89; Wedderburn, *Baptism* 75-76).

The other side of this death (with Christ), already stated in 3:1, is now restated in a variant formulation: "your life has been hidden with Christ in God." The thought once again is probably apocalyptic in character, as the

---

9. Levison 99-100 sees τὰ ἄνω as an allusion to paradise and the angelic host; but that would give too much ground to the practitioners of "angel worship" (2:18, 23) and ignores the obvious emphasis on Christ as the focus of τὰ ἄνω (3:1, 3-4). Nor is there any clear warning against spiritual elitism as such (*pace* Levison 102); unlike Romans and 1 John 2:19-20, there is no emphasis on "all who" or "you all."

next verse surely confirms.[10] The undisputed Paulines do not use the verb κρύπτω (though they do use the related adjective); but the theme of hiddenness has been a feature earlier in the letter, where the compounds ἀποκρύπτω and ἀπόκρυφος were used (1:26; 2:3). The "hiddenness" in mind here is therefore probably the hiddenness of the divine mystery (1:26) and of "all the treasures of wisdom and knowledge" (2:3; cf. Moule, *Colossians and Philemon* 112). That is to say, it refers to a hidden reality, what is not perceived by those who have not yet been let into the secret and so is meaningless or folly to them, but the reality that is actually determining the outworkings of history and is the true source of wisdom and knowledge (cf. 1 Cor. 2:6-16). As in both 1:26-27 and 2:2-3, the hidden reality focuses in Christ. It is because the Colossian believers are "with Christ" (see 2:12) that they share in this true reality in its hiddenness; and because Christ is bound up with God ("in God") they, too, are caught up in the ultimate determiner of all things. The perfect tense as usual indicates a continuing state which is the result of a past action (parallel in effect to the perfects in Rom. 6:5; Gal. 2:19; 6:14). "In God" is an unusual Pauline formulation (only in 1 Thes. 1:1 and 2 Thes. 1:1; cf. Eph. 3:9), but its christological weight is wholly of a piece with the Wisdom christology of the hymn in 1:15-20.

The main thrust, however, is again not toward some visionary or mystical preoccupation with what human eyes may or may not see on a journey to heaven. The concern is wholly practical and everyday-lifeish and focuses on their "life" (cf. Lincoln, *Paradise* 128; *pace* Grässer 161-66, who can only see different structures of thought that strain against each other). This, too, is not an invitation to understand "life" in mystical or apocalyptic terms, "whether in the body or out of the body I do not know" (2 Cor. 12:2-3). Rather, the "life" in view is that of Rom. 6:4, 10-11; 14:8; 2 Cor. 4:10-12; 5:15; 13:4; Gal. 2:19-20; and Phil. 1:21. That is to say, it is a life lived from day to day within the world of every day, but lived out of a hidden resource (Rom. 6:4; 2 Cor. 4:10-11; 13:4), a still center with Christ in God (Phil. 1:21), lived for God and his Christ (Rom. 6:10-11; 14:8; 2 Cor. 5:15), a life lived by faith in the Son of God (Gal. 2:19-20). Paul and Timothy were evidently wholly confident that this perspective, this hidden resource, would provide all the wisdom needed to cope with the challenges and problems of daily living.

3:4 ὅταν ὁ Χριστὸς φανερωθῇ, ἡ ζωὴ ἡμῶν, τότε καὶ ὑμεῖς σὺν αὐτῷ φανερωθήσεσθε ἐν δόξῃ. The other side of the thought of apocalyptic

---

10. Zeilinger, *Erstgeboren* 94-115; Gnilka, *Kolosserbrief* 174-75; Lincoln, *Paradise* 129; Wedderburn, *Theology* 52-53; Levison; Wolter 168-69. The category of "mysticism," as invoked by Dibelius, *Kolosser, Epheser, Philemon* 40, is likely to be more misleading here (see p. 202 above).

hiddenness is an apocalyptic unveiling. As also characteristic of Jewish apocalyptic, this unveiling is eschatological; it reveals what will happen at the end of time. In this case the content of the eschatological revelation is given in the well-established Christian tradition of Christ's parousia (his second coming; e.g., Mark 13:26; Acts 3:19-21; 1 Cor. 15:22; 1 Thes. 4:15-17). Whether the present writers shared this expectation with the same intensity as the earlier Christians is not clear (though see on 1:24 and 3:6); the present formulation could be read either way. That the parousia is mentioned only here in Colossians is also of ambiguous significance, since so many of the items included in the Pauline letters were determined by the circumstances addressed (see also O'Brien, *Colossians, Philemon* 168-69). The important point, however, is the assurance to the Colossian Christians that if they live out of the perspective and resource just spoken of (3:1-3), they will be vindicated in the parousia. Despite the present hiddenness of their "life," which might make their attitudes and actions in their present living somewhat bewildering to onlookers, they could nevertheless be confident that Christ, the focus of their life, would demonstrate to all the rightness of the choice they had made in baptism.

ʻΟ Χριστός is used five times in these four verses (three in the "with Christ" formulation). Here, the fourth time, a pronoun would have been more natural, so the repeated use of the name is obviously deliberate (Lightfoot 208). We could translate "this Christ," indicating both the reference to the "Christ" just spoken of and the suggestion that the name retains something of its character as a title.

Paul does not normally use φανερόω in reference to the parousia, but the verb does belong to Christian tradition in this connection (1 Pet. 5:4; 1 John 2:28; 3:2). This probably made it preferable to its near synonym ἀποκαλύπτω ("reveal"), which is the "classic" apocalyptic term and is used of revelation at the end of time by Paul (Rom. 8:18; 1 Cor. 3:13; 2 Thes. 2:3, 6, 8), but not of Christ's appearing (so only in Luke 17:30). That "hidden" versus "open" (κρυπτός, φανερός) is also the more natural antithesis (Deut. 29:29; Mark 4:22/Luke 8:17; Rom. 2:28-29; 1 Cor. 14:25) confirms that the motivation here is to draw out the contrast between present hiddenness (3:3) and future visibility (cf. P.-G. Müller, *EDNT* 3.413-14).

The identification (not just association) of Christ with the (real) life of believers ("who is our life") might seem at first a bold step beyond what has been said. But it is one of Paul's ways of emphasizing the centrality of Christ for believers, the way everything which gives the Christian meaning and identity focuses on Christ (cf. 1:27; also 1 Cor. 1:30; Eph. 2:14; 1 Tim. 1:1). Here it is simply the obverse of the "with Christ" formulation of 2:12, 20 and 3:1 and confirms that what is in view is an identification between Christ and believers which in practice amounts to the complete submission of the believers' selves to Christ as their Lord (cf. Aletti, *Épître aux Colos-*

siens 221). As in Gal. 2:19-20 and Phil. 1:21, the motif highlights the extent to which such a strong-minded person as Paul saw himself as nothing else but slave and agent of Christ. He could not imagine that it might be otherwise for his converts. Similarly Ignatius (*Ephesians* 3:2; *Magnesians* 1:2; *Smyrnaeans* 4:1). It should be noted that implications of both security and authority are bound up in the thought.

The final clause is a restatement, in terms appropriate to the flow of thought, of the Christian expectation that the climax and completion of the process of salvation would be its extension to the whole person, body included (Rom. 8:11, 23), and that the template of the resurrection body was already given in the resurrection of Christ (1 Cor. 15:45-49; Phil. 3:21). The formulation is not quite like anything else in the New Testament (the closest parallels are 1 Thes. 4:17 and 1 John 3:2), but that simply indicates that the conceptual portrayal of the end of time had not become fixed and allowed a variety of metaphors, which, like Paul's metaphors of salvation, overlapped and were not mutually consistent in all respects. The underlying motif, however, is the thought of restoration of the divine image, as intended in the initial creation of humanity, and of the risen Christ as the "firstborn" who gives the family image to the rest of the new humanity (see on 1:18 and 3:10).

Here, then, we can speak of Adam christology. It is implicit in the echo of Ps. 110:1 (3:1), which elsewhere in the New Testament is merged with Ps. 8:6 to give the picture of the exalted Christ as the one who fulfills the original intention in the creation of Adam (particularly 1 Cor. 15:25-27; Eph. 1:20-22; Heb. 1:13–2:8). And it is certainly present in the thought that this becoming like Christ involves a transformation into the heavenly glory (Rom. 5:2; 8:18, 21; 9:23; 1 Cor. 2:7; 1 Thes. 2:12; cf. Mark 12:25; 1 Pet. 5:1, 4), since the glory in view is both the glory Adam lost (Rom. 3:23) and the glory which is now Christ's (Rom. 8:17, 29-30; 2 Cor. 3:18; Phil. 3:21; 2 Thes. 2:14; Heb. 2:10; see also on 1:11 and 27). The scope of this Adam christology is neatly spanned by the three "with Christ" formulations of 3:1-4, covering as they do the three tenses of salvation: "raised with Christ" (past), "hidden with Christ" (present), "revealed with Christ" (future). This is the confidence which the Colossian believers can cherish despite the "hiddenness" of their present lives: that the work of glorification already begun in them has already been completed in Christ as a guarantee of its completion also in them.

General Guidelines and Practical Exhortations (3:5-17)

5 *Put to death, therefore, the parts*[1] *of you*[2] *which are "on the earth":
unlawful sex, uncleanness, passion, evil desire, and the*[3] *greed that is idolatry,*
6 *on account of which the wrath of God is coming* [4]*on the sons of disobedience.*[4] 7 *Among whom you also once walked, when you used to live in them.*
8 *But now you too put them all away, anger, rage, malice, slander, abusive
language from your mouth.* 9 *Do not lie*[5] *to one another, having put off* [6] *the
old nature with its practices,* 10 *and having put on*[6] *the new nature, which
is being renewed in knowledge in accordance with the image of him who
created it,* 11 *in which there is no*[7] *Greek and Jew, circumcision and uncircumcision, barbarian, Scythian, slave, free man, but Christ is all*[8] *and in all.*

12 *Put on therefore, as God's elect, holy and beloved, compassion,
kindness, humility, gentleness, patience,* 13 *putting up with one another and
forgiving each other, if anyone has a cause for complaint against another;
as the Lord*[9] *also forgave you, so must you.* 14 *And above all these things
put on love, which*[10] *is the bond of completeness.* 15 *And let the peace of*

---

1. The suggestion of Masson 142 that τὰ μέλη should be read as vocative has won no support, apart from Turner, *Insights* 104-5, since the thought of the body of Christ is not present at this point.

2. "Of you" is not part of the original text, but is implied, and so was added in the later textual tradition.

3. On the significance of the definite article see Harris 146-47.

4. This phrase is omitted by very important witnesses, particularly p[46] and B. It could have been inserted in (unconscious) echo of Eph. 5:6. But the beginning of the next verse seems to presuppose an antecedent reference to people: "among whom ["in which" would make the subse-quent "in them" tautologous] you also . . ." (see Metzger 624-25). Translations are also divided: the phrase is omitted by RSV, NEB/REB, and NIV and included by GNB, NJB, and NRSV; almost all commentators favor omission (recent exceptions include Lindemann, *Kolosserbrief* 55; Wright, *Colossians and Philemon* 135 n. 1).

5. For the possibility that the subjunctive (μὴ ψεύδησθε) in p[46] is original see Porter.

6. The aorists here could be taken as imperatival participles, "putting off," "putting on" (so Lightfoot 212-13; Lohse, *Colossians and Philemon* 141; Schweizer, *Colossians* 194 n. 43; Pokorný 168-69; Schnackenburg, *Botschaft* 2.77; Yates, *Colossians* 76), but it is more natural to read them as indicating the basis for the accompanying imperative (3:9) and present participle (3:10), as all translations and most commentators agree (see, e.g., Abbott 283-84; Masson 143 n. 6; R. P. Martin, *Colossians and Philemon* 106; Gnilka, *Kolosserbrief* 186; O'Brien, *Colossians, Philemon* 189; Harris 151; Aletti, *Épître aux Colossiens* 229). Eph. 4:22, 24 is parallel, but structured differently.

7. It was almost inevitable that some textual traditions would add "male and female" from Gal. 3:28.

8. Some manuscripts, including א*, omit the definite article, bringing the two "all things" references into conformity; but an allusion back to τὰ πάντα in the hymn (1:15-20) is probably intended.

9. To avoid possible confusion (to whom does "the Lord" refer?) it would appear that various scribes amended the text, mostly to "Christ," but in א* and Vulgate manuscripts to "God," and in one miniscule (33) to "God in Christ," perhaps in echo of Eph. 4:32 (Metzger 625).

10. ὅ ἐστιν rather than ὅς ἐστιν (see BDF §132.2; Lohse, *Colossians and Philemon* 148 n. 119).

Christ[11] arbitrate in your hearts, to which indeed you were called in one[12] body. And be thankful. 16 *Let the word of the Christ[13] dwell in you richly, teaching and warning each other in all wisdom,[14] singing psalms, hymns, and spiritual songs with thankfulness in your hearts to God.[15]* 17 *And everything, whatever it is, in word or in deed, do everything in the name of the Lord Jesus, giving thanks to God[16] the Father through him.*

3:1-4 has provided the perspective from which the daily life of the Colossian Christians should be lived out. Now follows more specific advice that should help them the better to carry out the thematic exhortation to "walk in him" (2:6). The doubled motif of "putting off" (3:8, 9) and "putting on" (3:10, 12) suggests the adoption of a pattern of parenesis fairly common in the earliest Christian churches (see on 3:8). Lists of virtues and vices were common in ethical systems of the ancient world (see on 3:5), the imagery of putting off/on was quite widely current (see on 3:8 and 10), and it is doubtful whether there is sufficient evidence of an already established catechetical structure in Christian writings.[17] Here in particular the adaptation of the pattern to the context is notable (Gnilka, *Kolosserbrief* 178-79; Yates, *Colossians* 65-67). And here it also becomes clear that the τὰ ἄνω perspective advocated by the authors differs from that of the Colossian philosophy (as least as represented in the letter) by reflecting high ethical standards and rich communal graces rather than strictness of ritual observances and ascetic practices. Particularly notable is the way the section climaxes in one of very few explicit references in the New Testament to Christian worship (3:16-17), presumably because the attractiveness of other worship was a factor at

11. Some later scribes preferred the more familiar "peace of God"; see on 3:15.

12. For some reason p[46] and B omit "one."

13. Again the unusual phrase "the word of Christ" has been altered at quite an early stage in some manuscripts to the more familiar "the word of God" or "the word of the Lord" (Metzger 625).

14. That "in all wisdom" should be taken with "teaching and warning" is now generally agreed (see, e.g., Abbott 290-91; O'Brien, *Colossians, Philemon* 208; Aletti, *Épître aux Colossiens* 241; Fee 652). Despite the arguments in favor of taking "psalms, hymns, and spiritual songs" also with "teaching and warning" (O'Brien 208-9; Pokorný 174 [bibliography in n. 83]; Fee 652-53 [bibliography in n. 64]), the picture of instruction carried out solely by diverse forms of sung praise seems rather strained (neither Eph. 5:19 nor 1 Cor. 14:26 is a close parallel at this point), and "psalms, hymns, and spiritual songs" reads much more naturally as the object of "singing," even though the result is a weighty final clause.

15. Here again we find a later alteration in some manuscripts to "Lord," influenced, perhaps, by Eph. 5:19 (Metzger 625).

16. The unusual formulation here has been amended by copyists by the addition of "and" to give the more typical "God and Father," as in Eph. 5:20 (Metzger 626).

17. As argued by P. Carrington, *The Primitive Christian Catechism* (Cambridge: Cambridge University, 1940); E. G. Selwyn, *The First Epistle of St Peter* (London: Macmillan, 1947) 363-466; supported by Cannon 70-82. But see my *Unity* 141-47.

Colossae (2:18, 23); also that the final call to "do everything in the name of the Lord Jesus" (3:17) brings us back to the thematic statement in 2:6-7 ("walk in the Lord") and leads into the repeated emphasis of the following section (3:20, 22-24; 4:1). As elsewhere, such parenesis has an important social function in helping to stabilize the community addressed.[18]

3:5 νεκρώσατε οὖν τὰ μέλη τὰ ἐπὶ τῆς γῆς, πορνείαν ἀκαθαρσίαν πάθος ἐπιθυμίαν κακήν, καὶ τὴν πλεονεξίαν, ἥτις ἐστὶν εἰδωλολατρία. Given the forcefulness of the repeated insistence that the Colossian believers had already "died" with Christ (2:12, 20; 3:3), the first specific exhortation is something of a surprise: "therefore kill off your members which are on the earth" (but see Bruce, *Colossians, Philemon, and Ephesians* 141-42). The verb νεκρόω, "make dead (νεκρός), put to death," does not occur often, but seems to be derived from medical usage in reference to the atrophy of part of a body through sickness: in old age the body dies little by little; a corpse is the body which has died (R. Bultmann, *TDNT* 4.894). Hence the use earlier by Paul of Abraham's aged body (Rom. 4:19; similarly Heb. 11:12, the only other occurrences of the verb in biblical Greek; cf., however, the noun in Rom. 4:19 and 2 Cor. 4:10): "dead (in a state of having been put to death)" in that normal bodily function had ceased.

This background also explains the use here of μέλη, literally "parts (of the body)." The term is not confined to physical parts; Aristotle, for example, speaks of the μέλος αἰσθανόμενον, "the organ of perception/understanding" (J. Horst, *TDNT* 4.556). But it does have a concreteness in denoting the means by which the body actually engages with other entities (Wolter 173-74). Hence Paul's earlier exhortations (Rom. 6:13, 19; also 7:5, 23; 1 Cor. 6:15). The call is not for the asceticism already dismissed in 2:18 and 23 (Lohmeyer 136; Caird 205). But the metaphor should be allowed its force: the person's interaction with the wider world as through organs and limbs is what is in view. It was precisely the interaction which had characterized the Colossians' old way of life which is now targeted (cf. *2 Baruch* 49:3: "the chained members that are in evil and by which evils are accomplished"; see further Levison 104-8). There is probably a deliberate echo of 3:2, where just the same phrase is used (τὰ ἐπὶ τῆς γῆς): to avoid "setting one's mind on what is on the earth" (3:2) is not achieved by dreamy reflection (see on 3:2) but requires forceful self-discipline ("put to death"). Despite the power of their having been identified with Christ in his death, there were still things, parts of their old lives, habits of hand and mind, which tied them "to the earth" and hindered the outworking of the "mind set on what is above." Since τὰ μέλη can also denote the body as a whole (BAGD s.v.

---

18. Cf. L. G. Perdue, "The Social Character of Paraenesis and Paraenetic Literature," in *Paraenesis: Acts and Form,* ed. L. G. Perdue and J. G. Gammie, *Semeia* 50 (1990) 5-39.

μέλος 1; cf. M. Völkel, *EDNT* 2.405), the exhortation is also to "put yourself to death in your belongingness to the earth," "everything in you that is earthly" (NJB). The exhortation is equivalent to that in Rom. 8:13 (Rom. 6:11 is less forceful) and complements the thought of 3:9 here (cf. Moule, *Colossians and Philemon* 114-16; Conzelmann 150).[19]

Paul and Timothy clearly did not harbor any illusions regarding their converts. They did not attempt to promote a Christian perspective which was unrelated to the hard realities of daily life. On the contrary, they were all too aware of the pressures which shaped people like the Colossian Christians and which still held a seductive attraction for them. They were concerned that the Colossian believers' death with Christ, the atrophy of old habits of evil, had not yet worked through the full extent of their bodily relationships.

The description of these "parts" of their old life (awkwardly set in apposition), both in this verse and in 3:8, is in some ways unsurprising, since "catalogues of vice" were standard items in ethical teaching of the time. They were particularly popular among the Stoics,[20] but common also in Judaism (e.g., Wis. 14:25-26; 4 Macc. 1:26-27; 2:15; 1QS 4:9-11; Philo, *De sacrificiis* 32; *2 Enoch* 10:4-5); in view of the possible links already noted between the Colossian Jewish praxis and the Essenes, the parallel with CD 4:17-19 (Lohse, *Colossians and Philemon* 138 n. 8) is perhaps worth particular note.[21] Early Christian usage is simply a reflection of this common way of listing vices to be avoided;[22] the format itself betrays no particular dependence on any contemporary philosophy or religion, though the scheme of five items in such a list may be traditional.[23] Nevertheless, such lists are never merely formal and always contain distinctive elements, presumably judged appropriate to the particular occasion.

So here, two features call for particular attention. One is the immediate focus on sexual sins. This is not always the case in the Christian lists (though cf. Mark 7:21; 1 Cor. 6:9; Gal. 5:19; *Didache* 5:1), but presumably indicates a considerable concern among the earliest Christian leadership at the con-

19. Schweizer, *Colossians* 182-88, followed by Gnilka, *Kolosserbrief* 179-81, argues for a more complex background in Platonic-Pythagorean thought, but the text does not require it; see also O'Brien, *Colossians, Philemon* 177-78; Aletti, *Épître aux Colossiens* 224 n. 22.

20. See, e.g., illustrations in A. J. Malherbe, *Moral Exhortation: A Greco-Roman Sourcebook* (Philadelphia: Westminster, 1986) 138-41.

21. Bibliography in Lohse, *Colossians and Philemon* 138 n. 8; brief review in D. Schroeder, "Ethical Lists," *IDBS* 546-47; O'Brien, *Colossians, Philemon* 179-81. "The most conspicuous agreements are to be found between the catalogues of Colossians and the rules of the Qumran sect" (Pokorný 164). See also Cannon ch. 3.

22. E.g., Mark 7:21-22; Rom. 1:29-31; 1 Cor. 6:9-10; 2 Cor. 12:20; Gal. 5:19-21; 1 Tim. 1:9-10; 2 Tim. 3:2-5; *1 Clement* 35:5; *Didache* 5:1-2; *Barnabas* 20:1-2.

23. Dibelius, *Kolosser, Epheser, Philemon* 41; Lohmeyer 135; Lohse, *Colossians and Philemon* 137; Schweizer, *Colossians* 185-87, who also speculates that the groups of five may be a further reflection of Pythagorean background ("Christianity" 251-52; but see p. 32 n. 36 above).

tinuing attractiveness within their churches of the looser sexual standards for men in Hellenistic society of the time (see F. Hauck and S. Schulz, *TDNT* 6.582-83; Jewish perception is summed up in *Aristeas* 152). The other is the strongly Jewish character of this list, as indicated by the association between sexual promiscuity and idolatry (see below).[24] Paul did not want his readers to follow the Colossian Jews in their ritual and worship, but their ethical standards were to be Jewish through and through.

Πορνεία originally denoted relations with a prostitute (πόρνη), but probably covers the whole range of unlawful sexual intercourse (BAGD), "sexual vice" (NJB), "sexual immorality" (GNB, NIV).[25] It stands first in the list of Mark 7:21 par. and Gal. 5:19 and is prominent in *Didache* 5:1; it is a particular concern in the *Testaments of the Twelve Patriarchs*, particularly *Reuben* and *Judah* (*Testament of Reuben* 1:6; 3:3; 4:6-8 — leads to idolatry; 4:11; 5:3, 5 — φεύγετε τὴν πορνείαν, etc.); in the DSS note, e.g., 1QS 1:6; 4:10 and CD 2:16. Πορνεία is linked with idolatry in the first list in the so-called "apostolic decree," which was designed to regulate relations between Christian Jews and Christian Gentiles (Acts 15:20, though it is subordinated in 15:29 and 21:25), thus underscoring both its importance for the Gentile mission as carried out by Jews and its correlation with idolatry in Jewish eyes. Paul's concern over it as a constant danger for many of his converts is indicated by its mention in several places (1 Cor. 5:1; 6:13, 18 — φεύγετε τὴν πορνείαν; 7:2; 2 Cor. 12:21; Gal. 5:19; 1 Thes. 4:3; also Eph. 5:3). In Rev. 2:21 the link between πορνεία and idolatry is again a major concern.

The second item in the list continues the same emphasis, since ἀκαθαρσία ("uncleanness"; "impurity" in NJB, NIV; "indecency" in NEB/REB, GNB) had by now almost entirely lost its earlier cultic connotation and bears a clear moral sense (as in Wis. 2:16; 1 Esd. 1:42), especially in reference to sexual immorality (*1 Enoch* 10:11; *Testament of Judah* 14:5; *Testament of Joseph* 4:6; see also BAGD). Presumably it was only because the word had become so separate from the cult that it could be used here, since otherwise it might have been thought to encourage the very attitude that was disparaged in 2:21 (cf. Isa. 52:11!). Note again the link between sexual impurity and idolatry in Rom. 1:24-25. Ἀκαθαρσία is almost exclusively Pauline in the New Testament (nine of the ten occurrences) and a natural associate with πορνεία in 2 Cor. 12:21; Gal. 5:19; and Eph. 5:3 (cf. Eph. 5:5 and Rev. 17:4).

"Passion" (πάθος), "lust" (NEB/REB, NIV, GNB), "uncontrolled pas-

---

24. See further Str-B 3.62-74; Easton; S. Wibbing, *Die Tugend- und Lasterkataloge im Neuen Testament* (BZNW 25; Berlin: Töpelmann, 1959).

25. See J. Jensen, "Does *Porneia* Mean Fornication?" *NovT* 20 (1978) 161-84; O'Brien, *Colossians, Philemon* 181.

sion" (NJB), is a less common member of such lists, but its two other New Testament occurrences (Rom. 1:26; 1 Thes. 4:5) indicate that it was for Paul a natural associate with the two preceding items, thus giving further emphasis to this primary concern over the danger of unrestrained sexual appetite (cf. again *Testament of Judah* 18:6; *Testament of Joseph* 7:8; also pseudo-Phocylides 194; see also BAGD).

"Desire" (ἐπιθυμία) can have a positive meaning (as in Phil. 1:23 and 1 Thes. 2:17), but more often it denotes desire for something forbidden, including sexual desire, as again in Rom. 1:24 and 1 Thes. 4:15. Otherwise the Paulines use it less specifically: the desires of sin (Rom. 6:12), "the desires of the flesh" (Rom. 13:14; Gal. 5:16, 24; Eph. 2:3), "deceitful desires" (Eph. 4:22), "youthful desires" (2 Tim. 2:22), "worldly desires" (Tit. 2:12), "slaves to desires" (Tit. 3:3). This negative meaning of "desire = lust" was familiar in the ancient world (e.g., Plutarch, *Moralia* 525AB; Susanna [Theodotion] 8, 11, 14, 20, 56; Josephus, *Antiquities* 4.130, 132); both Plato, *Leges* 9.854A, and Prov. 12:12; 21:26 speak of "evil desire" (BAGD s.v. 3). Wrong desire as the root of all sin was an established theologoumenon in Jewish thought, as reflected also in Rom. 7:7-8 and Jas. 1:15 (see my *Romans* 380).

"Greed" (πλεονεξία), literally "desire to have more" (πλέον-ἔχειν), so "covetousness, avarice, insatiableness" (BAGD), "consuming ambition" (C. Spicq, *Theological Lexicon of the New Testament* [Peabody: Hendrickson, 1994] 3.117-19), "ruthless greed" (NEB/REB), was generally recognized to be one of the most serious of vices, a threat to both individual and society (G. Delling, *TDNT* 6.266-70). It was thus an obvious member for inclusion in such vice lists (Mark 7:22; Rom. 1:29; Eph. 5:3; *1 Clement* 35:5; *Barnabas* 20:1). In Plato, *Symposium* 182D, the word is used of sexual greed and sums up what is primarily a list of sexual sins: the ruthless insatiableness evident when the sexual appetite is unrestrained in a man with power to gratify it (cf. 1 Thes. 4:4-6). Dibelius, *Kolosser, Epheser, Philemon* 42, suggests that the warning here is an application of Matt. 6:24/Luke 16:13.

"Which is idolatry" is attached to "greed." Εἰδωλολατρία may be a Christian formation; Paul is our earliest attestation (1 Cor. 10:14; Gal. 5:20; otherwise only 1 Pet. 4:3 in biblical Greek), though the term occurs also in *Testament of Judah* 19:1; 23:1 (both v.l.) and *Testament of Benjamin* 10:10, and its cognates in *Testament of Levi* 17:11 and *Sibylline Oracles* 3.38. The concern, however, is typically and peculiarly Jewish. The second of the ten commandments (Exod. 20:4-5; Deut. 5:8-9) summed up a Jewish antipathy to any attempt to make an image of God or gods, a concern which was deep-rooted and which colored Jewish attitudes to Gentiles throughout our period. Hence the classic polemics of Jewish monotheism against the syncretistic idolatry of other religions (Isa. 44:9-20; Wis. 12-15; Ep. Jer.; *Sibylline Oracles* 3.8-45). Also typically Jewish was the conviction that idolatry was closely tied to sexual license (Num. 25:1-3; Hos. 4:12-18; Ep. Jer. 43;

Wis. 14:12-27; *2 Enoch* 10:4-6; *Testament of Benjamin* 10:10 — πορνεία and εἰδωλολατρία cause alienation from God [ἀπηλλοτριώθησαν θεοῦ; cf. Col. 1:21]; reflected also in Rom. 1:23-27 and 1 Cor. 10:7-8), an attitude inherited by the first Christians (1 Cor. 6:9; Gal. 5:20; 1 Pet. 4:3; Rev. 21:8; 22:15; *Didache* 5:1). The assumption that πλεονεξία, particularly as sexual greed, is a form of idolatry is shared by Eph. 5:5.

It is worth noting that both of the early critiques of religion in the modern period — religion as projection of human needs and desires (Feuerbach) and the Father figure as a projection of suppressed sexuality (Freud) — are anticipated here. "Greed" is a form of idolatry because it projects acquisitiveness and personal satisfaction as objective go(o)ds to be praised and served. It is in fact idolatry thus understood which is the legitimate target for the critiques of Feuerbach and Freud. Religion understood essentially as response to the numinous and the beyond in the midst is less vulnerable.

3:6 δι᾽ ἃ ἔρχεται ἡ ὀργὴ τοῦ θεοῦ ἐπὶ τοὺς υἱοὺς τῆς ἀπειθείας. Typically Jewish also is the belief that such behavior (idolatry and sexual immorality) is the subject of God's judgment (cf. Rom. 1:32; 1 Cor. 5:9-13; 6:9-10; Gal. 5:19-21; 1 Thes. 4:3-6). The ὀργὴ τοῦ θεοῦ (divine "retribution" in REB, NJB) itself was not peculiar to Jewish theology. On the contrary, it was a familiar concept in the ancient world: divine indignation as heaven's response to human impiety or transgression of divinely approved laws, or as a way of explaining communal catastrophes or unexpected sickness or death (H. Kleinknecht, *TDNT* 5.383-92). Also common to all strands of religion in the ancient world was an awareness of the seeming irrationality and incalculability of this wrath. But in Israel's religion the fundamental premise of election by the one God provided the key means to resolve the problem of theodicy. God's wrath was directed against Israel itself for its failure to live in accordance with its covenant obligations, not least its lapses into idolatry and immorality (e.g., Exod. 32:10-12; Num. 25:1-4; Deut. 29:16-28; 2 Chron. 24:18; Jer. 7:16-20; 25:6; Ezekiel 22; Mic. 5:10-15; 1QS 2:15; 5:12; Matt. 3:7), but also against the other nations for failure to recognize Israel as Yahweh's people (e.g., Isa. 34:2; Jer. 10:25; 50:13; Zech. 1:15; see particularly J. Fichtner, *TDNT* 5.395-409).

The verb (ἔρχεται) could denote a wrath already in operation — that is, presumably, as in Rom. 1:18-32, in the consequences which follow from failure to acknowledge and worship God as God (Caird 205). In that case the wrath takes the form of God giving or allowing his human creatures what they want, leaving them to their own devices — the continuing avarice and abuse of sexual relations being its own reward. But the concept as taken over by the first Christians is more typically future oriented; so predominantly in Paul (Rom. 2:5, 8; 3:5; 5:9; 9:22; 1 Thes. 5:9). And the closest parallel (1 Thes. 1:10: τῆς ὀργῆς τῆς ἐρχομένης; cf. Matt. 3:7/Luke 3:7: "the coming wrath") suggests that this is what is in view here — "is going to come, is about to come" — a further indication that expectation of an imminent end may well have been still lively at this time (see also 1:24 and 3:4). The thought of final judgment was also familiar in Greek thought (F. Büchsel, *TDNT* 3.934), but again it is particularly prominent in Jewish tradition (e.g., Isa. 34:8; Dan. 7:9-11; Joel 2:1-2; Mal. 4:1; *Jubilees* 5:10-16; *1 Enoch* 90:20-27), not least as a day of "wrath" (Isa. 13:6-16; Zeph. 1:15, 18; 2:2-3; 3:8; for a full treatment of ὀργή θεοῦ in the New Testament see particularly G. Stählin, *TDNT* 5.422-47; briefly O'Brien, *Colossians, Philemon* 184-85).

"Disobedience" (ἀπείθεια) is, as the context indicates, disobedience to God, as always in the New Testament.[26] Again the idea is not peculiarly Jewish (see R. Bultmann, *TDNT* 6.10 n. 1), but the context is clearly so (disobedience understood in terms of sexual sins and idolatry), and the description "sons of disobedience" (as again in Eph. 2:2 and 5:6) is a Semitism (= disobedient persons; see also n. 4). As with the concept of "wrath," so with its correlative "disobedience," Jews who failed to recognize their covenant responsibilities to God could be included, with reference particularly to their failure to recognize that the gospel was the climax of God's covenant purpose (Rom. 10:21 = Isa. 65:2; 11:30-32). But here, as the talk of sexual immorality and idolatry makes clear, as also in the next verse, it is Gentiles who are primarily in mind. Either way, the larger theological point is straightforward: such self-projection, such making of self-gratification into an idol, will always be counted by God as disobedience, whether it happens among his own people or beyond the bounds of those who acknowledge him as God, a disobedience whose final end is the destruction of the self.

3:7 ἐν οἷς καὶ ὑμεῖς περιεπατήσατέ ποτε, ὅτε ἐζῆτε ἐν τούτοις. The point is that such behavior used to characterize the Colossian Christians' way of life: the aorist tense of the first verb sums up that previous behavior as a single event now past; the imperfect tense of the second verse, in contrast, indicates a sustained way of life. Ἐν οἷς, "among whom" (see n. 2), confirms that individual conduct is socially determined to a considerable degree: they lived that way because that was the pattern of behavior for most Gentile societies. NJB catches the sense well: "And these things made up your way of life when you were living among such people."

Περιεπατήσατε ("you walked") once again betrays a Jewish frame of reference (see on 1:10); the conversion of the Colossian Christians was also a conversion from a way of life to one more characteristically Jewish in its ethical norms and so also "worthy of the Lord" (1:10).[27] Ἐζῆτε ἐν τουτοῖς

26. Rom. 2:8; 10:21; 11:30-32; 15:31; also John 3:36; Acts 14:2; 19:9; Heb. 3:18; 4:6, 11; 11:31; 1 Pet. 2:8; 3:1, 20; 4:17.

27. "Again it is obvious how deeply determined are these sentences by Jewish dogmatism against heathenism" (Lohmeyer 139).

is a reminder that many of the first Christian converts had themselves indulged in such sexual license and greed: "you used to live in these ways" (cf. 1 Cor. 6:9-11 — "such were some of you"; Rom. 6:19-21; Tit. 3:3; 1 Pet. 4:3-4). Probably it was revulsion against such an ethos which attracted many Gentiles to the stronger morality of Judaism. But the pressures of the wider society were such that the temptation for Gentile Christians to relapse must have been fairly constant (cf. 1 Corinthians 5–6).

3:8 νυνὶ δὲ ἀπόθεσθε καὶ ὑμεῖς τὰ πάντα, ὀργήν, θυμόν, κακίαν, βλασφημίαν, αἰσχρολογίαν ἐκ τοῦ στόματος ὑμῶν. "But now. . . ." Νυνὶ δέ echoes the decisive νυνὶ δέ in 1:22: a fundamental shift in ethical norms and character of conduct has taken place, the equivalent in personal time and outworking of the epochal act of reconciliation on the cross (see on 1:22). Somewhat surprisingly, however, the verb which follows is in the imperative, where one might have expected the indicative, as usually in Paul (particularly Rom. 3:21; 6:22; 7:6; 11:30; 1 Cor. 15:20; Col. 1:22; Eph. 2:13; Tachau 124; Lona 94-95). With the balance between divine initiative and human response set out clearly already in 2:6-7 and 3:1-4, it is the responsibility of the Colossian Christians which is given first emphasis in the more specific parenesis; but the balance will be expressed again in 3:9-10.

The metaphor is of putting off or putting away; taking off clothes was again the obvious imagery (so Acts 7:58; as with ἀπεκδύομαι in Col. 2:15 and 3:9), but ἀποτίθεμαι (middle) was more widely used (LSJ). Hence in the New Testament it usually features in parenesis in the sense of putting away from oneself whatever would hinder the Christian walk: "the works of darkness" (Rom. 13:12), "the old self" (Eph. 4:22), "lying" (Eph. 4:25), "sin" (Heb. 12:1), "sordid avarice" (Jas. 1:21), or "every evil" (1 Pet. 2:1). "Putting off" vices was, indeed, if anything, a more Greek than Hebrew metaphor; Plutarch, *Coriolanus* 19.4, for example, advocates the putting away of ὀργήν, as here (see also BAGD s.v. ἀποτίθημι 1b; van der Horst 183-84). The frequency with which the imagery is used in New Testament parenesis could suggest a fairly regular element in early Christian catechesis (see the introduction to the comments on 3:5-17), although the imperative as such is used only here. The totality of the transformation required (τὰ πάντα) corresponds to the call for conversion in the Synoptic tradition carried over into a Hellenistic milieu (Gnilka, *Kolosserbrief* 184).

The imperative is the cue for another fivefold vice list (see on 3:5), again typically Jewish (Lohmeyer 139), though not so distinctively so. In this case the vices named focus on personal relationships within the Christian community, warning against the outbursts particularly of careless or malicious speech that can be so damaging to community relations.[28] Ὀργή is

---

28. Gnilka, *Kolosserbrief* 185, notes that when the warning against lying (3:9) is added to the concerns of the two lists (3:5, 8) some dependence on the Ten Commandments becomes evident,

now human "wrath" (in contrast to 3:6), with the implication that what is in view is such a powerful emotion that only God can be trusted to exercise it fairly. Hence such warnings as Rom. 12:19 — "do not take your own revenge, but give opportunity for [God's] wrath"; Jas. 1:19-20 — "let every-one be quick to hear, slow to speak, slow to anger (ὀργήν), for the anger of a man does not bring about the righteousness of God"; *1 Clement* 13:1 — "be humble-minded, putting aside (ἀποθέμενοι) all . . . anger"; and *Didache* 15:3 — "reprove one another, not in ὀργή." Most translations prefer "anger" here.

A regular associate with ὀργή in the Old Testament is θυμός, usually of God's anger (as also in *1 Enoch* 5:9; *Testament of Job* 43:11; Rom. 2:8; Rev. 16:19; 19:15; *1 Clement* 50:4). But the combination was also a natural one for human anger (as in Sir. 45:18; *Psalms of Solomon* 2:23; 16:10; Eph. 4:31; Josephus, *Antiquities* 20.108; see also BAGD s.v. θυμός 2). The two are almost synonymous, but θυμός probably indicates a more emotional response, "rage" (NIV), "bad temper" (REB), "quick temper" (Bruce, *Colossians, Philemon, and Ephesians* 145), "outbursts of anger" (cf. Light-foot 212).

Κακία means simply "badness, wickedness," though in this context it probably has a more specific reference, "malice, ill will" (BAGD s.v. 1b), "spitefulness" (JB), as in other lists (Rom. 1:29; Eph. 4:31; Tit. 3:3; 1 Pet. 2:1; *Didache* 5:1; *Barnabas* 20:1; cf. 1QS 4:11). Βλασφημία means "slander, defamation," another obvious member for a vice list (Mark 7:22; Eph. 4:31; 1 Tim. 6:4), familiar in wider Greek and directed both against others and against God (LSJ; see also O. Hofius, *EDNT* 1.220). Αἰσχρολογία occurs only here in biblical Greek and is not widely attested (also *Didache* 3:3 and 5:1). But its meaning is clear from its construction: αἰσχρός, "shameful, obscene," λόγιον, "saying" — hence "obscene language, abusive speech" (Lightfoot 212; BAGD), "dirty talk" (JB/NJB), "filthy language" (NIV). Jas. 3:1-12 contains what is in effect an exposition of this vice. Again we are given a glimpse into the character of the sort of human interaction which Paul and Timothy feared might all too easily be carried over into their churches. Habits of language may not die (3:5) quickly. "Banish them all from your lips!" (REB).

3:9 μὴ ψεύδεσθε εἰς ἀλλήλους, ἀπεκδυσάμενοι τὸν παλαιὸν ἄνθρωπον σὺν ταῖς πράξεσιν αὐτοῦ. The same concerns for relationships of mutual confidence and respect continue in a warning against lying to one another. Only here and in Eph. 4:25 within the Paulines is such a concern

---

strengthening the possibility that some of the earliest baptismal catechesis for Gentile converts made use of the decalogue as a framework. Similarly Lohmeyer 139 n. 3; Ernst, *Philipper, Philemon, Kolosser, Epheser* 226 on 3:8 (a kind of Jewish midrash on Deut. 5:17-18); Hartman, "Code" 239-42. Otherwise Aletti, *Épître aux Colossiens* 228.

voiced, though Paul on several occasions vouched formally for his own honesty: "I am not lying" (Rom. 9:1; 2 Cor. 11:31; Gal. 1:20; also 1 Tim. 2:7). But the concern was certainly present in other churches (Acts 5:3-4; Jas. 3:14; 1 John 1:6; *Didache* 3:5; Hermas *Mandates* 3.2). The antisocial effects of lying were common ground in Jewish and Greek ethics (see H. Conzelmann, *TDNT* 9.594-600). The present tense could be translated "Stop lying" (NEB), "Don't go on telling lies (as you used to)" (Bruce, *Colossians, Philemon, and Ephesians* 146). "In Col. 3:9a the imperative not to lie summarizes all the vices belonging to the old epoch (3:5-7)" (H. Giesen, *EDNT* 3.497).

Following the double imperative comes the aorist which looks back to the decisive step taken at conversion-initiation (see n. 6). The verb, ἀπεκδύομαι, is the same as in 2:15 and uses more clearly the imagery of stripping off clothes (see on 2:15; cf. ἀποτίθεμαι in 3:8). What has been stripped off is described as τὸν παλαιὸν ἄνθρωπον, "the old self" (with JB/NJB, GNB, NIV). Παλαιός is used consistently by Paul to denote what belonged to life prior to faith in Christ (1 Cor. 5:7-8), "the old covenant" (2 Cor. 3:14), and in this phrase, "the old self" (Rom. 6:6; also Eph. 4:22). The figure is clearly a way of indicating a whole way of life (more comprehensive than the τὰ μέλη of 3:5 and the ἐζῆτε ἐν τούτοις of 3:7), a way of life prior to and without Christ and characterized by the sort of vices listed in 3:5 and 8, here referred to as "its practices" (as in Rom. 8:13). The imagery is as vigorous as in 2:11: there Christ's body of flesh stripped off in death, here the equivalent attachment to a whole world of sentiment and attitude. In committing themselves to Christ in baptism they had stepped completely out of one whole life, equivalent to the "losing of life" that Jesus himself had demanded of his disciples (Mark 10:34-35). This event was the decisive starting point of all subsequent exhortation and moral seriousness. We may compare Diogenes Laertius 9.66 and Eusebius, *Praeparatio Evangelica* 14.18.26, who both record the philosopher Pyrrho's lament on how hard it was ἐκδῦναι τὸν ἄνθρωπον, "to put off the man," "to strip oneself of human weakness" (LCL), "to strip off one's human nature" (NDIEC 4.176; see further van der Horst 184-86). Also *Joseph and Asenath* 12:9, where Asenath the convert expresses her fear that "the wild old lion" (ὁ λεών ὁ ἄγριος ὁ παλαιός), the father of the Egyptian gods, that is, presumably, the devil, will persecute her (cf. 1 Pet. 5:8). The same fear is here, that any continuing attractiveness of their old way of life or intimidation from its practitioners (their old associates) would draw the Colossian converts away from their first resolve.

3:10 καὶ ἐνδυσάμενοι τὸν νέον τὸν ἀνακαινούμενον εἰς ἐπίγνωσιν κατ᾽ εἰκόνα τοῦ κτίσαντος αὐτόν. The complementary action to discarding old clothes is putting on new ones. Conversion was not simply a turning from an old way of life; it was also a positive embracing of a new way of life. The action of putting on a dry garment following baptism may be in mind (cf. Wedderburn, *Baptism* 338-39), but the word itself does not refer to baptism (*pace*, e.g., Merk 204-5; Ernst, *Philipper, Philemon, Kolosser, Epheser* 226; Wolter 178-79), as its use in imperatives addressed to the already baptized makes clear (3:12; Rom. 13:12, 14; Eph. 4:24; 6:11; cf. Yates, *Colossians* 66-67; Fee 647). The metaphor was quite common in Hebrew thought for putting on enabling graces from God (e.g., "righteousness" in Job 29:14; Ps. 132:9; Wis. 5:18; "strength and dignity" in Prov. 31:25; "the beauty of glory, the robe of righteousness" in Bar. 5:1-2; "faith" in Philo, *De confusione linguarum* 31; "virtues" in Philo, *De somnis* 1.225; see also Lohmeyer 140 n. 6; van der Horst 182; Meeks, "Body" 220 n. 32). Here, however, in parallel to "the old self" in 3:9, as in Eph. 4:22, 24, what has to be put on is "the new self," a new and distinctively Christian application of the metaphor.[29] Not simply individual virtues and graces are in view, but once again a whole personality and the social world and way of life that that implied (cf. the "new creation" in 2 Cor. 5:17 and Gal. 6:15). The thought is equivalent to "putting on Christ" in Rom. 13:14, as Col. 3:3-4 also implies. At its simplest, this means that the manner of Christ's living, as attested in the Jesus tradition, provided the pattern for this new self life (2:6-7), as the enabling of the risen Christ provided its means (1:9-11).

Even before the "indicative" gives way once again to the imperative (3:12), the aorist event of the conversion-initiation past is qualified by an ongoing present: the new self is in process of being renewed (ἀνα-καινούμενον), "constantly being renewed" (REB). Paul uses the same term in 2 Cor. 4:16 (the passive form occurs only in Paul and only in these two passages) for the experience of inner renewal which he found to accompany the physical affliction and attrition of his human resources which he underwent in the demanding circumstances of his missionary work. The equivalent noun appears also first in Paul, in Rom. 12:2, to denote the "renewal of mind" which Paul saw as integral to the ongoing transformation of the Christian and which was the key to being able to discern the will of God. The absence of any mention of the Spirit in all this is surprising (though see Fee 647) and increases the suspicion that Paul does not speak here with his own voice; but it could simply be that the particular imagery being used did not lend itself to incorporating references to the Spirit (as Rom. 12:2 and 13:14 may confirm).

Here the exhortation makes more explicit use of the motif of Adam

---

29. Lohse, *Colossians and Philemon* 142 n. 60; O'Brien, *Colossians, Philemon* 189-90, both citing Jervell 240. See also Gnilka, *Kolosserbrief* 187-88. Eph. 2:15 (cf. 4:13) develops the theme in a striking way. That a different word for "new" (καινός) is used in the Ephesians parallels is insignificant since the two words were more or less synonymous.

and creation, in terms both of knowledge and of the image of God, "an unavoidable allusion to Gen. 1:26f." (Wolter 180). For knowledge was at the heart of humanity's primal failure (Gen. 2:17; 3:5, 7), and humankind's failure to act in accordance with their knowledge of God by acknowledging him in worship was the central element in Paul's earlier analysis of the human plight, of "the old self" (Rom. 1:21). Renewal in knowledge of God, of the relation implied by that knowledge (see on 1:10), was therefore of first importance for Paul (cf. Pokorný 169); the parallel between Rom. 12:2 and Col. 1:9-10 is important for understanding the coherence of the theology here.

Likewise, the understanding of creation as God imprinting his image on humanity remained fundamental to both Judaism and Christianity (see on 1:15); ὁ κτίσας, "he who created," is, of course, God (as in Matt. 19:4; Rom. 1:25; Eph. 3:9; O'Brien, *Colossians, Philemon* 191). The idea that in the "fall" the divine image was lost or damaged may be implied here (Gnilka, *Kolosserbrief* 188), though its explicit expression is the product of subsequent Christian theology (contrast Gen. 5:1-3; 9:6; 1 Cor. 11:7; Jas. 3:9). For Jewish and early Christian theology it was Adam's share in divine glory which had been diminished (*Apocalypse of Moses* 20–21; Rom. 3:23; Scroggs 26-27, 35-36, 48-49, 55); though quite how 1 Cor. 11:7 relates to the idea of "the old self" is unclear (cf. Schweizer, *Colossians* 198 n. 55).[30] Perhaps more to the point here, "image" is a dynamic concept, as its use in reference to divine Wisdom and Christ (1:15) confirms. Consequently it does not imply a static status but a relationship, one in which the "image," to remain "fresh" (νέος, "new"), must continue in contact with the one whose image it is (cf. JB/NJB "which will progress towards true knowledge the more it is renewed in the image of its creator").[31] At all events the thought merges into Adam christology, where Christ as the divine image (see on 1:15) is the middle term between the creator and his first creation and his re-creation (cf. Rom. 8:29; 1 Cor. 15:49; 2 Cor. 3:18; 4:4; cf. Ignatius, *Ephesians* 20:1 — "the new man Jesus Christ"; cf. Scroggs 69-70). In this way Paul and Timothy in true Pauline style manage to hold together creation and salvation in the thought of Christ as both the creative power of God (1:15) and as the archetype for both creation and redeemed, renewed humanity (πρωτότοκος both "of all creation" and "from the dead," 1:15, 18b).

This has the effect of reminding the readers that Christian ethics is not a matter merely of individual resolve, but involves a corporate dimension; Adam christology leads directly into a theology of the body of Christ (cf.

---

30. See further my *Christology* 105-6.

31. Cf. Aletti, *Épître aux Colossiens* 231-32. Contrast Lohse, *Colossians and Philemon* 143, 146, who reads this clause as indicating that the image of God has already been given to the baptized person and that the divine act of creation referred to took place in baptism.

particularly Moule, *Colossians and Philemon* 119-20). But more to the point here, an Adam theology also has the effect of going behind the particularism of Israel's concept of election to a creation model more easily able to embrace Gentile as Gentile as well as Jew as Jew. This is important since transformation in accordance with the image of God could also have been an objective of the mystical practices implied in 2:18;[32] the point then would be that whereas the worship of the Colossian synagogue tended to reinforce national distinctiveness (see on 2:11, 16, 21), the objective here was more inclusive. That this line of exposition reflects the immediate concerns of the writer(s) at this point is confirmed by the next verse.

3:11 ὅπου οὐκ ἔνι Ἕλλην καὶ Ἰουδαῖος, περιτομὴ καὶ ἀκροβυστία, βάρβαρος, Σκύθης, δοῦλος, ἐλεύθερος, ἀλλὰ τὰ πάντα καὶ ἐν πᾶσιν Χριστός. The thought is clearly that Christ makes irrelevant ethnic, cultural, and social distinctions, that is, in practical terms, in the church (ὅπου, so Aletti, *Épître aux Colossiens* 232). This was a thought which Paul evidently cherished and to which he returned on several occasions:

1 Cor. 12:13   εἴτε Ἰουδαῖοι εἴτε Ἕλληνες εἴτε δοῦλοι εἴτε ἐλεύθεροι
Gal. 3:28   οὐκ ἔνι Ἰουδαῖος οὐδὲ Ἕλλην, οὐκ ἔνι δοῦλος οὐδὲ
               ἐλεύθερος, οὐκ ἔνι ἄρσεν καὶ θῆλυ
Col. 3:11   οὐκ ἔνι Ἕλλην καὶ Ἰουδαῖος, περιτομὴ καὶ ἀκροβυστία,
               βάρβαρος, Σκύθης, δοῦλος, ἐλεύθερος

The formulations are sufficiently varied to show that it was not a fixed formula so much as a cherished theme. Two variations are of particular significance here. (1) In Gal. 3:28 οὐκ ἔνι stresses the point in strong terms, ἔνι standing in place of ἔνεστιν (BDF §98) with the sense "it is possible" (BAGD s.v. ἔνειμι). Therefore, οὐκ ἔνι, "it is not possible, it cannot be" (NEB/REB "There is no question here of . . ."). Not simply particular ethnic distinctions have been abolished, but the very possibility of such distinctions having any continuing meaning has ceased to exist. Note also the linking καί in the first two couplets: it is not so much that the individual categories "Greek," "Jew," "circumcision," and "uncircumcision" are discounted as no longer meaningful; rather, it is that the way of categorizing humankind into two classes, "Greek and Jew," "circumcision and uncircumcision," is no longer appropriate. In contrast, the last two items ("slave, free") do not cover the complete range of human status, so we do not have "slave and free," breaking a parallelism which is a feature of the other two versions.

(2) Here in Colossians the focus is obviously primarily on ethnic, cultural distinctions, as the first six items, four of them unique to this version, clearly indicate (*pace* MacDonald 103-4, 145). Even more striking is the

---

32. Cf. particularly Morray-Jones, "Transformational Mysticism."

fact that the first four all focus on the Jew-Gentile division — with even
more emphasis than in Gal. 3:28, where that distinction is the principal issue
in the letter. This confirms both the Jewish character of the threat to the
Colossian church (with Lightfoot 214; *pace* Lohse, *Colossians and Philemon*
143 n. 70), and the earlier conclusion, that despite the absence of an explicit
argument as in Galatians, what was at stake in Colossae also was an attempt
(less forceful than in Galatia) to intimidate Gentile believers into admission
that Jewish practice and worship (as in Colossae) provided a more effective
access to knowledge of God (see also on 2:11, 16, 18, and 21).

"There is not any 'Greek and Jew,' 'circumcision and uncircumcision'. . . ." As already noted, it is quite appropriate to put quotation marks
around both pairs, since the phrases represent familiar ways of classifying
humanity into two categories. As the Greeks had tended to classify the people
of the world into "Greeks and barbarians," the latter covering all the rest
(see below), so Jews could lump all non-Jews together as "Greeks." The
fact that "Greeks" is used rather than "Gentiles = the (other) nations," which
would have been the more comprehensive term (given some awareness in
the Mediterranean world that there were regions where Hellenistic influence
had not penetrated), is simply a reminder of the pervasiveness of Hellenistic
culture in the Mediterranean basin. And this is the way Paul normally
expresses the contrast (Rom. 1:16; 2:9-10; 3:9; 10:12; 1 Cor. 1:22, 24; 10:32;
12:13; Gal. 3:28).

"Jew" ('Ιουδαῖος) was originally used by foreigners for a person
belonging to Judea ('Ιουδαία). But increasingly from the Maccabean period
it had come to be accepted and used by Jews themselves as a self-designation,
as a way of identifying themselves in relation to and in distinction from other
nationalities (note particularly the data in H. Kuhli, *EDNT* 2.194). That this
also involved a sense of distinctive religious identity is implied in the fact
that the word became the basis of the new name for the religion of the Jews,
"Judaism" ('Ιουδαϊσμος), which also emerged at this time (in literature first
in 2 Macc. 2:21; 8:1; 14:38). Equally significant is the fact that both the
Maccabean rebellion and the concept of "Judaism" emerged in response to
the threat of "Hellenism" ('Ελληνισμός, 2 Macc. 4:13). As used by Jews,
therefore, the distinction "Greek and Jew" would probably carry an overtone
or residue of disdain for things "Greek."

That "Greek and Jew" indicates a Jewish perspective (who else would
single out the "Jews" and lump all the rest together as "Greeks"?) is
confirmed by the second pair, "circumcision and uncircumcision." As already noted on 2:11, this again betrays a strongly Jewish perspective, one
in which the rite of circumcision is so highly valued that the rest of humanity
can be categorized by the fact that they have not received it. Here, too, we
should avoid the tendency of most translations to render the distinction as
"circumcised and uncircumcised"; it is the metonymy, whereby the ritual

act itself (or its absence!) can stand for whole nations, which indicates both the Jewish perspective and the fundamental importance of circumcision for Jewish self-understanding (see on 2:11).

Why should Paul and Timothy repeat what amounts to the same distinction (Greek and Jew, circumcision and uncircumcision)? The answer will be partly that the abolition of the boundaries between the two, with their limitation of Jewish Messiah and promise to those within the boundary marked by circumcision, had been a central feature of Paul's gospel from the beginning and was bound to come to expression in such a formulaic Pauline passage as this. But the distinctive doubling of the emphasis here, including the third otherwise gratuitous reference to the theme of circumcision versus uncircumcision in the letter (2:11, 13; 3:11; also 4:11) must surely indicate, first, that the primary challenge to the Colossian believers was posed by local Jews and, second, that it presupposed a valuation of circumcision which called the Christians' standing as beneficiaries of Jewish heritage into question. As before, the lack of any stronger polemic strengthens the suggestion that the challenge came in terms of a Jewish apologetic which simply expressed the superiority of more traditional Judaism and did not engage in vigorous proselytizing. But the message here is the same as when Paul confronts the more aggressive proselytizing in Galatia: the distinction between Jew and Greek, as marked out by circumcision, has been removed by Christ; the privileges of the Jewish people which have kept them separate from the other nations have been opened up to the Gentiles by the Jewish Messiah (cf. Gal. 5:6; 6:15).

The emphasis on removal of the significance of ethnic boundaries is continued in the next two items on the list. Here, however, the note of ethnic superiority (cultural or religious), which was only latent in the previous pairings, comes more to the surface. The very term βάρβαρος carried a derogatory significance. In its primary usage it referred to a speaker of a strange, unintelligible language (e.g., Ovid, *Tristia* 5.10.37; 1 Cor. 14:11). And from its early use in reference to the Medes and Persians, the historic foes of Greece, it carried a clear note of contempt (hence Roman unwillingness to be classed as βάρβαροι), though by now it simply denoted all non-Greeks (cf. Rom. 1:14).[33]

That a note of contempt is intended is confirmed by the addition of "Scythians," tribes which had settled on the northern coast of the Black Sea and which in earlier centuries had terrorized parts of Asia Minor and the Middle East (see K. S. Rubinson, *ABD* 5.1056-57). Their name was synonymous with crudity, excess, and ferocity: Σκύθης, "Scythian," had

---

33. See BAGD; Lightfoot 215-16; H. Windisch, *TDNT* 1.546-51; H. Balz, *EDNT* 1.197-98; M. Hengel, *Jews, Greeks and Barbarians* (London: SCM/Philadelphia: Fortress, 1980) 55-66; *NDIEC* 4.82.

the metaphorical sense of "rude, rough person," and the verb σκυθίζω, "behave like a Scythian," meant both "drink immoderately" and "shave the head" (from the Scythian practice of scalping their dead enemies; LSJ; O. Michel, *TDNT* 7.448). Josephus no doubt cites the common view when he refers to Scythians as "delighting in murder of people and little different from wild beasts" (*Contra Apionem* 2:26; see also Lightfoot 216-17). GNB quite properly renders the term as "savages." The point is again clear: in Christ there is no place for any such racial, ethnic, or cultural contempt among peoples and individuals; even the wild, repulsive Scythians are not ruled out of court.

The final pair and the first are the only ones to be repeated in all three of the passages where the formulation is used. But unlike the first, the last is not given prominence or elaborated. Probably, therefore, it was included not because the slave-free distinction was a factor in the Colossian situation causing concern to the writer(s) (though see 4:22-25),[34] but because the affirmation "no Jew or Greek, no slave or free" had become a more or less established credo of the Pauline churches. Perhaps it is there also partly in echo of the preceding items in the list, since "freedom" was such a fundamental element in Greek self-understanding over against the "barbarians."

Apart from ethnic differences (and gender differences in Gal. 3:28), the difference between slave and free was the other most fundamental division in society. Up to a third of those living in a city like Colossae may have been slaves. Slavery had not yet come to be thought of as immoral or necessarily degrading (it took the slave trade to bring this insight home to Western "civilization"). It was simply the means of providing labor at the bottom end of the economic spectrum (originally from the ranks of defeated enemies, but by now mainly through birth to slaves). To sell oneself as a slave was a device of last resort for someone in debt, and slaves of important masters could exercise significant influence themselves. Paul used slavery as a powerful metaphor in exhortation (Rom. 6:16-17; 1 Cor. 7:22; 2 Cor. 4:5; Phil. 2:7). Nevertheless, the distinction here was an unavoidable reminder that slavery was completely antithetical to the Greek idealization of freedom, with the slave defined as "one who does not belong to himself but to someone else" (Aristotle, *Politica* I.1254a.14) and as one who "does not have the power to refuse" (Seneca, *De beneficiis* 3.19). Not surprisingly, freedom (manumission) was the goal of every slave ("it is the slave's prayer that he be set free immediately," Epictetus 4.1.33) and, it should be added, was often achieved (K. H. Rengstorf, *TDNT* 2.261-64; H. Schlier, *TDNT* 2.487-88; *OCD* 994-96; S. S. Bartchy, *ABD* 6.58-73; see also on Phm. 16).

---

34. Here precisely the parallel with Galatians breaks down, since Colossians does not link "the elemental forces" with the theme of slavery (so prominent in Gal. 4:3, 9).

The point here, then, is once again that Christ has relativized all such distinctions, however fundamental to society, its structure, and its ongoing existence.

The final clause ("but Christ is all and in all") is a further variation of Gal. 3:28 ("for you are all one in Christ Jesus"). The variation was no doubt deliberate, intended to correlate the assertion here with the cosmic emphasis of the earlier hymn (1:16-20; see n. 8). It is precisely because of the cosmic scope of Christ's work, including above all his act of reconciliation (1:20), that such internal divisions and ways of categorizing peoples and individuals have ceased to have meaning as determinants of Christian self-perception, conduct, and relationships. The phrase is some-what surprising, since the equivalent phrase in 1 Cor. 15:28 refers to God (ἵνα ὁ θεὸς τὰ πάντα ἐν πᾶσιν; Eph. 1:23 is ambiguous). But here it is precisely the thought of Christ in a cosmic role, as embodying the creative power and rationality by which God created and sustains the cosmos, which is in mind. Anyone who recognizes God in Christ to that extent will find such human distinctions and boundaries relatively trivial and unimportant. If "Christ is everything and in everything," then nothing can diminish or disparage the standing of any one human in relation to another or to God.

3:12 ἐνδύσασθε οὖν, ὡς ἐκλεκτοὶ τοῦ θεοῦ ἅγιοι καὶ ἠγαπημένοι, σπλάγχνα οἰκτιρμοῦ χρηστότητα ταπεινοφροσύνην πραΰτητα μακροθυ-μίαν. The structure of the parenesis is not divided up neatly. The negative "put off" sequence was completed in 3:9, and the "put on" sequence began in 3:10. But 3:10-11 were more a statement of principle, the transformation of conversion-initiation being seen in the wholeness of its effect, the putting on of a completely fresh personality. Now we come to the particulars, the clothes, as it were, which the new person should wear. The verb (ἐνδύ-σασθε) is the same as in 3:10, though now clearly in the imperative. It is as a result of that decisive step and engagement with Christ (οὖν) that a whole set of particular consequences must follow. It is not clear whether behind these particulars there is conscious allusion to the picture of Christ in his ministry, as known to the Colossians in the Jesus tradition, in which they had been instructed. But that picture is implicit in the thematic state-ment of 2:6-7, and comparison with Gal. 5:22-23, bracketed as it is by 5:14, 24 and 6:2, gives some weight to the suggestion (cf. Aletti, *Épître aux Colossiens* 237).

Immediately striking is the fact that the appeal is based not simply on the event of conversion-initiation (οὖν), but on the status of the Colossians "as God's elect, holy and beloved." For these are all terms which individu-ally, but particularly in this combination, can be understood only from their reference to Israel. Ἐκλεκτός ("chosen, select") was familiar enough in Greek, but the idea of a people "chosen by God" was wholly and exclusively

Jewish, a fundamental feature of Israel's self-perception.[35] So too, as we have already seen, with ἅγιοι ("saints, holy ones"; see on 1:2). And though the idea of one beloved of the gods is familiar outside the Judeo-Christian tradition (cf. Dio Chrysostom 3.60; BAGD s.v. ἀγαπάω 1d), it is again a particular emphasis in Jewish self-understanding (e.g., Deut. 32:15; 33:26; Isa. 5:1, 7; 44:2; Jer. 12:7; 31:3; Bar. 3:37). The phrasing is so concentrated and has not yet become conventional (there are divergent parallels in Rom. 1:7; 1 Thes. 1:4; 2 Thes. 2:13) that the allusions must be deliberate and could hardly have been unnoticed by the recipients. The echo of the classic covenant text, Deut. 7:6-7, in particular, is striking (see further Wolter 184). More clearly than anywhere else in Colossians it is evident that the Gentile recipients of the letter were being invited to consider themselves full partic- ipants in the people and heritage of Israel.[36] Or to be more precise, the particular exhortations which follow assume and expect the Colossians to presuppose that the starting point for their praxis as Christians was the recognition that they stood before God as Israel stood before God. It is very likely that this assumption on the part of uncircumcised Gentiles (2:13) was a bone of contention with or provocation to the more traditional Jewish synagogues in Colossae.

The characteristics that these Gentile participants in Israel are to put on (see on 3:10) are again fivefold (see on 3:5) and are characteristic of, though not of course exclusive to, Jewish wisdom teaching (Wolter 185). Schweizer, *Colossians* 206 compares particularly 1QS 4:3. The σπλάγχνα are literally the "inward parts, entrails" (Acts 1:18), where the seat of the emotions was thought to be located (BAGD). It is thus a very emotive term, denoting something deeply felt (as in 2 Cor. 7:15; Phil. 1:8; Phm. 12; cf. εὔσπλαγχνος in Eph. 4:32 and 1 Pet. 3:8; and the verb, as in Matt. 20:34; Mark 1:41; 6:34; Luke 15:20; see also H. Köster, *TDNT* 7.555). Linked with οἰκτιρμός, "pity" (cf. Phil. 2:1 — σπλάγχνα καὶ οἰκτιρμοί; of God's mer- cies in Rom. 12:1 and 2 Cor. 1:3), the emotional content is even stronger; hence "heartfelt compassion" (so NJB; see further O'Brien, *Colossians, Philemon* 198-99). Compassion is a common theme in the *Testaments of the Twelve Patriarchs* and the principal theme specifically in the *Testament of*

---

35. E.g., 1 Chron. 16:13; Ps. 105:6; Isa. 43:20; 65:22; Tob. 8:15; Sir. 46:1; Wis. 4:15; *Jubilees* 1:29; *1 Enoch* 1:3, 8; 5:7-8; 93:2; CD 4:3-4; 1QM 12:1; 1QpHab 10:13; *Sibylline Oracles* 3.69. *Testament of Benjamin* 10:10 speaks analogously of "the chosen of the Gentiles." See further G. Schrenk, *TDNT* 4.181-84; also my *Partings* 21-23. In the New Testament cf. particularly Mark 13:20, 22, 27; Rom. 8:33; 2 Tim. 2:10; Tit. 1:1; 1 Pet. 1:1; 2:9; Rev. 17:14 (see also O'Brien, *Colossians, Philemon* 197-98). The term need not and should not be referred here to the angels in heaven (as by Lohmeyer 145).

36. Cf. Lightfoot 219: "All the three terms, ἐκλεκτοί, ἅγιοι, ἠγαπημένοι, are transferred from the Old Covenant to the New, from Israel after the flesh to the Israel after the Spirit" (similarly Scott 71; Houlden 206; Caird 207; Wright, *Colossians and Philemon* 141).

Zebulun (its Greek heading is ΠΕΡΙ ΕΥΣΠΛΑΓΧΝΙΑΣ ΚΑΙ ΕΛΕΟΥΣ; see further Köster, *TDNT* 7.550-52; W. H. Hollander and M. de Jonge, *The Testaments of the Twelve Patriarchs: A Commentary* [Leiden: Brill, 1985] 254-55); note particularly the phrase σπλάγχνα ἐλέους in 7:3 and 8:2, 6 (the same phrase as in Luke 1:78).

Χρηστότης, "goodness," "kindness" (so most translations), "generosity" (NJB) is a human grace also in 2 Cor. 6:6 and Gal. 5:22, but presumably seen as a reflection of God's "goodness" (as in Rom. 2:4), the more typical thought (BAGD), and so characteristic of the new self being renewed in accordance with the image of its creator (3:10). It refers to relationship with others, as the next term refers to one's self-estimate (Lightfoot 219). "Χρηστότης stands at the center [of the list], perhaps because it is considered the most important, a characteristic which also (at least in part) encompasses the others" (J. Zmijewski, *EDNT* 3.476; brief word studies of the terms are provided by O'Brien, *Colossians, Philemon* 199-201).

The presence of ταπεινοφροσύνη is surprising since it was used in reference to the somewhat disparaged practices of 2:18 and 23. This probably confirms that these earlier references were by no means out-and-out polemical in character, and the fact that the same thing is commended here must mean that a certain degree of similarity between the codes of religious practice in the Colossian groups in view was inevitable (both essentially Jewish in character). Here presumably it simply means "humility, modesty" (as in Phil. 2:3; Eph. 4:2; 1 Pet. 5:5; *1 Clement* 21:8; 31:4; 44:3), without reference to a spiritual discipline like fasting (see on 2:18). For Greek thought generally ταπεινοφροσύνη was too closely related to servility for it to be able to serve as a positive virtue (W. Grundmann, *TDNT* 8.1-4, 11-12), though in the sense of "modesty" it gained a positive ring (Gnilka, *Kolosserbrief* 194).

In Christian thought, in contrast, a natural associate is πραΰτης, "gentleness" (the two are closely linked in Matt. 11:29; 2 Cor. 10:1; Gal. 5:23; and Eph. 4:2; see also BAGD).[37] It was a virtue widely prized, though Greek thought recognized that, as with other virtues, it could be taken to extreme (F. Hauck and S. Schulz, *TDNT* 6.646). The Hebrew evaluation of such meekness is evident particularly in the Psalms (25:9; 34:2; 37:11, etc.) and Sirach (1:27; 3:17-18; 4:8, etc.). "It is the power that enables us, precisely in situations of conflict with our fellow, so to meet him that he experiences the criticism of his behavior (assuming that it is justified criticism) not as condemnation but as help" (Lindemann, *Kolosserbrief* 60-61). Since 2 Cor. 10:1 takes the "gentleness of Christ" as a model (see also H. Frankemölle, *EDNT* 3.146-47), we should perhaps see here again an echo

37. The English version of Schweizer, *Colossians* 205, has surprisingly translated his *"Sanftmut"* ("gentleness") with "weakness."

of Jesus tradition (cf. 2:6-7), with the same implication as in the case of χρηστότης, that this, too, is the outworking of renewal according to the image of God who is Christ.[38]

Equally natural as a companion of χρηστότης is μακροθυμία, "patience" (see on 1:11); the two are linked in Rom. 2:4; 2 Cor. 6:6; and Gal. 5:22 (cf. also Eph. 4:2 and *1 Clement* 42:2). As πραΰτης is best defined by contrast with its opposite (rudeness, harshness), so also μακροθυμία by its opposite (resentment, revenge, wrath; so Lightfoot 219).

Such virtues (or graces), particularly as in the combination here, can appear to encourage a "milksop" weakness as in people whose calling in life is to be a doormat for others — at least as those caught up in the cut and thrust of the rat race count strength. But in fact to live out such a character calls for a strength which is rarely seen in the marketplace (as Jesus demonstrated). And without such an attitude toward others no group of individuals can become and grow as a community, with a proper care for others and willingness to submerge one's own personal interests. This, it should be recalled, is the other side of the killing off and putting off of 3:5 and 8. Perhaps they in fact represent the two alternatives: a community which fails at 3:12 falls at 3:5 and 8.

3:13 ἀνεχόμενοι ἀλλήλων καὶ χαριζόμενοι ἑαυτοῖς ἐάν τις πρός τινα ἔχῃ μομφήν· καθὼς καὶ ὁ κύριος ἐχαρίσατο ὑμῖν, οὕτως καὶ ὑμεῖς. The theme struck in 3:12 is extended, highlighting still more clearly that quality of mutual relationships which any church (or community) needs to nurture if it is to thrive. Having stressed the personal qualities required (3:12), Paul and Timothy now focus on the actual relationships themselves. The precise connection with the preceding clause is unclear: the verbs here could denote the way in which the five positive qualities are to be "put on"; or the order of thought could be simply sequential. At the very least the implication is that the test of these qualities will be when other members of the community act thoughtlessly or inconsiderately.

Ἀνέχομαι has the sense of "endure, bear with, tolerate" (Mark 9:19 pars.; 2 Cor. 11:1, 19; Ignatius, *Polycarp* 1:2; Eph. 4:2 again is a close parallel; see BAGD and cf. Rom. 2:4). "Put up with" catches the sense of an acceptance requiring an effort of will because the actions or attitudes in question are immature and tiresome. Such a positive response is of a piece with the practical wisdom (as in Rom. 12:9–13:10) which small groups of Christians needed if they were to live without disturbance in unsympathetic and often hostile environments (cf. Conzelmann 152).

---

38. There is no reason why an element of *imitatio Christi* should be excluded here (cf. Lohmeyer 146; Jervell 251-54; R. P. Martin, *Colossians and Philemon* 112; Schweizer, *Colossians* 206-7; Bruce, *Colossians, Philemon, and Ephesians* 152-53; *pace* Merk 210-11; Lohse, *Colossians and Philemon* 147 n. 100).

Still more demanding is a situation where someone is at fault and deserving of blame or censure (μομφή, only here in biblical Greek, but see LSJ). Such a person must be forgiven (χαρίζομαι, the same verb as in 2:13). The implication of "forgiving each other" is that there will be not a few occasions when such forgiveness will be called for, that all members will be in the situation of having to forgive or needing forgiveness at some time or other, and that on many occasions there will be blame on both sides. Only such mutual respect and support, such recognition of mutual vulnerability, such valuing of each other beyond individual hurts and faults, it is also implied, would retain weaker or wavering members who otherwise might find the old way of life or the more traditional Jewish alternative too attractive.

The model here, as by implication in 3:12, is explicitly stated to be "the Lord" (cf. again particularly Eph. 4:32; 5:2, 25, 29; also Rom. 15:7). Presumably that means Christ (see, e.g., O'Brien, *Colossians, Philemon* 202; Wolter 186; Aletti, *Épître aux Colossiens* 238); in the Paulines, apart from Old Testament quotations, κύριος always denotes Christ. This adds to the untypically Pauline character of the thought, since the idea of Christ as forgiving sins is even more unusual than talk of forgiveness itself (see on 2:13); even in 2:13 the act of forgiveness is attributed to God. This could suggest that, unusually, ὁ κύριος here refers after all to God (the thought would then be directly parallel to that of Matt. 6:12, 14-15; 18:23-35; see also n. 9). But Jesus is recalled in the Jesus tradition as pronouncing sins forgiven and occasioning comment for doing so (Mark 2:5-7 pars.; Luke 7:47-49), with a similar correlation of forgiveness enabling a generous act in the latter case (cf. also Luke 23:34), so it is quite possible that Jesus as Lord was thought of also as the one who forgives (cf. Rom. 10:13; as presumably in 1 John 1:9).

The point, however, is to reinforce the interdependence between forgiving and being forgiven (as, again, in Matt. 6:12, 14-15; 18:23-35).[39] The two evidently hang together. It is the experience of having been forgiven which releases the generous impulses to forgive others (which is why the parable of Matt. 18:23-35 is so shocking), just as it is the refusal to forgive which betrays the reality that forgiveness has not been received, that the individual has not even recognized the need for forgiveness (hence again Matt. 6:14-15). A community has hope of holding together and growing together only when the need for forgiveness is recognized on each side where fault has been committed and only when forgiveness is both offered and received (hence Matt. 18:21-22/Luke 17:4).

---

39. Some think there is sufficient indication here of a conscious allusion to the Lord's Prayer (Scott 72-73; Hunter 50-51; Davies 139; Bruce, *Colossians, Philemon, and Ephesians* 155; cf. Gnilka, *Kolosserbrief* 196); this is disputed with surprising confidence by Lindemann, *Kolosserbrief* 61.

3:14 ἐπὶ πᾶσιν δὲ τούτοις τὴν ἀγάπην, ὅ ἐστιν σύνδεσμος τῆς τελει-
ότητος. It is not clear whether the intention was to continue the metaphor
of putting on clothes. This would be a natural reading of ἐπί and would allow
an extension of the metaphor into the second clause. So, most boldly, JB
"Over all these clothes, to keep them together and complete them, put on
love" (similarly Moule, *Colossians and Philemon* 123; NJB and NIV are
less ambitious). But though δεσμός ("something that ties or fastens") could
fit such an extended image, τελειότης ("completeness, perfection") is less
suitable, and the whole image would become too strained. It is better therefore to assume that while the verb "put on" (3:12) still determines the first
clause, the metaphor itself is not pursued further and it is the importance of
love as such which determines the second clause.

That ἀγάπη ("love") was the most important grace for Paul is clear
beyond dispute (Rom. 13:8-10; 1 Cor. 13:13; Gal. 5:6, 14, 22), with, once
again, the implication that it is Christ's self-sacrifice which provides the
model for such love (see on 1:4).[40] As in these passages, an echo of the Jesus
tradition (Mark 12:29-31) can hardly be excluded (Schrage, *Ethics* 210;
Wolter 186). It is because "love" sums up so effectively in one distinctive
Christian term the strong virtues and communal relationships that it is picked
out here (cf. 1 Cor. 13:4-7). Love is indeed like a "fastening," a σύνδεσμος,
which holds them together in a single coherent package (cf. *1 Clement* 49:2:
τὸν δεσμὸν τῆς ἀγάπης τοῦ θεοῦ). Nor is it accidental that σύνδεσμος was
used already in 2:19 in the more technical sense of "sinews, ligaments" of
the body (see on 2:19). For the point is the same, that at the end of the day
it is this love (and only this love) which is strong enough to hold together
a congregation of disparate individuals. An allusion to the Logos as the
δεσμός binding the cosmos together (so Gnilka, *Kolosserbrief* 197-98), however, does not seem necessary. More relevant is the much quoted report of
Simplicius, that the Pythagoreans regarded "friendship" as "the bond of all
the virtues" (e.g., BAGD, σύνδεσμος 1b; Bruce, *Colossians, Philemon, and
Ephesians* 156 n. 137), or the assertion in *Aristeas* 265 that friendship and
love (φιλανθρωπία καὶ ἀγάπησις) are "the bond of goodwill" (εὐνοίας
δεσμός); but "love" in the distinctive Christian sense is stronger. Plato at
one point speaks of law as the bond that holds a city together (*Leges* 921c);
for a Christian community, regulations would never be enough: only love
will suffice.

If τελειότης does not have a specific reference (to clothes perfectly
fitted and worn), it simply denotes the "completeness" and "maturity" (cf.
Heb. 6:1, the only other New Testament occurrence) of the community where

---

40. In response to J. T. Sanders's charge that love here has "lost any definite character"
(*Ethics* 68), Wedderburn, *Theology* 56, rightly replies by referring to the preceding verse: "love is
rather more likely 'Christ-shaped.' "

ἀγάπη is "on top of all." The genitive construction can indicate result or purpose,[41] but may not be quite so specific (Schweizer, *Colossians* 208; cf. RSV/NRSV "binds everything together in perfect harmony"; NIV "in perfect unity"; REB "to bind everything together and complete the whole"). Several commentators note the parallel with Matt. 5:43-48. The thought is probably also close to that in Eph. 4:13, where again it is Christ who provides the archetype of what such maturity and love-lived life should be (cf. Wis. 6:15: "to fix one's thought on her [Wisdom] is complete understanding [φρονήσεως τελειότης]"). See further on 1:28.

3:15 καὶ ἡ εἰρήνη τοῦ Χριστοῦ βραβευέτω ἐν ταῖς καρδίαις ὑμῶν, εἰς ἣν καὶ ἐκλήθητε ἐν ἑνὶ σώματι· καὶ εὐχάριστοι γίνεσθε. As elsewhere in Pauline thought, a close complement of love is peace (2 Cor. 13:11; Gal. 5:22; Eph. 4:2-3, where the same imagery is used, "the bond of peace"; 2 Tim. 2:22). Here it is "the peace of Christ," which some would regard as a mark of post-Pauline authorship (cf. 2 Thes. 3:16; Eph. 2:14) since elsewhere in Paul the thought is rather of the peace of God (Phil. 4:7; "the God of peace" in Rom. 15:33; 16:20; 2 Cor. 13:11; Phil. 4:9; 1 Thes. 5:23). The unusual absence of "the Lord Jesus Christ" in 1:2 from the normal greeting of "peace from God the Father and the Lord Jesus Christ" strengthens the suspicion at this point (see p. 43 n. 6 above). But either way does not make much difference, since the Christ of 1:15-20 and 2:9 is so much the embodiment of God's wisdom and fullness that it comes to the same thing.

Also unusual is the more clearly subjective tone given to the thought of "peace" here by the addition of "in your hearts" (the only close Pauline parallel is Phil. 4:7), since "heart" usually denotes the center and depth of personal experience (see on 2:2), whereas a strong corporate or social dimension is usually present in the Jewish idea of peace (see on 1:2).[42] The thought here, however, should not be reduced to a merely spiritualized or individualized sensation, for no doubt what was in mind was the state of peace achieved by Christ already spoken of in 1:20 (cf. W. Foerster, *TDNT* 2.414).[43] The confidence and calmness of the Colossian Christians was a reflection of that victory and reconciliation (1:20-22; 2:15); it was to this they had been "called." Here once more we should be ready to recognize something of a more titular force in the name "Christ" ("the Christ"), since in prophetic perspective the peace promised to God's covenant people was a hope for the future new age (Isa. 9:6-7; 54:10; Ezek. 34:25-31; 37:26; Mic.

41. Dibelius, *Kolosser, Epheser, Philemon* 43-44; Lohse, *Colossians and Philemon* 149; N. Turner, *GNTG* 3.212; Pokorný 172-73; Harris 164-65; discussion in Schmauch 80-82.

42. "In the OT . . . there is no specific text in which it [*šalom*] denotes the specifically spiritual attitude of inward peace" (G. von Rad, *TDNT* 2.406).

43. "The *pax Christiana* is to prevail in the church, as the *pax Romana* did in the world of Paul's day, allowing its inhabitants to pursue their respective callings without the constant threat of war" (Wright, *Colossians and Philemon* 143).

5:4; Hag. 2:9; Zech. 8:12; *1 Enoch* 5:7, 9; 10:17; 11:2; *Testament of Dan* 5:11). The peace the Colossian believers could experience in their hearts was further proof that they belonged to the people of the Messiah in the age of the Messiah already come (cf. Gnilka, *Kolosserbrief* 198-99).

As already observed (2:18), the verb βραβεύω is drawn from the athletic contest, meaning, first, "award a prize (βραβεῖον)" and so "act as judge or umpire, preside (at an election), arbitrate" (cf. Wis. 10:12; see Lightfoot 221), and then "direct, control" (LSJ). The broad sense here is clear enough, though not the precise meaning — "rule" (RSV/NRSV, NIV), "be arbiter" (NEB/REB). Here is the true arbiter ("peace"), not the Colossian Jews referred to in 2:18 (Aletti, *Épître aux Colossiens* 240). To be noted is the fact that the subject is "the peace of Christ," not "you"; this is something the Colossians have not to accomplish but to let happen — to let go any attempt to control and manipulate and to let the peace of Christ be the determiner — just as in the following clause peace is a call to which they can only respond. The metaphor is an attractive one: of the knowledge of what Christ has achieved and the inward calm tranquility which believers can enjoy in consequence, determining what courses should be followed in difficult decisions and how the tensions of community relations (cf. 3:13) may be resolved (cf. Rom. 14:17, 19; 1 Cor. 14:33). As Paul knew well, there were occasions when a sterner attitude was required (e.g., 1 Cor. 4:21 and Gal. 1:6-9), but in matters primarily of personal relationships (the theme of this passage) to "pursue what makes for peace" (Rom. 14:19) is a good rule.

It is to such peace, arbitrating in this way, that the Colossians had been "called." Καλέω is another characteristic Pauline term. In everyday speech it was used of an invitation to a meal or a summons to court (LSJ, BAGD). Here the stronger sense is implicit, as when the invitation to the banquet was given by a king or by a god (as in Matt. 22:3, 9 and *NDIEC* 1.5-6). And in this case it is the summons given by the one who has achieved peace (1:20) into that peace, the call to refugees and victims of the previous warfare into the area of peace which his death had won. The thought is also entirely Jewish and closely related to the theme of a chosen people (3:12), as we see particularly in deutero-Isaiah (Isa. 41:8-9; 42:6; 43:3-4; 48:12; 49:1; 51:2). The continued use of such themes close to the heart of Israel's self-understanding is significant and reinforces the view that what Paul and Timothy were trying to do was to mark out more carefully both the Jewish character of the Christian message and the Christian focus of the Jewish heritage.

The corporate dimension implicit in the talk of peace and of a people called is strengthened by the reminder that the call has in view "one body," that the one body is also the arena within which the peace of Christ comes to effect. This is the final variation on the complex body theme played in Colossians. And here, more than in any of the preceding variations, it is the main emphasis of the earlier Paulines (Rom. 12:5-8; 1 Corinthians 12) which is to the fore. That emphasis is on the body as a metaphor of unity, but precisely as a unity composed of the complementarity and integrated wholeness of different parts. In this case the primary influencing thought seems to be the common idea in the ancient world of the city or state as a body (the body politic), which served just the same function — that is, to inculcate a sense of mutual belonging and responsibility among the diverse constituents within the city or state, as in the famous fable of Menenius Agrippa in Livy, *Historia* 2.32 and Epictetus 2.10.4-5 (E. Schweizer, *TDNT* 7.1038-39, 1041, 1069; see also Dunn, "Body" 153-56). As in the earlier Paulines, the thought seems to be primarily of the local (Colossian) church as the one body (of Christ in Colossae), that is, the house church where they would meet for worship (3:16). But the same applies to the church now seen as the universal body of Christ (1:18a, 24; 2:19), a oneness which is itself an effect of the peace of Christ and which can only be sustained by that peace (hence again Eph. 4:3).

Almost as an afterthought[44] Paul and Timothy add "And be thankful," the adjective εὐχάριστος ("thankful") occurring only here in the New Testament, but common in inscriptions (BAGD). We could translate "Be thankful people," those who are characterized by their thankfulness, or indeed "keep being or becoming (γίνεσθε) thankful," the verb indicating an ongoing responsibility (cf. Abbott 290). As in 1:12 the inference is plain: a spirit of thanksgiving should be the basic attitude of the Colossian Christians; so again in 3:17, the double emphasis within three verses underlining the point. No doubt the themes of 3:13-15 are intertwined and interdependent: forgiveness and love of others, the peace of Christ, and thankfulness to God; without any one the others are unsustainable.

3:16 ὁ λόγος τοῦ Χριστοῦ ἐνοικείτω ἐν ὑμῖν πλουσίως, ἐν πάσῃ σοφίᾳ διδάσκοντες καὶ νουθετοῦντες ἑαυτούς, ψαλμοῖς ὕμνοις ᾠδαῖς πνευματικαῖς ἐν [τῇ] χάριτι ᾄδοντες ἐν ταῖς καρδίαις ὑμῶν τῷ θεῷ. The immediately preceding exhortations do not seem particularly to have been occasioned by the situation confronting the Colossian believers (contrast 3:1-4). They have a suitability and relevance to all churches of all times. Indeed, their relaxed character, if anything, suggests that the situation in Colossae fell well short of a crisis. One feature of the Colossian "philosophy" which seemingly was proving attractive, however, was its adherents' experience of worship, of a worship shared, it would appear, with the angels

---

44. However, J. M. Robinson, "Die Hodajot-Formel in Gebet und Hymnus des Frühchristentums," in *Apophoreta*, E. Haenchen FS (Berlin: Töpelmann, 1964) 194-235 (here 225), suggests that the call here functions as a sort of rubric or heading *(Überschrift)* for the following injunction (cf. 1 Thes. 5:18; Robinson is followed by R. P. Martin, *Colossians and Philemon* 114; Lindemann, *Kolosserbrief* 62).

(see 2:18, 23). Not surprisingly, therefore, this sequence of parenesis is rounded off by a description of the worship which the Colossian Christians should be enjoying and, by implication, should find sufficiently fulfilling — at least enough to reduce the attractiveness of the Jewish angel worship.

The elements of Christian worship commended are not altogether surprising: "the word of Christ," teaching and admonition, and singing and thanksgiving, elements which have been a feature of typical Christian worship from the beginning till now. But this is in fact one of only a handful of passages that give us some insight into the content and character of earliest Christian worship and enable us to say anything at all about it (the most obvious others are 1 Cor. 14:26 and Acts 2:42; cf. Ernst, *Philipper, Philemon, Kolosser, Epheser* 229). Quite how the elements are related to each other is not made clear: Is it a coordinated series, the instruction explaining how the indwelling takes place, the singing as the means of (cf. Eph. 5:19) or the response to the instruction? Or is it an uncoordinated series, the elements appearing in different combinations in different gatherings? Unfortunately, we cannot tell, though the first clause is certainly the principal clause. Nevertheless, for those with liturgical interests the details are of more than usual interest. The failure to mention or refer to any leaders here (prophets or teachers) may be significant (cf. Gnilka, *Kolosserbrief* 200) as indicating a responsibility for worship shared by all (see also my *Jesus* chs. 8-9).

The λόγος has already been identified as the gospel (1:5, 25). Ὁ λόγος τοῦ Χριστοῦ as a phrase occurs only here in the New Testament (in qualified form in Heb. 6:1), but "the word of the Lord" (1 Thes. 1:8; 2 Thes. 3:1; Acts 8:25; 12:24, etc.) is equivalent. As such it can denote both the word (gospel) of which (the) Christ is the content (so most; "the mode of Christ's presence in the community," Wolter 189), and the word which (the) Christ spoke (Jesus tradition);[45] there is no reason why the genitive form should be pressed to an either-or decision (either objective or subjective). This again would accord with the double emphasis of 2:6-7. Indeed, it would be surprising if the cross and resurrection provided the only subject of earliest Christian meditation, when there was (evidently) a fair amount of Jesus tradition which must have been known by the the earliest Christian churches.

The use of οἰκέω with ἐν- prefixed underlines the settled character of the "indwelling" envisaged: οἱ ἐνοικοῦντες elsewhere means "the inhabitants" (LSJ s.v. ἐνοικέω); as the rabbis later pointed out, he who dwells in a house is the master of the house, not just a passing guest (Str-B 3.239). As in 3:15 the subject of the imperative is not the readers, but something they must open up to and allow to do its work (cf. Lohmeyer 150). In this

45. Moule, "New Life" 492; Bruce, *Colossians, Philemon, and Ephesians* 157 n. 148 (see also on 3:13, 14 above). Contrast Gnilka, *Kolosserbrief* 199: the word of the earthly Jesus "plays no role" in Colossians.

context the ἐν ὑμῖν may also signify "among you," indicating an element of preaching/teaching in the communal gatherings of the Colossian Christians for worship and instruction (e.g., Masson 147 n. 5; Bruce, *Colossians, Philemon, and Ephesians* 157; Pokorný 173 n. 80; Fee 649). Πλουσίως ("richly") picks up the same theme of divine richness already announced in 1:27 and 2:2. There is a richness in "the word of Christ" which makes it an inexhaustible source of spiritual resource, intellectual stimulus, and personal and corporate challenge; but without the participants' positive response its "indwelling" might be feeble rather than rich (Schweizer, *Colossians* 209).

That a corporate context is envisaged, a sharing of the word of Christ within the gathered assembly, is confirmed by the next clause, where the "indwelling" of the word is further described or the complementary activity indicated: "in all wisdom [see n. 14] teaching and warning each other." The strong echo of 1:28 ("warning everyone and teaching everyone in all wisdom") can hardly be accidental (see on that verse). The most significant difference is that whereas 1:28 described the apostolic mission of proclaiming the gospel (though as a task shared with others, Timothy at least), here warning and teaching are seen as a corporate responsibility (Fee 649). Indeed, it is a striking feature of the Pauline corpus how much Paul insisted that the members of the churches to which he wrote should recognize their mutual responsibility to instruct and admonish (JB/NJB's "advise" is too weak) each other (Rom. 12:7; 15:14; 1 Cor. 14:26; 1 Thes. 5:14; 2 Thes. 3:15; note also Gal. 6:1-3). That it should be done "with all wisdom" is a crucial qualification (the wisdom more fully specified in 1:9). Nor should we forget that this counsel follows from the description of a forgiving, loving, and thankful congregation.

The third element of Christian worship is singing: "psalms, hymns, and spiritual songs." Their relation to the preceding clause is unclear (see n. 14), but the possibility that such hymns were vehicles of instruction cannot be ruled out. Prior to the invention of printing, hymns and songs were a necessary and invaluable means of implanting Christian teaching — and even after (it is often said that Methodism's distinctive theology is to be found primarily in the hymns of Charles Wesley).

Ψαλμός is derived from the verb ψάλλω, "pluck or play (a stringed instrument)," hence "a song sung to the harp" (LSJ). It was already well established as the description of the "psalms" of David (so the Psalm titles in LXX; also 2 Sam. 23:1; Luke 20:42; 24:44; Acts 1:20; 13:33). As its application to the first-century BCE *Psalms of Solomon* and the discovery of 1QH and 11QPs[a] (with six further psalms) have confirmed, the practice in Jewish circles of composing new psalms for use in worship continued into the New Testament period. Hengel observes ("Hymns" 81):

As there was no fixed number of syllables in the verses of psalms, it was impossible to follow a consistent pattern of melodic composition; a melodious tonal movement was possible only at certain points, say at the beginning and end of each verse; for the other variable parts of the verse it was necessary to maintain the same note. The form of such a psalm allowed many possibilities, ranging from short acclamatory liturgies to extended hymnic texts.

More or less synonymous was a ὕμνος, a "hymn" in praise of gods or heroes (LSJ); hence its use also in reference to David (e.g., 2 Chron. 7:6; 1 Esdr. 5:61; Neh. 12:24, 46-47; Josephus, *Antiquities* 9.269; always by Philo). The importance of such sung praise in Judaism is indicated by the accounts of the restoration of the cult by Judas Maccabeus (1 Macc. 4:54; 2 Macc. 1:30; Josephus, *Antiquities* 12.323; see further Schürer 2.288-91). But sung praise was a natural expression of worship, whether in separate gatherings (e.g., Mark 14:26; Qumran and the Therapeutae in Philo, *De vita contemplativa* 83-85) or of individuals in particular circumstances (e.g., *Testament of Joseph* 8:5; Acts 16:25), as much in the diaspora (Philo) as in the Temple. See further G. Delling, *TDNT* 8.489-98.

Given the near synonymity of the two terms it is not clear whether the latter can be clearly distinguished from the former, either here or in the only other occurrence of ὕμνος in the New Testament (the closely parallel Eph. 5:19). An attractive suggestion (Lightfoot 223) is that the "psalms" refer to praise drawn directly from the Scriptures (particularly the psalms of David), whereas the "hymns" are the more distinctively Christian compositions (the "new song" of Isa. 42:10?) which have been widely recognized within the New Testament itself, particularly the Magnificat and the Benedictus in Luke 1, but also the more disputed items in the Pauline corpus (Eph. 5:14; Phil. 2:6-11; Col. 1:15-20; 1 Tim. 3:16).[46] But the description here hardly enables this to be put forward as a firm claim. On the other hand, it would be surprising if a new movement as spiritually vital as Christianity did not produce its own hymnody, as the parallels with Qumran and the Therapeutae again confirm, not to mention the many renewal movements throughout the history of Christianity. The use of nonbiblical hymns in Christian worship does not seem to have been called into question before the third century (Delling, *TDNT* 8.503).

We can be a little more confident with regard to the third item, "spiritual songs" (again only here and in Eph. 5:19 in the New Testament, though ᾠδή is used of the heavenly worship in Rev. 5:9; 14:3; 15:3). It is true that ᾠδή is again more or less synonymous with the other two words, as the titles

---

46. See, e.g., R. P. Martin, *Worship in the Early Church* (London: Marshall/Grand Rapids: Eerdmans, 1964) 39-52; Deichgräber; J. T. Sanders, *Hymns;* Wengst, *Formeln* III Teil.

of the Psalms (LXX) and such passages as 2 Sam. 6:5; 22:1; 1 Macc. 13:51; and 1 Cor. 14:26 indicate (see Lohse, *Colossians and Philemon* 151 n. 148); but some range of songs is presumably in view, unless we assume that the authors are being needlessly tautologous.

The addition of πνευματικαῖς ("spiritual"), whether referring to all three items or only the last, almost certainly denotes or at least includes songs sung under immediate inspiration of the Spirit (charismatic songs, "inspired songs," JB/NJB). This is the implication of πνευματικός itself (see on 1:9), as the close parallel in 1 Cor. 14:15 (ψαλῶ τῷ πνεύματι), 26 also confirms (cf. *Testament of Job* 43:2(P); *1 Enoch* 71:11-12; see also on 2:18; H. Schlier, *TDNT* 1.164; Wolter 190-91).[47] We should also note that in Eph. 5:18-19 such singing is understood to be the result of being filled with the Spirit, in some ways like the uninhibited singing of those who are drunk (Eph. 5:18; cf. Acts 2:13-18), but expressive of a very different Spirit (see my *Jesus* 238). Whether glossolalic singing is envisaged is difficult to determine: the parallels in Acts 2:1-4 and 1 Cor. 14:15 would suggest so; but Paul probably thought of glossolalia as angel speech (1 Cor. 13:1; 14:2), and that might seem to put the Colossian Christian worship on the same level as the angel worship criticized in 2:18.[48] Given the use of πνευματικός already in 1:9 we should hesitate before attributing the reference here to a merely formal echo of earlier Pauline emphases. More probably we should recognize that a lively, spontaneous, charismatic worship (including glossolalia?) continued to be a feature of the Pauline churches (including those he had not himself founded or visited), at least for the full length of his own ministry.

The final clause probably emphasizes again the importance of thankfulness — χάρις in its regular extended sense of "thanks" (as in Rom. 6:17; 7:25; 2 Cor. 2:14; 8:16; 9:15; BAGD s.v. 5; so here all translations, most rendering it as "gratitude"). It is wholly to be expected that such singing would be a natural expression of gratitude to God; inspiration and thankfulness go hand in hand. The definite article, however, could imply a reference back to "the grace" spoken of in 1:6 (similarly 4:18);[49] the response of praise depends as much on God's grace as their initial reception of the gospel. As

47. Tertullian, *Apology* 39.18, describes the Christian *agapē* at the end of the second century: "Each is asked to stand forth and sing, as he can, a hymn to God, either one from the holy scriptures or one of his own composing/from his own heart." See also Dibelius, *Kolosser, Epheser, Philemon* 44-45, who suggests that ἐν πάσῃ σοφίᾳ may have the same reference as the λόγος σοφίας of 1 Cor. 12:8; Houlden 208; Dunn, *Jesus* 238-39.

48. If, despite n. 14 above, the psalms, hymns, and spiritual songs are to be regarded as a means of instruction, then glossolalia would be ruled out "since one neither teaches nor admonishes with unintelligible words" (Fee 654 n. 71).

49. Lightfoot 223-24; Dibelius, *Kolosser, Epheser, Philemon* 45; Masson 147-48 n. 7; Schweizer, *Colossians* 211; Gnilka, *Kolosserbrief* 201; Fee 654-55; but see already Abbott 291.

in 3:15, the addition of "in (or with) your hearts" underlines the importance of a worship rooted in the depths of personal experience and springing up from that source — heart worship and not merely lip worship (perhaps one further allusion to Isa. 29:13, in addition to 3:22).

3:17 καὶ πᾶν ὅ τι ἐὰν ποιῆτε ἐν λόγῳ ἢ ἐν ἔργῳ, πάντα ἐν ὀνόματι κυρίου Ἰησοῦ, εὐχαριστοῦντες τῷ θεῷ πατρὶ δι' αὐτοῦ. At the same time, this attitude of praise, worship, and thankfulness thus commended is not a merely inward attitude or confined to what happens when Christians gather for worship. The same attitude should lie behind and come to expression in everything done by Christians, both in their speech and in their actions. The point is labored to bring it home with more effect: *"everything, whatever* it is, in word or in deed, do *everything . . ."* (cf. 1 Cor. 10:31). There is no discontinuity envisaged between worship and daily living; on the contrary, the whole of daily life should be lived out in the same spirit — "your spiritual worship" (Rom. 12:1-2). The attitude is thoroughly Jewish, as the striking parallels in Sir. 47:8 and Mishnah *Aboth* 2:12 indicate (cited by Lohse, *Colossians and Philemon* 152 n. 160).

The phrase "in the name of the Lord" is formed directly on analogy from the Old Testament: no corresponding use has been found in secular Greek (BAGD s.v. ὄνομα 4cγ); whereas the phrase *bᵉšem YHWH* occurs regularly in Jewish Scripture (H. Bietenhard, *TDNT* 5.258-61) — another indication of the extent to which the first Christians understood what they were doing simply as an extension of Israel's ancestral religion. The fact that the Lord is here "the Lord Jesus" is a further indication of the significance of κύριος as attributed to Jesus. Not that Jesus is thought to have taken over, far less usurped, the role of Yahweh (see on 1:2 and 3); rather, that God has shared his sovereign role with Christ, as indicated more explicitly in Phil. 2:9-11 and 1 Cor. 8:5-6 (on the latter see my *Christology* 179-83). The link between 1 Cor. 8:6 and Col. 1:15-20 is important here (see further below). Nevertheless, the "pan-christology" (Aletti, *Épître aux Colossiens* 245) of this section is somewhat surprising, especially since the role of the Spirit in enabling Christian conduct (very prominent in Romans 8 and Galatians 5) is so completely overlooked.

The reason that it is Jesus who is named here, however, is perhaps as much Christian as christological. The naming of Christ's name by a group of people in the ancient Mediterranean world was a way of identifying themselves as much as him; they were thereby confessing their readiness to be known by reference to this Lord Jesus. And this was no light matter of labeling. The "name" was one of the chief ways in the ancient world by which a person could be known, by which her or his character could be disclosed, by which one could (as we might say) "get a handle" on another (see Bietenhard, *TDNT* 5.243, 250-51, 253-54). To identify oneself by reference to the Lord Jesus was therefore to stake all on his reputation and power. The particular formula here, "in the name of," elsewhere in the New Testament illustrates what this meant in practice — in exorcism or healing (e.g., Mark 9:38; Acts 3:6; 4:10), in baptism (Acts 2:38; 10:48), in preaching (Acts 9:27-28), or in formal discipline (1 Cor. 5:4; 2 Thes. 3:6). Exorcism, healing, and baptism presumably involved a formal invocation of the name, preaching and discipline more a consciousness of commissioning, of acting on behalf of, in the power of. At all events, both here and in Eph. 5:20 the thought is of those who have put themselves under the name of Jesus as Lord and who seek to do everything in consciousness of his commissioning and enabling. In this way an effective *inclusio* with the thematic 2:6-7 is achieved: to walk in Christ Jesus as Lord is to do everything in the name of the Lord Jesus. This is what should mark out the Colossian Christians, in life as in worship, not a hankering for worship with often unnamed angels (2:18).[50]

That there is this one further allusion to the alternative worship of the Colossian Jews is probable (despite Lohse, *Colossians and Philemon* 153 n. 169), as the main body of general parenesis is drawn to a conclusion with "giving thanks to God the Father through him." The worship and life just described are the most effective way of offering a worship which reaches to God. That God (not Christ) is the object of the praise is indicated in both 3:16 and 17. We note again how the role of Jesus even as Lord is simply that of mediator, the one through whom (δι' αὐτοῦ), not on account of whom (δι' αὐτόν), thanks are offered (O'Brien, *Colossians, Philemon* 212-13; see again on 1:3). Such a christology evidently sat comfortably in the minds of the writers (and readers) with the exalted christology of 1:15-20 and 2:9;[51] and as such, neither would be particularly strange or threatening to the monotheism of the Colossian Jews (or most Jews generally). Indeed, it is precisely in this (relatively speaking) less exalted role that the Christian message engaged most directly with the Colossian angel worship, in the Christian claim that effective worship to God the Father is offered "in the name of the Lord Jesus" and "through him."

The third reminder in three verses (3:15-17) of the importance of thankfulness simply underlines yet once more how fundamental is a spirit of gratefulness to God in the life of worship and discipleship. As Rom. 14:6 shows, a conscious concern to be thankful to God can be a valuable test of the acceptability of conduct even when that conduct is disapproved of by other Christians.

50. Dibelius, *Kolosser, Epheser, Philemon* 45, rejects this suggestion on the questionable grounds that the parenesis is general and not specific (but see pp. 199f. above).

51. "As Christ, according to Col. 1:15-20, was the mediator of the creation of everything and the reconciliation of everything (δι' αὐτοῦ), so he remains also the mediator between God and the community in the every day of the world" (Gnilka, *Kolosserbrief* 203).

Household Rules (3:18–4:1)

18 *Wives,*[1] *be subject to your husbands, as is fitting*[2] *in the Lord.* 19 *Husbands, love your wives and do not become embittered toward them.* 20 *Children, obey your parents in everything, for this is pleasing in the Lord.* 21 *Fathers, do not provoke*[3] *your children, that they may not lose heart.*

22 *Slaves, obey in everything*[4] *those who are your masters in terms of the flesh, not with eye service as men-pleasers, but with sincerity of heart, fearing the Lord.*[5] 23 *Whatever you do, put yourself wholly into it, as to the Lord and not to human beings,* 24 *knowing that you will receive from the Lord the reward of the inheritance.*[6] *The master you are slave to is Christ.*[6] 25 *For the wrongdoer will be paid back for the wrong done, and there is no favoritism.*[7] 1 *Masters, grant your slaves what is just and fair, knowing that you also have a master in heaven.*

The next main section of the parenesis is devoted to a sequence of household rules. It has the appearance of a free-standing unit (Crouch 9-13): it is not closely related to the context, the sentences are more abrupt and fall into a regular pattern (three pairs with reciprocal responsibilities, following the threefold form of address, instruction, motivation), and there are similar household codes in other early Christian writings (Eph. 5:22–6:9; 1 Pet. 2:18–3:7; with less close parallels in 1 Tim. 2:8-15; 6:1-2; Tit. 2:1-10; *Didache* 4:9-11; *Barnabas* 19:5-7; *1 Clement* 21:6-9; Ignatius, *Polycarp* 4:1–5:2; Polycarp, *Philippians* 4:2-3). This suggests that the Colossian code may have been derived from earlier traditional material, whether in form or content or both, and raises afresh the question whether this was simply a

---

1. The vocative expressed by the definite article with the nominative (αἱ γυναῖκες) is possible in Greek (BDF §147.3; Harris 178) but may be a Semitism (D. Daube, *The New Testament and Rabbinic Judaism* [London: Athlone, 1956] 102-3).

2. On the use of the imperfect with a present meaning here (ἀνῆκει) see BDF §358.2 and Harris 178-79.

3. Some manuscripts have replaced ἐρεθίζετε here with παροργίζετε ("provoke to anger") from the parallel passage in Eph. 6:4.

4. p[46] and some others omit "in everything," probably in (unconscious) echo of Eph. 6:5.

5. Fear of Christ is so unusual in the New Testament (only here) that p[46] and some other later hands have preferred to read θεόν (as elsewhere in the New Testament, particularly 1 Pet. 2:17).

6. Some witnesses attest understandable attempts to smooth the abruptness of the text at this point, by reading τοῦ κυρίου ἡμῶν Ἰησοῦ Χριστοῦ, ᾧ δουλεύετε ("of our Lord Jesus Christ, to whom you are slaves"). The view is popular that the verb should be read as imperative (e.g., Abbott 295; Lohse, *Colossians and Philemon* 161 n. 63; O'Brien, *Colossians, Philemon* 229; Harris 185-86; cf. NEB/REB): "Serve the Lord Christ." Otherwise Lightfoot 227.

7. A similar group of witnesses have again attempted to soften the abruptness of the text by adding παρὰ τῷ θεῷ at the end of the verse (cf. Eph. 6:7).

dollop of standard teaching inserted here (like an old sermon being "rerun") or whether it had any particular relation to the situation in Colossae.[8]

The debate as to where this material was derived from has rumbled on throughout most of the twentieth century,[9] but should probably now be regarded as settled. The model, insofar as there is one, was that of οἰκονομία, "household management" (Lührmann, "Sklave" 76-80; "Haustafeln"; Thraede, followed by Müller 284-90; and especially Balch, *Wives,* part I). In the classic definition of Aristotle, the household was the basic unit of the state.[10] As part of good ordering, therefore, it was necessary to deal with its basic relationships: "master and slave, husband and wife, father and children" (*Politica* I.1253b.1-14; Balch, *Wives* 33-34). That these became common concerns in thoughtful society is sufficiently clear from such examples as Dio Chrysostom's fragmentary oration on the theme (οἰκονομία), covering the same three relationships (LCL 5.348-51; Balch, *Wives* 28-29), Seneca's description of one department of philosophy as concerned to "advise how a husband should conduct himself toward his wife, or how a father should bring up his children, or how a master should rule his slaves" (*Epistle* 94.1; Balch, *Wives* 51), and Dionysius of Halicarnassus, who praises Roman household relationships using the same three pairs (in the same order as Colossians) and deals with duties of wives before those of husbands and those of children before those of fathers, as here (*Roman Antiquities* 2.25.4–26.4; Balch, *Wives* 55). That similar concerns were active in diaspora Judaism is evident, for example, from pseudo-Phocylides 175-227, Philo, *De decalogo* 165-67; *De specialibus legibus* 2.224-41, and the disputed extract *Hypothetica* 7.14 (preserved in Eusebius, *Praeparatio Evangelica* 8.7.14); and Josephus, *Contra Apionem* 2.199-208 (see particularly Crouch 74-90).

Study of such parallels, however, should be sufficient to warn us of the danger of speaking as though there was in the ancient world an established form of "household rules" from which Col. 3:18–4:1 has been derived (the Colossian code is itself the "purest" form!) or from which other similar passages have somehow deteriorated (the household rules are often simply part of a more widely ranging code of social behavior) — one of the standing dangers of a "form-critical" approach (Hartman, "Unorthodox Thoughts"). Rather, we should speak of common preoccupations among ethical and

8. However, there is little to be said, and no support, for the arguments of Munro and of Schmithals 119-20 that 3:18–4:1 (as also Eph. 5:21–6:9) or 3:15c–4:1 (respectively) are later additions to the Pauline text.

9. The debate is reviewed in most of the larger commentaries and recent literature mentioned below; see also the valuable review by D. Balch, "Household Codes," in *Greco-Roman Literature and the New Testament,* ed. D. E. Aune (Atlanta: Scholars, 1988) 25-50, and more briefly, J. T. Fitzgerald and D. L. Balch, *ABD* 3.80-81, 318-20 (with bibliography).

10. On "The Household in the Hellenistic-Roman World" see particularly Verner 27-81.

political thinkers which naturally included a focus on the theme of the good ordering of the household and its constituent parts.

The framework, then, is provided by the traditional concern for "household management." But we can also speak of characteristically Stoic features (particularly ἀνῆκεν and εὐάρεστον; see on 3:18 and 20; Dibelius, *Kolosser, Epheser, Philemon* 46, 48-49; Gnilka, *Kolosserbrief* 211-12).[11] And there are clearly Jewish features, particularly in the extent of the concern for the weaker members of the three pairings (as Lohmeyer 155 and Schweizer, "Weltlichkeit" 201-3 and "Traditional" 201-3, note, the exhortations are addressed not only to those who are male, adult, and free), in the actual form itself (address, instruction, motivation; cf. particularly Sir. 3:1),[12] and in the expanded section addressed to slaves (see, e.g., Müller 273-75 and further below). At the same time there are also clearly distinctive Christian features, most notably the sevenfold reference to "the Lord," that is, Christ (3:18, 20, 22-24; 4:1), not as a separate part of the code (duties toward God), but as providing the orientation of the whole,[13] and even the possibility of some dependence on some tradition of Jesus' own teaching (see on 3:20).[14]

Why should such a code be introduced here? Earlier speculation made much of the delay of the parousia and the need to combat a (potentially) anarchic enthusiasm or, alternatively(!), a second generation settling down to a more conformist ethic (cf., e.g., Crouch 146-51; Cannon 125-28; MacDonald 102-5). Perhaps we can see a transition from the earliest phase of the Christian mission, which had been more marked, perhaps, by breach with families (cf., e.g., Mark 3:31-35; 10:29; 13:12), even though the household unit (οἶκος) was a central feature of the Pauline churches from the first (Acts 16:15; 18:8; 1 Cor. 1:16; 16:15, etc.; Lührmann, "Haustafeln" 91-93). At all events, we can well understand that socially responsible Christian leaders, like their Hellenistic Jewish and Stoic counterparts, would wish to consider not merely how individuals should conduct themselves, but how Christian commitment to "the Lord" should affect the primary unit of community, the household. To become a member of the new family of Jesus (cf., e.g., Rom. 8:16-17, 29) did not involve displacement or justify neglect of household responsibilities, whether the believer belonged to a Christian or non-Christian

---

11. Schrage, *Ethics* 248-49, however, notes the absence of any argument based on natural law or on reason, in contrast to the Stoics.

12. Gnilka, *Kolosserbrief* 214-15; see also Crouch; Lohse, *Colossians and Philemon* 154-57; Verner 86-89.

13. Merk 220-24; Schweizer, "Weltlichkeit" 199-201; Gnilka, *Kolosserbrief* 226; Lindemann, *Kolosserbrief* 64, 68; Aletti, *Épître aux Colossiens* 249-50; usefully tabulated in Müller 268; *pace* Houlden 209-11; Yates, *Colossians* 79 — "vaguely christianized."

14. See L. Goppelt, "Jesus und die 'Haustafel'-Tradition," in *Orientierung an Jesus, J. Schmid FS*, ed. P. Hoffmann (Freiburg: Herder, 1973) 93-106, particularly 99-100; Schweizer, "Traditional" 202.

household; Christian discipleship was not disruptive of society's basic structure (Meeks, *Urban Christians* 106; MacDonald 108-9, 113-14).[15] Relationships within the family and household were themselves part of Christian vocation and the first place where responsibility to the Lord should come to expression and be put to the test.

In contrast, Sanders, *Ethics* 73-76, 79-80, assumes that a Christian writer must have wanted to encourage his readers to be ethically different from others; consequently he condemns the teaching here as "indistinguishable from the world." He quite fails to see that believers were being urged *not* to be different at this point, but to live fully in accord with high social ideals, widely esteemed as such by other ethicists of the time (cf. particularly Müller 304-10, 318). The perspective and enabling might be different, but the goals were shared (Schrage, "Haustafeln" 9). That others share their high standards of social behavior and vice versa should never be an embarrassment to Christians. On the contrary, the encouragement here is precisely to live responsibly within the pattern of everyday relationships, not to discount or abandon them. "The purpose of the *Haustafeln* is to subject the life of Christians to the Lordship of Christ within the institutions of the secular world" (Schrage, "Haustafeln" 21-22; also *Ethics* 252-57, here 252; Schweizer, "Traditional" 203-4), an ethic of "healthy 'worldliness'" (Schnackenburg, *Botschaft* 2.81, using Schweizer's phrase).

This would be important not least since the earliest churches were all "house churches" (see on 4:15), so that the model of the well-run household provided precedent for the well-run church (as we soon see in the Pastorals; though note Klauck's caution at this point, 46-47). With such motivation it would be natural to draw on rules of proven worth from the best contemporary social models. We should not ignore the fact that use of the model of "household management" betokens a similar concern for society and its good order (cf. Lindemann, *Kolosserbrief* 64). But it also had the bonus of demonstrating the good citizenship of the young churches, facilitating communication with the rest of society (Pokorný 177-80), and making possible an apologetic and evangelistic impact which should not be discounted (cf. Rom. 12:14–13:7; 1 Cor 7:16; 1 Pet. 3:15-16).

Whether all this meant a greater conformity to structures which ought to have been more radically questioned, too much compromise with conservative social tradition (Lührmann, "Haustafeln" 94), with what might now be described as "conventional middle-class morality" ("bürgerliche Ethik," Schulz 567-71), "a sanctification of the *status quo*" (Wedderburn, *Theology* 57), or even an increasing "paganizing" of the Christian ethic (Schweizer, *Colossians* 217-20; also "Traditional" 204-7; critiqued by Thraede 367), is

15. But Christian families are evidently in view here and not the situation of divided loyalties as in 1 Cor. 7:12-16 (Aletti, *Épitre aux Colossiens* 250).

certainly arguable. In the choice between revolution and transformation from within, Christianity chose the second; though we always need to bear in mind the political powerlessness of such small groups within the pervasiveness of Hellenistic culture and under the imperial might of Rome. Christianity certainly did not adopt more radical critiques of society (like the Cynics), or abandon society (like the Qumran Essenes), or pursue utopian dreams by encouraging slave rebellions, all of which could have resulted in the demise of Christianity within a few generations. No program for a new society was drawn up, not even one for the kingdom of God on earth. Instead Christianity recognized that it had perforce to live within an inevitably flawed and imperfect society and sought to live and witness within that society by combining that society's proven wisdom with commitment to its own Lord and the transforming power of the love which he had embodied (see also Houlden 213-14).

So far as more immediate relevance to the situation confronting the Colossian church is concerned we can say little. A reaction against the asceticism and "otherworldliness" of the Colossian Jews is certainly possible (O'Brien, *Colossians, Philemon* 219), but we do not know enough about the Colossian Jews' own household rules to make a firm comparison (were Col. 3:1-4 the only part of the letter extant we would be tempted to attribute a similar "otherworldliness" to the Colossian Christians!). There is no reason, however, why the presence of the household code here should not be explained by more general concerns for good order and good citizenship. And as for the continuing relevance of such household rules, we need to recall how much they were conditioned by and adapted to the situation of the times. They are not timeless rules (Lohse, *Colossians and Philemon* 156 n. 14, cites Conzelmann 153 to good effect) and can no more be transferred directly to the different circumstances of today than can the rules of, say, Susannah Wesley (mother of John and Charles) for bringing up children. It is the orientation and motivation indicated in the repeated references to the Lord ("in the Lord," "fearing the Lord," "to the Lord," "serving the Lord") which provide the fixed points for a continuing Christian ethic.

3:18 αἱ γυναῖκες, ὑποτάσσεσθε τοῖς ἀνδράσιν ὡς ἀνῆκεν ἐν κυρίῳ. Wives are addressed first (as in Eph. 5:22; in 1 Pet. 3:1 following slaves, but before husbands). It is important to note that it is wives and not women generally who are in view (as also in 1 Cor. 14:34). Women who were single, widowed, or divorced and of independent means could evidently function as heads of their own households, as in the case of Lydia (Acts 16:14-15), Phoebe, the first named "deacon" in Christian history and patron of the church at Cenchreae (Rom. 16:1-2), Chloe (1 Cor. 1:11), and presumably Nympha in Colossae itself (see on 4:15). The concern here is primarily for the household unit (Aletti, *Épître aux Colossiens* 251), with the implication that for Christians, too, its good ordering was fundamental to well-ordered human and social relationships. That wives are addressed first is presumably also a recognition that their relationship to their husbands was the linchpin of a stable and effective household.

The call for wives to be subject (ὑποτάσσομαι, "subject oneself, be subordinate to") is unequivocal, not even lightened by the prefixed call "Be subject to one another," or the addition "as the church is subject to Christ" (as in Eph. 5:21, 24).[16] The exhortation should not be weakened in translation in deference to modern sensibilities (cf. again 1 Cor. 14:34; so rightly Martin, *Colossians and Philemon* 119). But neither should its significance be exaggerated; "subjection" means "subordination," not "subjugation" (Schrage, *Ethics* 253; so also Aletti, *Épître aux Colossiens* 251-52). The teaching simply reflects the legal state of affairs, under Roman law at least, whereby the *paterfamilias* had absolute power over the other members of the family (*OCD* s.v. "patria potestas"). And while there were variations in Greek and Jewish law, the basic fact held true throughout the Mediterranean world that the household was essentially a patriarchal institution, with other members of the household subject to the authority of its male head (Verner 27-81). The exhortation here, therefore, simply conforms to current mores; the term itself is used by Plutarch, *Conjugalia praecepta* 33 (= *Moralia* 142E) and pseudo-Callisthenes 1.22.4 (in Lohse, *Colossians and Philemon* 157 n. 18; *RAC* 4.696; *NDIEC* 1.36; see also Müller 292-98; Schrage, *Ethics* 254). In contemporary legal terms the submission called for was of a piece with that called for in Rom. 13:1, 5 (cf. Tit. 2:5 with 3:1).[17] Those who, on the one hand, wish to criticize Paul and the first Christians for such conformity at this point should recall that it is only in the last hundred years of European civilization that the perception of the status of wives (and women) and their expected roles has been radically changed. Those who, on the other hand, wish to draw normative patterns of conduct from Scripture cannot ignore the degree to which the instruction simply reflects current social patterns, an unavoidably conformist rather than transformist ethic (cf. Conzelmann 153).

The one distinctively Christian feature is the additional words "as is fitting in the Lord" (Moule, *Colossians and Philemon* 128; Bruce, *Colossians, Philemon, and Ephesians* 162, 164). Ἀνήκει ("it is fitting") reflects the typical Stoic idea that one's best policy, indeed one's duty, was to live

16. G. Delling, *TDNT* 8.45 reads Col. 3:18 as though the Eph. 5:21 and 24 qualifications were in mind there. 1 Cor. 16:6 shows that the word could be used of voluntary submission, but it is not clear that a distinctive Christian note is sounded here in the word itself (as O'Brien, *Colossians, Philemon* 220-22, and those cited by him seem to want; contrast Kamlah, "'Υποτάσσεσθαι" 241-42 — a Jewish root); that surely comes with the ἐν κυρίῳ (Merk 215). The term itself (ὑποτάσσομαι) became the major theme of later codes (Crouch 34 and n. 94).

17. In theological terms cf. the subjection of Christ to God (1 Cor. 15:28); with which in turn cf. 1 Cor. 11:3 and again Eph. 5:23-24.

in harmony with the natural order of things (H. Schlier, *TDNT* 1.360 and 3.437-40), a sentiment shared by Hellenistic Judaism and the early Gentile mission (*Aristeas* 227; pseudo-Phocylides 80; Rom. 1:28; Eph. 5:4; Phm. 8; *1 Clement* 1:3)[18] — in this case, once again reflecting a patriarchal view of human society. But "in the Lord" implies a different perspective (*pace* Müller 310-16). It reflects both the claim that Christ is the fullest expression of the creative wisdom within the cosmos (1:15-20; 2:3) and the thematic statement that life should be lived in accordance with the traditions received regarding Jesus as Christ and Lord (2:6-7) — allusions lost in translations like "that is your Christian duty" (NEB/REB; cf. GNB).

The full phrase can function in two ways, either as an affirmation that husband headship of the household is "fitting" also within the community of those who own Jesus as Lord (Bruce, *Colossians, Philemon, and Ephesians* 163-64) or as a qualification that only that degree of subjection to the husband which is "fitting in the Lord" is to be countenanced. That the latter is not merely a modern reading of the exhortation can be deduced from the counsel provided by Paul earlier in 1 Cor. 7:15 and from the fact that it was Christian pressure which took the power away from fathers to expose unwanted infants some three centuries later (in 374; earlier Jewish and Christian protest in pseudo-Phocylides 185; Philo, *De specialibus legibus* 3.110; *Barnabas* 19:5). So now for a continuing Christian moral code we may say that "as is fitting in the Lord" is the fixed point while the limits of acceptable conduct within society are contingent on public sentiment of region and epoch (cf. Schweizer, *Colossians* 222).

3:19 οἱ ἄνδρες, ἀγαπᾶτε τὰς γυναῖκας καὶ μὴ πικραίνεσθε πρὸς αὐτάς. The corresponding responsibility of the husband is to love his wife. The ideal of a husband being tenderly solicitous for his wife was not distinctively Christian (classic expression in Musonius, *Orationes* 13A),[19] though how far reality matched the ideal in either case we are not in a position now to say. But again a distinctive Christian note comes through in the use of the verb ἀγαπάω, which, as elsewhere in the Paulines (Rom. 8:37; Gal. 2:20; Eph. 2:4; 5:2, 25), gains its characteristic emphasis from Christ's self-giving on the cross (see on 1:4 and 3:14).[20] Thus ἀγαπάω plays the role in 3:19 of "in the Lord" in 3:18 and 20 and is itself sufficient to refer the reader back to the traditions of Jesus as the Christ and Lord (2:6-7). This is one of the points in the parallel treatment of Ephesians at which the author

---

18. See further Crouch 37-73, 98-99.

19. In C. E. Lutz, "Musonius Rufus: 'The Roman Socrates,' " *Yale Classical Studies* 10 (1947) 3-147, here 88-89.

20. O'Brien, *Colossians, Philemon* 223, rightly refutes the claim of Crouch 111-13 (also Schulz 568-69; Wolter 199) that what is in view here is "the normal, human love of a husband for his wife"; see also Schrage, "Haustafeln" 12-15; Gnilka, *Kolosserbrief* 218. For the different language of other household rules see Schweizer, *Colossians* 222 n. 42.

"takes off" into a lyrical account of the love of Christ for his church (Eph. 5:25-33). The allusion to Christ as the model of love in action, it is true, did not alter the subordinate role attributed to the wife in 3:18, however much it might have conditioned that role and prevented abuse of the power of the *paterfamilias*. But it does remain significant that the talk here is not of authority and rights but of obligations and responsibilities (Schrage, "Haustafeln" 15). "It is humility and kindness, not superiority of status . . . which ought to dictate the conduct of the baptized" (Aletti, *Épître aux Colossiens* 253).

The verb πικραίνω (only here in the Paulines) is a vivid one. It comes from πικρός, which, from an original meaning of "pointed, sharp," gained the particular sense of "sharp, bitter" to the taste (W. Michaelis, *TDNT* 6.122; cf. Ruth 1:13, 20; Eph. 4:31; Heb. 12:15; Jas. 3:11); in Hermas, *Mandates* 10.2.3 it is the effect of ill-temper (ὀξυχολία). To be πικρός, "bitter, harsh," is a characteristic regularly attributed to a tyrannical over-lordship (Wolter 199, citing Philo, *Quod omnis probus liber sit* 106, 120; Josephus, *Contra Apionem* 1.210; 2.277; Philostratus, *Vita Apollonii* 7.3; Diogenes Laertius 4.46). Here, thus, we find the term used of the husband, rather than, as some might think more suitable, of the wife to describe her state under a harsh overlordship (as in 2 Kgs. 14:26). Most translate "Do not be harsh with them" (RSV, NEB/REB, NIV, GNB). But the passive voice here presumably implies that the bitterness is experienced by the husbands. What is in view, therefore, is probably the feeling of the dominant partner who can legally enforce his will on his wife but who will not thereby win her love and respect and can thus feel cheated and embittered at not receiving what he regards as his due (cf. Plutarch, *De cohibenda ira* 8 = *Moralia* 457A, cited in Lohse, *Colossians and Philemon* 158 n. 30). This is the likely outcome for anyone who stands on his rights alone and who knows and exercises little of the love called for in the first half of the verse.

3:20 τὰ τέκνα, ὑπακούετε τοῖς γονεῦσιν κατὰ πάντα, τοῦτο γὰρ εὐάρεστόν ἐστιν ἐν κυρίῳ. The legal status of children under Roman law was still more disadvantaged. Technically speaking, they were the property of the father; so, for example, the formalities for adoption were essentially the same as for the conveyance of property (*OCD* s.v. "patria potestas").[21] The child under age in fact was no better off than a slave (a point Paul had been able to put to good effect in Gal. 4:1-7); note how closely parallel are the instructions of 3:20 and 3:22 (cf. the advice of Sir. 30:1 and 42:5). This situation is presumably reflected in 3:21, where the responsibility for the

---

21. Dionysius of Halicarnassus sums the position up thus: "The law-giver of the Romans gave virtually full power to the father over his son, . . . whether he thought proper to imprison him, to scourge him, to put him in chains, and keep him at work in the fields, or to put him to death . . ." (*Roman Antiquities* 2.26.4; similarly Dio Chrysostom 15.20).

child is thought of as exclusively the father's. For although the mother was the main influence over her children till they were seven (cf. pseudo-Phocylides 208), the father was primarily responsible thereafter for the boys at least. In view of all this it is worth noting that children who were presumably still minors (cf. Eph. 6:4) are directly addressed; evidently they are thought of as both present in the Christian meeting where the letter would be read out and as responsible agents despite their youth (Schweizer, *Colossians* 223; Gnilka, *Kolosserbrief* 220). Responsibility in Christian relationships is not to be determined by legal standing.

Obedience[22] is called for in respect of both parents; those now primarily under their father's discipline should continue to respect their mother also. This is not an exclusively Jewish feature, since honoring parents was widely recognized as a virtue (e.g., Dionysius of Halicarnassus, *Roman Antiquities* 2.26.1-4; Plato, *Republic* 4.425b; Stobaeus, *Anthology* 3.1.80; 4.25.53 [in A. J. Malherbe, *Moral Exhortation: A Greco-Roman Sourcebook* (Philadelphia: Westminster, 1986) 91-93];[23] Epictetus 2.10.7; 3.7.26; see further Lincoln, *Ephesians* 401; Wolter 201). But it was given particular prominence within Jewish tradition, as enshrined in the fifth commandment (Exod. 20:12; Deut. 5:16) and repeatedly emphasized in Jewish writings of the period (e.g., Sir. 3:1-16; 7:27-28; Tob. 4:3-4; *Aristeas* 228; *Jubilees* 7:20; Philo, *De posteritate Caini* 181; *De ebrietate* 17). A stubborn and disobedient son, indeed, was liable to death by stoning (Lev. 20:9; Deut. 21:18-21; Philo, *De specialibus legibus* 2.232; Josephus, *Contra Apionem* 2.206). Κατὰ πάντα ("in everything") also reflects the customary respect in the ancient world for the wisdom of age. The assumption is that parents, acting as parents, will deal wisely and kindly with their children (cf. Matt. 7:9-11/Luke 11:11-13). This is the expected norm of good family and social relationships (so also Mark 7:10 par.; 10:19 pars.; cf. Rom. 1:30 and 2 Tim. 3:2). The counsel here, of course, does not envisage situations where the norm is breached by the parents or where a higher loyalty might need to be invoked (as in Luke 14:26).

The reason given is "for this is pleasing in the Lord." Εὐάρεστος, "acceptable, pleasing," will mean pleasing to God, as in the only two LXX uses of the word (Wis. 4:10; 9:10) and in the other Pauline uses (Rom. 12:1-2; 14:18; 2 Cor. 5:9; Phil. 4:18; only Tit. 2:9 otherwise; cf. Eph. 5:10 — εὐάρεστον τῷ κυρίῳ). Here a more conventional value (Gnilka, *Kolosserbrief* 220 refers to Epictetus 1.12.8 and 2.23.29) has been Christianized even

22. "In the Pauline homologoumena it [ὑπακούειν] is used exclusively of obedience to Jesus Christ and to the gospel. Its use here in conjunction with the orders of creation is a sign of the relatively later phase of Christian thought" (Pokorný 181 n. 26).

23. *Ioanis Stobaei Anthologium*, ed. C. Wachsmuth and O. Hense: vol. 3 = Hense vol. 1, vol. 4 = Hense vol. 2.

before the next phrase is added. "In the Lord," as in 3:18, roots the justification thus claimed in the tradition which formed the basis of Christian identity and conduct (translations like "the Christian way" in NEB/REB and "your Christian duty" in GNB again obscure the point). Here the tradition is that indicated in the preceding paragraph (the parallel passage Eph. 6:1-2 goes on to quote Exod. 20:12/Deut. 5:16 LXX explicitly); the thought is close to that of Philo, *De mutatione nominum* 40: "If you honor parents . . . you will be pleasing (εὐαρεστήσεις) before God." In other words, we no doubt have here (despite Merk 216-17) a conscious taking over of the particularly Jewish emphasis on honoring of parents. That the Lord is Christ here simply confirms that the traditions of Christ as Lord (2:6-7) will have included such Jesus tradition as Mark 7:10 and 10:19.[24] In the face of the challenge from the Colossian Jews it was no doubt important for the Christians to be able both to affirm their heritage of Jewish parenesis and to affirm it as "well-pleasing (to God) in the Lord (Jesus Christ)." Here, in other words, we can recognize a double apologetic slant in the parenesis: assurance to influential outsiders that the Christian message was not subversive and to Colossian Jews that the new movement was still faithful to Jewish praxis and ideals.

3:21 οἱ πατέρες, μὴ ἐρεθίζετε τὰ τέκνα ὑμῶν, ἵνα μὴ ἀθυμῶσιν. Indicative of his central role in the household, the head of the household is now addressed a second time, this time in his role as father (see also 4:1).[25] Corresponding to his responsibility to love his wife, the father has a responsibility not to "provoke" (ἐρεθίζω, usually in a bad sense [BAGD], though the only other New Testament usage, 2 Cor. 9:2, is positive), that is, "irritate" (NJB/GNB) or "embitter" (NIV; "exasperate" in NEB/REB; "drive to resentment" in JB) his children (see also Lohmeyer 157 n. 2). Here again the emphasis is not uniquely Christian (see, e.g., Menander, in Stobaeus, *Anthologia* 4.26.11-19; Plutarch, *De liberis educandis* 12, 14, 16 [= *Moralia* 8F-9A, 10D-E, 12C]; pseudo-Phocylides 150, 207 in Schweizer, *Colossians* 224 n. 51). It is striking, however, that the stress once again is not on the father's discipline or authority but on his duties (Schrage, *Ethics* 255) and that the only responsibility mentioned is this negative one, rather than that of bringing up and training the children (contrast Eph. 6:4 and *Didache* 4:9). If this is not merely coincidental, and reflects something of the situation in Colossae, it suggests that the primary concern was to avoid aggravation in

---

24. Schweizer, *Colossians* 215, asks whether the order (husbands and wives first) may reflect the influence of Mark 10:1-9 par., and Pokorný 182 wonders whether the tradition of Mark 10:13-16 par. may lie behind 3:21; see also Ernst, *Philipper, Philemon, Kolosser, Epheser* 233-34; but see also Gnilka, *Kolosserbrief* 210.

25. Πατέρες could, however, mean "parents" (BAGD s.v. πατήρ 1a; cf. Heb. 11:23; so also JB/NJB, GNB; Schweizer, *Colossians* 223), but the narrower focus reflects the *patria potestas* of the father (Gnilka, *Kolosserbrief* 220); cf., e.g., Mishnah *Kiddushin* 1:7.

the situation of stress addressed. That is to say, we may envisage a situation
where younger members of the Christian families were in a vulnerable
position. Either they felt attracted to the alternatives offered by the Colossian
Jews (since their parents were converts to such a characteristically Jewish
body, worshipers of the one God in the name of Messiah Jesus, and may
previously have been proselytes or God-fearers, the worship of the synagogue would seem to be closely related), and a too strong fatherly reaction
could have driven them away. Or they were embarrassed, as Gentiles and
among their fellow Gentiles, at belonging to such an ethnic sect as Christian
Judaism. It would take fatherly tact and not just a laying down of the law
to hold the different generations of the Christian family together.

This line of reflection is encouraged by the reason given: "in case they
lose heart" (REB; so also NJB, NRSV), that is, lose their θυμός, their strong
feeling and courage (LSJ), become timid (references in Lohmeyer 157 n. 3),
"go about their task in a listless, moody, sullen frame of mind" (Lightfoot
225). To belong to such a strange sect, a religion without a cult center, without
priest and sacrifice, must have exposed the younger members of the Christian
families of Colossae to some abuse from their fellows in the marketplace.
Without strong parental encouragement they could easily become "dis-
couraged" (RSV). The psychological sensitivity displayed here is remarkably
modern (see also Caird 209).

3:22 οἱ δοῦλοι, ὑπακούετε κατὰ πάντα τοῖς κατὰ σάρκα κυρίοις, μὴ
ἐν ὀφθαλμοδουλίᾳ ὡς ἀνθρωπάρεσκοι, ἀλλ᾽ ἐν ἁπλότητι καρδίας φοβού-
μενοι τὸν κύριον. The fourth group addressed are slaves (as in Eph. 6:5;
in reverse order in 1 Pet. 2:18). It is important to remember that they, too,
would be counted as part of the well-to-do household, an integral part of its
good functioning (like domestic servants in Victorian Britain).[26] The fact
that masters are addressed in 4:1 is a reminder that several at least of the
(no doubt small) Christian church in Colossae had slaves (see also on 3:11).
The treatment of slaves was therefore a topic inescapable in any set of rules
designed for the good regulation of households. What is interesting here is
that the first battery of instruction is directed to the slaves themselves,
whereas contemporary parallels confine themselves to advising the masters
or discussing what instruction should be given to slaves (Crouch 116-17).
Here, however, slaves are clearly members of the Christian congregation and
treated as responsible individuals (Moule, *Colossians and Philemon* 127;
Schweizer, *Colossians* 213). It was evidently another characteristic feature
of the early Christian churches that they contained as members of one body
both masters and slaves, presumably in some instances at least a *paterfami-*

---

26. See again Verner 47-63. "Even a comparatively modest household might be expected to
include two or three slaves" — so J. M. G. Barclay, "Paul, Philemon and Christian Slave-ownership," *NTS* 37 (1991) 161-86, here 166.

lias and (some of) his slaves from the same household (e.g., Philemon; see further pp. 300f. below). This, too, was not entirely distinctive in the ancient world,[27] but the "no slave or freedman" of 3:11 made the equal membership of master and slave a principle of far-reaching significance.

The instructions which follow are directed primarily to slaves' responsibility toward their masters (four verses), with only one verse directed to the masters (4:1). That probably indicates that there were more slaves than masters in the typical Pauline church (cf. 1 Cor. 1:26), strengthening the impression that Christianity initially drew its greatest numerical strength from the less advantaged groups in society (cf. Celsus's dismissive comment in Origen, *Contra Celsum* 3.44: "only slaves, women, and little children"). But ironically it seems to place the greater weight of responsibility in master-slave relations on the slave — a reminder that much of earliest Christian ethic is an ethic of the disadvantaged (cf. Rom. 12:14-21; 1 Pet. 2:11-25; Eph. 6:5-9 is a close echo of Col. 3:22–4:1). It is also a reminder that "the rules of the game" were (as always) dictated by the powerful. Christians who wanted as much freedom as possible within these structures to pursue a Christian calling as members of the church were wise to carry out their responsibilities as slaves with all diligence. This should not be criticized today as merely social conformism; those who live in modern social democracies, in which interest groups can hope to exert political pressure by intensive lobbying, should remember that in the cities of Paul's day the great bulk of Christians would have had no possibility whatsoever of exerting any political pressure for any particular policy or reform. In such circumstances a pragmatic quietism was the most effective means of gaining room enough to develop the quality of personal relationships which would establish and build up the microcosms (churches) of transformed communities.

The first responsibility of the slave as slave is to do the will of another: ὑπακούετε (Eph. 6:5); that, indeed, is at the heart of the distinction between slave and free (see on 3:11). Κατὰ πάντα ("in everything") adds nothing (it is omitted by Eph. 6:5), but underlines the completeness of the power of the master over his slave ("give entire obedience" in NEB/REB). But κατὰ σάρκα (the last of the "flesh" references in Colossians) does provide some qualification: "your masters" as determined by physical relationship, by the social ordering of this age, "according to human reckoning" (NJB). The qualification is not of the command just given; on the contrary, it heightens the sense of the slave's powerlessness in such relationships: even though their masters are masters κατὰ σάρκα, they must nevertheless be obeyed in everything. But it provides an effective reminder that even caught as they

27. See, e.g., S. Dill, *Roman Society from Nero to Marcus Aurelius* (London: Macmillan, 1904) 281; A. D. Nock, *Conversion* (London: Oxford University, 1933, 1961) 131-32; R. MacMullen, *Paganism in the Roman Empire* (New Haven: Yale University, 1981) 114.

were in such relationships, slaves could enjoy another set of relationships (κατὰ πνεῦμα) in which Christ was κύριος and all "in him" were brothers and sisters (including the earthly masters).

In terms of personal integrity it is important, however, that such obedience should be rendered conscientiously — "not with eye service as men-pleasers." Ὀφθαλμοδουλία occurs in Greek only here and in the parallel Eph. 6:6, but it is an effective construct and its meaning is fairly obvious as denoting service performed only to attract attention (BAGD), lacking in sincerity, going through the visible movements of work without any personal commitment to it (Masson 149 n. 8; Moule, *Colossians and Philemon* 130). Almost as unknown is ἀνθρωπάρεσκος (elsewhere in the New Testament again only in Eph. 6:6, but also in *2 Clement* 13:1), "someone who tries to please other human beings" even by sacrificing some principle (BAGD), so particularly apposite in reference to demagogues and those who "play to the gallery" (note the striking use in *Psalms of Solomon* 4:7, 8, 19; cf. also Gal. 1:10). The translations pick up different facets of the terms quite effectively — e.g., NRSV "not only while being watched and in order to please them"; REB "not merely to catch their eye or curry favour with them."

In contrast, Christian slaves should render their obedience "with sincerity of heart (ἁπλότητι καρδίας), fearing the Lord." The basic meaning of ἁπλότης is "simplicity" (as in 2 Sam. 15:11 and Josephus, *War* 2.151). Simplicity of life was an ideal for both Stoics and Cynics, but here the phrase ἁπλότης καρδίας ("sincerity of heart") certainly reflects the emphasis of Jewish wisdom that this is the way to seek God and live before him (1 Chron. 29:17; Wis. 1:1; *Testament of Reuben* 4:1; *Testament of Issachar* 3:8; 4:1; 7:7). It indicates a singleness of intention, a focus of purpose, springing from the center of motivation and concern (see on 2:2), so "wholeheartedly and without reservation" (T. Schramm, *EDNT* 1.123).

The addition of "fearing the Lord"[28] confirms the influence of Jewish wisdom (*Testament of Reuben* 4:1: ἐν ἁπλότητι καρδίας ἐν φόβῳ κυρίου), where "the fear of the Lord is the beginning of wisdom" (Ps. 111:10; Prov. 1:7; Sir. 1:14, 16, 18, 20, 27; see also, e.g., Pss. 34:9, 11; 112:1; Prov. 3:7; Sir. 2:7-9, 15-17; in Paul cf. Rom. 11:20; 2 Cor. 5:11; 7:1; also Eph. 5:1). What is meant therefore is more a reflective than an emotional fear (hence a translation like "reverence for the Lord," NEB/REB, NIV), though if the numinous sense of *mysterium tremendum et fascinans* (R. Otto) had wholly disappeared, something vital to the original force of "the fear of the Lord" would have been lost (see data in G. Wanke, *TDNT* 9.201-3; JB/NJB's "out of respect for the Master" is therefore too weak). The implication here is

---

28. "Fear" or "fear of the Lord" is a frequent motif in household rules (Eph. 6:5; 1 Pet. 2:18; Polycarp, *Philippians* 4:2; 6:3; *1 Clement* 21:6; *Didache* 4:9, 11; *Barnabas* 19:5, 7; Crouch 34 n. 95).

clear: the main motivation for such single-minded obedience is *not* the human relationship of slave to master (a servile fear, as in Rom. 8:15), but the obligation that, whatever one's position in human society, one should live as before the Lord and for the Lord (cf. 1 Cor. 7:17-24).[29] To be noted is the fact that the motif of fear is confined here to the relation between Christian and Christ, in contrast to Eph. 5:33; 6:5; 1 Pet. 2:18.

The further fact that now for the Christians "the Lord" is Christ (see n. 5) confirms not only the thematic role of 2:6-7 but also that the affirmation of Christ as Lord constituted for the first Christians a line of continuity and not breach with their Jewish heritage (cf. Mishnah *Aboth* 1:3). Here again the subtext is not only a policy of social quietism in order to avoid attracting hostile attention from the civil authorities, but also a theology of continuity with historic Jewish principles which should help counter the attractiveness of the Colossian synagogue.

3:23 ὃ ἐὰν ποιῆτε, ἐκ ψυχῆς ἐργάζεσθε ὡς τῷ κυρίῳ καὶ οὐκ ἀνθρώποις. This simply repeats what has just been said. The implication is that one of the chief dangers of the slave status was a lack of personal motivation which made all work a drudgery provided grudgingly, with lack of effort and always with a view to doing as little as one could get away with. Such an attitude can be sustained only at tremendous personal cost, with other aspects of the personality "switched off," withdrawn, or suppressed, or with a calculating motivation fed by resentment and bitterness. The danger was such that it required repeated warning. The alternative is a personal engagement with what one does, so that even what is done as the obedience of the slave can be a means of self-expression and of development of character and skill. "Whatever" (ὃ ἐάν), however, broadens out the scope beyond κατὰ πάντα (3:22) to include the actions and commitments engaged in beyond what the master required. One should put oneself into relationships within the slaves' quarters or in church as much as one does in serving one's master.

The ψυχή is the focus of human vitality, as the "heart" is the focus of human experiencing (see BAGD). The usual translation "soul" easily causes confusion because of the more typically Greek idea of the soul as the real person confined within the material body. The Hebrew idea is rather of the person as a vivified body, the whole person as animated by the breath of God (Gen. 2:7; cf. 1 Cor. 15:45). Here, however, the force of ἐκ ψυχῆς is much the same either way: action done from the vital heart of the person, with all the individual's life force behind it. The exhortation, therefore, probably echoes the elaboration of the Shema in Deut. 6:5 as reaffirmed by Jesus (Mark 12:30 pars.): "You shall love the Lord your God . . . ἐξ ὅλης

29. That "in the Lord" is not used of the third sequence of relationships (slaves and masters), as of the other two (3:18, 20), is no more significant than the fact that the phrase is used only of wives and children and not of husbands/fathers (despite Best, *One Body* 27 n. 1).

τῆς ψυχῆς. . . ." For similar exhortations we may compare Sir. 6:26 and 7:29 (further Lohmeyer 158 n. 6); also pseudo-Phocylides 50 (πᾶσιν δ' ἁπλόος ἴσθι τὰ δ' ἐκ ψυχῆς ἀγόρευε). How best to translate the phrase remains a problem: perhaps best is NEB/REB "put your whole heart into it" (similarly JB/NJB), "with his entire vital energy" (A. Sand, EDNT 3.502), but "gladly" (BAGD s.v. ψυχή 1αγ) does not seem sufficiently forceful.

The motivation will be strengthened by doing the "whatever" for the Lord (Christ), even when it is also to be done for human masters. If there is indeed an echo of Deut. 6:5, we should note again how easily the Christian writer thinks of the Lord to be loved "from the whole ψυχή" as Christ (see also on 3:22). Here, too, the thematic statement (2:6-7) continues to exert its influence.

3:24 εἰδότες ὅτι ἀπὸ κυρίου ἀπολήμψεσθε τὴν ἀνταπόδοσιν τῆς κληρονομίας. τῷ κυρίῳ Χριστῷ δουλεύετε. Further motivation should come from the prospect of future recompense. A central and well-emphasized (εἰδότες) part of the Christian hope is that from the same Lord whom they have been serving, they will receive the inheritance as a due return. That the "Lord" is Christ is self-evident from the context (on the absence of the article see Lightfoot 226). Here again there is no hesitation in attributing to Christ the role of final arbiter in the affairs of humankind. This is not simply the outworking of the high christology of the letter (once again 1:15-20; 2:9), but picks up earlier Pauline themes (as does 3:1). That Paul evidently saw no sharp distinction between the judgment seat of Christ (2 Cor. 5:10) and that of God (Rom. 14:10) is a further indication that he understood his christology as wholly of a piece with Jewish belief in God.

The noun ἀνταπόδοσις occurs only here in the New Testament (this is the only clause of the Colossian household rule on slaves that Eph. 6:8 omits), though note also ἀνταποδίδωμι (Luke 14:14; Rom. 11:35; 12:19) and ἀνταπόδομα (Luke 14:12; Rom. 11:9).[30] The sense of appropriate reward is strong (e.g., Judg. 9:16; 2 Sam. 19:37), usually in the sense of just punishment (e.g., Pss. 69:22; 91:8; 94:2; Jer. 51:57; Hos. 9:7), particularly at the eschaton (Isa. 34:8; 61:2; 63:4; 1 Enoch 22:11; Testament of Abraham 10:15; 12:15), but also of a good outcome (as in Ps. 19:11). The double prefix, "give back (ἀπό) in return (ἀντί)" ("exact requital," Lightfoot 227), suggests that the lot of many slaves was so harsh that the Christian promise of a future inheritance to compensate for such wholehearted obedience despite harsh treatment (cf. Philo, De specialibus legibus 2.90; 3.137-38; 1 Pet. 2:19-20) must have been very attractive to many slaves.

The description of the reward as "the inheritance (κληρονομία)," "the

---

30. Is there a play on ἀνδράποδα ("human-footed stock"), a term often used of slaves, on the analogy of τετράποδα ("four-footed stock")?

reward that is the inheritance" (genitive of content, BDF §167; Harris 185), "the inheritance as your reward" (RSV/NRSV), strikes an authentic Pauline note. As always in the earlier Paulines, it picks up the theme of the inheritance promised to Abraham, that is, primarily the land of Canaan (Gen. 15:7-8; 28:4; Deut. 1:39; 2:12, etc.), as consistently in Jewish usage (J. Herrmann and W. Foerster, *TDNT* 3.769-80). But the imagery lent itself to eschatological reference (Ps. 37:9; Isa. 54:17; J. H. Friedrich, *EDNT* 2.298) and was also spiritualized in the idea of "inheriting eternal life" (*Psalms of Solomon* 14:10; *1 Enoch* 40:9; *Sibylline Oracles* frag. 3, line 47; *Testament of Job* 18:6-7). The same trends are evident in the Jesus tradition (Mark 10:17 par.; Matt. 5:5; 19:29; 25:34; Luke 10:25) and in formulaic talk of "inheriting the kingdom" already established in the Paulines (1 Cor. 6:9-10; 15:50; Gal. 5:21; Eph. 5:5; see again Friedrich 299). Although this is the only mention of the theme in Colossians, the allusion to it already in 1:12 and the persistence of the theme in full Pauline strength into Ephesians (cf. Eph. 5:5 above; and 1:13-14 with 2 Cor. 1:22 and 5:5) strongly suggest that here also it carries all the overtones of the classic Pauline arguments in Galatians 3–4 and Romans 4. That is to say, once again we see that what was offered to Gentile slaves was a share in the inheritance promised to Abraham — that is, in the blessing promised to the nations through Abraham.

The paradox of slaves becoming heirs of God's kingdom would not be lost on the Colossians. Under Roman law slaves could not inherit anything; so it was only by being integrated into this distinctively Jewish heritage that their legal disability as slaves could be surmounted. This persistent Jewish character of the gospel preached to the Colossians would help explain both the further attraction to the Gentile Christians of the more elaborate Jewish worship practiced in Colossae and the degree of antipathy shown to the new movement by (some of) the Colossian Jews.

In a somewhat awkward addition (see n. 6) the reminder is given for a third time (also 3:22, 23) that it is the Lord Christ[31] whose slaves they are. Again the translations help bring out different facets of the thought: "Christ is the Master whose slaves you must be" (NEB/REB); "It is Christ the Lord that you are serving" (JB/NJB). The triple repetition suggests that slaves would need to keep reminding themselves that their loyalty to Christ transcended their loyalty to their masters, thus making it easier to bear the harsher features of their enslavement.

3:25 ὁ γὰρ ἀδικῶν κομίσεται ὃ ἠδίκησεν, καὶ οὐκ ἔστιν προσωπολημψία. The final motivating factor has a proverbial ring: "the wrongdoer will be paid back for the wrong he has done" (RSV, similarly

---

31. Apart from Rom. 16:18 this is the only time in the Paulines that we have this particular combination of titles; otherwise almost always "Lord Jesus Christ," though also "Lord Jesus." See also n. 6 above.

NRSV and REB). The verb κομίζομαι, "get back, receive (wages)," obviously overlaps with the thought of receiving the ἀνταπόδοσις in 3:24 and bears a similar implication that what is received matches that for which it is received, is indeed often in some sense the outworking of the thing itself. This "measure for measure" (Matt. 7:1-2 pars.) is a strong instinct in Jewish tradition, the *ius talionis* (Exod. 21:23-25; cf. Lev. 20:17 and Sir. 7:1), restored martyrs (2 Macc. 7:11, 29), the fitting punishment (Prov. 22:8; 2 Macc. 13:8; 1 Cor. 3:17), the talent with interest (Matt. 25:27; cf. Sir. 29:6), the things done in life (2 Cor. 5:10; Eph. 6:8; cf. *1 Enoch* 100:7), the promise fulfilled (Heb. 10:36; 11:13, 39), the outcome of faith (1 Pet. 1:9), or, in the closest parallel to the present passage, the wrongdoers receiving the reward of wrongdoing (ἀδικούμενοι μισθὸν ἀδικίας, 2 Pet. 2:13). So JB/NJB are justified in translating "Anyone who does wrong will be repaid in kind." The force of this warning or reassurance is twofold: it encouraged harshly treated slaves that their masters could not escape due judgment, in the final judgment if not in this life, and it warned the slaves themselves to maintain their own high standards of integrity so far as possible.[32] The teaching is not antithetical to the Pauline doctrine of justification by faith, but echoes Paul's own earlier teaching (Rom. 2:6-11; 1 Cor. 3:13-15; 2 Cor. 5:10).

The second half of the final encouragement is even more clearly proverbial, or rather a Jewish theologoumenon. To be sure, προσωπολημψία itself may be a Christian formulation, since apart from *Testament of Job* 43:13 (whose precise date is indeterminate) it first appears in the New Testament (Rom. 2:11; Eph. 6:9; Jas. 2:1; Polycarp, *Philippians* 6:1). But it clearly reflects the Hebrew idiom *naśa' panîm* = λαμβάνειν πρόσωπον = "raise/receive the face" of someone prostating himself, that is, accept and welcome him. But it was long established in an unfavorable sense, referring to unwarranted acceptance, that is, "favoritism" (REB/NIV) — a temptation particularly for judges (Lev. 19:15; Deut. 1:17; 16:19). In contrast, God is the model of impartiality (e.g., Deut. 10:17; 2 Chron. 19:7; Sir. 35:12-13;[33] *Jubilees* 5:16; 21:4; *Psalms of Solomon* 2:18).[34] The assurance, be it noted, is *not* that God (implied here; see n. 7) will be especially favourable to those who have worshiped him or believed in his Christ. It is rather that there is

---

32. The same verb, ἀδικέω, is used of Onesimus in Philemon 18, but there is no indication that Onesimus is in mind here (as has often been suggested, e.g., J. Knox, *Philemon among the Letters of Paul* [Nashville: Abingdon, ²1959/London: Collins, ²1960] 157-59; Percy, *Probleme* 402 n. 79); see also O'Brien, *Colossians, Philemon* 230-31. "The worst [!] of slavery was that it killed the sense of moral responsibility" (Scott 81).

33. Lohmeyer 159 n. 4 suggests that the passage here is almost a citation of Sir. 35:11-14 (LXX 32:13-14).

34. See further E. Lohse, *TDNT* 6.779-80; K. Berger, *EDNT* 3.179-80; J. M. Bassler, *Divine Impartiality: Paul and a Theological Axiom* (SBLDS 59; Chico: Scholars, 1982); Aletti, *Épître aux Colossiens* 255 n. 109.

a God-given justice among peoples and individuals determined by God and
that those who ignore or flout it cannot expect to escape the consequences,
whether slaves or masters (cf. again Eph. 6:9).

4:1 οἱ κύριοι, τὸ δίκαιον καὶ τὴν ἰσότητα τοῖς δούλοις παρέχεσθε,
εἰδότες ὅτι καὶ ὑμεῖς ἔχετε κύριον ἐν οὐρανῷ. As slaves have responsibilities toward their masters, so masters have responsibilities toward their
slaves. That their responsibilities are addressed in only one verse, against
the four verses of the preceding advice, may be less significant than at first
seems. For the exhortation to slaves was largely a reiteration of the counsel
to be conscientious in their work, whereas the *paterfamilias* is now addressed
for the third time — first as husband, then as father, now as master. The
greater his authority, the greater his responsibility. Even so, the brevity of
the counsel is striking, and, together with the surprising fact that slaves are
here directly addressed (see 3:22), marks out this Christian household rule
from parallels where slaveowners concerned for the well-being of their slaves
(and the more efficient running of their households) gave greater consideration to the question of how they should be treated. Whether anything can be
deduced from this is unclear (see again on 3:22); perhaps that the typical
Christian church of the first century had relatively few slaveowners, or that
the few who had been baptized in the name of Christ had done so in the full
recognition that "in Christ" there is no slave or free (3:11). Perhaps we can
at least infer that Christian slaves needed greater encouragement to live out
a positive relation to their non-Christian masters than the Christian masters
to their slaves.

Παρέχω is one of those loosely used, imprecise terms (like English
"do" or "put" or German *machen*), but here the middle form clearly means
to "grant" something to someone (BAGD s.v. 2b). The Christian master will
grant his slaves what is "just" (τὸ δίκαιον), in contrast to the injustice
envisaged in 3:25. As in 3:25, it is assumed that there is a recognized "good
practice" and humanitarian treatment of human beings (slaves included) that
goes beyond the strict requirement of the law, which regarded slaves as
chattels to be disposed of as their owners saw fit. It should be a special
concern of the strong to ensure justice. In this again there may be a conscious
dependence on Jewish tradition, which in general treated slaves more
favorably than most other traditions (Exod. 20:10; Lev. 25:43, 53; Sir. 4:30
— faultfinding, the temptation for the master, as eye service for the slave;
7:20-21; 33:31; Philo, *De specialibus legibus* 2.66-68, 89-91; 3:137-43;
pseudo-Phocylides 223-27).

The matching term, τὴν ἰσότητα, is a striking one. For it normally
means "equality" and was a fundamental term in Greek democracy and law
(G. Stählin, *TDNT* 3.345-48). But while we can find humanitarian treatment
urged for slaves, as in Seneca's well-known discourse on treating slaves as
human beings (*Epistle* 47), and while Philo can speak of masters "showing

the gentleness and kindness by which inequality is equalized (δι' ὧν ἐξιστοῦται τὸ ἄνισον," *De decalogo* 167), the idea of equality of treatment for slave and free *in law* was an impossible thought for the time. However tempting, then, the inference that Paul and Timothy here called for an effective abandonment of the legal status of slavery, it is much more probable that ἰσότης has the second sense of "equity, fairness" (Masson 150 n. 6). The two terms δίκαιος καὶ ἰσότης, in fact, are closely related elsewhere, though rarely in just this form: the righteous judge is one who is ἴσος (Plato, *Leges* 12.957c; Polybius 24.15.3); an inscription praises as ἴσος καὶ δίκαιος the man who is righteous in various public offices (*OGIS* I, 339.51); Plutarch discusses the relationship between δικαιοσύνη and ἰσότης (*Quaestiones convivales* 8.2.2; *Moralia* 719B); and Philo describes ἰσότης as the mother of δικαιοσύνη (*De specialibus legibus* 4.231).[35] Here, too, the appeal will be to what would generally be recognized as "just and fair," rather than assuming that the masters could be left to set their own standards (Stählin, *TDNT* 3.354-55).

The sanction is what we might expect given the emphasis of the preceding verses: as slaves should serve their masters as doing it for the Master, so masters should remember that they themselves have a Master in heaven. The sanction of ultimate judgment at the hands of God in and through Christ is the same as in 3:24-25. Whereas for slaves it was a comforting thought, for masters it was more of a threat; having the greater power in relation to their slaves, the possibility that they would abuse that power and therefore have greater liability in the final judgment was the greater. Here the ultimate sanction may be the only one that could be effective, given the legal power of the master over his slave. In the absence of such a sanction it is dubious whether humanly devised and managed legal systems can ever be strong enough to deter the abuse of equivalent power in the hands of the few who hold a stranglehold of financial or political or military power over others.

---

35. See further Lightfoot 228; Lohmeyer 159 n. 5; Lohse, *Colossians and Philemon* 162 n. 74.

Concluding Exhortations (4:2-6)

2 *Be continually devoted to prayer, being watchful in it with thanksgiving,*
3 *praying at the same time*[1] *also for us, that God will open for us a door for*
the word, to speak[2] *the mystery of Christ,*[3] *on account of which*[4] *I am in*
prison, 4 *that I might reveal it, as I ought to speak.*

5 *Walk with wisdom toward outsiders, buying up the time.* 6 *Let your*
speech be always with grace, seasoned with salt, so that you may know how
you ought to answer each one.

The second main section of the letter is rounded off with a twofold sequence
of exhortations. First comes a typical Pauline request for prayer for himself
and his ministry. As in other Pauline letters this indicates that the letter is
drawing to a close and matches the prayer of the opening (1:3, 9-10/4:2-4;
Rom. 1:9-10/15:30-32; Phil. 1:9-11/4:6; 1 Thes. 1:2-3/5:17, 25; 2 Thes.
1:3/3:1-2; Phm. 4-6/22; also Eph. 1:15-23/6:18-20); once again Eph. 6:18-20
is particularly close to Col. 4:2-4. Second comes what appears to be an
almost random series of exhortations, but probably expresses some of the
most persistent concerns remaining as the letter draws to a close (as in Rom.
16:17-20; 1 Cor. 16:13-18; Gal. 6:7-10; Phil. 4:8-9; 1 Thes. 5:12-22; 2 Thes.
3:6-13). Unusually they focus on relationships with others, but are not
particularly anxious in expression. This provides further confirmation that
the situation in Colossae was not so serious or so pressing as in Rome,
Galatia, or Thessalonica.

Houlden 215-16 notes a distinction between the role of the congregation and that of the apostle: the task of evangelism was the apostle's, and it
was a calling he was still anxious to fulfill, even in prison; the task of those
receiving the letter was to pray and watch and to live out their lives in and
in relation to the wider community in a positive fashion. This is a valid
observation, though the evangelistic overtones and opportunities implied in
4:5-6 (in ordinary everyday conversations) should not be ignored.

4:2 τῇ προσευχῇ προσκαρτερεῖτε, γρηγοροῦντες ἐν αὐτῇ ἐν
εὐχαριστίᾳ. As the letter opening began with assurance of Paul's prayer
for the Colossians, so the main section concludes with Paul's encouragement
that they should be faithful in prayer, for him as well (4:3). Here again we
may take it for granted that this was no mere formality but an expression of

---

1. ἅμα denotes the coincidence of two actions in time, so "at the same time, together"
(BAGD).

2. A adds "with boldness" in echo of Eph. 6:19.

3. B and some others read "of God" rather than "of Christ."

4. Some manuscripts read "on account of whom," which destroys the point of the sentence
(Lightfoot 229). Alternatively, we could read διό instead of δι' ὅ, as urged by Bockmuehl, "Note,"
which would link the clause to what follows ("For it is to this end that I have been imprisoned: in
order that I might manifest it . . ."); discussion in Aletti, *Épître aux Colossiens* 259-60.

the indispensability of prayer for Paul and the early Pauline mission; even in this letter we are still in the earliest years when traditions were being created and not merely parroted. Προσκαρτερέω has the basic sense of "persist at, remain with"; so with people, "be loyal to someone" (Acts 8:13; 10:7), and with things, "occupy oneself diligently with, pay persistent attention to" (W. Grundmann, TDNT 3.618-19). In the latter sense prayer is the most common single object of the verb in the New Testament: "busy oneself with, be busily engaged in, be devoted to" prayer, as here (Acts 1:14; 2:42; 6:4; Rom. 12:12); "persevere in prayer" (NEB/REB; similarly JB/NJB); the note is of perseverance and tenaciousness (EDNT 3.172). The thought is obviously of a piece with the idea of unceasing prayer (Rom. 1:9-10; 1 Thes. 5:17; Eph. 6:18); see also on 1:3.

The accompanying exhortation to "keep awake, be on the alert" (γρηγορέω) is drawn from the imagery of guard duty (Neh. 7:3; 1 Macc. 2:27; Mark 14:34, 37), but its metaphorical usage seems to be almost wholly Christian. The inspiration was almost certainly Christianity's sense of imminent expectation, which can be traced back to Jesus himself (Mark 13:35, 37; Matt. 24:42; 25:13; 1 Thes. 5:6; Rev. 3:3; 16:15) and which here still retains something of its earlier freshness.[5] Moreover, the link with prayer may echo the scene in the garden of Gethsemane from the passion narrative, which would no doubt be familiar in all the early Christian churches (Mark 14:38/Matt. 26:41), since there is no other obvious reason why the metaphor should be preserved here (Moule, Colossians and Philemon 132; Houlden 216; Caird 210). This should count therefore as a further indication that imminent expectation of the coming again of Christ had by no means disappeared at this stage of the Pauline churches. At the very least the sense of an impending threat requiring constant alertness is retained, and prayer functions as the vital channel of communication with the commander in chief.

The other accompanying exhortation is once again that their prayers should be made in a spirit of thanksgiving (ἐν εὐχαριστίᾳ). This repeated emphasis in Colossians makes it one of the most "thankful" documents in the New Testament (1:3, 12; 2:7; 3:17; 4:2). Here it provides an important balance to the call for watchfulness: they are to keep alert, not in a spirit of fear or anxiety, but with the confidence and assurance that their resources (in Christ) are more than equal to the potential challenges.

4:3 προσευχόμενοι ἅμα καὶ περὶ ἡμῶν, ἵνα ὁ θεὸς ἀνοίξῃ ἡμῖν θύραν

---

5. Conzelmann 155; O'Brien, Colossians, Philemon 237-38; cf. Lohmeyer 161; R. P. Martin, Colossians and Philemon 125-26; Schweizer, Colossians 231-32; Gnilka, Kolosserbrief 228; Pokorný 185, 187; pace Lohse, Colossians and Philemon 164-65; Lindemann, Kolosserbrief 69; Wolter 209. There is a sustained apocalyptic note through these verses: "keep awake . . . the mystery of Christ . . . that I might reveal it . . . δεῖ (the divinely ordained necessity) . . . buying up the καιρός . . . δεῖ (again). . . ." To treat the exhortation as purely a pastoral counsel ("Try to avoid falling asleep in your prayers; watch out for answers to your petitions") also loses sight of the determinative eschatological theology (cf. pp. 200f. above).

τοῦ λόγου λαλῆσαι τὸ μυστήριον τοῦ Χριστοῦ, δι' ὃ καὶ δέδεμαι. The assumption of 4:2 is that the Colossians will have no lack of subjects for prayer. The note of thanksgiving should be pervasive, and the theme of praise was well illustrated earlier in the letter (1:5, 12-20). Otherwise the primary concern was intercession (O'Brien, *Colossians, Philemon* 237). Paul had no embarrassment in understanding prayer as asking for things and on behalf of people (Jesus had so taught, e.g., Matt. 7:7-11/Luke 11:9-13). Such prayer expressed not a selfishness or acquisitiveness, but a recognition of dependence on God for the opportunities to serve him and the enabling to do so. So Paul does not hesitate, rather is eager to ask for prayer for himself and his work (as in Rom. 15:30-32; 2 Cor. 1:11; Phil. 1:19; 1 Thes. 5:25; 2 Thes. 3:1-2; Phm. 22; the parallel with Eph. 6:19-20 becomes very close for these two verses); the plural "us" is perhaps a reminder of the dual authorship of the letter, or that Paul's mission involved a substantial team (here including no doubt those to be mentioned in 4:7-14).

Characteristic of Paul is the request that the prayer should be for his missionary work — that God would open a door for the word (λόγος; see 1:5, 25; 3:16), that is, "give an opening for preaching" (NEB), "throw open a door for us to announce the message" (NJB), "give us a good opportunity to preach his message" (GNB); see also Harris 193-94. The metaphor was one which Paul evidently liked (1 Cor. 16:9; 2 Cor. 2:12; Acts 14:27). What might have been in mind is well illustrated in Phil. 1:12-14: opportunity to evangelize prison guards and visitors; would the hope of release from prison (as suggested by many) have been expressed by this metaphor?

The content envisaged here of his speaking (λαλέω; but it can have the force of "assert, proclaim," BAGD s.v. 2b) is "the mystery of [the] Christ," that is, the mystery which is Christ and which Christ has unveiled. This was certainly a primary theme of the letter itself (1:26-27; 2:2), so the request at this point is a way of reinforcing the emphasis of the letter. But, as in Ephesians, it indicates that this was a major feature of the Pauline message at this stage. One can well envisage the "apostle to the Gentiles" in prison reflecting on his life's work and seeing the simpler message of a gospel also for the Gentiles as more and more a key feature of the eschatological and cosmic scenario with which God's whole purpose for creation and humanity would reach its climax (see on 1:26 and 27). That this should continue to be the theme of his preaching in and from prison underlines the importance of the Jew-Gentile issue for the Pauline gospel and as the key to a more universal reconciliation (1:20).

Indeed, it was on account of this very gospel that he had been "bound," that is, not simply under "house arrest" but in prison, "fettered, in chains" (cf. 4:18; Mark 6:17; 15:7; Acts 12:6; 16:26; see also pp. 39-41 above).[6] This, of course, does not refer to the formal charge on which Paul had been

6. "A pseudepigraphic feature, intended to suggest authenticity" (Wolter 211); but imprisonment is surely in view, despite Yates, *Colossians* 82.

imprisoned, but indicates rather the Pauline perspective: since preaching this mystery was his primary raison d'être, this was also the reason for his imprisonment. It was this preaching which had incited the opposition to him and resulted in his imprisonment; but he also believed that the imprisonment was itself part of God's eschatological purpose to unfold the mystery (see also n. 4 above, and again Phil. 1:12-14). 2 Tim. 2:9 catches the Pauline mood well: "the gospel for which I suffer hardship, to the extent of being chained like a criminal; but the word of God is not chained."

4:4 ἵνα φανερώσω αὐτὸ ὡς δεῖ με λαλῆσαι. The second purpose clause (ἵνα) simply reinforces the first. The verb (φανερώσω) is the same as in 1:26: "reveal" (NRSV). It is tempting to avoid such a translation here (e.g., NIV "may proclaim it clearly"; NEB/REB "make the secret plain"), but on balance better to maintain a consistency of translation (1:26; 3:4) and to retain the apocalyptic sense of a mystery unveiled (cf. Zeilinger, *Erstgeborene* 112-13). The verse underlines Paul's own conviction that he had been given the primary privilege, as apostle to the Gentiles, to disclose the secret of God's overarching design in creation and salvation (Rom. 11:25-26; 1 Cor. 2:7; 4:1; Col. 1:27-29; Eph. 3:7-13).[7] This sense here is reinforced by δεῖ, indicating a predestined destiny and unavoidable compulsion (BAGD; as in Mark 9:11 par.; 13:10; Luke 4:43; Acts 3:21; 23:11; 1 Cor. 15:25; 2 Cor. 5:10; cf. 1 Cor. 9:16). It was this burning conviction and sense of destiny which no doubt sustained Paul through a ministry of astonishing exertion and suffering, made it so effective, and continues to give the Pauline letters such fascination. Such people are usually uncomfortable companions and can appear to be driven men; but Paul was evidently able both to retain sufficient equipoise and to inspire tremendous loyalty and commitment on the part of others.

4:5 ἐν σοφίᾳ περιπατεῖτε πρὸς τοὺς ἔξω τὸν καιρὸν ἐξαγοραζόμενοι. The final exhortation is directed to the Colossian believers' relations with their non-Christian neighbors and those they encountered at work and in the marketplace. As the last general exhortation of the letter it presumably tells us something about Paul and Timothy's concerns regarding those who would receive the letter: this is the point at which anything left unsaid earlier would be said now, the point at which the most important emphasis of the letter was likely to be reiterated to ensure that its thrust was not lost or averted (so particularly Gal. 6:11-16). It probably confirms therefore that the principal concerns of Paul and Timothy were not for the good order of the church in Colossae (as at Corinth), nor that deep, penetrating inroads had already been made into the church by persuasive teaching of other missionaries (as in Galatia), but that as a small group in a city where there were other larger,

---

7. "The person and the thing itself *(Sache)* have become so fully one that he himself appears as the giver of the revelation" (Lohmeyer 162); otherwise Bockmuehl, *Revelation* 191-92.

more established, and more self-confident groups, the Colossian Christians were vulnerable to the attractive appeal of these groups (particularly the Colossian Jews). They needed therefore to be both circumspect in their dealings with these others and to be ready to respond when questions were raised about their own faith (cf. MacDonald 100-101, 108-9).

The exhortation to "walk in wisdom" (ἐν σοφίᾳ περιπατεῖτε) is an effective summary of one of the main emphases of the letter, forming an *inclusio* with both 1:9-10 (ἐν πάσῃ σοφίᾳ . . . περιπατῆσαι) and 2:6-7 (ἐν αὐτῷ περιπατεῖτε), with the theme of wisdom prominent also in 1:28; 2:3, 23; and 3:16.[8] As in 1:28 and 2:3 in particular, the wisdom is related to the revelation of the mystery (cf. *4 Ezra* 14:26, 46; Gnilka, *Kolosserbrief* 230). It is just the same wisdom, with its double sense of God-given but also pragmatic wisdom, which should be expressed in all their dealings with outsiders (οἱ ἔξω). JB's "Be tactful" is a too limiting translation for the phrase; RSV/NRSV's "Conduct yourself wisely" is better (cf. Matt. 10:16 and 1 Thes. 4:12; 1 Cor. 10:32 is a more negative expression of the same concern). Οἱ ἔξω (Eph. 5:15 is again different) does indicate a sense of sectarian separateness from the world around (as in 1 Cor. 5:12-13 and 1 Thes. 4:12), the corollary to the sense of having been privileged with a revelation not more widely shared (as in Mark 4:11; cf. Matt. 11:25-27/Luke 10:21-22; *4 Ezra* 12:36; *2 Baruch* 48:3; the parallels in J. Behm, *TDNT* 2.575-76 are less close in substance). In the history of religions (not least Christianity) this has regularly involved a sense of being threatened by the world "outside" and a correlative introvertedness (the Qumran Essenes being a contemporary case in point).[9] But here the note comes in a sequence in which responsibility toward others is emphasized, including the obligation to make the revelation more widely known. To hold a balance between maintaining distinctive commitment and promoting genuine communication with others is never easy.

Quite what the attached clause (τὸν καιρὸν ἐξαγοραζόμενοι) means is not entirely clear. The verb ἐξαγοράζω would normally mean "buy" or "buy back," and so "redeem" (Gal. 3:13; 4:5); F. Büchsel argues that it refers to "intensive buying," that is, "buying which exhausts the possibilities available" (*TDNT* 1.128; cf. R. Dabelstein, *EDNT* 2.1; Moule, *Colossians and Philemon* 134; Harris 196-97). The likely meaning here, therefore, is "gain or reclaim time" which would otherwise be lost or slip away (cf. Dan. 2:8 LXX: καιρὸν ὑμεῖς ἐξαγοράζετε, "you are trying to gain time") or which is under the sway of evil (implied in Eph. 5:15; we recall that

8. The Ephesian parallel, Eph. 5:15, has ἀκριβῶς ("carefully") instead, but probably shows awareness of Col. 4:5 by adding μὴ ὡς ἄσοφοι ἀλλ' ὡς σοφοί.

9. See also W. A. Meeks, "The Man from Heaven in Johannine Sectarianism," *JBL* 91 (1972) 44-72.

αἰών can mean both a segment of time and an age or world hostile to God; see on 1:26). That καιρός often has the sense of significant time, in the New Testament eschatological time (as in Matt. 8:29; Mark 1:15; 13:33; Luke 21:8; Rom. 3:26; 8:18; 13:11; 1 Cor. 4:5; 7:29; 2 Cor. 6:2; 8:14; Gal. 6:10; 1 Pet. 1:5), also helps focus the thought on the present time as a unique climactic period in which every minute is precious (cf. J. Baumgarten, *EDNT* 2.233). This fits well with the Pauline sense of the period of his mission as a time pregnant with eschatological importance, to be used to the full in proclaiming the gospel (cf. particularly Rom. 11:13-15; 1 Cor. 4:9). The translations pick up one aspect of all this (NIV "make the most of every opportunity," NRSV "making the most of the time," REB "use your opportunities to the full"; though NJB "making the best of the present time" gives an overtone of resignation; see also BAGD s.v. ἐξαγοράζω 2), but the sense of eschatological urgency is lacking. Here again it is at least doubtful whether we should speak of a loss of imminent expectancy in Colossians.[10]

4:6 ὁ λόγος ὑμῶν πάντοτε ἐν χάριτι, ἅλατι ἠρτυμένος, εἰδέναι πῶς δεῖ ὑμᾶς ἑνὶ ἑκάστω ἀποκρίνεσθαι. The final exhortation explicitly envisages a church in communication with those around it, not cut off in a "holy huddle" speaking only "the language of Zion" to insiders (contrast Eph. 4:29), but engaged in regular conversation with others, and in such a way as to allow plenty opportunity to bear testimony to their faith. The counsel itself uses attractive imagery: "Let your spoken word [BAGD s.v. λόγος 1] be always [πάντοτε, as in 1:3] with grace." Here the last term certainly echoes the normal usage of χάρις in relation to speech, that is, "graciousness, attractiveness," that which delights and charms (cf. Ps. 45:2; Eccl. 10:12; Sir. 21:16; Josephus, *Antiquities* 18.208; Luke 4:22; Lightfoot 230; BAGD s.v. χάρις 1), though no Paulinist would intend such a usage to be independent of the χάρις manifested in Christ and fundamental to the Pauline gospel (see on 1:2, 6 and 3:16).

This slightly unexpected sense of agreeable speech is enhanced by the addition, ἅλατι ἠρτυμένος. The image is clear: salt that seasons, that is, makes more interesting what would otherwise be bland to the taste (Job 6:6; Mark 9:50; Luke 14:34; BAGD s.v. ἀρτύω). It was an obvious and familiar idiom: Timon (third century BC) calls the speech of the Academics ἀνάλιστος, "unsalted, insipid" (BAGD s.v. ἅλας 2); Plutarch speaks of a pastime or business "seasoned with the salt of conversation" and of wit as "the tastiest condiment of all," called by some "graciousness" (χάριτας, *Moralia* 514E-F, 685A, cited by Lohse 168 n. 39); in Latin *sales*

---

10. See also Lohmeyer 163; Masson 152 n. 6; and Houlden 217; cf. Gnilka, *Kolosserbrief* 231; Ernst, *Philipper, Philemon, Kolosser, Epheser* 240; Aletti, *Épître aux Colossiens* 261; *pace* Lohse, *Colossians and Philemon* 168.

Attici means "Attic wit" (e.g., Cicero, *Ad familiares* 9.15.2, cited by Bruce, *Colossians, Philemon, and Ephesians* 175 n. 22; see also Wolter 212).[11] The conversation envisaged, then, should be agreeable and "never insipid" (NEB/REB), "with a flavour of wit" (JB/NJB). "Those who are the salt of the earth [cf. Matt. 5:13; Mark 9:49-50; Luke 14:34-35] may reasonably be expected to have some savour about their language" (Bruce, *Colossians, Philemon, and Ephesians* 175); cf. Ignatius, *Magnesians* 10:2: "Be salted in him [Christ]."

The picture is as far as we can imagine from that of the Christian who has no interest in affairs outside those of faith or church and so no "small talk," no ability to maintain an interesting conversation. In contrast, it envisages opportunities for lively interchanges with non-Christians on topics and in a style which could be expected to find a positive resonance with the conversation partners. It would not be conversation which has "gone bad," but conversation which reflects the attractiveness of character displayed above all by Christ. Moreover, such advice envisages a group of Christians in a sufficiently positive relation with the surrounding community for such conversations to be natural, a group not fearful or threatened, but open to and in positive relationship with its neighbors (even as "outsiders," 4:5). Nor is there any hint of the persecution which is attested in other New Testament letters written to churches in Asia Minor (1 Pet. 4:12-19; Rev. 2:9-11, 13, etc.; the tone of 1 Pet. 3:15 is notably different in this respect), a fact which again suggests an earlier date. Rather, the picture evoked is one of social interaction and involvement in wider (Colossian) community affairs. Here, evidently, was a church not on the defensive against powerful forces organized against it, but expected to hold its own in the social setting of marketplace, baths, and meal table and to win attention by the attractiveness of its life and speech.

Such conversations, however, would regularly and quite naturally throw up opportunities to bear more specific Christian witness (cf. Pokorný 186-87) — not as something artificially added on to a "secular" conversation, nor requiring a special language or manner of speaking, but as part of a typical exchange of opinions and ideas. When asked about the distinctiveness of their faith and its lifestyle expression, the Christians should be ready to give an answer in each case (the δεῖ here implying both an obligation on their part and a givenness from God in the faith they should bear witness to).[12] Again it should be noted how integrated their faith was expected to be

---

11. W. Nauck, "Salt as a Metaphor in Instructions for Discipleship," *StTh* 6 (1952) 165-78, notes rabbinic parallels in which wisdom is likened to salt, an image taken up by several church fathers (see also Str-B 1.235).

12. Cf. Mishnah *Aboth* 2:14: "R. Eleazar said, 'Be alert to study the law and know how to make answer to an unbeliever' "; see further Str-B 3.765.

with their workaday lives in the city and how rounded the religion that could both charm a conversation partner by its quality and give testimony of faith as part of the same conversation. NJB adds a further dimension by translating "Be sensitive to the kind of answer each one requires."

CONCLUSION (4:7-18)

As was Paul's custom in his undisputed letters, so here the letter is rounded off with a sequence of personal messages, first, as most important, regarding Paul's own communication with the Colossians (4:7-9), then a series of greetings with personal comments attached (4:10-17), and finally a greeting, prayer request, and benediction in Paul's own hand (4:18).

4:7-9	travel plans	Rom. 15:22-32; 1 Cor. 16:1-18; 2 Cor. 13:1-10; Eph. 6:21-22; Phil. 4:10-18; 2 Tim. 4:9-18; Tit. 3:12-13; Phm. 22
4:10-15	greetings	Rom. 16:3-16; 1 Cor. 16:19-20; 2 Cor. 13:12-13; Phil. 4:21-22; 2 Tim. 4:19-21; Tit. 3:15; Phm. 23-24
4:16-17	final instructions	1 Cor. 16:15-18; 1 Thes. 5:27; 2 Tim. 4:21
4:18	personal note	Rom. 16:17-20(?); 1 Cor. 16:21-24; Gal. 6:11-18; 2 Thes. 3:17-18; Phm. 19 or 21
	final benediction	Rom. 16:20; 1 Cor. 16:23; 2 Cor. 13:13; Gal. 6:18; Eph. 6:24; Phil. 4:23; 1 Thes. 5:28; 2 Thes. 3:18; 1 Tim. 6:21; 2 Tim. 4:22; Tit. 3:15; Phm. 25

For a thesis of pseudonymous or post-Pauline authorship of some of the Pauline letters, the most puzzling feature is usually the very personal character of the final section (see also p. 37 above). Zeilinger, "Träger," tries to turn the personal notes to good account for such a thesis by arguing that the structure and content of 4:7-18 indicate that in Colossians the basic concern of the Pastorals, the preservation and defense of the apostolic tradition, was already being addressed. And the view is common that the post-Pauline authors used such material as a way of strengthening their own authority (e.g., MacDonald 126-30).

But, as we will see, the character of the detail makes much more sense if it was penned by Timothy while Paul was confined in prison (see pp. 37f. again); all we need envisage is Paul's approval in substance if not in detail and sufficient occasion for him to add 4:18 in his own hand. Eph. 6:21-22, on the other hand, is such a close echo of Col. 4:7-8 that it has probably been modeled on the latter. In the event, it was probably in this way that the tradition of such letters was established in the circle of Paul's associates and carried on into the Pastorals — the tradition, that is, of letters by Paul's immediate circle and incorporating authentic personal notes from Paul himself. In each case the concern would be not for personal legitimation so much as to claim the letter's authentic Pauline character — Pauline, that is, in continuity of personnel (after all, many of the lines of communication indicated under "travel plans" above were in fact maintained by Paul's associates acting in his name) and continuity of theological emphasis, however much developed to take account of changing circumstances (see also pp. 19f. above).

Yates, *Colossians* 84, draws attention to the social mix of those named — large householders (4:15), a doctor (4:14), those with sufficient financial freedom (or support) to travel on the business of the gospel (4:7, 10, 12), as well as slaves (4:9) — also to the task-oriented designations — "fellow worker," "servant/minister," "brother" — also "fellow slave" and "fellow prisoner."

Maintaining Communication (4:7-9)

7 *As for all my affairs, Tychicus will make them known to you. He is a beloved brother and faithful servant and fellow slave in the Lord.* 8 *I have sent[1] him to you for this very purpose, that you might know how we[2] are and that he might encourage your hearts;* 9 *and with him Onesimus, faithful and beloved brother, who is one of yourselves. They will make known to you everything which is happening here.*

4:7 τὰ κατ᾽ ἐμὲ πάντα γνωρίσει ὑμῖν Τύχικος ὁ ἀγαπητὸς ἀδελφὸς καὶ πιστὸς διάκονος καὶ σύνδουλος ἐν κυρίῳ. As the parallels listed above clearly indicate, Paul thought it of first importance, both in pastoral terms and in terms of building up support for his own work, to maintain as close contact with his churches as possible (in this case a church founded by one of his associates). Nor should we underestimate the importance of the bonds of personal friendship and the sense so evident in Paul's letters that he and his recipients were involved in each others' lives and committed to each other; Paul's affairs, everything to do with him (τὰ κατ᾽ ἐμὲ πάντα; see O'Brien, *Colossians, Philemon* 246), was evidently important to the Colossians: they would want to know how things were with him (cf. Phil. 1:12). To maintain such links was one of the chief reasons why Paul gathered around himself a team of associate workers and helpers. After all, when the scope of his missionary work is considered, the number of churches and the amount of travel involved, it would have been impossible for him to maintain anything but the most irregular contact otherwise. It is the extent to which the Pauline mission was a team effort which makes the problem of pseudonymity, the problem of letters written in his name from within his immediate circle, that much less pressing as a problem.

One of the most prominent of these associates was Tychicus. The name was not very common (*NDIEC* 2.109), though it appears nine times in inscriptions from Magnesia, further down toward the mouth of the Meander from Colossae (BAGD s.v. Τύχικος; Lightfoot 232). According to Acts 20:4 this Tychicus was also from the province of Asia. It is consistent with this information that the other references to Tychicus usually link him with that region: he was sent by Paul to Colossae (here) and to Ephesus (Eph. 6:21, and again in 2 Tim. 4:12). The exception is Tit. 3:12, where he is to be sent to Titus in Crete, presumably from Nicopolis in Epirus(?). If number of

---

1. A good example of "the epistolary aorist" (BDF §334), the tense reflecting when the letter was received, not when it was written; so it could be translated "I am sending."

2. Surprisingly some manuscripts read "you," resulting in some confusion in the tradition, perhaps initially a scribal slip, or some uncertainty in view of the undue repetition of the theme ("make known to you my affairs," "that you might know how we are," "make known to you everything here"); see Metzger 626.

mentions is significant, this would make Tychicus, along with Silvanus, one of Paul's closest associates after Timothy and Titus. That he appears only in deutero-Pauline letters is rather striking. It is unlikely that the circles from whom these letters were issued would have given such prominence to one who had not in fact been an associate of Paul himself. The more likely suggestion is that he was a late recruit by Paul (during his lengthy period in Ephesus most likely: Acts 19:10) who came into his own as one of the inner group only late in Paul's mission. But if this letter is pseudonymous it would suggest that Tychicus became still more prominent in (some) Pauline churches after his death and that one of the letter's important purposes was to legitimate him more widely as an authentic representative of the apostle (Gnilka, *Kolosserbrief* 234-35, 242; Pokorný 191).

Like Timothy, Tychicus is called a "brother" (see on 1:1), and like Epaphras he is called "beloved," "faithful or trustworthy servant," and "fellow-slave" (see on 1:7 and Lightfoot 232). The parallel terminology in the latter case suggests a deliberate attempt to rank Tychicus with, but no higher than, the Colossians' own Epaphras; similarly in the case of Onesimus (4:9). Almost by way of reflex action, the "in the Lord" formulation (see on 3:18) echoes the prominence of references to the Lord in the preceding parenesis (ten occurrences in 3:13–4:1) and ties in the final sequence of messages to the thematic concern of 2:6-7.

4:8 ὃν ἔπεμψα πρὸς ὑμᾶς εἰς αὐτὸ τοῦτο, ἵνα γνῶτε τὰ περὶ ἡμῶν καὶ παρακαλέσῃ τὰς καρδίας ὑμῶν. The point already implicit in 4:7 is stated expressly: Tychicus was being sent to give them news of Paul, and that, indeed, was the precise reason that Paul was sending him ("for this very purpose"); maintaining lively communication was sufficient reason of itself for the lengthy journey.[3] Of course, Tychicus may well have had other commissions as well (perhaps other Pauline churches to visit en route), but the wording is that of a gracious letter writer wanting the recipients to know how special they are to him. At the same time, with greater self-effacement, the singular of 4:7 ("my affairs") is replaced by a plural ("how we are," τὰ περὶ ἡμῶν); Timothy includes himself (1:2), but the ἡμῶν could also have wider reference. It is also assumed, and no doubt could be assumed, that the news would encourage or "reassure" (JB) the Colossians, "put fresh heart into" them (NEB/REB; for the same idiom see on 2:2). Here again we see how strong were the personal bonds which linked the members of these various churches, particularly with the mission teams which had founded them and their fellow churches elsewhere. It mattered to them how Paul and Timothy were faring.

4:9 σὺν Ὀνησίμῳ τῷ πιστῷ καὶ ἀγαπητῷ ἀδελφῷ, ὅς ἐστιν ἐξ ὑμῶν·

---

3. "His task is not to engage in the actual theological battle against the false teachers; that is left solely to the letter itself" (Lindemann, *Kolosserbrief* 72).

πάντα ὑμῖν γνωρίσουσιν τὰ ὧδε.   The party being sent to Colossae included Onesimus. Presumably as "one of yourselves" (like Epaphras, 4:12), this is the same Onesimus who is the subject of Philemon (see pp. 301ff. and on Phm. 10). He is mentioned here, however, almost as an afterthought: Tychicus is clearly more important, and it is he who has the primary task of passing on the news from Paul (and Timothy); the point was stated twice in 4:7-8 for emphasis. Moreover, Onesimus, having been mentioned as Tychicus's companion, is then given a fanfare similar to that for Tychicus: "faithful and beloved brother" (see on 1:1 and 1:7), but with a clear difference: Onesimus is not described as "servant" or "fellow slave" (contrast 4:7). Presumably Onesimus does not count as one of Paul's team of fellow workers; he is a Christian ("brother") and well regarded ("faithful and beloved"), but he carries no explicit responsibility in Paul's missionary and pastoral work. Whether this was because, as a slave of someone else, he could not act at Paul's bidding or with the freedom which one of Paul's coworkers needed, or because as a (former?) runaway slave his position was ambiguous, or because his relationship with Paul was one simply of friendship, depends in large part on how Phm. 10-22 is interpreted and is related to this verse (see further pp. 37f., 39f. above and 301ff. below).

Lest Onesimus be diminished in their eyes, however, for a third time, Paul (and Timothy) indicate that the purpose of Tychicus's and Onesimus's coming is to impart news: they (including Tychicus) "will tell you everything here." While it is clearly Tychicus who is to be the chief spokesperson, Onesimus, as one of their own, will no doubt have much to tell on his own part.

Greetings (4:10-17)

10 *Aristarchus, my fellow prisoner, greets you; also Mark, the cousin of Barnabas (concerning whom you have received instructions: if he comes to you, receive him);* 11 *also Jesus who is called Justus. They are of the circumcision,*[1] *these alone fellow workers for the kingdom of God, who have been a comfort for me.* 12 *Epaphras, who is one of yourselves, a servant of Christ (Jesus),*[2] *greets you; he always strives for you in his prayers, that you might stand mature and fully assured* [3]*in all the will of God.*[3] 13 *For I bear him witness that he has much labor*[4] *on your behalf and on behalf of those in Laodicea and those in Hierapolis.* 14 *Luke, the beloved doctor, greets you, and Demas.*

15 *Greet the brothers*[5] *in Laodicea, also Nympha*[6] *and the church in her*[6] *house.* 16 *And when the letter has been read among you, make sure*[7] *that it is read also in the church of the Laodiceans and that you also read the letter from Laodicea.* 17 *And say to Archippus, "See that you fulfill the ministry which you received in the Lord."*

Of considerable importance for the character and vitality of the first Christian churches was the fact that there was a network of personal friendships and relationships knitting them together. They were bound together not simply by a common experience of faith, but by the friendships of family and relations of the like-minded, of common interests and pursuits, of host and guest hospitality

1. On the slight difficulties of punctuation and rendition see Moule, *Colossians and Philemon* 137; Harris 208.

2. Here again we have the common confusion in the manuscript tradition as to whether the original text read "Christ" (alone), "Christ Jesus" (the best supported), or "Jesus Christ" (the least attested).

3. The final phrase of v. 12 can go with either "stand" or "fully assured" or with both (see Harris 210).

4. The word used here (πόνον) is little used in the New Testament (elsewhere only Rev. 16:10-11; 21:4), a fact which probably encouraged scribes to introduce what they must have judged to be more appropriate alternatives: κόπον ("trouble, hard work"), ζῆλον ("zeal"), πόθον ("longing, wish"), ἀγῶνα ("contest, struggle"); see Metzger 626.

5. See above, p. 43 n. 4.

6. Νυμφαν can be accented either Νύμφαν (from the feminine Νύμφα, "Nympha"), or Νυμφᾶν (from the masculine Νυμφᾶς, "Nymphas"). Since both names are attested in papyri and inscriptions (BAGD s.v. Νυμφαν; though the feminine form is more common [Lightfoot 240]), the decision depends on the gender of the following possessive pronoun. Here αὐτῆς ("her") is probably best attested (B and others), with the other readings (αὐτοῦ, "his," and αὐτῶν, "their") explained in part at least by the later scribal assumption that the leader of a house church could not have been a woman (see also Gnilka, *Kolosserbrief* 244; Metzger 627; αὐτοῦ is favored by Moule, *Colossians and Philemon* 28 n. 1; Masson 156 n. 6; Caird 212; αὐτῶν by Lightfoot 240-41; against Lightfoot see J. H. Moulton, *GNTG* 1.48).

7. For ποιέω ἵνα in the sense "cause that, bring it about that" see BAGD s.v. ποιέω Ibθ.

perhaps extending over many years. We should not think that such greetings came only through Paul, or only on the occasion of Paul's letters. Rather, we should assume that these friendships existed and thrived quite independently of Paul and that those here mentioned were simply taking the opportunity given by the journey of Tychicus and Onesimus to reaffirm and celebrate these friendships with the little touches of thoughtfulness and concern which keep friendships bright and fresh. It is one of the too little appreciated values of Paul's letters that they attest to the vitality of these early churches precisely in their character as a system of overlapping and interlocking circles of friendship, sustained, no doubt, as is well exemplified here (4:7, 9, 10, 15-17), by regular contact and communication (Schweizer, *Colossians* 243; cf. Meeks, *Urban Christians* 109). On the possibilities of social interaction while in custody which these verses imply see Rapske 347-67; on the parallels between this section and Philemon see pp. 37f. above.

4:10 ἀσπάζεται ὑμᾶς Ἀρίσταρχος ὁ συναιχμάλωτός μου καὶ Μᾶρκος ὁ ἀνεψιὸς Βαρναβᾶ (περὶ οὗ ἐλάβετε ἐντολάς, ἐὰν ἔλθῃ πρὸς ὑμᾶς, δέξασθε αὐτόν). Ἀσπάζομαι is the conventional word of the time for conveying greetings, not least at the end of letters (BAGD; MM; Weima 40-45); so here (four times in the next six verses; cf. particularly Rom. 16:3-23). The first mentioned is Aristarchus. The name was common (BAGD s.v. Ἀρίσταρχος), but it is probably fair to assume that this is the same Aristarchus from Thessalonica mentioned in Acts (19:29; 20:4; 27:2; but see Ollrog 46-47) and thus one of the few who accompanied Paul on his final journeys to Jerusalem and thence to Rome. He is included also in the greetings to Philemon, along with most of the group that is mentioned here — Epaphras, Mark, Luke, and Demas (Phm. 24) — the latter three all together described as Paul's "fellow workers" (συνεργοί).

Here, however, Aristarchus is named first and alone described as Paul's "fellow prisoner (of war)" (συναιχμάλωτος); in contrast, it is Epaphras who is named first and singled out as συναιχμάλωτος in Phm. 23. It is possible that the imagery is figurative (G. Kittel, *TDNT* 1.196-97; Caird 211; others in O'Brien, *Colossians, Philemon* 250; "Christ's captive," NEB/REB). But why then only Epaphras (in Philemon), Andronicus and Junia (Rom. 16:7), and Aristarchus (here) should be so designated is not clear, since the image is of a surrender to Christ which presumably was true of all believers — unlike the more specific commissioning implied in similar phrases ("fellow soldier" in Phil. 2:25 and Phm. 2; "fellow slave," see on 1:7). Alternatively, the reference to Aristarchus in Acts 27:2 could imply that he actually was a prisoner with Paul (though the account in Acts 21 on gives no indication of others than Paul arrested). Perhaps the references to four different people as Paul's "fellow prisoners" on three different occasions are best explained by the hypothesis that Paul's imprisonment was such as to permit certain of his associates to take turns sharing his confinement (Abbott 300; Dibelius,

Kolosser, Epheser, Philemon 107; Scott 115).[8] At all events, when taken in conjunction with 4:3 and 4:18, it is hard to avoid the conclusion that Paul alludes here to physical captivity (*EDNT* 3.297).[9] Moreover, the similarity of the references in Romans 16 and Philemon suggests that all three letters were written during the same imprisonment, when the regime was similar in that respect at least (see also on Phm. 23). In a culture dominated by ideas of honor and shame, the willingness to accept the stigma of prison (Rapske ch. 12: "The Shame of Bonds") would indicate a high degree of personal commitment to Paul on the part of those he designates his "fellow prisoners."

Second mentioned is Mark, who appears earlier in the Acts account as one well known in Christian circles: the "John called Mark" (Acts 12:12). According to Acts Mark was brought from Jerusalem (Acts 12:25) to become one of Paul's companions in the missionary expedition which he and Barnabas mounted from Antioch. But then, before Mark withdrew from the expedition in Pamphylia (15:38), occasioning a subsequent breach between Barnabas and Paul when Barnabas wanted to take Mark a second time (15:37-39). Paul himself says nothing of this here, and there are dark hints in Gal. 2:11-14 that the breach between Barnabas and Paul had other, much more serious causes (see my *Galatians, ad loc.*), though the two accounts (Acts and Galatians) may well be complementary rather than contradictory. In the undisputed Pauline letters Mark appears only in Phm. 24 (as here, one of Paul's "coworkers"). But he is also mentioned in 2 Tim. 4:11 in similarly friendly terms ("he is very useful to me for ministry"; cf. Col. 4:11). And he is one of a small handful who appear in letters outside the Pauline corpus as well, in 1 Pet. 5:13 (cf. Silvanus in 1 Pet. 5:12 and Timothy in Heb. 13:22), where the reference is still warmer ("my son Mark"). All this could suggest the pleasing picture of an earlier breach subsequently healed, with Mark coming to be a member of Paul's most intimate circle, and this is certainly how he is remembered in the tradition. At the very least, quite apart from the subsequent tradition that he wrote the second Gospel (Eusebius, *Historia Ecclesiastica* 3.39.14-16), Mark must rank as one of the few effective bridge figures between different strands of the early Christian mission (perhaps having been one of the casualties of the earlier disagreements).

The present passage adds significant information given us nowhere else, namely that Mark was Barnabas's "cousin" (ἀνεψιός; see Lightfoot 234-35). That in itself would be sufficient to explain why Mark was so well known. For Barnabas was evidently an important figure from the very

---

8. See discussion in Rapske ch. 12 and 371-74, 385-86 (Rapske 372-73 questions the hypothesis in reference to Aristarchus himself).

9. "One who looked on himself as a soldier of Jesus Christ, as Paul did, would not unnaturally think of himself during his captivity as a prisoner-of-war" (Bruce, *Colossians, Philemon, and Ephesians* 179).

beginnings of the Jerusalem church (Acts 4:36) and an absolutely key figure in ensuring that the breakthrough at Antioch did not itself become a breach (11:22-24), in the development in the church at Antioch itself (11:22; 13:1; 15:35), in bringing Saul the convert into the mainstream of the movement (9:27; 11:25-26), in leading the first missionary expedition from Antioch to the east of Colossae (13:2, 7; 14:12), and in the initial defense of the Gentile mission with Paul (15:2, 12, 22, 25; Gal. 2:1, 9). That he seems to have been well known to the Colossians, by name at least, also suggests both his stature within Christian circles and good communications between Galatia and the Lycus valley. The kinship of Barnabas and Mark could also explain why Barnabas was so sympathetic to Mark (Acts 15:37-39), or why Mark would have sided with Barnabas and the other Christian Jews at Antioch (Gal. 2:13), and so makes more understandable any part Mark played in the breach between Paul and Barnabas (though Ollrog 47-48 thinks that the positive reference to Mark here calls in question the Acts account).

The parenthetical note regarding Mark ("concerning whom you have received instructions — if he comes to you, receive him") is rather terse and bears a hint of mystery. In Paul the word ἐντολή ("command") almost always refers to divine commands (Rom. 7:8-13; 13:9; 1 Cor. 7:19; 14:37; also Eph. 2:15; 6:2; 1 Tim. 6:14); only here and in Tit. 1:14 is it used of human "commands" or "instructions." It is therefore a surprisingly forceful word to appear at this point (contrast letters of recommendation, as in Acts 18:27 and Rom. 16:1-2). And why should the Colossians need "instructions" ("commands") that they were to welcome Mark (cf. Phm. 21-22)? Would they not have done so for any Christian, particularly one of Paul's associates? Possibly there is a hint in the verb used (δέχομαι, "receive") that there would be some trepidation in the "receiving" of such a person (cf. the other passages in Paul which speak of "receiving" someone — 2 Cor. 7:5; 11:16; Gal. 4:14). There is also the conditional clause ("if he comes to you"), implying that Mark would not be journeying at Paul's behest or as part of Paul's team. In all this there may be sufficient hints that relations had not been entirely easy between Paul and Mark, or perhaps that previous disappointments had not entirely been forgotten and that awareness of this could have made the Colossians more guarded in their welcome than they otherwise would have been (cf. Lightfoot 35; Lohmeyer 167; Martin, Colossians and Philemon 131-32). At the same time it should be remembered that Mark is included in the commendatory words of v. 11 — "fellow workers . . . who have been a comfort for me" — strengthening the hypothesis that reconciliation had (recently?) taken place between the two.

Note also the implication that there had been previous communication regarding Mark — a further indication of a network of communication between the Pauline churches, sustained, no doubt, by travelers and traders as well as by those specifically on Christian business. It would be surprising (to put it no more strongly) if a "historicizing fiction" (Wolter 217) had been quite so pregnant with overtone and implication.

4:11 καὶ Ἰησοῦς ὁ λεγόμενος Ἰοῦστος, οἱ ὄντες ἐκ περιτομῆς, οὗτοι μόνοι συνεργοὶ εἰς τὴν βασιλείαν τοῦ θεοῦ, οἵτινες ἐγενήθησάν μοι παρηγορία. Third of those sending greetings is one "Jesus Justus." The first name is a reminder that "Jesus" (the Greek form of "Joshua") was a familiar name among Jews (cf. Luke 3:29; Matt. 27:16-17 v.l.; Acts 13:6; see further W. Foerster, *TDNT* 3.285-86). The surname, distinguishing this "Jesus" from others, was "Justus," itself a common name regularly borne by Jews and proselytes (Lightfoot 236), which appears as such also in Acts 1:23 (Joseph Barsabbas Justus) and Acts 18:7 (Titius Justus). The use of double names was common (*NDIEC* 1.89-96). We know no more of this man than what is told us here.

These three (Aristarchus, Mark, and Jesus Justus), or perhaps just the latter two (the inclusion of Aristarchus in Acts 20:4 may point to his being a Gentile; so Dibelius, *Kolosser, Epheser, Philemon* 51), are together described as "the ones who are from circumcision" (οἱ ὄντες ἐκ περιτομῆς). Similar phrases occur elsewhere in the Pauline corpus with a hint of menace or at least of hostility (Gal. 2:12; Tit. 1:10). Here it may simply denote Jews, the people marked out by the distinguishing feature of circumcision (see on 2:11), but probably with the hint that "those of the circumcision" were usually active in hostility to Paul's mission.[10] The reference presumably is intended to assure the Colossians that there were such Jews, or at any rate other Jews apart from himself, who, as Jews, were fully approving of and cooperative in the Gentile mission ("fellow workers"), despite, presumably, the disapproval of most of their compatriots (cf. Ollrog 45-46). This point is obscured by those who translate "Jewish Christians" (NEB/REB) or "Jewish converts" (GNB), which suggests that it was something more than their Jewishness which qualified them for mention here (but Paul does *not* say οἱ ὄντες ἐκ περιτομῆς ἐν Χριστῷ). Rather, it is precisely that they can be described as οἱ ὄντες ἐκ περιτομῆς pure and simple which gives the reference its significance.

That the reference is thus made strengthens the likelihood that any threats to the Colossian church's self-understanding came from the Colossian synagogue; why otherwise such a full reference added to them, when the notes added to Luke and Demas (equally "coworkers" in Phm. 24) are so brief (4:14)? And why mention these individuals, less well known to the Colossians, before he mentions their own Epaphras (4:12; contrast Phm. 23-24), unless he wanted to give particular prominence to them precisely because they were Jews? Furthermore, that the reference is made without

10. See particularly E. E. Ellis, "The Circumcision Party and the Early Christian Mission," *Prophecy* 116-28.

any sign of resentment or hostility to "the circumcision" (contrast Gal. 2:12 and Tit. 1:10) equally strengthens the suggestion that the threat from the Colossian synagogue was not at all so forceful as earlier in Galatia, nor was it making such an issue of circumcision as there.

There is a qualification, however. The writer adds: "these alone fellow workers for the kingdom of God" — that is, "these are the only Jews among my fellow workers for the kingdom of God" (NIV). The qualification is not very extensive: it refers only to Paul's "fellow workers" (there were many other Jews who had confessed Jesus as Lord), and since his circle of "co-workers" at previous and other times certainly included other Jews (e.g., Priscilla and Aquila, Timothy and Silvanus: Rom. 16:3, 21; 2 Cor. 1:24),[11] the reference here must be to those presently with him. In fact the immediate circle does not seem to have been very large (six names in 4:10-14), so that the note of evident sadness ("these only") is all the more striking. It under- lines the extent to which Paul was (or was perceived by his immediate circle to be) deeply concerned about the relative failure of his people to accept the gospel of Jesus Christ, and probably still more about the seemingly negative effect of the success of his Gentile mission on his fellow Jews — an echo of old disputes of which we still have record (Gal. 2:11-18; 5:1-12; 6:12-14; 2 Cor. 11:1-23; Phil. 3:2-21). That he could so express himself, without yielding the point that the gospel was as fully for Gentiles as Gentiles as for Jews as Jews, is a reminder of the complexity of Paul's personal involvement in the whole business. Presumably something at least of all this is in mind in the fact that it is just these fellow Jews who are described as having been or become such a "comfort" (παρηγορία, only here in the New Testament; see BAGD; MM; Lohse 173 n. 29) to Paul.

The phrase "(co)worker for the kingdom of God" is quite unusual in the Pauline letters. More typical is the use of the formulaic "inherit the kingdom of God" (1 Cor. 6:9-10; 15:50; Gal. 5:21; cf. Eph. 5:5 and the future references in 1 Thes. 2:12; 2 Thes. 1:5; 2 Tim. 4:1, 18); other pas- sages where the time reference is less clear (Rom. 14:17; 1 Cor. 4:20) are different; it may also be significant that Paul's two years in Rome are summed up in terms of him "testifying to" and "preaching the kingdom of God" (Acts 28:23, 31). The language here, then, could be a sign of another hand, or simply of a concept significant in the Jesus tradition which lent itself to quite diverse formulations; the Jesus tradition itself demon- strated this clearly enough, and, indeed, it may have been the richness of

---

11. On συνεργός ("fellow worker, coworker") see G. Bertram, *TDNT* 7.871-76; Ollrog, particularly 63-72 (also Ollrog in *EDNT* 3.303-4). Lohmeyer 167 sees a certain distancing in the fact that the phrase is "fellow worker for the kingdom of God," not "fellow worker with me," Paul's usual phrase elsewhere (Rom. 16:3, 9, 21; 2 Cor. 1:24; 8:23; Phil. 2:25; 4:3; 1 Thes. 3:2; Phm. 1, 24).

the usage (preserved in the Synoptic tradition) which encouraged the variation here. This suggestion is strengthened by the fact that the phrase is attached specifically to Jewish fellow workers, including one who, according to the Acts tradition, had been closely involved in the early days of the church in Jerusalem (Mark; see on 4:10). Whatever the precise facts, it is significant that Paul and his work can be summed up as "for the kingdom of God"; were it not to be understood as advancing God's purpose and the prospect of his rule, Paul presumably would not have wanted to do it. Also to be noted is the fact that no tension is even hinted at between the idea of "God's kingdom" and that of "the kingdom of his Son" (see on 1:13 and Ladd 509-10).

4:12 ἀσπάζεται ὑμᾶς Ἐπαφρᾶς ὁ ἐξ ὑμῶν, δοῦλος Χριστοῦ [Ἰησοῦ], πάντοτε ἀγωνιζόμενος ὑπὲρ ὑμῶν ἐν ταῖς προσευχαῖς, ἵνα σταθῆτε τέλειοι καὶ πεπληροφορημένοι ἐν παντὶ θελήματι τοῦ θεοῦ. Epaphras is now added to the list of those sending their greetings, mention of him delayed, perhaps, to give greater prominence to Paul's brother Jews (see on 4:11). Once mentioned, however, the commendation flows unstintingly — this despite, or just because, the recipients knew him so well, as one of their own number (perhaps he was a fellow citizen of Colossae), who had first taught them the gospel (see on 1:7). As before, he is described as a "slave," here explicitly of Christ Jesus, one of Paul's favorite self-designations and images of the total commitment involved in his concept of discipleship (see on 1:7), all the more potent an image following the household rules given in 3:22–4:1.

Epaphras's concern for the Colossians echoes that of Paul, the sentiments, indeed, almost a patchwork of Paul's earlier affirmation on his own behalf. He "always" (πάντοτε; 1:3) "wrestles" (ἀγωνιζόμενος; see on 1:29; cf. Phil. 1:30) "on your behalf in prayer" (ὑπὲρ ὑμῶν ἐν ταῖς προσευχαῖς; 1:3, 9) "that you might stand mature" (τέλειοι; see on 1:28) "and fully assured" (καὶ πεπληροφορημένοι; see on 2:2)[12] "in all God's will" (ἐν παντὶ θελήματι τοῦ θεοῦ; see on 1:9). Presumably it was important that their own apostle should be seen by them to share the same concerns for them as Paul himself, though also that the depth and sincerity of his concerns should not exceed that of Paul. The reuse of these earlier phrases and prayer-hopes presumably carries the same echoes as earlier to the threat envisaged as confronting the Colossian community: in particular, that "maturity, perfection" is to be attained by standing firm (σταθῆτε, the aorist passive perhaps suggesting divine enabling; cf. Rom. 14:4) within the Christian group and not by wandering off after other philosophies. Who

---

12. Some favor taking the verb as a synonym for πληρόω (BAGD s.v. πληροφορέω 1), making the parallel with 1:9 rather than with 2:2; see particularly R. P. Martin, *Colossians and Philemon* 133-34; O'Brien, *Colossians, Philemon* 254; the options are listed in Harris 210.

could make this prayer more knowledgeably and more effectively than their own Epaphras (cf. Ernst, *Philipper, Philemon, Kolosser, Epheser* 243-44)?[13]

Despite the fact that the image of Epaphras's concern is drawn on a Pauline template, it should not be doubted that Epaphras was indeed a man of prayer ("prays hard for you," NEB/REB; "never stops battling for you," JB/NJB; cf. Luke 22:44 — ἐν ἀγωνίᾳ) and that the churches he himself had established featured very prominently in his prayers (the classic examples of intercessory prayer in Jewish tradition were Abraham in Genesis 18 and Moses in Exodus 32; see Aletti, *Épître aux Colossiens* 268 n. 25). So, too, it should not be too surprising if Epaphras's hopes for his converts echoed Paul's, since he was himself, presumably, one of Paul's own converts. It is not least in significance that their ambition in both cases was not merely for individuals to be converted, but that they should stand firmly, "mature" (in the context of the letter that will mean also not being distracted by what the local Jews counted important in worship), that there should be an emotional depth and balance to their faith ("fully assured"), and that it should express itself in daily conduct where doing the will of God was the primary objective and yardstick (though REB's "fully determined to do the will of God" is rather free).

4:13 μαρτυρῶ γὰρ αὐτῷ ὅτι ἔχει πολὺν πόνον ὑπὲρ ὑμῶν καὶ τῶν ἐν Λαοδικείᾳ καὶ τῶν ἐν Ἱεραπόλει. Paul could commend Epaphras thus not simply because he knew the quality of Epaphras's spirituality by repute, but because he was himself an eyewitness of it (not least when they shared the same imprisonment? — Phm. 23). The degree of formality in the attestation (the usage rooted in courtroom procedure) adds a note of solemnity to the words ("I testify for him," NRSV). The writer(s) no doubt wished thereby to sustain and boost Epaphras's standing in the eyes of the Colossians, though there is no hint that Epaphras needed to be defended for some failure or loss of authority in the churches of the Lycus valley (Lohmeyer 169; Masson 156 n. 3). Again there is no need to doubt that Epaphras was as deeply concerned for the Colossian Christians as is claimed (almost "under oath"), or that the Colossians would have been heartened by the assurance that they remained so close to Epaphras's heart.

Again like Paul (see on 4:12), Epaphras had put himself to much effort on behalf of the Colossians and those in Laodicea (cf. 2:1). The main difference is the word used (there ἀγών; here πόνος). Both indicate considerable exertion, but in the case of πόνος what is usually in mind is the hard work of battle (classically in Homer; LSJ) or of physical labor, the consequence of the fall from paradise in both Greek (Onesicritus in BAGD) and Jewish thought (Ps. 90:10; Philo, *De opificio mundi* 167; *De legum allegoriae*

---

13. Gnilka, *Kolosserbrief* 240, suggests that not only the gospel but Epaphras himself may have been subjected to attacks by the "false teachers."

3.251; Josephus, *Antiquities* 1.49; *Adam and Eve* 25:1; *Testament of Issachar* 5:5); hence also it has the sense of "pain" (BAGD 2; as in the only other New Testament occurrences: see n. 4; cf. the English idiom "to take pains," BAGD); Aristophanes (*Pax* 1216) uses the same phrase (ἔχει πόνον πολύν) in the sense "involves much trouble" (LSJ). The present tense refers the "labor" to Epaphras's continuing prayers, or perhaps also to work done by Epaphras on the Colossians' behalf (business affairs[14] or ensuring a flow of regular visits by Christian teachers to Colossae); but not his original work of evangelism (since Paul himself had not previously visited the area, he could not speak of personally witnessing Epaphras's work there); nor in the light of the above would πόνος be a natural word to describe the pain of some rift between Epaphras and the Colossians (again Masson 156 n. 3). Whatever the precise reference, we are clearly intended to envisage Epaphras as spending much time and effort in his praying and working on behalf of his townsfolk and of the believers in the cities nearby.

Laodicea had been founded in the middle of the third century BC and came under Roman control as part of the province of Asia in 129. It was a financial, medical (*NDIEC* 3.56), and administrative center and enjoyed considerable prosperity at the beginning of the first century AD, and though it suffered from earthquakes in 17 and 60 it was wealthy enough to reestablish itself on both occasions (as Rev. 3:17 confirms; see also *NDIEC* 3.57-58). Josephus records a letter from the magistrates in Laodicea to the proconsul (dated about 45 BC) confirming the rights of their Jewish residents "to observe their sabbaths and perform their other rites in accordance with their native laws (κατὰ τοὺς πατρίους νόμους)" (*Antiquities* 14:241-43; see also pp. 21f. above and on 2:1).

Hierapolis stood six miles to the north of Laodicea, on the other side of the Lycus, on the road from Laodicea to Philadelphia. The failure to mention Hierapolis in 2:1 and 4:15-16 probably indicates that Epaphras's campaign there had been only partially successful in its early phase (see pp. 20f. and on 2:1). But there is an ancient tradition that sometime before 70, Philip and his daughters settled in Hierapolis; and Papias, an important link between apostolic and postapostolic generations, was bishop of Hierapolis about 125 (see further F. F. Bruce, *ABD* 3.195-96).

4:14 ἀσπάζεται ὑμᾶς Λουκᾶς ὁ ἰατρὸς ὁ ἀγαπητὸς καὶ Δημᾶς. The last two to be included in the list of greetings are Luke and Demas, who again are mentioned together with Epaphras, Mark, and Aristarchus in Phm. 24. Luke is also mentioned on one other occasion in the New Testament, in 2 Tim. 4:11 ("Luke alone is with me"), though there again Mark and Demas (also Tychicus) are named in close proximity (2 Tim. 4:10-12). The

---

14. Scott 90 suggests that it might have been to enlist the sympathy of wealthy Christians to assist their fellow Christians in Colossae who had lost everything in the great earthquake of 60.

present passage contains the only firm information about Luke, that, apart from being a close companion of Paul's (at least during his later imprisonment), and one of Paul's "coworkers" (Phm. 24), he was a doctor. That indicates a man of some learning and training (though at this time medicine was only just becoming a subject of systematic instruction; see *OCD*, "Medicine" 662). And since the title has a favorable ring here (contrast the typical criticism of doctors elsewhere in biblical tradition: 2 Chron. 16:12; Job 13:4; Jer. 46:11; Mark 5:26) we may assume that he was no charlatan but respected for genuine medical knowledge and healing skills. Beyond that we know nothing firm about Luke, though there is of course the long-established tradition that the Luke mentioned here was a regular companion of Paul in the main phase of his missionary work (the "we" passages in Acts) and the author of Luke-Acts (so particularly Eusebius, *Historia Ecclesiastica* 3.4.1-7; 3.24.14-15; 5.8.3; 6.25.6). The same traditions speak of Luke as an Antiochian (3.4.6), and others claim that Paul wrote Hebrews in Hebrew/Aramaic, which Luke then translated into Greek (3.38.2; 6.14.2). He has also been identified with the Lucius of Rom. 16:21 (e.g., Martin, *Colossians and Philemon* 136; but see Lightfoot 239). The note of affection here (ὁ ἀγαπητός, "dear friend" in JB/NJB, NEB/REB, NIV) indicates a closeness of relationship with Paul, a quality of friendship shared with Epaphras, Tychicus, and Onesimus (1:7; 4:7, 9).

In contrast the reference to Demas, a quite common name (BAGD s.v. Δημᾶς; *NDIEC* 1.70, 88-89) is brief, almost curt. It is notable that while the earlier names in the closest parallel list of greetings have some descriptive phrase or comment appended, to personalize what might otherwise be a mere catalogue, the later names lack such elaborations (Rom. 16:14-16). The appropriate inference is that Paul did not know the individuals so· well or feel so close to them. In this case Demas is not even described as "fellow worker" (as in Phm. 24). That all was not well between Paul and Demas is confirmed by one of the sadder personal notes in the Pauline corpus: "Demas, in love with the present world, has deserted me" (2 Tim. 4:10). Of Demas we hear nothing more in Christian tradition.

4:15 ἀσπάσασθε τοὺς ἐν Λαοδικείᾳ ἀδελφοὺς καὶ Νύμφαν καὶ τὴν κατ᾽ οἶκον αὐτῆς ἐκκλησίαν. The attention turns now from those giving the greetings to those to whom the greetings are addressed. That only two are named (Nympha and Archippus), in contrast to the longer list of those sending greetings (six named), is consistent with the information that Paul had never previously visited Colossae. But that there could be such personal contacts again suggests regular movement among the various churches. In particular, it is also assumed here that there were close links between the churches in Laodicea and Colossae (ten miles apart). Not only should there be an exchange of letters between them (4:16), but also, wholly exceptional within the New Testament (Lindemann, *Kolosserbrief*

76), the Colossians should themselves give their own greetings to the Laodiceans. On Laodicea see on v. 14 above and references there; on "brothers" see on 1:1 and p. 43 n. 4.

The only other one singled out for greetings is Nympha (see above, n. 6). Why she should be picked out is unclear. Almost all churches met in private homes for the first two centuries of Christianity's existence (explicitly indicated in Rom. 16:5; 1 Cor. 16:19; Phm. 2, as well as here; see also Acts 2:46; 5:42; 12:12; 16:15, 40; 18:7-8; 20:8, 20; Rom. 16:14-15, 23; *PGL* s.v. οἶκος 4). So there must have been at least one other house church in either Colossae or Laodicea (4:16). Indeed, we know of the church in Philemon's home (Phm. 1-2). This suggests the simple answer that Philemon's home was in Colossae, while Nympha's was in Laodicea.[15] In conveying Paul's greetings to the Laodiceans, the Colossians (consisting of or at least including those in the home church of Philemon) should make a special point of greeting Nympha and her home church ("especially Nympha . . ."; cf. Ignatius, *Polycarp* 8:2). In that case, since Nympha's home church is evidently only part of "the brothers in Laodicea," we have to assume at least one other house church in Laodicea itself (Meeks, *Urban Christians* 143). This suggests, in turn, that of the several (or at least two) churches in Laodicea, Nympha was the only one of the householders personally known to the writer(s); having greeted her personally, it was natural to extend the greeting to the church in her house. It is less likely that Nympha's was the only house church to have remained loyal to Paul, the others having been drawn into "the heresy" (Pokorný 194), since in that case we would have expected a much more vigorous treatment from Paul earlier in Colossians (as in Galatians). Whatever reconstruction of the situation we hazard, however, it remains surprising that there is no greeting to Philemon or to his house church in a letter to the Christians in Colossae; perhaps he was known to be absent on some business (see again pp. 37f. above).

Furthermore, since "the church (as a whole) in Laodicea" is also referred to in 4:16, it is evident that "church" can be used equally for the individual home-meeting and for the Christian community as a whole in a given place, as indeed, it would appear, for the totality of the Christian presence in the world (see on 1:18a). This holds wherever Nympha lived, since Colossae contained at least both the church in Colossae and the church in the home of Philemon. The point is that being "church" consists in believers worshiping and acting together, whether on the microcosmic or on the macrocosmic scale. "Wherever people meet together in the name of

---

15. Gnilka, *Kolosserbrief* 244, 248, suggests that Nympha's house church was in Hierapolis. But why then the different ways of describing the churches in the two cities (why not "the brothers in Hierapolis" or "the church in Hierapolis")? And why is Hierapolis not mentioned in the letter exchange of 4:16?

Jesus, they are a 'church' without the necessity of any quorum at all" (Schweizer, *Colossians* 241). They are "church" by virtue of their partici- pation in the body of Christ, not primarily by virtue of participation in an entity called "the Church (universal)."

Nympha as the named householder must have been either a widow or unmarried; it would hardly have been referred to as "her house" otherwise (see again n. 6 above). Though no doubt legally under the formal responsi- bility of her most significant male relative, she was evidently able to maintain her own household in substantial independence ("her house"). She must therefore have been a person of some means (provided by inheritance) and probably was able to maintain a household (also οἶκος; see BAGD s.v. 2), including personal slaves (Gnilka, *Kolosserbrief* 18-19 [cf. n. 18 below]; cf. 4:1).[16] At all events, her house was large enough to accommodate a meeting ("church") of (some of) the Laodicean believers. Judging by archaeological evidence from cities like Ostia and Pompeii in Italy, a typical well-to-do house could host only about thirty to fifty people (depending on the size of the house) for a meeting held in any comfort, though large villas of the wealthy elite could certainly hold more. We have no way of knowing how large the churches in Colossae and Laodicea were; on any count surprisingly few are named in the greeting (more from than to; contrast Romans 16), and we should recall that "the whole church" in the more important city of Corinth, one of Paul's chief centers of mission, could evidently meet in a single house (Rom. 16:23).[17] Moreover, as the householder and the only one named in connection with the church in her home, Nympha was probably the leader of the church there,[18] or at least she acted as host for the gathering and for the fellowship meal (including on at least some occasions the Lord's Supper). Certainly there is nothing in the New Testament as a whole which would tell against such an inference, though the inference itself is hardly certain (Aletti, *Épître aux Colossiens* 269).

4:16 καὶ ὅταν ἀναγνωσθῇ παρ' ὑμῖν ἡ ἐπιστολή, ποιήσατε ἵνα καὶ ἐν τῇ Λαοδικέων ἐκκλησίᾳ ἀναγνωσθῇ, καὶ τὴν ἐκ Λαοδικείας ἵνα καὶ

16. On women who held prominent positions or who could exercise significant influence during this period see, e.g., Trebilco ch. 5; D. W. J. Gill, "Acts and the Urban Elites," in Gill and Gempf 105-18 (here 114-17).

17. See further P. Stuhlmacher, *Der Brief an Philemon* (EKK; Benziger: Zurich, 1975) 70-75; Banks, *Community,* here particularly 41-43; J. Gnilka, *Der Philemonbrief* (HTKNT 10.4; Freiburg: Herder, 1982) 17-33, particularly 25-33; J. Murphy-O'Connor, *St. Paul's Corinth: Texts and Archeology* (Collegeville: Liturgical, 1983) 164-66. B. Blue, "Acts and the House Church," in Gill and Gempf 119-222, argues that a large house of the period could well accommodate a gathering of one hundred people (175; similarly Ellis, *Pauline Theology* 139-44). For bibliography on the early Christian house churches see Wolter 245-46, but he does not give enough consideration to the question of household furnishings, statuary, and partitions between rooms.

18. So also J. Hainz, *Ekklesia. Strukturen paulinischer Gemeinde-Theologie und Gemeinde-Ordnung* (BU 9; Regensburg: Pustet, 1972) 203; Klauck 45-46; Gnilka, *Theologie* 342.

ὑμεῖς ἀναγνῶτε. The ready implication of a close association between the churches in Colossae and Laodicea (the absence of Hierapolis is again noticeable; see on 4:13) is further strengthened by the next instruction, which gives a valuable insight into the way communication was maintained between Paul and his churches and among his churches. The current letter would be read among the Colossians, that is, read aloud (by Tychicus or Onesimus) at meetings of each of the house churches in Colossae (cf. 1 Thes. 5:27) or perhaps at a single (open-air?) meeting of the whole church called for the purpose (on reading aloud see BAGD s.v. ἀναγινώσκω 2). Without further delay, presumably (the cities were so close that any threat to the church in one would almost certainly be a threat to the other), it should be taken to Laodicea (again by Tychicus or Onesimus?), with the greetings of the Colossians (4:15), and read to a (single) gathering of the Laodicean church. Again presumably on their return, the party from Colossae would bring back a different letter sent initially to the Laodiceans, to be read to the Colossians.

How general was this practice with Paul's letters? We should hesitate to generalize too quickly from the case in point, since the cities of Colossae and Laodicea were so close. Nevertheless, it is significant that a letter written for a particular church should be regarded as of sufficiently wider relevance as to be read elsewhere. That suggests an awareness on the part of the author(s) that Paul's teaching, even in specific letters, was of not merely occasional or passing significance. In other words, we see here already the beginnings of that sense of the letters' importance that thereafter developed over the decades into an acknowledgment of their canonical status. Moreover, we begin to see something of the process by which, presumably, Paul's letters gained growing influence as a group; that is, by increasingly widespread circulation, different letters would not only gain wider recognition but also be put together with other letters. Whether this happened gradually over a period of time or at the initiative and instigation of a single individual we cannot tell. But either way, we gain some sense of how the different churches who owned Paul's influence must have seen themselves as a homogenous group (the Pauline churches) and how the influence of Paul must have continued and come to be embodied in the grouping of letters under his name. Those who saw themselves maintaining and continuing the Pauline tradition (in Ephesians and the Pastorals) presumably played a part in all this which is now impossible for us to reconstruct.

The mention of a letter to Laodicea provokes a further round of speculation. Possibly it was not *to* Laodicea but *from* Laodicea (τὴν ἐκ Λαοδικείας), that is, had been written in Laodicea by someone else. In this case, presumably, it would have been written to Paul; how else would the present writer(s) know about it? Or if it had been written to someone else but was well enough known to be familiar to the writer(s), would it not have already been known to the nearby Colossians? Or if it had been written by

Epaphras (in Laodicea; so Anderson, "Epistle"; Lohse 175 n. 47), would it not be referred to as Epaphras's letter? If, however, it is a letter to Laodicea but viewed (epistolary style) from the perspective of the Colossians, as seems more probable (Dibelius, *Kolosser, Epheser, Philemon* 52; Gnilka, *Kolosser-brief* 245; cf. also BDF §437), then we may assume that it is envisaged as coming likewise from Paul so that he, as author, could determine to whom it should be read.

In that case we have two possibilities. One is that the letter has been lost.[19] That would require us to qualify the reflections of the penultimate paragraph, since it would mean that some of Paul's letters were not valued so highly as to be carefully preserved, unless, that is, the loss was wholly accidental and unavoidable;[20] this seems to have been the case with some of Paul's correspondence with the Corinthian church (1 Cor. 5:9; 2 Cor. 2:3-4). The apocryphal *Letter to the Laodiceans*,[21] known from the fourth century on, was evidently written to make good the gap and was widely regarded as authentic for a thousand years in western Christianity (see C. P. Anderson, *ABD* 4.231-32).

The other possibility is that the letter to or from Laodicea has been preserved under some other name. The most obvious candidate would be Ephesians, so close to Colossians in so many respects. Ephesians was perhaps a circular letter, a letter passed "from" church to church rather than addressed to any one church in particular (Lightfoot 242, 272-98; Dibelius, *Kolosser, Epheser, Philemon* 56-57; others in Bruce, *Colossians, Philemon, and Ephesians* 184 n. 68). Other less plausible candidates include Philemon (Knox, *Philemon* 38-40, 59-61; Schweizer, *Colossians* 241?) and Hebrews.[22]

Either alternative opens up interesting corollaries for our understanding of how the Pauline corpus developed. But unfortunately it is not possible to reach any firm conclusion regarding "the letter from Laodicea."

4:17 καὶ εἴπατε Ἀρχίππῳ· βλέπε τὴν διακονίαν ἣν παρέλαβες ἐν κυρίῳ, ἵνα αὐτὴν πληροῖς. The final message is even more intriguing. Archippus, whose name was common and is attested in western Asia Minor in *CIG* 3143 and 3224 (BAGD), is the only one mentioned among the recipients of both

19. That it is a figment of the post-Pauline author's imagination (Lindemann, *Kolosserbrief* 77) leaves unanswered the question of what purpose such an invented detail would play in the later letter.

20. P. N. Harrison, "Onesimus and Philemon," *ATR* 32 (1950) 268-94, suggested that the letter may have been destroyed in the earthquake which seriously damaged the cities of the Lycus valley in 60.

21. It can be consulted in Lightfoot 285-97; Kiley 27-32; W. Schneemelcher, ed., *New Testament Apocrypha*, vol. 2 (Cambridge: James Clarke/Louisville: Westminster/John Knox, [2]1992) 42-46; J. K. Elliott, ed., *The Apocryphal New Testament* (Oxford: Clarendon, 1993) 543-46.

22. C. P. Anderson, "Hebrews among the Letters of Paul," *Studies in Religion* 5 (1975) 258-66. But see already Lightfoot 272-79.

Colossians and Philemon (Phm. 2). In the latter he appears to have been a member of Philemon's household, perhaps his son (a suggestion that goes back to Theodore of Mopsuestia; see Lightfoot 306 n. 7; Dibelius, *Kolosser, Epheser, Philemon* 103), and is described as Paul's "fellow soldier," as was Epaphroditus in Phil. 2:25. In other words, Archippus battled alongside in what Paul elsewhere describes as a war against spiritual opposition (2 Cor. 7:5; 10:3). That presumably indicates that Archippus shared in Paul's missionary work as one of his team (in Phil. 2:25 Epaphroditus is also described as a "fellow worker"), and presumably in some of the more challenging campaigns (hence the stronger metaphor; see further on Phm. 2).

What the present verse adds, however, is unclear. Archippus had evidently been given some special task. Διακονία can clearly be used of a particular act of "service" (cf. Rom. 12:7b; 15:31; 1 Cor. 12:5; 16:15; 2 Cor. 8:4; 9:1, 12-13; 2 Cor. 11:8; 2 Tim. 4:11), as well as the more sustained "ministry" (Rom. 11:13; 2 Cor. 4:1; 5:18; 6:3; 1 Tim. 1:12; 2 Tim. 4:5) of one who is counted a διάκονος, though there is general agreement that διακονία cannot yet have gained the technical sense of "diaconate" (see on 1:7). Here the former sense is evidently in mind, since it is a service which needed to be "fulfilled" (πληροῖς), that is, fully carried out (NEB/REB), brought to completion (NIV, NRSV, GNB). Like all Christian service in Paul's eyes διακονία was both gift (Rom. 12:7; 1 Cor. 12:5) and commission from the Lord Christ (the repetition of παραλαμβάνω makes an interesting and probably deliberate *inclusio* with 2:6).

What Archippus's commission was we cannot tell — perhaps a difficult or sensitive task which only he and Paul knew about (cf. Acts 19:22). Whether it implies that Archippus was the owner of Onesimus (Knox, "Philemon" 153; *Philemon* 49-51) depends on what we make of Phm. 1-2. The possibility that it had to do with the collection (W. Michaelis in Dibelius, *Kolosser, Epheser, Philemon* 53) depends on the dating of Colossians, and elsewhere Paul is hardly so coy on the subject. And why Paul would be so enigmatic, alternatively, about a commission to preach (O'Brien, *Colossians, Philemon* 259), to teach (Wright, *Colossians and Philemon* 161-62), or to take up Epaphras's role (Gnilka, *Kolosserbrief* 246) is unclear. At all events, Archippus seems to have been unwilling or unable (for some reason) to carry it through. That the whole community (all the recipients) have the responsibility of recalling Archippus to his task (particularly if he was a member of an important household in the community) conforms to Paul's concept of mutual responsibility and shared authority within the community, to which all, including the more important members, are to be subject (cf. particularly 3:16 and 1 Thes. 5:20-21; see further my *Jesus* 291-93). The character of the request, coming just before the personally written final phrases, makes its invention by a pseudonymous author less plausible and strengthens the impression that Paul himself was standing directly behind the letter.

A Final, Personal Greeting (4:18)

18 *The greeting, in my own hand, of Paul. Remember my fetters. Grace be with you.*

4:18 ὁ ἀσπασμὸς τῇ ἐμῇ χειρὶ Παύλου. μνημονεύετέ μου τῶν δεσμῶν. ἡ χάρις μεθ᾽ ὑμῶν. As was his custom in other letters, Paul ends the letter by appending a personal note in his own hand, a practice more widely attested in papyri letters.[1] The brevity in this case and its cramped character (contrast 1 Cor. 16:21-24; Gal. 6:11-18; 2 Thes. 3:17-18) suggest that it was added under difficult circumstances, when such a telegraphic note was all that he could (or was allowed to) contribute.

The first phrase is precisely that also used in 1 Cor. 16:21 and 2 Thes. 3:17 (otherwise Paul never so refers to himself by name in the conclusions to his letters). In 2 Thes. 3:17 it is explicitly presented as a mark of authentication (which adds an important twist to the issue of the pseudonymity of 2 Thessalonians), and presumably the phrase carries something of the same weight here. As such it must count in favor of the view that Paul himself actually held the stylus for these final words (see also on Phm. 19). At all events it reinforces the effect of the letter in providing a real substitute for the personal presence of the one absent (Aletti, *Épître aux Colossiens* 271).

The second phrase has a particular poignancy, reminding the Colossians that the letter had been sent by one held not simply in confinement but in shackles; perhaps it was the fetters themselves which made it difficult for Paul to add more than this brief scrawl.[2] The request was not simply for their pity but for an active concern, which would certainly include their prayers, but also might involve sending some support back to Paul, whether financial (cf. Gal. 2:10) or personal (as the Philippians sent Epaphroditus, Phil. 4:14-18). At the same time, it would add great weight to what he had written, the words of those who suffer for their beliefs, and particularly the last words of martyrs, being generally invested with greater significance for partisans of the same cause (cf. Moule, *Colossians and Philemon* 139; Martin, *Colossians and Philemon* 141; but see also O'Brien, *Colossians, Philemon* 260).

The final phrase is most characteristically and consistently Pauline in calling on God's grace to be with the Colossians (see the introduction to

---

1. A. Deissmann, *Light from the Ancient East* (New York: Doran, 1927) 170-72. Bruce, *Colossians, Philemon, and Ephesians* 186 n. 79, also notes that when Cicero used an amanuensis he indicated that the end of the letter was in his own hand ("hoc manu mea," *Ad Atticum* 13.28); see further Bahr 466-67; Richards 76-90; Weima 45-50 (with further bibliography 45 n. 3). For the possibility of literary activity while in prison see Rapske 342-46.

2. For what it meant to be held in manacles see Rapske 25-28, 31 and 206-9; on the varieties of custody in the Roman world see Rapske ch. 2.

4:7-18 and on Phm. 25; for χάρις see on 1:2). At the same time the phrase here is much more abrupt than any of its precedents: it usually has a fuller form like "the grace of our Lord Jesus be with you," and often with some other slight elaboration; only 1 and 2 Timothy copy the abruptness of Colossians. Again the brevity and the failure to follow Paul's normal practice of citing the title of Christ with its liturgical resonance strongly suggest that the words here were penned under considerable difficulty, so that only the most basic benediction could be given. If these were the final words which Paul himself wrote, as may well be the case, at least in full letter form, it is fitting that they focus in the word which so much expressed the heart of his gospel: "Grace be with you."

PHILEMON

BIBLIOGRAPHY

Commentaries

Bieder, W., *Der Philemonbrief* (Zurich: Zwingli, 1944)

Binder, H., *Der Brief des Paulus an Philemon* (THNT 11/2; Berlin: Evangelische, 1990)

Bruce, F. F., *The Epistles to the Colossians, to Philemon, and to the Ephesians* (NICNT; Grand Rapids: Eerdmans, 1984) = revision of (with E. K. Simpson), *Commentary on the Epistles to the Ephesians and Colossians* (NICNT; Grand Rapids: Eerdmans, 1958)

Caird, G. B., *Paul's Letters from Prison* (NCB; Oxford University, 1976)

Carson, H. M., *The Epistles of Paul to the Colossians and to Philemon* (TNTC; Grand Rapids: Eerdmans/London: Tyndale, 1960)

Collange, J.-F., *L'Épître de Saint Paul à Philémon* (CNT 11; Geneva: Labor et Fides, 1987)

Dibelius, M., *An die Kolosser, Epheser, an Philemon*, revised by H. Greeven (HNT 12; Tübingen: Mohr, [3]1953)

Ernst, J., *Die Briefe an die Philipper, an Philemon, an die Kolosser, an die Epheser* (RNT; Regensburg: Pustet, 1974)

Friedrich, G., "Der Brief an Philemon," in *Die kleineren Briefe des Apostels Paulus* (NTD 8; Göttingen: Vandenhoeck, [10]1965) 188-96

Gnilka, J., *Der Philemonbrief* (HTKNT 10/4; Freiburg: Herder, 1982)

Harris, M. J., *Colossians and Philemon* (EGGNT; Grand Rapids: Eerdmans, 1991)

Houlden, J. L., *Paul's Letters from Prison* (Harmondsworth: Penguin, 1970)

Leuken, W., "Die Briefe an Philemon, an die Kolosser und an die Epheser," *Die Schriften des Neuen Testaments*, Band II (Göttingen: Vandenhoeck, [3]1917) 339-58

Lightfoot, J. B., *The Epistles of St Paul: Colossians and Philemon* (London: Macmillan, 1875)

Lohmeyer, E., *Die Briefe an die Philipper, an die Kolosser und an Philemon* (KEK 9; Göttingen: Vandenhoeck, [13]1964)

Lohse, E., *Colossians and Philemon* (Hermeneia; Philadelphia: Fortress, 1971) = *Die Briefe an die Kolosser und an Philemon* (KEK 9/2; Göttingen: Vandenhoeck, 1968)

Martin, R. P., *Colossians and Philemon* (NCBC; London: Oliphants, 1974)

Metzger, B. M., *A Textual Commentary on the Greek New Testament* (London: United Bible Societies, [2]1975)

Moule, C. F. D., *The Epistles of Paul the Apostle to the Colossians and to Philemon* (CGT; Cambridge University, 1957)

Müller, J. J., *The Epistles of Paul to the Philippians and to Philemon* (NICNT; Grand Rapids: Eerdmans, 1955)

O'Brien, P. T., *Colossians, Philemon* (WBC 44; Waco: Word, 1982)

Radford, L. B., *The Epistle to the Colossians and the Epistle to Philemon* (WC; London: Methuen, 1931)

Schlatter, A., *Die Briefe an die Galater, Epheser, Kolosser und Philemon* (Erläuterungen zum NT 7; Stuttgart: Calwer, 1963)

Schmauch, W., *Beiheft* to Lohmeyer (KEK; Göttingen: Vandenhoeck, 1964)

Scott, E. F., *The Epistle of Paul to the Colossians, to Philemon and to the Ephesians* (MNTC; London: Hodder, 1930)

Stuhlmacher, P., *Der Brief an Philemon* (EKK; Zurich: Benziger, 1975)

Suhl, A., *Der Philemonbrief* (ZBK; Zurich: Theologische Verlag, 1981)

Vincent, M. R., *The Epistles to the Philippians and to Philemon* (ICC; Edinburgh: Clark, 1897)

Wall, R. W., *Colossians and Philemon* (Leicester and Downers Grove: Inter-Varsity, 1993)

Williams, A. L., *The Epistle of Paul the Apostle to the Colossians and to Philemon* (CGT; Cambridge University, 1907)

Wolter, M., *Der Brief an die Kolosser. Der Brief an Philemon* (ÖTKNT 12; Gütersloh: Gerd Mohn, 1993)

Wright, N. T., *The Epistles of Paul to the Colossians and to Philemon* (TNTC; Grand Rapids: Eerdmans/Leicester: Inter-Varsity, 1986)

Other Literature

Allen, D. L., "The Discourse Structure of Philemon: A Study in Text Linguistics," in *Scribes and Scriptures: New Testament Essays in Honor of J. Harold Greenlee*, ed. D. A. Black (Winona Lake: Eisenbrauns, 1992) 77-96.

Barclay, J. M. G., "Paul, Philemon and the Dilemma of Christian Slave-Ownership," *NTS* 37 (1991) 161-86

Bartchy, S. S., ΜΑΛΛΟΝ ΧΡΗΣΑΙ: *First-Century Slavery and the Interpretation of 1 Corinthians 7:21* (SBLDS 11; Missoula: Scholars, 1973)

Bellen, H., *Studien zur Sklavenflucht im römischen Kaiserreich* (Forschungen zur antiken Sklaverei 4; Wiesbaden: Steiner, 1971)

Birdsall, J. N., " 'Πρεσβύτης' in Philemon 9: A Study in Conjectural Emendation," *NTS* 39 (1993) 625-30

Bjerkelund, C. J., *Parakalô: Form, Funktion und Sinn der parakalô-Sätze in den paulinischen Briefen* (Oslo: Universitetsforlaget, 1967)

Bruce, F. F., *Paul: Apostle of the Free Spirit* (Exeter: Paternoster, 1977) = *Paul: Apostle of the Heart Set Free* (Grand Rapids: Eerdmans, 1977)

———, "St. Paul in Rome II: The Epistle to Philemon," *BJRL* 48 (1965-66) 81-97

Buckland, W. W., *The Roman Law of Slavery: The Condition of the Slave in Private Law from Augustus to Justinian* (Cambridge: Cambridge University, 1908; reprinted 1970)

Callahan, A. D., "Paul's Epistle to Philemon: Toward an Alternative *Argumentum*," *HTR* 86 (1993) 357-76

Church, F. F., "Rhetorical Structure and Design in Paul's Letter to Philemon," *HTR* 71 (1978) 17-33

Coleman-Norton, P. R., "The Apostle Paul and the Roman Law of Slavery," in *Studies in Roman Economic and Social History*, A. C. Johnson FS, ed. P. R. Coleman-Norton (Princeton: Princeton University, 1951) 155-77

Daube, D., "Onesimus," *HTR* 79 (1986) 40-43

Derrett, J. D. M., "The Functions of the Epistle to Philemon," *ZNW* 79 (1988) 63-91

Doty, W. G., *Letters in Primitive Christianity* (Philadelphia: Fortress, 1973)

Elliott, J. H., "Philemon and House Churches," *The Bible Today* 22 (1984) 145-50

Feeley-Harnik, G., "Is Historical Anthropology Possible? The Case of the Runaway Slave," in *Humanizing America's Iconic Book, Biblical Scholarship in North America* vol. 6 (Chico: Scholars, 1982) 95-126

Filson, F. V., "The Significance of the Early House Churches," *JBL* 58 (1939) 105-12

Gayer, R., *Die Stellung des Sklaven in den paulinischen Gemeinden und bei Paulus. Zugleich ein sozialgeschichtlich vergleichender Beitrag zur Wertung des Sklaven in der Antike* (Bern: Lang, 1976)

Getty, M. A., "The Theology of Philemon," in *SBLSP 1987* (Atlanta: Scholars, 1987) 503-8

Goodenough, E. R., "Paul and Onesimus," *HTR* 22 (1929) 181-83

Greeven, H., "Prüfung der Thesen von J. Knox zum Philemonbrief," *TLZ* 79 (1954) 373-78

Gülzow, H., *Christentum und Sklaverei in den ersten drei Jahrhunderten* (Bonn: Habelt, 1969)

Hahn, F., "Paulus und der Sklave Onesimus," *EvTh* 37 (1977) 179-85

Hainz, J., *Ekklesia. Strukturen paulinischer Gemeinde-Theologie und Gemeinde-Ordnung* (BU 9; Regensburg: Pustet, 1972) 199-209

Harrison, P. N., "Onesimus and Philemon," *ATR* 32 (1950) 268-94

Jang, L. K., *Der Philemonbrief im Zusammenhang mit dem theologischen Denken des Apostels Paulus* (diss., Bonn, 1964)

Kim, C.-H., *Form and Structure of the Familiar Greek Letter of Recommendation* (SBLDS 4; Missoula: Scholars, 1972)

Knox, J., *Philemon among the Letters of Paul* (Nashville: Abingdon, [2]1959/London: Collins, [2]1960)

Koester, H., *Introduction to the New Testament*. Vol. 2: *History and Literature of Early Christianity* (Philadelphia: Fortress, 1982)

Lampe, P., "Keine 'Sklavenflucht' des Onesimus," *ZNW* 76 (1985) 135-37

Laub, F., *Die Begegnung des frühen Christentums mit der antiken Sklaverei* (SBS 107; Stuttgart: KBW, 1982)

Lehmann, R., *Épître à Philémon: Le Christianisme primitif et l'esclavage* (Geneva: Labor et Fides, 1978)

Lührmann, D., "Wo man nicht mehr Sklave oder Freier ist," *WD* 13 (1975) 53-83

Lyall, F., "Roman Law in the Writings of Paul: The Slave and the Freedman," *NTS* 17 (1970-71) 73-79

Marshall, I. H. and Donfried, K., *The Theology of the Shorter Pauline Letters* (Cambridge: Cambridge University, 1993)

Martin, D. B., *Slavery as Salvation: The Metaphor of Slavery in Pauline Christianity* (New Haven: Yale University, 1990)

Martin, C. J., "The Rhetorical Function of Commercial Language in Paul's Letter to Philemon (Verse 18)," in *Persuasive Artistry: Studies in New Testament Rhetoric in Honor of George A. Kennedy,* ed. D. Watson (JSNTS 50; Sheffield: JSOT, 1991) 321-37.

Meeks, W. A., *The First Urban Christians: The Social World of the Apostle Paul* (New Haven: Yale University, 1983)

Merk, O., *Handeln aus Glauben. Die Motivierungen der paulinischen Ethik* (Marburg: Elwert, 1968)

Moule, C. F. D., *An Idiom-Book of New Testament Greek* (Cambridge: Cambridge University, [2]1959)

Nordling, J. G., "Onesimus Fugitivus: A Defense of the Runaway Slave Hypothesis in Philemon," *JSNT* 41 (1991) 97-119

O'Brien, P. T., *Introductory Thanksgivings in the Letters of Paul* (NovTSup 49; Leiden: Brill, 1977)

Ollrog, W.-H., *Paulus und seine Mitarbeiter* (WMANT 50; Neukirchen: Neukirchener, 1979)

Olson, S. N., "Pauline Expressions of Confidence in His Addressees," *CBQ* 47 (1985) 282-95

Petersen, N. R., *Rediscovering Paul: Philemon and the Sociology of Paul's Narrative World* (Philadelphia: Fortress, 1985)

Preiss, T., *Life in Christ* (London: SCM, 1954)

Rapske, B. M., "The Prisoner Paul in the Eyes of Onesimus," *NTS* 37 (1991) 187-203

Richardson, W. J., "Principle and Context in the Ethics of the Epistle to Philemon," *Int* 22 (1968) 301-16

Riesenfeld, H., "Faith and Love Promoting Hope: An Interpretation of Philemon v 6," in *Paul and Paulinism,* C. K. Barrett FS, ed. M. D. Hooker and S. G. Wilson (London: SPCK, 1982) 251-57

Sampley, J. P., *Pauline Partnership in Christ: Christian Community and Commitment in Light of Roman Law* (Philadelphia: Fortress, 1980)

————, "Societas Christi: Roman Law and Paul's Conception of the Christian Community," in *God's Christ and His People*, N. A. Dahl FS, ed. J. Jervell and W. A. Meeks (Oslo: Universitetsforlaget, 1977) 158-74

Schenk, W., "Der Brief des Paulus an Philemon in der neueren Forschung (1945-87)," *ANRW* 2.25.4 (1987) 3439-95

Schubert, P., *Form and Function of the Pauline Thanksgivings* (BZNW 20; Berlin: Töpelmann, 1939)

Schulz, S., *Neutestamentliche Ethik* (Zurich: Theologischer, 1987)

Schweizer, E., "Zum Sklavenproblem im Neuen Testament," *EvTh* 32 (1972) 502-6

Stowers, S. K., *Letter Writing in Greco-Roman Antiquity* (Philadelphia: Westminster, 1986)

Suhl, A., "Der Philemonbrief als Beispiel paulinischer Paränese," *Kairos* 15 (1973) 267-79

Weima, J. A. D., *Neglected Endings: The Significance of the Pauline Letter Closings* (JSNTS 101; Sheffield: JSOT, 1994)

Westermann, W. L., *The Slave Systems of Greek and Roman Antiquity* (Philadelphia: American Philosophical Society, 1955)

White, J. L., "The Structural Analysis of Philemon: A Point of Departure in the Formal Analysis of the Pauline Letter," *SBLSP* 1971 (Society of Biblical Literature, 1971) 1-47

Wickert, U., "Der Philemonbrief — Privatbrief oder apostolisches Schreiben?" *ZNW* 52 (1961) 230-38

Wiedemann, T., *Greek and Roman Slavery* (Baltimore: Johns Hopkins University/London: Croom Helm, 1981)

Wiles, G. P., *Paul's Intercessory Prayers* (SNTSMS 24; Cambridge: Cambridge University, 1974)

Wilson, A., "The Pragmatics of Politeness and Pauline Epistolography: A Case Study of the Letter to Philemon," *JSNT* 48 (1992) 107-19

Winter, S. C., "Methodological Observations on a New Interpretation of Paul's Letter to Philemon," *USQR* 39 (1984) 203-12

————, "Paul's Letter to Philemon," *NTS* 33 (1987) 1-15

Zmijewski, J., "Beobachtungen zur Struktur des Philemonbriefes," *BibLeb* 15 (1974) 273-96

INTRODUCTION

The letter to Philemon is unique within the New Testament. It is the only genuinely personal, that is, person-to-person, letter, even though the wider community is also in view (explicitly in vv. 2, 22, and 25 and in the background throughout). In contrast, the other New Testament letters are to churches as such, or consist of general exhortations, instructions, or a treatise dressed up as a letter. More important, Philemon provides insight both into the social realities of ancient society, in this case the relations between master and slave, which is surpassed only by 1 Corinthians, and into the way in which influence was brought to bear within the earliest churches between parties of differing social status.

THE AUTHOR

In the history of Christianity there have been no serious considerations brought against the letter's assertion that it was written by Paul (v. 1). To be sure, that it focuses on such an insignificant little episode from the great apostle's ministry made for its devaluation in the eyes of some in the early church, particularly in the fourth century. Apart from anything else, what relevance was it to the great theological debates of the period? To include it in the emerging canon would seem to give that episode a wholly disproportionate importance (Lightfoot 314-15; Callahan 365-67). Similar devaluation lies behind the only serious attack on its authenticity in modern times, by F. C. Baur (see, e.g., Vincent 159-60; Bruce, *Paul* 394-96).

Apart from such tendentious considerations, however, the authorship of Paul has been more or less universally accepted — and properly so. The style and vocabulary, as judged particularly by the opening and closing (vv. 1-7, 21-25), are characteristically Pauline, and overall the degree of variation lies well within the diversity of Paul's epistolary practice as attested by the undisputed letters.[1] That it is the only truly personal letter which we have from Paul and that the subject matter is so unique within the Pauline corpus

---

1. See particularly Schenk 3442-45; summary in S. S. Bartchy, *ABD* 5.306.

say nothing to the contrary: if we were to attempt to craft a person-to-person Pauline letter on the basis of what we know of his other letters, we might well end up with something like this; there is nothing in the letter which sets alarm bells ringing in the minds of those most familiar with Paul's manner of handling tricky situations elsewhere. Moreover, reasons for a later pseudepigrapher to bother to invent a letter of this sort and pass it off as Paul's are hard to imagine. In contrast, the only reason why a letter of such limited application should be retained as Paul's was that it was by Paul (Caird 213). The masterly blend of appeal and demand which is such a striking feature of the letter would be astonishingly artful if not by Paul himself; a letter written later to enhance Paul's authority (or that of Onesimus) would surely have been more forceful (on Onesimus see pp. 302ff. below and on v. 10). And the earliest testimony simply takes Paul's authorship for granted (see, e.g., Vincent 159).

We may be confident, therefore, that Philemon was authored by Paul, elsewhere so well known to current and later generations as the (Jewish) apostle to the Gentiles. Some indeed think that Philemon is also unique as having been entirely written by hand by Paul (see p. 343 n. 1 below), but it is more likely that the ἔγραψα indicates in v. 19 a few words written by Paul and in v. 21 Paul's normal habit of rounding off his letters in his own hand (see further the introduction to the comments on vv. 8-20 and on v. 19).

THE RECIPIENT

It is equally clear that the recipient was one person, Philemon (see on v. 1). What we can deduce about him is straightforward:

(1) He was well-to-do. He had a house large enough to host the church in the city where he lived (v. 2) and to provide a guest room (probably more than one; see on v. 22). He was a slaveowner, and we must assume owner of several slaves; had Onesimus been his only slave that would surely have been reflected in some way in what Paul says. On the relation to Philemon of Apphia and Archippus, see on v. 2.

(2) The inference is almost universal[2] that his home was in Colossae, primarily on the assumption that the Onesimus of v. 10, Philemon's (former) slave, is the Onesimus of Col. 4:9, who was so well known in Colossae

---

2. The suggestion that Philemon actually lived in Laodicea depends on the implausible hypothesis of Knox (followed by Winter, "Letter") that the master of Onesimus was Archippus and that the letter to Laodicea referred to in Col. 4:16 was none other than Philemon (see, e.g., the critiques of Greeven 375-78; Lohse 186-87; Bruce, *Colossians, Philemon, and Ephesians* 199-200; and Wright 165; see also below, p. 313 n. 6). Schenk 3482-83 surprisingly argues for Pergamon as the location of the addressees, chiefly on the grounds of correlation between v. 22 and 2 Cor. 1:8 and 2:12.

("one of yourselves"). The point is complicated by the issue of Pauline authorship of Colossians (see pp. 35ff. above), but not necessarily weakened. On Colossae see pp. 20ff. above.

(3) He was probably a successful businessman (see vv. 17 and 18), and he must have traveled from his home (presumably on business) to where he had encountered Paul, most likely in not too far distant Ephesus (v. 19).[3]

(4) He had been converted through Paul's ministry, though not necessarily in an immediately direct way (see on v. 19), and was close to Paul (ἀγαπητός; see on v. 1), presumably having spent at least some time in his company.

(5) He is also described as one of Paul's "fellow workers" (see on v. 1) and "partner" (see on v. 17). This must mean that Philemon was able to take time off from his business affairs to join Paul in his evangelistic work or in the business of maintaining communication with the churches thus established. In other words, though wealthy, he did not stay in the background content with a patronal role, but involved himself in the organizing of the mission and/or the churches (cf. Phoebe, Prisca, and Aquila in Rom. 16:1-5).

(6) We should probably infer that he was leader of the church which met in his home (see on v. 2). Since he was a successful businessman his experience and "know-how" must have been of considerable value to the infant church in Colossae (see also vv. 5 and 7). It says much for the relations within that church, that is, between Philemon and the other members in particular, that Paul should expect the letter to be read to the church as a whole (note the plurals in vv. 3, 22, and 25), a factor which influences the character of the whole appeal. "Although he is directly addressed, it is not as a private person that he is appealed to and petitioned" (Ollrog 104).[4]

THE OCCASION

It is clear that the letter's primary object is to intercede with Philemon on behalf of Philemon's slave Onesimus (see v. 16), himself from Colossae (according to Col. 4:9). A possible subsidiary reason is that Philemon himself needed to be boosted in the eyes of his church, since the departure of Onesimus may have suggested to some that Philemon was a cruel master (Lehmann 30); on the other hand, the praise bestowed on Philemon is not wholly out of line with Paul's practice in other letters and is consistent with

---

3. Despite Col. 2:1, Binder 31-32 thinks Paul may himself have been the founder of the church in Colossae, at which time he converted Philemon.

4. Winter, "Observations" 206, and "Letter" 1-2, argues that the letter is addressed to the church and is not a personal letter, but ignores the fact that a singular second person is sustained throughout the letter, including the thanksgiving and prayer (vv. 4-7) and the climactic request (vv. 21-22a).

the primary task of conciliating Philemon (see on vv. 4-7). Another possible reason is that the letter would also make clear to any authorities who made inquiry regarding the little *collegium* in the house of Philemon that it did not harbor or favor runaway slaves (Derrett); but that depends on the view that Onesimus was a runaway (see below).

That he was a slave tells us little about Onesimus himself.[5] Slavery was an established fact of life in the ancient world, and as many as a third of the inhabitants of most large urban centers would have been slaves. Onesimus was quite probably born into slavery: by this time children of women in slavery had become the primary source of slaves;[6] and the name Onesimus was common for slaves (see on v. 10). Another possibility is that he was sold (or sold himself) into slavery because of unpaid debt (see, e.g., Bartchy 45-49), but that would give a twist to the saga reflected in the letter which we might in that case expect to be hinted at in some way in the letter. Furthermore, we know that Phrygian slaves were notoriously unsatisfactory (see on v. 11). Yet we also know that slaves could be well educated, and if their masters were figures of substantial social significance and power, the slaves themselves could be entrusted with considerable responsibility in turn.[7] The fact that Onesimus had gained such a large place in Paul's affections and proved so useful to him (vv. 11-13; also Col. 4:9) suggests that he was a man of some ability. However, it may not matter much that we know so little about Onesimus himself; what the letter reveals as a witness to an early Christian attitude to slavery is not dependent on fuller knowledge on how Onesimus became a slave.

It is also clear that Onesimus had wronged his master in some way. The key verse here is 18, but it remains tantalizingly obscure. Since a slave had no legal rights, any matter in which Onesimus had denied Philemon his rights to use Onesimus's energies could be regarded as Onesimus acting unjustly toward Philemon (ἠδίκησεν). He was also financially in debt to

---

5. For what follows and on slavery more generally in the Greco-Roman world see the concise treatments of M. I. Finley, *OCD* 994-96; Gnilka 54-61; Barclay 165-70; and Bartchy, *ABD* 6.65-73; valuable documentation has been collected by Wiedemann. For more detailed and wide-ranging studies see Buckland; Westermann; M. I. Finley, ed., *Slavery in Classical Antiquity: Views and Controversies* (Cambridge: Heffer, 1960); and J. C. Dumont, *Servus: Rome et l'Esclavage sous la République* (Rome: École française, 1987). And for Asia Minor see E. S. Golubcova, "Sklaverei und Abhängigkeitsfirmen in Kleinasien," in *Die Sklaverei in den östlichen Provinzen des römischen Reiches im 1-3. Jahrhundert*, ed. L. P. Marinovic, et al. (Stuttgart: Steiner, 1992).

6. See, e.g., Buckland 397-400; Westermann 84-87, though this generalization needs careful qualification, as most recently by E. Hermann-Otto, *Ex Ancilla Natus: Untersuchungen zu den "Hausgeborenen" Sklaven und Sklavinnen im Westen des römischen Kaiserreiches* (Stuttgart: Steiner, 1994).

7. See D. B. Martin, *Slavery as Salvation* ch. 1. Everything we hear of Onesimus indicates that he was an urban household slave rather than a rural slave (on the distinction see Wiedemann 122).

Philemon (ὀφείλει), which most likely indicates robbery or embezzlement of funds entrusted to him.[8] It should be recalled, however, that Onesimus's physical removal of himself from Philemon's household would itself constitute an act of robbery, since as a slave he was technically Philemon's property (a stealer of himself, *Digest* 47.2.61) and since purchase of a slave could be a substantial investment (Binder 34; *NDIEC* 6.57; see further on v. 18).

The greatest unclarity lies over how Onesimus and Paul came together. Most envisage Onesimus fleeing from his master's house and heading for Ephesus (less than a week's journey away by foot) or, making use of his ill-gotten gains, for Rome (the capital city of the empire being better to hide in; so Lightfoot 310).[9] Once there, various scenarios could be imagined leading up to his first encounter with Paul. The most obvious would be through contacts he made once in Ephesus or Rome. That Onesimus, as a runaway slave guilty of robbery, was willing to meet Paul, however, would imply an interest in Paul or the Christian message already before their first encounter. Otherwise it would have been more sensible to seek asylum at some temple, such as the large temple dedicated to Artemis in Ephesus (cf. Acts 19:23-41), in the hope that the priests would act for him, in accordance with recognized custom.[10] More important, such an encounter resulting in Onesimus's conversion would surely have brought forth some expression of regret and repentance from Onesimus. In that case it is astonishing that Paul says nothing of it in his letter (contrast Pliny's letter to Sabinianus, cited below).[11]

The chief alternative scenario, that Onesimus had also been arrested and put in prison where he met Paul (e.g., Binder 35), raises more questions

8. Typical are Goodenough 183 ("this shrewd and peculating slave") and Gülzow 31 ("a hand in his master's till before his flight"); see also on v. 18. In contrast, Winter, "Letter" 2-5, ignores the clear allusion to *past* wrong and the weighty legal language of vv. 18-19, arguing that Onesimus had been sent to Paul in prison on behalf of the Colossian church (like Epaphroditus in Phil. 2:25; cf. Bruce, *Colossians, Philemon, and Ephesians* 197; Schenk 3466-75). As Barclay 164 notes, however, a non-Christian regarded by his master as "useless" "is hardly the sort of person whom Philemon or his church would commission to serve or assist Paul" (similarly Rapske 188-89).

9. For examples of the common problem of runaway slaves see Moule, *Colossians and Philemon* 34-37; Wiedemann 192; Nordling 99-106; *NDIEC* 1.140-41; 4.97; 6.55-60, 101-4. On the subject as a whole see Bellen.

10. See particularly Bellen 64-78 (summarized in Gnilka 71); examples also in Gülzow 32-35; Wiedemann 195-97. Cf. the earlier suggestion of Goodenough, developed by Bruce, *Paul* 400 (cf. Preiss 35), that Paul's hearth could be regarded as a legitimate place of asylum, now decisively critiqued by Rapske 193-95 (how could Paul's situation allow him to shelter a *fugitivus* or his commitment as a Christian allow him to claim that his hearth was an altar?).

11. The contrast was already observed by Knox 15-18, and lies at the root of his dissatisfaction with the runaway slave (*fugitivus*) hypothesis. Failure to meet this point (only partially met by Richardson 302-3; contrast 2 Cor. 2:7) is the principal weakness of Nordling's restatement of the "Onesimus *fugitivus*" hypothesis.

than it solves. What were the circumstances of Paul's imprisonment which would make such an encounter possible? If Paul was under loose "house arrest," a runaway slave certainly would not have been. And if both shared a more severe imprisonment, how could Paul, himself a prisoner, "send" a runaway back to Colossae (v. 12; Col. 4:8-9; see also Gayer 231-32; Rapske 191-92)?

In either case Onesimus's status as a fugitive slave *(fugitivus)* would put him very seriously in the wrong with Philemon, so that Paul's reference to it in the "if" clause of v. 18 would appear to be treating the matter rather lightly. And Paul, too, if he had in effect harbored a fugitive slave, had put himself also in the wrong with Philemon (to harbor a runaway was to be guilty of theft: *Digest* 11.4.1), in which case he, too, presumably needed to do more fence-mending with Philemon on his own behalf than we actually find in the letter.

The stumbling block with the principal theses so far considered is the assumption that Onesimus was legally at fault in going to Paul. There is, however, an explanation which avoids the problems caused by this assumption, namely the simpler hypothesis that Onesimus left his master's household with the express purpose of contacting Paul. It was in fact quite a common occurrence at this time for a slave who had put himself in the wrong with his master in some way to seek out a friendly third party to ask the latter to plead on his behalf with his offended master. Where the slave's goal was not to run away but to restore effective working relations with his master, legal opinion did not regard him as a *fugitivus* (*Digest* 21.1.17.5).[12] The much cited parallel of Pliny's letter to Sabinianus, albeit on behalf of one of the latter's freedmen, is an effective illustration of a no doubt quite often repeated train of events (*Epistle* 9.21).[13] In this case the "if" clause of v. 18

---

12. Already noted by Buckland 268: "It is not *fuga* to run to a friend of the master to secure intercession, and in this case mere failing to return is not *fuga:* there must be some definite act of flight." But Lampe's brief article has brought the point to the fore, going beyond the older view that Onesimus was a *fugitivus* seeking out Paul to intercede for him (as in Gayer 232-34). Lampe's argument is taken up and developed by Rapske 195-203 and Bartchy, *ABD* 5.307-8.

13. As translated in Stowers 160:

Your freedman with whom you said you were angry has been with me; he threw himself at my feet and clung to me with as much submission as he could have done at yours. He earnestly requested me with many tears, and even with all eloquence of silent sorrow, to intercede for him; in short, he convinced me by his whole behavior, that he sincerely repents of his fault. And I am persuaded he is thoroughly reformed, because he knows that he was wrong.

I know you are angry with him, and I know too, it is not without reason; but mercy is never more worthy of praise than when there is the justest cause for anger. You once loved this man, and, I hope, will again; in the meanwhile, let me only prevail with you to pardon him. If he should incur your displeasure hereafter, you will have so much the stronger a reason for your anger, as you show yourself willing to forgive him now. Allow something

would be an effective way of referring to an issue where Philemon thought he had a legitimate grievance against Onesimus but where Onesimus felt he was being blamed for something which was not wholly his fault (cf. Wolter 231, 275-76).

This would create an interesting dynamic in the three-way relationship which makes this letter so intriguing (more even than Petersen ch. 2 envisaged). For it would mean that Onesimus, not yet a Christian, had sought out his master's Christian mentor to intercede for him (cf. Gnilka 3, 44; Lampe 137). That tells us at once that it was Philemon's character as a Christian which Onesimus saw as likely to work most effectively in his favor. It also tells us that Philemon's regard for Paul would be well known within his household and that Philemon had not insisted that his whole household adopt his new faith, though conceivably Onesimus had been drawn into one or two of the meetings of the church in Philemon's house (cf. Lightfoot 310). That may suggest in turn, however, that Onesimus was ripe for conversion and that Paul was able to use the fact that Onesimus had come to plead with him precisely because Paul was a Christian. That is not to say that Paul's acting on behalf of Onesimus was a kind of trade-off for Onesimus becoming Christian; there is no hint of any such manipulation in the warmth of Paul's account (vv. 10-13). But the converting encounter between Paul and Onesimus should not be melodramatized by depicting the imprisoned apostle finding a way to penetrate the hard exterior of a determined runaway slave and thief.

At all events it is clear that Onesimus had been converted by Paul during his imprisonment (v. 10; *pace* Gnilka 3) and had become very close to Paul ("my own heart," v. 12), attending to Paul's varied needs while in prison (vv. 11, 13; see also Col. 4:9: "faithful and beloved brother"). How long a period passed between the initial meeting of Paul and Onesimus and this letter we have no means of knowing: it would depend on how accessible Paul was to visitors; presumably his confinement was relatively free, equivalent, perhaps, to the British remand stage in trial procedures (Stuhlmacher 21); it would depend also on how long it took for Onesimus to be converted,

---

to his youth, to his tears, and to your own gentle disposition: do not make him uneasy any longer, and I will add too, do not make yourself so; for a man of your kindness of heart cannot be angry without feeling great uneasiness.

I am afraid that if I add my prayers to his, I would seem to be compelling you rather than asking you to forgive him. Yet I will do it and in the strongest terms since I have rebuked him very sharply and severely, warning him that I will never intercede for him again. Although it was proper to say this to him, in order to frighten him, it was not intended for your hearing. I may possibly have the occasion to again intercede for him and obtain your forgiveness if the error is one which is suitable for my intercession and your pardon.

The text can also be found in Lightfoot 316-17; Dibelius 111; Knox 16-17; Lohse 196-97 n. 2. It is worth noting from *Epistle* 9.24, also to Sabinianus, that Pliny's plea was successful.

and on how quickly such a close relationship developed. But the more likely it is that Onesimus had sought out Paul to intervene on his behalf, the more likely it is that Onesimus was anxious to return (as v. 13 suggests).

All this bears on the interpretation of what it is that Paul asks of Philemon with regard to Onesimus. As a fugitive slave Onesimus could quite properly be punished by beatings, chains, branding, or worse.[14] But a potential crisis of that sort does not seem to be in view in the letter; how could Paul compensate (vv. 18-19) if such a penalty was in order? If, on the other hand, the nature and seriousness of Onesimus's wrongdoing were themselves an issue and if Onesimus's enlisting of Paul's good offices was itself not an unacceptable action, then the language used in vv. 15-17 is quite as might be expected (see there). Paul's main concern was for a positive reconciliation between the two (Wolter 233-34). So, too, Paul's readiness to let Philemon understand the breach in the way he chose (v. 18) displays the touch of an experienced mediator, recognizing as he did that in a master-slave dispute the master held all the cards. Likewise, the vagueness of the request and the fine mix of pressure and pleading in vv. 14-16 and 19-20 (see on these verses) allow Philemon to respond with dignity and generosity in a way that would both maintain and display his honor.[15] This would leave the door open to interpret the hint of hoping for something more (v. 21) in terms of Onesimus's manumission (a very substantial proportion of slaves were freed by their masters before their thirtieth birthdays; so Wiedemann 51; Bartchy, *ABD* 6.71; see also on v. 16 and Col. 3:11), or of his return (probably as a freedman) to Paul (see on v. 21).[16]

So far as Paul's attitude to slavery in general and its relevance to today is concerned, we need simply to remind ourselves what has already been noted on Col. 3:11, 22 and 4:1: (1) that in the ancient world slavery was accepted as an integral part of society and its economic working, (2) that while *treatment* of slaves was recognized as a moral question, the *fact* of slavery itself was not; it was only the revulsion against the slave trade in the modern period in Europe and North America which made slavery itself morally repulsive, (3) that in the absence of modern democracy it would not have been possible to conceive of an effective political protest against

14. See Lightfoot 312, 319-20; Vincent 163; Bellen 17-31; Wiedemann 193-94; Nordling 114-17; Rapske 189-90; Bartchy, *ABD* 5.307-8 (bibliography). On the violence and cruel punishments masters could inflict on their slaves, see also K. R. Bradley, *Slaves and Masters in the Roman Empire: A Study in Social Control* (Brussels: Latomus, 1984) ch. 4; though note also Bartchy 67-72.

15. Cf. particularly Barclay 170-75, though his analysis is weakened by his continued assumption of the traditional *fugitivus* hypothesis.

16. That the latter was the main objective of the letter is argued by Knox 18-27 and Ollrog 103-6 in particular: "the letter to Philemon is to be understood as a written request of Paul for a community delegate" (Ollrog 104). But the argument plays down too many other features of the text (see also Meeks's critique of Ollrog in *Urban Christians* 233 n. 65).

slavery, slave rebellions having consistently failed, and (4) that the most effective amelioration of the slave's lot had to depend on the master's kindly treatment of the slave and on his continuing positive patronage after the slave's manumission. In this context the most important counsel in the letter comes in v. 16: "no longer as a slave, but more than a slave, as a beloved brother, . . . both in the flesh and in the Lord." Such teaching put into practice from the heart would transform and enrich any social relationship, whatever its continuing outward form, and if sustained over time was bound to undermine and diminish any radical inequality between the partners. See also, e.g., Bartchy; Gayer 275-82, 296-309; Barclay 175-86; Marshall 189-91.

THE PLACE OF WRITING

This is the other great bone of contention among commentators on Philemon. Paul was obviously writing from prison (vv. 1, 9-10, 13, 22-23), but where was his prison? The three options remain, as always, Caesarea (Acts 24:26-27), Ephesus, and Rome. Despite the support of Dibelius 107 and Lohmeyer 3-4, the suggestion of Caesarea has largely fallen by the wayside. But the debate between the other two remains as divisive as ever. It should be noted that an Ephesian imprisonment would have to be dated in the middle of the 50s, while a Roman imprisonment would probably have been in the early 60s (see pp. 39-41 above). The main considerations on either side can be outlined briefly.[17]

The major factor in favor of Ephesus is its closeness to Colossae — less than a week's journey distant. To reach Rome meant a much longer journey, whether by sea, with all its hazards, or by tiring land journey (which could take several weeks). That Onesimus should contemplate a short journey to Ephesus is one thing; to Rome was an undertaking of quite a different order. On the other hand, if Philemon was fairly influential, Ephesus would be an obvious place for him to make inquiry, should he think Onesimus had run away or not know why he had departed; it would be quite possible for Philemon to initiate legal action against Onesimus before he even got to Paul. Even so, if these were the only considerations they would have to tell firmly in favor of Ephesus.

Also relevant here is Paul's request in v. 22: Paul hoped to be released and thus to be able to come (directly?) to Philemon, so Philemon should

---

17. For Ephesus see, e.g., G. S. Duncan, *St. Paul's Ephesian Ministry* (London: Hodder, 1929), here 72-75; Harrison 271-74, 281-82; Lohse 188; Stuhlmacher 21-22; Gnilka 4-5, referring to his fuller treatment in *Der Philipperbrief* (HTKNT 10.3; Freiburg: Herder, 1980) 18-24; Binder 22, 28-29; Wolter 238. For Rome see, e.g., Lightfoot 310-11; Vincent 161-62; E. Percy, *Probleme der Kolosser- und Epheserbriefe* (Lund: Gleerup, 1946) 467-74; Moule, *Colossians and Philemon* 21-25; Gülzow 30; O'Brien, *Colossians, Philemon* 269. See also above, p. 39 n. 48.

(immediately?) prepare his guest room for Paul's (imminent?) arrival. If all the question marks could be removed, the case for Ephesus would be almost overwhelming. However, we have to observe also a note of uncertainty in the hope Paul expresses (see on v. 22) and cannot exclude the possibility that Paul either had in mind a much more extensive itinerary (cf. Phil. 2:24) or that he spoke in partial jest ("Keep a room ready for me; you never know when I might turn up"). But here, too, the balance of probability would seem to favor the Ephesian hypothesis.

The relevance of the earthquake which caused so much damage in the Lycus valley in 60-61 is unclear, since it is quite possible to date (part at least of) a Roman imprisonment prior to that date. But until Colossae is properly excavated we are in no position to judge the strength of this argument (see also p. 23 above).

The major factors in favor of Rome are twofold. First, there is no firm record of an Ephesian imprisonment; the whole hypothesis rests on inferences of questionable weight (from 2 Cor. 1:8 and 11:23). And second, the traditions regarding the place of origin of Philemon uniformly attribute it to Rome, and these traditions go back at least to the fourth or fifth century in the versions (see Metzger 658-59). The problem is that the more that is attributed to an Ephesian imprisonment, in terms of the length of time Paul spent there — sufficient for news to reach Colossae, for Onesimus to travel there, and for the relation between Paul and Onesimus to blossom (not to mention anything relating to Philippians, the other undisputed Pauline prison epistle) — the more surprising it is that the imprisonment seems to have made so little lasting impact in the Christian memory.

In the end decisive weight may have to be given to the question of the relation of Colossians to Philemon (Martin, *Colossians and Philemon* 149; Bruce, *Colossians, Philemon, and Ephesians* 196). If Colossians is post-Pauline and the points of contact with Philemon (particularly Col. 4:9-14, 17 and Phm. 2, 23-24) have simply been derived from Philemon, then it adds nothing to the debate. But if Colossians was written on Paul's behalf during his final imprisonment (from which he was never released) and if the points of overlap between the two are to be understood as indicating one letter (Colossians) written shortly after the other, then Philemon is presumably tied with Colossians into a Roman imprisonment (see pp. 39ff. above; otherwise Binder 22-29). This is probably tantamount to concluding that if Colossians is post-Pauline, then the considerations in favor of an Ephesian origin for Philemon probably weigh the more strongly; whereas if Colossians was penned while Paul was still alive, then Philemon was also presumably written from Rome.

All in all, it is difficult to come to any final decision. Fortunately, however, the exposition of the letter depends only marginally on the conclusion regarding its place of writing, so that to that extent the issue can be left open.

THE STRUCTURE OF THE LETTER

The letter is a model of the normal structure of a personal letter, now so familiar to us from the multitude of papyri examples, though with the usual Pauline adaptations at beginning and end. It can be classified either as a letter of recommendation (cf. particularly Kim, here 123-28) or as a letter of mediation (Stowers ch. 11, also with illustrations).

ADDRESS AND GREETING (1-3)

THANKSGIVING AND PRAYER (4-7)

APPEAL TO PHILEMON (8-20)

IN CONCLUSION (21-25)

For further details see on v. 1 and the introductions to the other sections; also Schenk 3446-66, 3484-86.

ADDRESS AND GREETING (1-3)

1 *Paul, a prisoner[1] of Christ Jesus, and Timothy, our brother,[2] to Philemon,
our beloved[3] fellow worker, 2 and Apphia, our[4] sister, and Archippus, our
fellow soldier, and the church in your house.* 3 *Grace to you and peace from
God our Father and the Lord Jesus Christ.*

1 Παῦλος δέσμιος Χριστοῦ Ἰησοῦ καὶ Τιμόθεος ὁ ἀδελφὸς Φιλήμονι τῷ
ἀγαπητῷ καὶ συνεργῷ ἡμῶν.   As noted in the Introduction, this is the only
personal letter as such which we can definitely attribute to Paul's pen. It is
of interest, then, to note how Paul modified his opening greeting from the
more formal one used in most of his other letters. As in every other letter
in the Pauline corpus, and in accord with the normal convention of the time,
he gives the name of the sender, his own name, first (cf. Acts 15:23; 23:26;
Jas. 1:1; 1 Pet. 1:1; 2 Pet. 1:1; 2 John 1; 3 John 1; Jude 1; examples of
current practice in Gnilka 14; contrast Heb. 1:1 and 1 John 1:1). Particularly
in a personal letter, that is, a letter to one who knew Paul well, little more
would be needed to identify the author and to justify the presumption of
claim upon the recipient's interest which such a letter implied. It is possible
that Paul marked the intimacy thus claimed by writing the complete letter
in his own hand, in contrast to his normal practice (but see two paragraphs
below, on v. 19, and p. 343 n. 1). See further on Col. 1:1.

The first obvious difference from Paul's church letters is the self-
description appended to the name. Elsewhere, from Galatians on, it was
Paul's almost unvarying practice to "pull rank" by stressing his apostleship
(see again on Col. 1:1). The same is true, somewhat surprisingly, in the
personal letters which constitute the Pastorals (a sign that Paul's apostolic
authority was being evoked to back up Timothy and Titus). The only other
exception among the post-Thessalonian correspondence is Philippians — the
most uncomplicatedly friendly of all the churches to which Paul wrote. Here,
however, wholly unusually, Paul introduces himself simply as "prisoner of
Christ Jesus" (so also v. 9; Eph. 3:1; 4:1; 2 Tim. 1:8). Almost certainly Paul
had in mind his current physical imprisonment (as most agree; see, e.g.,
Dibelius 102; Martin, *Colossians and Philemon* 158; O'Brien, *Colossians,
Philemon* 271 with bibliography; hence RSV's "for Christ Jesus" and GNB's

    1. Some scribes not unnaturally thought it appropriate to insert "apostle" or "slave,"
characteristic elements in Paul's greetings elsewhere.
    2. NEB/REB again translate "colleague" as in Col. 1:1.
    3. The awkward "and" caused some scribes to insert "brother." Should we translate "our
dear friend and fellow worker" (so NEB/REB, NIV, GNB, NRSV) or ignore the "and" to translate
as above (RSV, JB/NJB)?
    4. Some scribes evidently thought that the greeting to Apphia should match that to Philemon
and added "beloved."

"for the sake of Christ Jesus"), not the otherwise plausibly Pauline idea that
Christ had taken him prisoner (but cf. 2 Cor. 2:14; Stuhlmacher 29-30). He
mentions his imprisonment at once since he evidently wishes to introduce a
theme on which he will play several times in the letter, no doubt because of
its emotive and persuasive power (vv. 9, 10, 13, 23; see also on Col. 4:18).
To see here in addition a veiled attempt to still "pull rank" when the term
"apostle" has been eschewed (Wickert 232; Hainz, *Ekklesia* 200-201) pushes
the evidence too far (contrast Wilson 113: "to emphasize . . . his social
solidarity with Onesimus"). On the double name Christ Jesus see again on
Col. 1:1.

As in Colossians, Paul adds the name of "Timothy, the brother" as
coauthor (see on Col. 1:1). This is more noteworthy here since Philemon is
such a personal letter. Why is Timothy named? Most likely because he was
such a close intimate of Paul and therefore fully privy to and supportive of
Paul's position in the delicate affairs which form the main subject of the
letter; quite possibly he had also come to know Philemon at the time of the
latter's conversion through Paul (v. 19), most likely in Ephesus (cf. Acts
19:22). Does the appearance of his name here, in such close parallel with
Col. 1:1, throw any more light on the relation between the two letters?
Certainly it must strengthen the case for seeing the two letters as written at
the same time and in the same circumstances (see pp. 37f. above). On the
other hand, Timothy is named in the greetings of several other letters (see
on Col. 1:1), which would seem to diminish the significance of the parallel
at this point. If, however, the two letters were written at the same time and
the arguments for the strictness of Paul's current imprisonment hold, we
would have to assume that, as with Colossians, the writer was Timothy
himself, even though the sentiments were Paul's (otherwise Binder 44).

After these briefest of self-introductions, the recipient is named: Philemon. This is the only time he is mentioned in the New Testament, but the
name was common (Lightfoot 301-2; *NDIEC* 3.91; 5.144). Like Epaphras,
Tychicus, Luke, and, perhaps significantly, Onesimus himself, Philemon is
called "the beloved one" (see n. 3 above and on Col. 1:7), preparing in effect
for the appeal in v. 16, that he should be willing to accept Onesimus in like
manner (see on that verse). He is also numbered in that select and important
band whom Paul designates as "fellow workers," which includes Prisca and
Aquila, Urbanus, Timothy (Rom. 16:3, 9, 21; 1 Thes. 3:2), Apollos (1 Cor.
3:9), Silvanus (2 Cor. 1:24), Titus (2 Cor. 8:23), Epaphroditus (Phil. 2:25),
Euodia, Syntyche, and Clement (Phil. 4:3), Aristarchus, Mark, and Jesus
Justus (Col. 4:11), and Demas and Luke (Phm. 24; see also on Col. 4:11).
On Philemon see further pp. 300f. above.

2 καὶ Ἀπφίᾳ τῇ ἀδελφῇ καὶ Ἀρχίππῳ τῷ συστρατιώτῃ ἡμῶν καὶ τῇ
κατ' οἶκόν σου ἐκκλησίᾳ. Linked with Philemon as recipient of the letter
is Apphia, whose name is found very frequently in western Asia Minor,

including Colossae itself (Lightfoot 304-6; Dibelius 111; BAGD s.v. Ἀπφία).
She is usually regarded as Philemon's wife, and this makes good sense, since
if Onesimus had been a household slave Philemon's wife would have had
much to do with him and therefore would have as much interest in the
Onesimus affair. She is called literally "the sister" (as Timothy was called
"the brother"). This presumably means that she also was a Christian, "our
sister" (though the possibility that she was Philemon's unmarried sister living
with him and responsible for his domestic affairs cannot be entirely dismissed). In contrast to the masculine ἀδελφός (see on Col. 1:1), the feminine
is rarely used for members of religious associations. This is surprising, since
women were active in religious cults of the time, particularly that of Isis.[5]
Nevertheless, the designation of a woman who also believed in Christ as
"sister" seems to have been particularly characteristic of Christianity (Rom.
16:1; 1 Cor. 7:15; 9:5; Jas. 2:15; Ignatius, *Polycarp* 5:1; *2 Clement* 12:5;
19:1; 20:2; Hermas, *Visions* 2.2.3; 2.3.1). Although the masculine still predominates in the New Testament and is often used in the plural when a
congregation made up of both sexes is addressed (as in Col. 1:2), the fact
that the feminine is used, as here, does suggest that a serious attempt was
made (and not least within the Pauline circle) to treat women as individuals
and as Christians in their own right.

Also linked with Philemon in the greeting is Archippus, often taken to
be Philemon's (and Apphia's) son (see on Col. 4:17), "an instance of legend
active when history fails" (Houlden 228). We may assume at least that he
is mentioned here either because he was a member of Philemon's household
or because he was the only other member of the church currently in Colossae
to be active in ministry, at least so as to warrant the title "fellow soldier"
(he is also subject of an enigmatic exhortation in Col. 4:17). The designation
"our [Paul's and Timothy's] fellow soldier" is applied only to Epaphroditus
elsewhere in the Pauline corpus (Phil. 2:25). Paul does not use military
metaphors for Christian service as much as is sometimes assumed: only,
strictly speaking, in 2 Cor. 10:1-6, itself not particularly typical of Paul's
concept of mission (O. Bauernfeind, *TDNT* 5.710-11). The image evoked by
the use of συστρατιώτης ("comrade-in-arms," NEB/REB) here and in Phil.
2:25, therefore, is probably more that of dedication and discipline than of
fierceness and warlike behavior. It probably indicates not that Archippus had
been one of Paul's mission team as such ("fellow worker"), but that he had,
like Epaphroditus, served under the banner of the gospel in a more independent commission, perhaps in Laodicea (Col. 4:17; Lightfoot 307), though in

5. S. B. Pomeroy, *Goddesses, Whores, Wives and Slaves: Women in Classical Antiquity* (New
York: Schocken, 1975) 217-26; R. MacMullen, *Paganism in the Roman Empire* (New Haven: Yale,
1981) 116-17; Meeks 24-25; R. S. Kraemer, *Maenads, Martyrs, Matrons, Monastics: A Sourcebook
on Women's Religion in the Greco-Roman World* (Philadelphia: Fortress, 1988) *passim*.

a cooperative and mutually supportive role with Paul.[6] Such a deduction makes the exhortation of Col. 4:17 all the more enigmatic!

The fourth and final greeting is to "the church in your (singular) house." The fact that the house is described as Philemon's alone need not count against the inferences drawn above (that Apphia and Archippus were related to Philemon and members of the same household). It simply reflects the fact that according to the law and custom of the time the senior male member of a household was its sole head, the *paterfamilias* with considerable authority (should he choose to use it) over all other members of the household (wife and children included). On home churches as the basic unit of early Christianity see on Col. 4:15; also Elliott. Somewhat surprising is the fact that Paul does not address them as "saints"; but he never so speaks of the members of a house church. That he does not address them as "the saints in Colossae" (as in Col. 1:2) may mean that Philemon's house church was not the only church in Colossae, or simply that the letter was for the members of Philemon's house church alone (see again on Col. 4:15).

At all events we should note that what might have seemed a purely personal matter between Philemon and Paul is shared not only with the family(?) members of the household (Apphia and Archippus), but also with the whole church which met in Philemon's house (a point often noted, e.g., Preiss 33-34; Gayer 247-48; Marshall 182). The assumption is that the letter would be read openly at a meeting of the house church (Hainz, *Ekklesia* 200; Gnilka 13). Of course, this was a not altogether subtle way of bringing pressure on Philemon,[7] but the very fact that it could be done indicates that Philemon was likely to recognize the church's right to take an interest in and even advise on the internal affairs of his own household (Friedrich 192); this was the character of their shared faith (v. 6). This is all the more striking since almost certainly slaves (Philemon's or others') would also be members of the house church (cf. Col. 4:22-25). If all this is so, we can deduce that in this case at least, the church in Philemon's home partook of something of the character of its meeting place; that is, it functioned in some real sense as an extended family. It is precisely the ambiguity of Onesimus's role as both a slave member of Philemon's household and a brother in Philemon's extended Christian family (v. 16) on which Paul evidently hoped to play with good effect.

3 χάρις ὑμῖν καὶ εἰρήνη ἀπὸ θεοῦ πατρὸς ἡμῶν καὶ κυρίου Ἰησοῦ Χριστοῦ. The actual greeting is Paul's normal one, the combined greeting

---

6. There is nothing in the text or the imagery to suggest that Archippus had replaced Epaphras as leader of the community (*pace* Lohmeyer 175; Scott 102; R. P. Martin 159; Hahn 183) or that Archippus was the real recipient of the letter (Knox 51-61), in which case he would surely have been given greater prominence (see also Gayer 224-27; p. 300 n. 2 above).

7. Petersen 99-100. The subtlety of the pressure is missed by Wickert: "In this 'private letter' Paul wants to be heard not as a private man but as apostle" (232, 238).

"grace and peace" being "a specifically Pauline characteristic of style" (Wolter 249). The formulaic character is indicated by the use of the normal plural "you," whereas the body of the letter is addressed to Philemon as such (singular "you"). For the first part of the greeting see on Col. 1:2. The only difference from Col. 1:2 is the retention of the normal "and the Lord Jesus Christ." As Paul's normal greeting the notable feature is that "the Lord Jesus Christ" is conjoined with "God our Father" in the benediction. This says much about the high regard in which Jesus Christ was already held, so that as "Lord," as God's supreme agent, even vice-regent, he could be seen as responsible with God the Father for bestowing such blessing. Nothing is made of this here or in the letter in terms of christology (though see vv. 8 and 9 in particular), but it is significant that the christology implied could already be taken so much for granted in a form of words already formalized and established. See also on Col. 1:3.

THANKSGIVING AND PRAYER (4-7)

4 *I give thanks to my God every time I make mention of you in my prayers,* 5 *hearing of your* ¹*love and faith*¹ *which you have for*² *the Lord Jesus and for all the saints,* 6 *that the shared experience of your faith might be effective in the knowledge of all the good*³ *that is among us*⁴ *for Christ.* 7 *For I*⁵ *have had much joy and encouragement from your love, brother, because the hearts of the saints have been refreshed through you.*

Again following normal practice (Doty 31-33; and see above, p. 55 n. 7), Paul at once offers a congratulatory thanksgiving and prayer on behalf of his readers. The following parallels show that in the thanksgiving Paul fell into a well-established pattern of his own: thanks to God, assurance of frequent remembrance in prayer, commendation of their faith and love:

Phm. 4-5   εὐχαριστῶ τῷ θεῷ μου πάντοτε μνείαν σου ποιούμενος
           ἐπὶ τῶν προσευχῶν μου, ἀκούων σου τὴν ἀγάπην
           καὶ τὴν πίστιν ἣν ἔχεις πρὸς τὸν κύριον Ἰησοῦν
           καὶ εἰς πάντας τοὺς ἁγίους

Rom. 1:8-9 εὐχαριστῶ τῷ θεῷ μου . . . ὅτι ἡ πίστις ὑμῶν . . . μνείαν
            ὑμῶν ποιοῦμαι πάντοτε ἐπὶ τῶν προσευχῶν μου . . .

1 Cor. 1:4 εὐχαριστῶ τῷ θεῷ μου πάντοτε περὶ ὑμῶν . . .

Phil. 1:3-4 εὐχαριστῶ τῷ θεῷ μου ἐπὶ πάσῃ τῇ μνείᾳ ὑμῶν πάντοτε
            ἐν πάσῃ δεήσει μου ὑπὲρ πάντων ὑμῶν

Col. 1:3-4 εὐχαριστοῦμεν τῷ θεῷ . . . πάντοτε περὶ ὑμῶν
            προσευχόμενοι, ἀκούσαντες τὴν πίστιν ὑμῶν ἐν
            Χριστῷ Ἰησοῦ καὶ τὴν ἀγάπην ἣν ἔχετε εἰς πάντας
            τοὺς ἁγίους

1 Thes. 1:2-3 εὐχαριστοῦμεν τῷ θεῷ πάντοτε περὶ πάντων ὑμῶν
            μνείαν ποιούμενοι ἐπὶ τῶν προσευχῶν ἡμῶν . . .
            ὑμῶν τοῦ ἔργου τῆς πίστεως καὶ τοῦ κόπου τῆς
            ἀγάπης

2 Thes. 1:3 εὐχαριστεῖν ὀφείλομεν τῷ θεῷ πάντοτε περὶ ὑμῶν . . . ἡ
            πίστις ὑμῶν καὶ . . . ἡ ἀγάπη . . . εἰς ἀλλήλους

1. Some manuscripts reverse the order of words, presumably assuming that it is more natural or Pauline to mention faith before love.

2. The unusual πρός evidently encouraged a popular alteration to εἰς, though one manuscript has ἐν Χριστῷ Ἰησοῦ (following Col. 1:4).

3. A few manuscripts add "work" ("every good work") to give a not very Pauline sentiment; cf. Bruce, *Colossians, Philemon, and Ephesians* 209.

4. A strong battery of witnesses read "among you," a natural alteration since the "us" is rather unexpected (see Metzger 657; Harris 252).

5. A good number of scribes again thought the singular was inappropriate and read "we."

The closest parallels are 1 Thes. 1:2-3 and, not surprisingly, Col. 1:3-4 (cf. also Eph. 1:15-16). See further Schubert ch. 2 and the introduction to the comments on Col. 1:3-8 above.

Although, strictly speaking, the thanksgiving and prayer end with v. 6, vv. 6 and 7 are linked structurally to v. 5, since they take up in turn (chiastically) the themes of Philemon's love and faith, which were introduced in v. 5. Verse 7 in particular, therefore, forms a transition to the body of the letter, but the thanksgiving as a whole is closely linked to the body of the letter by the repetition of key words: "love, beloved" (vv. 5, 7, 9, 16), "prayers" (vv. 4, 22), "sharing, partnership" (vv. 6, 17), "the good" (vv. 6, 14), "hearts" (vv. 7, 12, 20); "refresh" (vv. 7, 20), and the vocative "brother" (vv. 7, 20; Knox 19; Lohse 192 n. 5; Gayer 247; Wolter 251, 255). In this case at least the rhetorical technique of the Pauline letters (see particularly Church 21-24) seems to be neither contrived nor merely manipulative but a fulsome expression of genuine respect and regard.

4 εὐχαριστῶ τῷ θεῷ μου πάντοτε μνείαν σου ποιούμενος ἐπὶ τῶν προσευχῶν μου. This is one of Paul's most regular openings (Rom. 1:8-9; Phil. 1:3-4; Col. 1:3; Eph. 1:16), but the use of εὐχαριστέω in a thanksgiving prayer is quite conventional (MM; *NDIEC* 4.128). The relative brevity of the thanksgiving (the shortest of Paul's thanksgivings) gives the opening word a more dominant role (Schubert, 12; O'Brien, *Thanksgiving* 50). Τῷ θεῷ μου ("my God"), as in Rom. 1:8; 1 Cor. 1:4; Phil. 1:3, does not denote Paul's God as distinct from Philemon's, but rather underlines the personal character of Paul's devotion, probably in (un)conscious echo of typical Psalm speech (Pss. 3:7; 5:2; 7:1, 3, 6; 13:3; 18:2, 6, 21, 28-29, etc.). Unlike its occurrence in Colossians, εὐχαριστῶ is also singular, Timothy falling more obviously into the background in this case (see also vv. 9 and 19). On μνείαν σου ποιούμενος, "making mention of you" (Rom. 1:9; Eph. 1:16; 1 Thes. 1:2), see Moule, *Colossians and Philemon* 140-41; it indicates the actual speaking of Philemon's name in Paul's prayers (Gnilka 35). On that and the unceasing character of Paul's thanksgiving or remembrance see the comments on Col. 1:3 (GNB's "Every time I pray, I mention you and give thanks to my God" is rather free but quite acceptable). Again we should not regard this as mere literary flourish (cf. Wolter 252); Paul must have had an extensive prayer list and presumably spent some time each day naming before God all his churches, colleagues, and supporters. This would help maintain and strengthen the sense of a faith shared with "all the saints" (5-6).

5 ἀκούων σου τὴν ἀγάπην καὶ τὴν πίστιν ἣν ἔχεις πρὸς τὸν κύριον Ἰησοῦν καὶ εἰς πάντας τοὺς ἁγίους. Again the language is somewhat stereotyped. Paul elsewhere implies that the news of what had happened among his readers was broadcast widely (Rom. 1:8: "in all the world"; 1 Thes. 1:7-9); the parallel is again closest with Col. 1:4. But here again we should not assume a gratuitous flattery; rather we should see evidence of the network of communication among the Pauline churches which ensured that news of developments (and crises) was quite quickly spread to others, Paul himself being a central link in the network (cf. Rom. 15:17-19; 2 Cor. 7:14; 8:24; 9:2-3; 1 Thes. 2:19-20; 2 Thes. 1:4), the present tense indicating a regular flow of news (O'Brien, *Colossians, Philemon* 277, citing C. Spicq, *Agape in the New Testament* [St. Louis: Herder, 1963-66] 2.303; see also the introduction to the comments on Col. 4:10-17). Here it implies that Onesimus (as, presumably, one of Paul's chief informants) must have spoken warmly of his master (Scott 103; Caird 219). It also implies, as in Col. 1:4, that Philemon's main activity as a Christian had been in Colossae or the Lycus valley and that Paul himself had had no direct experience of it (though, *pace* Dibelius 103; Knox 55; Martin, *Colossians and Philemon* 160, it does not follow that Paul had never met the person thus commended; see on v. 19). For the themes of love and faith (the order is somewhat surprising: contrast Col. 1:3-4; 1 Thes. 1:2-3; 2 Thes. 1:3 above; and see n. 1 above) see on Col. 1:4. That it is only Philemon's love and faith which are mentioned (σου, singular "your") reflects the fact that the thrust of the letter is directed solely to Philemon, on whose decision alone its success depended; the thought is not of love and faith as Philemon's personal possession (Binder 47-48).

It is tempting to follow Col. 1:4 and apportion the love and faith between the phrases which follow in the relative clause, as does NIV with "your faith in the Lord Jesus and your love for all the saints" (similarly GNB), though it depends on reading the sentence chiastically (Suhl, "Philemonbrief" 270; Martin, *Colossians and Philemon* 160-61; Wiles 219-20; O'Brien, *Colossians, Philemon* 278-79 with bibliography; Harris 249-50; Wolter 253). But there is no reason why Paul should not have thought of both love and faith as the sum of the Christian lifestyle and therefore of both as related to both "the Lord Jesus" and "all the saints" (Vincent 178-79; Gnilka 35-36). If the thought of "faith to all the saints" is unexpected, it could be that the thought was already moving on to the next verse (which also reduces the plausibility of taking πίστις here in the sense of "faithfulness," as, e.g., Houlden 229 and Bruce, *Colossians, Philemon, and Ephesians* 208), just as the thought of "love to all the saints" is taken up in v 7. (see the comments there). At all events, the effect is to highlight the importance of Philemon's love, no doubt in preparation for v. 9 (cf. Wiles 220-21).

The prepositions are also somewhat surprising: one might have expected εἰς τὸν κύριον Ἰησοῦν καὶ πρὸς πάντας τοὺς ἁγίους. But the εἰς in reference to fellow Christians was the more regular Pauline usage (if we allow the evidence of Col. 1:4 and 2 Thes. 1:3), and the more surprising πρός (see n. 2 above; but cf. 1 Thes. 1:8) was chosen perhaps for stylistic variation (Moule, *Idiom-Book* 68; Turner, *GNTG* 3.256; cf. Rom. 3:30 and Gal. 2:16; see also Lightfoot 333). The two prepositions overlap in meaning anyway (cf. BDF §207.1) and can both be translated "for" (JB/NJB) or "to/toward." See again on Col. 1:4; on "the saints" see on Col. 1:2.

6 ὅπως ἡ κοινωνία τῆς πίστεώς σου ἐνεργὴς γένηται ἐν ἐπιγνώσει παντὸς ἀγαθοῦ τοῦ ἐν ἡμῖν εἰς Χριστόν. Slightly awkwardly the purpose clause follows from the subordinate clause of v. 4 ("making mention of you in my prayers"); most translations provide a more felicitous link by beginning a new sentence with "I pray. . . ." The subject of the prayer, however, is an intriguing phrase which has caused the translators some puzzlement: ἡ κοινωνία τῆς πίστεως, "the sharing of your faith" (RSV/NRSV, NIV), "your fellowship with us in our common faith" (NEB), "the faith you hold in common with us" (REB), "that this faith will give rise to a sense of fellowship" (JB), "your fellowship in faith" (NJB), "our fellowship with you as believers" (GNB). The puzzle is whether κοινωνία is something objective (the fellowship brought about by faith) or subjective (the experience of shared faith), and likewise whether πίστις is objective (the fellowship of a shared confession) or subjective (the shared experience of believing).

In both cases it is most likely the subjective sense which was in mind. By "faith" Paul almost always means the act and attitude of trust toward God and Christ (see again on Col. 1:4; the only likely exceptions being Gal. 1:23; 3:23-25; 6:10).[6] The first term, however, requires fuller analysis.

Κοινωνία was another word probably brought into Christian vocabulary by Paul (only three occurrences in LXX; thirteen of the nineteen New Testament occurrences in the undisputed Paulines; four of the remaining six in 1 John 1). For Paul it primarily denoted common participation in or sharing of something (1 Cor. 10:16 — in the body and blood of Christ; 2 Cor. 8:4 — in the service for the saints; 2 Cor. 13:13/14 and Phil. 2:1 — in the Holy Spirit; Phil. 1:5 — in the gospel; Phil. 3:10 — in Christ's sufferings). In each case the thought is of the act or subjective experience of sharing rather than of a condition or action created by the term qualified (*pace* Lightfoot 333; Wiles 222-23; Bruce, *Colossians, Philemon, and Ephesians* 208-9; O'Brien, *Colossians, Philemon* 280; Harris 251) — that is, the act of sharing in the Lord's Supper, *not* the congregation in which the Lord's Supper is celebrated (1 Cor. 10:16), the actual taking part in the collection, *not* the generosity which prompted it (2 Cor. 8:4), the experience of sharing the same Spirit, *not* the fellowship created by the Spirit (2 Cor. 13:13/14; Phil. 2:1), the shared experience of promulgating the gospel and of Christ's sufferings, *not* a quasi-title for a mission team or an order of spirituality (Phil. 1:5; 3:10); see also v. 17.

What Paul had in mind here, then, is almost certainly the subjective

---

6. Of other Pauline passages cited by BAGD s.v. πίστις 3, under the heading "body of faith or belief," Rom. 1:5 and 12:6 should not be included; see my *Romans* (WBC 38; Dallas: Word, 1988) *ad loc.* Contrast Binder 49.

experience of a faith shared in common.[7] The prayer is that this shared
experience of a common trust in Christ might be or become (γένηται)
ἐνεργής, "effective, active, powerful" (cf. the other two New Testament
instances: 1 Cor. 16:9; Heb. 4:12; also the verb in Gal. 5:6) in the knowledge
(ἐπίγνωσις, a term common in Colossians: 1:9-10; 2:2; 3:7; cf. also particu-
ularly Phil. 1:9) of all the good which was their common lot as Christians.
The thought is of the shared experience of faith as a dynamic relation with
the Lord Jesus which constantly fed their understanding and consciousness,
making them aware of how much they were benefiting as a result. The vague
phrase "all good" is presumably chosen to embrace all of what they together
and individually had experienced or come to recognize as theirs as a result
of their faith commitment (cf. Rom. 8:28; 10:15; 14:16; Phil. 1:6; Lohse
194); Stuhlmacher 34 and Gnilka 37 think that knowledge of God's will is
primarily in view (cf. again Col. 1:9).[8] The corporate character of the shared
faith is central to the thought; Paul had no desire to promote the idea of
religious faith as something private, that which a person enjoys alone and
practices as a separate individual. Moreover, the phrase underlines not only
the bonding character of this faith, but also the fact that this shared faith was
the basis and energy source of their common life and worship; without the
κοινωνία of the shared experience of faith, we might say, there could be no
"fellowship" in the more "objective" sense; alternatively, unless "the faith"
has the shared experience of believing as the primary bond, "the faith" will
lack the energy which Paul attributes to the κοινωνία τῆς πίστεως here. The
thought is primarily passive ("shared experience of faith"); but in this case
it can also have an active force ("the sharing of faith," RSV/NRSV, NIV;
cf. 2 Cor. 8:4; 9:13; Phil. 4:15), evoking the picture of the church gathered
in Philemon's house benefiting from Philemon's testifying of his own experience of faith, no doubt prompting other members in turn to share their
experience of faith (its ups and downs) in a way that was beneficial to them
all (cf. particularly Riesenfeld 254-55). Indeed, the primary sharing of faith
in mind may have been the reading of the letter itself and Philemon's and
the church's response to it.[9]

7. See particularly J. Y. Campbell, "*KOINONIA* and its Cognates in the New Testament,"
JBL 51 (1932), reprinted in *Three New Testament Studies* (Leiden: Brill, 1965) 1-28; F. Hauck,
TDNT 3.804-8; J. Hainz, *EDNT* 2.303-5, drawing on his larger study, *KOINONIA: "Kirche" als
Gemeinschaft bei Paulus* (BU 16; Regensburg: Pustet, 1982).

8. Note again the variety in translations: RSV: "I pray that the sharing of your faith may
promote the knowledge of all the good that is ours in Christ" (similarly NIV); NRSV: "I pray that
the sharing of your faith may become effective when you perceive all the good that we may do for
Christ" (similarly JB/NJB); NEB: ". . . may deepen the understanding of all the blessings that our
union with Christ brings us"; REB: ". . . may deepen your understanding of all the blessings which
belong to us as we are brought closer to Christ."

9. "The word group represented by κοινωνία can be seen as the key to the total understanding

That Paul thinks again only of Philemon's faith (again σου, "of you,"
singular) maintains the focus on Philemon as the leading actor in the script
here being written for him (cf. O'Brien, *Thanksgiving* 59-60). This may be
why Paul adds the awkward "among us" ("all the good that is among us"),
in order not to let the particular thrust directed to Philemon weaken the
corporate force of the imagery of shared faith. The individual awareness of
shared faith or act of sharing faith heightens the community's appreciation
of the good that they all share in Christ.

The final phrase is also awkward: εἰς Χριστόν. It could have an eschatological thrust (cf. 1 Cor. 1:7 and Phil. 1:6; Wickert 230 n. 2; Suhl,
"Philemonbrief" 271), though there is no reason to hear a note of menace
in it (Stuhlmacher 33 n. 55).[10] More likely it is a variant on ἐν Χριστῷ (see
BDF §§205-6, 218; O'Brien, *Colossians, Philemon* 281), perhaps reflecting
the influence of a train of thought on faith — faith as εἰς Χριστόν (though
the only exact parallel in Paul is Col. 2:5: see the comments there). Or else
it simply forms a characteristic Pauline flourish (as in Rom. 16:5; 2 Cor.
1:21; 11:3; Ernst 131). At all events, its basic force is clear: all that is spoken
of in the rest of the verse has its validity and effectiveness because of their
relation to Christ (Harris 253), or perhaps more specifically, by "bringing
us into (closer) relation to Christ" (Moule, *Colossians and Philemon* 142;
similarly Dibelius 103 and Wiles 225).

7 χαρὰν γὰρ πολλὴν ἔσχον καὶ παράκλησιν ἐπὶ τῇ ἀγάπῃ σου, ὅτι
τὰ σπλάγχνα τῶν ἁγίων ἀναπέπαυται διὰ σοῦ, ἀδελφέ. The compliment
to Philemon becomes even more fulsome, strengthened still further by the
personal warmth of the final ἀδελφέ (see on Col. 1:1), this verse together
with v. 20 being the only times Paul uses the vocative singular in all his
letters (giving greater force to the similar description of Onesimus in v. 16).
Paul himself has derived much joy (χαρά; see on Col. 1:11) and encouragement or comfort (παράκλησις; cf. Rom. 12:8; 15:4-5; 1 Cor. 14:3; 2 Cor.
1:3-7; 7:4, 7, 13; Phil. 2:1; 2 Thes. 2:16; O. Schmitz, *TDNT* 5.796-97) in
Philemon's love (again the singular). And not just Paul, but the hearts
(σπλάγχνα; see on Col. 3:12) of the saints (see on Col. 1:2) had been set at
rest or refreshed (ἀναπέπαυται; cf. 1 Cor. 16:18; 2 Cor. 7:13; BAGD s.v.
ἀναπαύω 1) through Philemon (again the singular σου).

Who "the saints" are in this case is unclear. They could, of course, be
the church in Colossae, though we noted the fact that Paul fails to speak of
the church in Philemon's house as "saints" (see on v. 2). But since Philemon

---

of the letter to Philemon; i.e. the letter is a concrete demonstration of what Paul understands by
κοινωνία" (Hainz, *EDNT* 2.304). But the language used ("sharing of faith . . . effective in the
knowledge of all the good . . .") tells against Winter's suggestion that what was in view was the
recipient sending Onesimus to Paul (Winter, "Letter" 3).

10. Lohse 194-95 renders it as "for the glory of Christ," but without adequate justification.

has already been described as "fellow worker" (v. 2), we may envisage Philemon as engaged in a wider ministry; v. 5 has already congratulated him on his love "to all the saints." The tense of the verb (ἀναπέπαυται, perfect) indicates some past ministry of Philemon which had had enduring results (the parallel with 2 Cor. 7:13 is thus particularly close). Possibly some particular visits were in mind that had brought a reinvigoration and refreshment to various churches, which would suggest that Philemon was a fine preacher. Or he had acted in such a way as to set various churches on a secure foundation, perhaps by financial aid or legal advice (Scott 105-6 again suggests it might have been help following the earthquake of 60), thus removing anxieties and giving them peace of mind, which would strengthen the impression that Philemon was a figure of some power and influence in wider society as well as in the church. Whatever the precise circumstances, the more emotional note implicit in the use of σπλάγχνα (rather than the much more common καρδία) should be noted; the emotional bonds between Philemon and "the saints" were strong. No doubt Paul hoped that this would be a factor in his favor when he came to make his appeal to Philemon in the next paragraph; hence also, presumably, the repeated mention of Philemon's love (vv. 6, 7). As Paul had been delighted and encouraged by the accounts he had received of Philemon's ministry (note again the network of communication implied), so he hoped for further delight and encouragement from Philemon's response to his request regarding Onesimus.

APPEAL TO PHILEMON (8-20)

8 *Therefore, though*[1] *I am bold enough in Christ to command you to do your duty,*[2] 9 *I would rather appeal to you on account of love, being as I am, Paul, an old man,*[3] *but now also prisoner of Christ Jesus.* 10 *I appeal to you for my son, of whom I became father while in chains — Onesimus.*[4] 11 *He was formerly useless to you, but now is indeed useful to you and to me.* 12 *I have sent*[5] *him back to you, that is, my own heart.*[6] 13 *I wanted*[7] *to keep him with me, so that on your behalf he might serve me in chains for the gospel,* 14 *but I resolved to do nothing without your consent, so that your goodness might not be by compulsion but of your own free will.*

15 *For perhaps it was for this reason he was separated from you*[8] *for a time, in order that you might have him back for ever,* 16 *no longer as a slave, but more than a slave, as a beloved brother, especially to me, but how much more to you, both in the flesh*[9] *and in the Lord.*[10] 17 *If therefore you*

---

1. The participial (ἔχων) is concessive (Moule, *Idiom-Book* 102).

2. Cf. the effective translations of REB ("Although in Christ I might feel free to dictate where your duty lies") and NJB ("Although in Christ I have no hesitations about telling you what your duty is").

3. The Greek clearly reads πρεσβύτης, "an old man" (JB/NJB, NIV, NRSV; so also Dibelius 104; Scott 107; G. Bornkamm, *TDNT* 6.683; Jang 32; Lohse 199). But many have argued that πρεσβευτής, "ambassador," should be read instead (RSV, NEB/REB, GNB; so also O'Brien, *Colossians, Philemon* 290 [bibliography]; cf. 2 Cor. 5:20; Eph. 6:20), principally on the ground of the appropriateness of the latter to the context and on the assumption of scribal indifference to the distinction between the two forms (Lightfoot 336-37; Lohmeyer 185 n. 2; though πρεσβύτης is attested in that sense unequivocally only in 2 Macc. 11:34; 1 Macc. 14:22; 15:17; as a variant reading in 2 Chron. 32:31 LXX[B]). The rendering is a major plank in Wickert's argument that Philemon is not a private but an apostolic letter (here 235) and in Petersen's analysis of the relationship between Paul and Philemon (125-28; " 'old man' is simply not a viable translation of *presbytes*" [128]); in direct contrast Koester 134-35. But it is not clear from the context whether Paul was appealing for respect or to authority (Gnilka 43; and why in a private letter would he call himself "ambassador" rather than his customary "apostle"?); and the assumption of scribal indifference is gratuitous (Stuhlmacher 37-38; and see now particularly Birdsall). Cf. Metzger 657.

4. On the fact that Ὀνήσιμον stands in the accusative, despite the genitive form of τοῦ ἐμοῦ τέκνου, see Schenk 3447-50.

5. Another very good example of the epistolary aorist (see also Col. 4:8), which could thus be translated "I am sending back."

6. The awkwardness of the Greek encouraged various improvements in the course of transmission, particularly the addition of προσλαβοῦ, "receive"; see Metzger 657-58. The ὃν . . . αὐτόν construction may be a Semitism (Moule, *Colossians and Philemon* 145; Lohse 201 n. 42).

7. ἐβουλόμην could be treated as equivalent to the optative: "I would have been glad to" (BAGD s.v. βούλομαι 1; RSV); "I should have liked" (BDF §359.2; Bruce, *Colossians, Philemon, and Ephesians* 214 n. 66; Harris 263; JB/NJB, NEB/REB; similarly GNB, NIV; cf. Acts 25:22).

8. Gnilka 50 objects to adding "from you," which he thinks was deliberately omitted: "Philemon should not be reminded of the injury he suffered."

9. Modern translations continue to shy away from translating σάρξ phrases with English "flesh." So here: "as a man" (NEB/REB, NIV), "as a blood-brother" (JB, explained by Bruce,

count me a partner, welcome him as you would me. 18 And if he has wronged you in any way or owes you anything, charge it to my account. 19 I, Paul, have written[11] with my own hand: I will repay; not to mention[12] that you owe me in addition your very self. 20 Yes, brother, let me have some benefit from you in the Lord; refresh my heart in Christ.

The actual appeal to Philemon is skillfully constructed: it plays affectively on the fact of Paul's imprisonment (vv. 9, 10, 13) and hints repeatedly at the other powerful constraints he might have brought to bear (vv. 8, 13-14, 19) in order to give greatest force to his primary grounds of appeal — love (vv. 9, 12, 16), personal ties (vv. 10, 13, 17), and the mutual obligations of the Christian family (vv. 10, 16, 20) — while at the same time taking care to go halfway toward Philemon by offering full restoration and compensation (vv. 15, 17-19). Paul's rhetorical skills are evident in his stated unwillingness to use the stronger arguments available to him (vv. 8-9, 14, 19) and manifest concern to leave Philemon free to act freely and honorably.[13]

Petersen has highlighted several aspects of Paul's rhetorical effectiveness: for example, the way in which Paul defers the negative information about Onesimus until he has presented the positive information that Onesimus has been converted and is being sent back (*Rediscovering Paul* 73), the juxtaposition of the two debts in vv. 18-19 (pp. 74-75), and the play on the theme of mutual brotherhood in vv. 16 and 20 (p. 78). Paul's rhetoric here, as elsewhere, should not be denigrated as manipulative and contrived. It is typical of a leader with a strong personality that he should sincerely want to encourage and leave it open to his audience to respond of their own free will, while at the same time being so convinced of the rightness of his own opinion that he naturally seeks to persuade them to share it. In the end it is Paul's courtesy and restraint which leaves the greatest impression here. Nor should we ignore the degree to which Paul's tactic reflects the social

---

Colossians, Philemon, and Ephesians 218), "on the natural plane" (NJB), "as a slave" (GNB); only RSV/NRSV have "in the flesh." This would be less objectionable if the resulting translations of such phrases were consistent within each translation, but this is rarely the case. The result is that an important feature of Paul's overall theological schema ("flesh") is obscured and distorted.

10. NEB/REB regularly translate such "in the Lord" phrases with "as (a) Christian," "as a fellow-Christian," thereby implying (falsely) that "Christian" was an already established and regularly used title.

11. Another example of the epistolary aorist, which could therefore be translated, "I am writing" (see p. 322 n. 5).

12. It is generally recognized that this final sentence begins with an ellipsis, with a main verb understood — e.g., literally, "I do this, or put it so, in order that I might not say to you that you also owe me yourself" (see Moule, *Idiom-Book* 145; Harris 274; Lohse 204-5 n. 75; against BDF §495.1).

13. Cf. Church 24-28; Daube 41; Bartchy, *ABD* 5.307; contrast Feeley-Harnik 117-23 ("Paul is using Onesimus to bring Philemon into line" [123]) with Wilson 115-17.

reality of his circumstances: if Philemon was a figure of social significance and power, then to press him over strongly with commands and threats might have been counterproductive in the loss of Philemon himself (cf. Petersen 142; see also n. 3 and on v. 17).

A further factor not to be ignored is the possibility that Paul's letters would have been read by the authorities before being allowed to be taken out of prison. A concern not to arouse suspicion or give unfriendly officials excuse to accuse him of disrupting the social fabric could also have weighed in Paul's choice of words and use of what was in effect Christian code language.

The length of this section is disputed. Most take it through v. 20, with the talk of "refreshing the heart" as a fitting climax, in deliberate echo of v. 7, though v. 21 could be seen as the conclusion to the body of the letter (e.g., Caird; JB/NJB, NIV, NRSV) as much as the recapitulation of the epilogue (but see the introduction to the comments on vv. 21-25). Others think that the epilogue begins with v. 17 (Gnilka 82-83; Wright). And the fact that Paul's personal autograph elsewhere always seems to introduce the letter closing (1 Cor. 16:21; Gal. 6:11; 2 Thes. 3:17; Col. 4:18) could be taken as argument for seeing v. 19 as the beginning of the epilogue,[14] though that is less likely since it follows so directly from v. 18 and since the function of the autograph in v. 19 is itself unusual in its setting as providing a legal guarantee (see there); in terms of Paul's typical practice the autograph indicating the letter closing is the ἔγραψα of v. 21. However, the thought of the letter is sufficiently integrated for such disagreements to be of little consequence.

Lohmeyer 181-83 sets out the passage in poetic form, but it is hardly likely that Paul set out to compose a poem as such. We should rather simply recognize that Paul's speaking (and writing) style, developed and shaped by long experience, naturally fell into a rhythmic pattern.

8 διὸ πολλὴν ἐν Χριστῷ παρρησίαν ἔχων ἐπιτάσσειν σοι τὸ ἀνῆκον. The opening greeting, thanksgiving and prayer having recalled and thus reestablished the relationship between Paul and Philemon, Paul can proceed to the business at hand. Διό, "therefore, for this reason, accordingly," is not Paul's normal transition to the body of a letter (usually γάρ or δέ).[15] But the expression of appreciation and commendation in v. 7 has already laid the ground for the central appeal of the letter, so that διό is entirely appropriate. Paul's appeal to Philemon is entirely on the basis of their previous relationship and of the mutual indebtedness of membership in Christian community.

14. E. R. Richards, *The Secretary in the Letters of Paul* (WUNT 2.42; Tübingen: Mohr, 1991) 173, 178-79; Weima 230-32.

15. Cf. J. T. Sanders, "The Transition from Opening Epistolary Thanskgivings to Body in the Letters of the Pauline Corpus," *JBL* 81 (1962) 348-62, here 355.

The implication of the διό is at once underlined. Paul could have tried a different tack. He could have spoken to Philemon "man to man," frankly, with an outspokenness which held nothing back, with παρρησία (BAGD 1; cf. H. Schlier, *TDNT* 5.883; H. Balz, *EDNT* 3.47). Παρρησία in this sense was rather strikingly characteristic of Christian confidence (details in O'Brien, *Colossians, Philemon* 287-88), which would be sufficient explanation of its usage here. But the word often also carries the implication of an unexpected "boldness" (Acts 4:13, 29; 2 Cor. 3:12; Phil. 1:20; Eph. 6:19), unexpected because of the disparity in status or condition of the speaker in comparison with the others mentioned in context (BAGD 3). In this case Paul would be acknowledging Philemon's social status and the unexpectedness of a prisoner in a Roman jail ordering a man of high social status about. This latter inference is probably strengthened by the use of ἐν Χριστῷ — literally "I have much in Christ boldness." Paul could be so confident because he would be speaking "in Christ," that is, as one who stood (with Philemon) in a higher or more important relationship (see on Col. 1:2) which took precedence over earthly obligations of client to patron or of subordinate to superior.[16] In other words, the appeal here is not to Paul's apostolic authority vis-a-vis Philemon;[17] the reminder of Philemon's debt to Paul will come later (v. 19). As one equally "in Christ," Philemon could be expected to acknowledge that an "in Christ" obligation transcended all others.

Had Paul taken that tack he could even have ordered Philemon how to act — ἐπιτάσσειν, a strong word denoting the authority of superior over inferior (BAGD; G. Delling, *TDNT* 8.36-37). But such abrupt assertion of authority was not Paul's preferred way: he never uses the verb elsewhere and refuses in 1 Cor. 7:6 and 2 Cor. 8:8 to issue an ἐπιταγή (see also on v. 9). The term used to denote what it is Paul could have ordered Philemon to do is an interesting one: τὸ ἀνῆκον, "what is proper, one's duty" (BAGD s.v. ἀνήκω), the obligation one owes to some constitutive principle which gives shape and meaning to existence (cf. Lohmeyer 183; see on Col. 3:18). The term is interesting because it implies that a transformation of such duty has taken place in Philemon. Since he was a prominent figure in Colossae, it might be thought that his duty was to uphold the laws which constituted orderly society and thus to deal with the case of an errant slave in a way which made it clear that slaves abandoning their masters were not to be tolerated. But here the implication is clearly that Paul was appealing to Philemon's duty ἐν Χριστῷ, his obligations and responsibilities having been transformed by his becoming Christian.

16. Cf. W. C. van Unnik, "The Christian's Freedom of Speech in the New Testament," *BJRL* 44 (1961-62) 466-88, here 474.

17. Rightly Gnilka 41-42, but against the common view (e.g., Scott 106; Friedrich 193; Ernst 133; Caird 221; Stuhlmacher 36-37).

The hesitation thus expressed may have been a common tactic in such pleas: Pliny in his letter to Sabinianus on a similar theme expresses himself in similar terms: "I am afraid that if I add my prayers to his, I would seem to be compelling you, rather than asking you to forgive him" (*Epistle* 9.21; cf. 9.24). Paul may also have been genuinely fearful lest Philemon fail to acknowledge his (Christian) duty (because it might put him in bad odor with other leading citizens in Colossae?). But it could equally be that Paul thought it inappropriate to nurture the fruit of loving relationships by laying down the law or appealing to duty. This would be consistent with what we know of Paul's exercise of authority in regard to his churches elsewhere: he sought less to manipulate and more to win consensus and to develop his readers' own sense of responsibility (see further my *Jesus* 278-80; contrast Hainz, *Ekklesia* 204-6).

9 διὰ τὴν ἀγάπην μᾶλλον παρακαλῶ, τοιοῦτος ὢν ὡς Παῦλος πρεσβύτης νυνὶ δὲ καὶ δέσμιος Χριστοῦ Ἰησοῦ. Paul's preferred approach, potentially more effective because of the alternative he spurned, was the appeal of love and to love. The verb παρακαλῶ is just the one we would expect in private correspondence (MM; Bjerkelund 34-58). In such a context its range of nuance strikes the right balance between obligation demanded and favor requested: "urge, exhort, appeal to, request, implore" (BAGD). Elsewhere, in the more formal contexts of his letters to churches, παρακαλῶ is also Paul's favorite term for urging particular behavior or action (Rom. 12:1; 15:30; 16:17; 1 Cor. 1:10; 4:16; 16:15; 2 Cor. 2:8; 10:1; Phil. 4:2; 1 Thes. 4:1, 10; 5:14; 2 Thes. 3:12; Eph. 4:1). As the same references (together with Rom. 12:8; 1 Cor. 14:31; 1 Thes. 4:18; 5:11) also indicate, παρακαλεῖν epitomizes the quality of discourse which should characterize the church in its discussion and debate — that is, not the demand of rights or threat of sanctions (it here stands in antithesis to ἐπιτάσσειν), but the exhortation, the appeal, the request within a community whose members trust and respect each other.[18]

Here the appeal can be all the more underplayed, since it is based on the love (ἀγάπη) on which Paul has already so effusively congratulated Philemon (vv. 5, 7), "because of that same love" (NEB/REB). Paul could be confident of the effectiveness of his appeal on the basis of love (διὰ τὴν ἀγάπην παρακαλῶ) because he had already received such encouragement from Philemon's love (παράκλησιν ἐπὶ τῇ ἀγάπῃ σου).[19] In his letter to

---

18. Bjerkelund 59-74, however, has also drawn attention to the use of παρακαλῶ in royal exhortation, where it is diplomatic but forceful (= "summon"), so that the contrast here with ἐπιτάσσω should not be exaggerated (119; similarly Petersen 131-33); but see again n. 3 above. The Roman Catholic Gnilka cites Luther appositely at this point: "When has the Pope ever acted so?" (42).

19. Lightfoot 335; Vincent 183; and Lohse 198-99 think the appeal is to love (ἀγάπη) as such; but see O'Brien, *Colossians, Philemon* 289.

Sabinianus Pliny is also able to appeal to Sabinianus's love or affection for his erring slave ("Amasti hominem et, spero, amabis"), though the weight of Pliny's appeal is as characteristically Stoic (in terms of clemency and self-control) as Paul's is Christian (among members of the new Christian family — "brother," vv. 1, 7, 16, 20; house church, v. 2; become father, v. 10).

The appeal to love is a cue for Paul to pursue a more sentimental tack by adding τοιοῦτος ὤν ("being as I am"; Lightfoot 335-36) ὡς (literally "in my character as," BAGD s.v. τοιοῦτος 2b) "Paul, an old man." If this is the correct rendering (see n. 3 above), it gives us valuable information about Paul's age. In a common reckoning of the "seven ages" of a man, the πρεσβύτης was the second oldest, from 50 to 56 (Philo, *De opificio mundi* 105; BAGD), though in other classifications the πρεσβύτης was the oldest and could be used for individuals in their 60s (Gnilka 43; Wolter 260). Depending on where Paul was when he wrote the letter (see pp. 307f. above), the former would put Paul's birth date somewhere in the first decade of the Christian era (see Stuhlmacher 38 n. 76). Since the term does not of itself imply someone near the end of his life or with failing powers (the seventh age is that of the γέρων), we should not see the appeal here as one for compassion — for the younger man (Philemon) to act out of pity for someone once so active and now so weak. Rather, since age usually brought with it the wisdom of experience, the appeal is for the respect that a younger member of the same family or circle should pay to the elder (cf. Lev. 19:32; Sir. 8:6; hence the evolution of the near synonym, πρεσβύτερος, from "older person" to synagogue or church leader, "elder"; see further G. Bornkamm, *TDNT* 6.651-80; R. A. Campbell, *The Elders: Seniority within Earliest Christianity* [Edinburgh: Clark, 1994]).

The tug to the heartstrings becomes more evident with the addition, "but now also a prisoner of Christ Jesus." "But now" does not necessarily imply that Paul's imprisonment had just begun (*pace* Martin, *Colossians and Philemon* 163). The same phrase ("prisoner of Christ Jesus") already used (unusually) in the address (see on v. 1) would no doubt conjure up for Philemon a picture of Paul in prison, with the restricted movement and conditions of which Philemon would presumably be aware. We should hesitate to judge Paul harshly for lowering the tone of the appeal, as if it were emotional blackmail; on the contrary, appeal to the emotions was standard practice in Greek rhetoric (see, e.g., Gnilka 40). What he was about to ask of Philemon was a considerable favor, with all sorts of potential ramifications for Philemon's standing and reputation in the church and the wider community. Paul himself presumably judged it appropriate to screw the emotional pitch to this height. More to the point, Paul knew Philemon as modern commentators cannot and no doubt had a good idea of how

Philemon was likely to react to such sentiments being read in public in the church of which he was a member as well as leader.

10 παρακαλῶ σε περὶ τοῦ ἐμοῦ τέκνου, ὃν ἐγέννησα ἐν τοῖς δεσμοῖς, Ὀνήσιμον. After the buildup, now comes the appeal itself, the repeated παρακαλῶ underlining the character of the approach being made. It is for[20] Onesimus, whom Paul calls "my own son." Paul uses the term elsewhere to denote those converted through his ministry (1 Cor. 4:14, 17; Gal. 4:19; cf. Phil. 2:22; 1 Thes. 2:11; 1 Tim. 1:2, 18; 2 Tim. 1:2; 2:1; Tit. 1:4). The verb γεννάω could be used equally of a mother "bearing" her child and of a father "becoming father of" his child (BAGD); so again elsewhere of Paul (1 Cor. 4:15; cf. the striking Gal. 4:19 — Paul suffers the labor pains!). The imagery of father and son was a natural one to describe the relation of pupil to teacher (cf. 2 Kgs. 2:12; Matt. 23:8-9) or one in a state of religious dependence on priest or sect leader (1QH 7:20-21) or mystagogue.[21] In this case Paul had been instrumental in bringing Onesimus to faith in Christ Jesus while Paul himself had been chained in prison. For the circumstances in which Paul had met Onesimus see pp. 303ff. above; and for what custody in manacles and/or fetters meant see B. Rapske, *The Book of Acts and Paul in Roman Custody* (Grand Rapids: Eerdmans, 1994) 25-28, 31, 206-9.

Paul leaves the name of the one being interceded for to the end, though (*pace* Caird 221 and Bruce, *Colossians, Philemon, and Ephesians* 213) Philemon must have been in no doubt as to whom he meant — Onesimus had brought the letter! Onesimus was one of the most common names throughout this period, typically (though by no means always) denoting a slave or someone of servile origin (Lightfoot 308; BAGD s.v. Ὀνήσιμος; *NDIEC* 1.89; 4.179-81; 5.113, 147), for obvious reasons (see on v. 11). Since the name appears to have been particularly common in Ephesus (*NDIEC* 4.179) the plausibility of the suggestion that this Onesimus later became bishop of Ephesus (Ignatius, *Ephesians* 1:3; 2:1; 6:2) is considerably weakened (argued by Knox 85-92 and Harrison 290-93; viewed with some sympathy by Moule, *Colossians and Philemon* 21; Stuhlmacher 19; Bruce, *Colossians, Philemon, and Ephesians* 200-202, also *Paul* 402-3, 406; but see Lightfoot 309, 314; Gnilka 6). See also Col. 4:9 and pp. 302ff. above.

11 τόν ποτέ σοι ἄχρηστον νυνὶ δὲ καὶ σοὶ καὶ ἐμοὶ εὔχρηστον. "Onesimus" means literally "useful." This allows Paul the appropriate pun, though if the experience of those whose names allow such puns today is

---

20. For περί in this sense, that is, designating the one to whom the request refers, not yet its content, see, e.g., Bjerkelund 120-21; Lohse 199 n. 23; O'Brien, *Colossians, Philemon* 290; and Wolter 261. In contrast, Bruce, *Colossians, Philemon, and Ephesians* 212-13; Winter, "Letter" 6-7, follow Knox 19-20 in suggesting that the appeal is "for my own child" in the sense "I am appealing to you to give me my own child"; but see Greeven 374 and Nordling 110-12; cf. Schenk 3466-67 n. 66.

21. F. Büchsel, *TDNT* 1.665-66; Str-B 3.340-41; for Qumran see Stuhlmacher 38 n. 81; for the mysteries see G. Schrenk, *TDNT* 5.954; Dibelius 105; see also Daube.

anything to go by, Onesimus must have been heartily sick of it by this time.[22] For similar wordplays using the same words see BAGD s.v. ἄχρηστος and Lohse 200 n. 35; ἄχρηστος occurs only here in the New Testament, εὔχρηστος elsewhere only in 2 Tim. 2:21 and 4:11 (of Mark). There may also be a pun on the name Χριστός, which could be pronounced like χρηστός: to be useful is to be like Christ (Lohmeyer 186; Lohse 200; Winter, "Letter" 4-5). In this case the language does not throw much more light on Onesimus's history. He had once been "without use" — that is, presumably, as an errant slave (though Callahan 361 points out that such disparagement of slaves is typical of slaveowning societies). But now (simply a temporal and not eschatological antithesis: see on Col. 1:22; cf. particularly Hermas, *Visions* 3.6.7) he was indeed of "good use" (as a Christian) to Philemon as well as Paul. The "good use" to Paul is further indicated in v. 13. What the "good use" to Philemon was is less clear. Possibly it is indicated also in v. 13: Onesimus had acted for Philemon, fulfilled Philemon's obligation of service to Paul ("on your behalf"; see on v. 13). But more likely what was in mind was the service Onesimus would be able to give to Philemon on his return, whether within his household or as a "beloved brother" in church (see v. 16), or indeed as Philemon's agent once more with Paul (vv. 13-14). "Perhaps the word-order emphasizes that Philemon will have to satisfy himself that Onesimus has become a different person" (O'Brien, *Colossians, Philemon* 292).

12 ὃν ἀνέπεμψά σοι, αὐτόν, τοῦτ' ἔστιν τὰ ἐμὰ σπλάγχνα. Philemon should be in no doubt as to Paul's personal involvement in what might otherwise have been simply a legal relation between master and slave, with the slave legally in the wrong and liable to serious punishment in consequence. Paul makes it clear that he is sending Onesimus back not because of such legal obligations,[23] but because of Onesimus's new status: wrongs done among fellow believers had to be sorted out as among fellow believers (v. 16; cf. 1 Cor. 6:1-8). It had been particularly hard for Paul to take this step, being as isolated as he was in prison (cf. vv. 23-24 and Col. 4:10-14), and because Onesimus had come to mean so much to him.

Here Paul screws the emotional intensity to a new pitch, calling Ones-

---

22. Onesimus was a Phrygian (from Colossae — so Col. 4:9), and, as already noted, Phrygian slaves were notoriously unsatisfactory (Lightfoot 310 n. 2). Ὀνήσιμος, synonymous with χρηστός, is derived from the verb ὀνίνημι, "profit, benefit, help"; see further on v. 20.

23. On the law governing runaway slaves see Bellen; Gnilka 71-81; p. 304 above. In Jewish law Deut. 23:15-16 pointed in a different direction (see discussion in Str-B 3.668-70). Moule, *Colossians and Philemon* 145; Houlden 230-31; and Winter, "Letter" 7 (following Knox 21); also Gnilka 46, think that the verb here has the technical sense of "refer back" or "refer up," as when a case is passed on to another tribunal (this is its force in all the other New Testament uses: Luke 23:7, 11, 15; Acts 25:21), but it is more likely that Paul plays with nicely judged sensitivity on the ambiguity of the term (cf. Nordling 108).

imus his very heart (JB's and NEB's "a part of myself" is inadequate, despite Moule, *Colossians and Philemon* 146 and Bruce, *Colossians, Philemon, and Ephesians* 214), using again the intensely emotive term σπλάγχνα (v. 7; see on Col. 3:12).[24] Even though others had remained loyal to him during his imprisonment, Onesimus had won a special place in Paul's heart (Caird 222), though no doubt the point is stressed here for Philemon's benefit. As one who had "refreshed the σπλάγχνα of the saints" (v. 7), Philemon would find it difficult to treat Paul's σπλάγχνα with anything but consideration and care (see also v. 20). Here again it would be too easy to accuse Paul of emotional blackmail: he was a man of deep emotional strength, as Philemon would no doubt be aware, and it would be natural if at this point in the letter's composition, where Onesimus's (and Philemon's) future hung in the balance, emotion should well up, expressive of both Paul's trepidation and his depth of feeling. Jang 65-70 notes the importance, at this point in the letter particularly, of the thought of "being for one another" as an expression of Paul's ecclesiology.

13 ὃν ἐγὼ ἐβουλόμην πρὸς ἐμαυτὸν κατέχειν, ἵνα ὑπὲρ σοῦ μοι διακονῇ ἐν τοῖς δεσμοῖς τοῦ εὐαγγελίου. The language Paul chooses suggests that the decision to send Onesimus back was not easily or quickly made. The imperfect tense ("I was wanting") implies a period during which Paul weighed the consequences of his action and during which the value of Onesimus's presence was a considerable factor in his deliberation (cf. Lightfoot 339). The ἐγώ ("I") indicates that it was Paul (not Onesimus) who remained so undecided for so long. Likewise πρὸς ἐμαυτόν might be better translated "for myself," indicating that Paul's appreciation of Onesimus's "usefulness" could all too easily in Paul's mind have outweighed the more speculative usefulness of Onesimus to Philemon (v. 11). Moreover, the infinitive κατέχειν would quite properly be translated "to hold back, prevent from leaving" (BAGD s.v. κατέχω 1), implying in turn that it was Onesimus who was anxious to return to make amends to and peace with his master and that Paul, far from pushing him to do so, was delaying his departure as long as he could because he found Onesimus so useful.[25] If such inferences are fairly to be read, they need not indicate mere selfishness on Paul's part ("for myself"), understandable in the circumstances, but again a real concern that Philemon might be unwilling or prevented (by social pressure) from treating Onesimus in a kindly manner.

The "for myself" is filled out. Onesimus would have continued to render Paul service (present tense). What that service might have been is not

---

24. "The I of Paul is enclosed in the thou of the slave" (Lohmeyer 187, who also cites *Testament of Joseph* 17:7 in comparison).

25. The alternative, that κατέχειν evokes the use of κατοχή for a god's detention of one who had fled to the god's temple for sanctuary (Gnilka 48), is more remote from the present context.

indicated, and the word could cover a wide range of acts of help and aid (see on Col. 1:7 — διάκονος; Col. 4:17 — διακονία). Possibly it retains something of its original imagery ("to wait on someone at table," BAGD s.v. διακονέω 1), thus indicating that Onesimus brought Paul his food and perhaps was even able to act in some degree as his personal slave. But the imagery would also cover a whole range of ministrations, including companionship and communication (Stuhlmacher 40). If the relatively limited description of Onesimus in Col. 4:9 is anything to go by ("faithful and beloved brother," not "beloved brother and faithful servant and fellow slave," as in 4:7), we may deduce that Onesimus's role was as Paul's helper, not having a regular ministry in church worship or evangelism apart from Paul (cf. Wickert 232 n. 6; Ollrog 104 n. 44 — "as a helper in the work of mission"; Gnilka 48 — "as servant in the gospel"; Winter, "Letter" 9, ignores the μοι).

'Υπὲρ σοῦ adds a further twist. The implication cannot be that Onesimus had been sent to Paul as a gift from Philemon, to serve Paul as he served Philemon; in that case a letter full of such trepidation and pleading would have been unnecessary. And to see it as a rebuke to Philemon, that Onesimus filled the role which Philemon himself had failed to provide, is not necessarily implied either (though see Vincent 186-87). In either case, the rendering "a substitute for you" (JB/NJB), "in your place" (GNB; similarly NIV) may be an overtranslation (but see A. Deissmann, *Light from the Ancient East* [New York: Doran, 1927] 335 n. 4; MM s.v. ὑπέρ 1[a]; H. Riesenfeld, *TDNT* 8.512-13). All that Paul probably meant is that Onesimus's service to Paul while a slave of Philemon could and should be regarded (in kindly light) as done on Philemon's behalf and at Philemon's willing behest. The formulation probably reflects something of the debate that Paul (and Onesimus) had had on the subject — a decisive point being that Onesimus could not continue to serve Paul "on behalf of" Philemon without Philemon's explicit approval; which in turn required a mending of fences between Philemon and Onesimus.

"In chains for the gospel" is another not too subtle attempt to remind Philemon that Paul's need (of Onesimus) was greater than Philemon's since Paul was in prison in chains: Onesimus could make up for some of Paul's lack of freedom of movement. Furthermore, Paul's commission to forward the gospel (see on Col. 1:5) was still active, and Onesimus could assist Paul in this in different ways. His usefulness to Paul "in chains for the gospel" outweighed his value to Philemon as a house slave. Passages from Ignatius are regularly quoted in comparison, particularly *Ephesians* 11:2: "In him I carry about my chains, the spiritual pearls in which may it be granted me to rise again through your prayers" (see further Lightfoot 339-40).

14 χωρὶς δὲ τῆς σῆς γνώμης οὐδὲν ἠθέλησα ποιῆσαι, ἵνα μὴ ὡς κατὰ ἀνάγκην τὸ ἀγαθόν σου ᾖ ἀλλὰ κατὰ ἑκούσιον. The impression given by v. 13 that Paul had taken some time to make up his mind on this affair is strengthened by the contrasting use here of the aorist ἠθέλησα, "I re-solved" (BAGD s.v. θέλω 2; Winter, "Letter" 8-9). Having deliberated for so long over what was the best and right thing to do, he came to his decision: that however much he wanted Onesimus to remain, it was more important to gain Philemon's consent. Γνώμη is well known in the sense "judgment, opinion" (LSJ III). But the idea of "consent" is present in a number of instances (2 Macc. 4:39; Josephus, *Antiquities* 7.60; Ignatius, *Polycarp* 4:1; 5:2; see also R. Bultmann, *TDNT* 1.717; Lohse 202 n. 15) and makes best sense here. At any rate what is implied is Paul's recognition of the need for a considered, emphatic, and favorable judgment on the subject by Philemon. The language may also suggest that Paul had reviewed other possible courses of action open to him, but in the end realized that without Philemon's willing agreement nothing that Paul decided with regard to Onesimus would be satisfactory or right.

The last inference is clarified a little further by the ἵνα clause. Among Paul's deliberations, perhaps chiefest among them, had been uncertainty on how best to approach Philemon (see also vv. 8-9). The resolution achieved had been in effect to throw himself (and Onesimus) on Philemon's mercy, limiting the pressure he brought to bear on Philemon to that of strong urging and emotive appeal. It was important not to provoke a confrontation, in which Philemon might have to choose between accepting Paul's authority (and thus losing face among his own circle of the influential well-to-do) or maintaining his social status at the cost of a rupture with Paul. Paul thus merely hints at the "compulsion" he might have brought (κατὰ ἀνάγκην; BAGD s.v. ἀνάγκη 1; see again v. 8), perhaps all too conscious of how weak that authority might be in such a confrontation. At all events, in terms of good relations and of how believers should act toward one another, it was more important that Philemon's consent should be given voluntarily, willingly (κατὰ ἑκούσιον; cf. 2 Cor. 9:7 and 1 Pet. 5:2; further Lohse 202 n. 53 and Wolter 267; "spontaneous" in JB/NJB and NIV is misleading).

What precisely Paul meant by τὸ ἀγαθόν σου, "your good deed" (NRSV), "your kindness" (NEB/REB), "act of kindness" (JB/NJB), is unclear (NIV's "favor" is less satisfactory). The term itself is unspecific, covering any action that would be generally approved of (cf. Rom. 2:10; 7:19; 12:9, 21; 13:3; 14:16; 16:19; Gal. 6:10; 1 Thes. 5:15; see further Gnilka 49, and also v. 6). Here it could refer to Philemon's willingness to receive Onesimus back as a brother, as he would receive Paul himself (vv. 16-17). It could refer to his readiness to wipe the slate clean over all that had passed (v. 18), that is, to forgive Onesimus and to take no further action against him, as he was fully entitled to do. Both actions would count as a single "good deed." That Paul also hinted at the possibility of Philemon returning Onesimus to Paul (so, e.g., Jang 34 and Gayer 241, 243-44) depends on what the final clause of v. 15 has in view, and v. 21 probably gives a broad hint that Philemon should also free Onesimus.

It should not escape notice that the language constitutes a gentle acknowledgment from Paul that if things went wrong he would be unable to bring any finally effective compulsion to bear on Philemon. Should Philemon respond positively to Paul's appeal it would be an act of goodness on his part. Those who see in Paul's earlier appeal a form of emotional manipulation should also acknowledge here that Paul in effect confesses his vulnerability and complete dependence on Philemon's goodwill. In the social relationships of a church existing in an unequal society there is a particular responsibility on the part of the powerful to act toward others in a spirit of goodness rather than standing on their rights.

15 τάχα γὰρ διὰ τοῦτο ἐχωρίσθη πρὸς ὥραν, ἵνα αἰώνιον αὐτὸν ἀπέχῃς. Nothing has been said thus far about the breach between Philemon and his slave Onesimus — nothing, that is, beyond the pun on Onesimus' name (v. 11). The strategy is, presumably, that the appeal to Philemon's love for Paul (v. 9), with its stress on how much Onesimus had come to mean to Paul (vv. 10, 12), and Paul's nicely judged deference to Philemon's rights in the matter (vv. 13-14) would mollify Philemon and soften the sense of hurt and anger he must have felt when Onesimus's wrongdoing was recalled. Now, however, Paul begins to grasp the nettle, but gently (Lohmeyer 188)!

He speaks soothingly — τάχα, "perhaps, possibly" (elsewhere in biblical Greek only in Wis. 13:6; 14:19; Rom. 5:7). He suggests that all that has happened so far has had a greater purpose behind it: ἐχωρίσθη, "divine passive," with God as implied subject; διὰ τοῦτο . . . ἵνα, "for this reason . . . in order that" — God's ways are ever mysterious (Gen. 50:20 is regularly cited as a parallel; cf. also Rom. 8:28). He introduces the thought of the breach between Philemon and Onesimus first as a "separation" — ἐχωρίσθη (the absolute use unusual in the New Testament but well enough attested in wider usage; BAGD s.v. χωρίζω 2b; JB/NJB's "deprived of" forces the sense somewhat).[26] And he plays it down by emphasizing its brevity: πρὸς ὥραν, "for an hour, a short time" (John 5:35; 2 Cor. 7:8; Gal. 2:5; *Martyrdom of Polycarp* 11:2).

In contrast, the prospect for Philemon is that he will now (Onesimus stands before him as he reads the words) have back a highly useful (v. 11) Onesimus αἰώνιον, which is presumably to be taken adverbially in the sense of "forever, permanently." The ambiguity of the αἰώνιον is part of Paul's "softly, softly" strategy. It is not clear whether he refers already to the new

---

26. "The word is chosen with rare tact. He does not say 'he ran away,' which might excite Philemon's anger; but 'he was separated,' and, by use of the passive, he puts Onesimus' flight into relation with the ordering of Providence" (Vincent 188); similarly the recent studies of Nordling 109 and Barclay 164.

relationship between Philemon and Onesimus, consequent upon the latter's conversion, as one that will last beyond death ("forever"; so most, particularly Gnilka 50-51), or rather to the restored and henceforth assuredly permanent relation of master to now dutiful slave ("permanently"; Moule, *Colossians and Philemon* 146, refers appositely to Exod. 21:6; H. Sasse, *TDNT* 1.209, to Deut. 15:17: οἰκέτης εἰς τὸν αἰῶνα, "slave for life"; Stuhlmacher 42; Binder 60). The verb shares in the ambiguity, since one could both "have" (that is, possess) a slave, and "have" a brother or a friend (BAGD s.v. ἔχω 2). The prefix (ἀπέχω) suggests a conscious echo of its technical commercial sense, "receive in full" (cf. Phil. 4:18; BAGD s.v. 1; MM), especially in view of the strong commercial imagery used in vv. 17-19; but that still leaves unclear whether what Philemon will receive back is a better slave or a loyal freedman (having been freed by Philemon) and client.

The uncertainty as to what it is Paul was asking of Philemon can never finally be settled. Perhaps Philemon knew well enough; there may be hints and allusions in the language of which the modern commentator is completely ignorant. Or possibly Paul felt that he could do no more than indicate a range of options in the hope that Philemon would act with the greatest generosity of heart. What Paul expected the *character* of the restored relationship to be certainly becomes clearer as Paul grasps the nettle more and more firmly. Initially, however, it was enough to highlight the contrast between the brief separation ("for an hour") and the constancy of the restoration ("forever"). The prospective highly favorable outcome would make the memory of past wrongs diminish in significance.

16 οὐκέτι ὡς δοῦλον ἀλλ᾽ ὑπὲρ δοῦλον, ἀδελφὸν ἀγαπητόν, μάλιστα ἐμοί, πόσῳ δὲ μᾶλλον σοὶ καὶ ἐν σαρκὶ καὶ ἐν κυρίῳ.   What this reunion of Onesimus with Philemon should mean begins to be spelled out along with the extent of the demand Paul was putting before Philemon. Once again, however, we have to ask: What was Paul asking for? A literal reading would suggest that he wanted Philemon to free Onesimus: "no longer as a slave" (Lohmeyer 189; Friedrich 196; Bruce, *Colossians, Philemon, and Ephesians* 217; S. S. Bartchy, *ABD* 5.308 and 6.71).[27] But it is just as possible to read the request as a plea for a transformed relationship between master and slave — still between master and slave, but transformed by the faith they shared in common (so particularly Schulz 416 and Binder 36-40).[28] This latter

27. Against the too hasty generalization of Moule, *Colossians and Philemon* 147, and Lohse 203 n. 63 (that in the mystery religions "a slave who had undergone the same initiation rites as his master, was no longer considered a slave, but stood alongside his former master as a free man"), see Stuhlmacher 46-47: "the mystery religions knew no programmatic abolition of slavery . . . a certain religious equality in the context of the cult community, but no more"; see also Gnilka 51-52; O'Brien, *Colossians, Philemon* 297.

28. Lohse 203 n. 59; O'Brien, *Colossians, Philemon* 297 cite H. von Soden, *Die Briefe an die Kolosser, Epheser, Philemon, die Pastoralbriefe* (Hand-Kommentar zum Neuen Testament 3.1;

alternative is strengthened by a possibly deliberate allusion to Exod. 21:6/Deut. 15:17 in v. 15 ("have back forever"; see on v. 15; and note also v. 11: more useful than ever), by the implication of the end of this verse that their relationship will continue to have a double dimension ("in the flesh and in the Lord"), and by the broader implication of such passages as Gal. 3:28 that relationships "in Christ" transcended even if they did not abolish distinctions of race, status, and gender (see also on Col. 3:11 and 4:1; cf. the also ambiguous 1 Cor. 7:20-24). "The renunciation of any punishment is obviously included and need not be expressly mentioned" (Gnilka 51).

Whether manumission (e.g., Jang 61-62; Koester 135) or simply for-giveness (Gülzow 39-40; Nordling 113-14) was in view (and again Paul may have been sufficiently uncertain of how much he could hope to sway Phile-mon as to leave the options open to Philemon, implying that either outcome would be acceptable), it is clear that Paul was much more hopeful that the new relationship between Philemon and Onesimus, since they were now both Christians, would be the determinative relationship: ὑπὲρ δοῦλον, "more than a slave" (see BAGD s.v. ὑπέρ 2), "a beloved brother."[29] After all, even if Philemon freed Onesimus, the latter would almost certainly have had to remain in a state of financial dependence on Philemon as his client ("have back forever"): under Greek law freedom might be only partial and limited with regard to employment and movement;[30] and economically there might be little difference between the secure relationship of the slave of a good master and the subservient client relationship of the impoverished

---

Leipzig: Mohr, [2]1893) 76: the particle " 'as' (ὡς) expresses the subjective evaluation of the rela-tionship without calling its objective form into question." See also Lightfoot 341; Vincent 188-89; Scott 110; Merk 228; Gayer 234-37; Wolter 233-35, 271-72: "according to Paul's view of things the legal relationship between master and slave remains undisturbed by the conversion of both to Christianity" (267); contrast the unrestrained comment of Preiss 40. Contrast still more the argument of Callahan 362-65, 368-76, who draws on mid-nineteenth-century American debate on slavery in maintaining that Onesimus was *not* Philemon's slave, but his *brother* (ἀδελφὸν . . . ἐν σαρκί); but that hardly explains the οὐκέτι ὡς δοῦλον (ἀδελφόν = ὑπὲρ δοῦλον), as the parallel with Xenophon, *Cyropaedia* 6.4.7 (cited by Callahan 371) itself confirms.

29. The degree to which Christianity accepted slaves as brothers, equal members of the body of Christ, was exceptional for the time (Gayer 237-40); for ἀδελφός see on Col. 1:1 and for ἀγαπητός see on Col. 1:7.

30. S. S. Bartchy, *ABD* 6.71:

Freedom was broken down into four elements: to represent oneself in legal matters; to be secure from seizure as property; to earn one's living as one chooses; and to live where one desires. More than ¼ of the 1,000+ manumission contracts inscribed on the sacred wall at Delphi fix limitations on at least two of these freedoms, usually of movement and employ-ment, by means of a so-called *paramone* clause that remained valid for a limited time (usually two to ten years). Such a freed slave could not be sold (and was thus legally a free person), but the freedman was still bound to the former owner in a variety of ways.

For examples of *paramonē* agreements see Wiedemann 46-49 (also 53-56); *NDIEC* 4.98-99. See also Lyall 78-79; Barclay 169 (with further references); the comments above on Col. 3:11.

freedman (Sabinianus, for whom Pliny pleaded, was actually a freedman; see pp. 302ff. above with n. 12 on p. 304). Either way, and this is the important point, whether as master to slave or as patron to client, the relationship of "beloved brother" (see further Wolter 272 and above on Col. 1:1 and 4:7) should be paramount. That would not change the social relationship of Onesimus's dependence on Philemon, but it would relativize it, infuse it with a family warmth, and make for heightened respect and consideration on both sides; Col. 4:1 and 1 Tim. 6:2 give some idea of what that would mean in practice (see further Stuhlmacher 42-45, 48; Barclay 177-82; and the fuller discussion in Bartchy, ΜΑΛΛΟΝ ΧΡΗΣΑΙ).

Paul cannot refrain from adding once again the note of personal involvement: μάλιστα ἐμοί ("most of all, especially to me"); for epistolary parallels in the papyri, see MM s.v. μάλιστα). Philemon was not to be allowed to forget that what was at stake was a three-way relation — Philemon, Onesimus, and Paul — not just that of Philemon and Onesimus. The more Philemon valued his relationship with Paul, the more Paul's relationship with Onesimus was bound to be a factor in Philemon's attitude to Onesimus. Πόσῳ δὲ μᾶλλον σοί, "how much more to you," presumably has in view the fact that Philemon had (now) a double relationship with Onesimus (whereas Paul knew Onesimus only ἐν κυρίῳ).

Here also the force of the double phrase (καὶ ἐν σαρκὶ καὶ ἐν κυρίῳ) is unclear, but it must denote a twofold relationship between Philemon and Onesimus. Ἐν σαρκί, as consistently in Paul, describes the world of human relationships, limited by human capacities, and constrained by human appetites and ambitions (cf. particularly Rom. 7:5; 8:8; 2 Cor. 4:11; 10:3; Gal. 2:20; Phil. 1:22; 3:3-4; E. Schweizer, *TDNT* 7.127; A. Sand, *EDNT* 3.231; see also on Col. 1:22). In this case it certainly denotes Philemon's relationship to Onesimus apart from their relationship as Christians — that is, as master to slave (cf. Col. 3:22; Eph. 6:5) or patron to client. That relationship continues, though, with Onesimus renewedly "useful" (v. 11) and as a "beloved brother." The fact that both are (now) Christians does not change the fact of their disparate social status; but clearly the relationship ἐν κυρίῳ should be the more important (cf. the repeated "in the Lord" and "Lord" references in Col. 3:18–4:1).

17 εἰ οὖν με ἔχεις κοινωνόν, προσλαβοῦ αὐτὸν ὡς ἐμέ. Somewhat surprisingly Paul now switches his appeal into a sustained commercial metaphor (vv. 17-19). This is no doubt in large part because slavery was itself a commercial transaction — the slave as a piece of property which could be bought and sold or stolen and compensated for. It was not that Paul was willing to reduce the affair among the three of them to the level of a mere commercial transaction (v. 16 was clear enough on that score). It was rather that there was inescapably a commercial dimension to the whole affair, so that the relationship between Philemon and Onesimus could not be restored

without the question of financial recompense being dealt with. The fact that Paul delayed raising the issue till this point in his letter suggests a degree of uncertainty as to Philemon's likely attitude: Would it be Philemon the brother "in the Lord" or Philemon the defrauded businessman ("in the flesh") who would respond? Paul had evidently not felt confident about raising the issue earlier, before he had "softened up" Philemon with the unstinting praise and emotive appeal of the earlier verses. That he goes on to emphasize with such force that he stood fully behind Onesimus as guarantor to make good Onesimus's wrongdoing (vv. 18-19; note the repeated use of the first person pronoun in vv. 17-20) confirms that this was the most sensitive area within their whole three-way relationship.

The note is struck by a further use of the κοινων- root (see on v. 6). Κοινωνός denotes "one who takes part in something with someone"; used absolutely, as here, it means "partner" (as also in 2 Cor. 8:23; BAGD; the usage of Luke 5:10, "partners" in a fishing business, is familiar in the papyri; see MM; cf. *NDIEC* 1.84-85; Wolter 273). Hence the sense "if then you have me as partner" (literally). The echo of legal contracts, with an implication of binding obligations upon the partner,[31] may be deliberate and ironic, since the appeal is to what Paul and Philemon share in common *as Christians,* and not as those legally bound to each other. The reference could be to their faith (as in v. 6): "partner in the faith" (NEB/REB), "if you grant me any fellowship with yourself" (NJB); in which case Paul's appeal is to Philemon simply, once again, as a brother "in the Lord" (Dibelius 106; Lohse 203-4). But since Philemon has already been designated "fellow worker" (v. 1), the effect of the reference here is to mark Philemon out as Paul marked out Titus in 2 Cor. 8:23: κοινωνὸς ἐμὸς καὶ συνεργός, "my partner and coworker" (Bruce, *Colossians, Philemon, and Ephesians* 218; O'Brien, *Colossians, Philemon* 299). The appeal, in other words, is to Philemon as a fellow evangelist or worker on behalf of the churches who looked to Paul for leadership. It is this further dimension of shared experience and shared ministry, with its evocation of mutual trust and collegiality between Paul and Philemon, and its implication that Philemon like Paul put the work of the gospel and care of the churches among his highest priorities, that gave Paul the stronger confidence that Philemon would know how to put the righting of Onesimus's wrong in its proper perspective.[32]

The stronger the shared bond evoked in the first part of the verse, the stronger the force of the second: Philemon should welcome (προσλαβοῦ) Onesimus as he would Paul (ὡς ἐμέ; the same appeal is used in the later

31. Sampley, "Societas" 170-71; *Partnership* 79-81; Winter, "Letter" 11-12, followed by Schenk 3474-75. Despite v. 19, however, it is not so clear that in this image Paul depicts himself as *senior* partner (as urged most forcibly by Petersen 103-8); the tentativeness of Paul's formulation in v. 17 suggests rather that Paul was conscious of the clash in social status and obligation precisely at this point.

32. See again J. Hainz, *EDNT* 2.304.

P. Oxy. 1.32 and *P. Osl.* 55, in Deissmann, *Light* 197-98, and Lohse 201 n. 45). Though Onesimus was a slave, and a slave liable to punishment for some misdemeanor, Philemon should receive him into his house (cf. Rom. 14:1; 15:7) as he would Paul his partner.[33] That implication gives the appeal an added edge, since it was a traditional assumption in Greco-Roman society that such a relationship was only possible between equals, and certainly not between master and slave (Wolter 274-75; note particularly Aristotle, *Ethica Nicomachea* 8.11.6-7; Plato, *Leges* 756E-757A; Seneca, *Epistle* 47.2). The appeal, it should be noted, is no longer merely that of strong sentiment (as in v. 12); it is now rather the appeal to one partner to accept the good faith and judgment of the other. Here Paul throws his own estimate of Onesimus into the scale, and does so precisely in his capacity as Philemon's partner in the business of the gospel. He counters his own uncertainty regarding Philemon's response by calling confidently on his investment in Onesimus: the returning Onesimus, also bearing Paul's letter, would be a worthy representative of Paul himself (cf. Preiss 36-37). "Here the real goal of the letter is reached. Everything up to this point prepares for this request" (Gayer 256).

18 εἰ δέ τι ἠδίκησέν σε ἢ ὀφείλει, τοῦτο ἐμοὶ ἐλλόγα. Such an appeal can only be made if the good faith can be demonstrated, should that be necessary. Onesimus had evidently wronged (ἠδίκησεν; the same verb as used in Col. 3:25) Philemon in some way not made explicit, or was financially in debt to Philemon (ὀφείλει; cf. Matt. 18:28, 30, 34; Luke 7:41; 16:5, 7; again regularly in the papyri: MM s.v. ὀφείλω). "If" presumably does not indicate that Paul was treating the matter lightly or that he had any uncertainty that Onesimus had told him the whole story. The letter itself attests to some serious breach between Philemon and Onesimus, and the immediately preceding expression of confidence in Onesimus as Paul's representative would prevent the "if" from being read as any kind of doubt regarding Onesimus's trustworthiness. But it neatly serves the purpose of taking for granted Philemon's view that Onesimus was guilty of serious misdemeanor, without wholly conceding that Philemon's judgment was entirely correct. The "if" has, indeed, the force of "whatever," the rhetorical effect being to underline the comprehensiveness of Paul's guarantee: "whatever wrong he has done or debt he has incurred. . . ."[34] For discussion of what the wrong was, whether something done by Onesimus prior to his flight (?) from Philemon's household or the flight

33. Προσλαμβάνω/ομαι itself can have the sense "take on as helper or partner" (LSJ s.v. 3; Bruce, *Colossians, Philemon, and Ephesians* 219 n. 87); but could Paul have meant this (Lohmeyer 190 n. 1)? Bruce (219 n. 88) suggests that Paul was speaking "playfully"; but the context is one of solemn seriousness, weighted with legal terminology.

34. C. J. Martin, "Rhetorical Function" 332-33, and Callahan 374 question whether v. 18 indicates Onesimus's guilt (even in Philemon's eyes); but the aorist (ἠδίκησεν) hardly indicates the possibility of Onesimus's *future* indebtedness (for travel and lodging), and the thesis hardly explains the vehemence of Paul's repeated assurance that he would repay whatever Onesimus owed.

itself, and whether robbery or some other financial irregularity was involved (so, e.g., Lightfoot 341; Dibelius 106; Caird 222-23; Stuhlmacher 49; Gnilka 84; Wright 187; Nordling 109-10), or simply Philemon's loss of Onesimus's services for a time (e.g., Lohse 204; Ernst 136; Martin, *Colossians and Philemon* 167), see pp. 302ff. above.

The resort to commercial technical terms is highlighted still further by Paul's use of ἐλλογέω, "charge it to my account" (once again many examples in the papyri: BAGD, MM). This sustained use of the language of commercial transaction suggests again that Paul was not entirely sure of his ground with Philemon and also that Philemon (not least as a slaveowner) was comfortable with the language of commerce. To leave Philemon as little reason as possible, should he even consider rejecting Paul's plea or dealing with it in a less than generous way, Paul stakes his own reputation for probity and fair dealing on the guarantee given here: whatever justifiable claim Philemon had on Onesimus in financial terms, Paul would meet it in full. This is an astonishing guarantee for someone with as little independent means as Paul, not to mention that he was in prison at the time. It can only mean that he would be able to call on wealthy backers who presumably knew both Paul and Onesimus, should the IOU be called in.[35] Alternatively, Paul could be so bold because, despite whatever misgivings he still had, he could not believe that Philemon would call in the debt. The issue is sharpened still further by the way Paul proceeds.

19 ἐγὼ Παῦλος ἔγραψα τῇ ἐμῇ χειρί, ἐγὼ ἀποτίσω· ἵνα μὴ λέγω σοι ὅτι καὶ σεαυτόν μοι προσοφείλεις. In an unusual step Paul evidently took the stylus in his own hand at this point and both signed his name ("Here is my signature: Paul," NEB/REB) and wrote out his personal guarantee ("Here, I will write this with my own hand: *I, Paul, will pay you back,*" GNB). It would be necessary to state what he was doing since the letter was not purely personal (where change of penmanship would be sufficient visual indication of the author's personal intervention; see Weima 46-47) but was for public reading. The step was unusual for Paul, since elsewhere his personal autograph marks the beginning of the letter's closing (see the introduction to the comments on vv. 8-20). But here it comes as the climax to Paul's appeal to Philemon, where he is pulling out all the stops and putting the full weight of his personal standing behind his words (cf. the "I, Paul" of 2 Cor. 10:1; Gal. 5:2; 1 Thes. 2:18). In this case the personal autograph

---

35. Again, the possibility that Paul was speaking in deliberately joking style (Dibelius 107; Gnilka 84, "Philemon must have laughed over the promise of a man who, as a prisoner, possessed not a penny in the world," echoing Oltramare, cited by Vincent 190) fails to give enough weight to the seriousness of the tone as confirmed by v. 19 (cf. Binder 62). Scott 111-12 also thinks that the words were "meant playfully," but notes some indications that Paul had funds at his command: according to Acts, the governor Felix hoped for a bribe (24:26), and in Rome Paul lived for two years at his own expense (28:30).

does not have the function of legitimating the letter as Paul's (see on Col. 4:18), but rather has a legal function as Paul's personal guarantee to Philemon on behalf of Onesimus.[36] The legal character of the procedure is put beyond doubt by Paul's use of ἀποτίνω, which occurs only here in the New Testament, but, once again, is common in the papyri as a legal technical term meaning "make compensation, pay the damages" (BAGD, MM). Paul was not content to make promises and provide mere reassurances; rather, he undertakes the formal legal responsibility to make good whatever wrong Onesimus has done Philemon.

However, to make trebly certain, Paul cannot refrain from once again recalling Philemon to the personal bond which held Paul and Philemon together. Only this time it is to remind Philemon not of their shared faith, or partnership in the gospel, but of Philemon's obligation to Paul (προσοφείλω, only here in biblical Greek, but again common in the papyri, "owe besides, in addition," MM). The climax of the appeal in legal terms is matched by the climax of the appeal in terms of personal relationship, albeit expressed still in terms of the commercial language which dominates the section. The effect of the ellipsis (see n. 12) is to drop in the mention as a kind of afterthought. It is a rhetorical trick, of course, but nonetheless evidences a certain hesitation on Paul's part to lean on Philemon too heavily. Its effect is to leave the main weight on the preceding legal guarantee, so that Philemon's hoped-for positive response would appear more as an act of graciousness on his part than as an unwilling repayment of a debt owed to Paul.

It is universally inferred that the obligation referred to is Philemon's conversion under Paul's ministry (cf. Rom. 15:27). In that case, that Paul does not call Philemon his son or put him alongside Onesimus in this respect (see v. 10) is surprising: Paul seems to pull out all available stops on Onesimus's behalf, and the appeal of Paul to Philemon as a father to a son would have carried great weight. It could be, however, that the influence of Paul on Philemon's conversion was not so direct — through a sermon preached, or even through a letter read, or (less likely as too indirect) through Epaphras's ministry, but not through personal counseling — so that the father-son imagery was less appropriate (Scott 112). The slightly more distant relationship which may thus be implied (cf. v. 5) should also give some cause for hesitation about speaking too glibly of Paul as Philemon's patron, so far as Philemon's Christian standing was concerned. In the world of patron-client networks, a signal act of service by a client to a patron did not necessarily involve a change in the relationship. This may also help explain the slight degree of diffidence Paul displays in referring to Philemon's

---

36. Cf. G. J. Bahr, "The Subscriptions in the Pauline Letters," *JBL* 87 (1968) 27-41, particularly 31 and 36.

indebtedness to him; despite that indebtedness, Philemon remained a much superior figure socially. It would also explain why Paul so formulates the plea as to leave the main weight on the legal guarantee just provided.

The issue which remains unclear in all this is whether Paul put so much of himself behind his appeal because he was confident of Philemon's response or because he was lacking precisely in such complete confidence. At the very least, such an offer from one "in chains," and from one in whose debt Philemon himself stood in significant measure, would make it hard for Philemon to act churlishly and easier for him to appear magnanimous. The strategy was brilliant — and from the fact that the letter was preserved, presumably successful.

20 ναὶ ἀδελφέ, ἐγώ σου ὀναίμην ἐν κυρίῳ· ἀνάπαυσόν μου τὰ σπλάγχνα ἐν Χριστῷ. Paul seems to be conscious of just how heavily he has leaned on Philemon and of the danger of some overload in the legal language used. So he makes a deliberate attempt to "lighten up" with this final plea. Ναί denotes affirmation or emphatic repetition of what has just been said ("Yes, indeed," BAGD), but now transposed into the language of the family ("brother"; see on v. 1), with its less formal appeal to mutual belonging and shared responsibilities and concerns. The lighter mood is heightened by the neat pun on Onesimus's name: on the matter of Onesimus (from ὀνίνημι, see also v. 11), Paul asks for some benefit from Philemon (ὀναίμην, middle optative of ὀνίνημι). That the request is somewhat conventional (BAGD s.v. ὀνίνημι; frequent in Ignatius: *Ephesians* 2:2; *Magnesians* 2; 12:1; *Romans* 5:2; *Polycarp* 1:1; 6:2) is not to the point: Paul deliberately chooses what was an unusual term for him (both the verb and the first person optative of any verb occur only here in the New Testament); Ignatius probably intended the same pun in *Eph.* 2:2, since he had in mind at that point their bishop Onesimus (Bruce, *Colossians, Philemon, and Ephesians* 221; otherwise Martin, *Colossians and Philemon* 168); and since Philemon as a man of education would doubtless be aware of the fact that the name Onesimus was derived from the word, the pun would not be lost on him (e.g., Lightfoot 343 and Wright 189; *pace* BDF §488.1; Lohse 205; Gnilka 87 n. 30; O'Brien, *Colossians, Philemon* 302). We should not ignore the fact, however, that the plea is equivalent to that for "the good action" of v. 14, that is, once again acknowledging that Paul could not enforce his wishes on Philemon and must look to him to act in kind and generous spirit: "Yes, brother, I am asking this favor of you" (REB).

Ἐν κυρίῳ reaffirms that the basis on which Paul makes his pleas is primarily that of their common standing "in the Lord" (v. 16). Likewise the appeal for Philemon to refresh his heart (the same emotive σπλάγχνα) is obviously a deliberate echo of v. 7 (see there): Philemon was so well known in this role, and that, in the end of the day, was all that Paul was asking for. Since the encouragement could come either from Onesimus's return to Paul (particularly Bruce, *Colossians, Philemon, and Ephesians* 220-21) or presumably also from news of Philemon welcoming Onesimus back, the language does not make clear what the benefit was that Paul hoped to receive in the whole affair (cf. Lohse 205).[37] The concluding ἐν Χριστῷ, following so closely on the ἐν κυρίῳ, reinforces the character of this final appeal, with the double implicit reminder that they all, Philemon as well, stood under the same master (cf. Col. 4:1), who was also the servant Christ (cf. Rom. 15:1-8).

37. Binder 64-65 stresses σου: "not from his money and his slave . . . [but] from *him*, from Philemon himself."

IN CONCLUSION (21-25)

*21 Confident of your obedience I have written[1] to you, knowing that you will
do even more than I say. 22 At the same time, make ready a guest room for
me; for I am hoping that through your prayers I may be granted to you.*

*23 Epaphras, who is my fellow prisoner in Christ Jesus,[2] greets you,
24 as do Mark, Aristarchus, Demas, and Luke, my fellow workers. 25 The
grace of the[3] Lord Jesus Christ be with your spirit.[4]*

If we are to look for a formal break between the body of the letter and the closure,
it probably comes between vv. 20 and 21: v. 20 brought the thought back to the
same point reached at the end of the thanksgiving (v. 7); and the lack of a linking
particle at v. 21 implies a break and a fresh start, with the letter's second ἔγραψα
also marking the beginning of the final autograph section (see also the introduction to the comments on vv. 8-20). So too, ἅμα δὲ καί in v. 22 is evidently a
deliberate attempt to link the plea for Onesimus with the personal request for
hospitality, so that a break between vv. 21 and 22 would disrupt the sequence.
The epilogue is thus fairly typical of Paul's practice elsewhere: a recapitulative
summary (v. 21; cf. particularly Gal. 6:11-18; 1 Cor. 16:22; 2 Cor. 13:11; see
further Weima 234-36), travel plans (v. 22),[5] greetings passed on (vv. 23-24),
and final benediction (v. 25; see the introduction to Col. 4:7-18).

1. Once again an epistolary aorist. Some (e.g., Lightfoot 342; Dibelius 107; Gnilka 87) think
that this second ἔγραψα may indicate that Paul wrote the whole letter.

2. An interesting suggested emendation (without textual support) is Ἰησοῦς in place of
Ἰησοῦ, thus including the Jesus Justus of Col. 4:11 (the only one missing from the parallel list in
Phm. 24) as one of the greeters. The text would then run: "Greetings from Epaphras, my fellow
prisoner in Christ, (also) Jesus, Mark . . ." (so Lohse 207 n. 16; Ollrog 49). The matter cannot be
determined by the "in Christ" or "in Christ Jesus" phrase; the latter is certainly more common in
Paul, but the former is also fairly common. More weighty is the consideration that Paul would hardly
have referred to "Jesus," unqualified, referring to someone other than Christ, for obvious reasons
(hence the fuller designation in Col. 4:11). And without any textual support the emendation cannot
stand (R. P. Martin 169; Stuhlmacher 55).

3. Typical of the tendency of the scribal tradition is the addition of "our" to conform the
text here to the fuller and more sonorous benediction. See Metzger 658.

4. Similarly with the addition of "Amen." See again Metzger 658. For the various subscriptions
added by subsequent scribes see also Metzger 658-59. They begin with the simple "to Philemon"; this
is elaborated by a reference to Rome as the place of writing; the most typical further elaborations
designate Onesimus the house slave as the letter bearer and indicate that the recipients were Philemon
and Apphia as owners of Onesimus and Archippus as deacon of the church in Colossae. The eleventh-
century miniscule 42 carries the further information that Onesimus later died as a martyr in Rome, but
the source of the information is unknown and its historical value very dubious.

5. See particularly R. W. Funk, "The Apostolic *Parousia:* Form and Significance," in
Christian History and Interpretation. John Knox FS, ed. W. R. Farmer, et al. (Cambridge: Cambridge
University, 1967) 249-68 = "The Apostolic Presence: Paul," in Funk, *Parables and Presence*
(Philadelphia: Fortress, 1982) 81-102; White 44; Doty 36-37; T. Y. Mullins, "Visit Talk in New
Testament Letters," *CBQ* 35 (1973) 350-58.

21 πεποιθὼς τῇ ὑπακοῇ σου ἔγραψά σοι, εἰδὼς ὅτι καὶ ὑπὲρ ἃ λέγω ποιήσεις. Paul has walked a difficult tightrope between covering the legal aspects of the affair and treating it as an in-house issue to be determined by other than the rules of the marketplace and law court. The effect has been to give Philemon the maximum amount of room to make his own decision, to act graciously precisely by discarding the legal option which has been put to him. Having set out the pieces on the board with such care, Paul, as it were, stands back and invites Philemon to make the decisive move. And having made it so much easier for Philemon to act generously, Paul can express his confidence that Philemon will do so.

Πεποιθώς, "being persuaded," however, should not be read as though it were some casual statement of confidence in Philemon; that would ring oddly with the weightiness of what has just preceded. Nor should it be devalued because of its undoubted rhetorical force (cf. Olson 289: "polite and friendly, if ironic, means for reinforcing the purpose for which the letter was written"). In fact, πείθομαι denotes the trust of someone who has been convinced that such trust is warranted. It could be translated "having been persuaded, believing"; and the perfect tense as usual will indicate a settled trust resulting from previous experience of Philemon as one in whom confidence could be placed (cf. particularly 2 Cor. 2:3; Gal. 5:10; Phil. 1:6, 14, 25; 2:24; 2 Thes. 3:4; R. Bultmann, *TDNT* 6.4-6). Paul stakes the success of his appeal on his earlier knowledge of Philemon (cf. again v. 20 with v. 7).

This presumably is why Paul also felt able to speak of his confidence in Philemon's "obedience" (τῇ ὑπακοῇ σου). The term is one he uses elsewhere in reference to his apostolic authority, as apostle to the Gentiles (Rom. 1:5; 15:18) and in dealing with challenges to that authority (2 Cor. 7:15; 10:5-6; 2 Thes. 3:14), though also in a friendly letter (Phil. 2:12). Here, at most, we might see an implicit threat, that a negative response from Philemon would seriously damage his relation with Paul by, in effect, calling into question Paul's right to appeal as he had on Onesimus's behalf. But if so Paul takes care to express himself in an unthreatening way, by calling for obedience as evidence, not so much of his authority as of his justified trust in Philemon (cf. Marshall 184-85). Some (Stuhlmacher 52; O'Brien, *Colossians, Philemon* 305; Binder 65) seek a solution in understanding the clause as a call for obedience to the will of God; but that would be even more manipulative in effect (cf. Hainz, *Ekklesia* 206-8). More in tune with the mood is Gnilka's suggestion (87-88) that the objectless "obedience" will here denote the "obedience of faith," obedience to the gospel, which is also the obligation to the practice of love (cf. v. 6).

A further factor to be borne in mind is that the word translated "obedience" (ὑπακοή) was little known outside Christian circles at the time (LSJ, MM). So within Christian circles the derivation of the verb ὑπακούω ("obey") from ἀκούω ("hear"), and the use of ὑπακούω in the LXX to translate *šama'* ("hear"), probably meant that ὑπακοή carried the overtone of a responsive obedience, of heedful hearing. In this case, implied in this concluding word on the whole affair is the expression of trust that Philemon as a Christian and man of sensitivity would hear all that Paul was saying and would respond as Paul wanted. JB/NJB ("your compliance"; also Harris 278) and NEB/REB ("meet my wishes") soften the more forceful term "obedience," but without being able to bring in any of these overtones; Dibelius 106 has *"Bereitwilligkeit"* ("readiness, willingness"), but see Wickert 233, approved by Lohse 206 n. 3; "the last word is obedience" (Petersen 133).

The attitude of mutual trust is climaxed by the final clause: "knowing that you will do even more than I say." No longer a matter of hope or even of trust, but of the knowledge that comes from personal acquaintance and mutual respect, Paul has no doubt that Philemon will act more generously than the circumstances warrant. Since he has talked so far only of Philemon receiving Onesimus back "forever" (vv. 15-17) and of forgiveness (or recompense, vv. 18-19), "even more" must mean something further, the most obvious alternatives being Philemon freeing Onesimus[6] and/or sending Onesimus back to Paul to continue to serve Paul[7] on Philemon's behalf (vv. 12-14).[8] But it is left entirely to Philemon to decide what is appropriate (Suhl, *Philemonbrief* 274-75; Gnilka 88; Koester 135; Collange 72).

22 ἅμα δὲ καὶ ἑτοίμαζέ μοι ξενίαν· ἐλπίζω γὰρ ὅτι διὰ τῶν προσευχῶν ὑμῶν χαρισθήσομαι ὑμῖν. In the more relaxed mood of the conclusion Paul appends his personal request. To maintain the link it is better to translate ἅμα δέ as "at the same time" (BAGD, RSV) rather than as a detached request, "one more thing" (NEB, NIV, NRSV); Paul implies that Philemon's treatment of Onesimus should be of a piece with his preparation for Paul's coming. Implicit also is the thought that Paul would visit Philemon's household, where he would no doubt expect to enjoy the company of both Philemon and Onesimus, on good relations with each other as Christian brothers. The request may be rather peremptory ("prepare for me"), but the context is one where guest friendship could be taken for granted, a token of the depth of their relationship. It should also be recalled that in the ancient world

6. Houlden 232; Caird 223; Bellen 80; Wright 189; Petersen 97-98; others in Stuhlmacher 53 n. 135.

7. Knox 24-25; Harrison 275-76, 287-88; Gayer 242-43; Wiles 216-17; Ollrog 104; O'Brien, *Colossians, Philemon* 306; Bruce, *Colossians, Philemon, and Ephesians* 221-22; Marshall 188. Stuhlmacher 53-54 notes that if Col. 4:7-9 can be drawn into evidence (as written later than Philemon), then it implies that Philemon did make Onesimus available (free?) for service to Paul and the Christian mission.

8. Contrast Church 30-32: "This has nothing to do with the return of Onesimus to Paul, or his manumission. It simply serves to trump Paul's argument in a flattering and very persuasive way"; Binder 65-66: more help from Philemon himself in his missionary work.

hospitality played a much larger role in traveling than today; inns were generally places to be avoided if at all possible, so that householders would generally expect to provide hospitality for their compatriots (cf. particularly Rom. 16:23; see further G. Stählin, *TDNT* 5.17-20). That Philemon had "a guest room" (ξενία; see BAGD; Stählin, *TDNT* 5.19 n. 137; cf. Acts 28:23; *Clementine Homilies* 12:2), not *"the* guest room," confirms that he was a man of means with a house capable of hosting more than one visitor at the same time (ἑτοίμαζε implies that the guest room is within Philemon's control).[9] The plural "you" of the next clause presumably embraces at least Apphia as well, as the one in charge of the household arrangements, if not the whole church which met in Philemon's house (so also v. 25).

Paul makes the request because he hopes to come to Philemon. Whereas ἐλπίς has a strong meaning, denoting full confidence in the future (see on Col. 1:5), ἐλπίζω, particularly where Paul is talking of his travel plans (Rom. 15:24; 1 Cor. 16:7; Phil. 2:19, 23; cf. 1 Tim. 3:14), seems to have something of the tentativeness of the more regular Greek usage (cf. LSJ; R. Bultmann, *TDNT* 2.519-20). Since the nature of Paul's affairs and the hazards of travel in the ancient Mediterranean world had upset his travel plans often enough (cf. Rom. 1:10-13; 15:30-32; 2 Cor. 1:15–2:12; 1 Thes. 3:1-5), a certain tentativeness would be understandable (contrast the πεποιθώς of v. 21; cf. on both counts Phil. 2:23-24).

This inference may be strengthened by the somewhat unexpected use of the verb χαρίζομαι ("show favor"). Although it can be used in the sense "release" (Acts 3:14; 25:11), the implication in both cases is of the judge acting improperly (cf. Plato, *Apologia* 35c: verdicts should express justice, not favor). Elsewhere the thought is of the release as an unexpected favor (Diodorus Siculus 13.59.3; Plutarch, *C. Gracchus* 4.3; *Papyrus Florentini* 61.61; Josephus, *Vita* 355; BAGD s.v. 1). And when used of divine action, as here, the note of unexpectedness is even stronger (*Testament of Joseph* 1:6). This chimes in with Paul's most regular use, denoting the unexpectedness of gracious giving (Rom. 8:32; 1 Cor. 2:12; Gal. 3:18; Phil. 1:29; 2:9; see also on Col. 2:13). So here, Paul's hope is that he would be given graciously as a favor to Philemon and the others; the popular translation "restored" (JB/NJB, NIV, NRSV, REB; NEB "will grant," RSV "granted") loses sight of this important nuance. In other words, Paul's expectations were not high,[10] and in the normal course of events he would have recognized the unlikelihood of his being able to come to Philemon; it would take an act of generosity on God's part, in which their (again plural) prayers would be

---

9. Bruce, *Colossians, Philemon, and Ephesians* 222 n. 100, notes that according to Theodoret, bishop of Cyrrhus (423–ca. 466), Philemon's house still survived.

10. Wiles 282; *pace* Lohse 207; Lohmeyer 192: "That the question of being freed from imprisonment depends on a judicial decision is completely overlooked."

important. If Col. 2:1 is post-Pauline but reflects the historical situation, it implies that Paul's wish was not granted (Stuhlmacher 55).

What we may properly deduce from this for Paul's situation at the time of writing the present letter is not clear. The more realistic the hope of visiting Philemon soon (why otherwise should Philemon make preparation right away?), the more likely the letter was written in Ephesus, only about four days' journey distant. Or should we see here something more of a "keeping up the spirits" throwaway remark: "before you know I may be needing your guest-chamber" (Scott 114)?[11] Moreover, the more hesitant the hope, with the implicit recognition that its fulfillment would depend on an unexpected act of generosity on God's part, the more distant and more difficult we may imagine Paul's situation to be. For the bearing of these considerations on the relation of Philemon to Colossians see pp. 37-40 above.

We should also note the corollary for Paul's theology of prayer. He asks for the prayers of Philemon, Apphia, Archippus, and the whole church (vv. 1-2) and assumes that they would be a factor in the success of his hoped-for visit ("through your prayers"). But there is no certainty that his hope will be fulfilled just because they pray for him; he does not presume to know what God's plans for him are; such deductions are best made with the benefit of hindsight (cf. v. 15). Nevertheless prayer remains important, presumably as a way of expressing support for Paul and of tuning into the will of God (cf. v. 6).

23 ἀσπάζεταί σε Ἐπαφρᾶς ὁ συναιχμάλωτός μου ἐν Χριστῷ Ἰησοῦ. The main business of the letter is complete. All that remains is for Paul to pass on, as usual, the greetings of those with him (see the introduction to Col. 4:7-18 and on 4:10), though, somewhat surprisingly, only Philemon is back in view ("you" singular; contrast vv. 22 and 25). Epaphras is given pride of place, a further indication that the letter was written to a place where he was thought of with special affection and regard, that is, the cities of the Lycus valley, which he had evangelized and worked for, and probably Colossae, his own city of birth or residence (see on Col. 1:7 and 4:12-13).

There is, however, a curious interchange between Epaphras and Aristarchus at this point. In Col. 4:10-13 it is Aristarchus who is given first mention, and he who is designated "fellow prisoner," with Epaphras following, commended for his "great labor" (though not designated "fellow worker"). Here, however, it is Epaphras who is named first and described as "fellow prisoner," and Aristarchus is mentioned merely as one, and not even the first, of the following group of "fellow workers" (v. 24). The most obvious explanation is that for Paul συναιχμάλωτος ("fellow prisoner") was the

11. F. J. A. Hort, *Prolegomena to St Paul's Epistles to the Romans and the Ephesians* (London: Macmillan, 1895), had earlier suggested that Paul spoke in "a playful way" (noted also by Harrison 281; R. P. Martin 147).

more honorific designation, so that the one to whom it is attached is naturally named first; in its only other occurrence in Paul (and the New Testament) it designates Andronicus and Junia, "outstanding among the apostles" (Rom. 16:7). But was it merely honorific, and so did Paul attach it to colleagues at random, the "in Christ Jesus" (see on Col. 1:2) being the more important part of the phrase, in which case it would simply be a further variation on "brother in the Lord" (= Christian)? That would hardly explain the restricted range of its usage. More likely, then, it denotes an actual imprisonment shared with Paul. In that case we have to imagine some kind of interchange between Aristarchus and Epaphras: Aristarchus (voluntarily) sharing Paul's imprisonment when Colossians was written(?), and Epaphras at Paul's side in prison when Philemon was written. That in turn need not imply a lengthy period separating the two letters; the interchange between Epaphras and Aristarchus could just have happened, or the shared imprisonment may have amounted to visits of short duration (see also on Col. 4:10).

24 Μᾶρκος, Ἀρίσταρχος, Δημᾶς, Λουκᾶς, οἱ συνεργοί μου. Attached to the greeting of Epaphras are greetings also (the verb is assumed) from Mark (see on Col. 4:10), Aristarchus (see on Col. 4:10), Demas, and Luke (see on Col. 4:14). All four are called "my fellow workers" (see on Col. 4:11 and Phm. 1). Since Philemon is named also as "fellow worker" (v. 1), their interest in Philemon is that of colleagues; the implication, of course, is that they share Paul's views on the matter of Onesimus.

It can hardly be accidental that just these four are mentioned, since it is just these four who are also included in the greetings in Col. 4:10-14 (see also n. 2 above):

Colossians	Philemon
Aristarchus	Epaphras
Mark	Mark
Jesus Justus	
Epaphras	Aristarchus
Luke	Demas
Demas	Luke

The obvious consistency is that Mark comes second in both lists, with Aristarchus and Epaphras exchanging places above and below him, and that Demas and Luke are last mentioned in both lists, though in different order. Only two explanations for the striking similarity of the lists can command real support: either the letters were written within a short time of each other, so that those close to Paul were the same, with only Jesus Justus having come or departed in the interval between; or the writer of Colossians derived his list from that in Philemon, with some random and imaginative changes (see further pp. 37f. above).

25 ἡ χάρις τοῦ κυρίου Ἰησοῦ Χριστοῦ μετὰ τοῦ πνεύματος ὑμῶν.
The final benediction takes its typical Pauline form, "the grace of the/our
Lord Jesus Christ be with you" (Rom. 16:20; 1 Cor. 16:23; 1 Thes. 5:28;
2 Thes. 3:18), with the final phrase expanded ". . . be with your spirit" (as
in Gal. 6:18 and Phil. 4:23; GNB translates these consistently as "be with
you all"); Col. 4:18 is more abrupt (see there). As such and in comparison
with the epistolary customs of the time (see Weima ch. 2) it marks the
distinctiveness of the Christian letter, with its characteristic Pauline emphasis
on χάρις, "grace" (see on Col. 1:2), from "the Lord Jesus Christ" (see on
Col. 1:3 and Phm. 3).

This is the only use of πνεῦμα in the letter, and it clearly refers to the
human spirit. Of course, the thought is not of grace to be with their spirit in
distinction from their body or mind. The thought is more Hebraic, with "your
spirit" meaning "you" (E. Schweizer, *TDNT* 6.435; Stuhlmacher 56), but
"you" as spiritual persons, "you" as open to the grace (and Spirit) of God
in and through your spirit (cf. Rom. 8:16), that is, precisely by virtue of the
fact that you function as persons in a spiritual dimension as well as in the
material and everyday dimension of reality (cf. v. 16: καὶ ἐν σαρκὶ καὶ ἐν
κυρίῳ). The plural "you" (ὑμῶν) denotes the regular distributive singular,
"your spirits" (BDF §140), but here may strengthen the sense that the church
in the house of Philemon should be one in spirit, not least in their response
(with Philemon) to the central request of the letter.

INDEX OF SUBJECTS

Admonish, 124, 236-37
Adoptionism, 102
Age, 119
Alienation, 105-6
Already/Not yet, 200-201
Angels, 27-28, 60, 76, 150
  of the Lord, 87
  worship of, 27-28, 76, 137, 150,
    179-84, 186-87, 191-92, 195,
    205-6, 235-36
Anger, 219
Apostle, 44, 47, 310-11
Apphia, 311-13
Archippus, 37-38, 287-88, 312-13
Aristarchus, 37, 275, 278, 311, 347-48
Assurance, 131

Baptism, 48, 68, 139, 159-60, 203, 220-21
Barbarian, 225
Barnabas, 276-77
Beloved, 64, 228, 311, 329
Benediction, 269
Blameless, 109
Bodily, 151-52
Body, 94-97, 177, 185-86, 196-98
  = church, 95-96, 117, 185-87
  = cosmos, 94-96, 118
  of flesh, 107-9, 117, 152, 157-58
  members of, 212-13, 220
  one body, 234-35
Boldness, 325
Brother, 47-49, 64, 272, 284, 329, 341

Calendar piety, 34
Calling, 234
Charismatic, 71
Chiasm, 54
Children, responsibility of, 243, 249-51
Christ:
  coming again, 207-8, 262

deity of, 88-90
died with, 158-59, 188-89, 199,
  202-3, 206
exalted, 203-4
firstborn, 89-90, 97-98, 209
hidden with, 206-7
= image of God, 87-88, 209
in Christ, 49-50, 57, 80-82, 91-92, 94,
  96-97, 106-7, 122, 131, 140-42,
  146, 152, 154, 160, 169, 199, 348
in you, 59, 121-23
is all, 227
as judge, 256
as Lord, 55-56, 72, 139-40, 244, 314
in the Lord, 247-48, 250-51, 341
as medium of creation, 90-91, 93-94
= Messiah, 45-47, 56, 139-40, 208, 233
model of conduct, 72, 140-41, 221, 227,
  229-31, 233
as mystery, 131, 139, 148, 263
preeminence over creation, 89-90,
  93-95, 98-99
resurrection of, 97-98;
  see also Resurrection
as Son, 79-80
= Wisdom, 88-91, 93-94, 99, 125, 139,
  148, 186; *see also* Wisdom, divine
word of, 235-37
Christian, 24, 45, 50
Christian heresy, 185
Christianity, 24-25
Christology, Adam, 50, 209, 222-23.
  See also Colossians, christology of
Church, 94-97, 104, 187
  house church, 245, 284-85, 313
Circumcision, 28, 34, 48, 145, 154-56,
  163-64, 278
  of Christ, 158
  and uncircumcision, 137, 154-56, 201,
  223-25

of flesh, 163-64
without hands, 156-57
Collection, 58
Colossae, 20-23, 37, 43, 63, 307-8, 347
  church in, 22-23
  Jewish community in, 21-22, 29-34,
    133-34, 147, 199, 234
  trouble at, 23-35, 65, 146-47;
    see also Colossian philosophy
Colossian errorists, 24-26, 35;
  see also Colossian philosophy
  false teaching, 24-26, 35, 129, 131-33,
    144; *see also* Colossian philosophy
  heresy, 24-26, 28, 35, 185, 284;
    see also Colossian philosophy
  hymn, 28, 83-87, 89, 105, 146
  philosophy, 24-35, 131, 147-48, 151,
    153, 174, 179, 190, 202, 235-36
    Jewish, 29, 35, 137, 171-74, 179-84,
      190-94, 197-98, 224-25, 228, 278
    syncretism, 27-28, 31, 33-34, 155-56,
      179-80; *see also* Gnosticism
Colossians:
  authorship of, 35-39, 43-45, 269-70
  christology of, 36, 86, 177;
    see also Christology
  date of, 39-41
  ecclesiology of, 36, 187;
    see also Body = church, Church
  eschatology of, 36, 76-80, 115-17,
    124-25, 161, 176-77
  overlap with Ephesians, 36-37, 106
  place of origin, 39-41
  relation to Philemon, 37-38, 308, 311
  structure of, 41-42
  theme of, 136-37
Commercial language, 337-40
Compassion, 228-29
Cross, 103-4, 136, 144-45, 154, 158, 162,
  165-66, 177, 199, 203
  as triumph, 166-70
Crucifixion, 170

Darkness, 77-78
Demas, 37, 275, 282-83, 311, 348
Desire/lust, 215
Disobedience, 217

Elect, 227-28
Elemental forces, 27, 137, 148-51, 153,
  168, 175, 182, 187-90
Encouragement, 130

Enemies, 105-6
Epaphras, 22-23, 43, 63-65, 129, 275,
  280-83, 311, 347-48
Ephesians, overlap with Colossians, 36-
  37, 106
Ephesus, 22-23, 35, 37-38, 43, 63, 129,
  307-8, 311
  imprisonment in, 38-40

Faith, 49, 56-57, 110-11, 136-38, 142,
  145, 162, 318-20
  household of, 52
  in Christ, 57, 135, 317
Faithful, 49, 65, 110
Father, responsibility of, 243, 251-52
Fellowship, 318-19
Flesh, 134, 196-98, 253, 336
  body of, 107-9
  circumcision of, 155
  mind of, 108, 184-85
  Paul's, 114-17
Food rules, 34, 172-74, 188, 190-91, 194
Forgiveness, 68, 81-82, 164-66, 231
Foundation, 111
Fruitbearing, 61-62, 67, 69, 72
Fullness, 27, 33, 99-102, 151-53

Galatia, 22, 277, 279
Galatian churches, 25, 33, 35, 136
  troublemakers, 25, 156, 174
Gentleness, 229
Glory, 59, 76, 123
  of God, 73-74, 121
Gnosticism (Christian), 26-34,
  100-101, 132, 201-2.
  See also Colossian syncretism
God:
  as deliverer, 77
  "energy" of, 127
  as Father, 51-52, 55, 314
  impartiality of, 258
  in God, 207
  object of worship, 241
  power of, 73-74
  will of, 46-47, 67-71
  wrath of, 216-17
Godfearers, 29
Gospel, 59-63, 123
Grace, 50-52, 57, 63, 67, 111, 266, 290,
  313, 349
Greed, 215-16
Greetings, 269

Head (of body), 153, 185-86
Heart, 130
Heavenly book, 164-66
Heavens, 59-60, 76-77, 92, 204-6
Hierapolis, 20-23, 63, 129, 282, 286
Holy, 48, 109.
  See also Saints
Hope, 58-60, 62, 111, 123
Hospitality, 345-47
Household rules, 36, 41, 242-46
  Christian character, 244-45, 247-48,
    254-57
  conservative character, 245-46
  Jewish character, 201, 250-51,
    254-59
  Stoic character, 244, 247-48
Humility, 178-79, 181, 188, 195, 229
  of angels, 182
  = fasting, 178, 181
Husband, 243, 248-49
Hymns, 237-38

Idolatry, 87, 172-73, 201, 215-16
Image, 222-23.
  See also Christ = image of God
Inheritance, 67, 75-76, 79, 174, 256-57

Jesus Justus, 278, 311
Jesus tradition, 138-41, 193-94, 221, 227,
    229-31, 244, 262
Jew/Greek, 223-24, 226
Jewish feasts, 30, 174-75
  sects, 30, 34
Joy, 75, 114, 320
Judaism:
  apocalyptic, 30-31, 34, 119-20, 122,
    132, 164, 180-81, 201-2, 204-8
  attractiveness to Christians, 29, 185,
    199, 264-65
  diaspora, 29-33
    not evangelistic, 32, 156
  mystical, 30-31, 34, 74, 148, 180-81,
    183, 205, 207
Judaizing, 34
Judgment, final, 217, 256-58
Justification, 81

Kindness, 229
Kingdom, 67-68, 77-79, 257, 279-80
  of Christ, 78-79
Knowledge, 27-28, 62-63, 76, 131-32
  of God, 67-69, 71-73, 87, 224

Laodicea, 20-23, 37, 48-49, 63, 97, 129,
    282-84, 286
  letter to, 286-87
Law, 70, 136, 165, 190-93
Lie, 219-20
Light, 68, 76-78
Lord, in the.
  See Christ as Lord
Love, 56-58, 65, 68, 130, 232-33, 248-49,
    317, 323, 326-27
Luke, 37, 275, 282-83, 311, 348
Lycus valley, 20-23, 29, 63, 129, 308, 347

Malice, 219
Mark, 37, 275-78, 311, 348
Master, responsibility of, 243, 259-60, 299
Messiah.
  See Christ = Messiah
Mystery, 28, 119-23, 131-32, 139, 263-65
Mystery cults, 27, 159-60
  initiation into, 182-83

Name of the Lord, 240-41
Nestorianism, 102
Nympha, 23, 283-85

Obedience, 250, 344-45
Old/new nature, 219-22
Onesimus, 37-38, 40, 272-73, 275, 283,
    286, 301-8, 311 and *passim,*
  particularly 328-31, 341
  Paul's request for, 332-36, 345
  Paul's son, 328

Patience, 74-75, 230
Paul:
  age of, 327
  concern for churches, 326
  coworkers, 271-72, 274-75, 278-79,
    283, 301, 311, 337
  imprisonment of, 39, 263-64, 275-76,
    281, 289, 304-5, 310-11, 323,
    327- 28, 331
  personal note, 289, 339-40
  rhetoric of, 323-24, 344
  travel plans, 269, 346
Pauline, 19, 36, 38-39, 41, 104, 114
Peace, 50-52, 103
  of Christ, 233-34
Peacemaker, 103
Perfection/maturity, 125-26, 232-33
Philemon, 23, 38, 284, 300-308, 311,
  and *passim*

social status of, 300-301, 321, 324-25,
    327-28, 333, 335-36, 340-41, 346
Philemon, letter of, 19, 37-38, 40
    authorship of, 299-300
    place of writing, 307-8
    relation to Colossians;
        see Colossians: relation to Philemon
    structure of, 309
Philosophy, 147-48.
    See also Colossian philosophy
Platonic, 176, 201, 205
Pleroma.
    See Fullness
Post-Pauline, 19, 37-39, 269
Prayer, 56, 261-63, 281-82, 315-16, 318,
    347
    for mission, 263
Principalities/Powers, 60, 92-93, 145, 153,
    169-70
Proclaim, 111-12, 123
Prophets, 236
Proselytes, 29, 48
Psalms, 237-38
Purity, 34, 190-92, 194
    impurity, 214
Put off/on, 199-200, 211, 218, 220-21, 227

Rage, 219
Reconciliation, 102-4,107-9
    cosmic, 104, 107, 122, 263
Redeem, 265-66
Redemption, 80-81
Repentance, 81
Resurrection, 154, 158, 162, 199, 203-4
    with Christ, 160-61, 188-89, 199, 203
Riches, 131
Righteousness, 76
Rome, 40-41
Rulers.
    See Principalities/Powers

Sabbath, 34, 174-75
Sacrificial interchange, 109-10
Saints, 48, 51, 56-58, 67-68, 75-77, 120-
    21, 228, 320-21
Salt, 266-67
Scythian, 225-26
Servant, 65, 112, 117-18
Sister, 312

Slave, 64-65, 243, 299
    fellow-slave, 64
    and free, 223, 226
    responsibility of, 252-59
    runaway, 303-4, 306
    treatment of, 259-60
Slavery, 226, 252, 301-7, 336-37
Songs, 237-39
Soul, 255-56
Spirit, Holy, 65-66, 70-71, 73, 79, 122-23,
    134, 136, 156, 158
Spirit, human, 134, 349
Spiritual, 66, 70-71, 238-39
Stoicheia.
    See Elemental forces
Suffering, 114-17
    servant, 116
Syncretism.
    See Colossian syncretism

Teach, 124, 142, 236-37
Teachers, 140-41
Temple tax, 22, 30
Thanksgiving, 41, 53-55, 62, 67-69, 75,
    111, 142-43, 235, 240-41, 315-16
Timothy, 38, 40, 45, 47, 49, 269, 311
Tradition, 136-44, 148, 248.
    See also Jesus tradition
Truth, 60-61, 63
Tychicus, 37-38, 40, 271-72, 275, 282-83,
    286, 311

Vice/virtue lists, 199-200, 213-14, 218-19,
    228, 230
    Christianized, 200
    sexual vice, 214-16, 218

Walk, 71, 111, 138, 140, 199, 217, 241,
    265
Wife, responsibility of, 243, 246-48
    subjection of, 247
Wisdom, 27-28, 31, 33, 70-71, 76, 124,
    131-32, 194-96, 265
    divine, 85-86, 88, 91, 93, 100-101, 117,
        122; see also Christ = Wisdom
    as intermediary, 88-89
    personified, 88-89
Works, good, 72
Worship, 211, 235-41

INDEX OF MODERN AUTHORS

Abbott, T. K., 58, 63, 67, 71, 72, 89, 103, 109, 116, 123, 125, 155, 162, 165, 167, 177, 190, 202, 210, 211, 235, 239, 242, 275
Agnew, F., 44
Aletti, J.-N., 29, 35, 37, 43, 49, 68, 71, 72, 76, 81, 84, 86, 88, 90, 91, 92, 93, 95, 102, 105, 110, 111, 113, 115, 121, 123, 130, 131, 142, 152, 157, 165, 166, 167, 175, 178, 190, 208, 210, 211, 213, 219, 222, 227, 231, 234, 240, 244, 245, 246, 247, 249, 258, 261, 266, 281, 285, 289
Anderson, C. P., 287
Argall, R. A., 27, 160, 182
Arnold, C. E., 21, 73, 93, 95, 186
Arzt, P., 55
Attridge, H. W., 181
Aune, D. E., 43

Bahr, G. J., 39, 289, 340
Balch, D. L., 243
Balchin, J. F., 83, 84, 85, 89
Balz, H., 152, 195, 225, 325
Bammel, E., 92
Bandstra, A. J., 128, 132, 149, 166, 168, 182
Banks, R., 48, 285
Barclay, J. M. G., 302, 303, 306, 307, 333, 335, 336
Barclay, M. G., 252
Barnett, P. W., 45
Bartchy, S. S., 226, 299, 302, 304, 306, 307, 323, 334, 335, 336
Barth, G., 56
Bassler, J. M., 258
Bauckham, R. J., 115
Bauer, W., 24
Bauernfeind, O., 312
Baugh, S. M., 84

Baumgarten, J., 266
Baur, F. C., 25-26, 299
Beasley-Murray, G. R., 158
Beasley-Murray, P., 95, 102
Bedale, S. M., 95
Behm, J., 124, 130, 185, 265
Beker, J. C., 116
Bellen, H., 303, 306, 329, 345
Benoit, P., 76, 83, 85, 102, 128, 151, 152
Berger, K., 51, 129, 164, 258
Bertram, G., 115, 127, 134, 135, 279
Best, E., 115, 152, 177, 255
Betz, H. D., 44
Betz, O., 157
Beyer, H. W., 65
Bietenhard, H., 180, 240
Binder, H., 301, 303, 307, 311, 317, 318, 334, 339, 342, 344, 345
Birdsall, J. N., 322
Bjerkelund, C. J., 326, 328
Blanchette, O. A., 166
Blinzler, J., 149
Blue, B., 285
Bockmuehl, M., 120, 128, 132, 182, 261, 264
Bornkamm, G., 27, 59, 147, 158, 201, 322, 327
Bowers, W. P., 113
Bradley, K. R., 306
Breytenbach, C., 168, 169
Brown, R. E., 120, 121
Bruce, F. F., 21, 22, 29, 31, 36, 38, 39, 40, 43, 55, 57, 61, 69, 75, 76, 82, 88, 100, 107, 109, 116, 125, 129, 146, 150, 157, 166, 167, 171, 176, 177, 178, 212, 219, 220, 230, 231, 232, 236, 237, 247, 248, 267, 276, 282, 287, 289, 299, 300, 303, 308, 315, 317, 318, 322, 328, 330, 334, 337, 338, 341, 342, 345, 346

355

Büchsel, F., 102, 217, 265, 328
Buckland, W. W., 302, 304
Bühner, J.-A., 44
Bujard, W., 35
Bultmann, R., 43, 58, 61, 81, 212, 217, 332, 344, 346
Burchard, C., 163
Burger, C., 83, 84, 85, 98, 146
Burney, C. F., 88

Caird, G. B., 24, 84, 88, 89, 93, 99, 131, 135, 175, 179, 212, 228, 252, 262, 274, 275, 300, 317, 324, 325, 330, 339, 345
Callahan, A. D., 299, 329, 335, 338
Campbell, J. Y., 319
Campbell, R. A., 327
Cannon, G. E., 146, 211, 213, 244
Carr, W., 29, 93, 149, 165, 167, 168, 169, 183, 195
Carrington, P., 211
Casey, P. M., 89
Cerfaux, L., 27, 101
Charlesworth, J. H., 81
Church, F. F., 323, 345
Cohen, S. J. D., 31
Collange, J.-F., 345
Collins, J. J., 32
Conzelmann, H., 27, 56, 63, 123, 135, 159, 161, 171, 175, 220, 230, 246, 247, 262
Coutts, J., 36
Crouch, J. E., 243, 244, 247, 248, 252, 254
Cullmann, O., 116, 140

Dabelstein, R., 265
Dahl, N. A., 46, 120
Daube, D., 242, 323, 328
Dautzenberg, G., 168
Davies, W. D., 88, 89, 231
de Jonge, M., 229
Deichgräber, R., 97, 146, 238
Deissmann, A., 289, 331, 338
Delling, G., 100, 125, 126, 130, 138, 149, 150, 174, 197, 215, 238, 247, 325
DeMaris, R. E., 21, 26, 33, 147, 149, 150, 179, 180, 182, 183, 195
Denis, A.-M., 164
Derrett, J. D. M., 302
Dibelius, M., 27, 43, 54, 57, 59, 71, 72, 76, 79, 86, 92, 100, 115, 119, 123, 126, 130, 134, 151, 157, 165, 166,

178, 182, 183, 184, 187, 200, 201, 202, 207, 213, 215, 233, 239, 241, 244, 275, 278, 287, 288, 305, 307, 310, 312, 317, 320, 322, 328, 337, 339, 343, 345
Dill, S., 253
Dion, P. E., 43
Dodd, C. H., 140
Doty, W. G., 43, 55, 315, 343
Duff, P. B., 169
Dumont, J. C., 302
Duncan, G. S., 307
Dunn, J. D. G., 68, 89, 107, 157, 235, 239
Dupont, J., 94, 100, 132, 171

Easton, B. S., 214
Eckart, K.-G., 68
Elliott, J. H., 313
Elliott, J. K., 287
Ellis, E. E., 48, 278, 285
Eltester, F.-W., 88, 92
Ernst, J., 48, 50, 58, 59, 62, 68, 85, 93, 100, 101, 117, 131, 134, 135, 139, 151, 157, 168, 175, 176, 187, 191, 219, 221, 236, 251, 266, 281, 320, 325, 339
Evans, C. A., 29, 100, 182, 183
Ewald, H., 39

Fee, G. D., 66, 71, 73, 211, 237, 239
Feeley-Harnik, G., 323
Feldman, L. H., 21, 30, 31
Feuerbach, L., 216
Feuillet, A., 84, 88, 90, 91, 94, 100
Fichtner, J., 216
Findeis, H.-J., 27, 77, 78, 102, 103, 104, 107, 202
Finley, M. I., 302
Fiorenza, E. S., 86
Fitzgerald, J. T., 243
Flemington, W. F., 116
Foerster, W., 30, 51, 76, 156, 177, 233, 257, 278
Fohrer, G., 70
Fossum, J., 88, 94
Fowl, S. E., 29, 87, 92, 102, 151, 152, 157, 196

Francis, F. O., 28, 29, 176, 180, 182, 183, 195
Frankemölle, H., 229
French, D., 22

Freud, S., 216
Fridrichsen, A., 116
Friedrich, G., 313, 325, 334
Friedrich, J. H., 75, 257
Funk, R. W., 343
Furnish, V., 39

Gabathuler, H. J., 83
Gardner, P. D., 160
Gayer, R., 304, 307, 313, 316, 332, 335, 338, 345
Giesen, H., 179, 220
Gill, D. W. J., 285
Glasson, T. F., 98
Gnilka, J., 21, 25, 27, 33, 37, 39, 47, 55, 59, 62, 66, 68, 71, 76, 78, 83, 85, 89, 92, 93, 94, 97, 102, 103, 112, 115, 119, 121, 123, 125, 128, 132, 134, 139, 146, 148, 150, 152, 157, 159, 165, 167, 171, 175, 176, 186, 187, 190, 194, 196, 203, 207, 210, 211, 213, 218, 221, 222, 229, 231, 232, 234, 236, 239, 241, 244, 248, 250, 251, 262, 265, 266, 272, 274, 281, 284, 285, 287, 288, 302, 303, 305, 307, 310, 313, 316, 317, 319, 322, 324, 325, 326, 327, 328, 329, 330, 331, 332, 334, 335, 339, 341, 343, 344, 345
Golubcova, E. S., 302
Goodenough, E. R., 303
Goodman, M., 32
Goppelt, L., 244
Gourges, M., 204
Grässer, E., 27, 201, 202, 203, 207
Greeven, H., 300, 328
Gruenwald, I., 182
Grundmann, W., 64, 73, 179, 229, 262
Gülzow, H., 303, 307, 335
Gundry Volf, J. M., 110
Gunther, J. J., 27

Habermann, J., 84, 86, 89
Hafemann, S. F., 169
Hahn, F., 313
Hainz, J., 285, 311, 313, 319, 320, 326, 337, 344
Hall, R. G., 154
Hanson, A. T., 116, 119, 167, 168
Hanssler, B., 196
Harnack, A., 88
Harrington, D. J., 34

Harris, J. R., 98
Harris, M. J., 43, 54, 61, 69, 91, 93, 101, 110, 128, 139, 142, 155, 165, 178, 202, 210, 233, 242, 257, 263, 265, 274, 280, 315, 317, 318, 320, 322, 323, 345
Harrison, P. N., 287, 307, 328, 345, 347
Hartman, L., 103, 219, 243
Hasler, V., 51
Hauck, F., 62, 126, 214, 229, 319
Hauck, H., 74
Hay, D. M., 204
Hegermann, H., 74
Helyer, L. R., 84, 94
Hemer, C. J., 22
Hengel, M., 86, 170, 225, 237
Hense, O., 250
Hermann-Otto, E., 302
Herrmann, J., 76, 257
Hester, J. D., 76
Hill, D., 81
Hockel, A., 90
Hofius, O., 219
Holladay, C. R., 32
Hollander, W. H., 229
Hollenbach, B., 196
Holtz, T., 119
Hooker, M. D., 26, 86, 133, 188
Hoppe, R., 68, 101
Horst, J., 212
Hort, F. J. A., 347
Houlden, J. L., 55, 86, 92, 102, 111, 119, 157, 175, 228, 239, 244, 246, 261, 262, 266, 312, 317, 329, 345
Hübner, H., 89, 96, 101, 116, 121, 125, 137, 196, 201
Hunter, A. M., 58, 200, 231
Hurtado, L. W., 86, 89, 180

James, M. R., 164
Jang, L. K., 322, 330, 332, 335
Jensen, J., 214
Jervell, J., 221, 230
Jewett, R., 130
Johnson, S. E., 21, 22

Kamlah, E., 115
Karlson, G., 134
Kasch, W., 93
Käsemann, E., 19, 68, 85, 86, 95
Kehl, N., 29, 89, 94, 100, 102, 182, 195
Kerényi, C., 120

Kern, O., 94
Kertelge, K., 81
Kiley, M., 26, 33, 35, 36, 38, 39, 287
Kim, C.-H., 309
Kirk, J. A., 44
Kittel, G., 275
Klauck, H.-J., 245, 285
Kleinknecht, H., 87, 216
Knox, J., 258, 287, 288, 300, 303, 305,
    306, 313, 316, 317, 328, 329, 345
Knox, W. L., 62, 90
Koester, H., 228, 229, 322, 335, 345
Kraabel, A. T., 31
Kraemer, R. S., 312
Krämer, H., 120
Kramer, W., 162
Kremer, J., 115
Kretzer, A., 138
Kselman, J. S., 81
Kuhli, H., 224
Kümmel, W. G., 35, 84
Kuschel, K.-J., 89, 95

Ladd, G. E., 280
Lähnemann, J., 26, 27, 33, 136, 138, 140,
    146, 151, 168, 187, 196
Lampe, P., 304, 305
Langkammer, H., 85
Larsson, E., 159
Lattke, M., 167
Lehmann, R., 301
Levison, J. R., 202, 206, 207, 212
Lightfoot, J. B., 20, 21, 22, 23, 30, 49, 55,
    57, 62, 69, 70, 71, 77, 78, 90, 92, 99,
    105, 109, 110, 113, 115, 125, 132,
    135, 145, 146, 148, 151, 152, 157,
    165, 167, 174, 178, 179, 186, 191,
    194, 195, 196, 202, 208, 210, 219,
    224, 225, 226, 228, 229, 230, 234,
    238, 239, 242, 252, 256, 260, 261,
    266, 271, 272, 274, 276, 277, 278,
    283, 287, 288, 299, 303, 305, 306,
    307, 311, 312, 317, 318, 322, 326,
    327, 328, 329, 330, 331, 335, 339,
    341, 343
Lincoln, A. T., 29, 76, 96, 119, 179, 182,
    183, 202, 203, 205, 207, 250
Lindemann, A., 28, 36, 37, 72, 123, 132,
    156, 165, 189, 197, 210, 229, 231,
    235, 244, 245, 262, 272, 283, 287
Loader, W. R. G., 204
Lohmeyer, E., 59, 68, 72, 73, 76, 78, 91,

94, 103, 111, 115, 119, 120, 121, 123,
    125, 128, 129, 135, 151, 165, 167,
    175, 176, 189, 190, 195, 200, 202,
    203, 212, 213, 217, 218, 219, 221,
    228, 230, 236, 244, 251, 252, 256,
    258, 260, 262, 264, 266, 277, 279,
    281, 307, 313, 322, 324, 325, 329,
    330, 333, 334, 346
Lohse, E., 19, 25, 27-28, 31, 33, 35, 36,
    37, 39, 43, 54, 55, 57, 59, 61, 63, 67,
    68, 70, 72, 73, 75, 76, 85, 87, 88, 89,
    92, 93, 94, 95, 100, 103, 109, 110,
    111, 116, 120, 121, 123, 124, 125,
    126, 128, 129, 130, 133, 134, 135,
    146, 147, 148, 150, 152, 156, 158,
    164, 165, 166, 175, 176, 179, 182,
    185, 190, 194, 201, 210, 213, 221,
    224, 230, 233, 239, 240, 241, 242,
    244, 246, 247, 249, 258, 260, 262,
    266, 279, 287, 300, 305, 307, 316,
    320, 322, 323, 326, 328, 329, 332,
    335, 337, 338, 339, 341, 342, 343,
    345, 346
Lona, H. E., 121, 151, 157, 160, 161, 162,
    206, 218
Löwe, H., 86, 116
Lührmann, D., 120, 121, 243, 244, 245
Luther, M., 326
Lutz, C. E., 248
Luz, U., 78
Lyall, F., 335
Lyonnet, S., 171, 180, 183

MacDonald, M., 36, 159, 223, 244, 245,
    265, 269
Mach, M., 180, 181
McKnight, S., 32
MacMullen, R., 253, 312
Malherbe, A. J., 124, 213, 250
Manns, F., 88, 89
Marshall, I. H., 103, 107, 307, 313, 344,
    345
Martin, C. J., 338
Martin, D. B., 64, 118, 302
Martin, R. P., 27, 31, 36, 39, 48, 59, 68,
    76, 83, 85, 89, 107, 109, 135, 145,
    146, 150, 158, 166, 175, 182, 210,
    230, 235, 238, 247, 262, 277, 280,
    283, 289, 308, 310, 313, 317, 327,
    339, 341, 343, 347
Marxsen, W., 27, 200
Masson, C., 43, 49, 57, 58, 71, 88, 93,

113, 134, 146, 152, 155, 157, 165,
171, 193, 197, 202, 210, 237, 239,
254, 260, 266, 274, 281, 282
Maurer, C., 27
Mayer, B., 59
Meeks, W. A., 35, 62, 86, 138, 139, 159,
160, 221, 245, 265, 275, 284, 306, 312
Merk, O., 221, 230, 244, 335
Merklein, H., 36, 39, 116
Metzger, B. M., 40, 55, 67, 83, 105, 128,
138, 145, 171, 202, 210, 211, 271,
274, 308, 315, 322, 343
Michaelis, W., 87, 249, 288
Michel, O., 147, 226
Michl, J., 103
Mitchell, S., 21, 22, 179
Mitton, C. L., 36
Moir, J., 171
Moore, G. F., 81
Morray-Jones, C. R. A., 74, 181, 184, 223
Morris, L., 81
Moule, C. F. D., 39, 40, 50, 54, 57, 63,
67, 83, 93, 100, 101, 103, 105, 113,
115, 122, 123, 128, 135, 139, 140,
149, 152, 157, 158, 161, 167, 171,
194, 196, 200, 207, 213, 223, 232,
236, 247, 252, 254, 262, 265, 274,
289, 303, 307, 316, 317, 320, 322,
323, 328, 329, 330, 334
Moulton, J. H., 146, 274
Müller, K., 244, 245, 247
Müller, P.-G., 208
Mullins, T. Y., 55, 343
Munck, J., 62, 116
Munderlein, G., 102
Munro, W., 243
Murphy-O'Connor, J., 285

Nauck, W., 267
Newsom, C., 181, 192
Newton, M., 191
Nielsen, C. M., 26, 116
Nock, A. D., 253
Norden, E., 83, 91
Nordling, J. G., 303, 306, 328, 329, 333,
335, 339

O'Brien, P. T., 22, 29, 36, 41, 43, 48, 55,
56, 59, 68, 69, 71, 72, 76, 83, 94, 97,
103, 109, 110, 111, 112, 115, 119,
129, 130, 132, 134, 138, 146, 158,
160, 161, 177, 194, 195, 196, 202,

208, 210, 211, 213, 214, 217, 221,
222, 228, 229, 231, 241, 242, 246,
247, 248, 258, 262, 263, 271, 275,
280, 288, 289, 307, 310, 316, 317,
318, 320, 322, 325, 326, 328, 329,
334, 337, 341, 344, 345
Ollrog, W.-H., 22, 37, 38, 63, 277, 278,
279, 301, 306, 331, 343, 345
Olson, S. N., 344
O'Neill, J. C., 85
Otramare, H., 339
Overfield, P. D., 100

Pagels, E. H., 168
Pardee, D., 43
Percy, E., 35, 71, 81, 86, 100, 161, 167,
179, 180, 186, 201, 258, 307
Perdue, L. G., 212
Petersen, N. R., 305, 313, 322, 323-24,
326, 337, 345
Pfitzner, V. C., 126
Plümacher, E., 150
Pöhlmann, W., 91
Pokorný, P., 19, 25, 28, 31, 39, 53, 55,
67, 68, 76, 78, 88, 89, 94, 100, 102,
111, 115, 124, 134, 139, 140, 146,
151, 152, 154, 157, 158, 159, 161,
177, 183, 191, 196, 200, 202, 210,
211, 213, 222, 233, 237, 245, 250,
251, 262, 267, 272, 284
Pomeroy, S. B., 312
Porter, S. E., 210
Preisker, H., 183
Preiss, T., 303, 313, 335, 338
Prestige, G. L., 88

Radl, W., 182
Ramsay, W. M., 20-21, 179, 182
Rapske, B. M., 275, 276, 289, 303, 304,
306, 328
Rebell, W., 157
Reicke, B., 22, 39, 196
Rengstorf, K. H., 64, 226
Reumann, J., 118
Reynolds, J., 31
Richards, E. R., 38, 39, 289, 324
Richardson, W. J., 303
Riesenfeld, H., 319, 331
Rigaux, B., 125
Robinson, J. M., 86, 235
Rogerson, J. W., 94
Roloff, J., 116, 187

Rowland, C., 29, 180, 182, 183, 195
Rubinson, K. S., 225
Rusam, D., 149

Sampley, J. P., 337
Sand, A., 130, 256, 336
Sanders, E. P., 31, 37, 81, 191
Sanders, J. T., 25, 31, 34, 86, 191, 200, 201, 232, 238, 245, 324
Sappington, T. J., 25, 26, 28, 29, 68, 86, 88, 125, 126, 128, 131, 146, 149, 164, 165, 167, 169, 175, 178, 181, 182, 183, 190
Sasse, H., 334
Saunders, E. W., 30
Schelkle, K. H., 47
Schenk, W., 26, 34, 35, 98, 102, 130, 175, 299, 300, 303, 309, 328, 337
Schenke, H. M., 27, 146
Schille, G., 146
Schlier, H., 64, 95, 142, 226, 239, 248, 325
Schmauch, W., 83, 233
Schmithals, W., 27, 243
Schmitz, O., 320
Schnackenburg, R., 86, 159, 201, 210, 245
Schneemelcher, W., 287
Schneider, G., 58, 89
Schniewind, J., 123
Scholem, G. G., 31
Schrage, W., 200, 232, 244, 245, 247, 248, 249, 251
Schramm, T., 254
Schrenk, G., 2, 101, 228, 328
Schroeder, D., 213
Schröger, F., 92
Schubert, P., 53, 55, 316
Schulz, S., 176, 200, 201, 214, 229, 245, 248, 334
Schürer, E., 21, 22, 30, 32, 172, 238
Schweizer, E., 32, 33, 35, 37, 38, 39, 43, 47, 61, 66, 74, 76, 78, 83, 85, 88, 90, 91, 92, 94, 95, 103, 115, 118, 134, 142, 149, 150, 156, 157, 160, 165, 166, 176, 179, 182, 186, 195, 200, 210, 213, 222, 228, 229, 230, 233, 235, 237, 239, 244, 245, 248, 250, 251, 252, 262, 275, 285, 287, 336, 349
Scott, E. F., 119, 130, 158, 168, 176, 228, 231, 276, 282, 313, 317, 321, 322, 325, 335, 339, 340, 347
Scroggs, R., 222
Seesemann, H., 71
Segal, A. F., 74, 183, 204

Sellin, G., 161
Selwyn, E. G., 211
Sheppard, A. R. R., 179
Simon, M., 179
Spicq, C., 57, 215, 317
Stählin, G., 217, 259, 260, 346
Stegemann, E., 33, 201
Steinmetz, F. J., 89, 201
Stommel, E., 159
Stowers, S. K., 43, 304, 309
Strecker, G., 27
Stuhlmacher, P., 285, 305, 307, 311, 319, 320, 322, 325, 327, 328, 331, 334, 336, 339, 343, 344, 345, 347, 349
Stuhlmann, R., 116
Suhl, A., 39, 317, 320, 345
Sumney, J., 33, 132, 182
Szabó, A., 179

Tachau, P., 107, 218
Tannehill, R. C., 157
Tannenbaum, R., 31
Thraede, K., 243, 245
Traub, H., 59
Trebilco, P., 21, 22, 29, 30, 31, 32, 179, 285
Turner, N., 91, 140, 210, 233, 317

van der Horst, P. W., 156, 218, 220, 221
van Kooten, G., 36
van Unnik, W. C., 325
Vawter, B., 68
Vermes, G., 181
Verner, D. C., 243, 244, 247, 252
Vielhauer, P., 27
Vincent, M. R., 299, 300, 306, 307, 317, 326, 331, 333, 335, 339
Völkel, M., 213
von Rad, G., 51, 233
von Soden, H., 334

Wachsmuth, C., 250
Wall, R. W., 47, 57, 64, 110, 128, 134, 152, 169, 178
Walter, N., 165
Wanke, G., 254
Wedderburn, A. J. M., 23, 31, 32, 38, 50, 92, 93, 94, 97, 102, 152, 157, 159, 160, 162, 167, 206, 207, 221, 232, 245
Wegenast, K., 139
Weima, J. A. D., 275, 289, 324, 339, 343, 349

Weiser, A., 65
Weiss, H., 165
Weiss, H.-F., 27, 89
Wengst, K., 85, 86, 139, 146, 162, 238
Westermann, W. L., 302
White, J. L., 43, 343
Wibbing, S., 214
Wickert, U., 311, 313, 320, 322, 331, 345
Wiedemann, T., 302, 303, 306, 335
Wikenhauser, A., 115
Wiles, G. P., 317, 318, 320, 345, 346
Wilken, R. L., 33
Williams, A. L., 180
Williamson, L., 168
Wilson, A., 311, 323
Windisch, H., 225
Wink, W., 29, 93, 149, 173, 189
Winter, S. C., 300, 301, 303, 320, 328,
    329, 331, 332, 337
Wischmeyer, O., 64
Wolter, M., 26, 31, 32, 37, 39, 46, 55, 58,

68, 69, 72, 73, 76, 82, 83, 86, 89, 91,
    92, 95, 99, 102, 103, 106, 112, 116,
    118, 123, 136, 150, 153, 157, 158,
    161, 163, 173, 179, 186, 189, 202,
    205, 207, 212, 221, 222, 228, 231,
    232, 236, 239, 249, 250, 262, 263,
    267, 278, 285, 305, 306, 307, 314,
    316, 317, 327, 328, 335, 336, 337, 338
Wright, N. T., 26, 33, 34, 39, 48, 85, 88,
    89, 94, 135, 147, 148, 155, 157, 165,
    175, 210, 228, 233, 288, 300, 324,
    339, 341, 345

Yamauchi, E. M., 21
Yates, R., 29, 37, 39, 47, 85, 89, 93, 96,
    118, 123, 145, 149, 158, 165, 166,
    167, 169, 210, 211, 221, 244, 263, 270

Zeilinger, F., 91, 146, 207, 264, 269
Zeller, D., 132
Zmijewski, J., 229

INDEX OF BIBLICAL AND OTHER ANCIENT WORKS

OLD TESTAMENT

Genesis
1:1	88
1:22	62
1:26	222
1:26-27	88
1:28	62
2:7	255
2:17	222
3:5	222
3:7	222
5:1	88
5:1-3	222
6:9	125
8:17	62
9:1	62
9:6	88, 222
9:7	62
15:6	57
15:7-8	257
16:7-12	87
17:9-14	154
17:11-14	155
17:20	62
18	281
20:6	190
22:11-12	87
28:4	257
49:3	97
49:10	59
50:20	333

Exodus
3:2-6	87
4:22	90
6:6	77
12:5	125
14:19-20	87
14:30	77

15:6	204
15:12	204
16:3	196
16:8	196
16:10	73
17:16	119
18:20	71
19:16-24	74
20:4-5	215
20:4-6	87
20:10	259
20:12	250, 251
21:6	334, 335
21:23-25	258
24:16-17	73
29:1	109
30:13-16	21
31:3	70, 71
31:16-17	174
32	281
32:10-12	216
32:32-33	164, 166
33:17-23	74
35:31	70, 71
35:35	70
40:15	119
40:34	73

Leviticus
1:3	109
1:10	109
4:20	81
4:26	81
4:31	81
4:35	81
5:2-3	190
5:3	191
5:6	81
5:10	81
5:13	81

5:16	81
5:18	81
7:19	190
7:21	190
7:26-27	172
9:23	73
11:1-23	172
11:8	190
11:24-28	190
13:45-46	191
15	191
19:15	258
19:17	47
19:32	327
20:9	250
20:17	258
21:7-8	48
21:17-21	181
25:19	196
25:43	259
25:53	259

Numbers
6:5-8	48
6:14	109
6:25-26	51
10:10	174
16:5-7	48
16:19-35	74
18:20	76
19:11-13	191
25:1-3	215
25:1-4	216
25:4	168

Deuteronomy
1:17	258
1:39	257
2:12	257
4:6	70

4:12	74	9:16	256
4:19	180	10:18	95
4:39-40	73	11:11	95
5:8-9	215		
5:8-10	87	**Ruth**	
5:15	174	1:13	249
5:16	250, 251	1:20	249
5:17-18	219		
6:5	256	**1 Samuel**	
7:6-7	228	3:7	72
7:8	80	18:22	178
9:26	80		
10:9	76	**2 Samuel**	
10:14	59	6:5	239
10:16	70, 156	7:14	78
10:17	258	15:11	254
12:12	76	15:26	178
12:16	172	19:37	256
12:23-24	172	20:1	76
13:4-5	71	22:1	239
13:5	77	22:24	109
14:3-21	172	22:44	95
15:12	47	23:1	237
15:15	80		
15:17	334, 335	**1 Kings**	
16:19	258	2:19	204
17:3	180	8:27	59
18:1	76	10:9	178
19:14	111	12:16	76
21:18-21	250	20:12	95
23:15-16	329		
28:13	95	**2 Kings**	
29:16-28	216	2:12	328
29:29	208	4:9	48
32:6	52	4:23	174
32:9	76	14:26	249
32:15	228		
32:36	64	**1 Chronicles**	
33:12	64, 79	16:13	228
33:26	228	22:12	70
		23:31	175
Joshua		29:17	254
14:3-4	76		
18:6-7	76	**2 Chronicles**	
19:9	76	1:10-12	70
19:49	76, 183	2:3	175
19:51	76, 183	2:6	59
24:29	64	6:18	59
		7:6	238
Judges		9:8	178
5:20	150	16:12	283
6:9	77	19:7	258

24:18	216		
31:3	175		
32:31	322		
35:3	48		
Nehemiah			
7:3	262		
9:6	59, 163		
10:32-33	21		
10:33	175		
12:24	238		
12:46-47	238		
13:26	79		
Esther			
10:3	119		
Job			
6:6	266		
8:10	70		
12:13	70		
13:4	283		
15:15	48		
23:11-12	193		
28	89		
28:20	70		
29:14	221		
38:7	150		
38:23	59		
39:17	70		
40:4	124		
Psalms			
3:7	316		
5:2	316		
7:1	316		
7:3	316		
7:6	316		
8:6	209		
9:10	72		
10:6	119		
13:3	316		
15:2	109		
16:3	48		
16:11	204		
17:7	204		
18:2	316		
18:6	316		
18:21	316		
18:23	109		
18:28-29	316		
19:11	256		

19:13	109	110:1-2	78	11:6-9	103
20:6	204	111:1	178	11:30-32	217
22	46	111:10	70, 254	13:6-16	217
24:1	99	112:1	254	28:16	111
25:9	229	118:15-16	204	29:13	193, 194, 240
29:1-2	181	119:43	61	29:14	70
30:3	163	132:9	221	30:27-28	115
34:2	229	139:7	100, 102	33:6	71
34:9	48, 254	143:10	69	33:15	71
34:11	254	146:10	178	34:2	216
35:13	178	147:14	51	34:8	217, 256
37:9	257	148:1-2	181	34:17	119
37:11	229			40:9	60
40:8	69	**Proverbs**		41:8	64, 79
44:3	204	1:7	70, 254	41:8-9	234
45:2	266	2:2-3	70	41:10	116
49:3	70	2:3-6	132	42:6	234
49:11	119	2:6	70	42:7	116
58:3	105	3:7	254	42:10	238
60:5	204	3:10	196	43:1	80
63:2	73	3:19	91	43:3-4	234
68:16	101	6:29	190	43:4	79
68:17	101	8:22	88, 90, 97	43:5	116
69	46	8:22-31	93	43:10	72
69:8	105	8:22-36	85	43:14	80
69:10	178	8:25	90	43:20	228
69:22	256	9:10	73	44:1	64
69:28	164, 166	10:10	103	44:2	228
72:1-7	51	12:12	215	44:9-20	215
73:23	204	21:26	215	44:22-24	80
77:8	119	22:8	258	45:3	132
81:3	174	28:18	71	48:12	234
85	51	31:25	221	49:1	234
86:11	71	31:30	72	49:1-6	116
88:3-6	163			49:8	116
89:3	64	**Ecclesiastes**		51:2	234
89:5	48	2:13	77	51:9	119
89:7	48	10:12	266	51:11	80
89:27	90			52:3	80
90:10	281	**Isaiah**		52:7	60
91:8	256	1:13	174	52:11	190, 214
94:2	256	1:13-14	175	52:15	116
97:2	74	5:1	228	53	46
98:1	204	5:7	228	54:10	51, 233
102:16	73	6:2-3	180	54:17	257
104:24	91	6:3	173	55:10-11	61
105:6	228	6:4-5	74	55:12	51
105:26	64	7:8-9	95	56:6	174
105:42	64	9:6	176	58:3	178
106:16	48	9:6-7	233	58:5	178
110:1	79, 139, 203, 204, 209	10:13	70	60:6	60
		11:2	70, 71	61:1	60

61:2	256	34:25-31	233	2:2	119
63:4	256	36:26-27	70	3	78
63:16	52	37:26	233		
65:2	217	40–41	183	**Amos**	
65:5	192	43:22-25	109	5:18	77
65:17	103	45:17	175	5:20	77
65:22	228	45:18	109		
65:25	103	45:23	109	**Jonah**	
66:18-19	73	46:3	174	2:6	163
66:20	47	46:4-6	109		
		46:6	174	**Micah**	
Jeremiah		46:13	109	5:4	233-34
1:9-10	142			5:10-15	216
2:2	58	**Daniel**		6:5	72
4:4	70, 156	1:3-16	172, 173		
7:16-20	216	1:17	70	**Zephaniah**	
8:2	180	2:8	265	1:5	180
8:16	99	2:18-19	120	1:15	217
10:16	76	2:21	70	1:18	217
10:25	216	2:27-30	120	2:2-3	217
12:7	228	3:35	64	3:8	217
12:9-10	76	5:14	70		
17:8	142	6:11	56	**Haggai**	
18:7-9	142	7:9	79, 92	2:9	234
19:13	180	7:9-11	217		
23:24	100	7:9-14	204	**Zechariah**	
24:6	142	7:10	164, 180	1:15	216
25:6	216	7:18	48	8:12	51, 234
31:3	228	7:21-22	115	14:5	48
31:9	52, 90	7:25-27	115		
31:20	64	8:10	150	**Malachi**	
31:28	142	8:13	48	1:6	52
31:31-34	70	8:24	48	4:1	217
42:10	142	10:2-3	182	4:4	64
46:11	283	10:3	172, 173		
50:13	216	11:32	73		
51:15	70	12:1	164		
51:19	76	12:1-3	115		
51:57	256	12:2	162		
		12:3	77	**APOCRYPHA**	
Lamentations		12:13	76		
5:6	196			**Tobit**	
		Hosea		1:3	47
Ezekiel		2:11	175	1:4	119
1:26-28	74	4:12-18	215	1:10-12	172
14:5	105, 106	8:1-3	73	4:3-4	250
14:7	105, 106	9:7	256	5:3	164
16:49	196	9:10	105	7:12	51
19:7	99	13:6	196	8:15	48, 225
22	216			9:5	164
30:12	99	**Joel**		12:18	46
31:7	142	2:1-2	217	13:2	163

13:3-4	52	18:9	48	44:17	125
				44:23	76
Judith		**Sirach**		45:18	219
4:9	178	1:4	70, 90, 93	45:22	76
8:29	70	1:14	254	46:1	228
12:2	172	1:16	254	47:8	240
12:19	172	1:18	254	50:23-24	51
		1:20	254	50:27	70
Additions to Esther		1:24-25	132		
14:17	172, 173	1:27	229, 254	**Baruch**	
		2:7-9	254	1:22	106
Wisdom of Solomon		2:15-17	254	3:9–4:4	85
1:1	254	3:1	244	3:15	132
1:4	100, 101	3:1-16	250	3:15–4:1	132
1:6-7	93, 94, 100	3:17-18	229	3:23	70
1:7	102	4:8	229	3:28-36	89
2:13	52	4:30	259	3:36–4:1	70, 89
2:16	52, 214	6:26	256	3:37	228
2:18	52	7:1	258	4:4	69
2:23	88	7:20-21	259	5:1-2	221
3:9	58	7:27-28	250		
4:10	79, 250	7:29	256	**Epistle of Jeremiah**	
4:15	228	8:6	327	43	215
5:5	76	11:34	105		
5:18	221	12:12	204	**Susanna**	
6:15	233	14:20	70	8, 11, 14, 20, 56	215
6:18	58	15:3	70		
6:22	132	17:3	88	**1 Maccabees**	
7:8	92	17:18	79	1:15	154
7:13-14	132	21:16	266	1:48	154
7:17	149	23:17	109	1:60-61	154
7:22–8:1	94	24	85	1:62-63	172
7:26	88	24:3	98	2:27	262
8:5	91	24:6	98	2:46	154
9:4-6	70	24:9	90	4:54	238
9:9-10	71	24:11	64	9:14	135
9:10	250	24:12	76, 141	10:34	175
9:17-19	71	24:23	89	13:51	239
10:12	234	24:23-26	70, 132	14:22	322
11:10	124	24:25-26	70	15:17	322
12–15	215	24:33	119		
12:2	124	29:6	258	**2 Maccabees**	
12:26	124	30:1	249	1:3	69
13:2	149	33:31	259	1:30	238
13:6	333	35:11-14	258	2:21	224
14:12-27	216	35:12-13	258	2:30	183
14:19	333	37:22-23	70	4:13	224
14:25-26	213	39:6	70, 71	4:39	332
15:2-3	69	39:9-10	70	6:9-10	154
16:13	163	40:15	142	7:11	258
16:16	73	42:5	249	7:22-23	163
17:20–18:4	77	43:26	93	7:29	258

8:1	224	5:5	257	25:13	262
11:34	322	5:9	103	25:27	258
12:45	59	5:12	75	25:31	78, 204
13:8	258	5:13	267	25:34	257
14:38	224	5:22-24	47	26:41	262
		5:43-48	233	27:16-17	278
3 Maccabees		5:47	47	27:34	191
1:3	165	5:48	126		
2:16	101	6:10	69, 79	**Mark**	
2:19-20	51	6:12	231	1:4	81
5:31	109	6:13	77	1:8	160
		6:14-15	231	1:11	79, 101, 102
4 Maccabees		6:20	59	1:15	57, 266
1:1-2	147	6:24	215	1:31	65
1:11	74	6:33	205	1:41	228
1:26-27	213	7:1-2	258	2:5-7	231
2:15	213	7:3-5	47	2:23–3:5	174
5:7	180	7:7-11	263	3:31-35	47, 244
5:22-24	147	7:9-11	250	3:35	69
7:9	74	7:21	69	4:8	62
8:11	59	8:29	266	4:11	265
9:8	74	10:16	265	4:22	132, 208
9:30	74	11:5	60	5:1-34	191
		11:25	132	5:26	283
1 Esdras		11:25-27	265	6:17	263
1:42	214	11:29	229	6:34	228
4:29	204	12:28	79	7:1-23	194
5:61	238	12:32	119, 176	7:3	185
		13:32	62	7:3-13	148
4 Ezra (= 2 Esdras 3–14)		13:41	78	7:4	145
4:33-43	116	15:1-20	194	7:7	193
5:13	182	15:2-9	148	7:8	137, 148
6:35	182	15:9	193	7:10	250, 251
6:58	90	15:17	193	7:19	193, 194
7:77	59	18:15	47	7:21-22	213
8:12	69	18:21	47	7:22	215, 219
8:44	88	18:21-22	231	9:7	79
10:38	120	18:23-35	231	9:11	264
12:36	265	18:28	338	9:19	230
14:5	120	18:30	338	9:35	65
14:22	71	18:34	338	9:38	241
14:26	265	18:35	47	9:49-50	267
14:39-40	71	19:4	222	9:50	266
14:46	265	19:21	126	10:1-9	251
		19:28	204	10:13-16	251
		19:29	257	10:17	257
NEW TESTAMENT		20:34	228	10:19	250, 251
		22:2	79	10:29	244
Matthew		22:3	234	10:30	119
1:19	168	22:9	234	10:34-35	220
3:7	216	23:8-9	328	10:37	204
3:11	115	24:42	262	10:38	115

10:38-39	160
10:43-45	65
12:6	79
12:25	209
12:29-31	232
12:30	255
12:36	204
13:10	264
13:12	244
13:20	228
13:22	228
13:26	208
13:27	228
13:33	266
13:35	262
13:37	262
14:26	238
14:34	262
14:36	69
14:37	262
14:38	262
14:58	156
14:62	204
15:7	263
15:26	78, 166
15:41	65

Luke

1	238
1:50	119
1:78	229
2:14	180
3:7	216
3:16	115
3:22	152
3:29	278
4:22	266
4:43	264
5:10	337
7:22	60
7:41	338
7:42-43	164
7:47-49	231
8:15	62
8:17	208
10:21	120
10:21-22	265
10:25	257
10:30-32	191
10:40	65
11:2	79
11:9-13	263

11:11-13	250
11:20	79
12:37	65
12:47	69
14:12	256
14:14	256
14:24	191
14:26	250
14:34	266
14:34-35	267
15:20	228
16:5	338
16:7	338
16:8	76
16:13	215
16:18	119
17:4	231
17:8	65
17:30	208
18:22	59
19:20	59
20:42	237
21:8	266
21:19	74
22:29	79
22:30	204
22:44	281
22:53	78
23:7	329
23:11	329
23:15	329
23:34	231
24:44	237
24:47	81

John

1:1-3	91
1:4-5	76
1:18	74
2:5	65
2:9	65, 191
3:19-21	76
3:36	217
5:18	204
5:21	162, 163
5:35	333
6:46	74
6:63	162
8:23	205
10:33	204
12:36	76
18:35-37	78

Acts

1:14	262
1:18	228
1:20	237
1:23	278
2:1-4	239
2:9-10	22
2:13-18	239
2:34-35	204
2:36	139
2:38	81, 241
2:42	236, 262
2:46	75, 284
3:1	56
3:6	241
3:7	135
3:14	346
3:19-21	208
3:21	264
4:10	241
4:13	325
4:29	325
4:36	277
5:3-4	220
5:42	284
6:2	65
6:4	262
6:7	62
7:58	218
8:13	262
8:20	193
8:25	236
9:27	277
9:27-28	241
10:3	56
10:7	262
10:10	191
10:14	172
10:36	60
10:43	81
10:48	241
11:3	172
11:22-24	277
11:25-26	277
11:26	30, 45
12:6	263
12:12	276, 284
12:24	62, 236
12:25	276
13:1	124, 141, 277
13:2	277
13:6	278

13:7	277	23:26	310	2:4	75, 81, 121, 229, 230
13:33	102, 237	24:24	135		
13:47	116	24:26	339	2:5	216
14:2	217	24:26-27	307	2:6-11	258
14:12	277	25:11	346	2:7	74, 205
14:15-17	52	25:21	329	2:8	216, 217, 219
14:22	115	25:22	322	2:9-10	224
14:27	263	26:16-18	116	2:10	332
15:2	277	26:18	77, 81, 135	2:11	258
15:12	277	26:23	98	2:12	173
15:20	214	27:2	275	2:12-16	166
15:22	277	28:23	279, 346	2:18	69, 70
15:23	310	28:30	339	2:21	124
15:25	277	28:31	279	2:25-27	154
15:29	214			2:28	155
15:35	277	**Romans**		2:28-29	156, 162, 208
15:37-39	276, 277	1:1	44, 46, 64	2:29	65, 158
16:1	47	1:3	197	3–4	106
16:5	135	1:3-4	86	3:5	216
16:14-15	246	1:4	98, 102	3:7	72
16:15	244, 284	1:5	318, 344	3:8	146
16:25	75, 238	1:7	43, 48, 64, 228	3:9	224
16:26	263	1:7-8	46	3:21	107, 218
16:40	284	1:8	54, 55, 56, 62	3:22	57, 125
17:14-15	47	1:8-9	53, 315, 316	3:23	123, 209, 222
17:22-31	52	1:9-10	69, 261, 262	3:24	63, 80, 161
17:30-31	61	1:10	46, 56	3:25	87, 103
18:7	278	1:10-13	346	3:26	57, 266
18:7-8	284	1:11-12	45	3:30	154, 317
18:8	244	1:11-15	113	4	57, 111, 155
18:9-10	116	1:13	47, 62, 129	4:1	197
18:23	22	1:14	225	4:7	81
18:27	277	1:16	73, 125, 224	4:9-12	154
19:1	22	1:16-17	138	4:11	125
19:1-3	30	1:18-32	106, 216	4:16	142
19:8-10	63	1:18–3:20	164	4:17	163
19:9	217	1:20	73, 87	4:19	212
19:10	22, 43, 272	1:21	73, 75, 106, 130, 222	4:24	162
19:20	62			4:25	87
19:22	47, 288, 311	1:23-27	216	5:1-5	58
19:23-41	43, 303	1:24	130, 215	5:2	209
19:26	22	1:24-25	214	5:3	114
19:29	275	1:25	222	5:3-4	74, 75
20:4	271, 275, 278	1:26	215	5:5	65, 159
20:8	284	1:28	248	5:6	189
20:11	191	1:29	215, 219	5:6-8	58
20:20	284	1:29-31	213	5:7	333
20:21	135	1:30	250	5:8	189
21:14	69	1:32	165, 216	5:9	216
21:25	214	2	106	5:10	102, 106, 107
23:11	264	2:1	173	5:12-21	164
23:14	191	2:3	173	5:14	177

5:15	63	8:13-14	70	11:13	45, 112, 118, 288
5:17	63	8:14-17	80	11:13-15	119, 266
6	203	8:15	161, 255	11:15	103
6–8	206	8:15-16	122, 131, 159	11:20	111, 254
6:2	189	8:15-17	79	11:22	110
6:3-11	50, 115	8:16	349	11:25	120, 129
6:4	67, 71, 76, 160, 207	8:16-17	244	11:25-26	121, 264
6:4-5	36	8:17	110, 114, 209	11:25-32	119
6:4-6	159	8:17-21	123	11:26	77
6:5	115, 161, 207	8:17-23	115	11:28	106
6:6	157, 220	8:17-25	59	11:30	107, 218
6:8	189	8:18	114, 208, 209, 266	11:30-32	217
6:10	189	8:18-23	115	11:33	132
6:10-11	207	8:19-23	103	11:35	256
6:11	213	8:21	193, 209	11:36	91, 92
6:12	215	8:23	77, 80, 122, 161,	12:1	65, 109, 228, 326
6:12-23	65		209	12:1-2	240, 250
6:13	80, 212	8:25	74	12:2	70, 119, 221, 222
6:16-17	226	8:26	122	12:3	118
6:17	239	8:27	130	12:4-5	50
6:18	64	8:28	319, 333	12:4-8	36
6:19	212	8:29	47, 98, 222, 244	12:5	50
6:19-21	218	8:29-30	209	12:5-8	235
6:22	64, 107, 218	8:31-35	58	12:6	318
6:23	57	8:32	346	12:7	124, 237, 288
7:1	47	8:33	228	12:8	72, 320, 326
7:4	47, 62	8:34	87, 189, 204	12:9	58, 106, 332
7:5	163, 212, 336	8:37	248	12:9–13:10	230
7:6	107, 189, 218	8:38-39	60	12:12	262
7:7-8	215	8:39	57	12:13	72
7:7-12	164	9:1	220	12:14	141
7:7–8:3	108	9:2	130	12:14-21	253
7:8-13	277	9:3	189, 197	12:14–13:7	245
7:14	163	9:5	197	12:19	64, 219, 256
7:19	332	9:6-11	111	12:21	332
7:23	212	9:8	197	13:1	247
7:24	77, 157	9:17	73	13:3	72, 106, 332
7:25	239	9:22	75, 216	13:4	184
8	200, 240	9:23	121, 209	13:5	247
8:1-2	50	9:33	111	13:8-10	232
8:3	158, 166	10:4	125	13:9	141, 277
8:4	70, 71	10:6-13	36	13:10	58
8:4-8	108	10:8	111	13:11	266
8:5	205	10:9	139, 142, 162	13:11-14	78
8:5-6	185	10:11	125	13:12	80, 218, 221
8:8	72, 336	10:12	224	13:13	71
8:9	122	10:13	55, 231	13:14	153, 197, 215, 221
8:10	122	10:14	57	14	174
8:11	36, 77, 115, 122,	10:14-15	111	14:1	338
	161, 162, 203, 209	10:15	319	14:3-6	173
8:12	47	10:21	217	14:4	280
8:13	108, 110, 213, 220	11:9	256	14:6	205, 241

14:8	207	16:12	64, 126	3:9	311
14:9	189	16:14-15	284	3:10	118
14:10	109, 256	16:14-16	283	3:10-12	111
14:14	141, 173, 194	16:16	95	3:10-14	142
14:15	130, 189	16:17	64, 326	3:11	111
14:16	319, 332	16:17-20	133, 261, 269	3:13	208
14:17	173, 192, 234, 279	16:18	257	3:13-15	258
14:18	250	16:19	332	3:17	258
14:19	234	16:20	233, 349	4:1	264
14:20	173	16:21	47, 279, 283, 311	4:5	266
14:21	173	16:23	48, 284, 285, 346	4:6	64, 184
14:23	111	16:25-26	121	4:8	78
15:1-2	72	16:26	120	4:9	45, 47, 116, 266
15:1-5	141			4:9-13	114
15:1-8	342	**1 Corinthians**		4:12	126
15:4-5	130, 320	1:1	44, 48	4:14	64, 328
15:6	55	1:2	48, 62, 95	4:15	50, 328
15:7	231, 338	1:3	43	4:16	326
15:8	65, 142	1:4	54, 55, 56, 57, 315,	4:17	47, 49, 64, 95, 124,
15:13	142		316		129, 328
15:14	124, 237	1:4-5	63	4:18	146
15:14-32	113	1:6	142	4:18-19	184
15:15	118	1:7	320	4:20	279
15:16	58, 65	1:7-9	86	4:21	234
15:17-19	56, 317	1:8	109, 142	5–6	218
15:18	344	1:10	133, 326	5:1	214
15:19	73, 119	1:11	246	5:2	184
15:20	111	1:12	133	5:3	173
15:20-21	116	1:16	244	5:3-4	134
15:22-32	269	1:17-18	104	5:4	241
15:24	346	1:18	60, 73	5:7-8	220
15:25	118	1:20	119	5:9	287
15:27	340	1:22	67, 69, 224	5:9-13	216
15:30	326	1:22-25	104	5:10	31, 189
15:30-32	261, 263, 346	1:23	46, 111	5:12-13	265
15:31	118, 217, 288	1:23-24	86	6:1-8	329
15:32	46	1:24	73, 224	6:9	213, 216
15:33	233	1:26	253	6:9-10	77, 213, 216, 257,
16	276	1:30	86, 104, 208		279
16:1	65, 95, 118, 312	2:1	123	6:9-11	79, 218
16:1-2	246, 277	2:1-4	13, 60, 133	6:13	193, 214
16:1-5	301	2:4-5	73	6:14	73, 162
16:2	139	2:6	119, 126	6:15	212
16:3	279, 311	2:6-16	207	6:16-18	107
16:3-16	269	2:6–3:4	126	6:18	214
16:3-23	275	2:7	120, 132, 209, 264	7:1	190
16:4-5	95	2:8	119	7:2	214
16:5	64, 284, 320	2:12	159, 346	7:4	107
16:6	126	2:12-13	71	7:6	325
16:7	275, 348	2:16	130	7:11	102
16:8	64	3:5	65, 112	7:12-16	245
16:9	64, 279, 311	3:6-7	62	7:15	248, 312

7:16	245	12:8	239	15:34	146
7:17	71	12:9	65	15:42	193
7:17-24	255	12:11	127	15:44	108
7:19	277	12:12	95	15:44-49	59
7:20-24	335	12:12-27	50	15:44-50	79
7:22	64, 226	12:13	50, 65, 223, 224	15:45	158, 162, 255
7:29	133, 266	12:14-26	186	15:45-49	209
7:32	72	12:21	96	15:47-49	161
7:37	111	12:27	95	15:49	222
8–10	172	12:28	141	15:50	77, 108, 133, 158,
8:1	184	13:1	239		193, 257, 279
8:4-6	36, 86	13:1–14:1	58	15:58	64, 111
8:5-6	55, 240	13:2	68	16:1	58
8:6	85, 91, 92	13:3	198	16:1-11	113
8:9	146	13:4	184	16:1-18	269
8:11	189	13:4-7	232	16:6	247
9:1-2	45, 63	13:11	205	16:7	346
9:5	312	13:12	73, 129	16:8	129
9:14	123	13:13	58, 232	16:9	263, 319
9:16	264	14:1-2	71	16:10	47, 129
9:17	118	14:2	239	16:12	48
9:24-27	177	14:3	320	16:13-18	261
9:25	126	14:11	225	16:14	130
9:27	110	14:15	239	16:15	118, 244, 288, 326
10:1	129	14:16	65	16:15-18	269
10:5	101	14:20	126	16:16	126
10:7-8	216	14:25	208	16:17	116
10:11-12	110	14:26	211, 236, 237, 239	16:18	320
10:12	146	14:31	326	16:19	284
10:14	64, 215	14:33	234	16:19-20	269
10:16	318	14:34	246, 247	16:21	324
10:18	197	14:37	277	16:21-24	269, 289
10:24	205	14:40	134	16:22	139, 343
10:27	31	15:1	138	16:23	349
10:31	240	15:2	111		
10:32	224, 265	15:3	138, 189	**2 Corinthians**	
10:33–11:1	72	15:5-11	44	1:1	44, 47, 48
11:2	138, 148	15:9	95	1:2	43
11:3	129, 247	15:10	63, 126	1:3	55, 228
11:7	88, 95, 222	15:11	111	1:3-7	53, 320
11:10	181	15:12	146, 161	1:4	130
11:14	124	15:14	148	1:5	142
11:16	95	15:15	162	1:5-7	114
11:22	95	15:20	107, 218	1:6	130
11:23	138	15:22	162, 208	1:7	142
11:25	103	15:23	98	1:8	129, 300, 308
12	36, 235	15:24	92	1:11	54, 263
12:1	71, 129	15:24-28	78, 79	1:15–2:12	346
12:3	65	15:25	204, 264	1:19-20	86
12:4	71	15:25-27	209	1:21	142, 320
12:5	288	15:27	158	1:22	159, 257
12:6	127	15:28	169, 227, 247	1:23–2:4	129

1:24 279, 311
2:3 344
2:3-4 287
2:4 58
2:7 303
2:7-10 164
2:8 58, 326
2:12 263, 300
2:14 168, 169, 239, 311
2:17 50
3:1 146
3:3 118, 156, 158
3:6 65, 67, 162
3:7-9 118
3:12 325
3:14 220
3:18 74, 209, 222
4:1 118, 288
4:4 87, 119, 222
4:5 139, 226
4:6 76
4:7 73
4:10 212
4:10-11 114
4:10-12 115, 207
4:11 336
4:14 109, 162
4:15 142
4:16 221
4:16–5:5 74, 115
4:17-18 114, 169
5:1 156
5:1-5 59
5:3 110
5:5 257
5:7 71
5:9 250
5:10 256, 258, 264
5:11 254
5:14-15 58
5:15 189, 207
5:17 50, 221
5:18 118, 288
5:18-20 102, 103, 107
5:19 83
5:20 322
5:21 110
6:1 63
6:1-2 116
6:2 266
6:3 118, 288
6:4 65

6:4-6 75
6:4-10 169
6:6 75, 229, 230
6:15 67
6:17 190
7:1 254
7:4 75, 114, 320
7:5 277, 288
7:7 320
7:8 129, 333
7:9-10 81
7:13 320, 321
7:14 317
7:15 228, 344
8:2 75
8:4 288, 318, 319
8:8 325
8:14 266
8:16 239
8:18 48
8:19-20 118
8:23 44, 279, 311, 337
8:24 317
9:1 288
9:2 251
9:2-3 317
9:3 48
9:5 48
9:7 130, 332
9:8 72, 142
9:10 62, 186
9:12-13 288
9:13 319
9:15 239
10:1 129, 229, 326, 339
10:1-6 312
10:2 146
10:3 129, 288, 336
10:5-6 344
10:7 129
10:13-16 45
10:15 62
11:1 230
11:1-23 279
11:2 109
11:3 320
11:8 288
11:16 277
11:19 230
11:23 65, 308
11:23-28 114
11:31 55, 220

12:1-7 30
12:2 50, 60
12:2-3 207
12:2-4 184
12:7 184
12:9 73
12:11-12 44
12:14 129
12:18 48
12:19 50
12:20 213
12:21 81, 214
13:1-10 269
13:4 73, 207
13:5 122
13:11 130, 205, 233, 343
13:12-13 269
13:13-14 318

Galatians
1:1 44, 46, 162
1:3 43
1:3-4 86
1:4 46, 106
1:6 63, 133
1:6-9 25, 86, 234
1:7 146
1:9 138
1:10 64, 72, 254
1:10–2:21 113
1:11-12 138
1:12 121, 124, 138
1:14 148
1:15 63
1:15-16 116, 122
1:20 220
1:22 50, 129
1:23 318
2 155
2:1 277
2:1-14 172
2:4 50, 57
2:5 61, 333
2:7 45
2:7-8 154
2:7-9 44
2:8 127
2:9 45, 118, 277
2:10 289
2:11 129
2:11-14 137, 276
2:11-18 279

2:12	146, 278, 279	5:2	112, 339
2:13	277	5:2-12	25, 137
2:14	61	5:4	110
2:16	317	5:4-5	111
2:16–3:26	57	5:4-6	111
2:17	65	5:5-6	58
2:19	115, 161, 189	5:5-12	156
2:19-20	207, 209	5:6	58, 225, 232, 319
2:19–3:1	136	5:10	344
2:20	50, 57, 129, 248,	5:11	104
	336	5:13	58
2:21	30, 189	5:13-19	137
3	57, 106	5:14	141, 227, 232
3:1-3	25	5:15	146
3:1-5	137, 139	5:16	70, 71, 140, 215
3:2-3	111	5:16-17	108, 197
3:2-5	159	5:16-21	79
3:4	184	5:16-26	137
3:5	186	5:18	70
3:8	122, 125	5:19	213, 214
3:13	265	5:19-21	213, 216
3:14	57, 122	5:20	215, 216
3:16	122	5:21	77, 257, 279
3:17	133	5:22	58, 62, 65, 75, 229,
3:18	346		230, 232, 233
3:19	137, 150	5:22-23	227
3:22	57	5:23	229
3:23-24	176	5:24	215, 227
3:23-25	150, 318	5:25	70
3:26	57, 125	5:25–6:2	140
3:26-29	50, 122	6:1-3	237
3:27	50, 153, 167	6:2	141, 227
3:28	125, 210, 223, 224,	6:6	141
	226, 227, 335	6:7-10	261
3:29–4:7	79	6:10	52, 72, 266, 318,
4:1-3	150		332
4:1-7	176, 249	6:11	324
4:3	137, 150, 226	6:11-16	264
4:5	265	6:11-17	25
4:8-9	150	6:11-18	269, 289, 343
4:8-10	25	6:12	104
4:9	73, 137, 149, 226	6:12-13	155, 197
4:9-10	150, 175, 189	6:12-14	136, 279
4:10	137	6:12-15	137
4:14	139, 277	6:14	115, 161, 189, 207
4:19	328	6:15	221, 225
4:23	197	6:17	114
4:26	205	6:18	349
4:29	197		
5	200, 240	**Ephesians**	
5–6	155	1:1	48
5:1-12	279	1:1-2	36

1:2	43		
1:3	55, 78		
1:4	10		
1:6	79		
1:7	67, 80, 81		
1:9	120		
1:9-10	121		
1:10	118		
1:13-14	79		
1:14	80		
1:15	36, 56, 57		
1:15-16	53, 69, 316		
1:15-23	261		
1:16	54, 316		
1:17	55		
1:17-23	72		
1:18	121		
1:19	73, 162		
1:19-20	127		
1:20	162, 204		
1:20-21	92		
1:20-22	209		
1:21	92, 119, 121, 176		
1:21-23	36		
1:22-23	96, 152, 158		
1:23	227		
2:1-2	163		
2:2	119, 217		
2:3	106, 215		
2:4	248		
2:5	36, 164		
2:6	161		
2:7	121		
2:8	106		
2:10	72		
2:11	155		
2:11-12	163		
2:12	105, 106		
2:13	107, 218		
2:13-18	103		
2:14	208, 233		
2:15	165, 221, 277		
2:16	102, 103		
2:18	67		
2:19	64		
2:20	111, 142		
3:1	310		
3:2	110, 118		
3:3	121		
3:3-4	120		
3:3-6	121		
3:6	64		

3:7	73, 127	5:21–6:9	243	1:15	146
3:7-13	264	5:22	246	1:19	263
3:8-9	120	5:22–6:9	36, 242	1:20	325
3:9	118, 119, 120, 207,	5:23-24	247	1:21	207, 209
	222	5:24	247	1:22	129, 336
3:10	92	5:25	231, 248	1:23	215
3:13	67, 69	5:25-33	249	1:24	129
3:14	67	5:27	109	1:25	344
3:16	73, 74, 121	5:29	231	1:27	71
3:17	100, 111, 122, 141	5:33	255	1:29	57, 346
3:19	153	6:1-2	251	1:30	129, 280
3:20	67, 69, 73	6:2	277	2:1	228, 318, 320
3:21	119	6:4	250, 251	2:1-2	130
4:1	71, 310, 326	6:4-5	242	2:2	205
4:2	75, 229, 230	6:5	252, 254, 255, 336	2:3	229
4:2-3	233	6:5-9	36, 253	2:5	205
4:3	235	6:6	69, 254	2:6	84
4:8	168	6:7	242	2:6-11	36, 238
4:10	60	6:8	256, 258	2:8	104
4:13	221, 233	6:9	258, 259	2:9	346
4:15-16	36, 186	6:10	73	2:9-11	55, 240
4:16	130, 186	6:11	221	2:10-11	103, 180
4:18	105, 106	6:12	60, 92	2:11	139
4:21	110	6:18	262	2:12	344
4:22	210, 215, 218, 220,	6:18-20	261	2:13	127
	221	6:19	120, 261, 325	2:15	109
4:24	106, 210, 221	6:19-20	263	2:16	116
4:25	218, 219	6:20	322	2:19	47, 346
4:29	266	6:21	271	2:22	328
4:30	80	6:21-22	36, 269	2:23-24	346
4:31	219, 249	6:22	130	2:24	308, 344
4:32	36, 210, 228, 231	6:24	269	2:25	44, 48, 63, 65, 275,
5:1	254				279, 288, 303, 311,
5:2	231, 248	**Philippians**			312
5:3	214, 215	1:1	47, 48, 64, 65, 118	2:30	110
5:4	248	1:2	43	3	106, 156
5:5	77, 78, 214, 216,	1:3	55	3:2	146
	257, 279	1:3-4	46, 53, 315, 316	3:2-21	279
5:6	148, 210, 217	1:3-11	53	3:3	156, 158, 162
5:7	64	1:4	54, 56, 67	3:3-4	197, 336
5:8	77	1:5	318	3:3-5	155
5:8-11	78	1:6	72, 78, 319, 320,	3:7-8	106
5:10	250		344	3:9	57
5:13-14	76	1:8	228	3:10	161, 318
5:14	238	1:9	69, 142, 319	3:10-11	114, 115
5:15	265	1:9-10	71	3:11	115
5:17	69	1:9-11	261	3:14	177, 205
5:18-19	239	1:11	62	3:15	126
5:19	211, 236, 238	1:12	271	3:18-20	189
5:19-20	36	1:12-14	263, 264	3:19	205
5:20	211, 241	1:13	50	3:21	108, 127, 161, 209
5:21	247	1:14	60, 344	4:2	326

4:3	279, 311
4:4-6	75
4:6	261
4:7	233
4:8-9	261
4:9	64, 138, 233
4:10-18	269
4:14-18	289
4:15	319
4:18	63, 250, 334
4:19	121
4:21-22	269
4:23	269, 349

Colossians

1:1	37, 43, 49, 63, 64, 69, 272, 273, 284, 310, 311, 320, 335, 336
1:1-2	36, 312
1:1-8	41
1:2	20, 23, 48, 49, 50, 55, 56, 58, 63, 65, 75, 80, 103, 107, 109, 120, 122, 125, 141, 142, 152, 174, 228, 233, 266, 272, 290, 313, 318, 320, 325, 348
1:2-3	240, 314, 349
1:3	46, 52, 53, 55, 75, 79, 140, 200, 241, 261, 262, 266, 280, 316
1:3-4	315, 316, 317
1:3-8	134, 316
1:3-9	54, 69
1:3-23	67, 75
1:4	36, 56, 57, 110, 122, 125, 130, 135, 138, 162, 232, 248, 316, 317, 318
1:4-5	65, 111
1:4-8	53
1:5	36, 58, 60, 63, 90, 123, 203, 236, 263, 331, 346
1:5-6	62
1:6	27, 51, 61, 72, 104, 112, 186, 239, 266
1:6-7	22, 43
1:7	45, 49, 60, 63, 112, 118, 272, 273, 275, 280, 283, 288, 311, 331, 335, 347
1:7-8	64
1:8	56, 58, 63, 65, 203
1:9	33, 47, 56, 72, 80, 124, 134, 145, 195, 200, 237, 239, 280
1:9-10	27, 88, 131, 200, 222, 261, 265, 319
1:9-11	72, 221
1:9-14	53, 130, 174
1:9-20	68
1:9–2:5	41
1:9–2:9	26
1:10	62, 71, 104, 106, 125, 126, 140, 186, 217, 222
1:10-11	127
1:11	73, 87, 110, 121, 123, 206, 209, 230, 320
1:11-12	79
1:12	29, 33, 34, 75, 77, 78, 94, 120, 134, 143, 174, 181, 183, 235, 257, 262
1:12-13	80
1:12-14	78, 81, 84
1:12-20	263
1:12-23	86
1:13	28, 76, 77, 93, 97, 102, 106, 169, 280
1:13-14	58, 87, 257
1:13-22	138
1:14	50, 80, 89, 92, 94, 102, 154, 164
1:15	30, 74, 87, 91, 93, 94, 97, 98, 102, 111, 222
1:15-17	91, 95
1:15-18	96, 108, 139, 195
1:15-20	28, 36, 52, 80, 83-86, 117, 120, 122, 124, 125, 131, 151, 167, 170, 177, 186, 200, 207, 210, 233, 238, 240, 241, 248, 256
1:15-23	105
1:15–2:5	53
1:16	60, 78, 90, 92, 102, 104, 111, 119, 153, 179
1:16-17	50
1:16-20	227
1:17	92, 93
1:18	50, 88, 91, 92, 93, 94, 97, 98, 102, 106, 107, 109, 118, 153, 185, 186, 187, 209, 222, 235, 284
1:18-20	99
1:19	33, 50, 69, 89, 123, 152
1:19-20	102
1:20	91, 92, 93, 104, 106, 107, 109, 111, 154, 169, 234
1:20-22	233
1:21	163, 216
1:21-22	33
1:21-23	84
1:21-32	106
1:22	96, 102, 108, 109, 117, 120, 124, 125, 129, 154, 157, 158, 185, 196, 218, 329, 336
1:23	59, 60, 65, 87, 117, 123, 126, 128, 138, 203
1:23-24	110
1:23-25	39
1:24	36, 96, 107, 108, 114, 115, 117, 119, 157, 161, 177, 196, 208, 217, 235
1:24-25	22, 69
1:24–2:5	112, 113, 128
1:24–4:1	105
1:25	33, 65, 117, 236, 263
1:25-26	47
1:25-27	66
1:25–2:3	28
1:26	118, 119, 264, 266
1:26-27	131, 132, 138, 151, 200, 207, 263
1:27	29, 59, 74, 80, 121, 123, 125, 139, 203, 208, 209, 237
1:27-28	36, 104
1:27-29	114, 264

1:28	27, 33, 50, 107, 109, 123, 138, 142, 195, 233, 237, 265, 280	2:10	27, 78, 92, 93, 96, 150, 152, 158, 177, 184	2:20-23	188, 206
1:29	73, 126, 162, 206, 280	2:11	27, 96, 107, 108, 152, 155, 159, 160, 163, 167, 168, 175, 180, 183, 196, 220, 223, 224, 225, 278	2:21	27, 28, 179, 190, 192, 194, 195, 196, 198, 203, 214, 223, 224
1:29–2:5	39			2:21-22	33, 163, 165
2:1	22, 43, 108, 114, 126, 157, 281, 282, 301, 347			2:22	141, 192, 193
				2:23	27, 28, 33, 71, 108, 113, 132, 147, 149, 179, 182, 194, 195, 205, 212, 229, 236, 265
2:1-5	133	2:11-12	36		
2:2	27, 33, 58, 69, 124, 130, 131, 139, 186, 233, 237, 254, 263, 272, 280, 319	2:11-13	28		
		2:11-14	33		
		2:11-15	110, 153	3:1	36, 77, 79, 110, 139, 161, 206, 208, 209, 256
		2:12	57, 59, 77, 98, 115, 160, 182, 203, 207, 208, 212		
2:2-3	71, 114, 200, 207	2:12-13	50, 157, 158, 189	3:1-2	201
2:2-6	138	2:13	29, 33, 36, 108, 155, 162, 225, 228, 231, 346	3:1-4	59, 202, 209, 218, 235, 246
2:3	27, 33, 50, 131, 138, 195, 248, 265			3:1-5	211
2:4	34, 114, 132, 147, 184, 192	2:14	164, 168	3:1–4:6	4, 26, 188, 199
		2:14-15	104, 190	3:2	28, 205, 212
2:4-5	131	2:15	27, 33, 36, 50, 78, 85, 92, 93, 97, 103, 141, 149, 157, 158, 164, 166, 179, 184, 189, 203, 218, 220, 233	3:3	132, 212
2:5	50, 57, 108, 114, 134, 142, 157, 162, 320			3:3-4	50, 201, 221
				3:3-5	153, 206
				3:4	36, 74, 123, 207, 217, 264
2:5-7	153				
2:6	55, 64, 65, 71, 72, 79, 128, 135, 142, 148, 194, 211, 288	2:16	27, 69, 78, 87, 114, 141, 150, 165, 171, 175, 177, 178, 180, 183, 191, 198, 223, 224	3:5	106, 161, 190, 201, 212, 219, 228, 230
				3:5-9	220
2:6-7	133, 199, 200, 212, 218, 221, 227, 230, 236, 241, 248, 251, 255, 256, 265, 272			3:5-17	210, 218
				3:5–4:6	202
		2:16-17	33	3:6	36, 182, 208, 216, 217, 219, 319
2:6-23	41, 188	2:16-18	163		
2:6–4:6	44, 136-37	2:16-23	26, 133, 148	3:8	106, 107, 190, 213, 218, 219, 230
2:7	75, 141, 262	2:17	108, 152, 176, 205		
2:8	25, 27, 32, 61, 69, 87, 114, 126, 133, 146, 153, 160, 168, 169, 171, 175, 182, 184, 189, 192, 194	2:17-18	171	3:8-10	211
		2:17-19	196	3:8-15	104
		2:18	27, 33, 60, 69, 76, 78, 87, 108, 114, 132, 150, 151, 171, 177, 184, 187, 191, 192, 204, 205, 206, 212, 223, 224, 229, 234, 236, 237, 241, 247	3:9	159, 167, 213, 219, 221
2:8-10	33			3:9-10	161, 218
2:8-15	145, 154, 167			3:10	27, 36, 88, 123, 153, 201, 209, 220, 228, 229
2:8-23	26, 34, 113, 144, 199-200				
				3:10-12	153, 227
2:9	27, 28, 52, 89, 101, 102, 152, 196, 233, 241, 256			3:11	28, 29, 34, 122, 155, 223, 225, 252, 253, 259, 306, 335
		2:18-19	28		
2:9-10	36, 69, 149	2:19	36, 96, 130, 153, 177, 185, 232, 235	3:11-12	33, 201
2:9-12	50, 151	2:20	27, 32, 33, 50, 87, 110, 122, 150, 161, 175, 184, 189, 208, 212	3:12	34, 36, 75, 120, 161, 211, 221, 232, 234, 320, 330
2:9-15	146, 169, 187				
2:9-23	202			3:12-13	230

3:12–4:1	140	4:7-9	271, 345	1:6	75, 114
3:13	164, 234	4:7-14	263	1:7-9	316
3:13-14	236	4:7-17	25, 37	1:8	62, 236, 317
3:13-16	235	4:7-18	41, 269, 290, 343,	1:9-10	52, 60, 61, 86
3:13–4:1	272		347	1:10	77, 162, 216
3:14	58, 65, 232, 248	4:8	130, 322	2:1	133
3:15	51, 96, 177, 211,	4:8-9	38, 304	2:2	129
	233, 236, 240, 241	4:9	49, 64, 272, 283,	2:4	72
3:15–4:1	243		300, 301, 302, 305,	2:6-7	45
3:16	27, 33, 36, 51, 124,		328, 329, 331	2:11	328
	142, 235, 263, 265,	4:9-10	270, 275	2:12	71, 77, 209, 279
	266, 288	4:9-14	308	2:13	60, 138
3:16-17	211, 241	4:10	22, 39, 280	2:14	50, 95
3:17	56, 75, 212, 235,	4:10-13	347	2:15	72
	240, 262	4:10-14	279, 329, 348	2:17	129, 215
3:18	141, 244, 246, 249,	4:10-17	274, 317	2:17–3:11	113
	251, 255, 325	4:11	29, 79, 225, 276,	2:18	112, 339
3:18-20	248		278, 311, 348	2:19-20	317
3:18–4:1	36, 47, 242, 243,	4:11-12	280	3:1-5	346
	336	4:12	23, 33, 47, 48, 63,	3:2	47, 65, 130, 279,
3:19	248		64, 69, 126, 131,		311
3:20	78, 212, 244, 249,		270, 273, 278	3:6	47
	255	4:12-13	60, 281	3:9-10	53, 69
3:21	249, 251	4:13	23, 43, 63, 128,	3:10	129
3:22	72, 108, 140, 240,		129, 286	3:12	130, 142
	249, 252, 255, 256,	4:14	64, 278, 282, 348	3:13	77
	259, 306, 336	4:14-15	270	3:14	130
3:22-23	257	4:15	23, 29, 245, 246,	4:1	72, 138, 141, 326
3:22-24	212, 244		286, 313	4:3	46, 69, 214
3:22–4:1	36, 253, 280	4:15-16	21, 95, 129, 282,	4:3-6	216
3:23	255		283	4:4-6	215
3:24	256, 258	4:15-17	275	4:5	215
3:24-25	36, 201, 260	4:16	44, 48, 284, 285	4:10	326
3:25	257, 259, 338	4:17	38, 69, 287, 308,	4:12	265
4:1	59, 140, 212, 244,		312, 313, 331	4:13	129
	252, 253, 259, 285,	4:18	38, 39, 44, 239,	4:14	189
	306, 335, 336, 342		263, 276, 289, 311,	4:14-17	59
4:2	56, 138, 201, 262,		324, 340, 349	4:15	133, 215
	263	4:22-25	226, 313	4:15-17	208
4:2-3	261			4:17	209
4:2-6	104, 261	**1 Thessalonians**		4:18	130, 326
4:3	39, 60, 262, 276	1:1	43, 47, 50, 207	5:4-8	78
4:3-4	121	1:1-3	46	5:6	262
4:3-18	39	1:2	53, 54, 56, 316	5:8	58
4:4	264	1:2-3	55, 69, 261, 315,	5:9	216
4:5	27, 33, 264, 265,		316, 317	5:10	189
	267	1:2–2:16	113	5:11	326
4:6	266	1:3	56, 58	5:12	124
4:6-7	80	1:4	228	5:12-22	261
4:7	49, 64, 65, 270,	1:5	65, 73, 131	5:13	130
	275, 283, 331, 336	1:5-6	159	5:14	124, 237, 326
4:7-8	36, 272, 273	1:5-8	60	5:15	76, 332

5:16-18	75	2:4	63	4:12	271
5:17	261, 262	2:7	220	4:17	119
5:18	46, 235	2:8-15	242	4:18	77, 279
5:20-21	288	3:8	118	4:19-21	269
5:22	106	3:9	111	4:22	269
5:23	233	3:10	109		
5:25	261, 263	3:13	57	**Titus**	
5:27	269, 286	3:14	346	1:1	63, 228
5:28	269, 349	3:16	84, 238	1:4	328
		4:1	111	1:6-7	109
2 Thessalonians		4:3	49, 63, 179, 190	1:10	278, 279
1:1	47, 207	4:6	111	1:14	277
1:2	43	4:10	126	2:1-10	242
1:3	54, 55, 56, 261,	4:12	49	2:5	247
	315, 317	5:8	111	2:9	250
1:3-12	53	6:1-2	242	2:12	215
1:4	317	6:2	336	3:1	247
1:5	77, 279	6:4	219	3:3	215, 218, 219
1:9-10	74	6:10	111	3:12	271
1:10	77	6:12	129	3:12-13	37, 269
1:11-12	69	6:14	277	3:15	269
2:3	208	6:21	111, 269		
2:6	208			**Philemon**	
2:6-7	116	**2 Timothy**		1	37, 47, 64, 279,
2:8	208	1:2	328		307, 309, 310, 348
2:12	173	1:8	310	1-2	300, 327, 347
2:13	228	1:13	57	1-3	301
2:14	209	2:1	328	1-7	299
2:15	148, 185	2:9	264	2	23, 38, 47, 275,
2:16	320	2:10	228		284, 288, 299, 308,
2:17	72, 130	2:14	196		311-12, 320, 321
3:1	236	2:15	109	3	43, 313-14, 349
3:1-2	261, 263	2:18	161	4	53, 56, 318
3:4	344	2:19	135	4-5	55, 315
3:6	138, 141, 148, 241	2:21	329	4-6	53, 261
3:6-13	261	2:22	215, 233	4-7	69, 301, 302, 316
3:12	326	2:25	63	5	56, 301, 321, 326,
3:14	344	3:2	250		340
3:15	124, 237	3:2-5	213	5-6	135
3:16	233	3:7	63	6	313, 318, 332, 337,
3:17	324	3:10	75		344, 347
3:17-18	269, 289	3:15	57	6-7	321
3:18	349	4:1	77, 279	7	301, 317, 320, 324,
		4:2	75		326, 327, 330, 341,
1 Timothy		4:5	288		344
1:1	208	4:7	129	7-20	343
1:2	328	4:8	59	8	248, 324
1:9-10	213	4:9-18	269	8-9	314, 332
1:12	288	4:9-21	37	8-10	323
1:16	75	4:10	119, 283	8-16	322
1:17	87	4:10-12	282	8-20	339
1:18	328	4:11	276, 282, 288, 329	8-21	300

Ref	Pages
9	310, 316, 317, 325, 326
9-10	307, 311
9-14	333
10	273, 300, 327, 340
10-11	328
10-13	302, 305
10-22	273
11	107, 330, 335, 336, 341
12	228, 304, 316, 338
12-14	329
12-20	323
13	307, 311, 332
13-21	306
14	316, 331-32, 341
15	333, 335, 347
15-19	345
16	226, 307, 311, 313, 316, 320, 327, 329, 334, 336, 341, 349
16-18	332
16-19	301
17	316, 318, 324
17-19	334, 336
17-20	323, 337
18	258, 302, 303, 304, 338
18-25	324
19	269, 289, 311, 316, 317, 325
20	316, 320, 327, 330, 341
20-21	344
20-22	343
21	269, 333, 346
21-22	113, 277, 301
21-25	299
22	40, 164, 261, 263, 269, 299, 300, 301, 316, 345, 347
22-23	307
22-24	308
23	43, 63, 64, 65, 276, 281, 347
23-24	37, 275, 278, 311, 329
23-25	269, 343
24	276, 279, 282, 283, 347, 348
25	290, 301, 346, 347, 349

Hebrews

Ref	Pages
1:1	310
1:1-4	85
1:3	84, 89, 94
1:13	204
1:13–2:8	209
2:5	176
2:9-10	115
2:10	91, 92, 209
3:18	217
4:6	217
4:11	217
4:12	319
4:14	185
5:5	102
5:12	149
6:1	232
6:2	145
6:5	119, 176
8:1	204
9:10	145
9:11	176
9:14	109
9:22	81
9:26	107
9:27	59
10:1	176
10:12-13	204
10:18	81
10:19	103
10:22	131
10:26	63
10:34	75
10:36	69, 258
11:12	212
11:13	258
11:14	205
11:23	251
11:27	87
11:31	217
11:39	258
12:1	74, 129, 218
12:2	75, 104, 204
12:11	75
12:14	176
12:15	249
13:14	205
13:21	69
13:22	276

James

Ref	Pages
1:1	310
1:2	75
1:3-4	74
1:15	215
1:19-20	219
1:21	218
1:22	133
2:1	258
2:15	312
2:20	148
3:1-12	219
3:9	88, 222
3:11	249
3:14	220
5:10-11	75
5:11	74
5:15	81

1 Peter

Ref	Pages
1:1	228, 310
1:2	51
1:3	55
1:5	266
1:6	75
1:9	258
1:19	109
2:1	218, 219
2:6	111
2:8	217
2:9	77, 78, 228
2:11-25	253
2:17	242
2:18	252, 254, 255
2:18–3:7	242
2:19-20	256
2:22	84
3:1	217, 246
3:8	228
3:15	267
3:15-16	245
3:17	69
3:18	162, 189
3:20	75, 217
3:22	204
4:3	215, 216
4:3-4	218
4:12-19	267
4:13	75
4:17	217
5:1	209
5:2	332
5:4	208, 209
5:5	229

5:8	220	3:14	30, 97	**Apocalypse of Moses**	
5:9	135	3:17	282	10:3	88
5:12-13	276	3:21	204	12:1	88
		4–5	180, 184	20–21	222
2 Peter		4:1-2	183	33:5	88
1:1	310	4:4	92, 204	35:2	88
1:2	51	5:6	204		
2:12	193	5:9	238	**Apocalypse of Zephaniah**	
2:13	258	6:9-11	116	3:6-9	164
3:10	149	7:17	79, 204	6:15	180
3:12	149	9:1	150	7:1-8	164
3:15	75	10:7	120	7:8	166
		11:16	204	8:3-4	181
1 John		13:10	74		
1	318	14:3	238	**Ascension of Isaiah**	
1:1	310	14:5	109	7–9	180
1:5	76	15:3	238	7:13–9:33	181
1:6	220	16:10-11	274	7:21	180
1:7	76	16:15	262		
1:9	81, 231	16:19	219	**2 Baruch**	
2:8	76	17:4	214	5:7	182
2:17	69	17:14	228	14:12	59
2:19-20	206	19:10	180	18:2	78
2:21	63	19:15	219	44:14-15	132
2:28	208	20:4	204	48:3	265
3:2	208, 209	20:12	164	48:42–52:7	202
		21:4	274	49:3	212
2 John		21:8	216	51:5	77
1	63, 310	22:1	79, 204	51:10	77
		22:3	79, 204	52:6	75, 114
3 John		22:9	180	54:13-14	132
1	310	22:15	216		
				3 Baruch	
Jude				3:1-2	183
1	310	**PSEUDEPIGRAPHA**		42:2	183
24	109				
		Adam and Eve		**1 Enoch**	
Revelation		13–15	180	1:3	228
1:4	51	14:1-2	88	1:8	77, 228
1:5	97	25:1	282	2:18	239
1:9	30	37:3	88	5:5-6	51
1:20	150			5:7	77, 234
2–3	129	**Apocalypse of Abraham**		5:7-8	228
2:9	49	9:7-10	182	5:9	219, 234
2:9-11	267	12:1-2	182	10:11	214
2:13	267	16:3	74	10:17	234
2:13-15	185	17	181	11:2	234
2:21	214	17–18	180	14	184
3:3	262	17:2	180	14:8-13	183
3:5	164, 166			14:18-23	180
3:9	49	**Apocalypse of Elijah**		14:21	74
3:10	74	1:10-11	92	18:1	132

18:14-16	150	8:5	172, 173	13:8		79
22:11	256	8:9	163	13:9		52, 124
36:4	180	8:10-11	77	14:4		141
36:39-40	180	11:18	81	14:10		257
40:9	257	12:1	163	16:10		219
42	132	12:9	220	17:13		106
43:1-2	150	15:10	59	18:4		79, 90
46:3	132	15:12	77			
48:5	180	20:7	163			
48:6	121			**Pseudo-Philo,**		
48:7	76	*Jubilees*		*Biblical Antiquities*		
49:3	100	1:23	156	13:6		179
49:3-4	101	1:29	103, 228	34:2		180
61:10	92	2:2	150			
61:10-12	180	2:8	150			
62:6	180	2:17-33	174	**Pseudo-Phocylides**		
62:7	121	5:10-16	217	50		256
62:9	180	5:16	258	80		248
71:11-12	239	7:20	250	150		251
75:1	150	21:4	258	175-227		243
86	150	22:9	51	185		248
89:61-64	164	23:22-31	115	194		215
89:70-71	164	23:26-29	103	207		251
90:20-27	217	50:6-13	174	208		250
91:16-17	103			223-27		259
92:4-5	77	*Letter of Aristeas*				
93:2	228	132	100	*Sibylline Oracles*		
100:7	258	142	192	3.8-45		215
102:5	109	152	214	3.38		215
103:2	120	227	248	3.47		257
104:2	77	228	250	3.69		228
106:19	120	256	147	3.592-93		192
108:3	166	265	232	4.107		30
108:7	164			4.150-51		30
108:11-15	78	*Odes of Solomon*				
		8:8	61	*Testament of Abraham*		
2 Enoch		11:2	157	10		184
3	183	38:17-22	141	10:7–11:7		164
4:1	150			10:15		256
10:4-5	213	*Prayer of Joseph*		11:10		166
10:4-6	216	3	90	12:7-18		164
19:1-4	150			12:15		256
20–21	180	*Psalms of Solomon*		13:9-14		164
20:1	92	2:18	258	13:11		150
22:8-9	158	2:23	219	14:12		81
24:3	120	3:8	178	14:14		81
53:2-3	164	4:7-8	254	16:3-4		87
65:2	88	4:19	254	17:12		167
		9:1	77			
Joseph and Asenath		9:7	81	*Testament of Asher*		
7:1	172	10:1-2	75, 114	1:6		178
8:3	163	11:1	60	6:5		106

Testament of Benjamin
6:4   100, 101
10:10   215, 216, 228

Testament of Dan
5:11   234
6:8   106

Testament of Gad
3:1   61
4:6   163

Testament of Isaac
4:1-6   182
5:4   182

Testament of Issachar
3:8   254
4:1   254
4:3   69
5:5   282
7:7   254

Testament of Job
11:11   164
18:6-7   257
42:8   81
43:1   164
43:2   239
43:11   219
43:13   258
48–50   181

Testament of Joseph
1:6   346
4:6   214
7:8   215
8:5   238
17:7   330

Testament of Judah
14:5   214
15:4   173
18:6   215
19:1   215
23:1   215

Testament of Levi
2:5-7   183
3:3-8   180
3:8   92
17:11   215

Testament of Moses
5–10   115
7:9-10   192

Testament of Naphtali
2:5   88

Testament of Reuben
1:6   214
1:10   173
3:3   214
4:1   254
4:6-8   214
4:11   214
5:3   214
5:5   214

Testament of Solomon
8:2-4   149

Testament of Zebulun
6:1   70
7:3   229
8:2   100, 101, 229
8:6   229

DEAD SEA SCROLLS

CD
2:16   214
3:14-15   175
3:18   81
4:3-4   228
4:17-19   213
6:20   47
7:1-2   47
10:14–11:18   174
19:4   71

1Q27   120

1QH
3:19   163
3:21-22   181
3:28-36   115
4:9-12   70
4:37   81
6:10-12   70
7:20-21   328
9:24-25   75, 114
11:7-10   70

11:10-12   76
11:10-13   181
12:11-13   70
16:11-12   70
18:14   60

1QM
1:1   78
1:8-14   78
3:5   48
7:4-6   181
12:1   228
13:1   47
13:5-16   78
15:4   47
15:7   47

1QpHab
7:1-5   125
7:5   120
9:2   108
10:13   228
11:13   156

1QS
1:6   214
1:9-10   78
2:2   125
2:15   216
3:9-11   125
3:17-21   184
3:23   120
3:24-25   78
4:3   70, 228
4:7-13   78
4:9-11   213
4:10   214
4:11   219
4:18   120
5:5   156
5:8-10   70
5:10   71
5:12   216
6–7   191
6:10   47
6:22   47
9:9-10   125
9:13   70
9:19   125
9:26–10:8   175
11:7-8   76
11:11-14   81

11:15-18   70

1QSa
1:18   47
2:8-9   181

1QSb
3:2   48
4:25-26   181

4Q169
2:6   108

4Q186   151

4Q286   184

4Q400-405   181

4Q400
1.i.14   192

4Q405
14–15i:3-4   183
23i:8-10   183

4QAmram   184

4QCD   181

4QMessAr   151

4QpNah   108

11QMelch
18   60

11QT
47   192

**RABBINIC
LITERATURE**

Aboth de Rabbi Nathan
12   182

Babylonian Talmud
Hagigah
14a   204

Mishnah *'Abodah Zarah*
2:3   173
5:2   173

Mishnah *Aboth*
1:1   138
2:12   240
2:14   267
1:3   255

Mishnah *Kiddushin*
1:7   251

Mishnah *Makshirin*
3:7-8   192

Shemoneh 'Esreh
2   163
6   81
13   76
19   51

Tosefta *Hullin*
2:18   180

**EARLY CHRISTIAN
WRITINGS**

Apocalypse of Paul
17   164

Apology of Aristides
14.4   179

Apostolic Constitutions
3.17   160

Barnabas
3:6   29
6:11   81
16:8   81
19:5   248, 254
19:5-7   242
19:7   254
20:1   215, 219
20:1-2   213

Chrysostom,
Homilia ad Judaeos
1   29

1 Clement
1:3   248
13:1   219
15:2   194
21:6   254
21:6-9   242
21:8   229
22:1   57
31:4   229
35:5   213, 215
42:2   230
43:1   57
44:3   229
49:2   232
50:3   78
50:4   219
64   75

2 Clement
12:5   312
13:1   254
19:1   312
20:2   312

Clement of Alexandria,
Stromata
6.5.41.2   179

Clementine Homilies
12:2   346

Didache
3:3   219
3:5   220
4:9   251, 254
4:9-11   242
4:11   254
5:1   213, 214, 216, 219
5:1-2   213
8:3   56
15:3   219

Diognetus
7:1   118

Eusebius
Historia Ecclesiastica
2.23.5   173

3.4.1-7   283
3.24.14-15   283
3.31.2-5   22
3.38.2   283
3.39.14-16   276
5.8.3   283
6.14.2   283
6.25.6   283

Praeparatio Evangelica
8.7.14   243
9.17.8-9   151
9.18.1   151
13.12.11   93
14.18.26   220

Gospel of Thomas
53   157

Gospel of Truth
20:24-34   166, 168
20:30-31   167

Hermas
Mandates
3.2   220
4.3.1   81
10.2.3   249

Similitudes
5.3.7   178-79

Visions
2.2.3   312
2.3.1   312
3.6.7   329
3.10.6   178
3.13.3   149

Ignatius
Ephesians
1:3   328
2:1   328
2:2   341
3:1   75
3:2   209
6:1   118
6:2   328
10:2   111
11:2   331
20:1   222

21:2   123

Magnesians
1:2   209
2   341
8:1   29
10:2   267
10:3   24, 29
11   123
12:1   341

Philippians
6:1   24

Polycarp
1:1   341
1:2   230
3:1   111
4:1   332
4:1–5:2   242
5:1   312
5:2   332
6:2   341
8:2   284

Romans
5:2   341

Smyrnaeans
4:1   209

Justin Martyr,
Dialogue with Trypho
8.4   175
47.4   29
48   194
78   194
140   194

Martyrdom of Polycarp
11:2   333

Origen
Comm. in Joann.
13.17   179

Contra Celsum
1.26   179
3.44   253
5.6   179

Homily on Leviticus
5:8   29

Selecta on Exodus
12:46   29

Polycarp, *Philippians*
4:2   254
4:2-3   242
6:1   258
6:3   254
12:2   77

Tertullian
Adversus Marcionem
5.19.6   109

Apology
39.18   239

**CLASSICAL AND
HELLENISTIC
LITERATURE**

Aelius Aristides,
Orationes
45.21   99-100

Apuleius, *Metamorphoses*
11.21   183

Aristophanes, *Pax*
1216   282

Aristotle
Ethica Nicomachea
1.3.4   133
1.13   70
8.11.6-7   338

Politica
I.1253b.1-14   243
I.1254a.14   226

Cicero
Ad Atticum
13.28   289

Ad familiares
9.15.2   267

Pro Flacco
28.68   21

Corpus Hermeticum
13.12   149

Dio Chrysostom
3.60 — 228
15.20 — 249
64.3 — 168

Diogenes Laertius
4.46 — 249
6.102 — 149
9.66 — 220

Dionysius of Halicarnassus, *Roman Antiquities*
2.25.4–26.4 — 243
2.26.1-4 — 250
2.26.4 — 249

Diodorus Siculus
13.59.3 — 346

Epictetus
1.8.7 — 133
1.12.8 — 250
2.10.4-5 — 235
2.10.7 — 250
2.23.29 — 250
3.7.26 — 250
4.1.33 — 226

Herodotus
2.104.2-3 — 154

Josephus

Antiquities
1.149 — 282
1.192 — 154
4.130 — 215
4.132 — 215
6.144 — 164
6.330 — 167
7.60 — 332
9.235 — 77
9.269 — 238
11.79 — 142
11.346 — 174
12.147-53 — 21
12.149 — 77
12.241 — 154
12.253 — 180
12.323 — 238
13.172 — 151

14.185-267 — 21
14.241-42 — 30
14.241-43 — 282
14.261 — 172
15.371 — 32
16.160-78 — 21
18.208 — 266
20.108 — 219

Contra Apionem
1.2-3 — 148
1.42 — 165
1.210 — 249
2.199-208 — 243
2.26 — 226
2.206 — 250
2.277 — 249
2.282 — 175

Vita
355 — 346

War
2.122 — 47
2.128 — 151
2.151 — 254

Justinian, *Digest*
11.4.1 — 304
21.1.17.5 — 304
47.2.61 — 303

Juvenal, *Satirae*
14.96 — 175

Life of Aesop
122 — 164

Lucian, *De Syriadea*
54 — 190

Marcus Aurelius, *Meditations*
4.23 — 91

Livy, *Historia*
2.32 — 235

Musonius, *Orationes*
13A — 248

Ovid, *Tristia*
5.10.37 — 225

Philo

De Abrahamo
34 — 125
119-20 — 176
272 — 95

De aeternitate mundi
107-9 — 149

De agricultura
50 — 90

De cherubim
9 — 133
68 — 138
125-26 — 91

De confusione linguarum
31 — 221
97 — 88
136 — 100
146 — 90
147 — 88
190 — 176

De decalogo
53 — 149
82 — 176
165-67 — 243
167 — 260

De ebrietate
17 — 250
30-31 — 90

De fuga
101 — 88
108-10 — 167
109 — 91
110 — 158
112 — 93
212 — 180

De gigantibus
22-27 — 71
47 — 100
52 — 165

De migratione Abrahami
12 — 176

De mutatione nominum
40 — 251

De opficio mundi
73 150
105 327
167 281

De plantatione
10 103
12 150
27 176
80 183

De posteritate Caini
181 250

De praemiis et poenis
104 59

De sacrificiis
32 213

De somnis
1.35-37 182
1.62-64 91
1.128 95
1.132 180
1.215 90
1.225 221
1.238 180
1.239 88
2.8 142
2.45 88

De specialibus legibus
1.1-11 156
1.45 74
1.305 156
2.66-68 259
2.89-91 259
2.90 256
2.192 103
2.224-41 243
2.232 250
3.110 248
3.137-38 256
3.137-43 259
3.205-6 192
4.231 260

De vita contemplativa
3 149
83-85 238

De vita Mosis
2.21 175
2.60 97
2.67-69 182

2.117-35 167
2.133 93
2.238 100

De virtutibus
62 90

Hypothetica
7.14 243

Legum Allegoriae
1.43 88, 97
1.55 165
2.55 158
3.4 100
3.100-103 176
3.251 281-82
245 21

Quaestiones in Genesin
1:53 158
3:46-62 156
4:97 90

Quaestiones in Exodum
2.117 95
2.118 93

Quis rerum divinarum heres
23 93
54 158
188 93
199 91
206 103

Quod deterius
54 91

Quod omnis probus liber sit
106 249
120 249

Philostratus, *Vita Apollonii*
7.3 249

Plato

Apologia
35c 346

Leges
9.854A 215
12.957C 260
756E-757A 338

921c 232

Republic
4.425b 250
6.509a 87

Symposium
182D 215

Theaetetus
162E 133
198B 138

Timaeus
31b-32a, 32c 94
92c 87

Pliny the Elder,
Historia Naturalis
5.105-6 21
5.145 20

Pliny the Younger,
Epistle 9
21 304, 326
24 305, 326

Plutarch
C. Gracchus
4.3 346

Comparatio Thesei et Romuli
4.4.3 169

Coriolanus
19.4 218

Moralia
8F-9A 251
10D-E 251
12C 251
142E 247
457A 249
514F 266
525AB 215
685A 266
719B 260

Quaestiones convivales
8.2.2 260

Polybius
24.15.3 260

Pseudo-Callisthenes
1.22.4   247

Seneca
De Beneficiis
3.19   226
4.8.2   99

De Providentia
4   114

Epistulae
47   259
47.2   338
65.8   91
94.1   243

Stobaeus, *Anthology*
3.1.80   250
4.25.53   250
4.26.11-19   251

Strabo
12.3.35.6   169
12.8.13   20
17.2.5   154

Tacitus
Annales
14.27.1   23, 129

Historiae
5.5.2   154

Vettius Valens
43.25-26   168

Xenophon
Anabasis
1.2.6   20

Cyropaedia
6.4.7   335

PAPYRI AND INSCRIPTIONS

Orphic fragment 168   94

Oxyrhyncus Papyrus 1
32   338

Papyrus Florentini 61
61   346

Papyrus Osloensis 55
      338